CONSUMER
BEHAVIOUR

Fourth

Canadian

Edition

Buying, Having, and Being

MICHAEL R. SOLOMON
AUBURN UNIVERSITY

JUDITH LYNNE ZAICHKOWSKY
SIMON FRASER UNIVERSITY

ROSEMARY POLEGATO
MOUNT ALLISON UNIVERSITY

CONSUMER BEHAVIOUR

Fourth

Canadian

Edition

Buying, Having, and Being

PEARSON

Education
Canada

Toronto

Library and Archives Canada Cataloguing in Publication

Solomon, Michael R.
    Consumer behaviour: buying, having, and being/Michael R. Solomon, Judith Lynne Zaichkowsky, Rosemary Polegato. —4th Canadian ed.

Includes index.
ISBN-13: 978-0-13-174040-2
ISBN-10: 0-13-174040-7

1. Consumer behaviour—Textbooks. I. Zaichkowsky, Judith Lynne. II. Polegato, Rosemary. III. Title.

HF5415.32.S64 2008   658.8'342   C2006-904883-5

Editor-in-Chief: Gary Bennett
Marketing Manager: Eileen Lasswell
Acquisitions Editor: Don Thompson
Developmental Editor: Joanne Scattolon
Production Editor: Leanne Rancourt
Copy Editor: Linda Bellio
Proofreader: Leanne Rancourt
Production Coordinator: Andrea Falkenberg
Indexer: Belle Wong
Page Layout: Debbie Kumpf
Photo and Permissions Research: Lisa Brant
Art Director: Julia Hall
Interior and Cover Design: Anthony Leung
Cover Image: FirstLight

Statistics Canada information is used with the permission of Statistics Canada. Users are forbidden to copy the data and redisseminate them, in an original or modified form, for commercial purposes, without the expressed permission of Statistics Canada. Information on the availability of the wide range of data from Statistics Canada can be obtained from Statistics Canada's Regional Offices, its World Wide Web site at http://www.statcan.ca, and its toll-free access number 1-800-263-1136.

All cases in the book were prepared as a basis for class discussion rather than to illustrate either effective or ineffective handling of an administrative situation.

 2 3 4 5   12 11 10 09 08
Printed and bound in Hong Kong.

Photo credits for part- and chapter-opening pages: p. 2: Courtesy of Samsung Electronics America, Inc.; p. 4: Mark Douet/Stone; p. 34: Used with permission of Boeri Sports USA; p. 36: Courtesy of Dairy Farmers of Canada. Photography: Philip Roston—Instil Productions; p. 66: Mike Derer/CP Photo Archive; p. 96: Courtesy of Yves Veggie Cuisine; p. 128: Robert Brenner/PhotoEdit; p. 156: J. Zaichkowsky and R. Polegato; p. 186: R. Polegato; p. 210: Riser/Getty Images; p. 242: Courtesy of Ask Jeeves Inc.; p. 244: © Gary Houlder/CORBIS; p. 280: Getty Images Inc.—Image Bank; p. 310: Ken Ross/Getty Images, Inc.—Taxi; p. 340: Philip Rostron—Instil Productions Inc.; p. 370: Courtesy of Evian; p. 372: R. Polegato; p. 402: Courtesy of Singapore Airlines; p. 434: Taxi/Getty Images Inc.—Taxi; p. 458: Used with permission of Ziba Designs; p. 460: J. Zaichkowsky; p. 482: Lonely Planet Images.

To All Our Students

Brief Contents →

Contents →

Contents

About the Authors

Michael R. Solomon is Human Sciences Professor of Consumer Behaviour in the Department of Consumer Affairs at Auburn University. Before joining Auburn in 1995, Professor Solomon was Chairman of the Department of Marketing in the School of Business at Rutgers University, New Brunswick, New Jersey. Prior to that appointment, he was a member of the faculty of the Graduate School of Business Administration at New York University. Professor Solomon earned BA degrees in Psychology and Sociology at Brandeis University, an MA and a Ph.D. in Sociology at Brandeis University, and an MA in Social Psychology at the University of North Carolina at Chapel Hill.

Professor Solomon's primary research interests include consumer behaviour and lifestyle issues, the symbolic aspects of products, the psychology of fashion and image, and services marketing. He has published many articles on these and related topics in academic journals. He is an Editorial Board Member of the *Journal of Consumer Research*, the *Journal of Retailing*, and *Psychology & Marketing*.

Professor Solomon received the first Cutty Sark Men's Fashion Award in 1981 for his research on the psychological aspects of clothing. He is the editor of *The Psychology of Fashion* and co-editor of *The Service Encounter: Managing Employee/Customer Interaction in Services Businesses*, both published in 1985 by Lexington Books.

Professor Solomon is also a frequent contributor to mass media. His feature articles have appeared in *Psychology Today, Gentleman's Quarterly*, and *Savvy*. He has been quoted in numerous national magazines and newspapers, including *Allure, Elle, Glamour, Mademoiselle, Mirabella, Newsweek, The New York Times Magazine, Self, USA Today*, and *The Wall Street Journal*. He has been a guest on *The Today Show, Good Morning America*, CNBC, Whittle Communications' Channel One, *Newsweek on the Air, Inside Edition*, and National Public Radio.

Professor Solomon has provided input to a variety of organizations on issues related to consumer behaviour. He has been a consultant to such companies as the Celanese Corporation, Levi Strauss & Company, Johnson & Johnson, Kayser-Roth, United Airlines, and Hakuhodo Advertising (Tokyo). He is also in demand as a speaker to many business groups on consumer behaviour and marketing topics. He lives with his wife, Gail; their three children, Amanda, Zachary, and Alexandra; and Chloe, their golden retriever, in Auburn, Alabama.

Judy Zaichkowsky is Professor of Marketing at the Faculty of Business Administration, Simon Fraser University. She received her Ph.D. from the University of California, Los Angeles, in 1984 in Marketing, with minors in Psychology and Statistics. She holds a Masters in Consumer Studies from the University of Guelph and received a Centenary Alumni award from the University of Guelph in 2003 for outstanding contributions to research. Her knowledge and expertise on the role of involvement in consumer research has had a major impact on the field of marketing. Her 1985 *Journal of Consumer Research* paper on the involvement construct is one of the top 10 cited articles in consumer behaviour and one of the most influential articles in the field of advertising. Professor Zaichkowsky sits on the review boards for the *Journal of Advertising*, the *Journal of Promotion Management, Psychology & Marketing*, and the *Journal of the Academy of Marketing Science*.

Besides this textbook, she is also the author of *Defending Your Brand Against Imitation: Consumer Behavior, Marketing Strategies and Legal Issues*, and the *Psychology Behind Trademark Infringement and Counterfeiting*, which deal with consumer and trademark infringement issues. Professor Zaichkowsky continues to research issues relating to brand imitation, trademark infringement, and design.

In addition to her own research success, Dr. Zaichkowsky brings a perspective that has been shaped by a wealth of experience that includes serving as MBA program director and teaching in the capacity of a visiting scholar and professor in many different countries. She is a member of the Board of Governors at Simon Fraser Unversity.

Rosemary Polegato is Professor of Commerce in the Faculty of Social Sciences at Mount Allison University. Before joining Mount Allison in 1994, Professor Polegato taught at St. Francis Xavier University, the University of Guelph, the University of Toronto, and the University of Western Ontario. She has taught numerous courses in the areas of Business Administration and Consumer Studies, including consumer behaviour (since 1976), marketing research, services and non-profit marketing, marketing management, international marketing, and policy. Professor Polegato earned a B.Sc. (H.E.) from St. Francis Xavier University, an M.Sc. from the University of Guelph, and an MBA and Ph.D. from the Ivey Business School.

Professor Polegato's research interests include cross-cultural consumer behaviour, arts and culture marketing, family decision making, and pedagogical effectiveness. She has published academic articles in these areas, and presents workshops to various audiences. Her publications appear in *Psychology & Marketing*, the *Journal of Advertising Research*, the *Journal of Consumer Affairs*, *Business Quarterly*, and the *Journal of Food Products Marketing*, as well as textbooks and published proceedings of several associations. In 1999, she received a Paul Paré Award for excellence in teaching, research, and service. During 2000–2002, she served as the Coordinator of Leadership at Mount Allison. She lives in Sackville, New Brunswick, with her spouse, Richard, and their tabby cat, Swirls.

Preface

This is the fourth Canadian edition of *Consumer Behaviour*. The changes over these four editions have really made this a unique text that captures the Canadian identity.

The textbook still carries Solomon's trademark of vastly interesting examples and issues. We have tried not to interfere with his winning style, but have definitely added our own "twist." Chapters 12, 13, 14, and 15 are presented with a distinctly Canadian focus. Throughout all the chapters, we have integrated successful Canadian stories.

We have also put our own personal twist on characters and examples of consumption. We realize that many students reading our book will be balancing jobs and families, and perhaps even seeking second careers. We are all consumers. As a result, many of the topics dealt with in this book are of both professional and personal relevance to the reader, whether he or she is a student, professor, or marketing practitioner. Nearly everyone can relate to the trials and tribulations associated with last-minute shopping, primping for a big night out, agonizing over an expensive purchase decision, fantasizing about a week in the Caribbean, celebrating a holiday, or commemorating a landmark event, such as a graduation, getting a driver's licence, or (dreaming about) winning the lottery.

APPROACH AND OBJECTIVE TO BUYING, HAVING, AND BEING

As the book's subtitle suggests, our version of this field goes beyond looking at the act of buying to having and being as well. Consumer behaviour is more than buying things; it also embraces the study of how having (or not having) things affects our lives and how our possessions influence the way we feel about ourselves and about each other—our state of being.

In addition to understanding why people buy things, we also try to appreciate how products, services, and consumption activities contribute to the broader social world we experience. Whether shopping, cooking, cleaning, playing basketball, hanging out at the beach, or even looking at ourselves in the mirror, our lives are touched by the marketing system. And, as if these experiences were not complex enough, the task of understanding the consumer multiplies geometrically when a multicultural perspective is taken. In addition to the numerous examples of marketing and consumer practices relating to consumers and companies, chapters contain boxes called "Multicultural Dimensions" that highlight cultural differences in consumer behaviour.

The book also emphasizes the importance of understanding consumers in formulating marketing strategy. Many (if not most) of the fundamental concepts in marketing are based on the practitioner's ability to know people. After all, if we don't understand why people behave as they do, how can we identify their needs? If we can't identify their needs, how can we satisfy those needs? If we can't satisfy people's needs, we don't have a marketing concept, so we might as well fold our tents and go home! To illustrate the potential of consumer research to inform marketing strategy, the text contains numerous examples of specific applications of consumer behaviour concepts by marketing practitioners, as well as examples of windows of opportunity where such concepts could be used—perhaps by alert strategists after taking this course! Many of these possibilities are highlighted in special features called "Marketing Opportunities."

This strategic focus is, however, tempered by an important qualification: Unlike some contemporary treatments of consumer behaviour, this book does not assume that everything marketers do is in the best interests of consumers or of their environment. Likewise, as consumers, we do many things that are not positive either. People are plagued by addictions, status envy, ethnocentrism, racism, sexism, and other "isms," and, regrettably, there are times when marketing activities—deliberately or not—encourage or exploit these human failings. This book deals with the totality of consumer behaviour, warts and all. Marketing mistakes or ethically suspect activities are also highlighted in special features labelled "Marketing Pitfalls."

FEATURES OF THE FOURTH CANADIAN EDITION

The fourth Canadian edition of *Consumer Behaviour* retains and updates the best elements of the previous edition.

 CBC Video Vignettes: Fifteen written video cases are provided at key points in the text, supported by exciting videos from CBC news programs. These videos and cases help to bring key concepts and issues to life in the classroom.

 Canadian/Regional Dimensions: Chapter 14 features several examples of consumer behaviour from a specifically Canadian perspective.

Case Appendix: Several written cases appear in an appendix at the end of the book. Some of these cases cross various chapters, which instructors should find useful.

 Multicultural Dimensions: These examples are reminders of cross-cultural differences in consumer behaviour.

 Net Profit: This boxed feature highlights recent developments of interest on the internet.

 The Tangled Web: This feature explores the downside of virtual consumer behaviour.

 Reality Check: These text boxes present the opinions of students from around the world on hot issues and topics in consumer behaviour.

Weblinks: We have included weblinks throughout each chapter. Web users are reminded that, although the sites are checked thoroughly prior to printing, addresses may change or be inaccessible or unavailable at a particular time.

ADDITIONAL LEARNING AIDS

Chapter-opening example: Each chapter starts with an interesting vignette that introduces the chapter material and helps spark student interest.

Full-colour figures, photographs, advertisements, and illustrations: Throughout each chapter, key concepts and applications are illustrated with strong, full-colour visual materials.

Key Terms: Key terms are highlighted within the text and listed at the end of each chapter with page references. All of the key terms are collected together in the glossary at the back of the book, and are boldfaced with their page references in the subject index.

Chapter Summary: This feature provides a concise review of the chapter's key topics.

Review Questions: These straighforward questions draw attention to key concepts and theories in each chapter.

Consumer Behaviour Challenge: Each chapter contains two sets of questions that challenge the student to apply the key issues covered: *Discussion Questions* encourage dialogue about important issues in consumer behaviour. *Experiential Exercises* connect learners directly to the marketplace and communities that provide the contexts for consumer behaviour. Many new questions have been added to this edition.

Indexes: A subject index and a product, service, corporate, and celebrity index reference all information and examples in the book.

SUPPLEMENTS

Consumer Behaviour, Fourth Canadian Edition, is accompanied by a complete supplements package.

Instructor's Resource CD-ROM: This comprehensive instructor's resource contains electronic versions of the following supplements: Instructor's Resource Manual, TestGen test-generating software, PowerPoint Slides, and the Image Library.

Instructor's Resource Manual with Video Guide: The Instructor's Resource Manual with Video Guide contains lecture notes, field project ideas, answers to the questions in each Consumer Behaviour Challenge, and informative case notes for the CBC Video Vignettes and case appendix.

TestGenerator: The test bank contains more than 1700 multiple-choice, true/false, and short-essay questions. Each question is rated by level of difficulty and includes a text page reference.

PowerPoint Slides: Over 150 transparency masters highlighting key concepts featured in the text are available electronically in PowerPoint.

Pearson Education Canada/CBC Video Library: Pearson Education Canada and the CBC have worked together to bring you segments from the CBC series *Venture, The National,* and *Marketplace.* Designed specifically to complement the text, this case collection is an excellent tool for bringing students in contact with the world outside the classroom. These programs have extremely high production quality and have been chosen to relate directly to chapter content. Please contact your Pearson Education Canada sales representative for details.

Companion Website: For a multitude of practice questions, key terms, and concepts, weblinks to related sites, newsgroups, CBC video updates and more, check out the *Consumer Behaviour,* 4/C/e, Companion Website at **www.pearsoned. ca/solomon**.

Image Library: The Image Library contains all the Canadian advertisements featured in this edition, as well as all the figures and tables.

Acknowledgments

The Canadian authors would like to thank Michael Solomon for continuing to provide updated, relevant material and interesting revisions. We thank our reviewers for their extensive and valuable comments: Alan Chapelle, Malaspina University College; Robert Palmer, Bishop's University; Robert Soroka, Dawson College; Perry Boome, Fanshawe College; Kalyani Menon, Wilfred Laurier University; May Aung, University of Guelph; Magdalena Cismaru, University of Regina; Allen Richert, Confederation College; Charles Royce, McGill University; and Cindy Stewart, University of British Columbia. We also owe much to our colleagues who wrote many interesting articles that were incorporated into this edition. We may have missed many additional important papers and hope our colleagues will point out to us where these can be added to the text for future editions. Work from many Canadian colleagues was a great help: Carmen Cullen, Brock University; Doug Olsen, University of Calgary; Louise Heslop, Judith Madill, and Nick Papadopoulous at Carleton University; Christopher Ross and Gad Saad at Concordia University; Karen Finlay, John Liefeld, and Marjorie Wall at University of Guelph; Donna Sears, McGill University (doctoral studies); Lanita Carter, Memorial University; Dierdre Grondin and Judy Ann Roy at University of New Brunswick; Stephen Arnold, Peggy Cunningham, and Shirley Taylor at Queen's University; Rhonda Watson, University of Regina; Tammi Feltham, University of Saskatchewan; Ida Berger, University of Toronto; Anne Lavack, University of Regina; and Brenda Gainer and Eileen Fischer at York University. Off-continent contributors include Benoit Heilbrunn at ESCP-EAP Paris and Espen Andersen at the Norwegian School of Management. Statistics Canada was also very helpful as a provider of Canadian data. A special thanks goes to Colleen Collins-Dodd, whose enthusiasm for finding interesting articles and applications for this text is unsurpassed.

We appreciate the work of the staff at Pearson Education Canada, including Laura Forbes, Joanne Scattolon, Leanne Rancourt, Marisa D'Andrea, Andrea Falkenberg, Debbie Kumpf, Anthony Leung, and Lisa Brant. Last but not least, the copy editor Linda Bellio was a delight to work with and caught many inconsistencies and flaws before production.

Michael R. Solomon
Judith L. Zaichkowsky
Rosemary Polegato

A Great Way to Learn and Instruct Online

The Pearson Education Canada Companion Website is easy to navigate and is organized to correspond to the chapters in this textbook. Whether you are a student in the classroom or a distance learner you will discover helpful resources for in-depth study and research that empower you in your quest for greater knowledge and maximize your potential for success in the course.

Companion
Website

[www.pearsoned.ca/solomon]

Enter

PEARSON
Prentice
Hall

Jump to... http://www.pearsoned.ca/solomon   Home | Search | Help | Profile

Companion
Website

Home >

Companion Website

Consumer Behaviour, Fourth Canadian Edition, by Solomon, Zaichkowsky, and Polegato

Student Resources

The modules in this section provide students with tools for learning course material. These modules include:

- Chapter Outline
- Chapter Summaries
- Weblinks
- Internet Exercises
- Self-Study Questions (Essay, Multiple Choice, and True/False)
- Comprehensive Cases
- Key Terms Net Search
- Net News
- Link to Video Central

In the self-study modules, students can send answers to the grader and receive instant feedback on their progress through the Results Reporter. Coaching comments and references to the textbook may be available to ensure that students take advantage of all available resources to enhance their learning experience.

Instructor Resources

A link to the protected Instructor's Central site provides instructors with additional teaching tools. Downloadable PowerPoint Presentations, Comprehensive Cases, and an Instructor's Manual are just some of the materials that may be available in this section. Where appropriate, this section will be password protected. To get a password, simply contact your Pearson Education Canada Representative or call Faculty Sales and Services at 1-800-850-5813.

SECTION → 1

Consumers in the Marketplace

This introductory section provides an overview of the field of consumer behaviour. Chapter 1 looks at how the field of marketing is influenced by the actions of consumers and how we as consumers are influenced by marketers. It describes the discipline of consumer behaviour and some of the different approaches to understanding what makes consumers tick. It also highlights the importance of the study of consumer behaviour to public policy issues such as addiction and environmentalism.

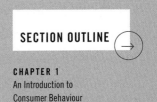

SECTION OUTLINE →

Gail is killing time before her accounting class by surfing the web in her room. Since she's been studying for her accounting and marketing exams, she realizes she hasn't looked at any interesting sites in weeks. Enough of the serious stuff, she decides. It's time for some *really* educational surfing. So, where to go first? Gail figures she'll start at one of the popular women's portals and see what happens. She goes to *www.ivillage.com*, where she checks her horoscope (cool! a good day to start a new relationship), scans a few beauty tips, and takes a Great Date quiz (uh-oh, this new guy, Bruce, she's been seeing may need to be replaced). Similar stuff is going on at *www.Oxygen.com*.

Gail decides to check out what "real people" are doing on the web. First she checks the clubs she belongs to at *www.collegeclub.com*—wow, more than 30 people from her campus are logged on right now! Looks like other students are studying as hard as she is! Then she clicks over to *www.camville.com* to decide which live web cam she'd like to peek in on today. The site has tons of them: cameras trained on real guys and women just doing their thing at work or at home. Most of these are pretty boring; there's even a "DissCam" site featuring a balding graduate student who can be observed writing his dissertation! Yawn. She finally settles on "DormCam," a live feed from a room with four residents just doing what students do. For a few minutes, she watches the riveting spectacle of one of the guys brushing his teeth and getting ready to go to class. Hey, it's not exactly an Eminem concert, but it sure beats studying for accounting!

An Introduction to Consumer Behaviour

INTRODUCTION

Consumer Behaviour: People in the Marketplace

This book is about people like Gail. It concerns the products and services they buy and use and the ways these purchases fit into their lives. This introductory chapter briefly describes some important aspects of the field of consumer behaviour and some of the essential explanations for how people interact with the marketing system.

For now, though, let's return to one "typical" consumer: Gail, the business major. This brief discussion allows us to highlight some aspects of consumer behaviour that will be covered in the rest of this book.

- As a consumer, Gail can be described and compared with other individuals in a number of ways. For some purposes, marketers might find it useful to categorize Gail in terms of her age, sex, income, or occupation. These are some examples of descriptive characteristics of a population, or *demographics*. In other cases, marketers would rather know something about Gail's interests in clothing or music, or the way she spends her leisure time. This sort of information comes under the category of *psychographics*, which refers to aspects of a person's lifestyle and personality. Knowledge of consumer characteristics plays an extremely important role in many marketing applications, such as defining the market for a product or deciding upon the appropriate techniques to employ when targeting a certain group of consumers.

- Gail's purchase decisions are heavily influenced by the opinions and behaviours of her friends. A lot of product information, as well as recommendations to use or avoid particular brands, is transmitted by conversations among real people, rather than by way of television commercials, magazines, or billboards, or even bizarre websites. The growth of the web has created thousands of online **consumption communities** where members share views and product recommendations about anything from Barbie dolls to BlackBerries. The bonds among Gail's group are cemented by the products they use in common. There is also pressure on each group member to buy things that will meet with the group's approval, and there is often a price to pay in the form of group rejection or embarrassment when one member does not conform to others' conceptions of what is good or bad, or "in" or "out."

- As members of a large society, people share certain cultural values or strongly held beliefs about the way the world should be structured. Other values are shared by members of *subcultures,* or smaller groups within the culture, such as French Canadians, teens, "prairie people," or even "Hell's Angels."

- When examining websites, Gail was exposed to many competing "brands." There were numerous sites that did not capture her attention at all, while there were others that she barely noticed or rejected because they did not fit the "image" with which she identified or to which she aspired. Using *market segmentation strategies* means targeting a brand only to a specific group of consumers rather than to everybody—even if it means that other consumers will not be interested in or may even deliberately avoid that brand.

- Brands often have clearly defined images or "personalities" created by product advertising, packaging, branding, and other marketing strategies that focus on positioning a product a certain way. The choice of a favourite website is very much a lifestyle statement: It says a lot about what a person is interested in, as well as something about the type of person he or she would like to be. People often choose a product because they like its image or because they feel that its personality somehow corresponds to their own. Moreover, a consumer may believe that when he or she buys and uses the product or service, its desirable qualities will magically "rub off" onto him or her.

- When a product succeeds in satisfying a consumer's specific needs or desires, it may be rewarded with many years of *brand loyalty,* a bond between product and consumer that is very difficult for competitors to break. Often a change in the consumer's life situation or self-concept is required to weaken this bond and thus create opportunities for competitors.

- Consumers' evaluations of products are affected by the products' appearance, taste, texture, or smell. We may be swayed by the shape and colour of a package, as well as by more subtle factors such as the symbolism used in a brand name, in an advertisement, or even in the choice of a cover model for a magazine. These judgments are affected by—and often reflect—how a society feels that people should define themselves at that point in time. If asked, Gail might not even be able to say exactly why she considered some websites and rejected others. Many product meanings are hidden below the surface of the packaging and advertising, and this book will discuss some of the methods used by marketers and social scientists to discover or apply these meanings.

- As Gail found, our opinions and desires increasingly are shaped by input from around the world, which is becoming a much smaller place because of rapid advancements in communications and transportation systems. In today's global culture, consumers often prize products and services that "transport" them to different places and allow them to experience the diversity of other cultures—even if only to watch others brush their teeth.

What Is Consumer Behaviour?

The field of **consumer behaviour** covers a lot of ground: *It is the study of the processes involved when individuals or groups select, purchase, use, or dispose of products, services, ideas, or experiences to satisfy needs and desires.* Consumers take many forms, ranging from an eight-year-old child begging her mother for a Groovy Girl doll to a large corporation's executive choosing a multimillion-dollar computer system. The items that are consumed can include anything from canned peas to a massage, democracy to hip hop music, and even other people (the images of rock stars, for example). Needs and desires to be satisfied range from hunger and thirst to love, status, or even spiritual fulfillment. And, as we'll see throughout this book, people can get passionate about a broad range of products. For example, maybe you're one of a growing number of "sneakerheads" who covet rare models and measure time not by years but by Air Jordan editions. If so, get your kicks at websites like ***www.instyleshoes.com*** and ***www.kickz.com.***[1]

CONSUMERS ARE ACTORS ON THE MARKETPLACE STAGE

The perspective of **role theory** is that much of consumer behaviour resembles actions in a play.[2] As in a play, each consumer has lines, props, and costumes that are necessary for a good performance. Since people act out many different roles, they sometimes alter their consumption decisions, depending on the particular "play" they are in at the time. The criteria that they use to evaluate products and services in one of their roles may be quite different from those used in another role.

CONSUMER BEHAVIOUR IS A PROCESS

In its early stages of development, the field of consumer behaviour was often referred to as *buyer behaviour,* reflecting an emphasis on the interaction between consumers and producers at the time of purchase. Marketers now recognize that consumer behaviour is an ongoing *process,* not merely what happens at the moment a consumer hands over money or a credit card and in turn receives a good or service.

The **exchange**, in which two or more organizations or people give and receive something of value, is an integral part of marketing.[3] Although exchange is an important part of consumer behaviour, the expanded view emphasizes the entire consumption process, which includes the issues that influence the consumer before, during, and after a purchase. Figure 1–1 illustrates some of the issues that are addressed during each stage of the consumption process.

CONSUMER BEHAVIOUR INVOLVES MANY DIFFERENT ACTORS

A consumer is generally thought of as a person who identifies a need or desire, makes a purchase, and then disposes of the product during the three stages in the consumption process. In many cases, however, different people may be involved in the process. The *purchaser* and *user* of a product might not be the same person, as when a parent picks out clothes for a teenager (and makes selections that can result

---

FIGURE 1–1   SOME ISSUES THAT ARISE DURING STAGES IN THE CONSUMPTION PROCESS

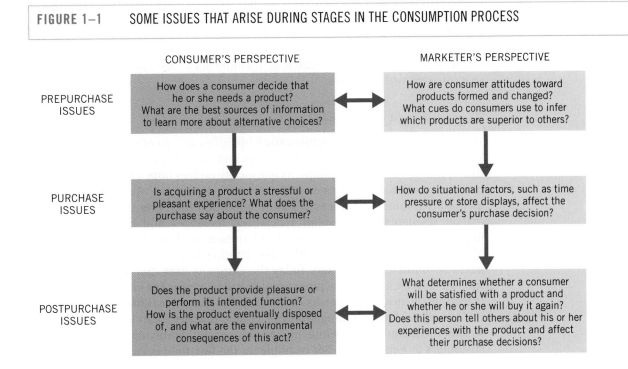

in "fashion suicide" in the view of the teen). In other cases, another person may act as an *influencer*, providing recommendations for or against certain products without actually buying or using them. For example, a friend accompanying a teen on a shopping trip might actually pick out the clothes that the teen decides to purchase.

Finally, consumers may be organizations or groups in which one person may make the decisions involved in purchasing products that will be used by many, as when a purchasing agent orders the company's office supplies. In other organizational situations, purchase decisions may be made by a large group of people—for example, company accountants, designers, engineers, sales personnel, and others—all of whom will have a say in the various stages of the consumption process. As we'll see in Chapter 12, one type of important organization is the family; different family members play pivotal roles in decision making regarding products and services used by all.

CONSUMERS' IMPACT ON MARKETING STRATEGY

Surfing cool websites can be a lot of fun (almost as much fun as actually making the purchases!). But, on the more serious side, why should managers, advertisers, and other marketing professionals bother to learn about consumer behaviour?

Very simply, *understanding consumer behaviour* is good business. A basic marketing concept states that firms exist to satisfy consumers' needs. These needs can be satisfied only to the extent that marketers understand the people or organizations that will use the products and services they are trying to sell—and that they do so *better* than their competitors.

Consumer response is the ultimate test of whether or not a marketing strategy will succeed. Thus, knowledge about consumers is incorporated into virtually every facet of a successful marketing plan. Data about consumers help marketers to define the market and to identify threats to a brand and opportunities for it. And, in the wild and wacky world of marketing, nothing is forever. This knowledge also helps to ensure that the product continues to appeal to its core market. The Sony Walkman is a good example of a successful product that needed to update its image. Although Sony revolutionized the mobile music experience and sold almost 300 million Walkmans in the process, recent research found that today's teens see portable cassette players as dinosaurs. The company's advertising agency followed 125 teens to see how they use products in their day-to-day lives. Now the product has been relaunched with a removable "Memory Stick" instead of a cassette player so it can work with MP3 files.

Segmenting Consumers

The process of **marketing segmentation** identifies groups of consumers who are similar to one another in one or more ways and then devises marketing strategies that appeal to one or more groups. As our society evolves from a mass culture where many consumers share the same preferences to a diverse one where we have almost an infinite number of choices, it's more important than ever to identify distinct market segments and develop specialized messages and products. It's also important to deliver those specialized messages through diverse channels. McDonald's now devotes one-third of its marketing budget to television—compared with two-thirds five years ago. Today the company uses that leftover money to sponsor closed-circuit sports programming and to pay for ads in custom-published magazines, in-store video networks, and websites like *www.iVillage.com*.[4]

As we'll see later, building loyalty to a brand is a very smart marketing strategy, so sometimes companies define market segments by identifying their most faithful customers or heavy users. For example, in the fast-food industry the loyal user accounts for only one of five customers but for about 60 percent of all visits to fast-food restaurants. Taco Bell developed the Chalupa, a deep-fried and higher-calorie version of its Gordita stuffed pita, to appeal to its frequent users, and Burger King came up with its Great American Burger for the same reason. The Checkers burger chain describes its core customer as a single male under age 30 who has a working-class job, loves loud music, doesn't read much, and hangs out with friends.[5] To attract the same customer, Hardee's recently unveiled its Monster Thickburger, which weighs in at 1418 calories. Comedian Jay Leno even joked that the burger comes in a cardboard box shaped like a coffin![6] Aside from frequent use of a product, there are many dimensions that can be used to slice up a larger market.

Demographics are statistics that measure observable aspects of a population, such as birth rate, age distribution, and income. Statistics Canada is a major source of demographic data on families. This information is available on the internet at *www.statcan.ca*. The changes and trends revealed in demographic studies are of great interest to marketers, because the data can be used to locate and predict the sizes of markets for many products, ranging from home mortgages to brooms and can openers. Imagine trying to sell baby food to a single male, or an around-the-world vacation to a couple making $15 000 a year!

Table 1–1 provides a statistical snapshot of the "typical" Canadian consumer, based on data compiled from Statistics Canada. As you go down this list, you will quickly see that many characteristics do not apply directly to you. How different are you from this consumer?

In this book, we'll explore many of the important demographic variables that make consumers the same as or different from others. We'll also consider other important characteristics that are not so easy to measure, such as *psychographics*—differences in consumers' personalities and tastes that can't be objectively measured. For now, let's summarize a few of the most important demographic dimensions, each of which will be developed in more detail in later chapters.

TABLE 1–1

A STATISTICAL PICTURE OF THE AVERAGE OR TYPICAL CANADIAN CONSUMER

- The typical Canadian is a woman who is 37.8 years old.
- The average Canadian worked approximately 37 hours per week in 2003.
- The average income of a Canadian was approximately $728 per week in 2005.
- In 2004 the average Canadian household spent $12 200 on shelter.
- In 2001 the typical Canadian household spent $86 per week at food stores.
- During 2001 this average household also spent $38 on restaurant meals per week.
- In 2001 the average Canadian ate 62.86 kg of red meat and 192 eggs.
- In 2004 the average household spent $897 on personal care.
- The average household spent $2506 on clothing purchases in 2004.
- During 2004 the typical household spent $297 on child-care expenses.
- In 2004 the average Canadian spent $1690 on healthcare.
- The average household spent $639 on entertainment in 2001.
- The average Canadian watched 21.4 hours of television per week during 2004.

Sources: Based on Statistics Canada, *Annual Demographic Statistics, 2002*, Cat. no. 91-213; Statistics Canada, *Labour Force Information, April 2003*, Cat. no. 71-001; Statistics Canada, *Survey of Household Spending, 2001*; Statistics Canada, *Food Consumption in Canada, 2001*, Cat. no. 32-229; Statistics Canada, *Food Expenditure in Canada, 2001*, Cat. no. 62-554-XIE; Statistics Canada, *Television Project, Fall 2001*, Cat. no. 87F0006XPE; Statistics Canada, *Average Household Expenditures, 2004*, Table 203-0001; CANSIM/StatsCan 2005—Earnings, Average Weekly, Cat. No. 72-002-X.

AGE

Consumers of different age groups obviously have very different needs and wants. Although people who belong to the same age group differ in many other ways, they do tend to share a set of values and common cultural experiences that they carry throughout life.[7] In some cases, marketers initially develop a product to attract one age group and then try to broaden its appeal later on. That's what the high-octane energy drink Red Bull is doing. Red Bull was aggressively introduced in bars, nightclubs, and gyms to the product's core audience of young people. Over time, the drink became popular in other contexts, and now the company is sponsoring the PGA European Tour to broaden its reach to older golfers (who probably aren't up to partying all night). It's also handing out free cans to commuters, cab drivers, and car-rental agencies to market the drink as a way to stay alert on the road.[8]

GENDER

Many products, from fragrances to footwear, are targeted at either men or women. Differentiating by gender starts at a very early age—even diapers are sold in pink versions for girls and blue for boys. In 2002, an all-female marketing team at Procter & Gamble, who jokingly call themselves "chicks in charge," introduced "Crest Rejuvenating Effects," the first mass-market toothpaste positioned just for women. Packaged in a teal tube nestled inside a glimmering "pearlescent" box, the toothpaste is sparkly and teal-toned, and tastes of vanilla and cinnamon.[9]

FAMILY STRUCTURE

A person's family and marital status is another important demographic variable because it has such a big effect on a consumer's spending priorities. Young singles and newlyweds are the most likely to exercise; to go to bars, concerts, and movies; and to consume alcohol. Families with young children are big purchasers of health foods and fruit juices, while single-parent households and those with older children buy more junk food. Home maintenance services are most likely to be used by older couples and dual-career couples.

SOCIAL CLASS AND INCOME

People who are grouped within the same social class are approximately equal in terms of their incomes and social standing in the community. They work in roughly similar occupations, and they tend to have similar tastes in music, clothing, art, and so on. They also tend to socialize with one another and share many ideas and values regarding the way life should be lived.[10] The distribution of wealth is of great interest to marketers because it determines which groups have the greatest buying power and market potential.

ETHNICITY

Multiculturalism and Canada go hand in hand. We are a country that comprises immigrants from all over the globe. Canada accepts nearly one million immigrants and refugees every four years, by far the highest per capita rate of immigration in the world.[11] We are diverse in our languages and in the cultural consumption that stems from our different ethnicities. For example, English is now a minority language in Vancouver. The growth of the Asian market in Canada has led to trilingual labelling of some products. Since Canadians blend together from many different racial and cultural backgrounds, we also blend together in our consumption heritage, as signified by food. As a culture, we are just as likely to enjoy eating sushi as pyrohy or lasagna. It is a rich experience to be a Canadian.

GEOGRAPHY

The climate changes drastically from region to region in Canada, which makes segmenting some products by region very obvious. For example, more snow blowers

I want to be...

a hockey player. A basketball star. An actor. I want to play the violin. Win an Olympic medal. At Air Canada, we take the dreams of children very seriously. That's why we're always ready to sponsor events like the BTI's Breakfast for Learning. After all, when kids get off to a good start, there's just no telling how far they'll go.

AIR CANADA ✦

← Many firms, like Air Canada, are recognizing racial diversity in their advertising.
Courtesy of Air Canada and Marketel.

and fur coats are sold east of the Rocky Mountains, more umbrellas and rain coats to the west. Humidifiers and dehumidifiers are a must in regions around the Great Lakes. On the Prairies, it is not unusual for people to have two or more freezers in their basements. Many people who live in farming regions preserve the food they produce for winter and year-round consumption.

Within regions, there are some different cultural pockets and hence differences in food tastes. New Brunswick has the highest consumption of sliced white bread, while Alberta leads in bubble-gum sales. Most corn flakes are sold on the Prairies, and linguini has its highest sales in Toronto. Quebecers consume the least amount of frozen french fries, preferring the real thing.[12]

LIFESTYLES: BEYOND DEMOGRAPHICS

Consumers also have very different lifestyles, even if they share other characteristics such as gender or age. The way we feel about ourselves, the things we value, the things we like to do in our spare time—all of these factors help to determine which products will push our buttons, or even those that will make us feel better. Based on a lifestyle analysis, Procter & Gamble developed the heartburn medicine Prilosec OTC with an ideal customer in mind. Her name is Joanne, and she's a mother over 35 who's more likely to get heartburn from a cup of coffee than from an overdose of pizza and beer. A P&G executive observed, "We know Joanne. We know what she feels. We know what she eats. We know what else she likes to buy in the store."[13]

Relationship Marketing: Building Bonds with Consumers

Marketers are carefully defining customer segments and listening to people in their markets as never before. Many of them have realized that a key to success is building relationships that will last a lifetime between brands and customers. Marketers who believe in this philosophy, called **relationship marketing**, are making an effort to interact with customers on a regular basis, giving them reasons to maintain a bond with the company over time.

Relationship building is made easy for us courtesy of **database marketing,** which involves tracking consumers' buying habits very closely and crafting products and messages tailored precisely to people's wants and needs based on this information. Wal-Mart collects massive amounts of information about the 100 million people who visit its stores each week, and the company uses this data to fine-tune its offerings. When the company analyzed how shoppers' buying patterns changed when major hurricanes were predicted in the southern United States, for example, it discovered that people do a lot more than just stock up on flashlights: sales of strawberry Pop-Tarts increased by about 700 percent. The top-selling product of all? Beer. Based on these insights, Wal-Mart loads trucks with toaster pastries and six-packs to stock local stores when a big storm approaches.[14]

Sophisticated companies, such as American Express, General Motors, and Kraft General Foods, are combining and constantly updating information from public records and marketing research surveys with data volunteered by consumers themselves when they return warranty cards, enter sweepstakes, or purchase from catalogues. These companies build complex databases that fine-tune their knowledge of what people are buying and how often.

MARKETING'S IMPACT ON CONSUMERS

For better or for worse, we all live in a world that is significantly influenced by the actions of marketers. We are surrounded by marketing stimuli in the form of advertisements, stores, and products competing for our attention and our dollars. Much of what we learn about the world is filtered by marketers, whether through the affluence depicted in glamorous magazine advertising or via the roles played by family members in commercials. Ads show us how we should act with regard to recycling, alcohol consumption, and even the types of houses and cars we wish to own. In many ways we are also "at the mercy" of marketers, since we rely on them to sell us products that are safe and that perform as promised, to tell us the truth about what they are selling, and to price and distribute these products fairly.

Marketing and Culture

Popular culture, consisting of the music, movies, sports, books, celebrities, and other forms of entertainment consumed by the mass market, is both a product of and an inspiration for marketers. Our lives are also affected in far-reaching ways, ranging from how we acknowledge cultural events such as marriage, death, or holidays to how we view social issues such as air pollution, gambling, and addictions. The Stanley Cup, holiday shopping, federal elections, newspaper recycling, and Barbie dolls are all examples of products and activities that touch many lives.

This cultural influence is hard to overlook, although many people do not seem to realize how much their views of the world around them—their movie and musical heroes, the latest fashions, food and decorating choices, and even the physical features that they find attractive or ugly in men and women—are affected by marketers.

For example, consider the product icons that marketers use to create an identity for their products. Various mythical creatures and personalities—from the Pillsbury Doughboy to Sasquatch—have been at one time or another central figures in popular culture. In fact, it is likely that more consumers could recognize such characters than could identify past prime ministers, business leaders, or artists. Although these figures never really existed, many of us feel as if we "know" them, and they certainly are effective *spokescharacters* for the products they represent. If you don't believe it, visit *www.toymuseum.com*.

The Meaning of Consumption

One of the fundamental premises of the modern field of consumer behaviour is that *people often buy products not for what they do, but for what they mean*. This principle does not imply that a product's basic function is unimportant, but rather that the roles products play in our lives go well beyond the tasks they perform. And the deeper meanings of a product may help it to stand out from other, similar goods and services: All things being equal, a person will choose the brand that has an image (or even a personality!) consistent with his or her underlying needs.

For example, although most people probably couldn't run faster or jump higher if they were wearing Nikes versus Adidas, many diehard loyalists swear by their favourite brand. These arch-rivals are largely marketed in terms of their images—

meanings that have been carefully crafted with the help of legions of rock stars, athletes, and slickly produced commercials—and many millions of dollars. So, when you buy a Nike "swoosh," you may be doing more than choosing footwear; you may also be making a lifestyle statement about the type of person you are or want to be. For a relatively simple item made of leather and laces, that's quite a feat!

Our allegiances to particular sneakers, musicians, or soft drinks help us to define our place in modern society, and these choices also help each of us to form bonds with others who share similar preferences. This comment by a participant in a focus group captures the curious bonding that can be caused by consumption choices: "I was at a Stanley Cup party, and I picked up an obscure drink. Somebody else across the room went 'yo!' because he had the same thing. People feel a connection when you're drinking the same thing."[15]

As we have already seen, one trademark of marketing strategies today is an emphasis on building relationships with customers. While the nature of these relationships can vary, researchers have found that, like friendships and love affairs, our relationships with brands evolve over time—some resemble deep friendships while others are more like exciting but short-lived flings.[16]

Following are some of the types of relationships consumers can have with a product:

- *Self-concept attachment:* The product helps to establish the user's identity.
- *Nostalgic attachment:* The product serves as a link with a past self.
- *Interdependence:* The product is a part of the user's daily routine.
- *Love:* The product elicits emotional bonds of warmth, passion, or other strong emotions.[17]

The Global Consumer

The majority of people on Earth live in urban centres. In fact, the number of megacities, defined as urban centres of 10 million people or more, is projected to grow to 26 in 2015.[18] Already, China boasts four shopping centres that are larger than the massive West Edmonton Mall, and within five years it will be home to seven of the world's largest malls.[19] One by-product of sophisticated marketing strategies is the movement toward a *global consumer culture*, where people around the world are united by their common devotion to brand-name consumer goods, movie stars, and celebrities.[20]

The rise of global marketing means that even smaller companies are looking to expand overseas—and this increases the pressure to understand how customers in other countries are the same as or different from the customers in the host country. In the restaurant industry, for example, Shakey's pizza restaurants are mushrooming in the Philippines, and food from the International House of Pancakes is selling like hot cakes in Tokyo. But menu changes are sometimes called for to please local palates: Schlotzsky's in Malaysia offers Smokey Mountain Chicken Crunch with "half-virgin" chicken, and diners in Bob's Big Boy in Thailand snap up Tropical Shrimp, deep fried with "exotic breading."[21] This book will pay special attention to the good and bad aspects of this cultural homogenization. Many chapters feature boxes called *Multicultural Dimensions* that spotlight some international aspect of consumer behaviour, an issue that will also be explored in depth in Chapter 17.

VIRTUAL CONSUMPTION

There's little doubt that the Digital Revolution is one of the most significant influences on consumer behaviour, and the web's impact will continue to expand as more and more people around the world hook in.

Electronic marketing has increased convenience by breaking down many of the barriers caused by time and location. You can shop 24 hours a day without leaving

Net Profit +

As new technologies develop, surfing the web by sitting in front of a PC will become the old model, eventually vanishing like the horse and buggy. **U-commerce** refers to the ubiquitous networks that will slowly but surely become a part of our society, whether in the form of wearable computers or customized advertisements beamed to us on our cell phones ("Hey, you're walking by McDonald's. Come on in for today's burger special.").[28]

Many products carry a plastic RFID tag containing a computer chip and a tiny antenna that lets the chip communicate with a network. Grocery items tell the store what needs to be restocked and which items are past their expiration dates. Your house will know when you're pulling into the driveway and will turn on the lights and start your favourite tunes spinning before you walk in the door. Already, IBM has introduced "smart" washers and dryers in some university dorms, which let students keep tabs on their laundry from anywhere they can access the internet—their dorm rooms, the library, or even a cell phone. Students can log on to a webpage to see whether there are machines free and receive email or a page when their load is finished.[29]

home; you can read today's newspaper without getting drenched when picking up a hard copy in a rainstorm; and you don't have to wait for the six o'clock news to find out what the weather will be like tomorrow—at home or around the globe. And, with the increasing use of handheld devices and wireless communications, you can get that same information—from stock quotes to the weather—even when you're away from your computer.[22]

And it's not all about businesses selling to consumers (**B2C commerce**). In addition, the cyberspace explosion has created a revolution in consumer-to-consumer activity (**C2C commerce**). Just as e-consumers are not limited to local retail outlets in their shopping, they are not limited to their local communities when looking for friends. Picture a small group of local collectors who meet once a month at a diner to discuss their shared interests over coffee. Now multiply that group by thousands, and include people from all over the world who are united by a shared passion for sports memorabilia, Barbie dolls, Harley-Davidson motorcycles, refrigerator magnets, or simulated neighbourhoods built using "The Sims Online" (where players can give characters real products including a computer with a Pentium 4 chip or McDonald's fries). Welcome to the new world of *virtual brand communities*. To appreciate the potential marketing power of these brand communities, consider the Hollywood Stock Exchange (***www.hsx.com***). This website offers a simulated entertainment stock market where traders predict the four-week box office take for each film. Major studios and actors cannot afford to ignore this customer community when making their "real" development and marketing decisions.

The popularity of chat rooms where consumers can discuss various topics with like-minded netizens around the world grows every day. News reports tell us of the sometimes wonderful and sometimes horrific romances that begin on the internet as people check out potential mates on sites such as ***www.lavalife.com.*** (In a recent month, 26 million people visited online dating sites!).[23] A Swiss company called ***www.skim.com*** even lets you log in to pursue someone you see in "RL" (real life). Each user is issued a six-digit number that he or she wears on jackets and backpacks sold by the company. When you see someone on the street or in a club you'd like to get to know better, you go to ***www.skim.com***, type in the person's number, and send him or her a message. If you're "lucky" enough to receive one, you can decide whether to respond.[24] The web also provides an easy way for consumers around the world to exchange information about their experiences with products. ***Amazon.com*** encourages shoppers to write reviews of books.

Will the web bring people closer together or drive each of us into our own private virtual world? A recent survey found that more than one-third of respondents who have access to the internet reported that they were online at least five hours a week. Sixty percent of internet users said they had reduced their television viewing, while one-third said they spent less time reading newspapers.

On the other hand, reports show that more than one-half of users surveyed felt that email actually strengthened family ties. Users reported far more offline social contact than non-users.[25] These results argue that people may be spending more time than ever with others. It's just that they are forming strong relationships over the internet instead of in person. But the author of the first survey disagreed. As he observed, "If I go home at 6:30 in the evening and spend the whole night sending email and wake up the next morning, I still haven't talked to my wife or kids or friends. When you spend your time on the internet, you don't hear a human voice and you never get a hug."[26] A follow-up study found that it works both ways—extroverts tend to make even more friends on the web, while introverts feel even more cut off from the rest of the world. This has been termed the "rich get richer" model of internet use.[27] So our new electronic world is both good and bad. Throughout this book, we'll look at some examples of the pros and the cons of virtual consumer behaviour in boxes called *Net Profit* and *The Tangled Web*.

Blurred Boundaries: Marketing and Reality

Marketers and consumers coexist in a complicated, two-way relationship. It's sometimes hard to tell where marketing efforts leave off and "the real world" begins. One result of these blurred boundaries is that we are no longer sure (and perhaps we don't care) where the line separating this fabricated world from reality begins and ends. In fact, sometimes we gleefully join in to further obscure it. A storyline in a recent *Wonder Woman* comic book features the usual out-of-this-world exploits of a vivacious superhero. But, it also includes the real-world marriage proposal of Todd McDevitt, the owner of a chain of comic book stores who persuaded DC Comics to let him woo his beloved in the issue.[30]

To what degree is the world of popular culture—and even consumers' perceptions of reality—shaped by the efforts of marketers? More than many of us believe, and this influence is increasing dramatically as companies experiment with new ways to command our attention.[31] The CBS reality adventure television program *Survivor* strands people on an island and lets them compete for products like a new pair of sneakers or a cold Budweiser—all provided courtesy of the show's sponsors.[32] And how about sleeping with corporations? Holiday Inn Family Suites Resort in Lake Buena Vista, Florida, offers rooms decorated in corporate themes, including the Orange Minute Maid suite and the Edy's Ice Cream suite. A Coca-Cola executive (there is a polar-bear motif in the Coca-Cola suite) comments, "Families ... feel like they can actually interact with our brands within a room."[33] Skiers at Whistler Mountain in British Columbia can play in a Nintendo GameCube terrain park and a Pontiac Race Centre and are greeted by hosts wearing Evian jackets. And how about marketing messages in the bathroom? One recent invention called the Wizmark gives marketers a new way to get your attention in there as well. The device is billed as an "interactive urinal communicator" that will play a message when activated by liquid.[34]

Marketing Ethics and Public Policy

In business, conflicts often arise between the goal of succeeding in the marketplace and the desire to conduct business honestly and to maximize the well-being of consumers by providing them with safe and effective products and services. Accordingly, many universities and corporations are now focusing very intently on teaching and reinforcing ethical behaviour.

BUSINESS ETHICS

Business ethics are essentially rules of conduct that guide actions in the marketplace—the standards against which most people in a marketplace judge what is right, wrong, good, or bad. These universal values include honesty, trustworthiness, fairness, respect, justice, integrity, concern for others, accountability, and loyalty.

Ethical business is good business. Consumers think better of products made by firms they feel are behaving ethically.[35] But just what is ethical behaviour? Sometimes it's not so easy to tell. For example, when you download songs from Kazaa, Morpheus, or other file-sharing programs, are you stealing? The film and recording industry thinks you are![36]

Notions of right and wrong do differ among people, organizations, and cultures. Some businesses, for example, believe it is all right for salespeople to persuade customers to buy even if it means giving them false information, while other firms feel that anything less than total honesty with customers is terribly wrong. Because each culture has its own set of values, beliefs, and customs, ethical business behaviours are defined quite differently around the world. For example, one recent study found that due to differences in values (more on this in Chapter 4), Mexican firms are less likely to have formal codes of ethics and more likely to bribe public officials than are American or Canadian companies. On the other hand, due to different attitudes about work and interpersonal relationships, Mexican companies are also more likely to treat lower-level employees better than do their NAFTA partners to the north.[37]

These cultural differences certainly influence whether business practices such as bribery are acceptable. In Japan, it's called *kuroi kiri* (black mist); in Germany, it's *schmiergeld* (grease money); Mexicans refer to *la mordida* (the bite); the French say *pot-de-vin* (jug of wine); and Italians speak of the *bustarella* (little envelope). They're all talking about *baksheesh*, the Middle Eastern term for a "tip" to grease the wheels of a transaction. Giving "gifts" in exchange for getting business from suppliers or customers is common and acceptable in many countries, even though this practice may be frowned upon in Canada. Recently, more than 800 business experts were asked to identify the countries where this practice is most flagrant. Russia and China emerged at the top of the list, and Taiwan and South Korea were close behind. The "cleanest" countries were Australia, Sweden, Switzerland, Austria, and Canada.[38]

PRESCRIBING ETHICAL STANDARDS OF CONDUCT

Professional organizations often devise a code of ethics for their members. For example, the American Marketing Association's Code of Ethics (see ***www.ama.org***) provides guidelines for conduct in many areas of marketing practice, some of which are as follows:[39]

- disclosure of all substantial risks associated with a product or service
- identification of added features that will increase the cost
- avoidance of false or misleading advertising
- rejection of high-pressure or misleading sales tactics
- prohibition of selling or fundraising under the guise of conducting market research

Whether intentionally or not, some marketers do violate their bond of trust with consumers. In some cases these actions are actually illegal, as when a manufacturer deliberately mislabels the contents of a package, or when a retailer adopts a bait-and-switch selling strategy whereby consumers are lured into the store with promises of inexpensive products with the sole intent of getting them to switch to higher-priced goods.

Unfortunately, unethical behaviour by big corporations is not always easily identified. For example, Coca-Cola's switch to large 600 mL bottles, sold exclusively in vending machines at educational sites, should give rise to alarm. Each bottle contains more than 15 teaspoons of sugar, supplying about 20 percent of an individual's daily recommended caloric intake. Yet research shows that the over-consumption of sugar leads to poorer grades for students, not to mention the medical problems of obesity and early on-set diabetes.

Rather than promoting responsible drinking, night clubs are now selling liquor by the bottle instead of the glass. These VIP lounges serve bottles of Grey Goose Vodka and mixer for $350, and customers pour themselves drinks that are much stronger than what the bartenders pour.[40]

Industry is increasingly coming to realize that ethical behaviour is good business in the long run, since consumer trust and satisfaction translates into years of loyalty. However, many problems remain. Sometimes consumers' buying behaviour is not consistent with their positive attitudes about ethical products. In a survey designed to measure people's willingness to pay for fair trade coffee, researchers found that most coffee drinkers were willing to pay an average price premium of 10 percent. Only 10 percent of respondents were willing to pay the current 27 percent price premium.[41] Throughout this book, ethical issues related to the practice of marketing are highlighted. Special boxes called *Marketing Pitfalls* feature questionable practices by marketers or the possible adverse effects on consumers of certain marketing strategies.

NEEDS AND WANTS: DO MARKETERS MANIPULATE CONSUMERS?

One of the most common and stinging criticisms of marketing is that marketing techniques (especially advertising) are responsible for convincing consumers that they "need" many material things and that they will be unhappy and somehow inferior people if they do not have these "necessities." The issue is a complex one and is certainly worth considering: Do marketers give people what they want, or do they tell people what they *should* want?

Welcome to Consumer Space

Who controls the market—companies or consumers? This question is becoming even more complicated as new ways of buying, having, and being are invented everyday. It seems that the "good old days" of *marketer space*, where companies called the shots and decided what they wanted their customers to know and to do, are dead and gone. As we saw with Gail's surfing decisions, many people now feel empowered to choose how, when, or *if* they will interact with corporations as they construct their own consumer space. In turn, companies need to develop and leverage brand equity in bold new ways to attract the loyalty of these consumer "nomads." People still "need" companies—but in new ways and *on their own terms*. As we'll see throughout the book, profound changes in consumer behaviour are influencing how people search for product information and evaluate alternative brands. In the brave new world of consumer space, we have the potential to shape our own marketing destinies.

Do Marketers Create Artificial Needs?

The marketing system has come under fire from both ends of the political spectrum. On the one hand, some believe that advertising contributes to the moral breakdown of society by presenting images of hedonistic pleasure, thus encouraging the pursuit of secular humanism. On the other hand, some leftists argue that the same deceitful promises of material pleasure function to buy off people who would otherwise be revolutionaries working to change the system.[42] Through advertising, the system creates demand that only its products can satisfy.

One such response to this argument is that a *need* is a basic biological motive, while a *want* represents one way society has taught us to satisfy that need. For example, while thirst is biologically based, we are taught to want Coca-Cola to satisfy that thirst rather than, say, goat's milk. Thus, the need is already there; marketers simply recommend ways to satisfy it. A basic objective of advertising is to create awareness that these needs exist, rather than to create the needs.

Are Advertising and Marketing Necessary?

As social critic Vance Packard wrote more than 40 years ago, "Large-scale efforts are being made, often with impressive success, to channel our unthinking habits, our purchasing decisions, and our thought processes by the use of insights gleaned from psychiatry and the social sciences."[43] The economist John Kenneth Galbraith felt that radio and television are important tools to accomplish this manipulation of the masses. Since virtually no literacy is required to use these media, they allow repetitive and compelling communications to reach almost everyone. This criticism may be even more relevant to online communications, where a simple click delivers a world of information to us.

Goods are arbitrarily linked to desirable social attributes. One influential critic even argued that the problem is that we are not materialistic enough; that

Marketing Pitfall

The charge that businesses create artificial needs is relevant in the case of gasoline marketing. Oil companies have attempted to convince consumers of the need for premium gasolines, even though this need has been questioned by many people. As one automotive engineer noted, "Oil company advertising has led people to the conclusion that more expensive fuels will make their car start easier, get more gas mileage, and last longer,... But in most cases this is untrue.... Your engine has to be designed to use that extra octane.... Otherwise,... the extra cost is just lining the pockets of the oil companies." The U.S. Federal Trade Commission estimates that 80 percent to 90 percent of the cars on the road run well on regular, unleaded gasoline. However, nearly a third of all motorists use midgrade or premium gasoline in their automobiles.[44] Fill 'er up!

is, we do not sufficiently value goods for the utilitarian functions they deliver but instead focus on the irrational value of goods for what they symbolize. According to this view, for example, "Beer would be enough for us, without the additional promise that in drinking it we show ourselves to be manly, young at heart, or neighbourly."[45]

One response to this particular argument is that products are designed to meet existing needs, and advertising merely helps to communicate the products' availability. According to the economics-of-information perspective, advertising is an important source of consumer information.[46] This view emphasizes the economic cost of the time spent searching for products, arguing that consumers are willing to pay for advertising because the information it provides reduces search time.

Do Marketers Promise Miracles?

Consumers are led to believe through advertising that products have magical properties; that is, products will do special and mysterious things for them that will transform their lives. They will be beautiful, have power over others' feelings, be successful, be relieved of all ills, and so on. In this respect, advertising functions as mythology did in primitive societies: It provides simple, anxiety-reducing answers to complex problems.

In response to this position, one could argue that advertisers simply do not know enough about people to manipulate them. Consider that the failure rate for new products ranges from 40 percent to 80 percent. In testimony, one advertising executive observed that, although people think advertisers have an endless source of magical tricks and scientific techniques to manipulate them, in reality the industry is successful when it tries to sell good products and unsuccessful when it sells poor ones.[47]

Public Policy and Consumerism

The welfare of the consumer is protected by many laws at the federal, provincial, and municipal levels. Regulations put forth by these governmental agencies sometimes overlap and are constantly changing. The main thrust of regulation is to protect the consumer from unfair business practices and to protect the broad interests of society. Laws involving "cooling off" periods for signing purchase agreements try to protect average consumers from getting into things they later regret. Other laws, such as the labelling of harmful products (e.g., cigarettes) and the prohibition of sales of certain substances (e.g., melatonin), are meant to protect the health of Canadians. Some of the various laws are outlined in Table 1–2.

The field of consumer behaviour can play an important role in improving our lives as consumers.[48] Many researchers assist in formulating or evaluating public policies such as those that ensure that products are labelled accurately, that people can comprehend important information presented in advertising, or that children are not exploited by program-length toy commercials masquerading as television shows.

Of course, to a large degree consumers depend on their governments to regulate and police safety and environmental standards. The extent of supervision may depend on such factors as the political climate in a country.

CONSUMER ACTIVISM?

Adbusters is a non-profit organization that advocates for "the new social activist movement of the information age."[49] Adbusters sponsors numerous initiatives, including Buy Nothing Day and TV Turnoff Week, intended to discourage rampant commercialism. These efforts, along with biting ads and commercials that lampoon advertising messages, are part and parcel of a strategy called **culture jamming** that aims to disrupt efforts by the corporate world to dominate our cultural landscape (see ***www.sniggle.net***).

Many firms choose to protect or enhance the natural environment as they go about their business activities, a practice known as **green marketing**. Some firms have focused their efforts on reducing wasteful packaging, as when Procter & Gamble introduced refillable containers for Downy fabric softener.[50] In other cases, successful marketers promise donations to charity as purchase incentives or donate their own money to good causes.[51]

TABLE 1–2

EXAMPLES OF FEDERAL GOVERNMENT LEGISLATION INTENDED TO ENHANCE CONSUMERS' WELFARE

Year	Act	Purpose
1949	National Trademark and True Labelling Act	Sets out who is authorized to use the national trademark "Canada Standards" and how it is to be used. The Act also empowers the Governor in Council to regulate how the content and quality of goods are required to be labelled or described when advertised.
1953	Food and Drugs Act	Protects consumers from purchasing food, cosmetics, drugs, and therapeutic devices that are passed off in a deceptive or misleading manner or pose a risk to human health.
1969	Hazardous Products Act	Fosters consumer safety through the banning of products that pose unacceptable hazards to the consumer. Products that have a limited potential to harm individuals because of improper care or use are required to be affixed with labels warning consumers of the nature of the danger.
1970	Motor Vehicle Safety Act	Establishes minimum safety standards for motor vehicles and their components through the setting of specific design and performance requirements.
1970	Consumer Packaging and Labelling Act	Sets out regulations for the packaging, labelling, and sale of prepackaged goods to consumers.
1970	The Textile Labelling Act	Requires all textile products that are offered for sale to consumers to bear labels attesting to the amount and types of generic fibres contained within the product. The Act also places conditions on the importation, advertising, and sale of these types of products.
1971	Weights and Measures Act	Establishes standardized forms of measurement for use in trade in Canada and assures the accuracy and correct use of all equipment used for this purpose.
1973	Precious Metals Marketing Act	Sets the quality and grading standards to be followed in the identification and marking of precious-metal items.
1986	Competition Act	Prohibits misleading advertising and deceptive marketing practices in promoting the supply or use of a product or service or any business interest.
2000	Personal Information Protection and Electronic Documents Act	Offers consumers the opportunity to know what information is being collected about them by regulated businesses, to opt out of businesses' information-collection practices, and to correct inaccurate information.

Sources: Based on *Revised Statutes of Canada, 1985* © Queen's Printer for Canada, Ottawa, 1985; Department of Consumer and Corporate Affairs, *Federal Legislation and Programs Relating to Consumer Protection*, March 1973, revised February 1975. Revised October 2003: *http://strategis.ic.gc.ca/epic/internet/inoca-bc.nsf/vwGeneratedInterE/Home.*

Social marketing refers to using marketing techniques normally employed to sell beer or detergent to encourage positive behaviours such as increased literacy and to discourage negative activities such as drunk driving.[52] A Swedish project aimed at curbing adolescent drinking illustrates social marketing at work. The

Swedish Brewer's Association invested 10 million Skr (about $7.5 million) in a co-operative effort with the Swedish Non-Violence Project to change teens' attitudes about alcohol consumption. Consumer researchers working on the project discovered that Swedish adolescents freely admitted that they "drink in order to get drunk" and enjoyed the feeling of being intoxicated, so trying to persuade them to give up alcohol would be a formidable task. However, the teens reported they also were afraid of losing control over their own behaviour, especially if there was a risk of being exposed to violence. And, while worries about the long-term health effects of drinking didn't concern this group (after all, at this age many teens believe they will live forever), female adolescents reported a fear of becoming less attractive as a result of prolonged alcohol consumption.

Based on these findings, the group commissioned to execute this project decided to stress a more realistic message of "drink if you want to, but within a safe limit. Don't lose control, because if you do, you might get yourself into violent situations." They made up the motto "Alco-hole in your head" to stress the importance of knowing one's limits. This message appeared on billboards, in video spots that depicted situations involving young drinkers getting out of control, and in school presentations given by young people.

THE DARK SIDE OF CONSUMER BEHAVIOUR

Despite the best efforts of researchers, government regulators, and concerned industry people, consumers' worst enemies are sometimes themselves. Individuals often are depicted as rational decision makers, calmly doing their best to obtain products and services that will maximize the health and well-being of themselves, their families, and their society. In reality, however, consumers' desires, choices, and actions often result in negative consequences to the individual or the society in which he or she lives.

Some consumer activities stem from social pressures, such as excessive drinking or cigarette smoking, and the cultural value placed upon money can encourage

→ Health Canada's approach to curbing smoking among the young is to limit the distribution system.
Courtesy of Health Canada.

The Tangled Web

Internet addiction is becoming a big problem in South Korea, which has the largest high-speed internet market penetration in the world. More than half of all South Korean households have high-speed internet connections, and the exploding web culture has "hooked" a huge number of young people on online gaming (80 percent of South Koreans under 25 play these games). Many of the gamers hang out in "PC bangs," which are coffeehouses and lounges featuring rows and rows of computers. South Korea is a group-oriented society where socializing in groups is the preferred form of interaction, but critics say the gaming industry is creating millions of addicts who are dropping out of school and (offline) group activities, and becoming uncommunicative and even violent due to the electronic games they play. Critics also claim that the PC bangs are turning into pickup joints, where teenagers swap pictures electronically and decide whether or not to meet. Reversing the usual pattern in a male-dominated society, the girls tend to be in charge; they send aggressive messages to boys and provide clues to help them figure out in which bang the girls are playing and where they are sitting.[56]

such activities as shoplifting or insurance fraud. Exposure to unattainable media ideals of beauty and success can create dissatisfaction with the self. Many of these issues will be touched upon later in the book, but for now let's review some dimensions of what has been called the "dark side" of consumer behaviour.

Addictive Consumption

Consumer addiction is a physiological or psychological dependency on products or services. This type of addiction includes addiction to alcohol, drugs, and cigarettes—and many companies profit from selling addictive products or by selling solutions to addiction. For example, bottled water mixed with nicotine called Nico Water is the latest in a string of tobacco products that has included candy-flavoured cigarettes and nicotine lollipops. The product's website touts it as a "safe nicotine drink for smokers trying to quit and smokers prohibited from smoking" in restaurants, offices, and airplanes. The company's CEO, responding to criticism about the potential of this product to hook kids, replied, "No one ever died of secondhand water."[53]

Although most people equate addiction with drugs, virtually any product or service can be seen as relieving some problem or satisfying some need to the point that reliance on it becomes extreme. There is even a Chapstick Addicts support group with approximately 250 active members![54]

Compulsive Consumption

For some consumers, the expression "born to shop" is quite literal. These consumers shop because they are compelled to do so, rather than because shopping is a pleasurable or functional task. **Compulsive consumption** refers to repetitive shopping, often excessive, done as an antidote to tension, anxiety, depression, or boredom. "Shopaholics" turn to shopping in much the same way as addicted people turn to drugs or alcohol.[55]

Compulsive consumption is distinctly different from impulse buying, which will be discussed in Chapter 10. The impulse to buy a specific item is temporary, and it centres on a specific product at a particular moment. In contrast, compulsive buying is an enduring behaviour that centres on the *process* of buying, not the purchases themselves. As one woman who spent $20 000 per year on clothing confessed, "I was possessed when I went into a store. I bought clothes that didn't fit, that I didn't like, and that I certainly didn't need."[57]

In some cases it is fairly safe to say that the consumer, not unlike a drug addict, has little or no control over consumption. The products, whether alcohol, cigarettes, chocolate, or diet colas, control the consumer. Even the act of shopping itself is an addicting experience for some consumers. Much negative or destructive consumer behaviour can be characterized by the following three common elements:[58]

1. The behaviour is not done by choice.
2. The gratification derived from the behaviour is short-lived.
3. The person experiences strong feelings of regret or guilt afterward.

Gambling is an example of a consumption addiction that touches every segment of consumer society. Whether it takes the form of casino gambling, playing the slots, betting on sports events with friends or through a bookie, or buying lottery tickets, excessive gambling can be quite destructive. Taken to extremes, gambling can result in lowered self-esteem, debt, divorce, and neglected children. According to one psychologist, gamblers exhibit a classic addictive cycle: They experience a high while in action and a depression when they stop gambling, which leads them back to the thrill of the action. Money is the substance that hard-core gamblers abuse.[59]

There are 62 casinos in Canada, 39 of which opened between 1995 and 2005. In addition, there are 87 000 slot machines and video lottery terminals, 250 racetracks and off-track betting theatres, 33 000 lottery ticket centres, and 25 000 charitable gaming licences. The result is windfall profits for provincial governments, which collected $7 billion—or $375 per adult—in 2004. As for the 1.2 million Canadians who struggled with gambling disorders and addiction, governments spent $63 per problem gambler on treatment programs. It seems the house always wins![60]

Illegal Activities

A survey conducted by the McCann-Erickson advertising agency revealed the following tidbits:[61]

- Ninety-one percent of people say they lie regularly. Thirty-three percent fib about their weight, 25 percent about their income, and 21 percent lie about their age. Nine percent even lie about their natural hair colour.
- Nineteen percent say they've snuck into a theatre to avoid paying admission.
- More than 60 percent of people say they've taken credit for making something from scratch when they have done no such thing. According to Pillsbury's CEO, this "behaviour is so prevalent that we've named a category after it—speed scratch."

CONSUMER THEFT

In North America, a retail theft is committed every five seconds. **Shrinkage** is the industry term for inventory and cash losses due to shoplifting and employee theft. This is a massive problem for businesses, and the cost is passed on to consumers in the form of higher prices (about 40 percent of the losses can be attributed to employees rather than shoppers). A family of four spends about $300 extra per year because of markups to cover shrinkage.[62] A comprehensive retail study found that the most frequently stolen products are cigarettes, athletic shoes, logo and brand name apparel, designer jeans, and undergarments. The average amount per theft is $58.43, up from $20.36 in 1995.[63] The problem is equally worrisome in Europe; in 2001 alone retailers apprehended 1.23 million shoplifters. Shrinkage was expected to cost European retailers more than $30 billion in 2002. The U.K. has the highest rate of shrinkage (as a percentage of annual sales), followed by Norway, Greece, and France. Switzerland and Austria have the lowest rates.[64]

Shoplifting increased by a third in a period of only four years. The large majority of shoplifting is *not* done by professional thieves or by people who genuinely need the stolen items.[65] About three-quarters of those caught are middle- or high-income people who shoplift for the thrill of it or as a substitute for affection. Shoplifting is common among adolescents. Research evidence indicates that teen shoplifting is influenced by such factors as having friends who shoplift. It is also more likely to occur if the adolescent does not believe that this behaviour is morally wrong.[66]

Still another growing form of fraud is the abuse of exchange and return policies. A number of big companies, including Guess, Staples, and Sports Authority, are using new software that lets them track a shopper's track record of bringing items back. They are trying to crack down on "serial wardrobers" who buy an outfit, wear it once and return it; customers who change price tags on items and then return one item for the higher amount; and shoppers who use fake or old receipts when making a return. The retail industry loses about $16 billion a year to these and other forms of fraudulent behaviour. Retail analysts estimate that about nine percent of all returns are fraudulent.[67]

ANTICONSUMPTION

Some types of destructive consumer behaviour can be thought of as **anticonsumption**, whereby products and services are deliberately defaced or mutilated.

Anticonsumption can range from product tampering, where innocent consumers are hurt or killed, to graffiti on buildings and subways. Anticonsumption can also take the form of political protest, in which activists alter or destroy billboards and other advertisements that promote what they feel are unhealthy or unethical acts. For example, some members of the clergy in areas heavily populated by minorities have organized rallies to protest the proliferation of alcohol advertising in their neighbourhoods.

CONSUMER BEHAVIOUR AS A FIELD OF STUDY

By now it should be clear that the field of consumer behaviour encompasses many things, from the simple purchase of a carton of milk to the selection of a complex networked computer system, and from the decision to donate money to a charity to devious plans to rip off a company or store. There's a lot to understand, and many ways to go about doing so.

Although people have certainly been consumers for a long time, it is only recently that consumption per se has been the object of formal study. In fact, although many business schools now require that marketing majors take a consumer behaviour course, most universities did not even offer such a course until the 1970s.

Interdisciplinary Influences on the Study of Consumer Behaviour

Consumer behaviour is being influenced by many different perspectives. Indeed, it is hard to think of a field that is more interdisciplinary. People with training in a very wide range of fields—from psychophysiology to literature—can now be found doing consumer research. Consumer researchers are employed by universities, manufacturers, museums, advertising agencies, and governments. Several professional groups, such as the Association for Consumer Research, have been formed since the mid-1970s.

To gain an idea of the diversity of interests of people who do consumer research, consider the list of professional associations that sponsor the field's major journal, the *Journal of Consumer Research*. It includes the American Home Economics Association, the American Statistical Association, the Association for Consumer Research, the Society for Consumer Psychology, the International Communication Association, the American Sociological Association, the Institute of Management Sciences, the American Anthropological Association, the American Marketing Association, the Society for Personality and Social Psychology, the American Association for Public Opinion Research, and the American Economic Association.

These diverse researchers approach consumer issues from different perspectives. You might remember a children's story about the blind men and the elephant. The gist of the story is that each man touched a different part of the animal and, as a result, the descriptions they gave of the elephant were quite different. This analogy applies to consumer research as well. A similar consumer phenomenon can be studied in different ways and at different levels, depending on the training and interests of the researchers studying it.

Figure 1–2 provides a glimpse at some of the disciplines working in the field and at the level at which each approaches research issues. These diverse disciplines can be roughly characterized in terms of their focus on micro versus macro consumer behaviour topics. The fields closer to the top of the pyramid concentrate on the individual consumer (micro issues), while those toward the base are more

FIGURE 1–2

THE PYRAMID OF
CONSUMER BEHAVIOUR

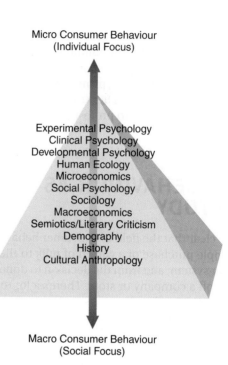

Micro Consumer Behaviour
(Individual Focus)

Experimental Psychology
Clinical Psychology
Developmental Psychology
Human Ecology
Microeconomics
Social Psychology
Sociology
Macroeconomics
Semiotics/Literary Criticism
Demography
History
Cultural Anthropology

Macro Consumer Behaviour
(Social Focus)

interested in the aggregate activities that occur among larger groups of people (macro issues), such as consumption patterns shared by members of a culture or subculture.

To demonstrate that the same marketing issue can be explored at different levels, let's look at the choice of selecting a magazine to buy. Table 1–3 lists research issues that might be of interest to each contributing discipline and provides examples of how these might be applied in the marketing of women's magazines.

The Issue of Strategic Focus

Many people regard the field of consumer behaviour as an applied social science. Accordingly, the value of the knowledge generated should be evaluated in terms of its ability to improve the effectiveness of marketing practice. Recently, though, some researchers have argued that consumer behaviour should not have a strategic focus at all; that is, the field should not be a "handmaiden to business." It should instead focus on the understanding of consumption for its own sake, rather than because the knowledge can be applied by marketers.[68] This rather extreme view is probably not held by most consumer researchers, but it has encouraged many to expand the scope of their work beyond the field's traditional focus on the purchase of consumer goods such as food, appliances, cars, and so on. And it has certainly led to some fiery debates among people working in the field!

The Issue of Two Perspectives on Consumer Research

One general way to classify consumer research is in terms of the fundamental assumptions the researchers make about what they are studying and how to study it. This set of beliefs is known as a **paradigm**. Like other fields of study, consumer behaviour is dominated by a paradigm, but some believe it is in the middle of a *paradigm shift,* which occurs when a competing paradigm challenges the dominant set of assumptions.

The basic set of assumptions underlying the dominant paradigm at this point in time is called **positivism** (or sometimes *modernism*). This perspective has significantly influenced Western art and science since the late sixteenth century. It emphasizes that human reason is supreme and that there is a single, objective truth

TABLE 1–3	
INTERDISCIPLINARY RESEARCH ISSUES IN CONSUMER BEHAVIOUR	
Disciplinary Focus	Magazine Usage Sample Research Issues
Experimental Psychology: product role in perception, learning, and memory processes	How specific aspects of magazines, such as their design or layout, are recognized and interpreted; which parts of a magazine are most likely to be read
Clinical Psychology: product role in psychological adjustment	How magazines affect readers' body images (e.g., do thin models make the average woman feel overweight?)
Microeconomics/Human Ecology: product role in allocation of individual or family resources	Factors influencing the amount of money spent on magazines in a household
Social Psychology: product role in the behaviour of individuals as members of social groups	Ways that ads in a magazine affect readers' attitudes toward the products depicted; how peer pressure influences a person's readership decisions
Sociology: product role in social institutions and group relationships	Pattern by which magazine preferences spread through a social group
Macroeconomics: product role in consumers' relations with the marketplace	Effects of the price of fashion magazines and expense of items advertised during periods of high unemployment
Semiotics/Literary Criticism: product role in the verbal and visual communication of meaning	Ways in which underlying messages communicated by models and ads in a magazine are interpreted
Demography: product role in the measurable characteristics of a population	Effects of age, income, and marital status of a magazine's readers
History: product role in societal changes over time	Ways in which our culture's depictions of "femininity" in magazines have changed over time
Cultural Anthropology: product role in a society's beliefs and practices	Ways in which fashions and models in a magazine affect readers' definitions of masculine versus feminine behaviour

that can be discovered by science. Positivism encourages us to stress the functions of objects, to celebrate technology, and to regard the world as a rational, ordered place with a clearly defined past, present, and future.

The emerging paradigm of **interpretivism** (or *postmodernism*) questions these assumptions. Proponents of this perspective argue that there is too much emphasis on science and technology in our society and that this ordered, rational view of consumers denies the complex social and cultural world in which we live. Others feel that positivism puts too much emphasis on material well-being and that its logical outlook is dominated by an ideology that stresses the homogeneous views of a culture dominated by white males.

Interpretivists instead stress the importance of symbolic, subjective experience and the idea that meaning is in the mind of the person—that is, individuals construct their own meanings based on their unique and shared cultural experiences, so that there are no single right or wrong answers. In this view, the world in which we live comprises a *pastiche,* or a mixture of images.[69] The value placed on products because they help us to create order in our lives is replaced by an appreciation of consumption as a set of diverse experiences.

The major differences between these two perspectives on consumer research are summarized in Table 1–4.

An interpretative framework for understanding marketing communications can be illustrated by an analysis of one of the best-known and longest-running advertising campaigns (1959–1978) of all time: the work done by the advertising agency Doyle Dane Bernbach for the Volkswagen Beetle. This campaign, widely noted for its self-mocking wit, found many ways to turn the Beetle's homeliness, smallness, and lack of power into positive attributes at a time when most car ads were emphasizing just the opposite. An interpretive analysis of these messages used concepts from literature, psychology, and anthropology to ground the appeal of this approach within a broader cultural context. The image created for the humble car was connected to other examples of what scholars of comedy call the "Little Man" pattern. This is a type of comedic character related to the clown or trickster, a social outcast who is able to poke holes in the stuffiness and rigidity of bureaucracy and conformity.

TAKING IT FROM HERE: THE PLAN OF THE BOOK

This book covers many facets of consumer behaviour, and many of the research perspectives briefly described in this chapter will be highlighted in later chapters. The plan of the book is simple: It goes from micro to macro. Think of the book as a sort of photograph album of consumer behaviour: Each chapter provides a "snapshot" of consumers, but the lens used to take each picture gets successively wider.

TABLE 1–4

POSITIVIST VERSUS INTERPRETIVIST APPROACHES TO CONSUMER BEHAVIOUR

Assumptions	Positivist Approach	Interpretivist Approach
Nature of reality	Objective, tangible Single	Socially constructed Multiple
Goal	Prediction	Understanding
Knowledge generated	Time free Context independent	Time bound Context dependent
View of causality	Existence of real causes	Multiple, simultaneous shaping events
Research relationship	Separation between researcher and subject	Interactive, co-operative, with researcher being part of phenomenon under study

Source: Adapted from Laurel A. Hudson and Julie L. Ozanne, "Alternative Ways of Seeking Knowledge in Consumer Research," *Journal of Consumer Research* 14 (March 1988): 508–521. Reprinted with the permission of The University of Chicago Press.

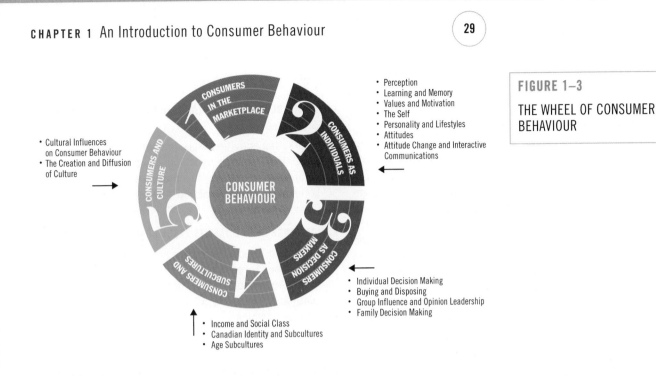

• Perception
• Learning and Memory
• Values and Motivation
• The Self
• Personality and Lifestyles
• Attitudes
• Attitude Change and Interactive
  Communications

• Cultural Influences
  on Consumer Behaviour
• The Creation and Diffusion
  of Culture

• Individual Decision Making
• Buying and Disposing
• Group Influence and Opinion Leadership
• Family Decision Making

• Income and Social Class
• Canadian Identity and Subcultures
• Age Subcultures

FIGURE 1–3

THE WHEEL OF CONSUMER BEHAVIOUR

The book begins with issues related to the individual consumer and expands its focus until it eventually considers the behaviours of large groups of people in their social settings. The topics to be covered correspond to the wheel of consumer behaviour presented in Figure 1–3.

Section II, "Consumers as Individuals," considers the consumer at his or her most micro level. It examines how the individual receives information from his or her immediate environment and how this material is learned, stored in memory, and used to form and modify individual attitudes—both about products and about the individual. Section III, "Consumers as Decision Makers," explores the ways in which consumers use the information they have acquired to make decisions about consumption activities, both as individuals and as group members. Section IV, "Consumers and Subcultures," further expands the focus by considering how the consumer functions as a part of a larger social structure. This structure includes the influence of different social groups to which the consumer belongs and with which he or she identifies, including social class, ethnic groups, and age groups. Finally, Section V, "Consumers and Culture," completes the picture as it examines marketing's impact on mass culture. These effects include the relationship of marketing to the expression of cultural values and lifestyles, how products and services are related to rituals and cultural myths, and the interface between marketing efforts and the creation of art, music, and other forms of popular culture that are so much a part of our daily lives.

CHAPTER SUMMARY

CONSUMER BEHAVIOUR IS A PROCESS.

• Consumer behaviour is the study of the processes involved when individuals or groups select, purchase, and use or dispose of products, services, ideas, or experiences to satisfy needs and desires.

CONSUMERS USE PRODUCTS TO HELP THEM DEFINE THEIR IDENTITIES IN DIFFERENT SETTINGS.

• A consumer may purchase, use, and dispose of a product, but these functions may also be performed by different people. In addition, consumers may be thought of as role players who need different products to help them play their various parts.

MARKETERS NEED TO UNDERSTAND THE WANTS AND NEEDS OF DIFFERENT CONSUMER SEGMENTS.

- Market segmentation is an important aspect of consumer behaviour. Consumers can be segmented along many dimensions, including product usage, demographics (the objective aspects of a population, such as age and sex), and psychographics (psychological and lifestyle characteristics). Emerging developments, such as the new emphasis on relationship marketing and the practice of database marketing, mean that marketers are much more attuned to the wants and needs of different consumer groups. This is especially important as people are empowered to construct their own consumer space—accessing product information where and when they want it and initiating contact with companies on the internet instead of passively receiving marketing communications.

THE WEB IS CHANGING CONSUMER BEHAVIOUR.

- The web is transforming the way consumers interact with companies and with each other. Online commerce allows us to locate obscure products from around the world, and consumption communities provide forums for people to share opinions and product recommendations. The benefits are accompanied by potential problems, including the loss of privacy and the deterioration of traditional social interactions as people log more time online.

CONSUMER BEHAVIOUR IS RELATED TO OTHER ISSUES IN OUR LIVES.

- Marketing activities exert an enormous impact on individuals. Consumer behaviour is relevant to our understanding of both public policy issues (for example, ethical marketing practices) and the dynamics of popular culture.

A WIDE RANGE OF SPECIALISTS STUDY CONSUMER BEHAVIOUR.

- The field of consumer behaviour is interdisciplinary; it comprises researchers from many different fields who share an interest in how people interact with the marketplace. These disciplines can be categorized by the degree to which their focus is micro (the individual consumer) versus macro (the consumer as a member of groups or of the larger society).

THERE ARE TWO MAJOR PERSPECTIVES ON UNDERSTANDING AND STUDYING CONSUMER BEHAVIOUR.

- There are many perspectives on consumer behaviour, but research orientations can be divided roughly into two approaches. The positivist perspective, which currently dominates the field, emphasizes the objectivity of science and the consumer as a rational decision maker. The interpretivist perspective, in contrast, stresses the subjective meaning of the consumer's individual experience and the idea that any behaviour is subject to multiple interpretations rather than having a single explanation.

KEY TERMS

Anticonsumption   p. 24

B2C commerce   p. 14

Business ethics   p. 15

C2C commerce   p. 14

Compulsive consumption   p. 22

Consumer addiction   p. 22

Consumer behaviour   p. 6

Consumption communities   p. 5

Culture jamming   p. 19

Database marketing   p. 11

Demographics   p. 9

Exchange   p. 7

Green marketing   p. 19

Interpretivism   p. 27

Marketing segmentation   p. 8

Paradigm   p. 26

Popular culture   p. 12

Positivism   p. 26

Relationship marketing   p. 11

Role theory   p. 7

Shrinkage   p. 24

Social marketing   p. 20

U-commerce   p. 13

REVIEW QUESTIONS

1. Provide a definition of consumer behaviour.
2. What are demographics? Give three examples of demographic characteristics.
3. What is the difference between a culture and a subculture?
4. Define market segmentation.
5. What is role theory, and how does it help us to understand consumer behaviour?
6. What do we mean by an exchange?
7. Why is it important for businesses to learn about their heavy users?
8. What is database marketing? Give an example of a company that uses this technique.
9. What is popular culture, and how does this concept relate to marketing and consumer behaviour?

10. The chapter states that "people often buy products not for what they do, but for what they mean." Explain the meaning of this statement and provide an example.

11. Describe two types of relationships a consumer can have with a product.

12. What is meant by the term "global consumer culture"?

13. What is the difference between B2B and B2C e-commerce?

14. The economics-of-information perspective argues that advertising is important. Do you agree? Why or why not?

15. Provide two examples of important legislation that relates to Canadian consumers.

16. Define social marketing and give an example of this technique.

17. Define consumer addiction and give two examples.

18. What is shrinkage, and why is it a problem?

19. Define anticonsumption, and provide two examples of it.

20. Name two different disciplines that study consumer behaviour. How would their approaches to the same issue differ?

21. What are the major differences between the positivist and interpretivist paradigms in consumer research?

CONSUMER BEHAVIOUR CHALLENGE

Discuss

1. This chapter states that people play different roles and that their consumption behaviours may differ, depending on the particular role they are playing. State whether you agree or disagree with this perspective, giving examples from your personal life. Try to construct a "stage set" for a role you play—specify the props, costumes, and script that you use to play a role (e.g., job interviewee, conscientious student, party animal).

2. Some researchers believe that the field of consumer behaviour should be a pure, rather than an applied, science; that is, research issues should be framed in terms of their scientific interest rather than their applicability to immediate marketing problems. Give your views on this issue.

3. Name some products or services that are widely used by your social group. State whether you agree or disagree with the notion that these products help to form the group bonds, supporting your argument with examples from your list of products used by the group.

4. Although demographic information on large numbers of consumers is used in many marketing contexts, some people believe that the sale of data on customers' incomes, buying habits, and so on constitutes an invasion of privacy and should be stopped. Comment on this issue from both a consumer's and a marketer's point of view.

5. List the three stages in the consumption process. Describe the issues that you considered in each of these stages when you made a recent important purchase.

6. State the differences between the positivist and interpretivist approaches to consumer research. For each type of inquiry, give examples of product dimensions that would be more usefully explored using that type of research rather than the other.

7. What aspects of consumer behaviour are likely to be of interest to a financial planner? To a university administrator? To a graphic arts designer? To a social worker in a government agency? To a nursing instructor?

8. Critics of targeted marketing strategies argue that this practice is discriminatory and unfair, especially if such a strategy encourages a group of people to buy a product that may be injurious to them or that they cannot afford. For example, community leaders in largely minority neighbourhoods have staged protests against billboards promoting beer or cigarettes in these areas. What are your views regarding this issue?

9. Do marketers have the ability to control our desires or the power to create needs? Is this situation changing as the internet creates new ways to interact with companies? If so, how?

Experiential Exercises

10. To what degree will consumers trade lower prices for less privacy? Car owners can now let insurance companies monitor their driving using a new technology in exchange for lower rates. Customers who sign up for Progressive's TripSense program get a device the size of a Tic Tac box to plug into their cars. The device will track speed and how many miles are driven at what times of day. Every few months, customers unplug the device from the car, plug it into a computer, download the data, and send it to the company. Depending on results, discounts will range from 5 percent to 25 percent. In Great Britain, a major insurer is testing a program called Pay as You Drive. Volunteers will get a device the size of a Palm computer installed in their cars. The gadget will use global positioning satellite technology to track where the car goes, constantly sending information back to the insurance company. Cars that spend more time in safer areas will qualify for bigger discounts.[70] Of course, the potential downside to these efforts is that the insurance companies may be able to collect data on where you have driven, how long you stayed in one location, and so on. Conduct a poll of 10 drivers of various ages where you describe these programs and ask respondents if they would participate in order to receive a discount on their insurance premiums. What reasons do they give pro and con? Do you find any differences in attitudes based on demographic characteristics such as age or gender?

11. While you're talking to car owners, probe to see what relationship (if any) they have with their vehicles. Do these feelings correspond to the types of consumer/product attachments we discussed in the chapter? How are these relationships manifested? (Hint: See if any of the respondents have nicknames for their cars, or if they "decorate" them with personal items.)

CBC VIDEO VIGNETTE

CONCEPTS AT WORK IN THE FUR INDUSTRY

Fur, with the image and price tag of a luxury good, stirs up emotions! Some of these emotions are positive, some are negative; almost all are felt strongly. Unlike most consumer goods, however, consumers are highly aware of its sources and characteristics. Thus, Canadian fur—where it comes from and where it goes to—has become a matter of global interest as stakeholders in the fur industry work to get their message out. Messages are frequently countervailing points to those of other players in the fur industry.

The global debate ebbs and flows as fur becomes more and less fashionable, and as each stakeholder group sharpens and articulates its view. Presently, fur is experiencing an upswing in global demand, which means higher prices for Canadian trappers. Fur trade activists, who held the industry at bay through the eighties and nineties, say that industry innovation and shifting points of view have pacified the buying and non-buying public. Traps are more humane and Canadian design is more creative than

the time when your grandmother's fur coat or your grandfather's beaver hat was produced. Further, domestic and international markets understand the fur trade to be part of Canada's heritage. Still, the debate and controversy continue.

Questions

1. Who buys Canadian fur clothing products? Briefly describe the buying process for the various consumer segments.
2. Who are the specific stakeholders in the Canadian fur industry? How does each stakeholder group affect demand for fur?
3. What is the interest of each stakeholder group? How do they communicate their respective messages?
4. Identify some specific actions or events that are likely to shift the dynamics of the upswing in demand for Canadian furs.

Resource: *Joan Leishman, "The Fur Industry," The National, CBC Air Date: January 10, 2003.*

NOTES

1. Olivia Ma, "Sneaker Freaks," *Newsweek* (August 16, 2004): 69.

2. Erving Goffman, *The Presentation of Self in Everyday Life* (Garden City, NY: Doubleday, 1959); George H. Mead, *Mind, Self, and Society* (Chicago: University of Chicago Press, 1934); Michael R. Solomon, "The Role of Products as Social Stimuli: A Symbolic Interactionism Perspective," *Journal of Consumer Research* 10 (December 1983): 319–339.

3. William F. Schoell and Joseph P. Guiltinan, *Marketing: Contemporary Concepts and Practices*, 4th ed. (Boston: Allyn & Bacon, 1990).

4. Anthony Bianco, "The Vanishing Mass Market," *BusinessWeek* (July 12, 2004): 61–67.

5. Jennifer Ordonez, "Cash Cows: Burger Joints Call Them 'Heavy Users'—But Not to Their Faces," *Wall Street Journal Interactive Edition* (January 12, 2000).

6. Steven Gray, "At Fast-Food Chains, Era of the Giant Burger (Plus Bacon) Is Here," *Wall Street Journal* (January 27, 2005).

7. Natalie Perkins, "Zeroing in on Consumer Values," *Advertising Age* (March 22, 1993): 23.

8. Hannah Karp, "Red Bull Aims at an Older Crowd," *Wall Street Journal* (June 7, 2004): B3.

9. Jack Neff, "Crest Spinoff Targets Women," *Advertising Age* (June 3, 2002): 1.

10. Richard P. Coleman, "The Continuing Significance of Social Class to Marketing," *Journal of Consumer Research* 10 (December 1983): 265–280.

11. Dan Gardner, "Immigration Ignored in Election Despite Its Impact on Future," *Vancouver Sun* (May 31, 1997): A6.

12. Eve Johnson, "Getting a Taste for Canada," *Vancouver Sun* (June 19, 1995): C1.

13. Sarah Ellison, "Prilosec OTC Blitz by P&G Represents New Drug Foray," *Wall Street Journal Interactive Edition* (September 12, 2003).

14. Constance L. Hays, "What Wal-Mart Knows About Customers' Habits," *New York Times on the Web* (November 14, 2004).

15. Quoted in "Bringing Meaning to Brands," *American Demographics* (June 1997): 34.

16. Jennifer Aaker, Susan Fournier, and S. Adam Brasel, "When Good Brands Do Bad," *Journal of Consumer Research* 31 (June 2004): 1–16.

17. Susan Fournier, "Consumers and Their Brands. Developing Relationship Theory in Consumer Research," *Journal of Consumer Research* 24 (March 1998): 343–73.

18. Brad Edmondson, "The Dawn of the Megacity," *Marketing Tools* (March 1999): 64.

19. David Barboza, "China, New Land of Shoppers, Builds Malls on Gigantic Scale," *New York Times on the Web* (May 25, 2005).

20. For a recent discussion of this trend, see Russell W. Belk, "Hyperreality and Globalization: Culture in the Age of Ronald McDonald," *Journal of International Consumer Marketing*, 8 3 and 4 (1995): 23–38.

21. Robert Frank, "When Small Chains Go Abroad, Culture Clashes Require Ingenuity," *Wall Street Journal Interactive Edition* (April 12, 2000).

22. Some material in this section was adapted from Michael R. Solomon and Elnora W. Stuart, *Welcome To Marketing.Com: The Brave New World Of E-Commerce* (Upper Saddle River, NJ: Prentice Hall, 2000).

23. Patricia Winters Lauro, "Marketing Battle for Online Dating," *New York Times on the Web* (January 27, 2003).

24. Tiffany Lee Brown, "Got Skim?" *Wired* (March 2000): 262.

25. Rebecca Fairley Raney, "Study Finds Internet of Social Benefit to Users," *New York Times on the Web* (May 11, 2000).

26. John Markoff, "Portrait of a Newer, Lonelier Crowd Is Captured in an Internet Survey," *New York Times on the Web* (February 16, 2000).

27. Lisa Guernsey, "Professor Who Once Found Isolation Online Has A Change Of Heart," *New York Times On The Web* (July 26, 2001).

28. Richard T. Watson, Leyland F. Pitt, Pierre Berthon, and George M. Zinkhan, "U-Commerce: Expanding The Universe of Marketing," *Journal of the Academy of Marketing Science* 30 (2002): 333–347.

29. "I.B.M. Unveils 'Smart' Laundry," *New York Times on the Web* (August 30, 2002).

30. Charles Sheehan, "Upcoming Comic Features Real-Life Marriage Proposal," *Montgomery Advertiser* (February 24, 2002).

31. "Goodbye Johnny, Hello Tic Tac," *Advertising Age* (May 25, 1992): 22; Cleveland Horton, "Hyundai Pulls Planned Ad in L.A. Beating Aftermath," *Advertising Age* (April 22, 1991): 2; Randall Rothenberg, "Does Integration Lead to Segregation? The Ethical Problems of Integrated Marketing," in *Integrated Marketing Communications*, eds. Jeri Moore and Esther Thorson (Hillsdale, NJ: Lawrence Erlbaum, 1992).

32. Marc Gunther, "Now Starring in Party of Five—Dr. Pepper," *Fortune* (April 17, 2000): 88 (2).

33. Rafer Guzman, "Hotel Offers Kids a Room with a Logo," *Wall Street Journal Interactive Edition* (October 6, 1999).

34. Jonathan Miller, "And Now, A Few Words from the Urinal," *New York Times* (September 30, 2004): E5.

35. Valerie S. Folkes and Michael A. Kamins, "Effects of Information About Firms' Ethical and Unethical Actions on Consumers' Attitudes," *Journal of Consumer Psychology* 8 (1999): 3, 243–259.

36. "Media Want Colleges to Fight Piracy," *New York Times on the Web* (October 11, 2002).

37. Jacqueline N. Hood and Jeanne M. Logsdon, "Business Ethics in the NAFTA Countries: A Cross-Cultural Comparison," *Journal of Business Research* 55 (2002): 883–890.

38. Barbara Crossette, "Russia And China Called Top Business Bribers," *New York Times on the Web* (May 17, 2002). For more details about the survey, see ***www.transparency.org***.

39. American Marketing Association, *Code of Ethics*, rev. ed. (Chicago: American Marketing Association, 1985).

40. Barney Gimble, "Buying by the Bottle," *Fortune* (February 6, 2005): 115–6.

41. Patrick de Pelsmacker, Liesbeth Driesen, and Glenn Rayp, "Do Consumers Care about Ethics? Willingness to Pay for Fair Trade Coffee," *The Journal of Consumer Affairs* 39, no. 2 (Winter, 2005): 363–385.

42. William Leiss, Stephen Kline, and Sut Jhally, *Social Communication in Advertising: Persons, Products, & Images of Well-Being* (Toronto: Methuen, 1986); Jerry Mander, *Four Arguments for the Elimination of Television* (New York: William Morrow, 1977).

43. Packard, *The Hidden Persuaders* (1957): 11; quoted in Leiss, Kline, and Jhally, *Social Communication*.

44. David Ivanovich, "Exxon to Run Commercials Saying Most Cars Don't Need Premium," *Houston Chronicle* (1997), accessed via Newslink, August 15, 1997.

45. Raymond Williams, "Advertising: The Magic System," in *Problems in Materialism and Culture* (London: New Left Books, 1962).

46. George Stigler, "The Economics of Information," *Journal of Political Economy* (1961): 69.

47. Quoted in Leiss, Kline, and Jhally, *Social Communication*.

48. For consumer research and discussions related to public policy issues, see Paul N. Bloom and Stephen A. Greyser, "The Maturing of Consumerism," *Harvard Business Review* (November/December 1981): 130–139; George S. Day, "Assessing the Effect of Information Disclosure Requirements," *Journal of Marketing* (April 1976): 42–52; Dennis E. Garrett, "The Effectiveness of Marketing Policy Boycotts: Environmental Opposition to Marketing," *Journal of Marketing* 51 (January 1987): 44–53; Michael Houston and Michael Rothschild, "Policy-Related Experiments on Information Provision: A Normative Model and Explication," *Journal of Marketing Research* 17 (November 1980): 432–449; Jacob Jacoby, Wayne D. Hoyer, and David A. Sheluga, *Misperception of Televised Communications* (New York: American Association of Advertising Agencies, 1980); Gene R. Laczniak and Patrick E. Murphy, *Marketing Ethics: Guidelines for Managers* (Lexington, MA: Lexington Books, 1985): 117–123; Lynn Phillips and Bobby Calder, "Evaluating Consumer Protection Laws: Promising Methods," *Journal of Consumer Affairs* 14 (Summer 1980): 9–36; Donald P. Robin and Eric Reidenbach, "Social Responsibility, Ethics, and Marketing Strategy: Closing the Gap Between Concept and Application," *Journal of Marketing* 51 (January 1987): 44–58; Howard Schutz and Marianne Casey, "Consumer Perceptions of Advertising as Misleading," *Journal of Consumer Affairs* 15 (Winter 1981): 340–357; Darlene Brannigan Smith and Paul N. Bloom, "Is Consumerism Dead or Alive? Some New Evidence," in *Advances in Consumer Research* 11, ed. Thomas C. Kinnear (Provo, UT: Association for Consumer Research, 1984): 369–373.

49. Adbusters Media Foundation, "Adbusters," (website) (Vancouver, British Columbia) (accessed June 27, 2002); available from ***http://secure.adbusters.org/orders/culturejam***.

50. "Concerned Consumers Push for Environmentally Friendly Packaging," *Boxboard Containers* (April 1993): 4.

51. Michal Strahilevitz and John G. Myers, "Donations to Charity as Purchase Incentives: How Well They Work May Depend on What You Are Trying to Sell," *Journal of Consumer Research* 24 (March 1998): 434–446.

52. Cf. Philip Kotler and Alan R. Andreasen, *Strategic Marketing for Nonprofit Organizations*, 4th ed. (Englewood Cliffs, NJ: Prentice Hall, 1991); Jeff B. Murray and Julie L. Ozanne, "The Critical Imagination: Emancipatory Interests in Consumer Research," *Journal of Consumer Research* 18 (September 1991): 192–244; William D. Wells, "Discovery-Oriented Consumer Research," *Journal of Consumer Research* 19 (March 1993): 489–504.

53. Wendy Koch, "Nicotine Water For Smokers Could Hook Kids," *USA Today Online* (May 23, 2002).

54. Laurie J. Flynn, "Web Site for Chap Stick Addicts," *New York Times on the Web* (November 1, 1999).

55. Thomas C. O'Guinn and Ronald J. Faber, "Compulsive Buying: A Phenomenological Explanation," *Journal of Consumer Research* 16 (September 1989): 154.

56. Howard W. French, "South Korea's Real Rage for Virtual Games," *New York Times on the Web* (October 9, 2002).

57. Quoted in Anastasia Toufexis, "365 Shopping Days Till Christmas," *Time* (December 26, 1988): 82; see also Ronald J. Faber and Thomas C. O'Guinn, "Compulsive Consumption and Credit Abuse," *Journal of Consumer Policy* 11 (1988): 109–121; Mary S. Butler, "Compulsive Buying: It's No Joke," *Consumer's Digest* (September 1986): 55.

58. Georgia Witkin, "The Shopping Fix," *Health* (May 1988): 73; see also Arch G. Woodside and Randolph J. Trappey III, "Compulsive Consumption of a Consumer Service: An Exploratory Study of Chronic Horse Race Track Gambling Behavior" (Working Paper #90–MKTG–04, A.B. Freeman School of Business, Tulane University, 1990); Rajan Nataraajan and Brent G. Goff, "Manifestations of Compulsiveness in the Consumer-Marketplace Domain," *Psychology & Marketing* 9 (January 1992): 31–44; Joann Ellison Rodgers, "Addiction: A Whole New View," *Psychology Today* (September/October 1994): 32 (11 pp.).

59. James Barron, "Are We All Really Losers with Gambling, a Spreading Social Addiction?" *New York Times* (May 31, 1989): A18.

60. "Full House," *Saturday Night* (Winter 2005): 11.

61. "Advertisers Face up to the New Morality: Making the Pitch," (Bloomberg), accessed via Newslink (July 8, 1997).

62. "Shoplifting: Bess Myerson's Arrest Highlights a Multibillion-Dollar Problem that Many Stores Won't Talk About," *Life* (August 1988): 32.

63. "New Survey Shows Shoplifting Is A Year-Round Problem," *Business Wire* (April 12, 1998).

64. "Customer Not King, But Thief," *Marketing News* (December 9, 2002): 4.

65. Catherine A. Cole, "Deterrence and Consumer Fraud," *Journal of Retailing* 65 (Spring 1989): 107–120; Stephen J. Grove, Scott J. Vitell, and David Strutton, "Non-Normative Consumer Behavior and the Techniques of Neutralization," in *Marketing Theory and Practice*, eds. Terry Childers et al. (1989 AMA Winter Educators Conference; Chicago: American Marketing Association, 1989): 131–135.

66. Anthony D. Cox, Dena Cox, Ronald D. Anderson, and George P. Moschis, "Social Influences on Adolescent Shoplifting—Theory, Evidence, and Implications for the Retail Industry," *Journal of Retailing* 69, 2 (Summer 1993): 234–246.

67. Stephanie Kang, "New Return Policy: Retailers Say 'No' to Serial Exchangers," *Wall Street Journal* (November 29, 2004): B1.

68. Morris B. Holbrook, "The Consumer Researcher Visits Radio City: Dancing in the Dark," in *Advances in Consumer Research* 12, eds. Elizabeth C. Hirschman and Morris B. Holbrook (Provo, UT: Association for Consumer Research, 1985): 28–31.

69. Alladi Venkatesh, "Postmodernism, Poststructuralism and Marketing" (paper presented at the American Marketing Association Winter Theory Conference, San Antonio, February 1992); see also A. Fuat Firat, "Postmodern Culture, Marketing and the Consumer," in *Marketing Theory and Application*, eds. T. Childers et al. (Chicago: American Marketing Association, 1991): 237–242; A. Fuat Firat and Alladi Venkatesh, "The Making of Postmodern Consumption," in *Consumption and Marketing: Macro Dimensions*, eds. Russell W. Belk and Nikhilesh Dholakia (Boston: PWS-Kent, 1993).

70. Kevin Maney, "Drivers Let Big Brother In To Get A Break," *Ethics* (August 9, 2004): 1B.

SECTION → 2

Consumers as Individuals

In this section we focus on the internal dynamics of consumer behaviour. We are constantly confronted with advertising messages, products, other people persuading us to buy something, and even reflections of ourselves. Each chapter in this section will consider a different aspect of the consumer—perceptions, memories, and attitudes—that is invisible to others but of vital importance to ourselves.

Chapter 2 describes the process of perception, in which information from the outside world about products and other people is absorbed by the individual and interpreted. Chapter 3 focuses on the ways this information is mentally stored and how it adds to our existing knowledge about the world during the learning process. Chapter 4 discusses our reasons or motivations for absorbing this information and how they are influenced by our values and needs.

Chapters 5 and 6 explore how our views about ourselves and our lifestyles affect what we do, want, and buy. Chapter 5 looks at the self and gender roles in our society; we are interested in the images we portray to others and the images we aspire to. Chapter 6 goes on to consider how people's individual personalities influence these decisions, and how the choices we make in terms of products, services, and leisure activities help to define our lifestyles.

Chapters 7 and 8 discuss how attitudes—our evaluations of all these products and ad messages—are formed and (sometimes) changed by marketers. When all of these "internal" parts are put together, the unique role of each individual consumer as a self-contained agent in the marketplace will be clear.

SECTION OUTLINE →

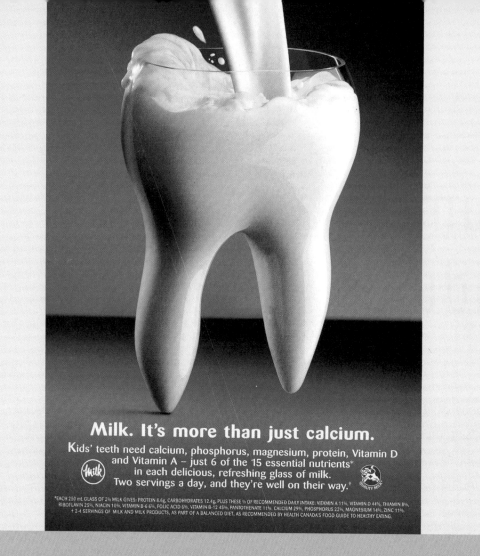

The European vacation has been wonderful, and this stop in Lisbon is no exception. Still, after two weeks of eating his way through some of the Continent's finest pastry shops and restaurants, Mike gets a craving for his favourite snack—President's Choice Decadent Chocolate Chip Cookies and an ice-cold carton of milk. He had stashed a package of the cookies in his backpack "just in case." This was the time to break it out.

He treks out of the hotel room to find the nearest grosa. When he heads to the small refrigerated section, though, he's puzzled—no milk here. Undaunted, Mike asks the clerk, *"Leite, por favor?"* The clerk quickly smiles and points to a rack in the middle of the store piled with little white square boxes. No, that can't be right—Mike resolves to work on his Portuguese. He repeats the question, and again he gets the same answer.

Finally, he investigates and, sure enough, he sees that the boxes, labelled with the brand name Parmalat, contain something called ultra heat treated (UHT) milk. Nasty! Who in the world would drink milk out of a little box that's been sitting on a warm shelf for who knows how long? Mike dejectedly returns to the hotel, his snack-time fantasies crumbling.

CHAPTER → 2

Perception

INTRODUCTION

Mike would be surprised to learn that many people in the world drink milk out of a box every day. UHT is Grade A pasteurized milk that has been heated until the bacteria causing spoilage are destroyed, and it can last for five to six months without refrigeration if its aseptic container is unopened.

Shelf-stable milk is particularly popular in Europe, where refrigerator space in homes and stores tends to be more limited than in Canada. Seven out of ten Europeans drink it routinely. The company is trying to crack the North American market as well, though analysts are dubious about its prospects. To begin with, milk consumption in Canada is declining steadily as teenagers choose soft drinks instead. Indeed, the Dairy Council of Canada pumped millions into an advertising campaign to promote milk drinking ("Got Milk?" ***www.gotmilk.com***).

But enticing Canadians to drink milk out of a box is even harder. In focus groups, consumers say they have trouble believing the milk is not spoiled or unsafe. They consider the square, quart-sized boxes more suitable for dry food, and some even feel the name Parmalat sounds too much like baby formulas such as Enfamil or Similac. Parmalat is trying to combat this resistance by introducing new containers featuring an image of an old-fashioned milk bottle.[1] So, while your McFlurry from McDonald's might be made with Parmalat, it's going to be a long, uphill battle to change Canadians' perceptions about the proper accompaniment to a bag of President's Choice Decadent Chocolate Chip Cookies.

Whether it's the taste of President's Choice Decadent Chocolate Chip Cookies, the sight of an Obsession perfume ad, or the sound of the music group Coldplay, we live in a world overflowing with sensations. Wherever we turn, we are bombarded by a symphony of colours, sounds, and odours. Some of the "notes" in this symphony, such as the loud barking of a dog, the shades of the evening sky, or the heady smell of a rose bush, occur naturally. Others come from people: The person sitting next to you in class might sport tinted blonde hair, bright pink pants, and a vanilla-chocolate scent.

Marketers certainly contribute to this commotion. Consumers are never far from advertisements, product packages, radio and television commercials, and billboards that clamour for their attention. Each of us copes with this bombardment by paying attention to some stimuli and tuning out others. And the messages to which we do choose to pay attention often wind up differing from what the sponsors intended, as we each put our "spin" on things by taking away meanings consistent with our own unique experiences, biases, and desires. This chapter focuses on the process of perception, in which sensations are absorbed by the consumer and used to interpret the surrounding world.

Sensation is the immediate response of our sensory receptors (eyes, ears, nose, mouth, and fingers) to such basic stimuli as light, colour, and sound. **Perception** is the process by which these sensations are selected, organized, and interpreted. The study of perception focuses on what we add to or take away from these raw sensations as we choose which to notice, and then go about assigning meaning to them.

Mike's encounter with milk in a box illustrates the perceptual process. He has learned to equate the cold temperature of refrigerated milk with freshness, so he experienced a negative physical reaction when confronted with a product that contradicted his expectations. Mike's evaluation was affected by factors such as the design of the package, the brand name, and even by the area in the grocery store in which it was displayed. These expectations are largely affected by a consumer's cultural background. Europeans do not necessarily have the same perceptions of milk, and as a result their reactions to the product are quite different.

Like computers, people undergo stages of information processing in which stimuli are input and stored. Unlike computers, however, consumers do not passively process whatever information happens to be present. Only a very small number of the stimuli in our environment are ever noticed. Of these, an even smaller number are attended to, and even these might not be processed objectively. The meaning of the stimulus is interpreted by the individual, who is influenced by his or her unique biases, needs, and experiences. As shown in Figure 2–1, three stages—exposure, attention, and interpretation—make up the process of perception. Before considering each of these stages, let's step back and consider the sensory systems that provide sensations to us in the first place.

SENSORY SYSTEMS

External stimuli, or *sensory inputs,* can be received on a number of channels. We may see a billboard, hear a jingle, feel the softness of a cashmere sweater, taste a new flavour of ice cream, or smell a leather jacket. The inputs picked up by our five senses constitute the raw data that generate many types of responses. For example, sensory data emanating from the external environment (hearing a song on the radio) can generate internal sensory experiences when the song on the radio triggers a young man's memory of his first dance and brings to mind the smell of his date's perfume or the feel of her hair on his cheek.

FIGURE 2–1   AN OVERVIEW OF THE PERCEPTUAL PROCESS

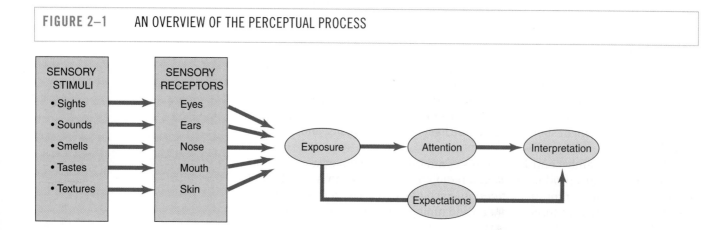

Starting to forget about "what's his name."

Find a little pleasure in the everyday.   HELLMANN'S REAL MAYONNAISE

← This Hellman's mayonnaise ad appeals to people's needs for pleasurable consumption.
The image of HELLMAN'S Real Mayonnaise appears with the permission of Unilever Canada.

The unique sensory quality of a product can play an important role in helping it to stand out from the competition, especially if the brand creates a unique association with the sensation. The Owens-Corning Corporation trademarked the colour pink for its fibreglass insulation material and adopted the Pink Panther cartoon character and pink flamingos to represent the company.[2] Harley-Davidson trademarked the distinctive "hog" sound of its revving motor.[3] These responses are an important part of **hedonic consumption**, or the multisensory, fantasy, and emotional aspects of consumers' interactions with products.[4]

Hedonic Consumption and the Design Economy

In recent years, the sensory experiences we get from products and services have become even more important when choosing among competing options. As manufacturing costs go down and the amount of "stuff" that people accumulate goes up, consumers increasingly want to buy things that will give them hedonic value in addition to simply doing what they're designed to do. A Dilbert comic strip poked fun at this trend when it featured a product designer who declared: "Quality is yesterday's news. Today we focus on the emotional impact of the product." All joking aside, the new focus on emotional experience is consistent with psychological research that finds that people prefer additional experiences over additional possessions as their incomes rise.[5]

In this environment, form *is* function. Two young entrepreneurs named Adam Lowry and Eric Ryan discovered that basic truth in the early days of 2000. They quit their day jobs to develop a line of house-cleaning products they called Method. Cleaning products—what a yawn, right?

Think again: For years companies like Procter & Gamble have plodded along, peddling boring boxes of soap powder to generations of people who suffered in silence, scrubbing and buffing, yearning for the daily respite of martini time. Lowry and Ryan gambled that they could offer an alternative—cleaning products in exotic scents like cucumber, lavender, and ylang-ylang that come in aesthetically pleasing bottles. The bet paid off. Within two years the partners were cleaning up, taking in more than $2 million in revenue. Shortly thereafter, they hit it big when Target contracted to sell Method products in its stores.[6]

There's a method to Target's madness. Design is no longer the province of an aesthete upper crust that never got close enough to a cleaning product to be revolted by it. The red-hot store chain has helped to make designers like Karim Rashid, Michael Graves, Philippe Starck, Todd Oldman, and Isaac Mizrahi household names. Mass-market consumers are thirsting for great design, and they're rewarding those companies that give it to them with their enthusiastic patronage and loyalty. From razor blades like the Gillette Sensor to computers like Apple and even to the lowly trash can, design *is* substance.

Ironically, even staid old P&G is starting to get the idea. Although it's a bit like turning a battleship, Procter & Gamble now recognizes the importance of integrating design into every product initiative. In the "good old days" (that is, a couple of years ago), design was basically an afterthought. Marketing meant appealing to customers in terms of efficiency rather than aesthetics. Now, Chairman-CEO A.G. Lafley wants P&G to focus on what he calls "the first moment of truth"—winning consumers in the store with packaging and displays. As a result, P&G now has a vice-president of design, strategy, and innovation who reports directly to the CEO. Her philosophy sums it up: "Competitive advantage comes not just from patents, but also from incorporating design into products, much like Apple, Sony or Dell."[7]

Vision

Marketers rely heavily on visual elements in advertising, store design, and packaging. Meanings are communicated on the visual channel through a product's size, styling, brightness, and distinctiveness from competitors' products. Philips is trying to give its products a younger feel by making them thinner and more colourful. Its audio products used to all be silver-coloured, but now each component comes in four colours, including a garish electric green.[8] Colours may even influence our emotions more directly. Evidence suggests that some colours (particularly red) create feelings of arousal and stimulate appetite, and others (such as blue) are more relaxing. Products presented against a backdrop of blue in advertisements are better liked than those shown with a red background, and cross-cultural research indicates a consistent preference for blue as consumers' favourite colour, whether they live in Canada or Hong Kong.[9] American Express chose to name its new card Blue after research showed the colour evokes a sense of excitement about the future. Its advertising agency named blue the colour of the new millennium because people associate it with sky and water, "providing a sense of limitlessness and peace."[10]

Colours are rich in symbolic value and cultural meanings. For example, red means good luck to the Chinese and is often the main colour in their celebrations. Such powerful cultural meanings make colour a central aspect of many marketing strategies. Some reactions to colour come from learned associations—in Western countries, black is the colour of mourning, while in some Eastern countries, notably Japan, white plays this role. In addition, the colour black is associated with power and may even have an impact on people who wear it. Teams in the National Hockey League who wear black uniforms are among the most aggressive; they consistently rank near the top of the league in penalties during the season.[11]

Some reactions to colour are due to biological differences. Women tend to be drawn to brighter tones and are more sensitive to subtle shadings and patterns, as women see colour better than men do. Men are 16 times more likely to be colour-

blind. Age also influences our response to colour. As we get older, our eyes mature and our vision takes on a yellow cast. Colours look duller to older people, so they prefer white and other bright tones. This helps to explain why mature consumers are much more likely to choose a white car—Lexus, which sells heavily in this market, makes 60 percent of its vehicles in white.

The trend toward brighter and more complex colours also reflects the increasingly multicultural makeup of Canada. For example, Hispanics tend to prefer brighter colours as a reflection of the intense lighting conditions in Latin America, since strong colours keep their character in strong sunlight.[12] That's why Procter & Gamble uses brighter colours in makeup it sells in Latin countries.[13]

Scientists and philosophers have been talking about the meanings of colours since the time of Socrates in the fifth century BC, but it wasn't until the early seventeenth century that Sir Isaac Newton was able to shine light through a prism and reveal the colour spectrum. Even then, Newton's observations weren't totally scientific; he identified seven major colours to be consistent with the number of planets known at that time, as well as the seven notes of the diatonic scale.

We now know that perceptions of a colour depend on both its physical wavelength and how the mind responds to that stimulus. Yellow, which is in the middle of wavelengths detectable by the human eye, is the brightest colour and attracts attention. The *Yellow Pages* were made yellow to heighten the attention level of bored telephone operators.[14] On the other hand, the colours we see are affected by our culture and the language we have learned to describe them. For example, the Welsh language has no words that correspond with green, blue, grey, or brown in English, but it uses other colours that English speakers don't (including one that covers part of green, part of grey, and the whole of our blue).[15]

Colour also plays a dominant role in webpage design; it directs a viewer's eye across the page, ties together design ideas, separates visual areas, organizes contextual relationships, creates mood, and captures attention. Saturated colours such as green, yellow, cyan, and orange are considered the best hues to capture attention, but don't overdo it: Extensive use of these hues can overwhelm people and cause visual fatigue.[16]

The choice of colour is frequently a key issue in package design. These choices used to be made casually. Today, however, colour is a serious business, and many companies realize that their colour choices can exert a big influence on consumers' assumptions about what is inside the package. When introducing a white cheese as a "sister product" to an existing blue Castello cheese, a Danish company launched it in a red package under the name of Castello Bianco. The red package was chosen to provide maximum visibility on store shelves. Although taste tests were very positive, sales were disappointing. A subsequent analysis of consumer interpretations showed that the red packaging and the name gave consumers the wrong impression about the product type and its degree of sweetness. Danish consumers had trouble associating the colour red with the white cheese. Also, the name Bianco connoted a sweetness that was incompatible with the actual taste of the product. It was relaunched in a white package and given the name "White Castello." Almost immediately sales more than doubled.[17]

Some colour combinations come to be associated so strongly with a corporation that they become known as the company's **trade dress**, and the company may even be granted exclusive use of these colours. For example, Eastman Kodak has successfully protected in court its trade dress of yellow, black, and red. As a rule, however, trade dress protection is granted only when consumers might be confused about what they are buying because of similar coloration of a competitor's packages.[18] Cadbury Adams Canada recently overhauled its packaging, adding its signature purple colour and logo to all its brands. Survey results showed that while consumers know Crème Eggs and Caramilk bars as Cadbury brands, people did not associate Crispy Crunch, Crunchie, and Mr. Big as Cadbury products. Therefore rebranding was necessary to bring association to all brands through the signature purple colour.[19] As well, successful businesses need to protect their brand equity from imitators. What strategies would you suggest to Cadbury and others to protect their identity from imitators?

Smell

Odours can stir emotions or create a calming feeling. They can evoke memories or relieve stress. Fragrance is processed by the limbic system, the most primitive part

Marketing Pitfall

See-food Diets—How Your Eyes Make You Lose and Gain Weight

Our eyes play tricks on us, and these perceptions can have calorie consequences.[20] When pouring or eating foods from larger boxes, the size of the box implicitly suggests that it's appropriate or "acceptable" to eat more—and we do! One study gave a number of moviegoers free medium-size or large-size popcorn buckets and revealed that they ate 45 percent more popcorn.[21] Even when 14-day-old popcorn was used, people still ate 32 percent more even though they said they hated the popcorn.[22] The same thing happens at parties. MBA students at a Super Bowl party were offered Chex Mix from either huge gallon-size bowls or from twice as many half-gallon bowls. Those dishing from the gallon-bowls ate 53 percent more.[23]

What's weird is that we also use our eyes and not our stomachs to tell us we're full. That's what gets us in trouble. In the "Bottomless Bowl" study, college students who ate from soup bowls that secretly refilled themselves from underneath the table ate 73 percent more soup than those eating from normal bowls.[24] The kicker is that the students estimated they ate the same amount, and even rated themselves as no more full. They used their eyes to tell them whether they had eaten enough. Since there was still food in their bowls, they believed they were not yet full.

These visual illusions also influence how much we pour and drink. Take drinking glasses, for example. When we pour into a glass, we tend to focus on the height of the liquid we are pouring and not the width.[25] If we are given two glasses that both hold 24 ounces, for instance, we will tend to pour over 30 percent more into the shorter, wider glass than the taller glass because we focus on the height and don't account for the width. Even the pros get tricked by this illusion. When 48 bartenders were asked to pour a "shot" of alcohol into either a wide tumbler or a tall highball glass, they poured 27 percent more gin, whisky, and vodka in the wide glasses than in the tall ones.[26]

Our eyes continue to trick us even when it comes to variety. When we see an assortment of foods, like at Thanksgiving dinner or at an all-you-can-eat buffet, this abundance suggests it's appropriate to eat more. College students who are given bowls of M&Ms that have ten colours of M&Ms will eat 26 percent more than those given the same size bowls with seven colours—even though all M&Ms taste the same. Also, students who were given six different flavours of jelly beans took and ate 85 percent more when they were mixed up than when they were neatly organized by flavour.[27] The bottom line: When it comes to how much we eat and drink, our eyes often have more to say than our stomachs.[28]

of the brain and the place where immediate emotions are experienced. Some of our responses to scents result from early associations that call up good or bad feelings, and that explains why businesses are exploring connections between smell, memory, and mood. One study found that consumers who viewed ads for either flowers or chocolate and who also were exposed to flowery or chocolatey odours spent more time processing the product information and were more likely to try different alternatives within each product category.[29]

The sense of smell is not just a physiological response to a stimulus. The labels we give to odours not only help us identify them, but also influence how we perceive them. Our cognitive processes for smell help to explain why the elderly are not as good at identifying odours as the young and why women can generally name more odours than men. In an experiment, 103 blindfolded women were asked to identify 80 different substances, but they could name only 36 odours accurately. In a follow-up study, the three most identifiable products were (1) Johnson's Baby Powder; (2) chocolate; and (3) coconut. These researchers concluded that women were better at identifying smells because they learn about them directly and deliberately.[30] Maybe as the genders share more household and child-rearing duties, men and women will become more equal in their ability to identify everyday odours.

At least to some extent, consumers' reactions to odours depend on their cultural background. There is a vast difference, culture to culture, in how people want to smell. The Germans like to layer it on, while American men don't like to smell "sissy," despite spending more time grooming than the French or Italians.[31] Many multinational companies adjust the scents of their products from country to country. Even Palmolive dish detergent has a different scent in Europe than in Canada. Vidal Sassoon products sold in Asia include a pine aroma that smells like floor cleaner to Americans.[32]

Scented marketing, now a $90-million business, is taking interesting turns as manufacturers find new ways to put scents into products, including men's suits, lingerie, detergents, and aircraft cabins. Cadillac even puts a scent it calls Nuance into its leather seats. The smell was created in a lab and selected by focus groups to best convey the smell of expensive upholstery. As a General Motors executive observed, "You pay the extra money for leather, you don't want it to smell like lighter fluid. You want it to smell like a Gucci bag."[33]

There is also evidence that certain smells appeal to the sexes. A vanilla smell diffused into a women's clothing store and a spicy, honey smell diffused into a men's clothing store almost doubled sales. When the scents were reversed, sales fell to levels below what they were when no scent was infused.[34]

Hearing

Consumers buy millions of dollars' worth of sound recordings each year; advertising jingles maintain brand awareness; and background music creates desired moods.[35] Many aspects of sound may affect people's feelings and behaviours. For example, a new technology, the HyperSonic Sound System (HSS), can even create a vending machine that can beckon you—and only you—with the sound of a fizzing soft drink from about 90 metres away. The process involves taking an audio signal from virtually any source, such as a stereo or computer, and converting it to an ultrasonic frequency that can be directed like a beam of light toward a target.[36]

Many aspects of sound affect people's feelings and behaviours. By decomposing brand names into individual sounds called *phonemes*, one study showed how even these cues affect consumer evaluations and convey unique meanings about inherent properties of the product. For instance, consumers infer that brands containing the vowel sound of short [i] weigh less than brands containing the vowel sound of [a].[37]

The Muzak Corporation (***www.muzak.com***) estimates that its recordings are heard by 80 million people every day. This so-called "functional music" is played in

→ Beauti-Tone Paint not only appeals primarily to the colour of childhood in this ad, but secondarily to the sound and touch of childhood.
Courtesy of Beauti-Tone Paint.

↑ Just as fabrics are prized for their textures, some types of liquor are rated according to their "feel." This ad for a premium Scotch whisky emphasizes the product's "smoothness" by equating its taste with the experience of gliding over ice.
Courtesy of William Grant & Sons, Inc.

stores, shopping malls, and offices to either relax or stimulate consumers. Research shows that workers tend to slow down during midmorning and midafternoon, so Muzak uses a system it calls "stimulus progression," in which the tempo of its music increases during those slack times. Muzak has been linked to reductions in absenteeism among factory workers. Even the milk output of cows and the egg output of chickens are claimed to increase under its influence.[39]

Touch

Although relatively little research has been done on the effects of tactile stimulation on consumer behaviour, common observation tells us that this sensory channel is important.[40] Moods are relaxed or stimulated on the basis of sensations of the skin, whether from a luxurious massage or the bite of a winter wind. Touch has even been shown to be a factor in sales interactions. In one study, diners who were touched by waiters gave bigger tips, and food demonstrators in a supermarket who lightly touched customers had better luck in getting shoppers to try a new snack product and to redeem coupons for the brand.[41]

New research is starting to identify the important role the *haptic* (touch) sense plays in consumer behaviour. Haptic senses appear to moderate the relationship between product experience and judgment confidence, confirming the common-sense notion that we're more sure about what we perceive when we can touch it. (Of course, this is a major problem for those who sell products online).[42] These researchers found that individuals who scored high on a "Need for Touch" (NFT) scale were especially influenced by this dimension. Those with a high need for touch responded positively to such statements as:

- When walking through stores, I can't help touching all kinds of products.
- Touching products can be fun.
- I feel more comfortable purchasing a product after physically examining it.[43]

Britain's ASDA grocery chain removed the wrapping from sample packages of several brands of toilet tissue in its stores so that shoppers could feel and compare textures. The result, the retailer says, was soaring sales for its own in-store brand, resulting in a 50 percent increase in shelf space for the line.[44]

Lubriderm Lotion restores lost moisture to heal and protect your skin.

←This ad for Lubriderm lotion relies on the vivid imagery of a rough tactile sensation to communicate a primary product benefit.
Courtesy of Warner Lambert Inc.

The Japanese take this idea of touch a step farther when they practise what they call **Kansei engineering**, a philosophy that translates customers' feelings into design elements. In one application of this practice, the designers of the Mazda Miata focused upon young drivers who saw the car as an extension of their bodies, a sensation they call the "horse and rider as one." After extensive research, the company discovered that making the stick shift exactly 9.5 cm long conveys the optimal feeling of sportiness and control.[46]

People associate the textures of fabrics and other products with underlying product qualities, and some marketers are exploring how touch can be used in packaging to arouse consumer interest. The perceived richness or quality of the material in clothing, bedding, or upholstery is linked to its "feel," that is, whether it is rough or smooth, flexible or inflexible. A smooth fabric like silk is equated with luxury, while denim is considered practical and durable. Some new plastic containers for household beauty items are incorporating "soft touch" resins that provide a soft, friction-like resistance when held. Focus group members who tested one such package for Clairol's Daily Defense shampoo described the sensations as almost sexy and were reluctant to let go of the containers![47]

Some of these tactile/quality associations are summarized in Table 2–1. Fabrics that comprise scarce materials or that require a high degree of processing to achieve their smoothness or fineness tend to be more expensive and thus are seen as being higher-class. Similarly, lighter, more delicate textures are assumed to be feminine. Roughness is often positively valued for men, while smoothness is sought by women.

TABLE 2–1

TACTILE OPPOSITIONS IN FABRICS

Perception	Male	Female	
High class	Wool	Silk	Fine
Low class	Denim	Cotton	↕
	Heavy ←——→ Light		Coarse

→ This Spanish ad for a hot chili–flavoured chip uses a novel visual image to communicate the ferocity of the product's flavour.
Tiempo BBDO Barcelona

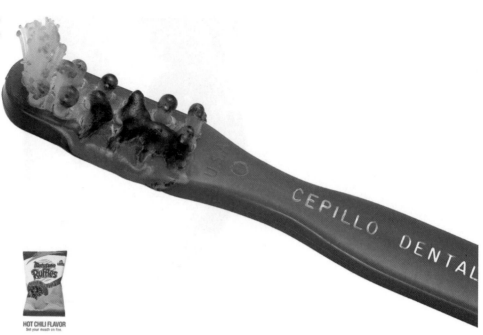

Taste

Our taste receptors obviously contribute to our experience of many products, and people form strong preferences for certain flavours.

Specialized companies called "flavour houses" keep busy trying to develop new tastes to please the changing palates of consumers. And scientists are right behind them, developing new devices to test these flavours. Alpha M.O.S. (***www.alpha-mos.com***) sells a sophisticated electronic tongue for tasting and is working on what its executives call an electronic mouth, complete with artificial saliva, to chew food and to dissect its flavour. Coca-Cola and Pepsi-Cola use the tongue to test the quality of corn syrups, while Bristol-Myers Squibb Company and Roche use the device to develop medicines that don't taste bitter.[48]

→ The wineries of Niagara-on-the-Lake educate the wine drinker with visuals that evoke all five senses in the enjoyment of wine.
Courtesy of Wineries of Niagara-on-the-Lake, Canada.

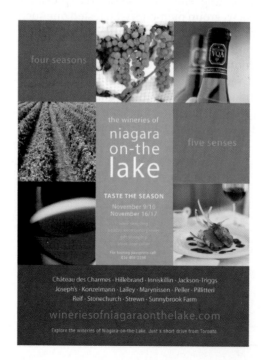

Changes in our culture also determine the tastes we find desirable. For example, consumers' greater appreciation of different ethnic dishes has contributed to increased desires for spicy foods, so the quest for the ultimate pepper sauce is a hot taste trend. The "heat" of peppers is measured in units called Scovilles. In 1912, Wilbur Scoville asked a five-person panel to see how much sugar water it would take to eliminate the hotness of a pepper. How's this for a hot tip: It takes 7497 litres of sweetened water to neutralize a teaspoon of Da' Bomb, which claims to be the hottest sauce ever made.[49]

At the other extreme of sensation, Japanese beverage companies are catching onto a new fad among younger Japanese consumers who are becoming more health conscious and want to avoid harmful additives—bland watery drinks. Beverage manufacturers there are working hard to make fruit drinks that you can see through. Stores are stacked with cartons of "near waters," mineral waters with just a touch of flavour. Sapporo sells a watered-down iced coffee, while Asahi Breweries makes a beer that is as clear as water with a name that sums up this new trend: Beer Water.[50] While that may not sound too appealing, perhaps it's good for washing down some hot sauce!

EXPOSURE

Exposure is the degree to which people notice a stimulus that is within range of their sensory receptors. Consumers concentrate on some stimuli, are unaware of others, and even go out of their way to ignore some messages. We are capable of noticing stimuli that come within range for even a very short time—*if* we choose to do so. That's the reasoning behind Cadillac's new ads for cars that can go from zero to 60 miles an hour in less than five seconds. Rather than use the traditional 30 seconds to communicate this message, the company ran five-second commercials to make its point.[51]

However, getting a message noticed in such a short time (or even in a longer one) is no mean feat. An experiment by a Minneapolis bank illustrates consumers' tendencies to miss or ignore information in which they are not interested. After a state law was passed that required banks to explain details about money transfers in electronic banking, the Northwestern National Bank distributed a pamphlet to 120 000 of its customers at considerable cost to provide the required information, which was hardly exciting bedtime reading. In 100 of the mailings, a section in the middle of the pamphlet offered readers $10 merely for finding that paragraph. Not a single person claimed the reward.[52]

Before we consider what people may choose not to perceive, let's consider what they are capable of perceiving.

Sensory Thresholds

If you have ever blown a dog whistle and watched pets respond to a sound you cannot hear, you know that there are some stimuli that people simply are not capable of perceiving. And, of course, some people are better able to pick up sensory information than others. The science that focuses on how the physical environment is integrated into our personal, subjective world is known as **psychophysics**.

THE ABSOLUTE THRESHOLD

When we define the lowest intensity of a stimulus that can be registered on a sensory channel, we speak of a *threshold* for that receptor. The **absolute threshold** refers to the minimum amount of stimulation that can be detected on a sensory channel. The sound emitted by a dog whistle is too high to be detected by human ears, so this stimulus is beyond our auditory absolute threshold. The absolute threshold is an important consideration in designing marketing stimuli. A billboard might have the most entertaining copy ever written, but this genius is wasted if the print is too small for passing motorists to see from the highway.

Marketing Opportunity

Companies such as the Anglo-Dutch Unilever and France's Picard are attempting to change consumers' perceptions of its frozen foods. In supermarkets across the United Kingdom, increasing numbers of shoppers head for the chiller cabinet first rather than the freezer. The chilled food section is where much of the innovation in convenience food is happening and where manufacturers compete most aggressively for space. Shoppers perceive chilled food as fresher and healthier—even though the champions of frozen food note that food picked or prepared and immediately frozen keeps its nutritional value and does not rely on preservatives the way that some chilled or ambient (tinned) food does. Still, many British shoppers view frozen food as inferior—something you serve as a last resort.[53] Makers of frozen foods are trying to fight back by designing new logos and packaging with warmer, more contemporary designs that imply the food is the product of natural sunlight rather than factory freezing.[54]

THE DIFFERENTIAL THRESHOLD

The **differential threshold** refers to the ability of a sensory system to detect changes in a stimulus or differences *between* two stimuli. The minimum change in a stimulus that can be detected is also known as the **JND**, which stands for *just noticeable difference.*

The issue of when and if a change will be noticed by consumers is relevant to many marketing situations. Sometimes a marketer may want to ensure that a change is noticed, such as when merchandise is offered at a discount. In other situations, the fact that a change has been made is downplayed, as in the case of price increases or when a product is downsized.

A consumer's ability to detect a difference between two stimuli is relative. A whispered conversation that might be unintelligible on a noisy street can suddenly become public and embarrassing knowledge in a quiet library. It is the relative difference between the decibel level of the conversation and its surroundings,

→ Campbell's Soup has been gradually modifying its label for the last 125 years. Consumers rushed to hoard classic Campbell's Soup cans when the company decided to retire the label in 1999. The new cans featured photos of actual soup in the bowl, but the design retained the distinctive red-and-white colours and unique script to avert a consumer backlash.
Courtesy of Campbell Soup Company.

rather than the loudness of the conversation itself, that determines whether the stimulus will register.

In the nineteenth century a psychophysicist named Ernst Weber found that the amount of change that is necessary to be noticed is systematically related to the original intensity of the stimulus. The stronger the initial stimulus, the greater the change must be for it to be noticed. This relationship is known as **Weber's law** and is expressed in the following equation:

$$K = \frac{\triangle I}{I}$$

where

K = the constant increase or decrease necessary for the stimulus to be noticed (this varies across the senses)

$\triangle I$ = the minimal change in intensity of the stimulus required to be just noticeable to the person (JND)

I = the intensity of the stimulus before the change occurs

For example, consider how Weber's law might work with respect to a product that has had its price decreased for a special sale. A rule of thumb used by some retailers is that a markdown should be at least 20 percent to make an impact on shoppers. If so, a pair of socks that retails for $10 should be put on sale for $8 (a $2 discount). However, a sports coat selling for $100 would not benefit from a mere $2 discount; it would have to be marked down to $80 to achieve the same impact.

The main point of Weber's law is that the ratios, not the absolute differences, are important in describing the least perceptible differences in sensory discrimination. The differential threshold varies not only with consumers' sensitivity and type of stimuli, but also with the absolute intensity of the stimuli being compared. The use of Weber's law in selling goods is important. Manufacturers and brand managers endeavour to determine the relevant just noticeable difference for their products for two reasons: first, so that reductions in product size, increases in product price, or changes in packaging are not readily discernible to the public; and second, so that product improvements are perceived by the public. Can you give an example of each from your own buying experience?

Subliminal Perception

Most marketers are concerned with creating advertising messages above consumers' thresholds. There is, however, another side to this story. A good number of consumers appear to believe that many advertising messages are in fact designed to be perceived unconsciously, or below the threshold of recognition. Another word for threshold is *limen*, and stimuli that fall below the limen are termed *subliminal*. **Subliminal perception** thus occurs when the stimulus is below the level of the consumer's awareness.

Subliminal perception is a topic that has captivated the public for more than 50 years, despite the fact that there is virtually no proof that this process has any effect on consumer behaviour. In fact, most examples of subliminal perception that have been "discovered" are not subliminal at all; they are quite visible. Remember, if you can see it or hear it, it is *not* subliminal, because the stimulus is above the level of conscious awareness! Nonetheless, the continuing controversy about subliminal persuasion has been important in shaping the public's beliefs about advertising and the ability of marketers to manipulate consumers against their will.

The public's fear of unconscious manipulation began with a widely popularized experiment that was performed in a New Jersey drive-in movie theatre in September 1957. During a showing of the movie *Picnic,* a firm called the Subliminal Projection Company inserted messages that said "Drink Coca-Cola" and "Eat

Popcorn" for 1/3000 second every 5 seconds. This rate was too fast for viewers to be aware that they had seen the images. Supposedly, sales of popcorn increased by almost 20 percent and consumption of Coke by almost 60 percent.

These claims created an uproar as journalists and social critics expressed fears that social scientists would team up with advertisers to invade privacy and control consumers against their will. As one magazine put it at the time, consumers' minds had been "broken and entered."[55] This experiment was never replicated and has been criticized repeatedly. The design of the study was flawed in that other possible effects on consumption, such as the movie itself, the weather during the showing, and so on, could not be ruled out. Indeed, the executive responsible for the test later admitted that he had made up the results to revive his failing research firm![56]

SUBLIMINAL TECHNIQUES

Subliminal messages supposedly can be sent on both visual and aural channels. *Embeds* are tiny figures that are inserted into magazine advertising by using high-speed photography or airbrushing. These hidden figures, usually of a sexual nature, supposedly exert strong but unconscious influences on innocent readers. To date, the only real impact of this interest in hidden messages is to make consumers (and students of consumer behaviour) look a bit more closely at print ads—perhaps seeing whatever their imaginations lead them to see.

In addition to these subliminal visual messages, many consumers and marketers seem to be fascinated by the possible effects of messages hidden on sound recordings. An attempt to capitalize on subliminal auditory perception techniques is found in the growing market for self-help cassettes. These tapes, which typically feature the sound of waves crashing or some other natural setting, supposedly

→ This Seagram's ad pokes fun at the belief that advertisers frequently embed pleasurable images in the ice cubes in pictures of drinks. *Courtesy of The House of Seagram.*

contain subliminal messages to help the listener stop smoking, lose weight, gain confidence, and so on. Despite the rapid growth of this market, there is little evidence that any subliminal stimuli transmitted on the auditory channel can bring about desired changes in behaviour.[57] In a major study conducted to obtain a definitive answer on the effect of subliminal persuasion, groups of people were recruited to a double-blind weight loss experiment involving tapes with subaudible messages. One group had real weight loss messages in their tapes, while the other group just listened to the ocean. After many weeks of listening to the tapes, there were no differences in weight loss between the two groups.[58]

Along with the interest in hidden self-help messages on recordings, some consumers have become concerned about rumours of satanic messages recorded backward in rock songs. However, humans do not have a speech perception mechanism operating at an unconscious level that is capable of decoding a reversed signal.

DOES SUBLIMINAL PERCEPTION WORK? EVALUATING THE EVIDENCE

Some research by clinical psychologists suggests that people can be influenced by subliminal messages under very specific conditions, though it is doubtful that these techniques would be of much use in most marketing contexts. To be effective, messages must be tailored very specifically to individuals rather than to a mass audience, as required by advertising.[59] These messages should also be as close to the liminal threshold as possible. Other discouraging factors include the following:

- There are wide individual differences in threshold levels. In order for a message to avoid conscious detection by consumers who have a low threshold, it would have to be so weak that it would not reach those who have a high threshold.

- Advertisers lack control over consumers' distance and position from a screen. In a movie theatre, for example, only a small portion of the audience would be in exactly the right seats to be exposed to the subliminal message.

- The consumer must be paying absolute attention to the stimulus. People watching a television program or a movie typically shift their attention periodically and might not even be looking when the stimulus is presented.

- Even if the desired effect is induced, it operates only at a very general level. For example, a message might increase a person's thirst, but not necessarily for a specific drink. Because basic drives are affected, marketers could find that, after all the bother and expense of creating a subliminal message, demand for competitors' products increases as well!

Clearly, there are better ways to get our attention. Let's see how.

ATTENTION

As you sit in a lecture, you might find your mind wandering (yes, even you!). One minute you are concentrating on the instructor's words, and the next you catch yourself daydreaming about the upcoming weekend. Suddenly, you tune back in as you hear your name being spoken. Fortunately, it's a false alarm—the professor has called on another "victim" who has the same first name. But she's got your attention now!

Attention refers to the extent to which processing activity is devoted to a particular stimulus. As you know from sitting through both interesting and "less interesting" lectures, this allocation can vary, depending on the characteristics of both the stimulus (i.e., the lecture itself) and the recipient (i.e., your mental state at the time).

Although we live in an information society, it's possible to have too much of a good thing. Consumers are often in a state of *sensory overload*; that is, they are exposed to far more information than they are able or willing to process. In our society, much of this bombardment comes from commercial sources, and the competition for our attention is increasing steadily. The average adult is exposed to about 3500 pieces of advertising information every single day—up from about 560 a day 30 years ago. Many younger people in particular (80 percent, by one estimate) have developed the ability to *multitask*, or process information from more than one medium at a time as they attend to their cell phones, TV, instant messages, and so on.[60]

Still, many people (perhaps the teens' parents?) are getting fed up. In one recent survey, 54 percent of respondents said they "avoid buying products that overwhelm them with advertising and marketing"; 60 percent said their opinion of advertising "is much more negative than just a few years ago"; and 69 percent said they "are interested in products and services that would help them skip or block marketing."[61] Those folks might be interested in a new product called TV-B-Gone, a plastic $19.99 keychain fob that, as the pitch goes, "turns off virtually any television!"[62]

Because the brain's capacity to process information is limited, consumers are very selective about what they pay attention to. The process of **perceptual selectivity** means that people attend to only a small portion of the stimuli to which they are exposed. Consumers practise a form of psychic economy, picking and choosing among stimuli to avoid being overwhelmed. How do they choose? Both personal and stimulus factors help to decide.

PERSONAL SELECTION FACTORS

Experience, which is the result of acquiring stimulation, is one factor that determines how much exposure to a particular stimulus a person accepts. *Perceptual filters* based on consumers' past experiences influence what they decide to process.

Perceptual vigilance is a factor in selective exposure. Consumers are more likely to be aware of stimuli that relate to their current needs. These needs may be conscious or unconscious. A consumer who rarely notices car ads will become very much aware of them when he or she is in the market for a new car. A newspaper ad for a fast-food restaurant that would otherwise go unnoticed becomes significant when one glances at the paper in the middle of a five o'clock class.

The flip side of perceptual vigilance is *perceptual defence*. This means that people see what they want to see—and don't see what they don't want to see. If a stimulus is threatening to us in some way, we may not process it, or we may distort its meaning so that it is more acceptable. For example, a heavy smoker may block out images of cancer-scarred lungs because these vivid reminders hit a bit too close to home.

Another factor affecting exposure is **adaptation**—that is, the degree to which consumers continue to notice a stimulus over time. The process of adaptation occurs when consumers no longer pay attention to a stimulus because it is so familiar. Almost like drug addiction, a consumer can become "habituated" and require increasingly stronger "doses" of a stimulus for it to continue to be noticed. For example, a consumer en route to work might read a billboard message when it is first installed, but after a few days it becomes part of the passing scenery. Generally, several factors can lead to adaptation:

- *Intensity:* Less-intense stimuli (soft sounds or dim colours) habituate because they have less of a sensory impact.
- *Duration:* Stimuli that require relatively lengthy exposure in order to be processed tend to habituate because they require a long attention span.
- *Discrimination:* Simple stimuli tend to habituate because they do not require attention to detail.
- *Exposure:* Frequently encountered stimuli tend to habituate as the rate of exposure increases.
- *Relevance*: Stimuli that are irrelevant or unimportant will habituate because they fail to attract attention.

← The photograph in this ad for *Pensions & Investments Age* illustrates how visual stimuli can cause advertising clutter—the sensory overload to which consumers are exposed in the marketplace.
Courtesy of Pensions & Investments Age. Concept: W. Bisson; Copy: W. Bisson; Design: J. Hunt, Donna Klein.

STIMULUS SELECTION FACTORS

In addition to the receiver's "mindset," characteristics of the stimulus itself play an important role in determining what gets noticed and what gets ignored.[64] These factors need to be understood by marketers, who can apply them to their messages and packages to boost their chances of cutting through the clutter and commanding attention. This idea even applies to getting animals' attention. A British ad agency did a TV commercial aimed at felines that used fish and mouse images and sounds to attract catty consumers. In trials, 60 percent of cats showed some form of response to the ad, from twitching their ears to tapping the television screen.[65]

In general, stimuli that differ from others around them are more likely to be noticed (remember Weber's law). This *contrast* can be created in several ways:

- *Size:* The size of the stimulus itself in contrast to the competition helps to determine whether it will command attention. Readership of a magazine ad increases in proportion to the size of the ad.

- *Colour:* As we've seen, colour is a powerful way to draw attention to a product or to give it a distinct identity. For example, Black & Decker has a line of tools, called DeWalt, targeted at the residential construction industry. The new line was coloured yellow instead of black, which made them stand out against other "dull" tools.[66]

- *Position:* Not surprisingly, stimuli that are in places where we're more likely to look stand a better chance of being noticed. That's why the competition among suppliers to have their products displayed at eye level in stores is so heated. In magazines, ads that are placed toward the front of the issue, preferably on the right-hand side, also win out in the race to get readers' attention. (Hint: The next time you read a magazine, notice which pages you're more likely to spend time looking at.)[67]

  One recent study found that the noticeability of warning labels on alcoholic beverages was improved by placing the message on the front label in a horizontal position and by reducing surrounding clutter.[68] Another study that tracked consumers' eye movements as they scanned telephone directories also illustrates the importance of a message's position. Consumers scanned listings in alphabetical order, and they noticed 93 percent of quarter-page display ads but only 26 percent of plain listings. Their eyes were drawn to colour ads first, and these were viewed longer than black-and-white ones. In addition, subjects spent 54 percent more time viewing ads for businesses they ended up choosing, which illustrates the influence of attention on subsequent product choice.[69]

Reality Check ✓

The slogan for the movie *Godzilla* was "Size does matter." Should this be the slogan for North America as well? Many marketers seem to believe so. The average serving size for a fountain drink has gone from 350 mL to 590 mL. An industry consultant explains that the 950 mL Big Gulp is so popular because "people like something large in their hands. The larger the better." Hardee's Monster Burger, complete with two beef patties and five pieces of bacon, weighs in at 63 grams of fat and more than 900 calories. Clothes have ballooned: Kickwear makes women's jeans with 40-inch-diameter legs. The standard for television sets used to be 19 inches, now it's 32 inches. Hulking SUVs have replaced tiny sports cars as the status vehicle.

One consumer psychologist theorizes that consuming big things is reassuring: "Large things compensate for our vulnerability," she says. "It gives us insulation, the feeling that we're less likely to die."[70]

What's up with our fascination with bigness? Is this a uniquely North American preference? Do you believe that "bigger is better"? Is this a sound marketing strategy?

> I believe that the importance of size is product-specific. For example, the larger portions of food and drink give consumers the idea of value for money. However, there are products for which their "smallness" is just as important. Men comparing mobile phones are not going to boast about how big theirs is!
>
> *Pamela Gillen, Dublin City University, Ireland*

> What exactly are the Americans trying to prove? That their stomachs are in fact bigger than their eyes? I find that eating out in some places in the U.S. is somewhat an "appetite repressant" mainly due to the negative psychological effect that the sight of mountains of food piled sky high can have.
>
> *Nicole Schragger, Edinburgh University, Scotland*

> I think Americans value their possessions and money in a much different way than most other cultures. By this I mean Americans view the items they buy and the money they spend as an extension of themselves....Many Americans are raised with the idea of pursuing their goals by whatever means possible and then enjoying their rewards. As a result, Americans have gained the mindset of "getting more for your money." As a result of this American mindset, many more Americans are overweight and out of shape....We are also becoming a wasteful society, producing more than half the world's waste and pollution. These are the negative results of the "bigger is better" attitude and are not likely to go away.
>
> *Jennifer Freet, George Mason University, U.S.*

> I am not sure that bigness is only noticeable in U.S., but compared to Europe, everything there is disproportionate: roads, space, buildings, economy, and number of obese people....
>
> *Astrid Spielrein, ASSAS University Paris II, France*

> I believe that bigger is better to a great extent. A lot of this belief has to do with the fact that I grew up in Canada, the second-largest land mass, where there are very few geographical limitations placed on what one can consume....Additionally, my ethnic heritage is Pakistani and the Pakistanis definitely believe that bigger is better. To them, large houses, cars, and televisions are a sure sign of wealth and prosperity...
>
> *Sabrina Aslam, Simon Fraser University, Canada*

> "Size does matter" seems to be America's slogan. When I went to a restaurant in America, I was surprised by the size of a dish. "Am I supposed to eat all this?" was my question. I got used to it, and also gained a lot of weight. Then when I went back to Japan, I could not take the fact that everything was so small. It seemed stingy.
>
> *Mai Sasaki, Keio University, Japan*

- *Novelty:* Stimuli that appear in unexpected ways or places tend to grab our attention. These places include the backs of shopping carts, tunnels, sports stadiums, and movies.[71]

  A recent promotion to introduce Vanilla Coke in Europe illustrates how effective novelty can be. Coke put a big wooden box in shopping malls and told people to stick their head in it. The brave souls who complied were rewarded with a bottle of the stuff. This request tied into TV commercials for the new product that told viewers to "Reward your curiosity."[72] Another example of novelty attracting consumers' attention is Naked Grape wine produced by Vincor. Point of sale and advertising taglines say "It takes Confidence to go Unoaked." Sales have soared for this wine, which retails for less than $10.[73]

INTERPRETATION

Interpretation refers to the meanings that people assign to sensory stimuli. Just as people differ in terms of the stimuli that they perceive, the eventual assignment of meanings to these stimuli varies as well. Two people can see or hear the same event, but their interpretations of it can be like night and day, depending on what they had expected the stimulus to be.

Consumers assign meaning to stimuli based on the schema, or set of beliefs, to which the stimulus is assigned. Certain properties of a stimulus will more likely evoke a schema than others. (This process is known as *priming*.) A brand name can communicate expectations about product attributes and can colour consumers' perceptions of product performance by activating a schema. Identifying and evoking the correct schema is crucial to many marketing decisions because this determines what criteria will be used to evaluate the product, package, or message. Extra Strength Maalox Whip Antacid flopped even though a spray can is a pretty effective way to deliver the product. But to consumers, aerosol whips mean dessert toppings, not medication.[74] On the other hand, when menu items in a college cafeteria were given descriptive labels (e.g., "Red Beans with Rice" versus "Traditional Cajun Red Beans with Rice," and "Chocolate Pudding" versus "Satin Chocolate Pudding") so that diners had more information about each option and were able to better categorize them, sales increased by more than 25 percent.[75]

Stimulus Organization

People do not perceive a single stimulus in isolation; they tend to view it in terms of relationships with other events, sensations, or images. When RJR Nabisco introduced a version of Teddy Grahams (a children's product) for adults, restrained packaging colours were used to reinforce the idea that the new product was for grownups, but sales were disappointing. The box was then changed to a bright yellow to convey the idea that this was a fun snack, and buyers' more positive association between a bright primary colour and taste led adults to start buying the cookies.[76]

Our brains tend to relate incoming sensations to others already in memory based on some fundamental organizational principles. These principles are based on work in **Gestalt psychology**, a school of thought maintaining that people derive meaning from the *totality* of a set of stimuli, rather than from any individual stimulus. The German word *gestalt* means, roughly, "whole," "pattern," or "configuration," a perspective best summarized by the saying "the whole is greater than the sum of its parts." The importance of a gestalt is underscored when consumers' interpretations of stimuli are affected by aesthetic, symbolic, or sensory qualities. Set in a context that is painfully familiar to most students, the Colombian coffee ad shown below demonstrates the formation of a meaningful image from the individual coloured circles on a Scantron sheet when viewed in totality. A piecemeal perspective that analyzes each component of the stimulus separately will be unable to capture the

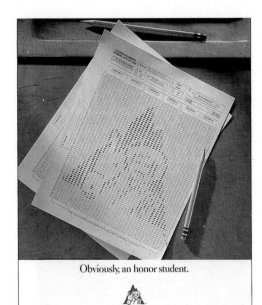

Obviously, an honor student.

← This ad for Colombian coffee illustrates gestalt principles of perception, in which the individual parts (the coloured circles) are seen as a whole (the familiar symbol used to promote Colombian coffee).
Courtesy of the National Federation of Coffee Growers of Colombia.

FIGURE 2–2

PRINCIPLES OF STIMULUS ORGANIZATION DERIVED FROM GESTALT PSYCHOLOGY

PRINCIPLE OF CLOSURE   PRINCIPLE OF SIMILARITY   PRINCIPLE OF FIGURE-GROUND

total effect. The gestalt perspective provides several principles relating to the way stimuli are organized. Three of these principles, or perceptual tendencies, are illustrated in Figure 2–2.

The gestalt **principle of closure** implies that consumers tend to perceive an incomplete picture as complete. That is, we tend to fill in the blanks based on our prior experience. This principle explains why most of us have no trouble filling in the blanks in an incomplete message or reading a neon sign even if one or two of its letters are burned out. The principle of closure is also at work when we hear only part of a jingle or theme. Utilization of the principle of closure in marketing strategies encourages audience participation, which increases the chance that people will attend to the message.

The **principle of similarity** tells us that consumers tend to group together objects that share similar physical characteristics; that is, they group like items into sets to form an integrated whole. Green Giant relied upon this principle when the company redesigned the packaging for its line of frozen vegetables. It created a "sea-of-green" look to unify all of its different offerings.

Another important gestalt concept is the **figure-ground principle**, in which one part of a stimulus will dominate (the *figure*) while other parts recede into the background. This concept is easy to understand if one thinks of a photograph with a clear and sharply focused object (the figure) in the centre. The figure is dominant, and the eye goes straight to it. The parts of the configuration that will be perceived as figure or ground can vary, depending on the individual consumer as well as other factors. Similarly, in marketing messages that use the figure-ground principle, a stimulus can be made the focal point of the message or merely the context that surrounds the focus.

→This J&B ad illustrates use of the principle of closure, in which people participate in the ad by mentally filling in the gaps.
Reprinted with permission by The Paddington Corporation ©.

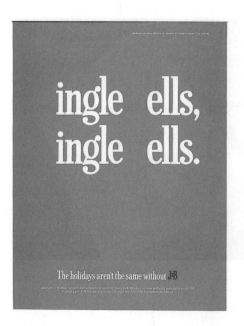

THE EYE OF THE BEHOLDER: INTERPRETATION BIASES

The stimuli we perceive are often ambiguous; it's up to us to determine the meaning based on our past experiences, expectations, and needs. The process of "seeing what you want to see" was demonstrated in a classic experiment where students at Princeton and Dartmouth viewed a movie of a particularly rough football game between the two schools. Although everyone was exposed to the same stimulus, the degree to which students saw infractions, and the blame they assigned for those they did see, was quite different, depending on which college they attended.[77]

As this experiment demonstrates, consumers tend to project their own desires or assumptions onto products and advertisements. This interpretation process can backfire for marketers, as occurred in 1992 when Planters Lifesavers Company introduced a vacuum-packed peanuts package called Planters Fresh Roast. The idea was to capitalize on consumers' growing love affair with fresh roast coffee by emphasizing the freshness of the nuts in the same way. A great idea—until irate supermarket managers began calling to ask who was going to pay to clean the peanut goop out of their stores' coffee-grinding machines.[78]

Semiotics: The Symbols Around Us

When we try to "make sense" of a marketing stimulus, whether a distinctive package, an elaborately staged television commercial, or perhaps a model on the cover of a magazine, we do so by interpreting its meaning in the light of associations we have with these images. For this reason, much of the meaning we take away is influenced by what we make of the symbolism we perceive. After all, on the surface many marketing images have virtually no literal connection to actual products.

For assistance in understanding how consumers interpret the meanings of symbols, some marketers are turning to a field of study known as **semiotics**, which examines the correspondence between signs and symbols and their role in the assignment of meaning.[79] Semiotics is important to the understanding of consumer behaviour since consumers use products to express their social identities. Products have learned meanings, and we rely on advertising to help us figure out what those meanings are. As one set of researchers put it, "advertising serves as a kind of culture/consumption dictionary; its entries are products, and their definitions are cultural meanings."[80]

From a semiotic perspective, every marketing message has three basic components: an object, a sign or symbol, and an interpretant. The relationship between them (as exemplified by Molson's "I am Canadian" ad) is diagrammed in Figure 2–3. The **object** is the product that is the focus of the message (Canadian brand of beer). The **sign** is the sensory imagery that represents the intended meanings of the object (Joe representing the typical Canadian male). The **interpretant** is the meaning derived (true Canadian identity).

According to semiotician Charles Sanders Peirce, signs are related to objects in one of three ways: They can resemble objects, be connected to them, or be conventionally tied to them.[81] An *icon* is a sign that resembles the product in some way (for example, Bell Telephone uses an image of a bell to represent itself). An *index* is a sign that is connected to a product because they share some property (the pine tree on some of Procter & Gamble's Spic and Span cleanser products conveys the shared property of fresh scent). A **symbol** is a sign that is related to a product through either conventional or agreed-upon associations (the tiger in AGF ads provides the conventional association with fearlessness that is carried over to the company's approach to investments).

A lot of time, thought, and money goes into creating brand names and logos that will clearly communicate a product's image (even when a name like Exxon is generated by a computer!). The Nissan Xterra combines the word "terrain" with the

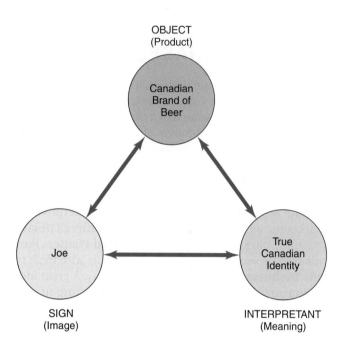

letter X, which is associated by many young people with extreme sports, to give the brand name a cutting-edge, off-road feel. The choice of a logo is even more difficult when the brand has to travel across cultures. For example, as Chinese business becomes more global, companies are refashioning ancient Chinese pictograms into new corporate logos that resonate with both Eastern and Western images. Chinese pictograms really are icons, because the ancient symbols were once graphic depictions of the words they signify. For example, China Telecom's logo features two interlocking letter Cs that together form the Chinese character for China but also represent the concept of "customer" and "competition," the firm's new focus. In addition, the symbol also resembles the horns of an ox, a hard-working animal. The software company Oracle recently redid its logo for the Chinese market by adding three Chinese characters that signify the literal translation of the word *oracle:* "writing on a tortoise shell." The expression dates back to ancient China, when prophecies were scrawled on bones. The California firm was enthusiastic about the translation because it conveyed Oracle's core competency: data storage.[82]

One of the hallmarks of modern advertising is that it creates a condition that has been termed **hyperreality**. Hyperreality refers to the "becoming real" of what is initially simulation of "hype." Advertisers create new relationships between objects and interpretants by inventing new connections between products and benefits.

In a hyperreal environment, over time the true relationship between the symbol and reality is no longer possible to discern. The "artificial" associations between product symbols and the real world may take on lives of their own. Consider for example the region of Switzerland that has been renamed "Heidiland" by tourism marketers in honour of the supposed birthplace of the imaginary Swiss girl. In the town of Maienfeld, new Heidi attractions are flourishing. A Heidi trail leads to a Heidi refreshment stand and then to a man who poses full-time as Heidi's grandfather. Initially officials refused to permit "Welcome to Heidiland" highway signs, because Swiss law allows only real place names. The number of tourists making a pilgrimage to the "home" of this mythical character apparently changed their minds.[83] In our hyperreal world, Heidi lives!

Perceptual Positioning

As we've seen, a product stimulus is often interpreted in the light of what we already know about a product category and the characteristics of existing brands.

Perceptions of a brand comprise both its functional attributes (its features, price, and so on) and its symbolic attributes (its image and what we think it says about us when we use it). We'll look more closely at issues like brand image in later chapters, but for now it's important to keep in mind that our evaluation of a product typically is the result of what it means rather than what it does. This meaning, as perceived by consumers, constitutes the product's *market position*—and it may have more to do with our expectations of product performance as communicated by its colour, packaging, or styling than with the product itself. How does a marketer determine where a product actually stands in the minds of consumers? One technique is to ask them what attributes are important to them and how they feel competitors rate on these attributes.

This information can be used to construct a perceptual map—a vivid way to paint a picture of where products or brands are "located" in consumers' minds. GRW Advertising created the perceptual map shown in Figure 2–4 for HMV music stores, a British company that operates stores in large North American cities. The agency wanted to know more about how its target market, which represents frequent buyers of CDs, perceived the different stores they might patronize. GRW plotted perceptions of such attributes of competitors as selection, price, service, and hipness on an imaginary street map. Tower Records is located where Selection Street runs past Hip Highway and the High Awareness Interstate, while small independent stores are at a point where Local Taste Alley goes past Hip Highway and Customer Service Court. Based on this research, the firm determined that HMV's strengths were service, selection, and the stores' ability to cater to local taste because store managers can order their own stock. This map was used in the strategic decision to specialize in music products as opposed to competing by offering other items sold by the competition, such as video games, fragrances, and computer CD-ROMs.[84]

PERCEPTION STREET MAP

FIGURE 2–4

HMV PERCEPTUAL MAP

→ This repositioning strategy, based on renaming fish species, is built on the belief that a fish by another name will gain greater consumer acceptance.

Article reprinted with permission of Andrew Allentuck. Photos left to right: G. Van Ryckerorsel/Valen Photos; Stephen J. Kraseman/Valen Photos; Todd Gipstein/Corbis/Magma.

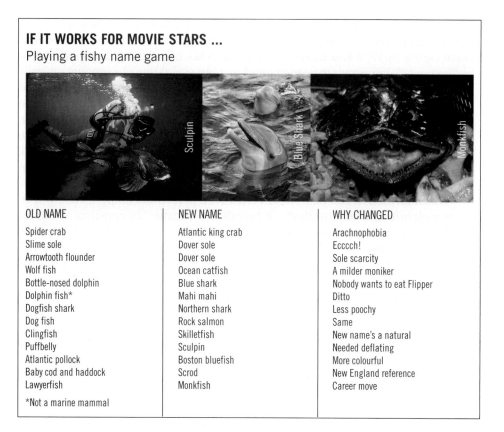

IF IT WORKS FOR MOVIE STARS ...
Playing a fishy name game

OLD NAME	NEW NAME	WHY CHANGED
Spider crab	Atlantic king crab	Arachnophobia
Slime sole	Dover sole	Ecccch!
Arrowtooth flounder	Dover sole	Sole scarcity
Wolf fish	Ocean catfish	A milder moniker
Bottle-nosed dolphin	Blue shark	Nobody wants to eat Flipper
Dolphin fish*	Mahi mahi	Ditto
Dogfish shark	Northern shark	Less poochy
Dog fish	Rock salmon	Same
Clingfish	Skilletfish	New name's a natural
Puffbelly	Sculpin	Needed deflating
Atlantic pollock	Boston bluefish	More colourful
Baby cod and haddock	Scrod	New England reference
Lawyerfish	Monkfish	Career move
*Not a marine mammal		

A **positioning strategy** is a fundamental part of a company's marketing efforts as it uses elements of the marketing mix (product design, price, distribution, and marketing communications) to influence the consumer's interpretation of its meaning. For example, although consumers' preference for the taste of one product over another is important, this functional attribute is only one component of product evaluation.[85] Coca-Cola found this out the hard way when it committed its (in)famous New Coke marketing blunder in the 1980s. New Coke was preferred to Pepsi in blind taste tests (in which the products were not identified) by an average of 45 percent to 55 percent in 17 markets, yet New Coke ran into problems when it replaced the older version. Consumers' impassioned protests and letter-writing campaigns eventually forced the company to bring back "Coke Classic." People do not buy a cola for taste alone; they are buying intangibles like brand image as well. Coca-Cola's unique position as part of a fun-loving lifestyle is based on years of marketing efforts that involve a lot more than taste alone. In 2000 Pepsi revived its Pepsi Challenge. The original promotion was widely believed to have been a driving force behind Coke's disastrous introduction of its sweeter New Coke.[86]

POSITIONING DIMENSIONS

There are many dimensions that can be used to establish a brand's position in the marketplace.[87] These include the following:

- *Price leadership:* L'Oréal's brand face cream is sold in upscale beauty shops, while its Plentitude brand is available for one-sixth the price in discount stores.
- *Attributes:* Bounty paper towels are "the quicker picker upper."
- *Product class:* The Mazda Miata is a sporty convertible.
- *Occasions:* Wrigley's gum is an alternative at times when smoking is not permitted.
- *Users:* Levi's Dockers are targeted primarily at men in their twenties, thirties, and forties.
- *Quality:* At Ford, "Quality is Job 1."[88]

CHAPTER SUMMARY

PERCEPTION IS A THREE-STAGE PROCESS THAT TRANSLATES RAW STIMULI INTO MEANING.

- Perception is the process by which physical sensations such as sights, sounds, and smells are selected, organized, and interpreted. The eventual interpretation of a stimulus allows it to be assigned meaning. A perceptual map is a widely used marketing tool that evaluates the relative standing of competing brands along relevant dimensions.

PRODUCTS AND COMMERCIAL MESSAGES OFTEN APPEAL TO OUR SENSES, BUT MANY OF THEM WILL NOT SUCCEED.

- Marketing stimuli have important sensory qualities. We rely on colours, odours, sounds, tastes, and even the "feel" of products when evaluating them. Not all sensations make their way successfully through the perceptual process. Many stimuli compete for our attention, and the majority are not noticed or accurately comprehended. People have different thresholds of perception. A stimulus must be presented at a certain level of intensity before it can be detected by an individual's sensory receptors. In addition, a consumer's ability to detect whether two stimuli are different (the differential threshold) is an important issue in many marketing contexts, such as changing a package design, altering the size of a product, or reducing its price.

THE DESIGN OF A PRODUCT TODAY IS A KEY DRIVER OF ITS SUCCESS OR FAILURE.

- In recent years, the sensory experiences we get from products and services have become even more important when choosing among competing options. Consumers increasingly want to buy things that will give them hedonic value in addition to functional value. They often believe that most brands perform similarly, so they weigh a product's aesthetic qualities heavily when they choose.

SUBLIMINAL ADVERTISING IS A CONTROVERSIAL—BUT LARGELY INEFFECTIVE—WAY TO TALK TO CONSUMERS.

- A lot of controversy has been sparked by so-called subliminal persuasion and related techniques, by which people are exposed to visual and audio messages below the threshold. Although evidence of subliminal persuasion's effectiveness is virtually non-existent, many consumers continue to believe that advertisers use this technique. Some of the factors that determine which stimuli get perceived (above the threshold level) are the amount of exposure to the stimulus, how much attention it generates, and how it is interpreted. In an increasingly crowded stimulus environment, advertising clutter occurs when too many marketing-related messages compete for attention.

THE STIMULI WE DO PAY ATTENTION TO ARE INTERPRETED ACCORDING TO LEARNED PATTERNS AND EXPECTATIONS.

- A stimulus that is attended to is not perceived in isolation; it is classified and organized according to principles of perceptual organization. These principles are guided by a gestalt, or overall pattern. Specific grouping principles include closure, similarity, and figure-ground relationships. The final step in the process of perception is interpretation. Symbols help us to make sense of the world by providing us with an interpretation of a stimulus that is often shared by others. The degree to which the symbolism is consistent with our previous experience affects the meaning we assign to related objects.

THE SCIENCE OF SEMIOTICS HELPS US TO UNDERSTAND HOW SYMBOLS ARE USED TO CREATE MEANING.

- Marketers try to communicate with consumers by creating relationships between their products or services and desired attributes. A semiotic analysis involves the correspondence between stimuli and the meanings of signs. The intended meaning may be literal (e.g., an icon such as a street sign with a picture of children playing). The meaning may be indexical; it relies on shared characteristics (e.g., the red in a stop sign means danger). Finally, meaning can be conveyed by a symbol, in which an image is given meaning by convention or by agreement of members of a society (e.g., stop signs are octagonal, while yield signs are triangular). Marketer-created associations often take on a life of their own as hype is assumed to be real; this condition is known as hyperreality.

KEY TERMS

Absolute threshold   p. 47

Adaptation   p. 52

Attention   p. 51

Differential threshold   p. 48

Exposure   p. 47

Figure-ground principle   p. 56

Gestalt psychology   p. 55

Hedonic consumption   p. 39

Hyperreality   p. 58

Interpretant   p. 57

Interpretation   p. 54

JND (just noticeable difference)   p. 48

Kansei engineering   p. 45

Object   p. 57

Perception   p. 38

Perceptual selectivity   p. 52

Positioning strategy   p. 60

Principle of closure   p. 56

Principle of similarity   p. 56

Psychophysics   p. 47

Semiotics   p. 57

Sensation   p. 38

Sign   p. 57

Subliminal perception   p. 49

Symbol   p. 57

Trade dress   p. 42

Weber's law   p. 49

REVIEW QUESTIONS

1. Define hedonic consumption and provide an example.
2. Does the size of a package influence how much of the contents we eat? How?
3. How does the sense of touch influence consumers' reactions to products?
4. Identify and describe the three stages of perception.
5. What is the difference between an absolute threshold and a differential threshold?
6. Does subliminal perception work? Why or why not?
7. "Consumers practise a form of 'psychic economy.'" What does this mean?

8. Describe two factors that can lead to stimulus adaptation.
9. Define a "schema" and provide an example of how this concept is relevant to marketing.
10. "The whole is greater than the sum of its parts." Explain this statement.
11. List the three semiotic components of a marketing message, giving an example of each.
12. What do we mean by the idea of hyperreality?
13. What is a positioning strategy? What are some ways marketers can position their products?

CONSUMER BEHAVIOUR CHALLENGE

Discuss

1. Many studies have shown that our sensory detection abilities decline as we grow older. Discuss the implications of the absolute threshold for marketers attempting to appeal to seniors.
2. Assuming that some forms of subliminal persuasion may have the desired effect of influencing consumers, do you think the use of these techniques is ethical? Explain your answer.
3. Do you believe that marketers have the right to use any or all public spaces to deliver product messages? Where would you draw the line in terms of places and products that should be restricted?

Experiential Exercises

4. Interview three to five male and three to five female friends regarding their perceptions of both men's and women's fragrances. Construct a perceptual map for each set of products. Based on your map of perfumes, do you see any areas that are not adequately served by current offerings? What (if any) gender differences did you detect regarding both the relevant dimensions used by raters and the placement of specific brands along these dimensions?

5. Assume that you are a consultant for a marketer who wants to design a package for a new premium chocolate bar targeted at an affluent market. What recommendations would you make in terms of package elements, such as colour, symbolism, and graphic design? Give the reasons for your suggestions.
6. Using magazines archived in the library, track the packaging of a specific brand over time. Find an example of gradual changes in package design that may have been below the JND.
7. Visit a set of websites for one type of product (e.g., personal computers, perfumes, laundry detergents, or athletic shoes) and analyze the colours and other design principles employed. Which sites "work" and which don't? Why?
8. Look through a current magazine and select one ad that captures your attention over the others. Give the reasons why.
9. Find ads that utilize the techniques of contrast and novelty. Give your opinion of the effectiveness of each ad and whether the technique is likely to be appropriate for the consumers targeted by the ad.

CBC ⊛ VIDEO VIGNETTE

CONCEPTS AT WORK FOR BEER NECESSITIES

Beer is a favourite beverage of many Canadians! We have been brewing this beverage Canadian-style for more than a century, but surprisingly few of us really know what we're drinking when we open "a cold one." Under Canadian law, requirements for listing ingredients are rather lenient compared with those for other food and beverage products. Breweries, which generally promote beer on lifestyle dimensions, are not much help, nor are our own taste buds. Taste tests continue to demonstrate that beer drinkers have difficulty identifying their favourite beer.

Beer experts are aware of the limitations of consumers' perceptual acuity when it comes to beer. Periodically, questions are raised about the need for the ingredient lists and expiry dates that are mandatory in other countries where beer is also a popular beverage. These experts also remind us that a trained palate can distinguish among the myriad beer brands and that some beers may actually be better than others. However, there is no guarantee that your favourite brand will be the number one contender! Or that the marketing communications strategies used by large and small breweries will be any more enlightening.

Questions

1. What is the difference between experts and novices in how they perceive beer?
2. Describe the structure of the Canadian beer industry and the marketing strategies used to reach the Canadian beer market.
3. Why are breweries against putting "best before" dates on their products?

4. What kind of consumer protection do beer consumers have in Canada and other countries? Why do you think countries use different approaches?

Resource: "True Brew," Marketplace #4, CBC Air Date: October 21, 1998.

What are the perceived differences among Canadian beers?
Courtesy of Moosehead.

NOTES

1. Cathy Sivak, "Purposeful Parmalat: Part 1 of 2" *Dairy Field*, 182 (9): 1+ (September 1999); "North Brunswick, N.J.-based food company signs deal with online grocer," *Home News Tribune* (East Brunswick, NJ) (March 21, 2000).

2. Glenn Collins, "Owens-Corning's Blurred Identity," *New York Times* (August 19, 1994): D4; Owens-Corning Fiberglass Corp., 774 F.2d 1116 (Fed Cir 1985).

3. Anna D. Wilde, "Harley Hopes to Add Hogs Roar to Its Menagerie," *Wall Street Journal* (June 23, 1995): B1; Associated Press, "Harley Growls About Exclusive Rights on Potato-Potato-Potato Sound," *Vancouver Sun* (March 29, 1996): D1.

4. Elizabeth C. Hirschman and Morris B. Holbrook, "Hedonic Consumption: Emerging Concepts, Methods, and Propositions," *Journal of Marketing* 46 (Summer 1982): 92–101.

5. Virginia Postrel, "The New Trend in Spending," *New York Times on the Web* (September 9, 2004).

6. Emily Cadei, "Cleaning Up: S.F. Duo Putting a Shine on its Product Line," *San Francisco Business Times* 17, no. 16.

7. Quoted in Jack Neff, "P&G Boosts Design's Role in Marketing," *Advertising Age* (February 9, 2004): 52.

8. Gabriel Kahn, "Philips Blitzes Asian Market as It Strives to Become Hip," *Wall Street Journal Interactive Edition* (August 1, 2002).

9. Amitava Chattopadhyay, Gerald J. Gorn, and Peter R. Darke, "Roses Are Red and Violets Are Blue—Everywhere? Cultural Universals and Differences in Colour Preference Among Consumers and Marketing Managers," unpublished manuscript, University of British Columbia, Fall 1999; Joseph Bellizzi and Robert E. Hite, "Environmental Color, Consumer Feelings, and Purchase Likelihood," *Psychology &*

Marketing 9 (1992): 347–363; Ayn E. Crowley, "The Two-Dimensional Impact of Color on Shopping," *Marketing Letters* (1993) V4 N1, 59–67; Gerald J. Gorn, Amitava Chattopadhyay, and Darren W. Dahl, "Effects of Color as an Executional Cue in an Ad: It's in the Shade," *Management Science* 43, 10 (October 1997): 1387–1397.

10. Quoted in Adam Bryant, "Plastic Surgery at AmEx," *Newsweek* (October 4, 1999): 55.

11. Mark G. Frank and Thomas Gilovich, "The Dark Side of Self and Social Perception: Black Uniforms and Aggression in Professional Sports," *Journal of Personality and Social Psychology* 54, 1 (1988): 74–85.

12. Pamela Paul, "Color By Numbers," *American Demographics* (February 2002): 31–36.

13. Paulette Thomas, "Cosmetics Makers Offer World's Women an All-American Look with Local Twists," *Wall Street Journal* (May 8, 1995): B1.

14. Marc Gobé, *Emotional Branding: The New Paradigm for Connecting Brands to People* (New York: Allworth Press, 2001).

15. Dirk Olin, "Color Cognition," *New York Times on the Web* (November 30, 2003).

16. Mike Golding and Julie White, *Pantone Color Resource Kit* (Hayden Publishing: New York, N.Y., 1997); Caroline Lego, *Effective Web Site Design: A Marketing Strategy for Small Liberal Arts Colleges*, Coe College, unpublished honours thesis, 1998; T. Long, "Human Factors Principles for the Design of Computer Colour Graphics Display," *British Telecom Technology Journal* 2, 3 (July 1994): 5–14; Morton Walker, *The Power of Color* (Avery Publishing Group: Garden City, NY, 1991).

17. "Ny emballage og nyt navn fordoblede salget," *Markedsforing* 12 (1992): 24. Adapted from Michael R. Solomon, Gary Bamossy, and Soren Askegaard, *Consumer Behavior: A European Perspective*, 2nd ed. (London: Pearson Education, 2001).

18. Ronald Alsop, "Color Grows More Important in Catching Consumers' Eyes," *Wall Street Journal* (November 29, 1984): 37; Meg Rosen and Frank Alpert, "Protecting Your Business Image: The Supreme Court Rules on Trade Dress," *Journal of Consumer Marketing* 11, 1 (1994): 50–55.

19. Rebecca Harris, "Sweet Rebranding," *Marketing Magazine* (November 7, 2005): 43.

20. Brian Wansink, *Mindless Eating: The Hidden Persuaders that Cause Us to Lose and Gain Weight* (New York: Bantam-Dell, 2006).

21. Brian Wansink and SeaBum Park, "At the Movies: How External Cues and Perceived Taste Impact Consumption Volume," *Food Quality and Preference* 12, no. 1 (January 2001): 69–74.

22. Brian Wansink and Junyong Kim, "Bad Popcorn in Big Buckets: Portion Size Can Influence Intake as Much as Taste," *Journal of Nutrition Education and Behavior* 37, no. 5 (September 2005): 242–245.

23. Brian Wansink and Matthew M. Cheney, "Super Bowls: Serving Bowl Size and Food Consumption," *Journal of the American Medical Association* 293, no. 14 (April 13, 2005): 1727–1728.

24. Brian Wansink, James E. Painter, and Jill North, "Bottomless Bowls: Why Visual Cues of Portion Size May Influence Intake," *Obesity Research* 13, no. 1 (January 2005): 93–100.

25. Priya Raghubir and Aradna Krishna, "Vital Dimensions in Volume Perception: Can the Eye Fool the Stomach?" *Journal of Marketing Research* 36 (August 1999): 313–326.

26. Brian Wansink and Koert van Ittersum, "Bottoms Up! The Influence of Elongation and Pouring on Consumption Volume", *Journal of Consumer Research* 30, no. 3 (December 2003): 455–463.

27. Barbara E. Kahn and Brian Wansink, "The Influence of Assortment Structure on Perceived Variety and Consumption Quantities," *Journal of Consumer Research* 30, no. 4 (March 2004): 519–533.

28. This section was contributed by Professor Brian Wansink of Cornell University and is reprinted here with his kind permission.

29. Deborah J. Mitchell, Barbara E. Kahn, and Susan C. Knasko, "There's Something in the Air: Effects of Congruent or Incongruent Ambient Odor on Consumer Decision Making," *Journal of Consumer Research* 22 (September 1995): 229–238; for a review of olfactory cues in store environments, see also Eric R. Spangenberg, Ayn E. Crowley, and Pamela W. Henderson, "Improving the Store Environment: Do Olfactory Cues Affect Evaluations and Behaviors?" *Journal of Marketing* 60 (April 1996): 67–80.

30. William S. Cain, "Educating Your Nose," *Psychology Today* (July 1981): 48–56.

31. Barbara Carton, "Thank Carl Klumpp for the Swell Smell of Right Guard," *Wall Street Journal* (May 11, 1995): A1.

32. Thomas, "Cosmetics Makers Offer World's Women an All-American Look with Local Twists."

33. Danny Hakim, "New Luxury-Car Specifications: Styling. Performance. Aroma," *New York Times on the Web* (October 25, 2003).

34. "The Smell of Sales," *Marketing Magazine* (August 1, 2005): 6.

35. Gail Tom, "Marketing with Music," *Journal of Consumer Marketing* 7 (Spring 1990): 49–53; J. Vail, "Music as a Marketing Tool," *Advertising Age* (November 4, 1985): 24. For empirical work on the effects of music on consumer behaviour, see James J. Kellaris and Robert J. Kent, "An Exploratory Investigation of Responses Elicited by Music Varying in Tempo, Tonality, and Texture," *Journal of Consumer Psychology* 2, 4 (1994): 381–401; James J. Kellaris, Anthony D. Cox, and Dena Cox, "The Effect of Background Music on Ad Processing: A Contingency Explanation," *Journal of Marketing* 57, 4 (October 1993): 114–125.

36. Reno Jamie and Croal N'Gai, "Hearing is Believing" *Newsweek* (August 5, 2002): 44–46.

37. E. Yorkston and G. Menon, "A Sound Idea: Phonetic Effects of Brand Names on Consumer Judgments," *Journal of Consumer Research* 31, no. 1 (June 2004): 43–51.

38. Larry M. Greenberg, "A City Smells Perfume and Holds Its Nose," *Wall Street Journal*, July 28, 1999: B1.

39. Otto Friedrich, "Trapped in a Musical Elevator," *Time* 110 (December 10, 1984): 3.

40. See Leslie Davis Burns and Sharron J. Lennon, "The Look and the Feel: Methods for Measuring Aesthetic Perceptions of Textiles and Apparel," in M.R. DeLong and A.M. Fiore, *Aesthetics of Textiles and Clothing: Advancing Multi-Disciplinary Perspectives* (Monument, CO: International Textile and Apparel Association, 1994): 120–130.

41. Jacob Hornik, "Tactile Stimulation and Consumer Response," *Journal of Consumer Research* 19 (December 1992).

42. Cf. Alka Varma Citrin, Donald E. Stern, Eric R. Spangenberg, and Michael J. Clark, "Consumer Need for Tactile Input an Internet Retailing Challenge," *Journal of Business Research* 56 (2003): 915–922.

43. J. Peck and T.L. Childers, "Individual Differences in Haptic Information Processing: The 'Need for Touch' Scale," *Journal of Consumer Research* 30, no. 3 (2003): 430–442.

44. Sarah Ellison and Erin White, "'Sensory' Marketers Say the Way to Reach Shoppers Is the Nose," *Advertising* (November 24, 2000): 1–3.

45. Douglas Heingartner, "Now Hear This, Quickly," *New York Times on the Web* (October 2, 2003).

46. Material adapted from a presentation by Glenn H. Mazur, QFD Institute, 2002.

47. Anonymous, "Touch Looms Large as a Sense that Drives Sales," *Brand Packaging* (May/June 1999): 39–40.

48. John Tagliabue, "Sniffing And Tasting With Metal And Wire," *New York Times Online* (February 17, 2002).

49. Dan Morse, "From Tabasco to Insane: When You're Hot, It May Not Be Enough," *Wall Street Journal Interactive Edition* (May 15, 2000).

50. Yumiko Ono, "Flat, Watery Drinks Are All the Rage as Japan Embraces New Taste Sensation," *Wall Street Journal Interactive Edition* (August 13, 1999).

51. Stuart Elliott, "TV Commercials Adjust to a Shorter Attention Span," *New York Times on the Web* (April 8, 2005).

52. "$10 Sure Thing," *Time* (August 4, 1980): 51.

53. Clare Dowdy, "A Fresh Look Inside the Shop Freezer," *The Financial Times* (March 24, 2004).

54. Elaine Sciolino, "Foie Gras in the Freezer? Just Don't Tell Anyone!" *New York Times* (December 19, 2002).

55. *New Yorker* (September 21, 1957): 33.

56. Erv Wolk, "Can Subliminal Ads Work for You?" *Modern Floor Coverings* (June 1986): 23.

57. Philip M. Merikle, "Subliminal Auditory Messages: An Evaluation," *Psychology & Marketing* 5, 4 (1988): 355–372.

58. Eric R. Spangenberg, Carl Obermiller, and Anthony G. Greenwald, "A Field Test of Subliminal Self-Help Audio-Tapes," *Journal of Public Policy and Marketing* 11, 2 (1992): 26–36.

59. Joel Saegert, "Why Marketing Should Quit Giving Subliminal Advertising the Benefit of the Doubt," *Psychology & Marketing* 4 (Summer 1987): 107–120. See also Dennis L. Rosen and Surendra N. Singh, "An Investigation of Subliminal Embed Effect on Multiple Measures of Advertising Effectiveness," *Psychology & Marketing* 9 (March/April 1992): 157–173. For a more recent review, see Kathryn T. Theus, "Subliminal Advertising and the Psychology of Processing Unconscious Stimuli: A Review of Research," *Psychology & Marketing* (May/June 1994): 271–290.

60. Jennifer Pendleton, "Multi Taskers," *Advertising Age* (March 29, 2004): S8.

61. Stuart Elliott, "New Survey on Ad Effectiveness," *New York Times on the Web* (April 14, 2004).

62. Seth Schiesel, "Vigilante on the TV Frontier," *New York Times on the Web* (November 4, 2004).

63. Mylene Mangalindon, "Some Bulk E-Mailers Make a Healthy Living on a Steady Diet of Spam," *Wall Street Journal Europe* (November 13, 2002), A2.

64. Roger Barton, *Advertising Media* (New York: McGraw-Hill, 1964).

65. Lucy Howard, "Trying to Fool a Feline," *Newsweek* (February 8, 1999): 8.

66. Quoted, without headline, *Atlanta Journal-Constitution*, accessed via Newslink May 2, 1998.

67. Suzanne Oliver, "New Personality," *Forbes* (August 15, 1994): 114.

68. Adam Finn, "Print Ad Recognition Readership Scores: An Information Processing Perspective," *Journal of Marketing Research* 25 (May 1988): 168–177.

69. J. Craig Andrews and Richard G. Netemeyer, "Alcohol Warning Label Effects: Socialization, Addiction, and Public Policy Issues," in Ronald P. Hill, ed. *Marketing and Consumer Research in the Public Interest* (Thousand Oaks, CA: Sage, 1996): 153–175.

70. Stuart Elliott, "When Up Is Down, Does It Sell?" *New York Times* (February 21, 1992): D1.

71. Gerald L. Lohse, "Consumer Eye Movement Patterns on Yellow Pages Advertising," *Journal of Advertising* XXVI, 1 (Spring 1997): 61–73.

72. Erin White and David Pringle, "New Ads for Vanilla Coke Reward Curiosity in Europe," *Wall Street Journal Interactive Edition* (October 30, 2002).

73. Eve Lazarus, "Grape Exposure," *Marketing Magazine* (October 31, 2005): 6.

74. Robert M. McMath, "Image Counts," *American Demographics* (May 1998): 64.

75. Brian Wansink, James Painter, and Koert van Ittersum, "Descriptive Menu Labels' Effect on Sales," *Cornell Hotel and Restaurant Administration Quarterly* (December 2001): 68–72.

76. Anthony Ramirez, "Lessons in the Cracker Market: Nabisco Saved New Graham Snack," *New York Times* (July 5, 1990): D1.

77. Albert H. Hastorf and Hadley Cantril, "They Saw a Game: A Case Study," *Journal of Abnormal and Social Psychology* 49 (1954): 129–134. Cf. also Roberto Friedmann and Mary R. Zimmer, "The Role of Psychological Meaning in Advertising," *Journal of Advertising* 17, 1 (1988): 31–40.

78. Robert M. McMath, "Chock Full of (Pea)nuts," *American Demographics* (April 1997): 60.

79. See David Mick, "Consumer Research and Semiotics: Exploring the Morphology of Signs, Symbols, and Significance," *Journal of Consumer Research* 13 (September 1986): 196–213.

80. Teresa J. Domzal and Jerome B. Kernan, "Reading Advertising: The What and How of Product Meaning," *Journal of Consumer Marketing* 9 (Summer 1992): 48–64.

81. Arthur Asa Berger, *Signs in Contemporary Culture: An Introduction to Semiotics* (New York: Longman, 1984); Mick, "Consumer Research and Semiotics"; Charles Sanders Peirce, in *Collected Papers*, eds. Charles Hartshorne, Paul Weiss, and Arthur W. Burks (Cambridge, MA: Harvard University Press, 1931–1958).

82. Gabriel Kahn, "Chinese Characters Are Gaining New Meaning as Corporate Logos," *Wall Street Journal Interactive Edition* (July 18, 2002).

83. Ernest Beck, "A Minefield in Maienfeld: 'Heidiland' Is Taking Over," *Wall Street Journal Interactive Edition* (October 2, 1997).

84. Stuart Elliott, "Advertising: A Music Retailer Whistles a New Marketing Tune to Get Heard Above the Cacophony of Competitors," *New York Times* (July 2, 1996): D7; Personal Communication, GRW Advertising, April 1997.

85. See Tim Davis, "Taste Tests: Are the Blind Leading the Blind?" *Beverage World* (April 1987) 3: 43.

86. Betsy McKay, "Pepsi to Revive a Cola-War Barb: The Decades-Old Blind Taste Test," *Wall Street Journal Interactive* (March 21, 2000).

87. Adapted from Michael R. Solomon and Elnora W. Stuart, *Marketing: Real People, Real Choices* (Englewood Cliffs, NJ: Prentice Hall, 1997).

88. William Echikson, "Aiming at High and Low Markets," *Fortune* (March 22, 1993): 89.

It's Tuesday morning, and all is routine in James's apartment. Wake up, stagger to the bathroom, and then head to the fridge for some cold orange juice. Jump in the shower, shave, pull on pants, and search the closet for a clean shirt. Turn on the TV to check the weather for the day.

What he sees on the screen is unbelievable! A jumbo passenger jet has flown into one of the World Trade Center towers in New York City and exploded. James cannot believe his eyes. Then minutes later, another jet hits the second tower, and it too is turned into a fiery inferno. James finds these events impossible to comprehend, even as he watches. He listens to the panic in the voices of the television reporters, relaying messages of missing planes and another crash at the Pentagon in Washington, D.C. What is happening? Why are passenger jets crashing into buildings, killing thousands of people?

September 11, 2001, the day the world changed forever, is seared into the memory of people all around the globe.

CHAPTER → 3

Learning and Memory

THE LEARNING PROCESS

James and most of the world will have memories of where they were and what they were doing the morning of September 11, 2001. Many people will add this event to their memories of where they were when John F. Kennedy was assassinated or when Princess Diana died. The development of vivid memories, along with their associations to objects, feelings, and opinions, is relevant to the study of how brand networks are formed. Many marketers realize that long-standing, learned connections between products and memories are a potent way to build and keep brand loyalty. Some companies are bringing their old trademark characters out of retirement, including the Campbell Soup Kids, the Pillsbury Doughboy, Betty Crocker, and Planters' Mr. Peanut.[1] Several familiar faces returned in major advertising campaigns recently, including the Jolly Green Giant (born in 1925), Charlie the Tuna (who first appeared in 1961), and even Charmin's Mr. Whipple, who was brought out of retirement in 1999.[2] In this chapter, we'll explore how learned associations among feelings, events, and products—and the memories they evoke—are an important aspect of consumer behaviour.

Learning refers to a relatively permanent change in behaviour that is caused by experience. This experience does not have to affect the learner directly; we can learn *vicariously* by observing events that affect others.[3] We also learn even when we are not trying. Consumers recognize many brand names and can hum many product jingles, even those for product categories they themselves do not use. This casual, unintentional acquisition of knowledge is known as *incidental learning*.

Learning is an ongoing process. Our knowledge about the world is constantly being revised as we are exposed to new stimuli and receive ongoing feedback that allows us to modify behaviour in other, similar situations at a later time. The concept of learning covers a lot of ground, ranging from a consumer's simple association between a stimulus such as a product logo (Coca-Cola) and a response ("refreshing soft drink") to a complex series of cognitive activities (writing an essay on learning for a consumer behaviour exam). Psychologists who study learning have advanced several theories to explain the learning process. These theories range from those focusing on simple stimulus-response connections (behavioural theories) to perspectives that regard consumers as complex problem solvers who learn abstract rules and concepts by observing others (cognitive theories). Understanding these theories is important to marketers as well, since basic learning principles are at the heart of many consumer purchase decisions.

→ Many classic advertising campaigns consist of product slogans that have been repeated so many times that they are etched in consumers' minds. The ad shown here brags about the high awareness of the Chiquita banana jingle ("I'm Chiquita banana, and I'm here to say …").
Used by permission of Chiquita Brands, Inc.

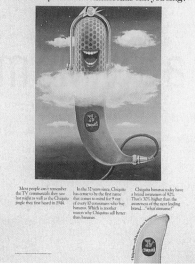

BEHAVIOURAL LEARNING THEORIES

Behavioural learning theories assume that learning takes place as the result of responses to external events. Psychologists who subscribe to this viewpoint do not focus on internal thought processes. Instead, they approach the mind as a "black box" and emphasize the observable aspects of behaviour.

This view is represented by two major approaches to learning: classical conditioning and instrumental conditioning. People's experiences are shaped by the feedback they receive as they go through life. Similarly, consumers respond to brand names, scents, jingles, and other marketing stimuli based upon the learned connections they have formed over time. People also learn that actions they take result in rewards and punishments, and this feedback influences the way they will respond in similar situations in the future. Consumers who receive compliments on a product choice will be more likely to buy that brand again, while those who get food poisoning at a new restaurant will not likely patronize it in the future.

Classical Conditioning

Classical conditioning occurs when a stimulus that elicits a response is paired with another stimulus that initially does not elicit a response on its own. Over time, this second stimulus causes a similar response because it is associated with the first stimulus. This phenomenon was first demonstrated in dogs by Ivan Pavlov, a Russian physiologist doing research on digestion in animals, and is shown in Figure 3–1.

Pavlov induced classically conditioned learning by pairing a neutral stimulus (a bell) with a stimulus known to cause a salivation response in dogs (he squirted

FIGURE 3–1

DIAGRAM OF THE CLASSICAL CONDITIONING PROCESS

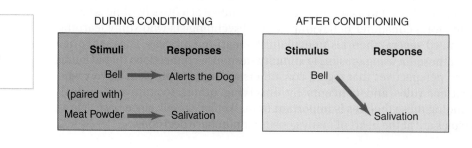

dried meat powder into their mouths). The powder was an **unconditioned stimulus (UCS)** because it was naturally capable of causing the response. Over time, the bell became a **conditioned stimulus (CS)**; it did not initially cause salivation, but the dogs learned to associate the bell with the meat powder and began to salivate at the sound of the bell only. The drooling, caused by a sound now linked to feeding time, was a **conditioned response (CR)**.

This basic form of classical conditioning demonstrated by Pavlov applies primarily to responses controlled by the autonomic (e.g., salivation) and nervous (e.g., eye blink) systems. That is, it focuses on visual and olfactory cues that induce hunger, thirst, or sexual arousal. When these cues are consistently paired with conditioned stimuli, such as brand names, consumers may learn to feel hungry, thirsty, or aroused when later exposed to the brand cues.

Classical conditioning can have similar effects for more complex reactions too. Even a credit card becomes a conditioned cue that triggers greater spending, especially since it is a stimulus that is present only in situations where consumers are spending money. People learn that they can make larger purchases when using credit cards, and they also have been found to leave larger tips than they do when using cash.[4] Small wonder that American Express reminds us, "Don't leave home without it."

REPETITION

Conditioning effects are more likely to occur after the conditioned and unconditioned stimuli have been paired a number of times.[5] Repeated exposures increase the strength of stimulus-response associations and prevent the **decay** of these associations in memory. Recent research indicates that the interval between exposures may influence the effectiveness of this strategy as well as the type of medium that is used to communicate the stimulus-response associations; the most effective repetition strategy seems to be a combination of spaced exposures that alternate in terms of media that are more and less involving, such as television advertising complemented by print media.[6] Many classic advertising campaigns consist of product slogans that have been repeated so many times they are etched in consumers' minds.

Conditioning will not occur or will take longer if the CS is only occasionally presented with the UCS. One result of this lack of association may be **extinction**, which occurs when the effects of prior conditioning are reduced and finally disappear. This can occur, for example, when a product is *overexposed* in the marketplace so that its original allure is lost. The Lacoste polo shirt (sold by Izod), with its distinctive crocodile crest, is a good example of this effect. When the once-exclusive crocodile started to appear on baby clothes and many other items, it lost its cachet and was soon replaced by other contenders, such as the Ralph Lauren polo player.[7] Now that Izod is being more careful about where its logo appears, the brand is starting to regain its "cool" in some circles.

STIMULUS GENERALIZATION

Stimulus generalization refers to the tendency of stimuli similar to a CS to evoke similar, conditioned responses.[8] For example, Pavlov noticed in subsequent studies that his dogs would sometimes salivate when they heard noises that only resembled the sound of a bell (keys jangling, for instance). People react to other, similar stimuli in much the same way as they respond to an original stimulus. A drugstore's bottle of private-brand mouthwash deliberately packaged to resemble Listerine mouthwash may evoke a similar response among consumers who assume that this "me-too" product shares other characteristics of the original.

Indeed, consumers in one study on shampoo brands tended to rate those with similar packages as similar in quality and performance as well.[9] This "piggybacking" strategy can cut both ways: When the quality of the me-too product turns out to be lower than that of the original brand, consumers may exhibit even more positive feelings toward the original; however, if the quality of the two competitors is

→ American Airlines uses an obvious reference to classical conditioning effects.
Used with permission of American Airlines. American Airlines is a registered trademark of American Airlines.

perceived to be about equal, consumers may conclude the price premium they are paying for the original is not worth it.[10] In addition, consumers' learned associations with a large corporation can influence what they believe about its products. The company's overall reputation has been shown to have a particularly strong impact on brand evaluations, and to a lesser extent its reputation for social responsibility can also affect these individual brand ratings.[11]

In a recent twist on this principle, some companies are using a strategy called **masked branding**, which deliberately hides a product's true origin. For example, General Motors distanced itself from its reputation for bad service by creating the Saturn brand and packaging it as a product made by a small-town company run by ordinary people, and Levi Strauss markets its Red Tab line to appeal to young consumers who don't want to be associated with an "old" brand.[12] Rickard's Red beer is positioned to compete with microbreweries, and the label lists the manufacturer as the Capilano Brewing Co., although in reality the beer is made by Molson's.

STIMULUS DISCRIMINATION

Stimulus discrimination occurs when a stimulus similar to a CS is *not* followed by a UCS. In these situations, reactions are weakened and will soon disappear. Part of the learning process involves learning to respond to some stimuli but not to other, similar stimuli. Manufacturers of well-established brands commonly urge consumers not to buy "cheap imitations" because the results will not be what they expect.

Marketing Applications of Classical Conditioning

Many marketing strategies focus on the establishment of associations between stimuli and responses. Behavioural learning principles apply to many consumer phenomena, ranging from the creation of a distinctive brand image to the perceived link between a product and an underlying need.

The transfer of meaning from an unconditioned stimulus to a conditioned stimulus explains why "made-up" brand names like Coca-Cola or IBM can exert such powerful effects on consumers. When nonsense syllables (meaningless sets of letters) are paired with such evaluative words as beauty or success, the meaning is transferred to the nonsense syllables. This change in the symbolic significance of initially meaningless words shows that complex meanings can be conditioned by fairly simple associations.[13]

These conditioned associations are crucial to many marketing strategies that rely on the creation and perpetuation of positive **brand equity**, in which a brand has strong positive associations in a consumer's memory and commands a lot of loyalty as a result.[14] As we will see in the following chapters, a product with brand equity holds a tremendous advantage in the marketplace.

REPETITION

One advertising researcher argues that scheduling more than three exposures is a waste. The first creates awareness of the product, the second demonstrates its relevance to the consumer, and the third serves as a reminder of the product's benefits.[15] However, even this bare-bones approach implies that repetition is needed to ensure that the consumer is actually exposed to (and processes) the ad at least three times. As we saw in the last chapter, this exposure is by no means guaranteed, since people tend to tune out or distort many marketing communications. Marketers attempting to condition an association must ensure that the consumers they have targeted will be exposed to the stimulus a sufficient number of times to make it "stick."

On the other hand, it is possible to have too much of a good thing. Consumers can become so used to hearing or seeing a marketing stimulus that they no longer pay attention to it. This problem, known as *advertising wearout,* can be alleviated by varying the way in which the basic message is presented. For example, the tax-preparation firm H&R Block (***www.hrblock.com***) is famous for its long-standing "Another of the 17 reasons to use H&R Block … " campaign.

CONDITIONING PRODUCT ASSOCIATIONS

Advertisements often pair a product with a positive stimulus to create a desirable association. Various aspects of a marketing message, such as music, humour, or imagery, can affect conditioning. In one study, for example, subjects who viewed a photograph of pens paired with either pleasant or unpleasant music were more likely later to select the pen that appeared with pleasant music.[16]

The behaviour of consumers can also be conditioned. In studies involving the effect of music on the consumption behaviour of people in supermarkets or restaurants, consumption was found to be influenced. Slow music in grocery stores led to longer visits and more money being spent.[17] Slow music in restaurants had no impact on food consumption, but patrons did tend to have one extra drink, on average.[18]

The order in which the conditioned stimulus and the unconditioned stimulus are presented can affect the likelihood that learning will occur. Generally speaking,

Marketing
Opportunity   !

The choice of a great brand name is so important that companies often hire specialists called naming consultants to come up with a winning selection. These experts often try to find *semantic associations* that click because they evoke some desirable connection. That strategy brought us names like Qualcomm ("quality" and "communications"), Verizon ("horizon," as in forward-looking), and Intel ("intelligent" and "electronics"). The name "Viagra" rhymes with "Niagara," the famous waterfall. People associate water with both sexuality and life, and Niagara Falls is a honeymoon mecca. Philip Morris has renamed itself Altria Group, Inc. to convey its expansion beyond cigarettes into packaged foods and brewing. The word *Altria* means high, which is a controversial choice; one brand consultant comments, "I'm not sure 'high' is right for a company with many mood-altering products in its brand portfolio."[24]

Appropriate semantic combinations are getting harder to find, so some consultants are trying to appeal to consumers' more basic instincts by focusing on links between the raw sounds of vowels and consonants (called *phonemes*) and emotional responses. To get at these associations, researchers usually give subjects pairs of nonsense names that differ in only a single phoneme, such as Paressa and Taressa, where the phonemes that differ are *p* and *t*, and ask which word sounds faster, more daring, nicer, and so on. They've found that sounds that come to a full stop (*p, b, t,* and *d*) connote slowness, while *f, v, s,* and *z* are fast. The words *Prozac* and *Amazon* convey a sense of speed (of recovery or of delivery). When naming consultants were asked to label a new handheld personal digital assistant (PDA), they first thought of "Strawberry," because the little keyboard buttons resembled seeds. They liked the "berry" part of the name because they knew that people associated the letter *b* with reliability, and a berry communicated smallness compared to other PDAs. But a linguist pointed out that "straw" is a slow syllable, and the product needed to have a fast connotation. Voila! The BlackBerry PDA was born.[25]

the unconditioned stimulus should be presented prior to the conditioned stimulus. The technique of *backward conditioning,* such as showing a soft drink (the CS) and then playing a jingle (the UCS), is generally not effective.[19] Because sequential presentation is desirable for conditioning to occur, classical conditioning is not very effective in static situations, such as in magazine ads, where (in contrast to TV or radio) the marketer cannot control the order in which the CS and the UCS are perceived.

Just as product associations can be formed, they can also be *extinguished.* Because of the danger of extinction, a classical conditioning strategy may not be as effective for products that are frequently encountered, since there is no guarantee they will be accompanied by the CS. A bottle of Pepsi paired with the refreshing sound of a carbonated beverage being poured over ice may seem like a good example of conditioning. Unfortunately, the product would also be seen in many other contexts where this sound was absent, reducing the effectiveness of the conditioning strategy.

By the same reasoning, a novel tune should be chosen over a popular one to pair with a product, since the popular song might also be heard in many situations in which the product is not present.[20] Music videos in particular may serve as effective UCSs because they often have an emotional impact on viewers, and this effect may transfer to ads accompanying the video.[21]

APPLICATIONS OF STIMULUS GENERALIZATION

The process of stimulus generalization is often central to branding and packaging decisions that attempt to capitalize on consumers' positive associations with an existing brand or company name. The marketing value of an admired stimulus is clearly demonstrated at universities with winning sports teams, where loyal fans snap up merchandise, from clothing to bathroom accessories, emblazoned with the school's name. This business did not even exist 30 years ago, when schools were reluctant to commercialize their images. Today, it's a different story. Many university administrators crave the revenue they receive from sales of products that range from sweatshirts to drink coasters. Strategies based on stimulus generalization include the following:

- *Family branding,* in which a variety of products capitalize on the reputation of a company name. Companies such as Virgin, Campbell's, Heinz, and General Electric rely on their positive corporate images to sell different product lines.

- *Product line extensions,* in which related products are added to an established brand. Dole, which is associated with fruit, was able to introduce refrigerated juices and juice bars, while Sun Maid went from raisins to raisin bread. Meanwhile, Procter & Gamble is cleaning up with its Mr. Clean brand of liquid cleanser, aggressively putting the name on new products such as Mr. Clean Magic Eraser, for removing crayon marks from walls and scuff marks from chair rails, and Mr. Clean AutoDry, for leaving a freshly washed car spot-free without hand drying.[22]

- *Licensing,* in which well-known names are "rented" by others. This strategy is increasing in popularity as marketers try to link their products and services with well-established brands. *Prevention* magazine is introducing vitamins, *Runners World* magazine is putting its name on jogging suits. *Maxim* magazine, which already brought out its own brand of hair colour for men two years ago, is now thinking of putting its name on nightclubs and frozen food. And *Vibe* magazine is producing a line of Vibe sheets and will be bringing out a line of greeting cards featuring quotes from the songs of music celebrities.

- *Look-alike packaging,* in which distinctive packaging designs create strong associations with a particular brand. This link is often exploited by makers of generic or private-label brands that wish to communicate a quality image by putting their products in very similar packages. Imitating the look of an existing successful brand is common in today's crowded marketplace. However, one study found that a negative experience with an imitator brand increased evaluations of the original brand. A positive experience with the imitator had the opposite effect of decreasing evaluations of the original brand.[23]

→ President's Choice Decadent Chocolate Chip Cookie is a popular PC product among the wide array under the PC label. This private brand illustrates both stimulus generalization through family branding and stimulus discrimination through positioning vis-à-vis competitors using distinctive packaging.
Courtesy of Loblaws.

A related problem happens when fake products masquerade as the real thing. "Knock-offs" of well-known products are a problem around the world. For example, Converse's Chuck Taylor All Stars are a favourite among Brazilian kids, and only the United States and Japan post higher sales of these athletic shoes. One small problem: Though most wearers don't know it, all of the All Stars sold in Brazil are fakes. The sneakers look genuine, down to the circle with the five-pointed blue star on the high-top model. A local company registered the All Star trademark as its own back in 1979 and has been selling about one million pairs each year since for about one-third of the U.S. price.[26]

Instrumental Conditioning

Instrumental conditioning, also known as *operant conditioning,* occurs as the individual learns to perform behaviours that produce positive outcomes and to avoid those that yield negative outcomes. This learning process is most closely associated with the psychologist B.F. Skinner, who demonstrated the effects of instrumental conditioning by teaching animals to dance, play ping-pong, and so on by systematically rewarding them for desired behaviours.[27]

Under classical conditioning, people respond involuntarily and fairly simply. Under instrumental conditioning, people respond deliberately to obtain a goal; the reasons for their responses may be more complex. The desired behaviour may be learned over a period of time, as intermediate actions are rewarded in a process called **shaping**. For example, the owner of a new store may award prizes to shoppers just for coming in, hoping that over time they will continue to drop in and eventually buy something.

Also, classical conditioning involves the close pairing of two stimuli. Instrumental learning occurs as a result of a reward received *following* the desired behaviour and takes place over a period in which a variety of other behaviours are attempted and abandoned because they are not reinforced. A good way to remember the difference is to keep in mind that in instrumental learning the response is performed because it is *instrumental* to gaining a reward or avoiding a punishment. Consumers over time come to associate with people who reward them and to choose products that make them feel good or satisfy some need.

Instrumental learning occurs in one of three ways. When the environment provides **positive reinforcement** in the form of a reward, the response is strengthened and appropriate behaviour is learned. For example, a woman who gets compliments after wearing Obsession perfume will learn that using this product has the desired effect, and she will be more likely to keep buying the product. **Negative reinforcement** also strengthens responses so that appropriate behaviour is learned. A perfume company, for example, might run an ad showing a woman sitting home alone on a Saturday night because she did not use its fragrance. The message conveyed is that she could have *avoided* this negative outcome if only she had used the perfume. In contrast to situations wherein we learn to do certain things to avoid unpleasantness, **punishment** occurs when a response is followed by unpleasant events (such as being ridiculed by friends for wearing an offensive-smelling perfume). We learn not to repeat these behaviours.

When trying to understand the differences among these mechanisms, keep in mind that outcomes from a person's response to behaviour can be either positive or negative and that these outcomes or anticipated outcomes can be applied or removed. That is, under conditions of both positive reinforcement and punishment, the person receives a reaction after doing something. In contrast, negative reinforcement occurs when someone avoids a negative outcome; removing something negative is pleasurable and hence also rewarding. (On your credit card bill, interest is a negative reinforcement. So if you pay your bill on time, you will not be subject to interest payments.)

Finally, when a positive outcome is no longer received, extinction of the behaviour is likely to occur, and the learned stimulus-response connection will not be maintained (as when a woman no longer receives compliments on her perfume). Thus, either positive or negative reinforcement *strengthens* the future link between a response and an outcome because of the pleasant experience. This tie is *weakened* under conditions of both punishment and extinction because of the unpleasant experience. The relationships among these four conditions are easier to understand by referring to Figure 3–2.

An important factor in operant conditioning is the set of rules by which appropriate reinforcements are given for a behaviour. The issue of what is the most effective *reinforcement schedule* to use is important to marketers, because it relates to the amount of effort and resources they must devote to rewarding consumers in order to condition desired behaviours. Several schedules are possible:

- *Fixed-interval reinforcement:* After a specified time period has passed, the first response that is made brings the reward. Under such conditions, people tend to respond slowly right after being reinforced, but their responses speed up as the time for the next reinforcement looms. For example, consumers may crowd into a store for the last day of its seasonal sale and not reappear until the next sale.

- *Variable-interval reinforcement:* The time that must pass before reinforcement is delivered varies around some average. Since the person does not know exactly when to expect the reinforcement, responses must be performed at a consistent rate. This logic is behind retailers' use of so-called secret shoppers—people who

Net Profit +

Marketing researchers frequently face the problem of consumers' reluctance to disclose personal information in surveys. Can online techniques help to overcome this barrier? Perhaps, if automated questioning can be made to resemble human interactions. One study found that when a computer appears to possess characteristics normally associated with human behaviour, such as using everyday language and taking turns in conversations, consumers respond favourably and form a relationship with the machine. In other words, they transfer rules they have learned in human interaction to a human-machine context. The research found that consumers are more likely to divulge personal information when the computer divulges information first, and that the degree of intimate disclosure gradually escalates. For example, the computer may disclose the fact that there are times when it crashes for no apparent reason and then ask the consumer to reciprocate by disclosing something about himself or herself. And those consumers who had engaged in self-disclosure and reciprocity with a computer were likely to evaluate products described online more favourably than those that had not engaged in this interaction.[28] So, go give your computer a nice big hug!

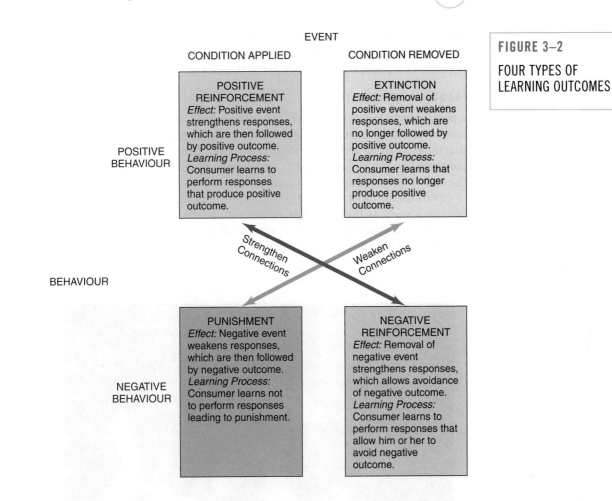

FIGURE 3–2

FOUR TYPES OF
LEARNING OUTCOMES

periodically test for service quality by posing as customers at unannounced times. Since store employees never know exactly when to expect a visit, they must maintain high-quality service and standards constantly, "just in case."

- *Fixed-ratio reinforcement*: Reinforcement occurs only after a fixed number of responses. This schedule motivates people to continue performing the same behaviour over and over. For example, a consumer might keep buying at the same store to earn a prize after collecting frequent buyer points.

- *Variable-ratio reinforcement*: The behaviour of a person is reinforced after a certain number of responses, but he or she does not know how many responses are required. People in such situations tend to respond at very high and steady rates, and this type of behaviour is very difficult to extinguish. This reinforcement schedule is responsible for consumers' attraction to slot machines. They learn that, if they keep throwing money into the machine, they will eventually win something—if they don't go broke first!

Applications of Instrumental Conditioning Principles

Principles of instrumental conditioning are at work when a consumer is rewarded or punished for a purchase decision. Business people shape behaviour by gradually reinforcing consumers for taking appropriate actions. For example, a car dealer might encourage a reluctant buyer just to sit in a floor model, then suggest a test drive, and then try to close the deal.

REINFORCEMENT OF CONSUMPTION

Marketers use many ways to reinforce the behaviour of consumers, ranging from a simple "thank you" after a purchase to substantial rebates and follow-up phone calls. For example, a life insurance company obtained a much higher rate of policy renewal among a group of new customers who received a thank-you letter after each payment compared with a control group that did not receive any reinforcement.[29]

FREQUENCY MARKETING

A popular technique known as **frequency marketing** (*www.frequencymarketing.com*) reinforces the behaviour of regular purchasers by giving them prizes with values that increase along with the amount purchased. This operant learning strategy was pioneered by the airline industry, which introduced "frequent-flyer" programs in the early 1980s to reward loyal customers.

Perhaps the most enthusiastic fan of frequency marketing is David Phillips. He became known as the Pudding Guy because he earned a lifetime of free airplane rides after noticing a frequent-flyer offer on a chocolate pudding package. Realizing that he could earn 500 miles for every 10 UPC symbols redeemed, he invested about

→ Rewarding customers with frequent-flyer miles is an effective way to reinforce customers and build brand loyalty.
Used with permission of American Airlines and the OneWorld Airline Consortium.

www.oneworld.com

It's natural to want to be rewarded.   oneworld

Loyalty should be rewarded. So if you're a frequent flyer member of one of our airlines, you can earn and redeem miles on the other seven. After all, **one**world™ revolves around you.

AmericanAirlines   Aer Lingus   BRITISH AIRWAYS   CATHAY PACIFIC

FINNAIR   IBERIA   LANCHILE   QANTAS

$3000 and 50 hours of his time to buy enough pudding to win 1.25 million frequent-flyer miles from American Airlines. He donated the pudding to local food banks; in exchange for free pudding, workers agreed to peel off the labels as they dished out the pudding. The final tally: 12 150 cups of pudding.[30] Whipped cream with that?

Frequent buyer programs are not just about consumers earning free trips and merchandise. Retailers can use related databases to refine everything from their merchandise mix to their marketing strategy based on their detailed knowledge of consumers and their purchases. Costs are lowered by the ability to design focused and personalized marketing communications to the prime customer; customer retention programs are more effective; product launches and redesigns are more likely to be successful; and blunders are prevented. In Canada, for example, a Shell station slated for conversion to self-serve was left as full-serve because a major reason its customers (more than half were women) used the station was that it offered full service. A&P won back its customers and avoided a strategic error when response to a pilot self-serve deli in one store showed that customers overwhelmingly wanted a full-service deli and would go elsewhere to get the service, as well as do their other shopping![31]

COGNITIVE LEARNING THEORY

In contrast to behavioural theories of learning, **cognitive learning theory** stresses the importance of internal mental processes. This perspective views people as problem solvers who actively use information from the world around them to master their environment. Supporters of this viewpoint also stress the role of creativity and insight during the learning process.

Is Learning Conscious or Not?

A lot of controversy surrounds the issue of whether or when people are aware of their learning processes. While behavioural learning theorists emphasize the routine, automatic nature of conditioning, proponents of cognitive learning argue that even these simple effects are based on cognitive factors; that is, expectations are created that a stimulus will be followed by a response (the formation of expectations requires mental activity). According to this school of thought, conditioning occurs because subjects develop conscious hypotheses and then act on them.

On the one hand, there is some evidence for the existence of unconscious procedural knowledge. People apparently do process at least some information in an automatic, passive way, which is a condition that has been termed *mindlessness*.[32] When we meet someone new or encounter a new product, for example, we have a tendency to respond to the stimulus in terms of existing categories, rather than taking the trouble to formulate different ones. Our reactions are activated by a *trigger feature*—some stimulus that cues us toward a particular pattern. For example, men in one study rated a car in an ad as superior on a variety of characteristics if a seductive woman (the trigger feature) was present, despite the fact that the men did not believe the woman's presence actually had an influence on their evaluations.[33] Indeed, a controversial book published in 2005 argues that we often make snap judgments that result in superior decisions compared to those we think about a lot because we rely on our "adaptive unconscious" to guide us.[34]

Nonetheless, many modern theorists are beginning to regard some instances of conditioning as cognitive processes, especially where expectations are formed about the links between stimuli and responses. Indeed, studies using *masking effects*, wherein it is difficult for subjects to learn CS/UCS associations, show substantial reductions in conditioning.[35] An adolescent girl may observe that women on television and in real life seem to be rewarded with compliments and attention when they smell nice and wear alluring clothing. She figures out that the probability of these rewards occurring is greater when she wears perfume, and so she deliberately wears a popular scent to obtain the reward of social acceptance.

Observational Learning

Observational learning occurs when people watch the actions of others and note the reinforcements they receive for their behaviours; learning occurs as a result of *vicarious* rather than direct experience. This type of learning is a complex process; people store these observations in memory as they accumulate knowledge, perhaps using this information at a later point to guide their own behaviours. This process of imitating the behaviour of others is called *modelling*. For example, a woman shopping for a new kind of perfume may remember the reactions a friend received upon wearing a certain brand several months earlier, and she will base her behaviour on her friend's actions.

The modelling process is a powerful form of learning, and people's tendencies to imitate others' behaviours can have negative effects. Of particular concern is the potential of television shows and movies to teach violence to children. Children may be exposed to new methods of aggression by models (e.g., cartoon heroes) in the shows they watch. At some later point, the child may imitate these behaviours when he or she becomes angry.

A classic study demonstrates the effect of modelling on children's actions. Kids who watched an adult stomp on, knock down, and otherwise torture a large inflated "Bobo doll" repeated these behaviours when later left alone in a room with the doll; children who did not witness these acts did not.[36]

For observational learning in the form of modelling to occur, four conditions must be met.[37] These factors are summarized in Figure 3–3.

1. The consumer's attention must be directed toward the appropriate model whom, for reasons of attractiveness, competence, status, or similarity, it is desirable to emulate.

2. The consumer must remember what the model says or does.

3. The consumer must convert this information into actions.

4. The consumer must be motivated to perform these actions.

Applications of Cognitive Learning Principles

Consumers' ability to learn vicariously by observing how the behaviour of others is reinforced makes the lives of marketers much easier. Because people do not have to be reinforced directly for their actions, marketers do not necessarily have to reward

---

FIGURE 3–3   COMPONENTS OF OBSERVATIONAL LEARNING

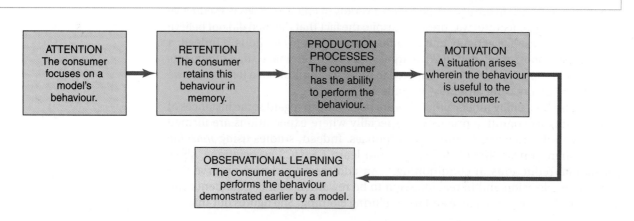

or punish them for purchase behaviours. Instead, they can show what happens to models who use or do not use their products, in the knowledge that consumers will often be motivated to imitate these actions at a later time. For example, a perfume commercial may depict a woman surrounded by a throng of admirers who are providing her with positive reinforcement for using the product. Needless to say, this learning process is more practical than providing the same personal attention to each woman who actually buys the perfume!

Consumers' evaluations of models go beyond simple stimulus-response connections. For example, a celebrity's image often provokes more than a simple reflexive response of good or bad;[38] it is a complex combination of many attributes. In general, the degree to which a model will be emulated depends upon his or her social attractiveness. Attractiveness can be based upon several components, including physical appearance, expertise, or similarity to the evaluator.

THE ROLE OF MEMORY IN LEARNING

Memory involves a process of acquiring information and storing it over time so that it will be available when needed. Contemporary approaches to the study of memory employ an information-processing approach. They assume that the mind is in some ways like a computer: Data are input, processed, and output for later use in revised form. In the **encoding** stage, information is entered in a way the system will recognize. In the **storage** stage, this knowledge is integrated with what is already in memory and "warehoused" until needed. During **retrieval**, the mind accesses the desired information.[39] The memory process is summarized in Figure 3–4.

Many of our experiences are locked inside our heads and may surface years later if prompted by the right cues. Marketers rely on consumers to retain information they have learned about products and services, trusting that they will later apply it when they decide to buy. During the consumer decision-making process, this *internal memory* is combined with *external memory*—which includes all of the product details on packages, in shopping lists, and through other marketing stimuli—to permit brand alternatives to be identified and evaluated.[40] The grocery shopping list is a good example of a powerful external memory aid. When consumers use shopping lists, they buy approximately 80 percent of the items on the list, and the likelihood of a particular list item being purchased is higher if the person who wrote the list also participates in the shopping trip. Marketers also found that the likelihood of purchasing a list item increased with household size and is marginally greater during holiday periods. This means that if marketers can induce a consumer to plan to buy an item in advance of shopping, the probability of the item being purchased is high. One suggested way to encourage purchasing would be to provide peel-off stickers on packages so that when the consumer notices the supply is low, the consumer can peel off the label and place it directly onto a shopping list.[41]

Research supports the idea that marketers can distort a consumer's recall of a product experience. What we think we "know" about products can be influenced by advertising messages to which we are exposed after using the products. This *postexperience advertising* is more likely to alter actual memories when it is very similar to or activates memories about the actual experience. For example, advertising can make a remembered product experience more favourable than it actually was.

FIGURE 3–4   THE MEMORY PROCESS

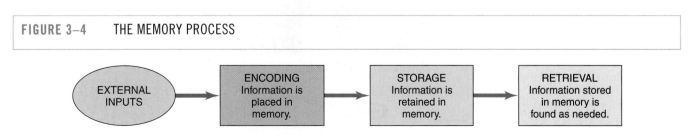

→ This fragrance ad emphasizes that products can evoke memories of earlier experiences.
Courtesy of COMPAR.

Encoding of Information for Later Retrieval

The way information is *encoded*, or mentally programmed, helps to determine how it will be represented in memory. In general, incoming data that are associated with other information already in memory stand a better chance of being retained. For example, brand names that are linked to physical characteristics[42] of a product category (Coffee Mate creamer or Sani-Flush toilet bowl cleaner) or that are easy to visualize (Tide detergent or Jaguar cars) tend to be more easily retained in memory than more abstract brand names.[43]

However, memory for brand names may interact with one's involvement in the product class. Low-involvement products, such as household cleaners, seem to benefit from descriptive names by being easier to remember. There is no evidence that descriptive names for high-involvement products, such as automobiles, are remembered any better than non-descriptive names.[44]

→ This Kraft cheese ad uses a play on words to link the product to consumers' pre-existing knowledge, increasing the chances that brand information will be stored in memory.
Kraft® is a registered trademark of Kraft General Foods, Inc. Used with permission.

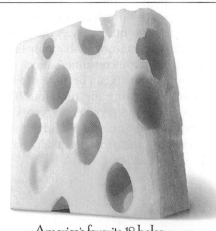

TYPES OF MEANING

A consumer may process a stimulus simply in terms of its *sensory meaning,* such as its colour or shape. When this occurs, the meaning may be activated when the person sees a picture of the stimulus. We may experience a sense of familiarity upon seeing an ad for a new snack food we tasted recently, for example. In many cases, though, meanings are encoded at a more abstract level. *Semantic meaning* refers to symbolic associations, such as the idea that rich people drink champagne.

PERSONAL RELEVANCE

Episodic memories are those that relate to events that are personally relevant.[45] As a result, a person's motivation to retain these memories will likely be strong. Couples often have a song that reminds them of their first date or their wedding. The memories that might be triggered upon hearing this song would be quite different and unique for them and are called *flashbulb memories.*

One method of conveying product information is through a *narrative* or a story. Much of the social information that an individual acquires is represented in memory this way. Therefore, utilizing this method in product advertising can be an effective marketing technique. Narratives persuade people to construct a mental representation of the information they are viewing. Pictures aid in this construction and allow for a more developed and detailed mental representation.[46] Recent research supports the idea that brands are more likely to be positively evaluated and purchased when they connect to a consumer through a narrative.[47]

Memory Systems

According to the information-processing perspective, there are three distinct memory systems: sensory memory, short-term memory (STM), and long-term memory (LTM). Each plays a role in processing brand-related information. The interrelationships of these memory systems are summarized in Figure 3–5.

Sensory memory permits storage of the information we receive from our senses. This storage is very temporary; it lasts a couple of seconds at most. For example, a person might be walking past a doughnut shop and get a quick, enticing whiff of something baking inside. While this sensation would last for only a few seconds, it would be sufficient to allow the person to determine whether he or she should investigate further. If the information is retained for further processing, it passes through an *attentional gate* and is transferred to short-term memory.

FIGURE 3–5   RELATIONSHIPS AMONG MEMORY SYSTEMS

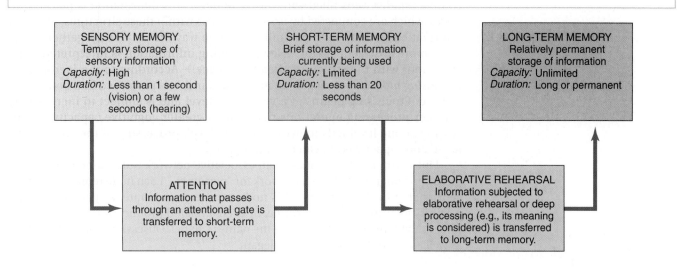

Short-term memory also stores information for a limited period of time, and its capacity is limited. As with the RAM in a computer, this system can be regarded as *working memory;* it holds the information we are currently processing. Verbal input may be stored *acoustically* (in terms of how it sounds) or *semantically* (in terms of its meaning).[48]

The information is stored by combining small pieces into larger ones in a process known as *chunking.* A chunk is a configuration that is familiar to the person and can be manipulated as a unit. For example, a brand name can be a chunk that summarizes a great deal of detailed information about the brand.

Initially, it was believed that STM was capable of processing between five and nine chunks of information at a time, and for this reason phone numbers were designed to have seven digits.[49] It now appears that three to four chunks is the optimum size for efficient retrieval (ten-digit phone numbers can be remembered because the individual digits are chunked, so we may remember a three-digit exchange as one piece of information).[50]

Long-term memory is the system that allows us to retain information for a long period of time. For information to enter into long-term memory from short-term memory, *elaborative rehearsal* is required. This process involves thinking about the meaning of a stimulus and relating it to other information already in memory. Marketers sometimes assist in the process by devising catchy slogans or jingles that consumers repeat on their own.

Storing Information in Memory

Relationships among the types of memory are a source of some controversy. The traditional perspective, known as *multiple-store,* assumes that STM and LTM are separate systems. More recent research has moved away from the distinction between the two types of memory, instead emphasizing the interdependence of the systems. This work argues that, depending upon the nature of the processing task, different levels of processing occur that activate some aspects of memory rather than others. These approaches are called **activation models of memory**.[51] The more effort it takes to process information (so-called deep processing), the more likely it is that information will be placed in long-term memory.

ASSOCIATIVE NETWORKS

Activation models propose that an incoming piece of information is stored in an *associative network* containing many bits of related information organized according to some set of relationships. The consumer has organized systems of concepts relating to brands, stores, and manufacturers.

These storage units, known as **knowledge structures**, can be thought of as complex spider webs filled with pieces of data. This information is placed into *nodes,* which are connected by *associative links* within these structures. Pieces of information that are seen as similar in some way are chunked together under some more abstract category. New, incoming information is interpreted to be consistent with the structure already in place.[52] According to the *hierarchical processing model,* a message—an ad, for instance—is processed in a bottom-up fashion: Processing begins at a very basic level and is subject to increasingly complex processing operations that require greater cognitive capacity. If processing at one level fails to evoke the next level, processing of the ad is terminated and capacity is allocated to other tasks.[53]

Links form between nodes as an associative network is developed. For example, a consumer might have a network for "perfumes." Each node represents a concept related to the category. This node can be an attribute, a specific brand, a celebrity identified with a perfume, or even a related product. A network for perfumes might include concepts like the names Chanel, Obsession, and Calvin Klein, as well as attributes like sexy and elegant.

When asked to list perfumes, the consumer would recall only those brands contained in the appropriate category. This group constitutes that person's **evoked set**. The task of a new entrant that wants to position itself as a category member (a new luxury perfume, for example) is to provide cues that facilitate its placement in the appropriate category. A sample network for perfumes is shown in Figure 3–6.

SPREADING ACTIVATION

A meaning can be activated indirectly; energy spreads across nodes of varying levels of abstraction. As one node is activated, other nodes associated with it also begin to be triggered. Meaning thus spreads across the network, bringing up concepts including competing brands and relevant attributes that are used to form attitudes toward the brand.

This process of **spreading activation** allows consumers to shift back and forth between levels of meaning. The way a piece of information is stored in memory depends upon the type of meaning assigned to it. This meaning type will, in turn, determine how and when the meaning is activated. For example, the *memory trace* for an ad could be stored in one or more of the following ways:

- brand-specific—in terms of claims made for the brand
- ad-specific—in terms of the medium or content of the ad itself
- brand identification—in terms of the brand name
- product category—in terms of how the product works, where it should be used, or experiences with the product
- evaluative reactions—in terms of whether "that looks like fun"[54]

LEVELS OF KNOWLEDGE

Knowledge is coded at different levels of abstraction and complexity. *Meaning concepts* are individual nodes (e.g., elegant). These may be combined into a larger unit, called a *proposition* (also known as a *belief*). A proposition links two nodes together to form a more complex meaning, which can serve as a single chunk of information. For example, a proposition might be that "Chanel is a perfume for elegant women."

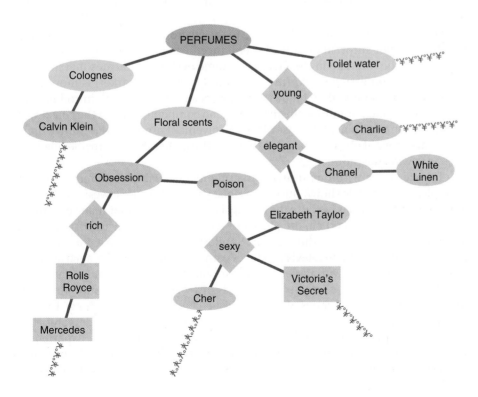

FIGURE 3–6

AN ASSOCIATIVE NETWORK FOR PERFUMES

Propositions are, in turn, integrated to produce a complex unit known as a *schema*. As was noted in Chapter 2, a **schema** is a cognitive framework that is developed through experience. Information that is consistent with an existing schema is encoded more readily.[55] The ability to move up and down among levels of abstraction greatly increases processing flexibility and efficiency. For this reason, young children, who do not yet have well-developed schemas, are not able to make as efficient use of purchase information as older children.[56]

One type of schema that is relevant to consumer behaviour is a *script*—a sequence of procedures that is expected by an individual. For example, consumers learn service scripts that guide expectations and purchasing behaviour in business settings. Consumers learn to expect a certain sequence of events and may become uncomfortable if the service departs from the script. A service script for your visit to the dentist might include events such as: (1) driving to the dentist, (2) reading old magazines in the waiting room, (3) hearing your name called and sitting in the dentist's chair, (4) having the dentist put a funny substance on your teeth, (5) having the dentist clean your teeth, and so on. This desire to follow a script helps to explain why such service innovations as automatic bank machines and self-service gas stations initially met with resistance by some consumers, who had trouble adapting to a new sequence of events.[57]

Retrieving Information for Purchase Decisions

Retrieval is the process of accessing information from long-term memory. As evidenced by the popularity of the TV show *Who Wants to Be a Millionaire*, people have a vast quantity of information stored in their heads that is not necessarily available on demand. Although most of the information entered in long-term memory does not go away, it may be difficult or impossible to retrieve unless the appropriate cues are present.

FACTORS INFLUENCING RETRIEVAL

Some differences in retrieval ability are physiological. Older adults consistently display inferior recall ability for current items, such as prescription information, though events that happened to them when they were younger may be recalled with great clarity.[58]

Other factors are situational, relating to the environment in which the message is delivered. Not surprisingly, recall is enhanced when the consumer pays more attention to the message in the first place. Some evidence indicates that information about a *pioneering brand* (the first brand to enter a market) is more easily retrieved from memory than follower brands because the product's introduction is likely to be distinctive and, for the time being, no competitors divert the consumer's attention.[59] In addition, in the case of low-involvement products, descriptive brand names are more likely to be recalled than are those that do not provide adequate cues as to what the product is.[60]

The viewing environment of a marketing message also can affect recall. For example, commercials shown during baseball games yield the lowest recall scores among sports programs because the activity is stop-and-go rather than continuous. Unlike football or basketball, the pacing of baseball gives many opportunities for attention to wander, even during play. Similarly, General Electric found that its commercials fare better in television shows with continuous activity, such as stories or dramas, compared with variety shows or talk shows that are punctuated by a series of acts.[61] Finally, a large-scale analysis of TV commercials found that commercials shown first in a series of ads are recalled better than those shown last.[62]

Recent research on *postexperience advertising effects* underscores how powerful marketing communications can be in shaping our daily experiences. Language and imagery from ads we have seen recently can become confused with our own experiential memories so that we may come to believe that what we saw in advertising actually was our own experience with products. One study showed that when consumers were exposed to advertising after they had directly experienced a product, the ad altered their recollections of the experience.[63]

STATE-DEPENDENT RETRIEVAL   In a process termed *state-dependent retrieval,* people are better able to access information if their internal state is the same at the time of recall as it was when the information was learned. This phenomenon, called the *mood congruence effect,* underscores the desirability of matching a consumer's mood at the time of purchase when the marketer is planning exposure to marketing communications. A consumer is more likely to recall an ad, for example, if his or her mood or level of arousal at the time of exposure is similar to that in the purchase environment. By recreating the cues that were present when the information was first presented, marketers can enhance consumers' recall.[64]

FAMILIARITY AND RECALL   As a general rule, prior familiarity with an item enhances its recall. Indeed, this is one of the basic goals of marketers who are trying to create and maintain awareness of their products. The more experience a consumer has with a product, the better use that person is able to make of product information.[65]

However, there is a possible fly in the ointment. As noted earlier in this chapter, some evidence indicates that extreme familiarity can result in inferior learning and recall. When consumers are highly familiar with a brand or an advertisement, they may attend to fewer attributes because they do not believe that any additional effort will yield a gain in knowledge.[66] For example, when consumers are exposed to the technique of *radio replay,* where the audio track from a television ad is replayed on the radio, they do very little critical, evaluative processing and instead mentally replay the video portion of the ad.[67]

SALIENCE AND RECALL   The **salience** of a brand refers to its prominence or level of activation in memory. As noted in Chapter 2, stimuli that stand out in contrast to their environment are more likely to command attention, which, in turn, increases the likelihood that they will be recalled. Almost any technique that increases the novelty of a stimulus also improves recall (a result known as the *von Restorff effect*).[68] This effect explains why unusual advertising or distinctive packaging tends to facilitate brand recall.[69]

Introducing a surprise element into an ad (like the Energizer Bunny, who unexpectedly marches through a commercial) can be particularly effective in aiding recall, even if the stimulus is not relevant to the factual information being presented.[70] In addition, so-called *mystery ads,* where the brand is not identified until the end of the ad, are more effective at building associations in memory between the product category and that brand—especially in the case of relatively unknown brands.[71]

←A picture is worth a thousand words: Product icons—like the Jolly Green Giant, who has appeared in ads and on packaging for more than 30 years—are a significant factor in product recognition.
Courtesy of Pillsbury.

PICTORIAL VERSUS VERBAL CUES   Is a picture worth a thousand words? There is some evidence for the superiority of visual memory over verbal memory, but this advantage is unclear because it is more difficult to measure recall of pictures.[72] However, the available data indicate that information presented in picture form is more likely to be recognized later.[73] Certainly, visual aspects of an ad are more likely to grab a consumer's attention. In fact, eye-movement studies indicate that about 90 percent of viewers look at the dominant picture in an ad before they bother to view the copy.[74]

Although pictorial ads may enhance recall, they do not necessarily improve comprehension. One study found that television news items presented with illustrations (still pictures) as a backdrop result in improved recall for details of the news story, even though understanding of the story's content does not improve.[75] The use of ethnic images in advertising was studied in Canada. The results of two experiments suggested print advertisers should be careful in using ethnic names and pictures where the product is not specifically matched to that subculture.[76]

FACTORS INFLUENCING FORGETTING

Marketers obviously hope that consumers will not forget about their products. However, in a poll of more than 13 000 adults, more than half were unable to remember any specific ad they had seen, heard, or read in the last 30 days.[77] Forgetting is obviously a problem for marketers.

Early memory theorists assumed that memories fade because of the simple passage of time. In a process of decay, the structural changes in the brain produced by learning simply go away. Forgetting also occurs because of **interference**; as additional information is learned, it displaces earlier information.

Stimulus-response associations will be forgotten if consumers subsequently learn new responses to the same or similar stimuli in a process known as *retroactive interference*. On the other hand, prior learning can interfere with new learning, a process termed *proactive interference*. Since pieces of information are stored in memory as nodes that are connected to one another by links, a meaning concept that is connected by a larger number of links is more likely to be retrieved. But, as new responses are learned, a stimulus loses its effectiveness in retrieving the old response.[78]

These interference effects help to explain problems in remembering brand information. Consumers tend to organize attribute information by brand.[79] Additional attribute information regarding a brand or similar brands may limit a person's ability to recall old brand information. Recall may also be inhibited if the brand name comprises frequently used words. These words cue competing associations and result in less retention of brand information.[80]

In one study, brand evaluations deteriorated more rapidly when ads for the brand appeared with messages for other brands in the same category than when the ad was shown with ads for 12 dissimilar products.[81] By increasing the salience of a brand, marketers can impair the recall of other brands.[82] However, calling a competitor by name can result in poorer recall for one's own brand.[83]

Finally, a phenomenon known as the *part-list cueing effect* allows marketers to utilize the interference process strategically. When only a portion of the items in a category are presented to consumers, the omitted items are not as easily recalled. For example, comparative advertising that mentions only a subset of competitors (preferably those that the marketer is not very worried about) may inhibit recall of the unmentioned brands with which the product does not compare favourably.[84]

Products as Memory Markers

Products and ads can themselves serve as powerful retrieval cues. Indeed, the three types of possessions most valued by consumers are furniture, visual art, and photos. The most common explanation for this attachment is the ability of these things to call forth memories of the past.[85] Studies find that valued possessions can evoke thoughts about people and prior events on several dimensions, including friends and loved ones, sensory experiences, and memories of breaking away from parents or former partners.[86] In fact, researchers are just beginning to probe the effects of *autobiographical memories* on buying behaviour. These memories appear to be one way that advertisements create emotional responses. Ads that succeed in getting us to think about our own past also appear to get us to like these ads more—especially if the link between the nostalgia experience and the brand is strong.[87] Products are particularly important as life-markers when our sense of past is threatened, as when a consumer's current identity is challenged due to some change in role caused by divorce, moving, graduation, and so on.[88] Our possessions often have *mnemonic* qualities that serve as a form of external memory by prompting consumers to retrieve episodic memories. For example, family photography allows consumers to create their own retrieval cues, with the 11 billion amateur photos taken annually forming a kind of external memory bank for our culture.

THE MARKETING POWER OF NOSTALGIA

Nostalgia has been described as a bittersweet emotion, where the past is viewed with both sadness and longing. References to "the good old days" are increasingly common, as advertisers call up memories of distant youth—feelings they hope will translate to what they're selling today. A stimulus is at times able to evoke a weakened response much later, an effect known as *spontaneous recovery*. This re-established connection may explain consumers' powerful nostalgic reactions to songs or pictures they have not been exposed to in many years.

Why are nostalgia appeals so welcomed by consumers? According to one consumer analyst, "We are creating a new culture, and we don't know what's going to happen. So we need some warm fuzzies from our past."[89] Or this strategy may work because more than half of adults think things were better in the past than they are today, according to research by Roper Starch Worldwide.[90] In the aftermath of September 11, consumers seem to be craving the comfort of items from the past even more. Marketers such as Ford, General Electric, S.C. Johnson, and Sears are sponsoring campaigns that celebrate their heritage. Once-popular products like Breck shampoo, Sea & Ski sun-care lotion, and the Care Bears are being revived.[91]

A **retro brand** is an updated version of a brand from a prior historical period (like the PT Cruiser we'll talk about in Chapter 17). These products trigger nostalgia, and researchers find that they often inspire consumers to think back to an era where (at least in our memories) life was more stable, simple, or even utopian; they let us "look back through rose-coloured glasses."[92]

Mitchum antiperspirant is trying to appeal to men in their late 20s or early 30s by reminding them of days gone by when they sewed their wild oats. The brand is distributing drink coasters to bars frequented by men of this age with sayings like "If you let your buddy have the hot one, you're a Mitchum man," and "If you can see the inner beauty of the girl dancing on the bar, you're a Mitchum man."[93]

MEMORY AND AESTHETIC PREFERENCES

We like ads and products that remind us of our past; prior experiences also determine what we like now. *The Nostalgia Index* indicates that people's tastes in such products as movies and clothing are influenced by what was popular during certain critical periods of their youth. For example, liking a specific song appears to be related to how old a person was when that song was popular. On average, songs that were popular when an individual was 23.5 years old are the most likely to be favoured;[94] favourite movie stars and fashion models are usually those who were popular when that individual was 26 and 33 years old, respectively.[95] Men, but not women, also show evidence of nostalgic attachment to cars from their youth.[96]

Marketing Opportunity !

What could be more nostalgic than a good old-fashioned pajama party—for grown-ups? Sleepwear makers, cosmetics companies, and event planners report that adult sleepovers are hot. Beauty-products maker Jaqua Girls is doing well with its "Pajama-Rama" kit, which includes nail polish, peppermint foot soak, and invitations ("Come over and get beautiful!"), and a record label recently released *For a Girls Night In*, a CD with music from *The Sleeping Beauty*. Even the website ***www.match.com*** is getting into the act by sponsoring coed pajama parties for singles at chic hotels.[97] And what to do when you get tired of pillow fights? How about playing "The Chick Game," where you reveal secrets to questions like "Who is the one that got away?" or "Heels! The Game that Heals," where you move shoe-shaped tokens around a board with spaces including Children Clean Room and Shop All Day. (Sample question: "Name one time a man's opinion was important to you.")

Measuring Memory for Marketing Stimuli

Because advertisers pay so much money to place their messages in front of consumers, they are naturally concerned about whether people will actually remember these messages at a later point. It seems that they have good reason to be. In one study, fewer than 40 percent of television viewers made positive links between commercial messages and the corresponding products; only 65 percent noticed the brand name in a commercial; and only 38 percent recognized a connection to an important point.[98]

Even more sadly, only 7 percent of television viewers can recall the product or company featured in the most recent television commercial they watched. This figure represents less than half the recall rate recorded in 1965 and may be attributed to such factors as the increase of 30- and 15-second commercials and the practice of airing television commercials in clusters rather than in connection with single-sponsor programs.[99]

RECOGNITION VERSUS RECALL

One indicator of good advertising is, of course, the impression it makes on consumers. But how can this impact be defined and measured? Two basic measures of impact are *recognition* and *recall*. In the typical recognition test, subjects are shown ads one at a time and asked whether they have seen them before. In contrast, free-recall tests ask consumers to think independently of what they have seen, without being prompted for this information first; obviously, this task requires greater effort on the part of respondents. For example, Intermedia Advertising Group is a research firm that measures advertising effectiveness by monitoring the ability of the TV viewing population to remember an ad within 24 hours. The firm assigns a recall index to each ad to indicate the strength of its impact. Scores for 2002 attest to the power of a memorable character in aiding recall. Ads with well-known celebrities like Britney Spears tend to have very high recall rates.[100]

Under some conditions these two memory measures tend to yield the same results, especially when the researchers try to keep the viewers' interest in the ads constant.[101] Generally, though, recognition scores tend to be more reliable and do not decay over time the way recall scores do.[102] Recognition scores are almost always better than recall scores, because recognition is a simpler process and more retrieval cues are available to the consumer.

Both types of retrieval play important roles in purchase decisions. Recall tends to be more important in situations where consumers do not have product data at their disposal, and so they must rely upon memory to generate this information.[103] On the other hand, recognition is more likely to be an important factor in a store, where consumers are confronted with thousands of product options and information (i.e., where external memory is abundantly available) and where the task may simply be to recognize a familiar package. Unfortunately, package recognition and familiarity can have a negative consequence in that warning labels may be ignored, since their existence is taken for granted and not really noticed.[104]

THE STARCH TEST

A widely used commercial measure of advertising recall for magazines is called the Starch Test, a syndicated service founded in 1932. This service provides scores on a number of aspects of consumers' familiarity with an ad, including such categories as "noted," "associated," and "read most." It also scores the impact of the component parts of an overall ad, giving such information as "seen" for major illustrations and "read some" for a major block of copy.[105] Such factors as the size of the ad, whether it appears toward the front or the back of the magazine, if it is on the right or left page, and the size of illustrations play an important role in affecting the amount of attention given to an ad as determined by Starch scores.

Net Profit +

The head office for John Fluevog Shoes, a world-famous, fashion-forward shoe store, is located on Granville Street in Vancouver, British Columbia. Fluevog stores are also found in Boston, San Francisco, Seattle, Toronto, and New York. Fluevog's success illustrates the power of applying learning theories effectively. The store name, for example, is just difficult—and interesting—enough to pronounce to be easy to remember. (The family name was adopted from the Norwegian village from which they emigrated to Canada.) They sell memorable (i.e., fun and imaginative) styles, with names like Lounge Lizards, Swingers, Wok 'n Roll, Angels, Demerol (yes, it's a nurse's Fluevog), and Granny Glamour, to a primarily youthful market (aged 18 to 50 years, 60 percent female).

Fluevog carries the strategy to be distinctive through to store décor and marketing communications. Each store is designed to fit with its neighbourhood and the previous life of that neighbourhood. The Toronto store retained some fixtures and furnishings from its diner days, while the San Francisco store is reminiscent of a smoking parlour with overstuffed couches. Fluevog stays away from runway placements and conventional promotions, opting for wacky ads, pocket-sized catalogues, in-store fashion shows and sample sales, angels moulded on shoe soles, and poetry enclosures in shoes. The company's website (*www.fluevog.com*) attracts about 2 million visits each month.[106]

PROBLEMS WITH MEMORY MEASURES

Although the measurement of an ad's memorability is important, the ability of existing measures to accurately assess these dimensions has been criticized for several reasons.

RESPONSE BIASES   Results obtained from a measuring instrument are not necessarily due to what is being measured, but rather to something else about the instrument or the respondent. This form of contamination is called a **response bias**. For example, people tend to give "yes" responses to questions, regardless of what is asked. In addition, consumers often are eager to be "good subjects" by pleasing the experimenter. They will try to give the responses they think the experimenter is looking for. In some studies, the claimed recognition of bogus ads (ads that have not been seen before) is almost as high as the recognition rate of real ads.[107]

MEMORY LAPSES   People are also prone to unintentionally forgetting information. Typical problems include *omitting* (the leaving out of facts), *averaging* (the tendency to "normalize" things and not report extreme cases), and *telescoping* (the inaccurate recall of time).[108] These distortions call into question the accuracy of various product usage databases that rely upon consumers to recall their purchases and consumption of food and household items. In one study, for example, people were asked to describe what portion of various foods—small, medium, or large—they ate in a normal meal. However, different definitions of medium were used (e.g., 3/4 cup versus 1-1/2 cups). Regardless of the measurement specified, about the same number of people claimed they normally ate medium portions.[109]

MEMORY FOR FACTS VERSUS FEELINGS   Although techniques are being developed to increase the accuracy of memory scores, these improvements do not address the more fundamental issue of whether recall is necessary for advertising to have an effect. In particular, some critics argue that these measures do not adequately tap the impact of "feeling" ads, where the objective is to arouse strong emotions rather than to convey concrete product benefits. Many ad campaigns, including those for Hallmark cards, Chevrolet, and Pepsi (*www.pepsi.com*), use this approach. An effective strategy relies on a long-term build up of feeling rather than on a one-shot attempt to convince consumers to buy the product.[110]

Also, it is not clear that recall translates into preference. We may recall the benefits touted in an ad but not believe them. Or the ad may be memorable because it is obnoxious, and the product becomes one we "love to hate." The bottom line is that while recall is important, especially for creating brand awareness, it is not necessarily sufficient to alter consumer preferences. To accomplish this, marketers need more sophisticated attitude-change strategies. These issues will be discussed in Chapters 7 and 8.

CHAPTER SUMMARY

IT'S IMPORTANT FOR MARKETERS TO UNDERSTAND HOW CONSUMERS LEARN ABOUT PRODUCTS AND SERVICES.

- Learning is a change in behaviour that is caused by experience. Learning can occur through simple associations between a stimulus and a response or via a complex series of cognitive activities.

CONDITIONING RESULTS IN LEARNING.

- Behavioural learning theories assume that learning occurs as a result of responses to external events. Classical conditioning occurs when a stimulus that naturally elicits a response (an unconditioned stimulus) is paired with another stimulus that does not initially elicit this response. Over time, the second stimulus (the conditioned stimulus) comes to elicit the response as well.

LEARNED ASSOCIATIONS CAN GENERALIZE TO OTHER THINGS, WHICH IS IMPORTANT TO MARKETERS.

- This response can also extend to other, similar stimuli in a process known as stimulus generalization. This process is the basis for such marketing strategies as licensing and family branding, in which a consumer's positive associations with a product are transferred to other contexts.

THERE IS A DIFFERENCE BETWEEN CLASSICAL AND INSTRUMENTAL CONDITIONING.

- Operant or instrumental conditioning occurs as the person learns to perform behaviours that produce positive outcomes and avoid those that result in negative outcomes. While classical conditioning involves the pairing of two stimuli, instrumental learning occurs when reinforcement is delivered following a response to a stimulus. Reinforcement is positive if a reward is delivered following a response. It is negative if a negative outcome is avoided by not performing a response. Punishment occurs when a response is followed by unpleasant events. Extinction of the behaviour will occur if reinforcement is no longer received.

OBSERVATION OF OTHERS' BEHAVIOUR CAN RESULT IN LEARNING.

- Cognitive learning occurs as the result of mental processes. For example, observational learning takes place when the consumer performs a behaviour as a result of seeing someone else performing it and being rewarded for it.

MEMORY SYSTEMS WORK.

- Memory refers to the storage of learned information. The way information is encoded when it is perceived determines how it will be stored in memory. The memory systems known as sensory memory, short-term memory, and long-term memory each play a role in retaining and processing information from the outside world.

OUR KNOWLEDGE OF INDIVIDUAL PRODUCTS IS INFLUENCED BY OTHER PRODUCTS WE ASSOCIATE WITH THEM.

- Information is not stored in isolation; it is incorporated into knowledge structures where it is associated with other related data. The location of product information in associative networks and the level of abstraction at which it is coded help to determine when and how this information will be activated at a later time. Some factors that influence the likelihood of retrieval include the level of familiarity with an item, its salience (or prominence) in memory, and whether the information was presented in pictorial or written form.

PRODUCTS HELP US TO RETRIEVE MEMORIES FROM OUR PAST.

- Products also play a role as memory markers; they are used by consumers to retrieve memories about past experiences (autobiographical memories) and are often valued for their ability to do so. This function also contributes to the use of nostalgia in marketing strategies.

MARKETERS MEASURE OUR MEMORIES ABOUT PRODUCTS AND ADS.

- Memory of product information can be measured through either recognition or recall techniques. Consumers are more likely to recognize an advertisement if it is presented to them than to recall one without having any cues. However, neither recognition nor recall automatically or reliably translates into product purchases.

KEY TERMS

REVIEW QUESTIONS

1. What is the difference between an unconditioned stimulus and a conditioned stimulus?
2. How can marketers use repetition to increase the likelihood that consumers will learn about their brand?
3. Why is it not necessarily a good idea to advertise a product in a commercial where a really popular song is playing in the background?
4. What is the difference between classical conditioning and instrumental conditioning?
5. How do different types of reinforcement enhance learning? How does the strategy of frequency marketing relate to conditioning?
6. What is the major difference between behavioural and cognitive theories of learning?
7. Name the three stages of information processing.
8. What is external memory and why is it important to marketers?
9. Give an example of an episodic memory.
10. Why do phone numbers have seven digits?
11. List three types of memory and explain how they work together.
12. How is associative memory like a spider web?
13. How does the likelihood that a person will be willing to use an ATM machine relate to a schema?
14. Why does a pioneering brand have a memory advantage over follower brands?
15. If a consumer is familiar with a product, seeing an ad for it can work both ways by either enhancing or diminishing recall. Why?
16. How does learning new information make it more likely that we'll forget things we've already learned?
17. Define nostalgia and explain why it's such a widely used advertising strategy.
18. Name the two basic measures of memory and describe how they differ from one another.
19. List three problems with measures of memory in the field of advertising.

CONSUMER BEHAVIOUR CHALLENGE

Discuss

1. In his 2005 book, *Blink: The Power of Thinking without Thinking*, author Malcolm Gladwell argues that hallowed marketing research techniques like focus groups are ineffective. According to Gladwell, we usually react to products quickly and without much conscious thought, so it's better to simply solicit consumers' first impressions rather than getting them to think at length about why they buy. What's your position on this issue?

2. Some diehard fans were not pleased when the Rolling Stones sold the tune "Start Me Up" for about $4 million to Microsoft, which wanted the classic song to promote its Windows 95 launch. The Beach Boys sold "Good Vibrations" to Cadbury Schweppes for its Sunkist soft drink, and Bob Dylan sold "The Times They Are A-Changin'" to Coopers & Lybrand (now PricewaterhouseCoopers).[111] Other rock legends have refused to play the commercial game, including Bruce Springsteen, the Grateful Dead, Led Zeppelin, Fleetwood Mac, R.E.M., and U2. According to U2's manager, "Rock 'n roll is the last vestige of independence. It is undignified to put that creative effort and hard work to the disposal of a soft drink or beer or car."[112] Singer Neil Young is especially adamant about not selling out; in his song "This Note's for You," he croons, "Ain't singing for Pepsi, ain't singing for Coke, I don't sing for nobody, makes me look like a joke." What's your take on this issue? How do you react when one of your favourite songs turns up in a commercial? Is this use of nostalgia an effective way to market a product? Why or why not?

Experiential Exercises

3. Devise a "product jingle memory test." Compile a list of brands that are or have been associated with memorable jingles, such as Chiquita Banana or Alka-Seltzer. Read this list to friends, and see how many jingles are remembered. You may be surprised at the level of recall.

4. Identify some important characteristics of a product with a well-known brand name. Based on these attributes, generate a list of possible brand extension or licensing opportunities. Include some that would most likely not be accepted by consumers.

CBC VIDEO VIGNETTE

CONCEPTS AT WORK FOR LOYALTY CARDS

Many companies offer reward programs in the form of loyalty cards; some offer cross-category redemption opportunities and status programs. In fact, there are enough loyalty cards out there to inspire many casual conversations: "How many loyalty cards do you have in your wallet?" "How many points have you racked up?" Loyalty cards enable Canadians of all walks of life to save money, get free merchandise or services, access exclusive offers, and enjoy the status of being a member. More than three-quarters of Canadians belong to at least one loyalty program, so that whether they are purchasing a coffee, an airline ticket, their groceries for the week, drugstore items, or clothing, they can benefit from their membership.

What do the companies that issue cards hope to gain from their loyalty programs? They can expand their customer database with your personal information, including not only demographics, such as your name and the ages of your children, but also what you buy and when. This information can be used to predict subsequent purchases for target segments. Promotions can be tailored and even spot-delivered to specific consumers. The goal is to increase sales revenue.

But do loyalty programs exemplify a balanced marketplace relationship? "Consumer cadets" and some researchers don't think so. They raise concerns about the misuse of consumers' information, personal information on receipts falling into the wrong hands, and the cost to consumers of seeing a company's file of information. They also doubt whether consumers are actually saving money. And the next step may be embedding Radio Frequency Identification (RFID) chips into loyalty cards that can track the movements of customers while shopping in a store.

Will you use a loyalty card today? If so, who will be happy that you did?

Questions

1. Identify one grocery store and one drug store loyalty card. What benefits do consumers expect to get from these loyalty cards?
2. What are the benefits of loyalty cards to the companies that issue them? Do any of these benefits also accrue to the loyalty card holders?
3. Do consumers receive the benefits they expect from loyalty cards?
4. Do loyalty cards foster brand loyalty in the marketplace, or do they merely elicit a conditioned response from consumers? Explain your answer.

Resources: "Loyalty Cards," Marketplace, CBC Air Date: October 24, 2004; Francois Pariseau, "Global Loyalty," Marketing Magazine (February 20, 2006): 22.

"I'm not that loyal."

Reprinted by permission of Michael F. Eddenden

NOTES

1. Stuart Elliott, "At 75, Mr. Peanut Is Getting Expanded Role at Planters," *New York Times* (September 23, 1991): D15.
2. Todd Pruzan, "Brand Illusions," *New York Times on the Web* (September 12, 1999).
3. Robert A. Baron, *Psychology: The Essential Science* (Boston, MA: Allyn & Bacon, 1989).
4. Richard A. Feinberg, "Credit Cards as Spending Facilitating Stimuli: A Conditioning Interpretation," *Journal of Consumer Research* 13 (December 1986): 348–356.
5. R.A. Rescorla, "Pavlovian Conditioning: It's Not What You Think It Is," *American Psychologist* 43 (1988): 151–160; Elnora W. Stuart, Terence A. Shimp, and Randall W. Engle, "Classical Conditioning of Consumer Attitudes: Four Experiments in an Advertising Context," *Journal of Consumer Research* 14 (December 1987): 334–339; Terence A. Shimp, Elnora W. Stuart, and Randall W. Engle, "A Program of Classical Conditioning Experiments Testing Variations in the Conditioned Stimulus and Context," *Journal of Consumer Research* 18, 1 (June 1991): 1–12.
6. C. Janiszewski, H. Noel, and A.G. Sawyer, "A Meta-Analysis of the Spacing Effect in Verbal Learning: Implications for Research on Advertising Repetition and Consumer Memory," *Journal of Consumer Research* 30, no. 1 (2003): 138–149.
7. "Anemic Crocodile," *Forbes* (August 15, 1994): 116.
8. Baron, *Psychology*.
9. James Ward, Barbara Loken, Ivan Ross, and Tedi Hasapopoulous, "The Influence of Physical Similarity of Affect and Attribute Perceptions from National Brands to Private Label Brands," in *American Marketing Educators' Conference*, eds. Terence A. Shimp et al. (Chicago, IL: American Marketing Association, 1986), 51–56.
10. Judith Lynne Zaichkowsky and Richard Neil Simpson, "The Effect of Experience with a Brand Imitator on the Original Brand," *Marketing Letters* 7, 1 (1996): 31–39.
11. Tom J. Brown and Peter A. Dacin, "The Company and the Product: Corporate Associations and Consumer Product Responses," *Journal of Marketing* 61 (January 1997): 68–84.

12. Janice S. Griffiths and Mary Zimmer, "Masked Brands and Consumers' Need for Uniqueness," *American Marketing Association* (Summer 1998): 145–153.

13. Chris T. Allen and Thomas J. Madden, "A Closer Look at Classical Conditioning," *Journal of Consumer Research* 12 (December 1985): 301–315; Chester A. Insko and William F. Oakes, "Awareness and the Conditioning of Attitudes," *Journal of Personality and Social Psychology* 4 (November 1966): 487–496; Carolyn K. Staats and Arthur W. Staats, "Meaning Established by Classical Conditioning," *Journal of Experimental Psychology* 54 (July 1957): 74–80.

14. Kevin Lane Keller, "Conceptualizing, Measuring, and Managing Customer-Based Brand Equity," *Journal of Marketing* 57 (January 1993): 1–22.

15. Herbert Krugman, "Low Recall and High Recognition of Advertising," *Journal of Advertising Research* (February/March 1986): 79–86.

16. Gerald J. Gorn, "The Effects of Music in Advertising on Choice Behavior: A Classical Conditioning Approach," *Journal of Marketing* 46 (Winter 1982): 94–101.

17. Ronald Milliman, "Using Background Music to Affect the Behavior of Supermarket Shoppers," *Journal of Marketing* 46 (Summer 1982): 86–91.

18. Ronald Milliman, "The Influence of Background Music on the Behavior of Restaurant Patrons," *Journal of Consumer Research* 13 (September 1986): 286–289.

19. Calvin Bierley, Frances K. McSweeney, and Renee Vannieuwkerk, "Classical Conditioning of Preferences for Stimuli," *Journal of Consumer Research* 12 (December 1985): 316–323; James J. Kellaris and Anthony D. Cox, "The Effects of Background Music in Advertising: A Reassessment," *Journal of Consumer Research* 16 (June 1989): 113–118.

20. Frances K. McSweeney and Calvin Bierley, "Recent Developments in Classical Conditioning," *Journal of Consumer Research* 11 (September 1984): 619–631.

21. Basil G. Englis, "The Reinforcement Properties of Music Videos: 'I Want My ... I Want My ... I Want My ... MTV'" (paper presented at the meetings of the Association for Consumer Research, New Orleans, 1989).

22. Anand Natarajan, "Branding: Interiors by Smith & Wesson," *BusinessWeek* (November 10, 2003): 16; James B. Arndorfer, "Starbucks Wakes Up to Liquor Possibilities," *Advertising Age* (November 22, 2004): 4; Claudia Deutsch, "Will Real Men Buy Mr. Clean?" *New York Times on the Web* (September 24, 2003); Jane L. Levere, "Huggies and Pampers Seek to Extend Brands into Toiletries," *New York Times on the Web* (January 18, 2005).

23. Zaickhowsky and Simpson, "The Effect of Experience with a Brand Imitator on the Original Brand."

24. Quoted in Stuart Elliott, "A Name Change at Philip Morris," *New York Times on the Web* (November 19, 2001).

25. Sharon Begley, "StrawBerry Is No BlackBerry: Building Brands Using Sound," *Wall Street Journal Interactive Edition* (August 26, 2002).

26. Miriam Jordan, "In Wooing Brazil's Teenagers, Converse Has Big Shoes to Fill," *Wall Street Journal Interactive Edition* (July 18, 2002).

27. For a comprehensive approach to consumer behaviour based on operant conditioning principles, see Gordon R. Foxall, "Behavior Analysis and Consumer Psychology," *Journal of Economic Psychology* 15 (March 1994): 5–91.

28. Youngme Moon, "Intimate Exchanges: Using Computers to Elicit Self-Disclosure from Consumers," *Journal of Consumer Research* 26 (2000) 3: 323–339.

29. Blaise J. Bergiel and Christine Trosclair, "Instrumental Learning: Its Application to Customer Satisfaction," *Journal of Consumer Marketing* 2 (Fall 1985): 23–28.

30. Jane Costello, "Do Offers of Free Mileage Sell? The Proof Is in Pudding Guy," *Wall Street Journal Interactive* (January 24, 2000).

31. David Menzies, "Loyalty Cards Are a Mine of Data," *Financial Post Magazine*, (October 1998): 74, 77–79. Ann M. Raider, "Programs Make Results Out of Research," *Marketing News* (June 21, 1999): 14.

32. Ellen J. Langer, *The Psychology of Control* (Beverly Hills, CA: Sage, 1983).

33. Robert B. Cialdini, *Influence: Science and Practice*, 2nd ed. (New York, NY: William Morrow, 1984).

34. Malcolm Gladwell, *Blink: The Power of Thinking without Thinking* (New York: Little, Brown, 2005).

35. Allen and Madden, "A Closer Look at Classical Conditioning"; see also Shimp, Stuart, and Engle, "A Program of Classical Conditioning Experiments Testing Variations in the Conditioned Stimulus and Context."

36. Terence A. Shimp, "Neo-Pavlovian Conditioning and Its Implications for Consumer Theory and Research," in *Handbook of Consumer Behavior*, eds. Thomas S. Robertson and Harold H. Kassargian (Upper Saddle River, NJ: Prentice Hall, 1991).

37. Albert Bandura, *Social Foundations of Thought and Action: A Social Cognitive View* (Englewood Cliffs, NJ: Prentice Hall, 1986); Baron, *Psychology*.

38. Shimp, "Neo-Pavlovian Conditioning and Its Implications for Consumer Theory and Research."

39. R.C. Atkinson and R.M. Shiffrin, "Human Memory: A Proposed System and Its Control Processes," in *The Psychology of Learning and Motivation: Advances in Research and Theory*, eds. K.W. Spence and J.T. Spence (New York, NY: Academic Press, 1968), pp. 89–195.

40. James R. Bettman, "Memory Factors in Consumer Choice: A Review," *Journal of Marketing* (Spring 1979): 37–53. For a study that explored the relative impact of internal versus external memory on brand choice, cf. Joseph W. Alba, Howard Marmorstein, and Amitava Chattopadhyay, "Transitions in Preference over Time: The Effects of Memory on Message Persuasiveness," *Journal of Marketing Research* 29 (November 1992): 406–417. For other research on memory and advertising, see H. Shanker Krishnan and Dipankar Chakravarti, "Varieties of Brand Memory Induced by Advertising: Determinants, Measures, and Relationships," in *Brand Equity & Advertising: Advertising's Role in Building Strong Brands*, eds. David A. Aaker and Alexander L. Biel (Hillsdale, NJ: Lawrence Erlbaum Associates, 1993), pp. 213–231; Bernd H. Schmitt, Nader T. Tavassoli, and Robert T. Millard, "Memory for Print Ads: Understanding Relations among Brand Name, Copy, and Picture," *Journal of Consumer Psychology* 2, 1 (1993): 55–81; Marian Friestad and Esther Thorson, "Remembering Ads: The Effects of Encoding Strategies, Retrieval Cues, and Emotional Response," *Journal of Consumer Psychology* 2, 1 (1993): 1–23; Surendra N. Singh, Sanjay Mishra, Neeli Bendapudi, and Denise Linville, "Enhancing Memory of Television Commercials through Message Spacing," *Journal of Marketing Research* 31 (August 1994): 384–392.

41. Lauren G. Block and Vicki G. Morwitz "Shopping Lists as an External Memory Aid for Grocery Shopping: Influences on List Writing and List Fulfillment," *Journal of Consumer Psychology* 8, no.4 (1999): 343–375.

42. Kathryn R. Braun, "Postexperience Advertising Effects on Consumer Memory," *Journal of Consumer Research* (March 25, 1999): 319–334.

43. Kim Robertson, "Recall and Recognition Effects of Brand Name Imagery," *Psychology & Marketing* 4 (Spring 1987): 3–15.

44. Judith Lynne Zaichkowsky and Padma Vipat, "Inferences from Brand Names," in *European Advances in Consumer Research*, eds. W. Fred Van Raaij and Gary J. Bamossy (Provo, UT: Association for Consumer Research, 1993), Vol. 1, 534–540.

45. Endel Tulving, "Remembering and Knowing the Past," *American Scientist* 77 (July/August 1989): 361.

46. Rashmi Adaval and Robert S. Wyer, Jr., "The Role of Narratives in Consumer Information Processing," *Journal of Consumer Psychology* (1998) 7(3): 207–246.

47. Jennifer Edson Escalas, "Narrative Processing: Building Consumer Connections to Brands," *Journal of Consumer Psychology* 14, no. 1&2 (2004): 168–180.

48. Baron, *Psychology*.

49. George A. Miller, "The Magical Number Seven, Plus or Minus Two: Some Limits on Our Capacity for Processing Information," *Psychological Review* 63 (1956): 81–97.

50. James N. MacGregor, "Short-Term Memory Capacity: Limitation or Optimization?" *Psychological Review* 94 (1987): 107–108.

51. See Catherine A. Cole and Michael J. Houston, "Encoding and Media Effects on Consumer Learning Deficiencies in the Elderly," *Journal of Marketing Research* 24 (February 1987): 55–64; A.M. Collins and E.F. Loftus, "A Spreading Activation Theory of Semantic Processing," *Psychological Review* 82 (1975): 407–428; Fergus I.M. Craik and Robert S. Lockhart, "Levels of Processing: A Framework for Memory Research," *Journal of Verbal Learning and Verbal Behavior* 11 (1972): 671–684.

52. Walter A. Henry, "The Effect of Information-Processing Ability on Processing Accuracy," *Journal of Consumer Research* 7 (June 1980): 42–48.

53. Anthony G. Greenwald and Clark Leavitt, "Audience Involvement in Advertising: Four Levels," *Journal of Consumer Research* 11 (June 1984): 581–592.

54. Kevin Lane Keller, "Memory Factors in Advertising: The Effect of Advertising Retrieval Cues on Brand Evaluations," *Journal of Consumer Research* 14 (December 1987): 316–333. For a discussion of processing operations that occur during brand choice, see Gabriel Biehal and Dipankar Chakravarti, "Consumers' Use of Memory and External Information in Choice: Macro and Micro Perspectives," *Journal of Consumer Research* 12 (March 1986): 382–405.

55. Susan T. Fiske and Shelley E. Taylor, *Social Cognition* (Reading, MA: Addison-Wesley, 1984).

56. Deborah Roedder John and John C. Whitney, Jr., "The Development of Consumer Knowledge in Children: A Cognitive Structure Approach," *Journal of Consumer Research* 12 (March 1986): 406–417.

57. Michael R. Solomon, Carol Surprenant, John A. Czepiel, and Evelyn G. Gutman, "A Role Theory Perspective on Dyadic Interactions: The Service Encounter," *Journal of Marketing* 49 (Winter 1985): 99–111.

58. Roger W. Morrell, Denise C. Park, and Leonard W. Poon, "Quality of Instructions on Prescription Drug Labels: Effects on Memory and Comprehension in Young and Old Adults," *The Gerontologist* 29 (1989): 345–354.

59. Frank R. Kardes, Gurumurthy Kalyanaram, Murali Chandrashekaranm, and Ronald J. Dornoff, "Brand Retrieval, Consideration Set Composition, Consumer Choice, and the Pioneering Advantage" (unpublished manuscript, University of Cincinnati, 1992).

60. Zaichkowsky and Vipat, "Inferences from Brand Names."

61. Krugman, "Low Recall and High Recognition of Advertising."

62. Rik G.M. Pieters and Tammo H.A. Bijmolt, "Consumer Memory for Television Advertising: A Field Study of Duration, Serial Position, and Competition Effects," *Journal of Consumer Research* 23 (March 1997): 362–372.

63. Braun, "Postexperience Advertising Effects on Consumer Memory."

64. Keller, "Memory Factors in Advertising …."

65. Eric J. Johnson and J. Edward Russo, "Product Familiarity and Learning New Information," *Journal of Consumer Research* 11 (June 1984): 542–550.

66. Eric J. Johnson and J. Edward Russo, "Product Familiarity and Learning New Information," in *Advances in Consumer Research 8*, ed. Kent Monroe (Ann Arbor, MI: Association for Consumer Research, 1981): 151–155; John G. Lynch and Thomas K. Srull, "Memory and Attentional Factors in Consumer Choice: Concepts and Research Methods," *Journal of Consumer Research* 9 (June 1982): 18–37.

67. Julie A. Edell and Kevin Lane Keller, "The Information Processing of Coordinated Media Campaigns," *Journal of Marketing Research* 26 (May 1989): 149–164.

68. Lynch and Srull, "Memory and Attentional Factors in Consumer Choice …."

69. Joseph W. Alba and Amitava Chattopadhyay, "Salience Effects in Brand Recall," *Journal of Marketing Research* 23 (November 1986): 363–370; Elizabeth C. Hirschman and Michael R. Solomon, "Utilitarian, Aesthetic, and Familiarity Responses to Verbal versus Visual Advertisements," in *Advances in Consumer Research 11*, ed. Thomas C. Kinnear (Provo, UT: Association for Consumer Research, 1984): 426–431.

70. Susan E. Heckler and Terry L. Childers, "The Role of Expectancy and Relevancy in Memory for Verbal and Visual Information: What Is Incongruency?" *Journal of Consumer Research* 18 (March 1992): 475–492.

71. Russell H. Fazio, Paul M. Herr, and Martha C. Powell, "On the Development and Strength of Category-Brand Associations in Memory: The Case of Mystery Ads," *Journal of Consumer Psychology* 1, 1 (1992): 1–13.

72. Hirschman and Solomon, "Utilitarian, Aesthetic, and Familiarity Responses to Verbal versus Visual Advertisements."

73. Terry Childers and Michael Houston, "Conditions for a Picture-Superiority Effect on Consumer Memory," *Journal of Consumer Research* 11 (September 1984): 643–654; Terry Childers, Susan Heckler, and Michael Houston, "Memory for the Visual and Verbal Components of Print Advertisements," *Psychology & Marketing* 3 (Fall 1986): 147–150.

74. Werner Krober-Riel, "Effects of Emotional Pictorial Elements in Ads Analyzed by Means of Eye Movement Monitoring," in *Advances in Consumer Research 11*, ed. Thomas C. Kinnear (Provo, UT: Association for Consumer Research, 1984): 591–596.

75. Hans-Bernd Brosius, "Influence of Presentation Features and News Context on Learning from Television News," *Journal of Broadcasting & Electronic Media* 33 (Winter 1989): 1–14.

76. Robert M. MacGregor and Stuart J. McKelvie, "Effects of Ethnic Imagery on Recall of Brand Names," *Canadian Journal of Administrative Sciences* (September 1990): 1–9.

77. Raymond R. Burke and Thomas K. Srull, "Competitive Interference and Consumer Memory for Advertising," *Journal of Consumer Research* 15 (June 1988): 55–68.

78. Burke and Srull, "Competitive Interference and Consumer Memory for Advertising."

79. Johnson and Russo, "Product Familiarity and Learning New Information."

80. Joan Meyers-Levy, "The Influence of Brand Names Association Set Size and Word Frequency on Brand Memory," *Journal of Consumer Research* 16 (September 1989): 197–208.

81. Michael H. Baumgardner, Michael R. Leippe, David L. Ronis, and Anthony G. Greenwald, "In Search of Reliable Persuasion Effects: II. Associative Interference and Persistence of Persuasion in a Message-Dense Environment," *Journal of Personality and Social Psychology* 45 (September 1983): 524–537.

82. Alba and Chattopadhyay, "Salience Effects in Brand Recall."

83. Margaret Henderson Blair, Allan R. Kuse, David H. Furse, and David W. Stewart, "Advertising in a New and Competitive Environment: Persuading Consumers to Buy," *Business Horizons* 30 (November/December 1987): 20.

84. Lynch and Srull, "Memory and Attentional Factors in Consumer Choice …."

85. Russell W. Belk, "Possessions and the Extended Self," *Journal of Consumer Research* 15 (September 1988): 139–168.

86. Morris B. Holbrook and Robert M. Schindler, "Nostalgic Bonding: Exploring the Role of Nostalgia in the Consumption Experience," *Journal of Consumer Behavior* 3, no. 2 (December 2003): 107–127.

87. Hans Baumgartner, Mita Sujan, and James R. Bettman, "Autobiographical Memories, Affect and Consumer Information Processing," *Journal of Consumer Psychology* 1 (January 1992): 53–82; Mita Sujan, James R. Bettman, and Hans Baumgartner, "Influencing Consumer Judgments Using Autobiographical Memories: A Self-Referencing Perspective," *Journal of Marketing Research* 30 (November 1993): 422–436.

88. Russell W. Belk, "The Role of Possessions in Constructing and Maintaining a Sense of Past," in *Advances in Consumer Research* 16, eds. Marvin E. Goldberg, Gerald Gorn, and Richard W. Pollay (Provo, UT: Association for Consumer Research, 1989): 669–678.

89. Quoted in Keith Naughton and Bill Vlasic, "Nostalgia Boom," *Business Week* (March 23, 1998): 59–64, p. 59.

90. Diane Crispell, "Which Good Old Days," *American Demographics* (April 1996): 35.

91. Stuart Elliot, "Ads from the Past with Modern Touches," *New York Times on the Web* (September 9, 2002); Julia Cosgrove, "Listen up, Sucka, the 80s Are Back," *Business Week* (August 5, 2002): 16.

92. Stephen Brown, Robert V. Kozinets, and John F. Sherry, "Teaching Old Brands New Tricks: Retro Branding and the Revival of Brand Meaning," *Journal of Marketing* 67, no. 3 (July 2003): 19–33.

93. Nat Ives, "Creating Ads for Older Lads," *New York Times on the Web* (April 25, 2005).

94. Morris B. Holbrook and Robert M. Schindler, "Some Exploratory Findings on the Development of Musical Tastes," *Journal of Consumer Research* 16 (June 1989): 119–124.

95. Holbrook and Schindler, "Some Exploratory Findings on the Development of Musical Tastes"; Morris B. Holbrook and Robert M. Schindler, "Market Segmentation Based on Age and Attitude toward the Past: Concepts, Methods, and Findings Concerning Nostalgic Influences on Consumer Tastes," *Journal of Business Research* 37 (September 1996)1: 27–40.

96. Robert M. Schinlder and Morris B. Holbrook, "Nostalgia for Early Experience as a Determinant of Consumer Preferences," *Psychology & Marketing* 20, no. 4 (April 2003): 275–302; Holbrook and Schindler, "Some Exploratory Findings on the Development of Musical Tastes." Holbrook and Schindler, "Market Segmentation Based on Age and Attitude toward the Past …."

97. Lauren Lipton, "Nightlife, with Nighties Pajama Parties Catch on with Women, Retailers; Snoring at the Sleepover," *Wall Street Journal Interactive Edition* (January 9, 2004).

98. "Only 38% of T.V. Audience Links Brands with Ads," *Marketing News* (January 6, 1984): 10.

99. "Terminal Television," *American Demographics* (January 1987): 15.

100. Vanessa O'Connell, "Toys 'R' Us Spokesanimal Makes Lasting Impression: Giraffe Tops List of Television Ads Viewers Found the Most Memorable," *Wall Street Journal Interactive Edition* (January 2, 2003).

101. Richard P. Bagozzi and Alvin J. Silk, "Recall, Recognition, and the Measurement of Memory for Print Advertisements," *Marketing Science* (1983): 95–134.

102. Adam Finn, "Print Ad Recognition Readership Scores: An Information Processing Perspective," *Journal of Marketing Research* 25 (May 1988): 168–177.

103. Bettman, "Memory Factors in Consumer Choice: A Review."

104. Mark A. deTurck and Gerald M. Goldhaber, "Effectiveness of Product Warning Labels: Effects of Consumers' Information Processing Objectives," *Journal of Consumer Affairs* 23, 1 (1989): 111–125.

105. Finn, "Print Ad Recognition Readership Scores …."

106. Louise Aird, "Sole Man," Blitz on the Business of Media Communications in BC, (May/June 1999), 10: 1, 4, 5; Virginia Leeming, "San Francisco Is Latest Fluevog Shoe-in," *Vancouver Sun* (October 21, 1997): C5.

107. Surendra N. Singh and Gilbert A. Churchill, Jr., "Response-Bias-Free Recognition Tests to Measure Advertising Effects," *Journal of Advertising Research* (June/July 1987): 23–36.

108. William A. Cook, "Telescoping and Memory's Other Tricks," *Journal of Advertising Research* 27 (February/March 1987): 5–8.

109. "On a Diet? Don't Trust Your Memory," *Psychology Today* (October 1989): 12.

110. Hubert A. Zielske and Walter A. Henry, "Remembering and Forgetting Television Ads," *Journal of Advertising Research* 20 (April 1980): 7–13.

111. Thomas F. Jones, "Our Musical Heritage Is Being Raided," *San Francisco Examiner* (May 23, 1997).

112. Kevin Goldman, "A Few Rockers Refuse to Turn Tunes into Ads," *New York Times* (August 25, 1995): B1.

Good food for life!

As Jamie scans the menu at the trendy vegetarian restaurant Susan has dragged him to, he reflects on what a man will give up for love. Susan is a diehard vegan; she even has a carrot in a fist tattooed on her ankle. She's slowly but surely working on Jamie to forsake those juicy steaks and burgers for tofu and beans. Jamie is bound and determined to make this relationship work, but he sure would like to join his friends at The Keg.

Susan is totally into vegetarianism; she claims that eating this way not only cuts out unwanted fat, but also is good for the environment. Just his luck to fall head-over-heels for a vegan. As Jamie gamely tries to decide between the stuffed artichokes with red pepper vinaigrette and the grilled marinated zucchini, visions of a flaming grill loaded with a 24-ounce T-bone steak dance before his eyes.

CHAPTER 4

Motivation and Values

INTRODUCTION

It is estimated that 7 percent of the general population is vegetarian and that an additional 10 percent to 20 percent of consumers are interested in vegetarian options in addition to their traditional fare of meat. The same study also indicates that women aged 15 to 25 are the group of people who most frequently eliminate meat from their diets.[1] To reach these veggie-lovin' consumers, many companies have developed meat-free products and services. For example, every week Vancouver-based Yves Veggie Cuisine (***www.yvesveggie.com***) makes 125 tonnes of soy-based meat look-alikes. British Columbia absorbs 30 percent of that; the rest goes to the United States.[2]

In addition, some major food companies like Pillsbury are marketing meat-free food like "The Green Giant Harvest Burger," and another company, ConAgra, offers a line of meatless meals called "Life Choice."[3] Magazines, such as *The Canadian Vegetarian Magazine, Vegetarian Times* (***www.vegetariantimes.com***), and *Veggie Life* (***www.veggielife.com***), as well as organizations such as the Vegetarian Resource Group (***www.vrg.org***), respond to the growing interest in vegetarianism.

The forces that drive people to buy and use products are generally straight-forward, as when a person chooses what to have for lunch. As hard-core vegetarians demonstrate, however, even the consumption of basic food products may be related to wide-ranging beliefs about what is appropriate or desirable. In some cases these emotional responses create a deep commitment to the product. Sometimes people are not even fully aware of the forces that drive them toward some products and away from others. Often these choices are influenced by the person's values—his or her priorities and beliefs about the world.

To understand motivation is to understand *why* consumers do what they do. Why do people choose to bungee jump off a bridge or go whitewater rafting in the Yukon, while others spend their leisure time playing chess or gardening? We do everything for a reason, whether to quench a thirst, to kill boredom, or to attain some deep spiritual experience. Marketing students are taught from day one that the goal of marketing is to satisfy consumers' needs. However, this insight is useless unless we can discover *what* those needs are and why they exist. A popular beer commercial asks the question, "Why ask why?" In this chapter we'll find out.

THE MOTIVATION PROCESS

Motivation refers to the processes that cause people to behave as they do. It occurs when a need is aroused that the consumer wishes to satisfy. Once a need has been activated, a state of tension exists that drives the consumer to attempt to reduce or eliminate the need.

This need may be utilitarian (a desire to achieve some functional or practical benefit, as when a person requires a pair of durable sneakers), or it may be hedonic (an experiential need, involving emotional responses or fantasies, as when someone buys special running shoes for a triathlon event). The desired end state is the consumer's **goal**. Marketers try to create products and services that will provide the desired benefits and permit the consumer to reduce this tension.

Whether the need is utilitarian or hedonic, a discrepancy exists between the consumer's present state and some ideal state. This gulf creates a state of tension. The magnitude of this tension determines the urgency the consumer feels to reduce the tension. This degree of arousal is called a **drive**. A basic need can be satisfied any number of ways, and the specific path a person chooses is influenced by his or her unique set of experiences and by the values instilled by the culture in which the person has been raised.

These personal and cultural factors combine to create a want, which is one manifestation of a need. For example, hunger is a basic need that must be satisfied by all; the lack of food creates a tension state that can be reduced by the intake of such products as cheeseburgers, double-fudge Oreo cookies, raw fish, or bean sprouts. The specific route to hunger reduction is culturally determined.

Once the goal is attained, tension is reduced and the motivation recedes (for the time being). Motivation can be described in terms of its strength, or the pull it exerts on the consumer, and its direction, or the particular way the consumer attempts to reduce motivational tension.

→ A want is a manifestation of a need. This ad from Singapore reminds us that consumer society tempts us with wants.
Courtesy of M&C Saatchi, Singapore

MOTIVATIONAL STRENGTH

The degree to which a person is willing to expend energy to reach one goal as opposed to another reflects his or her underlying motivation to attain that goal. Many theories have been advanced to explain why people behave the way they do. Most share the basic idea that people have some finite amount of energy that must be directed toward certain goals.

Biological versus Learned Needs

Early work on motivation ascribed behaviour to instinct, the innate patterns of behaviour that are universal in a species. This view is now largely discredited. For one thing, the existence of an instinct is difficult to prove or disprove. The instinct is inferred from the behaviour it is supposed to explain (this type of circular explanation is called a *tautology*).[4] It is like saying that a consumer buys products that are status symbols because he or she is motivated to attain status, which is hardly a satisfying explanation.

Drive Theory

Drive theory focuses on biological needs that produce unpleasant states of arousal (such as your stomach grumbling during a morning class). We are motivated to reduce the tension caused by this arousal. Tension reduction has been proposed as a basic mechanism governing human behaviour.

In marketing, tension refers to the unpleasant state that exists if a person's consumption needs are not fulfilled. People may be grumpy if they haven't eaten, or dejected or angry if they cannot afford that new car. This state activates goal-oriented behaviour that attempts to reduce or eliminate this unpleasant state and return to a balanced one, called **homeostasis**.

Those behaviours that are successful in reducing the drive by eliminating the underlying need are strengthened and tend to be repeated. (This aspect of the learning process was discussed in Chapter 3.) Your motivation to leave class early to grab a snack would be greater if you hadn't eaten in 24 hours than if you had eaten only two hours earlier. If you did sneak out and had indigestion after, say, wolfing down a package of chips, this behaviour would be less likely to be repeated the next time you wanted a snack. A person's degree of motivation, then, depends upon the distance between his or her present state and the goal.

Drive theory, however, runs into difficulties when it tries to explain some facets of human behaviour that run counter to its predictions. People often do things that increase a drive state rather than decrease it. For example, people may delay gratification. If you know you are going out for a lavish dinner, you might decide to forgo a snack earlier in the day even though you are hungry at that time.

Expectancy Theory

Most current explanations of motivation focus on cognitive factors rather than biological ones to understand what drives behaviour. **Expectancy theory** suggests that behaviour is largely pulled by expectations of achieving desirable outcomes—*positive incentives*—rather than pushed from within. We choose one product over another because we expect this choice to have more positive consequences for us. Thus, the term *drive* is used here more loosely to refer to both physical and cognitive processes.

MOTIVATIONAL DIRECTION

Motives have direction as well as strength. They are goal oriented in that specific objectives are desired to satisfy a need. Most goals can be reached by a number of routes, and the objective of marketers is to convince consumers that the alternative they offer provides the best chance to attain the goal. For example, a consumer who decides that he needs a pair of jeans to help him reach his goal of being accepted by others or of projecting an appropriate image can choose among Levi's, Wranglers, Guess, Calvin Klein, and many other alternatives, each of which promises to deliver certain benefits.

Needs versus Wants

The specific way a need is satisfied depends upon the individual's unique history and learning experiences and his or her cultural environment. The particular form of consumption used to satisfy a need is termed a **want**. For example, two classmates may feel their stomachs rumbling during a lunchtime lecture. If neither person has eaten since the night before, the strength of their respective needs (hunger) would be about the same. However, the way each person goes about satisfying this need might be quite different. The first person may be a health-conscious individual who fantasizes about gulping down a big handful of trail mix, while the second person may be equally aroused by the prospect of a greasy cheeseburger and fries.

Types of Needs

People are born with a need for certain elements necessary to maintain life, such as food, water, air, and shelter. These are called *biogenic needs.* People have many other needs, however, that are not innate. *Psychogenic needs* are acquired in the process of becoming a member of a culture. These include the need for status, power, affiliation, and so on. Psychogenic needs reflect the priorities of a culture, and their effect on behaviour will vary in different environments. For example, Hong Kong consumers may be driven to devote a good chunk of income to products that permit them to display their wealth and status, while their Japanese counterparts may work equally hard to ensure that they do not stand out from the group. These differences in cultural values will be discussed later in this chapter.

Consumers can also be motivated to satisfy either utilitarian or hedonic needs. The satisfaction of utilitarian needs implies that consumers will emphasize the objective, tangible attributes of products, such as kilometres per litre of gas in a car; the amount of fat, calories, and protein in a cheeseburger; and the durability of a pair of blue jeans. Hedonic needs are subjective and experiential, leading consumers to rely on a product because it meets their needs for excitement, self-confidence, or fantasy, perhaps to escape the mundane or routine aspects of life.[5] Of course, consumers may be motivated to purchase a product because it provides *both* types of benefits. For example, a mink coat may be bought because of the luxurious image it portrays *and* because it keeps the wearer warm throughout the long cold winter.

Motivational Conflicts

A goal has *valence,* which means that it can be positive or negative. A positively valued goal is one toward which consumers direct their behaviour; they are motivated to *approach* the goal and will seek out products that will be instrumental in attaining it. However, not all behaviour is motivated by the desire to approach a goal. As we saw in Chapter 3, sometimes consumers are motivated to *avoid* a negative outcome. They will structure their purchases or consumption activities to reduce the chances of attaining this end result. For example, many consumers work hard to avoid rejection, a negative goal. They will stay away from products that they associate with social disapproval. Products such as deodorants and mouthwash frequently rely upon consumers' negative motivation by depicting the onerous social consequences of underarm odour or bad breath.

Because a purchase decision may involve more than one source of motivation, consumers often find themselves in situations where different motives, positive and negative, conflict with one another. Since marketers are attempting to satisfy consumers' needs, they can also help by providing possible solutions to these dilemmas. As shown in Figure 4–1, three general types of conflict can occur: approach-approach, approach-avoidance, and avoidance-avoidance.

APPROACH-APPROACH CONFLICT

In an approach-approach conflict, a person must choose between two desirable alternatives. A student might be torn between going home for the holidays and going on a ski trip with friends. Or he or she might have to choose between two CDs.

The **theory of cognitive dissonance** is based on the premise that people have a need for order and consistency in their lives and that a state of tension is created when beliefs or behaviours conflict with one another. The conflict that arises when choosing between two alternatives may be resolved through a process of cognitive dissonance reduction, in which people are motivated to reduce this inconsistency (or dissonance) and thus eliminate unpleasant tension.[6]

A state of dissonance occurs when there is a psychological inconsistency between two or more beliefs or behaviours. It often occurs when a consumer must make a choice between two products, both of which possess good and bad qualities. By choosing one product and not the other, the person gets the bad qualities of the chosen product and loses out on the good qualities of the unchosen one.

This loss creates an unpleasant, dissonant state that the person is motivated to reduce. People tend to convince themselves after the fact that choices they made were smart ones by finding additional reasons to support the alternatives they chose, or perhaps by "discovering" flaws with the options they did not choose. A marketer can resolve an approach-approach conflict by bundling several benefits together. For example, Miller Lite's claim that it is "less filling" *and* "tastes great" allows the drinker to "have his beer and drink it too."

APPROACH-AVOIDANCE CONFLICT

Many of the products and services we desire have negative consequences attached to them as well. We may feel guilty or ostentatious when buying a status-laden product like a mink coat or feel like a glutton when contemplating a bag of potato chips. When we desire a goal but wish to avoid it at the same time, an approach-avoidance conflict exists.

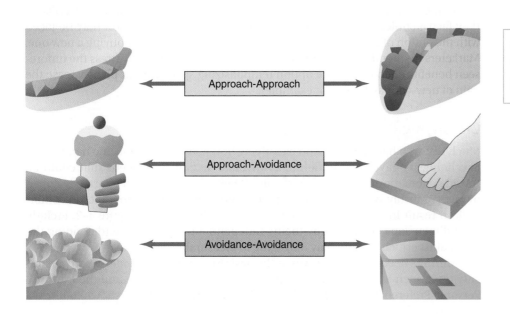

FIGURE 4–1

THREE TYPES OF MOTIVATIONAL CONFLICT

Approach-Approach

Approach-Avoidance

Avoidance-Avoidance

→ Haagen-Dazs promises the pleasure of eating ice cream without the caloric overload.
Courtesy of Nestle Canada

97% fat free Häagen-Dazs.
(We left in 3% so you could still be a little naughty.)

The Newest Pure Pleasure

FIGURE 4–2

TYPES OF NEEDS DEFINED BY MURRAY

Types of Needs Defined by Murray

Biogenic	Food
	Water
	Air
	Sleep
	Sex
	Shelter
Psychogenic	Dominance
	Superiority
	Emotional Stability
	Achievement
	Compliance
	Order
	Autonomy
	Affiliation
	Analysis
	Dependence
	Self-Depreciation
	Exhibition
	Assistance
	Change
	Endurance
	Aggression
	Defendence
	Play

Some solutions to these conflicts include the proliferation of fake furs, which eliminate guilt about harming animals while still allowing you to make a fashion statement, and the success of diet foods, such as Weight Watchers *(www.weightwatchers.com)* brands, which promise good food without the calories. Many marketers try to overcome guilt by convincing consumers that they are deserving of luxuries (such as when the model for L'Oréal cosmetics claims, "Because I'm worth it!").

AVOIDANCE-AVOIDANCE CONFLICT

Sometimes consumers find themselves caught "between a rock and a hard place": they face a choice between two undesirable alternatives. A person may be faced with the option of either throwing more money into an old car or buying a new one. Marketers frequently address this conflict through messages that stress the unforeseen benefits of choosing one option (emphasizing special credit plans to ease the pain of new-car payments, for example).

Classifying Consumer Needs

Much research has been done on classifying human needs. On the one hand, some psychologists have tried to define a universal inventory of needs that could be traced systematically to explain virtually all behaviour. One such effort, developed by Henry Murray, delineates a set of psychogenic needs that (sometimes in combination) result in specific behaviours. These needs, shown in Figure 4–2, include such dimensions as autonomy (being independent), defendence (defending the self against criticism), and play (engaging in pleasurable activities).[7]

Murray's need structure serves as the basis for a number of widely used personality tests, such as the Thematic Apperception Technique (TAT) and the Edward's Personal Preference Schedule (EPPS). In the TAT, test subjects are shown four to six

← This ambiguous picture would be suitable for the TAT.
Photo courtesy of Judy Zaichkowsky.

ambiguous pictures and asked to write answers to four *directing* questions about the pictures. These questions are: (1) What is happening? (2) What has led to this situation? (3) What is being thought? and (4) What will happen? The subject is allowed four minutes of writing time to answer these questions for each story. Each answer is then content-analyzed for references to certain needs and scored whenever that need is mentioned.

The theory behind the test is that people will freely project their own subconscious needs onto the ambiguous picture. By getting their responses to the picture, you are really getting at the person's true needs for achievement or affiliation or whatever other needs may dominate. Murray believed that everyone has the same basic set of needs but that individuals differ in how they priority rank them.

SPECIFIC NEEDS AND BUYING BEHAVIOUR

Other motivational approaches have focused on specific needs and their ramifications for behaviour. For example, individuals with a high *need for achievement* strongly value personal accomplishment.[8] They place a premium on products and services that signify success, because these consumption items provide feedback about the realization of their goals. These consumers are good prospects for products that provide evidence of their achievements. One study of working women found that those who were high in achievement motivation were more likely to choose clothing they considered businesslike and less likely to be interested in apparel that accentuated their femininity.[9] Some other important needs that are relevant to consumer behaviour include the following:

- *Need for affiliation* (to be in the company of other people):[10] This need is relevant to products and services that alleviate loneliness and that are consumed among groups of people at places such as athletic venues, bars, and shopping malls.

- *Need for power* (to control one's environment):[11] Many products and services, ranging from "souped-up" muscle cars to hotels, restaurants, and resorts, that promise to respond to the customer's every whim allow consumers to feel that they have mastery over their surroundings.

- *Need for uniqueness* (to assert one's individual identity):[12] This need is satisfied by products that pledge to accentuate a consumer's distinctive qualities. For example, Cachet perfume claims to be "as individual as you are."

MASLOW'S HIERARCHY OF NEEDS

One influential approach to motivation was proposed by the psychologist Abraham Maslow. Maslow's approach is a general one originally developed to understand personal growth and the attainment of "peak experiences."[13] Maslow formulated a hierarchy of biogenic and psychogenic needs, in which levels of motives are specified. A hierarchical approach implies that the order of development is fixed—that is, a certain level must be attained before the next, higher one is activated. This universal approach to motivation has been adopted by marketers because it (indirectly) specifies certain types of product benefits people might be looking for, depending upon the different stages in their development and/or their environmental conditions.

These levels are summarized in Figure 4–3. At each level different priorities exist in terms of the product benefits a consumer is looking for. Ideally, an individual progresses up the hierarchy until his or her dominant motivation is a focus on "ultimate" goals, such as justice and beauty. Unfortunately, this state is difficult to achieve (at least on a regular basis); most of us have to be satisfied with occasional glimpses of peak experiences.

For most Canadians, the biogenic or physiological needs are regularly and easily satisfied. Thus, the higher-level needs are usually dominant. Safety and security become the next driving force of behaviour. These needs are concerned with much more than physical safety. They include order, stability, routine, familiarity, and certainty—the knowledge, for example, that the individual will eat dinner not only on that day and the following day but also far into the future. Safety needs are met by unions, social welfare programs, and insurance policies.

Social needs are met by seeking warm and satisfying human relationships. When the social needs are more or less satisfied, the esteem or ego needs emerge. Inwardly directed ego needs reflect an individual's need for self-acceptance, self-

↑ Alcan appeals to Canadian consumers' need for food safety.
Supplied by ALCAN FOIL PRODUCTS.

FIGURE 4–3

LEVELS OF NEEDS IN THE MASLOW HIERARCHY

UPPER-LEVEL NEEDS

Relevant Products

	Level	Example
Hobbies, travel, education	**SELF-ACTUALIZATION** Self-Fulfillment, Enriching Experiences	U.S. Army—"Be all you can be."
Cars, furniture, credit cards, stores, country clubs, liquors	**EGO NEEDS** Prestige, Status, Accomplishment	Royal Salute Scotch—"What the rich give the wealthy."
Clothing, grooming products, clubs, drinks	**BELONGINGNESS** Love, Friendship, Acceptance by Others	Pepsi—"You're in the Pepsi generation."
Insurance, alarm systems, retirement, investments	**SAFETY** Security, Shelter, Protection	Allstate Insurance—"You're in good hands with Allstate."
Medicines, staple items, generics	**PHYSIOLOGICAL** Water, Sleep, Food	Quaker Oat Bran—"It's the right thing to do."

LOWER-LEVEL NEEDS

Gardening

Since 1939

is all about give'n take, about sharing and learning. That's why we'd like to share our 2000 seed catalogue with you. Not only is it full of hundreds of flower, vegetable and herb varieties suited to our Canadian growing seasons, it's also loaded with planting information, tips, and knowledge that we've learned over the past six decades.

Please take advantage of this offer and order your free Vesey's seed catalogue today.

Vesey's
Seeds for Canadian Gardens

Dept. CG0, York
Prince Edward Island
C0A 1P0
1 (800) 363-7333
catalog@veseys.com

←This Vesey's ad appeals to fulfilling social and self-actualization needs through gardening.
Courtesy of Vesey's Seed Ltd.

esteem, achievement, and success. Outwardly directed ego needs include the needs for prestige, reputation, status, and recognition from others. Most people spend most of their lives trying to fill their ego needs and never move on to the fifth level of self-actualization. This need refers to individuals' desire to fulfill their own potential, to become everything they are capable of becoming, so that they are totally and completely satisfied with their lives.

In summary, Maslow's need hierarchy predicts that higher-order needs become the driving force behind human behaviour as the consumer's lower-level needs are satisfied. The theory says, in effect, that satisfaction does not motivate behaviour; dissatisfaction does. It is important to note that lower needs are never totally satisfied but are ongoing. We do not need to satisfy one need totally before the next level of need motivates our behaviour. Sometimes certain behaviours satisfy two needs at once. For example, a Mercedes might satisfy the safety need and the ego need for prestige. You might be surprised at how often these needs are expressed. Consumers' feelings about the activity of gardening were classified according to Maslow's hierarchy and were found to express needs at all levels. This is shown in Table 4–1.

TABLE 4–1	
MASLOW'S HIERARCHY OF GARDENING	
Need	Expression of Need
Physiological	I like to work in the soil.
Safety	I feel safe in the garden.
Social	I can share my produce with others.
Esteem	I can create something of beauty.
Self-actualization	My garden gives me a sense of peace.

Source: Adapted from Kansas State University, Horticulture Department, 1992, cited in "Survey Tells Why Gardening's Good," *Vancouver Sun* (April 12, 1997): B12.

Although Maslow's theory is very interesting and applicable to marketing, it has certain problems. There is no measurement tool for researchers to test the need hierarchy empirically. Also, they cannot measure precisely how well satisfied one need is before the next higher need becomes operational.

Another problem with taking Maslow's hierarchy too literally is that its assumptions may be particular to Western culture. People of other cultures may question the order of the levels as specified. Many Asian cultures operate on the premise that the welfare of the group (belongingness needs) is more highly valued than needs of the individual (esteem needs).

The point is that this hierarchy is widely applied in marketing because it reminds us that consumers may have different need priorities at different times and stages of their lives—not because it *exactly* specifies a consumer's progression up the ladder of needs.

CONSUMER INVOLVEMENT

Do consumers form strong relationships with products and services? If you don't believe so, consider these recent events:

- A consumer in Brighton, England, loves a local restaurant called All In One so much that he had its name and phone number tattooed on his forehead. The owner remarked, "I'm not going to give him free pizza, because he did it on his own free will. But whenever he comes in, he'll go straight to the front of the queue."[14]

- *Lucky* is a new magazine devoted to shopping for shoes and other fashion accessories. The centrefold of the first issue featured rows of makeup sponges. The editor observes, "It's the same way that you might look at a golf magazine and see a spread of nine irons. *Lucky* is addressing one interest in women's lives, in a really obsessive, specific way."[15]

These examples illustrate that people can get pretty attached to products.

As we have seen, a consumer's motivation to attain a goal influences his or her desire to expend the effort necessary to attain the products or services believed to be instrumental in satisfying that objective. However, not everyone is motivated to the same extent; that is, one person might be convinced that he or she can't live without the latest style or modern convenience, while another is only marginally interested in these items. **Involvement** can be defined as "a person's perceived relevance of the object based on their inherent needs, values and interests."[16] The word

Rezepte gegen die Langeweile: www.kartoffel.ch

← The Swiss Potato Board is trying to increase involvement with its product. The ad reads, "Recipes against boredom."
Used with permission of Swisspatat.

"object" is used in the generic sense and refers to a product (or brand), an advertisement, or a purchase situation. Consumers can find involvement in all these "objects."

Since involvement is a motivational construct, it can be triggered by one or more of the different antecedents shown in Figure 4–4. The antecedents can be something about the person, something about the object, or something about the situation. On the right side of Figure 4–4 are the results or consequences of being involved with the "object." When consumers are intent on doing what they can to satisfy a need, they will be motivated to pay attention to and process any information felt to be relevant to achieving their goals.

Involvement can be viewed as the motivation to process information.[17] To the degree that there is a perceived link between a consumer's needs, goals, or values and product knowledge, the consumer will be motivated to pay attention to product information. When relevant knowledge is activated in memory, a motivational state is created that drives behaviour (e.g., shopping). As involvement with a product increases, people devote more attention to ads related to the

FIGURE 4-4

CONCEPTUALIZING INVOLVEMENT

Source: J.L. Zaichkowsky, "Conceptualizing Involvement," *Journal of Advertising* 15, no. 2 (1986), pp. 2–14.

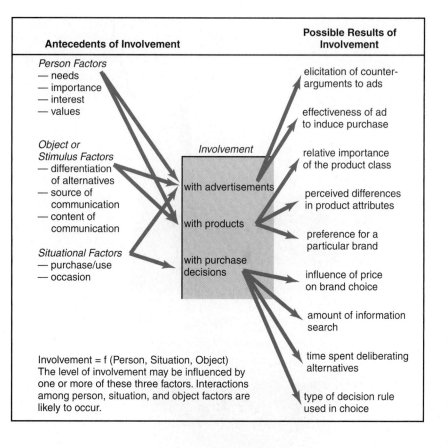

Involvement = f (Person, Situation, Object)
The level of involvement may be influenced by one or more of these three factors. Interactions among person, situation, and object factors are likely to occur.

product, exert more cognitive effort to understand these ads, and focus their attention on the product-related information in them.[18]

Levels of Involvement: From Inertia to Passion

The type of information processing that will occur thus depends upon the consumer's level of involvement. It can range from *simple processing*, in which only the basic features of a message are considered, all the way to *elaboration*, in which the incoming information is linked to pre-existing knowledge systems.[19]

A person's degree of involvement can be conceived as a continuum, ranging from absolute lack of interest in a marketing stimulus at one end to obsession at the other. Consumption at the low end of involvement is characterized by **inertia**, where decisions are made out of habit, because the consumer lacks the motivation to consider alternatives. At the high end of involvement we can expect to find the type of passionate intensity reserved for people and objects that carry great meaning to the individual.

When consumers are truly involved with a product, an ad, or a website, they enter what has been called a **flow state**. This state is the Holy Grail of web designers who want to create sites that are so entrancing the surfer loses all track of time as he or she becomes engrossed in the site's contents (and hopefully buys stuff in the process!). Flow is an optimal experience characterized by:

- a sense of playfulness
- a feeling of being in control
- concentration and highly focused attention
- mental enjoyment of the activity for its own sake
- a distorted sense of time
- a match between the challenge at hand and one's skills[20]

← This advertisement draws consumers in with the familiar format used for nutrition information, and keeps them involved through the use of emotive language.

Reprinted with permission of Canada Bread Company Limited.

A more sophisticated view of involvement recognizes that, besides the level of involvement, there may be a *type* of involvement. A person may be emotionally or affectively involved with an object (such as an advertisement), or rationally or cognitively involved with a product or purchase situation, and so on. The advertising industry has long held this view and advocates different types of advertising strategies, depending upon the level and type of involvement. This is shown in Figure 4–5.

CULT PRODUCTS

A devoted Starbucks fan, a humble computer programmer by day, is on a mission to visit every Starbucks in the world. In the seven years that he's been on his quest, he's been to almost all of the approximately 5000 stores Starbucks operates around the world. This is no mean feat given the rate at which the company is opening new outlets to satisfy its loyal drinkers—an average of about 10 stores a week. This corporate growth is so remarkable that it prompted *The Onion*, an online satirical newspaper, to publish the (fake) headline: "New Starbucks Opens in Rest Room of Existing Starbucks."[21] **Cult products** command fierce consumer loyalty, devotion—and maybe even worship by consumers who are very highly involved with a brand. These items take many forms, from Apple computers and Harley-Davidson motorcycles to Tim Hortons donuts, Jones Soda, and Beanie Babies, not to mention

TYPE OF INVOLVEMENT

		Cognitive	Affective
Level of Involvement	**High**	• Car • New products Media: print, information based	• Jewellery • Motorcycles Media: TV, image based
	Low	• Ground beef • Household cleansers Media: 10 sec. IDs, POS reminder	• Candy • Liquor Media: POS attention grabbing

FIGURE 4–5

FOOTE, CONE, AND BELDING'S INVOLVEMENT AND PRODUCT TYPOLOGY

Source: Adapted from Richard Vaughn, "How Advertising Works: A Planning Model," *Journal of Advertising Research* 20 (October 1980): 31. See also Judith Lynne Zaichkowsky, "The Emotional Side of Product Involvement," in *Advances in Consumer Research* 14, eds. Paul Anderson and Melanie Wallendorf (Provo, UT: Association for Consumer Research), pp. 32–35.

consumers' devotion to recording artists and sports teams.[22] What else explains the willingness of many women (like Carrie on the TV show *Sex and the City*) to shell out up to $3400 for a pair of shoes designed by Manolo Blahnik?

The Many Faces of Involvement

As previously defined, involvement can take many forms. Involvement can be cognitive, as when a "webhead" is motivated to learn all she can about the latest specs of a new multimedia PC, or emotional, as when the thought of a new Armani suit gives a clotheshorse goosebumps.[23] To complicate matters further, advertisements, such as those produced for Nike or Adidas (*www.adidas.com*), may themselves be involving for some reason (because they make us laugh or cry, or inspire us to work harder). It seems that involvement is a fuzzy concept, because it overlaps and means different things to different people. Indeed, the consensus is that there are actually three broad types of involvement—related to the product, to the message, or to the situation.[24]

PRODUCT INVOLVEMENT

Product involvement is related to a consumer's level of interest in a particular product. Many sales promotions are designed to increase this type of involvement. For example, when LifeSavers announced that it was going to eliminate the pineapple flavour unless consumers went to the LifeSavers' website and voted to keep it, more than 400 000 consumers heard the call and saved the flavour.[25]

Perhaps the most powerful way to enhance product involvement is to invite consumers to play a role in designing or personalizing what they buy. **Mass customization** is the customization and personalization of products and services for individual customers at a mass production price.[26] Improved manufacturing techniques in many industries are allowing companies to produce made-to-order products for many customers at a time. Customers love it: today around 40 percent of Lands' End shoppers choose a customized garment over the standard-sized equivalent even though these items cost at least $20 more and take about three to four weeks to arrive. At *www.nike.com*, buyers can specify a unique palette of colours or even words that will appear on their shoes, while websites like *www.venturoma. com* and *www.reflect.com* let the shopper create her own blend of massage oils, skin creams, or body washes. MasterFoods is letting candy lovers go online to choose one of 13 colours and add a personal slogan that will appear on one side of the M&M's candy shell.[27]

MESSAGE-RESPONSE INVOLVEMENT

Vigilante marketing, where freelancers and fans film their own commercials for favourite products and post them on websites, is hot. In one unauthorized spot produced by a teacher that got media attention in magazines like *Wired* and on advertising blogs like *AdRants*, an iPod Mini zips around to the song "Tiny Machine" by the Darling Buds.[28] This devotion to creating a commercial is an extreme example of *message-response involvement*, or advertising involvement, which refers to the consumer's interest in processing marketing communications.[29] Television is considered a low-involvement medium because it requires a passive viewer who exerts relatively little control over content (remote-control "zipping" notwithstanding). In contrast, print media demand high involvement. The reader is actively involved in processing the information and is able to pause and reflect on what he or she has read before moving on.[30] The role of message characteristics in changing attitudes is discussed further in Chapter 8.

A variety of marketers are experimenting with novel ways to increase consumers' involvement with different message formats. Procter & Gamble is going so far as to create a new medium by printing trivia questions and answers on its Pringles snack chips using ink made of blue or red food colouring, while a company called Speaking Roses International has patented a technology to laser print words, images, or logos on flower petals.[31]

In the online space, food companies are developing video games based on their products to boost involvement (more on this in Chapter 17):

- Lipton produced its first new ad for Cup-a-Soup in more than a decade as a game called "Beat the 3 p.m. Slump." Located on Lipton's website, you play an office worker who winds through cubicles gobbling up Cup-a-Soups to beat the green blobs chasing you (the slumps).[32]

- Kraft's ***www.nabiscoworld.com*** offers games featuring 17 of its brands, plus classic games such as chess, mah-jong, and backgammon. In the company's Ritz Bits sumo wrestling game, players control either the Creamy Marshmallow or the Chocolatey Fudge cracker in a belly-smacking showdown, which results in the "S'more"-flavoured cracker.

- In another Kraft game, users are Planters peanut vendors at a baseball game; they have to throw bags of nuts at spectators in a ballpark festooned with Planters logos.

- In a LifeSavers "boardwalk bowling" game, players try to roll balls over a LifeSavers logo through holes shaped like the candies.

- PepsiCo Inc.'s Frito-Lay unit hosts an auction site for kids and kids' sports teams at ***www.eploids.com.*** The currency is Ploids, which kids get from bags of chips.[33]

Other firms are creating customized advertising messages that directly relate to the consumer's specific environment. For example, online weather sites are starting to offer ads that are triggered by the local weather; they run only when the current weather or forecast meets certain conditions. Accordingly, an advertiser could sell air conditioners on a hot day in Toronto or snow tires during a blizzard in Regina.[34]

PURCHASE SITUATION INVOLVEMENT

Purchase situation involvement refers to differences that may occur when buying the same object for different contexts. Here the person may perceive a great deal of social risk or none at all. What people think when they consume the product for themselves, or when they know others will consume the product they buy, is not always obvious or intuitive. For example, when you want to impress someone, you may try to buy a brand or product with a certain image that you think reflects good taste. When you have to buy a gift for someone in an obligatory situation, such as a wedding gift for a cousin you do not really like, you may not care what image the gift portrays, or you may actually pick something cheap that reflects your desire to distance yourself from that cousin.[35] Again, some smart retailers are waking up to the value of increasing purchase situation involvement by appealing to hedonic shoppers who are looking to be entertained or otherwise engaged in addition to simply "buying stuff."[36] We'll learn more about how they're doing this via the creation of themed retailing venues and other strategies in Chapter 10.

Measuring Involvement

The measurement of involvement is important for many marketing applications. For example, research evidence indicates that a viewer who is more involved with a television show will also respond more positively to commercials contained in that show and that these spots will have a greater chance of influencing his or her purchase intentions.[37] One of the most widely used measures of the state of involvement is the scale shown in Table 4–2. It is the most widely used because it is context-free and therefore applicable to products, advertisements, and purchase situations.[38]

Net Profit +

Marketers in the online world can increase message-response involvement by letting web surfers design their own sites. The **skin** is a graphical interface that acts as both the "face" and the control panel of a computer program. Rather than settling for the boring skins that come with most programs, many people prefer to make and trade their own unique ones. According to the product manager for "Real Player," "This kind of customization is a huge factor in driving product use.... We're getting into a world where one size doesn't fit all, and one of the great benefits of technology is having the experience tailored to you." In addition to the more than 15 million skins that have been created for "Real Player," many other games, including "The Sims" and the multi-player "Unreal Tournament" have websites devoted to user-created skins. Players swap skins of the Incredible Hulk or Rambo or even playable skins of themselves. Movie companies and record labels now routinely commission artists to create promotional skins for films like *Blow* and *Frequency* and for music artists like U2 and Britney Spears.[39]

| TABLE 4–2 |

A SCALE TO MEASURE INVOLVEMENT

To me [object to be judged] is		
1. important	__:__:__:__:__:__:__	unimportant*
2. boring	__:__:__:__:__:__:__	interesting
3. relevant	__:__:__:__:__:__:__	irrelevant*
4. exciting	__:__:__:__:__:__:__	unexciting*
5. means nothing	__:__:__:__:__:__:__	means a lot to me
6. appealing	__:__:__:__:__:__:__	unappealing*
7. fascinating	__:__:__:__:__:__:__	mundane*
8. worthless	__:__:__:__:__:__:__	valuable
9. involving	__:__:__:__:__:__:__	uninvolving*
10. not needed	__:__:__:__:__:__:__	needed

*Indicates item is reverse scored. For example, a score of 7 for item no. 1 (important/unimportant) would actually be scored as 1.

Note: A check mark ✔ or an ✗ is placed in the appropriate space on each line of the semantic differential scale. Totalling the 10 items gives a score from a low of 10 to a high of 70. Items 1, 3, 5, 8, and 10 measure a more cognitive involvement, while items 2, 4, 6, 7, and 9 seem to capture a more affective type of involvement.

Source: Judith Lynne Zaichkowsky, "The Personal Involvement Inventory: Reduction, Revision, and Application to Advertising," *Journal of Advertising* 23, no. 4 (December 1994): 59–70.

Teasing out the Dimensions of Involvement

A pair of French researchers devised a scale to measure the antecedents of product involvement. Recognizing that consumers can be involved with a product because it is a risky purchase or because its use reflects upon or affects the self, they advocate the development of an *involvement profile* containing five components:[40]

1. the personal interest a consumer has in a product category
2. the perceived importance of the potential negative consequences associated with a poor choice of the product (risk importance)
3. probability of making a bad purchase
4. pleasure value of the product category
5. sign value of the product category

These researchers asked a sample of women to rate a set of 14 product categories on the above facets of involvement. The results are shown in Table 4–3. These data indicate that no single component captures consumer involvement, since this quality can occur for different reasons. For example, the purchase of a durable product, such as a vacuum cleaner, is seen as risky because one can be stuck with a bad choice for many years. However, the vacuum cleaner does not provide pleasure (hedonic value), nor is it high in sign value (i.e., its use is not related to the person's self-concept). In contrast, chocolate is high in pleasure value but is not seen as risky or closely related to the self. Dresses and bras, on the other hand, appear to be involving for a combination of reasons.

Segmenting by Involvement Levels

A measurement approach that segments involvement by levels allows consumer researchers to capture the diversity of the involvement construct, and it also allows for involvement to be used as a basis for market segmentation. For example, a yogourt manufacturer might find that, even though its product is low in sign value for one group of consumers, it is highly related to the self-concept of another market segment, such as health-food enthusiasts or avid dieters. The company could then adapt its strategy to account for the motivation of different segments to process information about the product.

One study looked at the roles of affective versus cognitive involvement and of level of involvement (high versus low) in promoting Canadian universities. The researchers found that students with a high level of cognitive involvement conducted an intense search for information about universities, while those students who had a low level of cognitive involvement and were affectively involved made their university choice based mainly on emotional factors.[41]

Note also that involvement with a product class may vary across cultures. Although the sample of French consumers shown in Table 4–3 rated champagne high in both sign value and personal value, the ability of champagne to provide pleasure or be central to self-definition might not transfer to other countries—to those with Islamic cultures, for example.

Strategies to Increase Involvement

Although consumers differ in their levels of involvement with respect to a product message, marketers do not have to just sit back and hope for the best. By being aware of some basic factors that increase or decrease attention, they can take steps to increase the likelihood that product information will get through. The marketer can enchance the consumer's motivation to process relevant information fairly easily by using one or more of the following techniques:[42]

- Appeal to consumers' hedonic needs. For example, ads with sensory appeal generate higher levels of attention.

- Use novel stimuli, such as unusual cinematography, sudden silences, or unexpected movements in commercials.

TABLE 4–3

INVOLVEMENT PROFILES FOR A SET OF FRENCH CONSUMER PRODUCTS

	Importance of Negative Consequences*	Subjective Probability of Mispurchase	Pleasure Value	Sign Value
Dresses	121	112	147	181
Bras	117	115	106	130
Washing machines	118	109	106	111
TV sets	112	100	122	95
Vacuum cleaners	110	112	70	78
Irons	103	95	72	76
Champagne	109	120	125	125
Oil	89	97	65	92
Yogourt	86	83	106	78
Chocolate	80	89	123	75
Shampoo	96	103	90	81
Toothpaste	95	95	94	105
Facial soap	82	90	114	118
Detergents	79	82	56	63

* Note that the first two antecedents, personal interest and the importance of negative consequences, are combined in these data.

Source: Gilles Laurent and Jean-Noël Kapferer, "Measuring Consumer Involvement Profiles," *Journal of Marketing Research* 22 (February 1985): 45, Table 3. By permission of the American Marketing Association.

- Use prominent stimuli, such as loud music and fast action, to capture attention in commercials. In print formats, larger ads increase attention. Also, viewers look longer at coloured pictures than at those in black and white.
- Include celebrity endorsers to generate higher interest in commercials. This strategy will be discussed in Chapter 8.
- Build a bond with consumers by maintaining an ongoing relationship with them.

VALUES

A **value** is a belief that some condition is preferable to its opposite. Many people avidly pursue products and services that will make them look young, believing that this is preferable to appearing old. A person's set of values plays a very important role in his or her consumption activities, since many products and services are purchased because they will (it is believed) help attain a value-related goal.

Two people can believe in the same behaviours (e.g., vegetarianism), but their underlying belief systems may be quite different (e.g., animal activism versus health concerns). The extent to which people share a belief system is a function of individual, social, and cultural forces. Advocates of a given belief system often seek out others with similar beliefs, so that social networks overlap and, as a result, believers tend to be exposed to information that supports their beliefs (e.g., "tree-huggers" rarely hang out with loggers).[43]

Core Values

More than 8.2 million women in 50 countries read versions of *Cosmopolitan* in 28 different languages. Adapting the *Cosmo* credo of "Fun, Fearless Female" in all these places gets a bit tricky. Different cultures emphasize varying belief systems that define what it means to be female, feminine, or appealing—and what is considered appropriate to see in print on these matters. In India, you won't come across any *Cosmo* articles about sexual positions. Publishers of the Chinese version aren't even permitted to mention sex at all, so articles about uplifting cleavage are replaced by uplifting stories about youthful dedication. Ironically, there isn't much down and dirty material in the Swedish edition either—but for the opposite reason: The culture is so open about this topic that it doesn't grab readers' attention the way it would in North America.[44]

Every culture has a set of values that it imparts to its members. People in one culture might feel that being a unique individual is preferable to subordinating one's identity to the group, while another culture may emphasize the virtues of group membership. A study by Wirthlin Worldwide, for example, found that the most important values to Asian executives are hard work, respect for learning, and honesty. In contrast, North American respondents emphasize the values of personal freedom, self-reliance, and freedom of expression.[45] And, of course, a

→ Fluevog shoes appeal to the value of individuality.
Courtesy of Fluevog Shoes.

culture's values do change over time—not necessarily in positive ways. Right now in Japan, young people are working hard to adopt more Western values and behaviours—which explains why the current fashion for young people is bleached blond hair, chalky makeup, deep tans, and luxury goods.

These differences in values often explain why marketing efforts that are a big hit in one country can flop in another. For example, a hugely successful advertisement in Japan promoted breast cancer awareness by showing an attractive woman in a sundress drawing stares from men on the street as a voice over says, "If only women paid as much attention to their breasts as men do." The same ad flopped in France because the use of humour to talk about a serious disease offended the French.[46]

In many cases, values are universal. Who does not desire health, wisdom, or world peace? What sets cultures apart is the *relative importance*, or ranking, of these universal values. This set of rankings constitutes a culture's **value system**.[47]

Every culture is characterized by its members' endorsement of a value system. These end states may not be equally endorsed by everyone, and in some cases values may even seem to contradict one another. (North Americans appear to value both conformity and individuality and seek to find some accommodation between the two.) Nonetheless, it is usually possible to identify a general set of *core values* that uniquely define a culture. These beliefs are taught to us by *socialization agents*, including parents, friends, and teachers. The process of learning the beliefs and behaviours endorsed by one's own culture is termed **enculturation**. In contrast, the process of learning the value system and behaviours of another culture (often a priority for those who wish to understand consumers and markets in foreign countries) is called **acculturation**.

Core values such as equality, youthfulness, achievement, materialism, and activity have been claimed to characterize most Western cultures, but even these basic beliefs are subject to change. For example, the emphasis on youth is eroding as the population ages (see Chapter 15).

Application of Values to Consumer Behaviour

Despite their importance, values have not been widely applied to direct examinations of consumer behaviour. One reason is that such broad-based concepts as

Multicultural Dimensions

The values treasured by a culture create opportunities for new products that might seem strange or a bit excessive to foreigners. Consider the "toilet wars" now underway in Japan, as companies vie with each other to produce the most sophisticated and luxurious bathroom fixture. Why the commotion over commodes? As one marketing executive explains, in a Japanese house "the only place you can be alone and sit quietly is likely to be the toilet." Take cramped living conditions, and then factor in a love of new technology. Now, add a strong cultural emphasis on cleanliness: Many Japanese wear gloves to protect themselves from strangers' germs and some ATM machines dispense cash that has been sanitized (yes, banks literally "launder" their money!). Nearly half of Japanese homes already have toilets with

a water jet spray that washes and massages the buttocks. Let the games begin:

> It all started when Matsushita unveiled a toilet seat equipped with electrodes that send a mild electric charge through the user's buttocks, yielding a digital measurement of body-fat ratio.
> Engineers from INAX counterattacked with a toilet that glows in the dark. When in use, the toilet plays any one of six soundtracks, including chirping birds, rushing water, tinkling wind chimes, or the strumming of a traditional Japanese harp.
> Matsushita retaliated with a $3000 throne that greets a user by flipping its lid and by blasting its twin air nozzles that provide air conditioning in the summer and heat in the winter.

> Toto weighed in with the Wellyoull model that automatically measures the user's urine sugar levels by making a collection with a little spoon held by a retractable, mechanical arm.

What's next? Matsushita is working on devices to measure weight, heartbeat, blood pressure, and other health indicators; the toilet will send results to a doctor via a built-in cell phone connected to the internet. Also in the works are talking toilets equipped with microchips that will greet each user with a personalized message such as words of encouragement from mom, and soon people will be able to give their toilets simple verbal commands.[48]

freedom, security, or inner harmony are more likely to affect general purchasing patterns than to differentiate among brands within a product category. For this reason, some researchers have found it convenient to distinguish among such broad-based *cultural values* as security or happiness, such *consumption-specific values* as convenient shopping or prompt service, and such *product-specific values* as ease of use or durability.[49] For example, people who value group affiliation and approval have been shown to place more importance on style and brand name when evaluating the desirability of clothing products.[50]

Since values drive much of consumer behaviour (at least in a very general sense), it could be said that virtually *all* types of consumer research ultimately are related to the identification and measurement of values. This section will describe some specific attempts by researchers to measure cultural values and apply this knowledge to marketing strategy.

The Rokeach Value Survey

The psychologist Milton Rokeach identified a set of **terminal values**, or desired end states, that apply (to various degrees) to many different cultures. The *Rokeach Value Survey*, a scale used to measure these values, also includes a set of **instrumental values**, which comprise actions needed to achieve these terminal values.[51] These two sets of values appear in Table 4–4.

There are a great many differences in the importance of these values to different cultures. Since it is these values that underlie, motivate, and guide our behaviour, by understanding the difference in the importance of values, we can understand what motivates people's behaviour. For example, freedom is a very basic and important value in the United States, emanating from the history of the country. A war was fought for "freedom" from Britain, and another was fought to "free" the

---

TABLE 4–4

TWO TYPES OF VALUES IN THE ROKEACH VALUE SURVEY

Instrumental Values	Terminal Values
Ambitious	A comfortable life
Broadminded	An exciting life
Capable	A sense of accomplishment
Cheerful	A world at peace
Clean	A world of beauty
Courageous	Equality
Forgiving	Family security
Helpful	Freedom
Honest	Happiness
Imaginative	Inner harmony
Independent	Mature love
Intellectual	National security
Logical	Pleasure
Loving	Salvation
Obedient	Self-respect
Polite	Social recognition
Responsible	True friendship
Self-controlled	Wisdom

Source: Richard W. Pollay, "Measuring the Cultural Values Manifest in Advertising," *Current Issues and Research in Advertising* (1983): 71–92. Reprinted by permission of the University of Michigan Division of Research.

slaves. The phrases "freedom" of expression, "free" to bear arms, and "freedom" of speech are the basis of the American constitution and reflect U.S. culture. In contrast, Canadians focus on equality. Equal access to health care and education, and "equality" of the provinces and territories underlie Canadian cultural values.

The List of Values (LOV) Scale

Although some evidence indicates that these global values do translate into product-specific preferences and differences in media usage, the Rokeach Value Survey has not been widely used by marketing researchers.[52] As an alternative, the *List of Values (LOV) Scale* was developed to isolate values with more direct-marketing applications.

This instrument identifies nine consumer segments based on the values they endorse and relates each to differences in consumption behaviours. These segments include consumers who place a priority on such values as a sense of belonging, excitement, warm relationships with others, and security. For example, people who endorse the value of a sense of belonging are more likely to read *Reader's Digest* and *TV Guide*, drink and entertain frequently, prefer group activities, and be older than are people who do not endorse this value as highly. In contrast, those who endorse the value of excitement prefer *Wallpaper* and are younger than those who do not.[53]

The Means-End Chain Model

Another research approach that incorporates values is termed a means-end chain model. This approach assumes that very specific product attributes are linked at levels of increasing abstraction to terminal values. The individual has valued end states, and he or she chooses among alternative means to attain these goals. Products are thus valued as the means to an end. Through a technique called **laddering**, consumers' associations between specific attributes and general consequences are uncovered. Consumers are helped to climb up the "ladder" of abstraction that connects functional product attributes with desired end states.[54]

To understand how laddering works, consider the purchase of a diamond ring to symbolize an upcoming marriage. Concrete attributes like size and clarity of the stone are parlayed into abstract and emotional values of love and self-esteem. The diamond industry is very good at keeping an artificially high price on a luxury good by linking the size of the diamond to the size of your paycheque, to the size of your love, and to your self-worth.

The notion that products are consumed because they are instrumental in attaining more abstract values is central to one application of this technique, called the *Means-End Conceptualization of the Components of Advertising Strategy (MECCAS)*. In this approach, researchers first generate a map depicting relationships between functional product or service attributes and terminal values. This information is then used to develop an advertising strategy by identifying elements such as those that follow:[55]

- *message elements*—the specific attributes or product features to be depicted
- *consumer benefits*—the positive consequences of using the product or service
- *executional framework*—the overall style and tone of the advertisement
- *leverage point*—the way the message will activate the terminal value by linking it with specific product features
- *driving force*—the end value upon which the advertising will focus

This technique was the foundation for an advertising strategy for Federal Express. The researchers developed a "hierarchical value map" for secretaries, an important group of decision makers in the category of overnight delivery services. As shown in Figure 4–6, concrete attributes of competitive services, such as having

FIGURE 4-6

SECRETARIES' HIERARCHICAL VALUE MAP FOR OVERNIGHT DELIVERY SERVICES

Source: Adapted from Thomas J. Reynolds and Alyce Byrd Craddock, "The Application of the MECCAS Model to the Development and Assessment of Advertising Strategy: A Case Study," *Journal of Advertising Research* (April/May 1988): 43–54.

a drop box or on-time delivery, were successively related to more abstract benefits, such as "makes me look good" or "saves time." These intermediate levels were then linked, or laddered, to reveal their relationships to the terminal values of peace of mind and self-esteem.

Based on these results, an advertisement was created. Its message elements emphasized Federal Express's satellite communications network. The consumer benefit was the reliability of the service, which made work easier. The executional framework of the ad was a humorous one: In the ad, a secretary is trying to track down an overnight delivery. She and her boss are interrupted and taken to view the Federal Express satellite system. As a result, the secretary sees the benefit of using the company. The leverage point is that using this service allows the secretary to be in control, which in turn provides peace of mind, the driving force (terminal value). A visit to Federal Express's website (*www.fedex.com*) will give you some insight into the sophistication of their operations.

Syndicated Surveys

A number of companies track changes in values through syndicated, large-scale surveys. The results of these studies are then sold to marketers, who pay a fee to receive regular updates on changes and trends.

This approach originated in the mid-1960s, when Playtex was concerned about sagging girdle sales.[56] The company commissioned the market research firm of Yankelovich, Skelly & White to determine the cause. Their research determined that sales had been affected by a shift in values regarding appearance and naturalness. Playtex went on to design lighter, less restrictive garments, while Yankelovich went on to track the impact of these types of changes in a range of industries. Gradually, the firm developed the idea of one big study to track attitudes. In 1970, the Monitor was introduced. It is based on two-hour interviews with 4000 respondents.

This survey attempts to pick up changes in values; for example, it reported a movement among consumers toward simplification and away from hype, as people

TABLE 4–5

NEW WORLD TEEN STUDY

Segment	Key Countries	Driving Principles	Overview	Marketing Approach
Thrills and Chills	Germany, England, Lithuania, Greece, the Netherlands, South Africa, United States, Belgium, Canada, Turkey, France, Poland, Japan, Italy, Denmark, Argentina, and Norway	Fun, friends, irreverence, and sensation	Stereotype of the devil-may-care, trying-to-become-independent hedonist. For the most part, they come from affluent or middle-class parents, live mainly in developed countries, and have allowance money to spend.	Respond to sensory stimulation. Tend to get bored easily, so stale advertising messages will escape their notice. They want action ads with bells and whistles, humour, novelty, colour, and sound. Edgier than their peers. Constantly seek out the new. First ones to hear of the newest technology or the hippest website. Experimenting is second nature. Wear all sorts of body rings and wear their hair in different shades.
Resigned	Denmark, Sweden, Korea, Japan, Norway, Germany, Belgium, the Netherlands, Argentina, Canada, Turkey, England, Spain, France, and Taiwan	Friends, fun, family, and low expectations	Resemble the thrills-and-chills teens, often decorating their bodies with rings and dye. However, they are alienated from society and very pessimistic about their chances for economic success. The punk rockers of the world, who sometimes take drugs and drink to excess. Respond to heavy metal and grunge music that emphasizes the negative and angry side of society.	Do not have as much discretionary income to spend as teens in other segments. Infrequent consumers save for some fast food, low-ticket clothes items, tobacco, and alcohol. They are drawn to irony and to ads that make fun of the pompousness of society.
World Savers	Hungary, Philippines, Venezuela, Brazil, Spain, Colombia, Belgium, Argentina, Russia, Singapore, France, Poland, Ukraine, Italy, South Africa, Mexico, and England	Environment, humanism, fun, and friends	A long list of do-good global and local causes that spark their interest. The intelligentsia in most countries who do well in school. They are the class and club leaders who join many organizations. They attend the same parties as the thrills-and-chills kids, but they are more into romance, relationships, and strong friendships. Eagerly attend concerts, operas, and plays. They exhibit a joie de vivre about life and enjoy dancing or drinking at bars and cafés with friends. They love the outdoors as well, including camping, hiking, and other sports activities.	Attracted by honest and sincere messages that tell the truth. Offended by any ad that puts people down or makes fun of another group. Piggyback a promotion with a worthwhile cause.
Quiet Achievers	Thailand, China, Hong Kong, Ukraine, Korea, Lithuania, Russia, and Peru	Success, anonymity, anti-individualism, and social optimism	Value anonymity and prefer to rest in the shadows. They are the least rebellious of all the groups, avoid the limelight, and do not ever want to stand out in the crowd. These are the bookish and straight kids who study long hours and are fiercely ambitious and highly goal-directed. Their top priority is to make good grades in school and use higher education to further their career advancement. Most of the quiet achievers live in Asia, especially Thailand and China. But these	Love to purchase stuff. Part of the reward for working diligently is being able to buy products. Their parents will defer to their children's needs when it comes to computers and other technological products that will aid in homework. This group is also keen on music; they are inner directed and adept at creating their own good times. Prefer ads that address the benefits of a product. They are embarrassed by ads that

TABLE 4–5 Continued

Segment	Key Countries	Driving Principles	Overview	Marketing Approach
			somewhat stereotypical studious types also exist in the United States, where they are sometimes regarded as being techies or nerds.	display rampant sexuality. And they do not respond to the sarcastic or the irreverent.
Boot-strappers	Nigeria, Mexico, United States, India, Chile, Puerto Rico, Peru, Venezuela, Colombia, and South Africa	Achievement, individualism, optimism, determination, and power	Most dreamy and childlike of the six segments. They live sheltered and ordered lives that seem bereft of many forms of typical teen fun and wild adult-emulating teen behaviour. Spend a lot of time at home, doing homework and helping around the house. Eager for power; they are the politicians in every high school who covet the class offices. They view the use of authority as a means for securing rewards, and they are constantly seeking out recognition. Geographically, many of these teens come from emerging nations such as Nigeria and India. In the United States, bootstrappers represent one in every four teens. Moreover, they represent 40 percent of young African Americans. A major error of U.S. marketers is to misread the size and purchasing power of this ambitious African-American segment.	Young yuppies in training. They want premium brands and luxury goods. Bootstrappers are also on the lookout for goods and services that will help them get ahead. They want to dress for success, have access to technology and software, and stay plugged-in to the world of media and culture to give them a competitive edge. They are attracted by messages that portray aspirations and possibilities for products and their users.
Upholders	Vietnam, Indonesia, Taiwan, China, Italy, Peru, Venezuela, Puerto Rico, India, Philippines, and Singapore	Family, custom, tradition, and respect for individuals	Traditions act as a rigid guideline, and these teens would be hard-pressed to rebel or confront authority. They are content to rest comfortably in the mainstream of life, remaining unnoticed. The girls seek mostly to get married and have families. The boys perceive that they are fated to have jobs similar to their fathers. Predominant in Asian countries, such as Indonesia and Vietnam, that value old traditions and extended family relationships. Teens in these countries are helpful around the home and protective of their siblings. Moreover, many upholders are in Catholic countries where the Church and tradition guide schooling, attitudes, and values.	Advertisers and marketers have had success selling to upholders using youthful, almost childlike communication and fun messages. These are teens who still watch cartoons and are avid media consumers. They are highly involved in both watching and playing sports, particularly basketball and soccer. More than any other group, they plan to live in their country of birth throughout adulthood. Essentially, upholders are homebodies. They are deeply rooted in family and community and they like to make purchase decisions that are safe and conform to their parents' values. Brands that take a leadership stance will attract upholders for their risk-free quality, value, and reliability.

Source: Adapted from "The Six Value Segments of Global Youth," *Brandweek* 11, no. 21 (May 22, 2000): 38, based on data initially presented in *The $100 Billion Allowance: How to Get Your Share of the Global Teen Market* by Elissa Moses (New York: John Wiley & Sons, 2000).

try to streamline their hectic lives and reduce their concerns about gaining the approval of others through their purchases. People who are **voluntary simplifiers** believe that once basic material needs are sated, additional income does not add to happiness. Instead of adding yet another SUV to the collection in the garage, simplifiers are into community building, public service, and spiritual pursuits.[57] Voluntary simplifiers range from senior citizens who downsize their homes to young, mobile professionals who don't want to be tied down to their possessions. These sentiments snowballed after the tragedy of September 11, 2001, when many people became more reflective and less materialistic. In the months that followed, stories abounded of successful careerists who gave it all up to spend time with their families.

Today, many other syndicated surveys also track changes in values. Some of these are operated by advertising agencies to allow them to stay on top of important cultural trends and help them to shape the messages they craft on behalf of their clients. The VALS2™ segmentation system (more on this in Chapter 6), New Wave (the Ogilvy & Mather advertising agency), the Lifestyles Study conducted by the DDB World Communications Group, and the Ipsos-Reid Group in Canada survey changes in values of specific groups or industry segments.

As we'll see in later chapters, it's often useful to go beyond simple demographics like people's ages to understand the values and preferences a group of people might have in common. This philosophy applies to understanding the youth market. We'll show in Chapter 15 that, as much as adults would like to lump all kids together, there are in fact important differences among them in terms of what they value. These priorities may mean that a young person has more in common with another young person halfway around the globe than with the guy sitting in the next seat in homeroom.

The New World Teen Study surveyed more than 27 000 teenagers in 44 countries and identified six value segments that characterize young people from Cairo to Caracas. Companies like Coca-Cola and Royal Philips Electronics have used the results of this massive segmentation exercise to develop ads that appeal to youth around the world. Table 4–5 (pages 120 and 121) summarizes some of the findings from this study.

Materialism: "He Who Dies with the Most Toys, Wins"

Although most people don't literally worship material goods, "things" do play a central role in many people's lives and can influence their value systems. **Materialism** refers to the importance people attach to worldly possessions.[58] We sometimes take the bounty of products and services for granted, until we remember how recent this abundance is. For example, in 1950 two of five homes did not have a telephone, and in 1940 half of all households still did not possess complete indoor plumbing.

Today, though, many consumers now energetically seek "the good life," which abounds in material comforts. Most young people can't imagine a life without cell phones, iPods, and other creature comforts. In fact, one way to think about marketing is as a system that provides a certain standard of living to consumers. To some extent, then, our lifestyles are influenced by the standard of living we have come to expect and desire—either by personal experience or because of the affluent lifestyles we see on TV and in movies.[59] Materialistic values tend to emphasize the well-being of the individual versus the group, which may conflict with family or religious values. That conflict may help to explain why people with highly material values tend to be less happy.[60]

North Americans inhabit a materialistic society in which people often gauge the worth of themselves and others in terms of how much they own (see Chapter 13). The popular bumper sticker "He Who Dies with the Most Toys, Wins" is a comment on this philosophy.

Shift in Values in the Aftermath of 9/11

September 11, 2001, forced a dramatic and public re-examination of consumer values. The threats to safety and security had a direct impact on businesses ranging from travel and hospitality (e.g., both United Airlines and Air Canada were forced to file for bankruptcy protection) to home improvement products and takeout foods as people seek the sanctuary of their homes rather than venturing out as much as they did before.

Even television programming has been affected; conventional situation comedies and family-oriented shows have re-emerged as favourites after many years of decline.[61] Following the attacks, many luxury goods marketers such as high-end auto dealers reported a surge in purchases, as some people seemed to be splurging in a "you can't take it with you mentality."[62]

One of the biggest value shifts is related to consumers' willingness to sacrifice their privacy for security. Polls taken since 9/11 indicate that a large majority favour wider use of facial-recognition systems, and they want closer monitoring of banking and credit-card transactions. Many high-tech surveillance tools that were deemed too intrusive before September 11, including the FBI's "Carnivore" internet eavesdropping system, are being unleashed. Cameras equipped with facial-recognition software can pick out known criminals in a crowd at airports, stadiums, and other public areas. Cars and cell phones equipped with location-finding technology make it possible to track down people to within about three metres. Meanwhile, sophisticated X-ray machines that can see through people's clothes may be more widely deployed at airports, in government buildings, and even in corporate lobbies.[63]

CHAPTER SUMMARY

IT'S IMPORTANT FOR MARKETERS TO RECOGNIZE THAT PRODUCTS CAN SATISFY A RANGE OF CONSUMER NEEDS.

- Marketers try to satisfy consumer needs, but the reasons any product is purchased can vary widely. The identification of consumer motives is an important step in ensuring that the appropriate needs will be met by a product. Traditional approaches to consumer behaviour have focused on the abilities of products to satisfy rational needs (utilitarian motives), but hedonic motives (such as the needs for exploration or fun) also play a role in many purchase decisions.

- As demonstrated by Maslow's hierarchy of needs, the same product can satisfy different needs, depending upon the consumer's state at the time (i.e., whether basic physiological needs have already been satisfied). In addition to his or her objective situation, the consumer's degree of involvement with the product must be considered.

THE WAY WE EVALUATE AND CHOOSE A PRODUCT DEPENDS ON OUR DEGREE OF INVOLVEMENT WITH THE PRODUCT, THE MARKETING MESSAGE, AND/OR THE PURCHASE SITUATION.

- Product involvement can range from very low, where purchase decisions are made via inertia, to very high, where consumers form very strong bonds with what they buy. In addition to considering the degree to which consumers are involved with a product, marketing strategists also need to assess the extent of involvement with marketing messages and with the purchase situation.

OUR DEEPLY HELD CULTURAL VALUES DICTATE THE TYPES OF PRODUCTS AND SERVICES WE SEEK OUT OR AVOID.

- Consumer motivations often are driven by underlying values. In this context, products take on meaning because they are seen as being instrumental in helping the person to achieve some goal that is linked to a value, such as individuality or freedom. Each culture is characterized by a set of core values to which many of its members adhere.

CONSUMERS VARY IN THE IMPORTANCE THEY ATTACH TO WORLDLY
POSSESSIONS, AND THIS ORIENTATION IN TURN HAS AN IMPACT
ON THEIR PRIORITIES AND BEHAVIOURS.

- Materialism refers to the importance people attach to
worldly possessions. Although many people can be
described as being materialists, there are indications of
a value shift within a sizable portion of the population—
especially in the aftermath of 9/11.

KEY TERMS

Acculturation   p. 116

Cult products   p. 109

Drive   p. 98

Enculturation   p. 116

Expectancy theory   p. 99

Flow state   p. 108

Goal   p. 98

Homeostasis   p. 99

Inertia   p. 108

Instrumental values   p. 117

Involvement   p. 106

Laddering   p. 118

Mass customization   p. 110

Materialism   p. 122

Motivation   p. 98

Skin   p. 111

Terminal values   p. 117

Theory of cognitive dissonance   p. 101

Value   p. 114

Value system   p. 116

Vigilante marketing   p. 110

Voluntary simplifiers   p. 122

Want   p. 100

REVIEW QUESTIONS

1. What is motivation, and how is this idea relevant to marketing?
2. Describe three types of motivational conflicts, citing an example of each from current marketing campaigns.
3. Explain the difference between a need and a want.
4. What is cognitive dissonance?
5. Name the levels in Maslow's hierarchy of needs, and give an example of a marketing appeal that's focused at each level.
6. What is consumer involvement? How does this concept relate to motivation?
7. Why would marketers want their customers to enter into a flow state when shopping for their products?
8. List three types of consumer involvement, giving an example of each.
9. What are some strategies marketers can use to increase consumers' involvement with their products?
10. What are values, and why should marketers care?
11. What is the difference between enculturation and acculturation?
12. Describe at least two alternative techniques marketing researchers have used to measure values.

CONSUMER BEHAVIOUR CHALLENGE

Discuss

1. "University students' concerns about the environment and vege-tarianism are just a passing fad; a way to look 'cool.'" Do you agree? Why or why not?

2. Some market analysts see a shift in values among young people. They claim that the people in this generation have not had a lot of stability in their lives. They are fed up with superficial relation-ships and are yearning for a return to tradition. This change is reflected in attitudes toward marriage and family. One survey of 22- to 24-year-old women found that 82 percent thought mother-hood was the most important job in the world. *Brides* magazine reports a swing toward traditional weddings—80 percent of brides today are tossing their garters. Daddy walks 78 percent of them down the aisle.[64] So, what's your take on this? Are young people indeed returning to the values of their parents (or even their grandparents)? How have these changes influenced your perspective on marriage and family?

3. Core values evolve over time. What do you think are the 3-5 core values that best describe Canadians now?

4. "High involvement is just a fancy term for expensive." Do you agree? Why or why not?

Experiential Exercises

5. Devise separate promotional strategies for an article of clothing, each of which stresses one of the levels of Maslow's hierarchy of needs.

6. Collect a sample of ads that appeal to consumers' values. What value is being communicated in each ad, and how is this done? Is this an effective approach to designing a marketing communica-tion?

7. Describe how a man's level of involvement with his car would affect how he is influenced by different marketing stimuli. How might you design a strategy for a line of car batteries for a seg-ment of low-involvement consumers, and how would this strategy differ from your attempts to reach a segment of men who are very involved in working on their cars?

8. Interview members of a celebrity fan club. Describe their level of involvement with the "product" and devise some marketing opportunities to reach this group.

CBC VIDEO VIGNETTE

CONCEPTS AT WORK FOR ELECTRIC CARS

Monte Gisborne wanted a product not sold in Canada—an electric car. He was so motivated by his desire to make the world a little better for his daughter and her generation that he converted his Pontiac Firefly into the Electrifly at a cost of about $20 000. The car burns no gasoline at all; instead, it is powered by 24 batteries and a solar panel (to power the radio and windshield wipers). The car costs about $15 per month to run and is expected to run for 10 years, or 100 000 kilometres, before the batteries need replacing. The 75-horsepower engine can take the car up to 140 kilo-metres per hour. All in all, Gisborne's custom-designed electric car is very much like a gas-fuelled car, except that it takes about a minute to discon-nect the car from the power source before he can leave his driveway.

Some critics accuse the producers of electric cars of switching the source of pollution from the tail pipe to the power plant. Car manufacturers are also less than enthusiastic about the concept. General Motors, for example, leased their electric model, called the GM EV1, in California and

Arizona, but discontinued it in August 2000 because there was not a viable demand for it. So, despite continued interest and anticipation by some interest groups and the high involvement of consumers like Monte Gisborne, the electric car has yet to "turn the corner" in the vehicle market.

Questions

1. Describe the values and motivations of the consumer who would most likely buy an electric car.

2. How satisfactorily does the electric car fulfill a consumer's desire to (a) reduce pollution and (b) have personal transportation?

3. Develop a hierarchical value map and propose a MECCAS for a manu-facturer of electric cars.

4. What has to happen before a company, such as General Motors, will be able to find viable demand for electric cars?

Resource: "Electric Cars," Marketplace #6, CBC Air Date: November 12, 2002.

NOTES

1. "Eating Trends Study Reveals Few Canadians Practice Vegetarianism," *Beef Information Centre Report*, 1999; "Perspectives on Vegetarianism," *Rapport*, Fall 1998, 13, 4.

2. Eve Johnson, "When a Hot Dog Is not a Hot Dog," *Weekend Post* (July 24, 1999): 22.

3. Chip Walker, "Meet the New Vegetarian," *American Demographics* (January 1995): 9 (2); Marilyn Chase, "Pretty Soon the Word 'Organic' on Foods Will Mean One Thing," *Wall Street Journal Interactive Edition* (August 18, 1997).

4. Robert A. Baron, *Psychology: The Essential Science* (Needham, MA: Allyn & Bacon, 1989).

5. Russell W. Belk, Guliz Ger, and Søren Askegaard, "The Fire of Desire: A Multisited Inquiry into Consumer Passion," *Journal of Consumer Research* 30 (December 2003): 326–351.

6. Leon Festinger, *A Theory of Cognitive Dissonance* (Stanford, CA: Stanford University Press, 1957).

7. See Paul T. Costa and Robert R. McCrae, "From Catalog to Classification: Murray's Needs and the Five-Factor Model," *Journal of Personality and Social Psychology* 55, 2 (1988): 258–265; Calvin S. Hall and Gardner Lindzey, *Theories of Personality*, 2nd ed. (New York, NY: John Wiley, 1970); James U. McNeal and Stephen W. McDaniel, "An Analysis of Need-Appeals in Television Advertising," *Journal of the Academy of Marketing Science* 12 (Spring 1984): 176–190.

8. See David C. McClelland, *Studies in Motivation* (New York, NY: Appleton-Century-Crofts, 1955).

9. Mary Kay Ericksen and M. Joseph Sirgy, "Achievement Motivation and Clothing Preferences of White-Collar Working Women," in *The Psychology of Fashion*, ed. Michael R. Solomon (Lexington, MA: Lexington Books, 1985): 357–369.

10. See Stanley Schachter, *The Psychology of Affiliation* (Stanford, CA: Stanford University Press, 1959).

11. Eugene M. Fodor and Terry Smith, "The Power Motive as an Influence on Group Decision Making," *Journal of Personality and Social Psychology* 42 (1982): 178–185.

12. C.R. Snyder and Howard L. Fromkin, *Uniqueness: The Human Pursuit of Difference* (New York, NY: Plenum Press, 1980).

13. Abraham H. Maslow, *Motivation and Personality*, 2nd ed. (New York, NY: Harper & Row, 1970).

14. Quoted in "Forehead Advertisement Pays Off," *Montgomery Advertiser* (May 4, 2000): 7A.

15. Quoted in Alex Kuczynski, "A New Magazine Celebrates the Rites of Shopping," *New York Times on the Web* (May 8, 2000).

16. Judith Lynne Zaichkowsky, "Measuring the Involvement Construct in Marketing," *Journal of Consumer Research* 12 (December 1985): 341–352.

17. The literature offers numerous approaches to the construct of involvement. See also Peter H. Bloch, "Involvement Beyond the Purchase Process: Conceptual Issues and Empirical Investigation," in *Advances in Consumer Research* 8, ed. Kent Monroe (Provo, UT: Association for Consumer Research, 1981): 61–65; George S. Day, *Buyer Attitudes and Brand Choice Behavior* (Chicago: Free Press, 1970); Michael J. Houston and Michael L. Rothschild, "Conceptual and Methodological Perspectives on Involvement," in *Research Frontiers in Marketing: Dialogues and Directions*, ed. S.C. Jain (Chicago, IL: American Marketing Association, 1978), 184–187; John L. Lastovicka and David Gardner, "Components of Involvement," in *Attitude Research Plays for High Stakes*, eds. John C. Maloney and Bernard Silverman (Chicago, IL: American Marketing Association, 1979), 53–73; Andrew Mitchell, "Involvement: A Potentially Important Mediator of Consumer Behavior," in *Advances in Consumer Research* 6, ed. William L. Wilkie (Provo, UT: Association for Consumer Research, 1979), 191–196.

18. Richard L. Celsi and Jerry C. Olson, "The Role of Involvement in Attention and Comprehension Processes," *Journal of Consumer Research* 15 (September 1988): 210–224.

19. Anthony G. Greenwald and Clark Leavitt, "Audience Involvement in Advertising: Four Levels," *Journal of Consumer Research* 11 (June 1984): 581–592.

20. Mihaly Csikszentmihalyi, *Flow: The Psychology of Optimal Experience* (New York: Harper Collins, 1991); Donna L. Hoffman and Thomas P. Novak, "Marketing in Hypermedia Computer-Mediated Environments: Conceptual Foundations," *Journal of Marketing* (July 1996), 60; 50–68.

21. Daniel Roth, "This Just In: Seeing World on Ten Coffees a Day," *Fortune on the Web* (June 28, 2004).

22. Robert W. Pimentel and Kristy E. Reynolds, "A Model for Consumer Devotion: Affective Commitment with Proactive Sustaining Behaviors," *Academy of Marketing Science Review [Online]* 5 (2004), available at http://www.amsreview.org/articles/pimentel05-2004.pdf.

23. Judith Lynne Zaichkowsky, "The Emotional Side of Product Involvement," in *Advances in Consumer Research* 14, eds. Paul Anderson and Melanie Wallendorf (Provo, UT: Association for Consumer Research): 32–35.

24. For a recent discussion of interrelationships between situational and enduring involvement, see Marsha L. Richins, Peter H. Bloch, and Edward F. McQuarrie, "How Enduring and Situational Involvement Combine to Create Involvement Responses," *Journal of Consumer Psychology* 1, 2 (1992): 143–153.

25. Rob Wherry, "Stunts For Blue Chips," *Forbes* (November 11, 1999): 232.

26. Joseph B. Pine II and James H. Gilmore, *Markets of One: Creating Customer-Unique Value through Mass Customization* (Boston: Harvard Business School Press, 2000), accessed on May 30, 2005, at http://www.managingchange.com/masscust/overview.htm.

27. Julie Schlosser, "Cashing in on the New World of Me," *Fortune* (December 13, 2004): 244–250.

28. Nat Ives, "Advertising: Unauthorized Campaigns Used by Unauthorized Creators Become a Trend," *New York Times on the Web* (December 23, 3004).

29. Rajeev Batra and Michael L. Ray, "Operationalizing Involvement as Depth and Quality of Cognitive Responses," in *Advances in Consumer Research* 10, eds. Alice Tybout and Richard Bagozzi (Ann Arbor, MI: Association for Consumer Research, 1983), 309–313.

30. Herbert E. Krugman, "The Impact of Television Advertising: Learning Without Involvement," *Public Opinion Quarterly* 29 (Fall 1965): 349–356.

31. "Read My Chips? Pringles Has Plans to Print Jokes, Trivia on Its Potatoes Associated Press," *Wall Street Journal on the Web* (May 20, 2004): C13; David Serchuk, "A Rose with Another Name," *Forbes* (December 27, 2004): 52.

32. Sarah Sennott, "Gaming the Ad," *Newsweek* (January 31, 2005): E2.

33. Joseph Pereira, "Junk-Food Games Online Arcades Draw Fire for Immersing Kids in Ads; Ritz Bits Wrestling, Anyone?" *Wall Street Journal* (May 3, 2004): B1.

34. Carl Bialik, "Weather Sites Run Ads Based on Local Conditions," *Wall Street Journal Interactive Edition* (August 21, 2003).

35. For more information on the involvement construct see "Special Issue on Involvement," *Psychology and Marketing* 10, 4 (July/August 1993).

36. Mark J. Arnold and Kristy E. Reynolds, "Hedonic Shopping Motivations," *Journal of Retailing* 79 (January 2003): 77–95.

37. Kevin J. Clancy, "CPMs Must Bow to Involvement Measurement," *Advertising Age* (January 20, 1992): 26.

38. Judith Lynne Zaichkowsky, "RPII Reduction, Revision and Application to Advertising," *Journal of Advertising* 23, 4 (December 1994): 59–70.

39. David Kushner, "From the Skin Artist, Always a Free Makeover," *New York Times on the Web* (March 21, 2002).

40. For an English translation of this scale, see Jean-Noël Kapferer and Gilles Laurent, "Further Evidence on the Consumer Involvement Profile: Five Antecedents of Involvement," *Psychology & Marketing* 10, 4 (July/August 1993): 347–356; Gilles Laurent and Jean-Noël Kapferer, "Measuring Consumer Involvement Profiles," *Journal of Marketing Research* 22 (February 1985): 41–53 (this scale was recently validated on an American sample as well). Cf. William C. Rodgers and Kenneth C. Schneider, "An Empirical Evaluation of the Kapferer-Laurent Consumer Involvement Profile Scale," *Psychology & Marketing* 10, 4 (July/August 1993): 333–345.

41. Carmen W. Cullen and Scott J. Edgett, "The Role of Involvement in Promoting Canadian Universities," *Journal of Promotion Management* 1, 2 (1991): 57–71.

42. Deborah J. MacInnis, Christine Moorman, and Bernard J. Jaworski, "Enhancing and Measuring Consumers' Motivation, Opportunity, and Ability to Process Brand Information from Ads," *Journal of Marketing* 55 (October 1991): 332–353.

43. Ajay K. Sirsi, James C. Ward, and Peter H. Reingen, "Microcultural Analysis of Variation in Sharing of Causal Reasoning about Behavior," *Journal of Consumer Research* 22 (March 1996): 345–332.

44. David Carr, "Romance, in Cosmo's World, Is Translated in Many Ways," *New York Times on the Web* (May 26, 2002).

45. Paul M. Sherer, "North American and Asian Executives Have Contrasting Values, Study Finds," *Wall Street Journal* (March 8, 1996): B12.

46. Sarah Ellison, "Sexy-Ad Reel Shows What Tickles in Tokyo Can Fade Fast in France," *Wall Street Journal Interactive Edition* (March 31, 2000).

47. Milton Rokeach, *The Nature of Human Values* (New York, NY: Free Press, 1973).

48. James Brooke, "Japanese Masters Get Closer to the Toilet Nirvana," *New York Times on the Web* (October 8, 2002).

49. Donald E. Vinson, Jerome E. Scott, and Lawrence R. Lamont, "The Role of Personal Values in Marketing and Consumer Behavior," *Journal of Marketing* 41 (April 1977): 44–50; John A. McCarty and L.J. Shrum, "The Role of Personal Values and Demographics in Predicting Television Viewing Behavior: Implications for Theory and Application," *Journal of Advertising* 22, 4 (December 1993): 77–101.

50. Gregory M. Rose, Aviv Shoham, Lynn R. Kahle, and Rajeev Batra, "Social Values, Conformity, and Dress," *Journal of Applied Social Psychology* 24, 17 (1994): 1501–1519.

51. Milton Rokeach, *Understanding Human Values* (New York, NY: Free Press, 1979). See also J. Michael Munson and Edward McQuarrie, "Shortening the Rokeach Value Survey for Use in Consumer Research," in *Advances in Consumer Research* 15, ed. Michael J. Houston (Provo, UT: Association for Consumer Research, 1988), 381–386.

52. B.W. Becker and P.E. Conner, "Personal Values of the Heavy User of Mass Media," *Journal of Advertising Research* 21 (1981): 37–43; Vinson, Scott, and Lamont, "The Role of Personal Values ...."

53. Sharon E. Beatty, Lynn R. Kahle, Pamela Homer, and Shekhar Misra, "Alternative Measurement Approaches to Consumer Values: The List of Values and the Rokeach Value Survey," *Psychology & Marketing* 2 (1985): 181–200; Lynn R. Kahle and Patricia Kennedy, "Using the List of Values (LOV) to Understand Consumers," *Journal of Consumer Marketing* 2 (Fall 1988): 49–56; Lynn R. Kahle, Basil Poulos, and Ajay Sukhdial, "Changes in Social Values in the United States during the Past Decade," *Journal of Advertising Research* 28 (February/March 1988): 35–41. See also Wagner A. Kamakura and Jose Afonso Mazzon, "Value Segmentation: A Model for the Measurement of Values and Value Systems," *Journal of Consumer Research* 18, 2 (September 1991): 208–218.

54. Thomas J. Reynolds and Jonathan Gutman, "Laddering Theory, Method, Analysis, and Interpretation," *Journal of Advertising Research* 28 (February/March 1988): 11–34; Beth Walker, Richard Celsi, and Jerry Olson, "Exploring the Structural Characteristics of Consumers' Knowledge," in *Advances in Consumer Research* 14, eds. Melanie Wallendorf and Paul Anderson (Provo, UT: Association for Consumer Research, 1986), 17–21.

55. Thomas J. Reynolds and Alyce Byrd Craddock, "The Application of the MECCAS Model to the Development and Assessment of Advertising Strategy: A Case Study," *Journal of Advertising Research* (April/May 1988): 43–54.

56. "25 Years of Attitude," *Marketing Tools* (November/December 1995): 38–39.

57. Amitai Etzioni, "The Good Society: Goals Beyond Money," *The Futurist* 35, no. 4 (2001); D. Elgin, *Voluntary Simplicity: Toward a Way of Life that Is Outwardly Simple, Inwardly Rich* (New York: Quill, 1993); Ascribe Higher Education News Service, "PNA Trend in Consumer Behavior Called 'Voluntary Simplicity' Poses Challenges for Marketers" (December 6, 2001).

58. Susan Schultz Kleine and Stacy Menzel Baker, "An Integrative Review of Material Possession Attachment," *Academy of Marketing Science Review*, no. 1 (2004): 1–39.

59. L. J. Shrum, James E. Burroughs, and Aric Rindfleisch, "Television's Cultivation of Material Values," *Journal of Consumer Research* 32 (December 2005): 473–480.

60. James E. Burroughs and Aric Rindfleisch, "Materialism and Well-Being: A Conflicting Values Perspective," *Journal of Consumer Research* 29 (December 2002): 348–370.

61. Bill Carter, "Mom, Dad and the Kids Reclaim TV Perch," *New York Times on the Web* (October 15, 2002).

62. J. Cosgrove, "What-The-Hell Consumption," *Businessweek* (2001): 12. For a study that examined value changes following a terrorist attack (the Oklahoma City bombing), see Dwight D. Frink, Gregory M. Rose, and Ann L. Canty, "The Effects of Values on Worries Associated with Acute Disaster: A Naturally Occurring Quasi-Experiment," *Journal of Applied Social Psychology* (forthcoming).

63. M. France et al., "Privacy in an Age of Terror," *Business Week* (November 5, 2001): 83.

64. Helene Stapinski, "Y Not Love?" *American Demographics* (February 1999): 62–68.

Leafing through *Glamour* and *Cosmopolitan* during her lunch hour, Rhoda is struck by all the articles about ways to be more attractive by dieting, exercising, and wearing sexy clothes. Rhoda looks at the models in the many advertisements for perfumes, apparel, and makeup. Each woman is more glamorous and beautiful than the last. She could swear that some of them must have had breast implants and other assorted "adjustments." Women just don't look that way in real life.

Rhoda entertains the thought that maybe she should look into cosmetic surgery, even though she's never considered herself unattractive. Who knows? Maybe a new nose or liposuction will improve her looks. On second thought, though, is it even worth it? Rhoda may be one of the 90 percent of Canadian women who believe it's a person's inner qualities that count.[1]

CHAPTER → 5

The Self

PERSPECTIVES ON THE SELF

Many products, from cars to cologne, are bought because people are trying to highlight or hide some aspect of the self. This chapter focuses on the self. We'll consider how consumers' feelings about themselves shape their consumption practices, particularly as they strive to fulfill their society's expectations about how males or females should look and act.

Does the Self Exist?

Although it seems natural to think about each consumer as having a self, this concept is actually a relatively new way of regarding people and their relationships with society. The idea that each single human life is unique, rather than a part of a group, developed only in late medieval times (between the eleventh and fifteenth centuries). The notion that the self is an object to be pampered is even more recent. In addition, the emphasis on the unique nature of the self is much greater in Western societies.[2] Many Eastern cultures instead stress the importance of a collective self, in which the person's identity is derived in large measure from his or her social group.

Both Eastern and Western cultures see the self as divided into an inner, private self and an outer, public self. But where these conceptions of self differ is in terms of which part is seen as the "real you": The West tends to subscribe to an independent construal of the self, which emphasizes the inherent separateness of each individual; non-Western cultures, in contrast, tend to focus on an interdependent self, where a person's identity is largely defined by the relationships he or she has with others.[3] For example, a Confucian perspective stresses the importance of "face"—others' perceptions of the self and maintaining one's desired status in their eyes. One dimension of face is *mien-tzu*—reputation achieved through success and ostentation. Some Asian cultures developed explicit rules about the specific garments and even colours that certain social classes and occupations were allowed to display, and these live on today in Japanese style manuals that provide very detailed instructions for dressing and for addressing people of different social status.[4]

Self-Concept

The **self-concept** refers to the beliefs a person holds about his or her attributes and how he or she evaluates these qualities. Although one's overall self-concept may be positive, there are certainly parts of the self that are evaluated more positively than others.

The self-concept is a very complex structure. It comprises many attributes, some of which are given greater emphasis in determining overall self-attitude. Attributes of self-concept can be described along such dimensions as their content (e.g., facial attractiveness versus mental aptitude), positivity or negativity (i.e., self-esteem), intensity, stability over time, and accuracy (i.e., the degree to which one's self-assessment corresponds to reality).[5] As will be seen later in this chapter, consumers' self-assessments can be quite distorted, especially with regard to their physical appearance.

SELF-ESTEEM

Self-esteem refers to the positivity of your attitude toward yourself. People with low self-esteem do not expect that they will perform very well, and they will try to avoid embarrassment, failure, or rejection. In developing a new line of snack cakes, Sara Lee found that consumers low in self-esteem preferred portion-controlled snack items because they felt they lacked self-control.[6] In contrast, people with high self-esteem expect to be successful, will take more risks, and are more willing to be the centre of attention.[7] Self-esteem often is related to acceptance by others. As you probably remember from your own experience, high-school students who hang out in high-status "crowds" seem to have higher self-esteem than their classmates (even though this may not be deserved!).[8]

Marketing communications can influence a consumer's level of self-esteem. Exposure to ads can trigger a process of *social comparison,* wherein the person tries to evaluate his or her self by comparing it with other people's and those of media images. This form of comparison appears to be a basic human motive, and many marketers have tapped into this need by supplying idealized images of happy, attractive people who just happen to be using their products. One study illustrates this process of social comparison. It showed that female college students do tend to compare their physical appearance with that of models who appear in advertising. Furthermore, the study participants who were exposed to beautiful women in advertisements afterward expressed lowered satisfaction with their *own* appearance, as compared with other participants who did not view ads with models.[9] Another study demonstrated that young women's perceptions of their body shapes and sizes can be altered after they are exposed to as little as 30 minutes of television programming.[10] Similar findings have been reported for young men.[11]

Self-esteem advertising attempts to change product attitudes by stimulating positive feelings about the self.[12] One strategy is to flatter the consumer, as when Virginia Slims cigarettes says, "You've come a long way, baby."

REAL AND IDEAL SELVES

In South Korean shopping malls, teenage girls line up at photo machines that provide high-tech makeovers with options including glamour lighting, a hair-blowing breeze, and virtual plastic surgery. At the Beauty Plus booth, for example, the fashion model wannabees can digitally trim jawlines, puff up lips, eliminate blemishes, and give themselves Western-style eyelids (this is the most popular option at booths in Seoul).[13]

When a consumer compares some aspect of herself to an ideal, this judgment influences her self-esteem. A consumer might ask, "Am I as attractive as I would like to be?" "Do I make as much money as I should?" and so on. The **ideal self** is a person's conception of how he or she would like to be, while the **actual self** is our more realistic appraisal of the qualities we do and don't have.

The ideal self is partly moulded by elements of the consumer's culture, such as heroes or people depicted in advertising, that serve as models of achievement or appearance.[14] Products may be purchased because they are believed to be instrumental in helping the consumer achieve the goal of emulating these models. Some products are chosen because they are perceived to be consistent with the consumer's actual self, while others are used to help in reaching the standard set by the ideal self.

FANTASY: BRIDGING THE GAP BETWEEN THE SELVES

Although most people experience a discrepancy between their real and ideal selves, for some consumers this gap is larger than for others. People for whom this gap is wide are especially good targets for marketing communications that employ *fantasy appeals*.[15] A **fantasy** or daydream is a self-induced shift in consciousness, which is sometimes a way of compensating for a lack of external stimulation or a means of coping with problems in the real world.[16]

Many products and services are successful because they appeal to consumers' tendencies to fantasize. These marketing strategies allow us to extend our vision of ourselves by placing us in unfamiliar, exciting situations or by permitting us to "try on" interesting or provocative roles. The thousands of personal websites people create to make a statement about themselves relate to the motivation to project a version of the self (perhaps an idealized one) into popular culture. A recent study investigated why consumers create personal websites and how those web space strategies compare to the self-presentation strategies of real life.

The authors of the study found that many of these personal sites are triggered by such events as graduation or promotion, a desire for personal growth (mastering of technology, search for a job, etc.) or advocacy (homage to a favourite artist or product). The creators choose every element of the site carefully, selecting images and text that symbolize something about their self-identity, and many of them digitize their physical selves as part of their self-presentation. Furthermore, the sites often reveal intimate aspects of the self that people wouldn't necessarily share in "RL" (real life).[17]

Multiple Selves

In a way, each consumer is really a number of different people. We have as many selves as we have different social roles. Depending upon the situation, we act differently, use different products and services, and even vary in terms of how much we like ourselves. A person may require a different set of products to play a number of desired roles. One may choose to consume beer with close friends but opt for a sophisticated Chardonnay when in business company. Each of us plays many roles, and each role has its own script, props, and costumes.[18]

The self can be thought of as having different components or *role identities,* and only some of these are active at any given time. Some identities (husband, boss, or student) are more central to the self than others, but other identities (stamp collector, dancer, or advocate for the homeless) may be dominant in specific situations. Strategically, this means a marketer may want to take steps to ensure the appropriate role identity is active before pitching products needed to play that particular role. One obvious way to do that is to place advertising messages in contexts where people are likely to be well aware of that role identity—for example, by promoting fitness and energy products at a marathon.

SYMBOLIC INTERACTIONISM

If each person potentially has many social selves, how does each develop, and how do we decide which self to "activate" at any point in time? The sociological tradition of **symbolic interactionism** stresses that relationships with other people play a large part in forming the self.[19] This perspective maintains that people exist in a symbolic environment and that the meaning attached to any situation or object is determined by the interpretation of the symbols. As members of society we learn to agree on shared meanings. Thus, we "know" that a red light means stop and that the "golden arches" means fast food.

Like other social objects, the meanings of consumers themselves are defined by social consensus. The consumer interprets his or her own identity, and this assessment is continuously evolving as he or she encounters new situations and people. In symbolic interactionist terms, we *negotiate* these meanings over time. Essentially, the consumer poses the question, "Who am I in this situation?" The answer to this question is greatly influenced by those around us and is really an answer to the question, "Who do other people think I am?" We tend to pattern our behaviour on the perceived expectations of others in a form of *self-fulfilling prophecy*. By acting the way we *assume* others expect us to act, we often wind up confirming these perceptions.

THE LOOKING-GLASS SELF

This process of imagining the reactions of others toward us is known as "taking the role of the other," or the **looking-glass self**.[20] According to this view, a process of *reflexive evaluation* occurs when the individual attempts to define the self, and it operates as a sort of psychological sonar: We take readings of our own identity by "bouncing" signals off others and trying to project what impression they have of us. The looking-glass image we receive will differ depending upon whose views we are considering. Like the images in distorted mirrors in a fun house, our appraisal of who we are can vary, depending upon whose perspective we are taking and how accurately we are able to predict their evaluations of us.

Self-Consciousness

There are times when people seem to be painfully aware of themselves. If you have ever walked into a class in the middle of a lecture and noticed that all eyes were on you, you can understand this feeling of self-consciousness. In contrast, consumers sometimes behave with little self-consciousness. For example, people may do things in a stadium, during a riot, or at a party that they would never do if they were highly conscious of their behaviour.[21]

→ The dynamics of this advertisement appeal to consumers who want to be perceived as well-behaved individuals.
Courtesy of Pharmasave.

WELL BALANCED

It's a reality – paying the mortgage, dentist appointments, car repairs, grocery shopping, house cleaning, paying bills, cooking dinner, exercise, self improvement, time with your loved ones, not to mention time for yourself!

Fitting it all in is a balancing act.

Pharmasave is here to support you in your search for a well balanced life with health and wellness services, preventative consultations, premium quality herbals, natural source vitamins, health and beauty products, even cards and gifts for that birthday you forgot last week!

Live well with
PHARMASAVE   *www.pharmasave.com*

Some people seem, in general, to be more sensitive to the image they communicate to others, although we all know people who act as if they're oblivious to the impression they are making! A heightened concern about the nature of one's public "image" also results in more concern about the social appropriateness of products and consumption activities.

Several measures have been devised to quantify this tendency. Consumers who score high on a scale of *public self-consciousness* are also more interested in clothing and tend to be heavier users of cosmetics.[22] A similar measure is *self-monitoring*. High self-monitors are more attuned to how they present themselves in their social environments, and their product choices are influenced by their estimates of how these items will be perceived by others.[23] Self-monitoring is assessed by the extent of a consumer's agreement with such statements as "I guess I put on a show to impress or entertain others" or "I would probably make a good actor."[24]

High self-monitors are more likely than low self-monitors to evaluate products consumed in public in terms of the impressions they make on others.[25] Similarly, some recent research has looked at aspects of *vanity*, such as a fixation on physical appearance or on the achievement of personal goals.[26]

CONSUMPTION AND SELF-CONCEPT

It is easy to see how the consumption of products and services contributes to the definition of the self. For an actor to play a role convincingly, he or she needs the correct props, stage setting, and so on. Consumers learn that different roles are accompanied by *constellations* of products and activities that help to define these roles.[27] Some "props" are so important to the roles we play that they can be viewed as a part of the *extended self.* Taking this to extremes, a British marketing firm is paying five people to transform themselves into human billboards for a fantasy superhero. This so-called identity marketing technique requires each participant to legally change his or her name for one year to Turok, the hero of a video game series about a time-travelling American Indian who slays bionically enhanced dinosaurs. A company spokesman notes, "It's not a gimmick.... Every form of their identity will have to change for this to work. They'll be walking, talking, living, breathing advertisements."[28]

Products that Shape the Self: You Are What You Consume

Recall that the reflected self helps to shape self-concept, which implies that people see themselves as they imagine others see them. Since what others see includes a person's clothing, jewellery, furniture, car, and so on, it stands to reason that these products also help to determine the perceived self. A consumer's products place him or her into a social role, which helps to answer the question, "Who am I now?"

People use an individual's consumption behaviours to help them make judgments about who that person is. In addition to considering a person's clothes, grooming habits, and so on, we make inferences about personality based on a person's choice of leisure activities (squash versus bowling), food preferences (vegetarians versus "steak-and-potatoes" people), cars, home-decorating choices, and so on. People who are shown pictures of someone's living room, for example, are able to make surprisingly accurate guesses about that consumer's personality.[29] In the same way that a consumer's use of products influences others' perceptions, the same products can help to determine his or her *own* self-concept and social identity.[30]

A consumer exhibits *attachment* to an object to the extent that it is used by that person to maintain his or her self-concept.[31] Objects can act as a sort of security blanket by reinforcing our identities, especially in unfamiliar situations. For example, students who decorate their residence rooms with personal items are less likely to drop out of university. This coping process may protect the self from being diluted in a strange environment.[32]

Using consumption information to define the self is especially important when an identity is yet to be adequately formed, as occurs when a consumer plays a new or unfamiliar role. **Symbolic self-completion theory** predicts that people who have an incomplete self-definition tend to complete this identity by acquiring and displaying symbols associated with it.[33] Adolescent boys, for example, may use "macho" products like cars and cigarettes to bolster their developing masculinity; these products are a sort of "social crutch" to be leaned upon during a period of uncertainty.

The contribution of possessions to self-identity is perhaps most apparent when these treasured objects are lost or stolen. One of the first acts performed by institutions that want to repress individuality and encourage group identity, such as prisons or convents, is to confiscate personal possessions.[34] Victims of burglaries and natural disasters commonly report feelings of alienation, of depression, or of being "violated." One consumer's comment after being robbed is typical: "It's the next worst thing to being bereaved; it's like being raped."[35] Burglary victims exhibit a diminished sense of community and fewer feelings of privacy and take less pride in their houses' appearance than do their neighbours.[36]

The dramatic impact of the loss of possessions is highlighted by studying post-disaster conditions, when consumers may literally lose almost everything but the clothes on their backs during a fire, an ice storm, a flood, or an earthquake. Some people are reluctant to undergo the process of recreating their identities by acquiring all new possessions. Interviews with disaster victims reveal that some are reluctant to invest the self in new possessions and so become more detached about what they buy. This comment from a woman in her fifties is representative of this attitude: "I had so much love tied up in my things. I can't go through that kind of loss again. What I'm buying now won't be as important to me."[37]

Self/Product Congruence

Because many consumption activities are related to self-definition, it is not surprising to learn that consumers demonstrate consistency between their values and attitudes and the things they buy.[38] **Self-image congruence models** predict that products will be chosen when their attributes match some aspect of the self.[39] These models assume a process of cognitive matching between these attributes and the consumer's self-image.[40]

→ In emphasizing the notion that looking the right way gives one confidence, this Yes Clothing ad relies on symbolic self-completion theory to appeal to consumers.

© *Philippe Berthome for No Comment!*

Although results are somewhat mixed, the ideal self appears to be more relevant as a comparison standard for highly expressive social products, such as perfume. In contrast, the actual self is more relevant for everyday, functional products. These standards are also likely to vary by usage situation. For example, a consumer might want a functional, reliable car to commute to work every day, but a flashier model with more "zing" when going out on a date in the evening.

Research tends to support the idea of congruence between product usage and self-image. One of the earliest studies to examine this process found that car owners' ratings of themselves tended to match their perceptions of their cars. Pontiac drivers, for example, saw themselves as more active and flashier than did Volkswagen drivers.[41] Congruity also has been found between consumers and their most-preferred brands of beer, soap, toothpaste, and cigarettes relative to their least-preferred brands, as well as between consumers' self-images and their favourite stores.[42] Some specific attributes that have been found to be useful in describing some of the matches between consumers and products include rugged/delicate, excitable/calm, rational/emotional, and formal/informal.[43]

Although these findings make some intuitive sense, we cannot blithely assume that consumers will always buy products whose characteristics match their own. It is not clear that consumers really see aspects of themselves in down-to-earth, functional products that don't have very complex or humanlike images. It is one thing to consider a brand personality for an expressive, image-oriented product like perfume and quite another to impute human characteristics to a toaster.

Another problem is the old "chicken-and-egg" question: Do people buy products because they are seen as similar to the self, or do they *assume* that these products must be similar because they have bought them? The similarity between a person's self-image and the images of products purchased does tend to increase with ownership, so this explanation cannot be ruled out.

The Extended Self

Recently a young man named John Freyer sold all his possessions on eBay to see whether our "stuff" really defines who we are. These treasures included an open box of taco shells, half a bottle of mouthwash, and his sideburns packaged in a plastic bag (yes, it seems people will buy just about anything!). Those who bought the artifacts he listed for sale registered them on a website called ***www.allmylifeforsale.com***. Freyer then undertook a decidedly non-spiritual odyssey as he set out to "visit" all of his possessions in their new homes around the world—including a bag of Porky's BBQ Pork Skins that wound up in Japan.[44] As noted earlier, many of the props and settings consumers use to define their social roles in a sense become a part of their selves. Those external objects that we consider a part of us comprise the **extended self**. In some cultures people literally incorporate objects into the self—that is, they lick new possessions, take the names of conquered enemies (or, in some cases, eat them), or bury the dead with their possessions.[45]

We don't usually go that far, but many people do cherish possessions as if they were a part of them. Consider shoes, for example: You don't have to be Carrie of *Sex and the City* fame to acknowledge that many people feel a strong bond to their footwear. One study found that people commonly view their shoes as magical emblems of self, Cinderella-like vehicles for self-transformation. Based upon data collected from consumers, the study concluded that (like their sister Carrie) women tend to be more attuned to the symbolic implications of shoes than men. A common theme that emerged was that a pair of shoes obtained when younger— whether a first pair of leather shoes, a first pair of high heels, or a first pair of cowboy boots—had a big impact even later in life. These experiences were similar to those that occur in such well-known fairytales and stories as Dorothy's red shoes in *The Wizard of Oz*, Karen's magical red shoes in Hans Christian Anderson's *The Red Shoes*, and Cinderella's glass slippers.[46]

→ The exhibits of the Bata Shoe Museum document how footwear throughout the ages has been employed as an extension of self.
Bata Shoe Museum, Toronto.

THE BATA SHOE MUSEUM

327 BLOOR STREET WEST, TORONTO, ONTARIO, CANADA M5S 1W7

In addition to shoes, of course, many material objects, ranging from personal possessions and pets to national monuments or landmarks, help to form a consumer's identity. Just about everyone can name a valued possession that has a lot of the self "wrapped up" in it, whether it is a beloved photograph, a trophy, an old shirt, a car, or a cat. Indeed, it is often possible to construct a pretty accurate "biography" of someone just by cataloguing the items on display in his or her bedroom or office.

Understanding the importance of the extended self helps to explain why in Japan something as seemingly inconsequential as the mishandling of a business card can be a deal killer. Japanese business people view their business cards as an

→ Our pets often become part of our extended selves. This Brazilian pet food ad plays on the popular belief that over time pets and their owners start to resemble each other.
Courtesy of Cesar c/o Almap/ BBDO Communicacaoes Ltda.

extension of their selves, and they expect them to be treated respectfully (see CBC Video Vignette, Chapter 16). A business card should not be bent or serve double duty as a toothpick. Arriving in Japan without an ample stock of business cards is akin to arriving barefoot. There is an elaborate, solemn etiquette connected to the giving and receiving of cards. The card should be studied, not shoved into a coat pocket to file later.[49] Japanese people take the failure to follow these rules as a personal insult.

In one study on the extended self, people were given a list of items that ranged from electronic equipment, facial tissues, and television programs to parents, body parts, and favourite clothes. They were asked to rate each in terms of its closeness to the self. Objects were more likely to be considered a part of the extended self if "psychic energy" was invested in them by expending effort to obtain them or because they were personalized and kept for a long time.[50]

Consumers define themselves by referring to four levels of the extended self. These range from very personal objects to places and things that allow people to feel as if they are rooted in their environments.[51]

1. *Individual level:* Consumers include many of their personal possessions in self-definition. These products can include jewellery, cars, clothing, and so on. The saying "you are what you wear" reflects the belief that one's things are a part of what one is.

2. *Family level:* This part of the extended self includes a consumer's residence and the furnishings in it. The house can be thought of as a symbolic body for the family and is often a central aspect of identity.

3. *Community level:* It is common for consumers to describe themselves in terms of the neighbourhood or town from which they come. For farm families or residents with close ties to a community, this sense of belonging is particularly important.

4. *Group level:* Our attachments to certain social groups also can be considered a part of self. A consumer may feel that landmarks, monuments, or sports teams are a part of the extended self.

GENDER ROLES

Gender identity is a very important component of a consumer's self-concept. People often conform to their culture's expectations about what those of their gender should do. Of course, these guidelines change over time, and they can differ radically across societies. It's unclear to what extent gender differences are innate versus culturally shaped, but they're certainly evident in many consumption decisions!

Consider the differences market researchers have observed when comparing the food preferences of men and women. Women eat more fruit. Men are more likely to eat meat; as one food writer put it, "Boy food doesn't grow. It is hunted or killed." Men are more likely to eat Frosted Flakes or Corn Pops, while women prefer multigrain cereals. Men are big root-beer drinkers; women account for the bulk of bottled-water sales.

And the genders differ sharply in the quantities of food they eat. When researchers at Hershey's discovered that women eat smaller amounts of candy, the company created a white chocolate confection called Hugs, one of the most successful food introductions of all time. On the other hand, men are more likely to take their food and drink in larger servings.[52]

Gender Differences in Socialization

In many societies, males are controlled by **agentic goals**, which stress self-assertion and mastery. Females, on the other hand, are taught to value **communal goals**, such as affiliation and the fostering of harmonious relations.[53]

→This ad for Bijan (*www.bijan.com*) illustrates how gender-role identities are culturally bound by contrasting the expectations of how women should appear in two different countries.
Courtesy of Bijan. Photographer Jim Koch.

Every society creates a set of expectations regarding the behaviours appropriate for men and women and finds ways to communicate these priorities. For example, an activity such as gift shopping is widely regarded as "women's work."[54] This training begins very young; even children's stories reinforce gender roles. A recent analysis showed that, although stereotypical depictions have decreased over time, female characters in children's books are still far more likely to take on nurturing roles, such as baking and gift-giving. In stories, the adult who prepares the birthday celebration is virtually always the mother; often no adult male is present at all. On the other hand, the male figure in these stories is often cast in the role of a miraculous provider of gifts.[55]

When Mattel decided to develop a new brand of building toy called Ello™ to appeal to girls, its designers began by watching the play patterns of five- to ten-year-old girls. The new toy features interconnecting plastic squares, balls, triangles, squiggles, flowers, and sticks, in pastel colours and with rounded corners that let users snap pieces together to create houses, people, jewellery, and picture frames. As one of the developers observed, "Boys enjoy stacking blocks and working towards a goal, such as finishing a building. Their play is more physically active, and they like to create conflict between characters. Girls don't like repetitive stacking. They prefer to create relationships between characters, building communities and decorative spaces."[56]

GENDER VERSUS SEXUAL IDENTITY

Gender role identity is a state of mind as well as body. A person's biological gender (i.e., male or female) does not totally determine whether he or she will exhibit **sex-typed traits**, or characteristics that are stereotypically associated with one gender or the other. A consumer's subjective feelings about his or her sexuality are crucial as well.[57]

Unlike maleness and femaleness, masculinity and femininity are *not* biological characteristics. A behaviour considered masculine in one culture may not be viewed as such in another. For example, the norm that males should be "strong" and repress tender feelings ("Real men don't eat quiche") and that male friends avoid touching each other (except in "safe" situations, such as on the football field) is not universal. In some Latin and European cultures it is common for men to hug one another. Each society determines what "real" men and women should and should not do.

eram·

Aucun corps de femme n'a été exploité dans cette publicité.

399 F Alexandre Matthieu pour eram

← This French shoe ad pokes fun at ads that demean women by proclaiming: "No woman's body was exploited in the making of this advertisement."
Courtesy of Eram and Devarrieuxvillaret Ad Agency.

SEX-TYPED PRODUCTS

A popular book was entitled *Real Men Don't Eat Quiche*. Many products (in addition to quiche) also are *sex-typed*. They take on masculine or feminine attributes, and consumers often associate them with one gender or another.[58] The sex-typing of products is often created or perpetuated by marketers (e.g., Princess telephones, boys' and girls' bicycles, and Luvs colour-coded diapers). FisherGirl is reeling in female fishing enthusiasts with the colour pink, which represents the fighting power of women against breast cancer. The company designed a line of fishing rods and accessories just for women, with lighter reels and a smaller handle than typical rods. The company donates a portion of sales to the Breast Cancer Foundation.[59]

Androgyny

Masculinity and femininity are not opposite ends of the same dimension. **Androgyny** refers to the possession of both masculine and feminine traits.[60]

Researchers make a distinction between gender-typed people, who are stereotypically masculine or feminine, and androgynous people, whose mixture of characteristics allows them to function well in a variety of social situations. And, of course, the "normality" of sex-typed behaviours varies across cultures. For example, while acceptance of homosexuality varies in Asian cultures, it doesn't occur to most Asians to assume that a man with some feminine qualities is gay. A recent survey of Korean consumers found that more than 66 percent of men and 57 percent of women under 40 were living self-described "androgynous" lifestyles—with men having more traditionally female traits, and women having more traditionally male ones, than they might have had years ago. But the respondents didn't link that with sexual orientation. While the Koreans nickname males with feminine interests "flower men," they don't consider this to be a derogatory term.[61]

Differences in gender-role orientation can influence responses to marketing stimuli, at least under some circumstances.[62] For example, research evidence indicates that females are likelier to undergo more elaborate processing of message content, so they tend to be more sensitive to specific pieces of information when forming a judgment, while males are more influenced by overall themes.[63] In addition, women with a relatively strong masculine component in their gender-role identity prefer ad portrayals that include non-traditional women.[64] Some research indicates that gender-typed people are more sensitive to the gender-role depictions of characters in advertising, although women appear to be more sensitive to gender-role relationships than men.

In one study, subjects read two versions of a beer advertisement, one couched in masculine terms and the other in feminine ones. The masculine version contained phrases like "X beer has the strong, aggressive flavour that really asserts itself with good food and good company . . .," while the feminine version made claims like "Brewed with tender care, X beer is a full-bodied beer that goes down smooth and gentle. . . ." People who rated themselves as highly masculine or highly feminine preferred the version that was described in very masculine or in feminine terms.[65]

Sex-typed people in general are more concerned with ensuring that their behaviour is consistent with their culture's definition of gender appropriateness.

Recently, researchers developed a scale to identify "non-traditional males" (NTMs) who exhibit stereotypical female tendencies. The scale included statements such as these:

- I enjoy looking through fashion magazines.
- In our family, I take care of the chequebook and pay the bills.
- I am concerned about getting enough calcium in my diet.
- I am good at fixing mechanical things.
- I would do better than average in a fistfight.

Not too surprisingly, strong differences emerged between men who answered the scale along traditional gender-role lines versus those who had a non-traditional orientation. When asked how they would like to be seen by others, NTMs were more likely than TMs to say that they would like to be considered stylish, sophisticated, up to date, and trendsetting. They were also more likely to say that they would like to be seen as sensitive, spiritual, affectionate, organized, and thrifty, but less likely to say they would like to be seen as "outdoorsy."[66]

Female Roles

In the 1949 movie *Adam's Rib*, Katharine Hepburn played a stylish and competent lawyer. This film was one of the first to show that a woman can have a successful career and still be happily married. Today the evolution of a new managerial class of women has forced marketers to change their traditional assumptions about women as they target this growing market.

Younger women's views of themselves are quite different from those of their mothers, who fought the good fight for feminism 30 to 40 years ago. To some extent they may take for granted certain rights that their mothers had to fight for. After all, they have grown up with female role models who are strong leaders, they participate to a much greater degree in organized sports, and they spend a lot of time on the internet, where factors like gender, race, and social status tend to disappear. In one study, only 34 percent of girls aged 13 to 20 years labelled themselves as feminists—even though they strongly endorsed the principles of the feminist movement! Ninety-seven percent of the same respondents believed a woman should receive the same pay for the same work a man does; 92 percent agreed that a woman's lifestyle choices should not be limited by her gender; and 89 percent said a woman can be successful without either a man or children. But, 56 percent also believed that "a man should always open the door for a woman."[68]

These changes have forced marketers to re-examine their strategies. Burton Snowboards Company was one of the early learners. When the company started to offer high-quality clothing and gear made specifically for women, female snowboarders snapped them up. Burton also changed the way it promotes these products. It recently redesigned its website after getting feedback from female riders. Now, models in the women's section are shot from the bottom looking up, which makes them look more empowered. In contrast, the photos in the men's section feature tighter shots of the gear itself, because Burton's research showed that males were more interested in the technical details.[69]

Announcing the death of traditional role stereotypes is premature. This is certainly true in traditional Islamic countries like Saudi Arabia, where women are required to be completely covered in public and are not allowed to work as salespeople in stores open to the public (even if the store sells female intimate apparel).[70]

Male Roles

Although the traditional conception of the ideal male as a tough, aggressive, muscular man who enjoys "manly" sports and activities is not dead, society's definition of the male role is evolving. Like women, men receive mixed messages about how they are supposed to behave and feel. It's more common these days to see men holding babies or being involved in meaningful relationships with women or with male friends in advertisements.

In a display of "what's good for the goose is good for the gander," men are concerned as never before with their appearance. Men spend $7.7 billion on grooming products globally each year. Skin cleansers, moisturizers, sunscreens, depilatories, and body sprays are available especially for men, largely from European companies. Unilever spent $90 million to launch its Axe body spray after its research showed that a sizable number of men would put on a spritz or two in addition to their usual deodorant.

Men are showing a willingness to use other traditionally feminine products, such as depilatories, to give them that smooth-torso look (depilatory sales increased by 16 percent between 2001 and 2002).[71] Many of these same guys also are colouring their hair; men between the ages of 18 to 24 years are 64 percent more likely to dye their hair than the average adult male.[72] Other vanity products introduced in recent years include Bodyslimmers underwear, which suck in the waist, and Super Shaper Briefs, which round out the buttocks.

Indeed, no doubt one of the biggest marketing buzzwords over the past few years is the **metrosexual**, a straight urban male who exhibits strong interests and knowledge regarding product categories such as fashion, home design, gourmet cooking, and personal care that run counter to the traditional male sex role. A gay writer named Mark Simpson actually coined the term way back in a 1994 article when he "outed" British soccer star and pop icon David Beckham as a metrosexual. Simpson noted that Beckham is " . . . almost as famous for wearing sarongs and

Marketing Pitfall

Marketers continue to grapple with gender portrayal in advertising. Women protest about sexual objectification and being cast in traditional roles, while men now object to being portrayed as idiots, incompetent at household tasks, and deserving victims of violence.[73] The Canadian Advertising Foundation compiled Gender Portrayal Guidelines to guide advertisers in areas that have been most problematic. The goal is to guide advertisers in reflecting the changing roles of men and women in their communications. Specifically, the Guidelines are meant to help creators of advertising develop positive images of men and women and to eliminate systemic gender discrimination. In brief, the interpretation guide advises that:

1. Caution should be taken that the overall impression, as well as the individual elements, of an ad does not violate the guidelines.
2. Some clauses are particularly directed at the portrayal of women, because the guidelines recognize that the risk of being portrayed negatively is greater for women than for men.
3. Humour, works of art, and historical settings should not be used as an excuse to stereotype men or women or to portray behaviour that is unacceptable today.
4. Sensitivity should be demonstrated in choosing media for certain product categories, such as intimate or personal products.[74]

pink nail polish and panties belonging to his wife, Victoria (aka Posh from the Spice Girls), as he is for his impressive ball skills."[75]

   Although it's unclear just how pervasive this new stereotype really is (despite the popularity of TV shows like *Queer Eye for the Straight Guy*), clearly many men's attitudes and behaviours are changing. Marketers also refer to such style-obsessed shoppers as *prosumers* or *urban influentials*—educated customers who are willing and able to focus their attention on their personal appearance and living environment. And this evolution is by no means confined to North American men: In the U.K., sales of male grooming products grew 560% over the last five years. Gillette India's research found that Indian men now spend an average of 20 minutes in front of the mirror each morning, higher than the 18-minute average for Indian women.[76]

Gay, Lesbian, Bisexual, and Transgender Consumers

The proportion of the population that is gay and lesbian is difficult to determine, and efforts to measure this group have been controversial.[77] However, the respected research company Yankelovich Partners Inc., which has tracked consumer values and attitudes since 1971 in its annual Monitor survey, now includes a question about sexual identity in its survey. This was the first commercial survey to use a sample that reflects the population as a whole instead of polling only smaller or biased groups (such as readers of gay publications) whose responses may not be representative of all consumers. About six percent of respondents described themselves as "gay/homosexual/lesbian."

The results, therefore, help to paint a more accurate picture of the potential size and attractiveness of this segment. For example, contrary to earlier surveys that reported homosexuals to be far more affluent than the general population, this study found few differences in household income. On the other hand, additional findings underscore the potential desirability of this segment for marketers: Homosexuals are twice as likely as heterosexuals to have attended graduate school, are more concerned about physical fitness and self-improvement, experience more stress in their daily lives (making them good prospects for security systems and vacations), and are much more likely to be self-employed. This means that they are an excellent market for fax machines, cellular phones, and other high-tech products.[78] In a 1997 Simmons study of readers of gay publications, the results showed that gays were 12 times more likely to be in professional jobs, twice as likely to own a vacation home, 8 times more likely to own a computer notebook, and 94 percent more likely to use a product or service advertised in a gay publication.[79]

In the mid-1990s, IKEA broke new ground by running a TV spot featuring a gay couple who purchased a dining room table at the store.[80] For many consumers, gay culture is more familiar largely due to the prominence of gay people in popular shows like *Queer Eye for the Straight Guy* and *Will & Grace*, and due to the decisions by stars like Ellen DeGeneres and Rosie O'Donnell to openly discuss their sexuality. And, while it has been common for years for companies to run ads in gay publications (often unbeknownst to their straight customers), now major marketers including American Express, Audi, Cartier, General Motors, Volkswagen, and Wrigley are using openly gay and lesbian celebrities in campaigns aimed at the wider general audience. They are hiring personalities like the singers kd lang and Melissa Etheridge, the designers Isaac Mizrahi and Todd Oldham, the actor John Cameron Mitchell, and the former football player Esera Tuaolo, along with all five members of the cast of *Queer Eye for the Straight Guy*.[81]

A readers' survey by a lesbian-oriented publication called *Girlfriends* magazine found that 54 percent hold professional/managerial jobs, 57 percent have partners, and 22 percent have children. But lesbian women are harder to reach than gay men, since they don't tend to concentrate in urban neighbourhoods or in bars and don't read as many gay publications. Some marketers have chosen to focus instead on such venues as women's basketball games and women's music festivals.[82] Acting on research that showed lesbians are four times as likely as the average consumer to own one of their cars, Subaru of America decided to target this market in a big way.

← Absolut started advertising to gays in the 1970s and has strong brand recognition in the gay community.
XTRA! Inhouse design. Sharpe Blackmore Inc.

Fed up because you don't get mistaken for a svelte supermodel on the street? A provocative campaign by Dove that started in Europe featuring women with imperfect bodies in their underwear may help. One ad reads, "Let's face it. Firming the thighs of a size 8 supermodel wouldn't have been much of a challenge." The advertising was prompted by Unilever's research that found many women didn't believe its products worked because the women shown using them were so unrealistic.[87] Dove also sponsored a survey of 1800 women to assess how they felt about their looks. Overall, they found that women were satisfied with who they are; these positive feelings were even stronger in subgroups among younger women and wealthier women. Fifty-two percent of women between the ages of 18 and 39 said that "looking beautiful" describes them very well, while 37 percent of women ages 40 and older feel the same. And, 75 percent of the women agree that beauty does not come from a woman's looks but from her spirit and love of life. Only 26 percent feel that women's beauty is evaluated according to reasonable standards in our society.[88]

And, in one of the first mainstream pitches to directly address the controversy over gay marriage, Grand Marnier, a French cognac, launched print ads that read, "Your sister is finally getting remarried. Her fiancée's name is Jill."[83]

BODY IMAGE

A person's physical appearance is a large part of his or her self-concept. **Body image** refers to a consumer's subjective evaluation of his or her physical self. This image is not necessarily accurate. A man may think of himself as being more muscular than he really is, or a woman may feel she appears fatter than is the case. In fact, it is not uncommon to find marketing strategies that exploit consumers' tendencies to distort their body images by preying upon insecurities about appearance, thereby creating a gap between the real and ideal physical self and, consequently, the desire to purchase products and services to narrow that gap. Indeed, the success of the photo chain Glamour Shots, which provides dramatic makeovers to customers (90 percent of them women) and then gives them a pictorial record of their pinup potential, can be traced to the fantasies of everyday people to be supermodels—at least for an hour or two.[84]

Body Cathexis

A person's feelings about his or her body can be described in terms of **body cathexis**. *Cathexis* refers to the emotional significance of some object or idea to a person, and some parts of the body are more central to self-concept than others. One study of young adults' feelings about their bodies found that these respondents were the most satisfied with their hair and eyes and had the least positive feelings about their waists. These feelings also were related to usage of grooming products. Consumers who were more satisfied with their bodies were more frequent users of such "preening" products as hair conditioner, blow-dryers, cologne, facial bronzer, tooth polish, and pumice soap.[85]

Ideals of Beauty

A national survey of 1000 women found that only 2 percent of Canadian women believe physical characteristics define true beauty. More than 90 percent said qualities such as a positive attitude (35 percent), being nice to others (31 percent), and high self-esteem (30 percent) are what really make someone attractive. About 40 percent said spending time with family and friends contributes most to their sense of self, while 34 percent said it was learning new things, and 23 percent said making a difference in the community.[86]

A person's satisfaction with the physical image he or she presents to others is affected by how closely that image corresponds to the image valued by his or her culture. An **ideal of beauty** is a particular model, or exemplar, of appearance. Female ideals of beauty include physical features (large lips or small lips, big breasts or small breasts) as well as such aspects as clothing styles, cosmetics, hairstyles, skin tone (pale versus tan), and body type (petite, athletic, or voluptuous).

IS BEAUTY UNIVERSAL?

Recent research indicates that preferences for some physical features over others are "wired in" genetically and that these reactions tend to be the same among people around the world. Specifically, people appear to favour features associated with good health and youth, attributes linked to reproductive ability and strength. These characteristics include large eyes, high cheekbones, and a narrow jaw.

Another cue that apparently is used by people across ethnic and racial groups to signal sexual desirability is whether the person's features are balanced. In one

← Dove's use of real women in its advertising has contributed to changes in how we think about ideals of beauty.
Courtesy of Unilever Home and Personal Care.

study, men and women with greater facial symmetry started having sex three to four years earlier than people whose facial features were lopsided! Men also are more likely to use a woman's body shape as a sexual cue, and it has been theorized that this is because feminine curves provide evidence of reproductive potential. During puberty, a typical female gains almost 35 pounds of "reproductive fat" around her hips and thighs that supply the approximately 80 000 extra calories needed for pregnancy. Most fertile women have waist-hip ratios of 0.6 to 0.8, an hourglass shape that also happens to be the one men rank highest.[89] Other positively valued female characteristics include a higher than average forehead, fuller lips, a shorter jaw, and a smaller chin and nose. Women, on the other hand, favour men with a heavy lower face (an indication of high concentration of androgens that create strength), those who are slightly above-average height, and those with a prominent brow. Women prefer men with more feminine facial features, but when they are ovulating they prefer more masculine ones.[90]

Of course, the way these faces are "packaged" still varies enormously, and that's where marketers come in: Advertising and other forms of mass media play a significant role in determining which forms of beauty are considered desirable at any point in time. An ideal of beauty functions as a sort of cultural yardstick. Consumers compare themselves to some standard (often advocated by fashion media) and are dissatisfied with their appearance.

IDEALS OF BEAUTY OVER TIME

In retrospect, periods of history tend to be characterized by a specific "look" or ideal of beauty. For example, in sharp contrast to today's emphasis on health and vigour, in the early nineteenth century it was fashionable to appear delicate to the point of looking ill. The poet Keats described the ideal woman of that time as "a milk white lamb that bleats for man's protection." Other popular looks have included the voluptuous, lusty woman as epitomized by Lillian Russell; the athletic Gibson Girl of the 1890s; and the small, boyish flapper of the 1920s, exemplified by Clara Bow.[91]

In much of the nineteenth century the desirable waistline for American women was 18 inches (45 cm), a circumference that required the use of corsets pulled so tight that they routinely caused headaches, fainting spells, and possibly even the uterine and spinal disorders common among women of the time. Although modern women are not quite as "straightlaced," many still endure such indignities as high

Multicultural Dimensions

The question of whether beauty is universal is central in the debate about whether to standardize or localize marketing strategy as a company does business across cultures. A study of cross-cultural comparisons across five European cities—Hamburg, London, Madrid, Milan, and Paris—showed that it is difficult to achieve sameness of meaning for even international products and beauty types in women. Indeed, there were cross-cultural differences in the meanings of "healthy" and "beautiful" as conveyed in words (nine descriptors), beauty types (two contemporary women models), and products (water and perfume). Interestingly, not only were there differences among the five cities for the three components studied, but there were also differences in the extent to which the three components reinforced one another. London was the only city for which there was a reasonable matchup among the respective words, both beauty types, and both products for both the "beautiful" and the "healthy" themes.[92] The potential for international standardization is clearly very limited. Meanings encoded in words, beauty types, and products need to be developed carefully and simultaneously to communicate a consistent and focused message in international marketing strategies.

heels, body waxing, eye lifts, and liposuction. In addition to the millions spent on cosmetics, clothing, health clubs, and fashion magazines, these practices remind us that the desire to conform to current standards of beauty—rightly or wrongly—is alive and well.

The ideal body type of Western women has changed radically over time, and these changes have resulted in a realignment of *sexual dimorphic markers*—those aspects of the body that distinguish between the sexes. For example, using heights and weights from winners of the Miss America pageant, nutrition experts concluded that many beauty queens are in the undernourished range. In the 1920s, contestants had a body mass index in the range now considered normal—20 to 25. Since then, an increasing number of winners have had indexes under 18.5, which is the World Health Organization's standard for undernutrition.[93]

The first part of the 1990s saw the emergence of the controversial "waif" look, where successful models (most notably Kate Moss) were likely to have bodies resembling those of young boys. The pendulum seems to be shifting back a bit, as the more buxom, hourglass figure popular in the 1950s (exemplified by the Marilyn Monroe ideal) has reappeared.[94] One factor leading to this change has been the opposition to the use of overly thin models by feminist groups, who charge that these role models encourage starvation diets and eating disorders among women who want to emulate the look.[95] These groups have advocated boycotts against companies like Coca-Cola and Calvin Klein, which have used wafer-thin models in their advertising. Some protesters have even taken to pasting stickers over these ads that read "Feed this woman" and "Give me a cheeseburger." The Rylstone and District chapter of the Women's Institute (popularized in the 2003 movie *Calendar Girls*) are taking a different tack by creating calendar parodies of supermodels. The middle-aged British women pose nude with good nature and quiet elegance; Miss April pots African Violets under the caption, "Guard your tender blooms against late frosts."[96]

We can also distinguish among ideals of beauty for men in terms of facial features, musculature, facial hair, and so on—who could confuse Tom Cruise with George Clooney? In fact, one recent national survey that asked both men and women to comment on male aspects of appearance found that the dominant standard of beauty for men is a strongly masculine, muscled body, though women tend to prefer men with less muscle mass than men themselves strive to attain.[97] Advertisers appear to have the males' ideal in mind—a recent study of men appearing in advertisements found that most sport the strong and muscular physique of the male stereotype.[98]

→This ad for Hanes Smooth Illusions pantyhose claims to provide women who want to change their shape with an alternative to surgery.
Courtesy of Sara Lee Corporation.

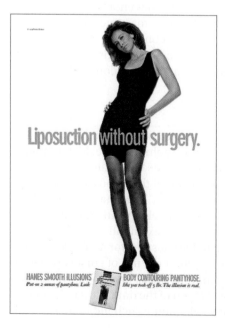

Betting that men are becoming every bit as body-conscious as women, manufacturers including Seven for All Mankind, Miss Sixty, and Diesel are introducing figure-enhancing jeans for men in styles that would have been deemed too risky even a few years ago. The new styles feature many of the same touches that designers have brought to women's jeans: low-rise cuts, stretchy fabrics, bleached-out colours. Chip and Pepper lowered the back pockets on one men's style by several inches to make pear-shaped guys look less . . . pear-like, and Diesel's slim-fitting "Bumix" jean features a "sexy under-crotch enforcement."[99]

Working on the Body

Because many consumers are motivated to match up to some ideal of appearance, they often go to great lengths to change aspects of their physical selves. From cosmetics to plastic surgery, tanning salons to diet drinks, a multitude of products and services are directed toward altering or maintaining aspects of the physical self in order to present a desirable appearance. It is difficult to overstate the importance of the physical self-concept (and the desire by consumers to improve their appearance) to many marketing activities.

HAIR AND THE SELF

Grant McCracken has provided a complete analysis of how our hair forms the basis for the presentation of self-image and how it can be used as a tool to transform or change one's image.[100] Haircuts are a regular part of the consumption process. Many people, especially men, adhere to a four-week schedule for the grooming ritual. However, much of McCracken's discussion focuses around women, as he found men to be much vainer about their hair and more reluctant to discuss the topic. This may be because, genetically, men are more prone to lose their hair. To compensate for this male phenomenon, male folklore such as "baldness is a sign of virility" has evolved. Men are also secretive about dyeing their hair. It is obvious they do it, but it is not a hot topic on the golf course.

So McCracken concentrates his analysis on women. Both hair styles and hair colour are used to project images that match the needs and social structure of the era and the individual. A blonde is not simply a blonde: She is a bombshell (Mae West), sunny (Goldie Hawn), brassy (Cybill Shepherd), dangerous (Sharon Stone), a society leader (Ivana Trump), or cool (Grace Kelly). Brunettes are said to be self-confident, because no one cares about their hair colour; it is never a topic of discussion; therefore, personalities are diversified rather than stereotyped. Redheads are said to be "hot-headed" and "energetic," as typified by Lucille Ball. Red is the tint of choice for French women. There are no subtleties in the projection of the redhead's image.

The preference for long hair or short hair is reflective of the social situation. Long flowing hair is said to very sexy and maybe even dangerous. Short hair is said to be "boyish" or a signal that a woman is simplifying her life. Men are said to find the "pixie" cut unthreatening and attractive. But they seem to draw the line at women shaving their heads completely bald. This style is said to portray a tough image, which is hostile and provocative.

Whenever we want to transform our image, we change our hair along with our clothes. With changes in age, lifestyle, careers, and even partners comes an inevitable change in colour or style of hair.

FATTISM

As reflected in the expression "you can never be too thin or too rich," our society has an obsession with weight. The pressure to be slim is continually reinforced, both by advertising and by peers. North Americans in particular are preoccupied with how much they weigh. We are continually bombarded by images of thin, happy people.

How realistic are these appearance standards? Fashion dolls, such as the ubiquitous Barbie, reinforce an unnatural ideal of thinness. The dimensions of these dolls, when extrapolated to average female body sizes, are unnaturally long and thin.[101] If the traditional Barbie doll were a real woman, her dimensions would be 38-18-34! In 1998, Mattel conducted "plastic surgery" on Barbie to give her a less pronounced bust and slimmer hips, but she is still not exactly dumpy.[102] One reason for Mattel's change is to meet the growing competition from other doll makers who are responding to the public's desire for more down-to-earth figures. Emme, a full-figure fashion doll based on the voluptuous supermodel, is extremely popular. Visitors to the model's website can read about Emme's acceptance of her weight: "There is nothing more freeing after many years of not feeling comfortable in my own skin and going on every diet you could imagine, than to learn that I wasn't crazy... millions of other women and men felt the same way.... I've learned that after many years of trying to fit into others' ideals of beauty, I had to learn that my own image of beauty was perfect just as it is, as long as I took care of myself."[103]

The desire to be thin has had a big impact on consumers' lifestyles and eating habits. A number of companies specifically target the weight conscious: Weight Watchers International, the largest weight-loss company, developed a program called Quick Success that recognizes the new lifestyles of busy working women. This program includes eating guidelines for working lunches and cocktail parties.[104]

A similar program in Australia is called "Gut Busters." This program is for men only. The middle bulge is obvious in men who drive trucks or sit at a desk all day. The "Gut Buster" program is designed to focus particularly on male-dominated food habits. Instead of reaching for a cheeseburger and fries at a truck stop or fast-food outlet, men are conditioned to accept something less fatty and easier to digest, but more "feminine" by food image, such as fruit and salads. In Canada, Harvey Brooker Weight Loss for Men offers a similar program in Toronto and Montreal. Many of the clients are executives who have suffered through rich lunches and dinners and long hours at a desk.

BODY IMAGE DISTORTIONS

Although many people perceive a strong link between self-esteem and appearance, some consumers unfortunately exaggerate this connection even more and make great sacrifices to attain what they consider to be a desirable body image. Women tend to be taught to a greater degree than men that the quality of their bodies reflects their self-worth, so it is not surprising that most major distortions of body image occur among females.

Men's opinions do not tend to differ in ratings of their current figure, their ideal figure, and the figure they think is most attractive to women. In contrast, women rate both the figure they think is most attractive to men and their ideal figure as much thinner than their actual figure.[105] In one survey two-thirds of university women admitted resorting to unhealthy behaviour to control weight. Advertising messages that convey an image of slimness help to reinforce these activities by arousing insecurities about weight.[106]

A distorted body image has been linked to the rise of eating disorders. People with *anorexia* always see themselves as fat and virtually starve themselves in the quest for thinness. This condition often results in *bulimia*, which involves two stages. First, binge eating occurs (usually in private), where more than 5000 calories may be consumed at one time. The binge is then followed by induced vomiting, abuse of laxatives, fasting, and/or overly strenuous exercise—a "purging" process that reasserts the woman's sense of control.

Most eating disorders are found in white, upper-middle-class teenaged and university-aged girls. Victims often have brothers or fathers who are hypercritical of their weight, and these disorders are also associated with a history of sexual abuse.[107]

Eating disorders have also been documented in men. They are common among male athletes, such as jockeys and boxers, and male models, who must also conform to various weight requirements.[108] In general, though, most men who have distorted body images consider themselves to be too light rather than too heavy: Society has

taught them that they must be muscular to be masculine. Men are more likely than women to express their insecurities about their bodies by becoming addicted to exercise. In fact, striking similarities have been found between male compulsive runners and female anorexics. These include a commitment to diet and exercise as a central part of one's identity and susceptibility to body-image distortions.[109]

COSMETIC SURGERY

There is no longer much (if any) psychological stigma associated with having cosmetic surgery; it is commonplace and accepted among many segments of consumers.[110] In fact, men now account for as much as 20 percent of plastic-surgery patients. Popular operations for men include the implantation of silicon pectoral muscles (for the chest) and calf implants to fill out "chicken legs."[111]

Some women feel that larger breasts will increase their allure and so undergo breast-augmentation procedures. The importance of breast size to self-concept resulted in an interesting and successful marketing strategy undertaken by an underwear company. While conducting focus groups on bras, an analyst noted that small-chested women typically reacted with hostility when discussing the subject. They unconsciously covered their chests with their arms as they spoke, and they felt that their needs were ignored by the fashion industry. To meet this overlooked need, the company introduced a line of A-cup bras called "A-OK" and depicted wearers in a positive light. A new market segment was born.

BODY DECORATION AND MUTILATION

The body is adorned or altered in some way in every culture. Decorating the self serves a number of purposes:[112]

- *To separate group members from non-members:* The Chinook Indians of North America pressed the head of a newborn between two boards for a year, permanently altering its shape. In our society teens go out of their way to adopt distinctive hair and clothing styles that will separate them from adults.

- *To place the individual in the social organization:* Many cultures engage in puberty rites, wherein a boy symbolically becomes a man. Young men in Ghana paint their bodies with white stripes to resemble skeletons, symbolizing the death of their child status. In Western culture, this rite may involve some form of mild self-mutilation or engagement in dangerous activities.

- *To place the person in a gender category:* The Tchikrin Indians of South America insert a string of beads in a boy's lip to enlarge it. Western women wear lipstick to enhance femininity. At the turn of the twentieth century, small lips were fashionable because they represented women's submissive role at that time.[113] Today, big red lips are provocative and indicate an aggressive sexuality. Some women, including a number of famous actresses and models, receive collagen injections or lip inserts to create large, pouting lips (known in the modelling industry as "liver lips").[114]

- *To enhance gender-role identification:* The modern use of high heels, which podiatrists agree are a prime cause of knee and hip problems, backaches, and fatigue, can be compared with the traditional Asian practice of foot binding to enhance femininity. As one doctor observed, "When they [women] get home, they can't get their high-heeled shoes off fast enough. But every doctor in the world could yell from now until Doomsday, and women would still wear them."[115]

- *To provide a sense of security:* Consumers often wear lucky charms, amulets, rabbits' feet, and so on to protect them from the "evil eye."

- *To indicate desired social conduct:* The Suya of South America wear ear ornaments to emphasize the importance placed in their culture on listening and obedience. In Western society, some gay men may wear an earring in the left or right ear to signal what role (submissive or dominant) they prefer in a relationship.

- *To indicate high status or rank:* The Hidatsa Indians of North America wear feather ornaments that indicate how many people they have killed. In our society, some people wear glasses with clear lenses, even though they do not have eye problems, to enhance their perceived status.

TATTOOS

Tattoos—both temporary and permanent—are a popular form of body adornment. This body art can be used to communicate aspects of the self to onlookers and may serve some of the same functions that other kinds of body painting do in primitive cultures. Tattoos (from the Tahitian *ta-tu*) have deep roots in folk art. Until recently, the images were crude, consisting primarily of either death symbols (such as a skull), animals (especially panthers, eagles, and snakes), pinup women, or military designs. More current influences include science-fiction themes, Japanese symbolism, and tribal designs.

→ Sta-Prest incorporates the message of individuality in this message through the inclusion of an eye-catching, indigo-blue tattoo that coordinates with its denim jeans.
Levi Strauss Europe/Bartle Bogle Hegarty.
Photographer: Nadav Kander.

STA-PREST® Denim Pants

A tattoo may be viewed as a fairly risk-free way of expressing an adventurous side of the self. One recent trend is for middle-aged women to get one to commemorate a milestone, like a big birthday, a divorce, or becoming an "empty nester." So, now these skin designs are more of a fashion statement than a declaration of rebellion—especially since 10 percent of North Americans have one.[116] When the Edmonton Oilers started to look like Stanley Cup contenders in 2006, one Edmonton family all got the Oilers logo tattooed on their body in support of their team. What are you waiting for?

BODY PIERCING

Decorating the body with various kinds of metallic inserts also has evolved from a practice associated with some fringe groups and natives in third world countries to become a popular fashion statement. Piercing can and is being done on all parts of the body. There are more than a million websites related to the practice of body piercing. This popularity is not pleasing to hard-core piercing fans, who view the practice as a sensual consciousness-raising ritual and are concerned that people now do it simply because it's trendy. As one customer waiting for a nipple piercing remarked, "If your piercing doesn't mean anything, then it's just like buying a pair of platform shoes."[117]

CHAPTER SUMMARY

THE SELF-CONCEPT IS STRONGLY RELATED TO CONSUMER BEHAVIOUR.

- Consumers' self-concepts are reflections of their attitudes toward themselves. Whether these attitudes are positive or negative, they will help to guide many purchase decisions; products can be used to bolster self-esteem or to "reward" the self.

PRODUCTS OFTEN PLAY A PIVOTAL ROLE IN DEFINING THE SELF-CONCEPT.

- Many product choices are dictated by the consumer's perception of a similarity between his or her personality and attributes of the product. The symbolic interactionist perspective on the self states that each of us actually has many selves, and a different set of products is required as props to play each role. Many things other than the body can also be viewed as part of the self. Valued objects, cars, homes, and even attachments to sports teams or national monuments are used to define the self when these are incorporated into the extended self.

GENDER-ROLE IDENTITY IS DIFFERENT THAN GENDER, AND SOCIETY'S EXPECTATIONS OF MASCULINITY AND FEMININITY HELP TO DETERMINE THE PRODUCTS WE BUY THAT ENABLE US TO BE CONSISTENT WITH THESE EXPECTATIONS.

- A person's gender-role identity is a major component of self-definition. Conceptions about masculinity and femininity, largely shaped by society, guide the acquisition of "gender-typed" products and services.

- Advertising and other media play an important role in socializing consumers to be male and female. Although traditional women's roles have often been perpetuated in advertising depictions, this situation is changing somewhat. The media do not always portray men accurately, either.

THE WAY WE THINK ABOUT OUR BODIES (AND THE WAY OUR CULTURE TELLS US WE SHOULD THINK ABOUT THEM) IS A KEY COMPONENT OF SELF-ESTEEM.

- A person's conception of his or her body also provides feedback to self-image. A culture communicates certain ideals of beauty, and consumers go to great lengths to attain these. Many consumer activities involve manipulating the body, whether through dieting, cosmetic surgery, or tattooing.

OUR DESIRE TO LIVE UP TO CULTURAL EXPECTATIONS OF APPEARANCE CAN BE HARMFUL.

- Sometimes these activities are carried to an extreme, as people try too hard to live up to cultural ideals. One example is found in eating disorders, wherein women in particular become obsessed with thinness.

EVERY CULTURE DICTATES CERTAIN TYPES OF BODY DECORATION AND/OR MUTILATION THAT HELP TO IDENTIFY ITS MEMBERS.

- Body decoration and/or mutilation may serve such functions as separating group members from non-members, or marking the individual's status or rank within a social organization or within a gender category (e.g., homosexual), or even providing a sense of security or good luck.

KEY TERMS

Actual self   p. 130

Agentic goals   p. 137

Androgyny   p. 139

Body cathexis   p. 144

Body image   p. 144

Communal goals   p. 137

Extended self   p. 135

Fantasy   p. 131

Ideal of beauty   p. 144

Ideal self   p. 130

Looking-glass self   p. 132

Metrosexual   p. 141

Self-concept   p. 129

Self-image congruence models   p. 134

Sex-typed traits   p. 138

Symbolic interactionism   p. 131

Symbolic self-completion theory   p. 134

REVIEW QUESTIONS

1. How do Eastern and Western cultures tend to differ in terms of how people think about the self?
2. List three dimensions by which we can describe the self-concept.
3. Compare and contrast the real versus the ideal self. List three products for which each type of self is likely to be used as a reference point when a purchase is considered.
4. What does "the looking-glass self" mean?
5. How do feelings about the self influence the specific brands people buy?
6. Define the extended self and provide three examples.

7. What is the difference between agentic and communal goals?
8. Is masculinity/femininity a biological distinction? Why or why not?
9. Give two examples of gender-typed products.
10. What is body cathexis?
11. Have ideals of beauty in Canada changed over the last 50 years? If so, how?
12. What is fattism?
13. How did tattoos originate?

CONSUMER BEHAVIOUR CHALLENGE

Discuss

1. The "metrosexual" is a big buzzword in marketing—but is it real or just media hype? Do you see men in your age group changing their ideas about acceptable interests for males (e.g., home design, cooking, etc.)?
2. How prevalent is the western ideal among your peers? How do you see this ideal evolving now (if at all)?
3. Some historians and social critics say our obsession with thinness is based less on science than on morality. These critics argue that the definition of obesity has often arbitrarily shifted throughout history. Indeed, being slightly overweight was once associated with good health (as we've seen, in some parts of the world it still is) in a time when many of the most troubling diseases were wasting diseases like tuberculosis. Plumpness used to be associated with affluence and the aristocracy (King Louis XIV of France padded his body to look more imposing), while today it is associated with the poor and their supposedly bad eating habits.[118] What do you think?
4. Should fast-food restaurants be liable if customers sue them for contributing to their obesity?
5. How might the creation of a self-conscious state be related to consumers who are trying on clothing in dressing rooms? Does the act of preening in front of a mirror change the dynamics by which people evaluate their product choices? Why?

6. Is it ethical for marketers to encourage infatuation with the self?
7. To date, the bulk of advertising targeted to gay consumers has been placed in exclusively gay media. If it were your decision, would you consider using mainstream media as well to reach gays, who constitute a significant proportion of the general population? Or, remembering that members of some targeted segments have serious objections about this practice, especially when the product (e.g., liquor or cigarettes) may be viewed as harmful in some way, do you think gays should be singled out at all by marketers?
8. Some consumer advocates have protested the use of superthin models in advertising, claiming that these women encourage others to starve themselves to attain the "waif" look. Other critics respond that the media's power to shape behaviour has been overestimated and that it is insulting to people to assume that they are unable to separate fantasy from reality. What do you think?
9. Does sex sell? There's certainly enough of it around, whether in print ads, television commercials, or on websites. Perhaps the appropriate question is not does sex sell, but *should* sex sell? What are your feelings about the blatant use of sex to sell products? Do you think this tactic works better when selling to men than to women? Does exposure to unbelievably attractive men and women models only make the rest of us "normal" folks unhappy and insecure? Under what conditions (if any) should sex be used as a marketing strategy?

Experiential Exercises

10. Watch a set of ads on television featuring men and women. Try to imagine the characters with reversed roles (i.e., the male parts played by women and vice versa). Can you see any differences in assumptions about gender-typed behaviour?

11. Construct a "consumption biography" of a friend or family member. Make a list of or photograph his or her favourite possessions, and see whether you or others can describe this person's personality just from the information provided by this catalogue.

12. Interview victims of burglaries, or people who have lost personal property in floods, ice storms, or other natural disasters. How do they go about reconstructing their possessions, and what effect does the loss appear to have on them?

13. Locate additional examples of self-esteem advertising and evaluate the probable effectiveness of these appeals. Is it true that "flattery gets you everywhere"?

CBC ⏺ VIDEO VIGNETTE

CONCEPTS AT WORK FOR TATTOOS

"Tattoo" is thought to be a Tahitian word derived from the sound of the use of a traditional tattoo tool. The word worked its way into the English language when Captain Cooke introduced the technique from the South Pacific to the English aristocracy. Indeed, most of the history of tattoos belongs to those who were noble, famous, or infamous. Today, they are much more common. It is estimated that one in seven, or 45 million, people in North America have a tattoo. In the United States, about one-third of young adults 25 to 29 years old have at least one tattoo.

Tattoos are more than skin deep. The symbolism and colour of this body décor can be linked to personality, concepts of self, emotions, and gender. Stories abound of when, where, for what reason, and by whom a tattoo was acquired. Although there are pockets of resistance among individuals and employers, they have become commonplace. Because they are generally permanent, consumers should be cautious about choosing their tattoo artist and the design.

The tendency for people to talk about their tattoos led advertisers to the idea of using skin space to promote brands. These walking billboards take the form of washable logos on foreheads, hair shaved into the designs of logos, and yes, even permanent tattoos on people with the stature and personality consistent with a particular brand image. Negotiable rates have encouraged some consumers to sell their epidermal real estate on the internet and to volunteer to represent specific brands through a contract with companies, such as TatAD Marketing Group Limited. If you change your mind because you no longer love Lucy or your loyalty has shifted to another brand, you can have the tattoo removed—for a fee, of course!

Questions

1. Why do consumers decorate and mutilate their bodies?
2. Why do consumers choose to get tattoos?
3. How have the reasons for getting tattoos changed over time and cultures?
4. What is the future of tattoos in terms of the various ways in which consumers can decorate and mutilate their bodies?

*Resources: "Tattoos," The National, CBC Air Date: November 25, 2004; Sarah Staples, "Tattoos become the New Flesh Trade," The National Post, November 25, 2004: A2. For more information, see **www.vanishingtattoo.com**.*

NOTES

1. Catherine Dawson March, "No More Ugly Duckling Feelings," *Globe and Mail* (April 5, 2003): F11.

2. Harry C. Triandis, "The Self and Social Behavior in Differing Cultural Contexts," *Psychological Review* 96, 3 (1989): 506–520; H. Markus and S. Kitayama, "Culture and the Self: Implications for Cognition, Emotion, and Motivation," *Psychological Review* 98 (1991): 224–253.

3. Markus and Kitayama, "Culture and the Self ...."

4. Nancy Wong and Aaron Ahuvia, "A Cross-Cultural Approach to Materialism and the Self," in *Cultural Dimensions of International Marketing*, ed. Dominique Bouchet (Denmark: Odense University, 1995), 68–69.

5. Morris Rosenberg, *Conceiving the Self* (New York, NY: Basic Books, 1979); M. Joseph Sirgy, "Self-Concept in Consumer Behavior: A Critical Review," *Journal of Consumer Research* 9 (December 1982): 287–300.

6. Emily Yoffe, "You Are What You Buy," *Newsweek* (June 4, 1990): 59.

7. Roy F. Baumeister, Dianne M. Tice, and Debra G. Hutton, "Self-Presentational Motivations and Personality Differences in Self-Esteem," *Journal of Personality* 57 (September 1989): 547–575; Ronald J. Faber, "Are Self-Esteem Appeals Appealing?" in *Proceedings of the 1992 Conference of The American Academy of Advertising*, ed. Leonard N. Reid (1992): 230–235.

8. B. Bradford Brown and Mary Jane Lohr, "Peer-Group Affiliation and Adolescent Self-Esteem: An Integration of Ego-Identity and Symbolic-Interaction Theories," *Journal of Personality and Social Psychology* 52, no. 1 (1987): 47–55.

9. Marsha L. Richins, "Social Comparison and the Idealized Images of Advertising," *Journal of Consumer Research* 18 (June 1991): 71–83; Mary C. Martin and Patricia F. Kennedy, "Advertising and Social Comparison: Consequences for Female Preadolescents and Adolescents," *Psychology & Marketing* 10, 6 (November/December 1993): 513–530.

10. Philip N. Myers, Jr. and Frank A. Biocca, "The Elastic Body Image: The Effect of Television Advertising and Programming on Body Image Distortions in Young Women," *Journal of Communication* 42 (Summer 1992): 108–133.

11. Charles S. Gulas and Kim McKeage, "Extending Social Comparison: An Examination of the Unintended Consequences of Idealized Advertising Imagery," *Journal of Advertising* 29 (Summer 2000): 17–28.

12. Jeffrey F. Durgee, "Self-Esteem Advertising," *Journal of Advertising* 14, 4 (1986): 21.

13. J.C. Herz, "Flash Face-Lift," *Wired* (March 2002): 45.

14. Sigmund Freud, *New Introductory Lectures in Psychoanalysis* (New York, NY: Norton, 1965).

15. Harrison G. Gough, Mario Fioravanti, and Renato Lazzari, "Some Implications of Self Versus Ideal-Self Congruence on the Revised Adjective Check List," *Journal of Personality and Social Psychology* 44, 6 (1983): 1214–1220.

16. Steven Jay Lynn and Judith W. Rhue, "Daydream Believers," *Psychology Today* (September 1985): 14.

17. Hope Jensen Schau and Mary Gilly, "We Are What We Post? Self-Presentation in Personal Web Space," *Journal of Consumer Research* 30 (December 2003): 385–404.

18. Erving Goffman, *The Presentation of Self in Everyday Life* (Garden City, NY: Doubleday, 1959); Michael R. Solomon, "The Role of Products as Social Stimuli: A Symbolic Interactionism Perspective," *Journal of Consumer Research* 10 (December 1983): 319–329.

19. George H. Mead, *Mind, Self and Society* (Chicago, IL: University of Chicago Press, 1934).

20. Charles H. Cooley, *Human Nature and the Social Order* (New York, NY: Scribner's, 1902).

21. J.G. Hull and A.S. Levy, "The Organizational Functions of the Self: An Alternative to the Duval and Wicklund Model of Self-Awareness," *Journal of Personality and Social Psychology* 37 (1979): 756–768; Jay G. Hull et al., "Self-Consciousness and the Processing of Self-Relevant Information," *Journal of Personality and Social Psychology* 54, 3 (1988): 452–465.

22. Arnold W. Buss, *Self-Consciousness and Social Anxiety* (San Francisco, CA: W.H. Freeman, 1980); Lynn Carol Miller and Cathryn Leigh Cox, "Public Self-Consciousness and Makeup Use," *Personality and Social Psychology Bulletin* 8, 4 (1982): 748–751; Michael R. Solomon and John Schopler, "Self-Consciousness and Clothing," *Personality and Social Psychology Bulletin* 8, 3 (1982): 508–514.

23. Morris B. Holbrook, Michael R. Solomon, and Stephen Bell, "A Re-Examination of Self-Monitoring and Judgments of Furniture Designs," *Home Economics Research Journal* 19 (September 1990): 6–16; Mark Snyder, "Self-Monitoring Processes," in *Advances in Experimental Social Psychology*, ed. Leonard Berkowitz (New York, NY: Academic Press, 1979): 851–928.

24. Mark Snyder and Steve Gangestad, "On the Nature of Self-Monitoring: Matters of Assessment, Matters of Validity," *Journal of Personality and Social Psychology* 51 (1986): 125–139.

25. Timothy R. Graeff, "Image Congruence Effects on Product Evaluations: The Role of Self-Monitoring and Public/Private Consumption," *Psychology & Marketing* 13, 5 (August 1996): 481–499.

26. Richard G. Netemeyer, Scot Burton, and Donald R. Lichtenstein, "Trait Aspects of Vanity: Measurement and Relevance to Consumer Behavior," *Journal of Consumer Research* 21 (March 1995): 612–626.

27. Michael R. Solomon and Henry Assael, "The Forest or the Trees? A Gestalt Approach to Symbolic Consumption," in *Marketing and Semiotics: New Directions in the Study of Signs for Sale*, ed. Jean Umiker-Sebeok (Berlin: Mouton de Gruyter, 1987): 189–218.

28. Quoted in "Video Game Company Tries Human Branding," *New York Times on the Web* (August 12, 2002).

29. Jack L. Nasar, "Symbolic Meanings of House Styles," *Environment and Behavior* 21 (May 1989): 235–257; E.K. Sadalla, B. Verschure, and J. Burroughs, "Identity Symbolism," in *Housing, Environment and Behavior* 19 (1987): 599–687.

30. Solomon, "The Role of Products as Social Stimuli … "; Robert E. Kleine III, Susan Schultz-Kleine, and Jerome B. Kernan, "Mundane Consumption and the Self: A Social-Identity Perspective," *Journal of Consumer Psychology* 2, 3 (1993): 209–235; Newell D. Wright, C.B. Claiborne, and M. Joseph Sirgy, "The Effects of Product Symbolism on Consumer Self-Concept," in *Advances in Consumer Research* 19, eds. John F. Sherry, Jr. and Brian Sternthal (Provo, UT: Association for Consumer Research, 1992): 311–318; Susan Fournier, "A Person-Based Relationship Framework for Strategic Brand Management," Doctoral Dissertation, Department of Marketing, University of Florida, 1994.

31. A. Dwayne Ball and Lori H. Tasaki, "The Role and Measurement of Attachment in Consumer Behavior," *Journal of Consumer Psychology* 1, 2 (1992): 155–172.

32. William B. Hansen and Irwin Altman, "Decorating Personal Places: A Descriptive Analysis," *Environment and Behavior* 8 (December 1976): 491–504.

33. R.A. Wicklund and P.M. Gollwitzer, *Symbolic Self-Completion* (Hillsdale, NJ: Lawrence Erlbaum, 1982).

34. Erving Goffman, *Asylums* (New York, NY: Doubleday, 1961).

35. Quoted in Floyd Rudmin, "Property Crime Victimization Impact on Self, on Attachment, and on Territorial Dominance, CPA Highlights," *Victims of Crime Supplement* 9, 2 (1987): 4–7.

36. Barbara B. Brown, "House and Block as Territory" (paper presented at the Conference of the Association for Consumer Research, San Francisco, 1982).

37. Quoted in Shay Sayre and David Horne, "I Shop, Therefore I Am: The Role of Possessions for Self Definition," in *Earth, Wind, and Fire and Water: Perspectives on Natural Disaster*, eds. Shay Sayre and David Horne (Pasadena, CA: Open Door Publishers, 1996), 353–370.

38. Deborah A. Prentice, "Psychological Correspondence of Possessions, Attitudes, and Values," *Journal of Personality and Social Psychology* 53, 6 (1987): 993–1002.

39. Sak Onkvisit and John Shaw, "Self-Concept and Image Congruence: Some Research and Managerial Implications," *Journal of Consumer Marketing* 4 (Winter 1987):

13–24. For a related treatment of congruence between advertising appeals and self-concept, see George M. Zinkhan and Jae W. Hong, "Self-Concept and Advertising Effectiveness: A Conceptual Model of Congruency, Conspicuousness, and Response Mode," in *Advances in Consumer Research* 18, eds. Rebecca H. Holman and Michael R. Solomon (Provo, UT: Association for Consumer Research, 1991), 348–354.

40. C.B. Claiborne and M. Joseph Sirgy, "Self-Image Congruence as a Model of Consumer Attitude Formation and Behavior: A Conceptual Review and Guide for Further Research" (paper presented at the Academy of Marketing Science Conference, New Orleans, 1990).

41. Al E. Birdwell, "A Study of Influence of Image Congruence on Consumer Choice," *Journal of Business* 41 (January 1964): 76–88; Edward L. Grubb and Gregg Hupp, "Perception of Self, Generalized Stereotypes, and Brand Selection," *Journal of Marketing Research* 5 (February 1986): 58–63.

42. Ira J. Dolich, "Congruence Relationship Between Self-Image and Product Brands," *Journal of Marketing Research* 6 (February 1969): 80–84; Danny N. Bellenger, Earle Steinberg, and Wilbur W. Stanton, "The Congruence of Store Image and Self Image as It Relates to Store Loyalty," *Journal of Retailing* 52, 1 (1976): 17–32; Ronald J. Dornoff and Ronald L. Tatham, "Congruence Between Personal Image and Store Image," *Journal of the Market Research Society* 14, 1 (1972): 45–52.

43. Naresh K. Malhotra, "A Scale to Measure Self-Concepts, Person Concepts, and Product Concepts," *Journal of Marketing Research* 18 (November 1981): 456–464.

44. Leslie Walker, "More than the Sum of His Stuff," *Washington Post* (August 11, 2001): E1.

45. Ernest Beaglehole, *Property: A Study in Social Psychology* (New York: Macmillan, 1932).

46. Russell W. Belk, "Shoes and Self," *Advances in Consumer Research* (2003): 27–33.

47. Jeffrey Ball, "Religious Leaders to Discuss SUVs With GM, Ford Officials," *Wall Street Journal Interactive Edition* (September 17, 2002).

48. David R. Shoonmaker, "Book Review: High and Mighty: SUVs—The World's Most Dangerous Vehicles and How They Got that Way," *American Scientist* (January/February 2003): 69; Keith Bradsher, *High and Mighty: SUVs—The World's Most Dangerous Vehicles and How They Got that Way* (New York: Public Affairs, 2002).

49. James Brooke, "Learning to Avoid a Deal-Killing Faux Pas in Japan," *New York Times on the Web* (September 17, 2002).

50. M. Csikszentmihalyi and Eugene Rochberg-Halton, *The Meaning of Things: Domestic Symbols and the Self* (Cambridge, MA: Cambridge University Press, 1981).

51. Russell W. Belk, "Possessions and the Extended Self," *Journal of Consumer Research* 15 (September 1988): 139–168.

52. Diane Goldner, "What Men and Women Really Want... to Eat," *New York Times* (March 2, 1994): C1, 2.

53. Joan Meyers-Levy, "The Influence of Sex Roles on Judgment," *Journal of Consumer Research* 14 (March 1988): 522–530.

54. Eileen Fischer and Stephen J. Arnold, "More than a Labor of Love: Gender Roles and Christmas Gift Shopping," *Journal of Consumer Research* 17 (December 1990): 333–345.

55. Kimberly J. Dodson and Russell W. Belk, "Gender in Children's Birthday Stories," in *Gender, Marketing, and Consumer Behavior*, ed. Janeen Costa (Salt Lake City, UT: Association for Consumer Research, 1996), 96–108.

56. Quoted in Lisa Bannon, "Mattel Sees Untapped Market for Blocks: Little Girls," *Wall Street Journal* (June 6, 2002): B1.

57. Eileen Fischer and Stephen J. Arnold, "Sex, Gender Identity, Gender Role Attitudes, and Consumer Behavior," *Psychology & Marketing* 11, 2 (March/April 1994): 163–182.

58. Clifford Nass, Youngme Moon, and Nancy Green, "Are Machines Gender Neutral? Gender-Stereotypic Responses to Computers with Voices," *Journal of Applied Social Psychology* 27, 10 (1997): 864–876; Kathleen Debevec and Easwar Iyer, "Sex Roles and Consumer Perceptions of Promotions, Products, and Self: What Do We Know and Where Should We Be Headed," in *Advances in Consumer Research* 13, ed. Richard J. Lutz (Provo, UT: Association for Consumer Research, 1986): 210–214; Joseph A. Bellizzi and Laura Milner, "Gender Positioning of a Traditionally Male-Dominant Product," *Journal of Advertising Research* (June/July 1991): 72–79.

59. Rebecca Harris, "Girls Gone Fishing," *Marketing Magazine* (January 9, 2006): 6.

60. Sandra L. Bem, "The Measurement of Psychological Androgyny," *Journal of Consulting and Clinical Psychology* 42 (1974): 155–162; Deborah E.S. Frable, "Sex Typing and Gender Ideology: Two Facets of the Individual's Gender Psychology that Go Together," *Journal of Personality and Social Psychology* 56, 1 (1989): 95–108.

61. Geoffrey A. Fowler, "Asia's Lipstick Lads," *Wall Street Journal Interactive Edition* (May 27, 2005).

62. See D. Bruce Carter and Gary D. Levy, "Cognitive Aspects of Early Sex-Role Development: The Influence of Gender Schemas on Preschoolers' Memories and

Preferences for Sex-Typed Toys and Activities," *Child Development* 59 (1988): 782–792; Bernd H. Schmitt, France Le Clerc, and Laurette Dube-Rioux, "Sex Typing and Consumer Behavior: A Test of Gender Schema Theory," *Journal of Consumer Research* 15 (June 1988): 122–127.

63. Carol Gilligan, *In a Different Voice: Psychological Theory and Women's Development* (Cambridge, MA: Harvard University Press, 1982); Joan Meyers-Levy and Durairaj Maheswaran, "Exploring Differences in Males' and Females' Processing Strategies," *Journal of Consumer Research* 18 (June 1991): 63–70.

64. Lynn J. Jaffe and Paul D. Berger, "Impact on Purchase Intent of Sex-Role Identity and Product Positioning," *Psychology & Marketing* (Fall 1988): 259–271; Lynn J. Jaffe, "The Unique Predictive Ability of Sex-Role Identity in Explaining Women's Response to Advertising," *Psychology & Marketing* 11, 5 (September/October 1994): 467–482.

65. Leila T. Worth, Jeanne Smith, and Diane M. Mackie, "Gender Schematicity and Preference for Gender-Typed Products," *Psychology & Marketing* 9 (January 1992): 17–30.

66. Qimei Chen, Shelly Rodgers, and William D Wells, "Better than Sex: Identifying Within-—Gender Differences Creates more Targeted Segmentation," *Marketing Research* (Winter 2004): 17–22.

67. Courtney Kane, "Men Are Becoming the Ad Target of the Gender Sneer," *New York Times on the Web* (January 28, 2005).

68. Gardyn Rebecca, "Granddaughters of Feminism," *American Demographics* (April 2001): 43–47.

69. Rebecca, "Granddaughters of Feminism."

70. Craig S. Smith, "Underneath, Saudi Women Keep Their Secrets," *New York Times on the Web* (December 3, 2002).

71. Jack Neff, "Marketers Rush into Men's Care Category," *Advertising Age* (July 29, 2002): 6.

72. "Peroxide Tales," *American Demographics* (July/ August 2002): 9.

73. Meg Murphy, "Menswar," *National Post* (June 26, 1999): 3.

74. "Gender Portrayal Guidelines," Canadian Advertising Foundation (May 1994; reprinted September 1996).

75. "Defining Metro. Sexuality," *Metrosource* (September/October/November 2003).

76. Kala Vijayraghavan, "It's a Man's World," *The Economic Times New Delhi* (March 9, 2005): 8; "Peroxide Tales," *American Demographics* (July-August 2002): 9; Jack Neff, "Marketers Rush into Men's Care Category," *Advertising Age* (July 29, 2002): 6; Warrant St. John, "Metrosexuals Come Out: They're Straight, Hip and Moisturized Men—Every Marketer's Dream," *New York Times* (June 22, 2003): 5.

77. Projections of the incidence of homosexuality in the general population often are influenced by assumptions of the researchers, as well as the methodology they employ (e.g., self-report, behavioural measures, fantasy measures). For a discussion of these factors, see Edward O. Laumann et al., *The Social Organization of Homosexuality* (Chicago, IL: University of Chicago Press, 1994).

78. Stuart Elliott, "A Sharper View of Gay Consumers," *New York Times* (June 9, 1994): D1 (2).

79. Laura Koss-Feder, "Out and About," *Marketing News* (May 25, 1998): 1(2).

80. Kate Fitzgerald, "IKEA Dares to Reveal Gays Buy Tables, Too," *Advertising Age* (March 28, 1994); Cyndee Miller, "Top Marketers Take Bolder Approach in Targeting Gays," *Marketing News* (July 4, 1994): 1; Michael Wilke, "Big Advertisers Join Move to Embrace Gay Market," *Advertising Age* (August 4, 1997): 1.

81. Stuart Elliott, "More Gay Celebrities in Ads," *New York Times on the Web* (March 10, 2004).

82. Ronald Alsop, "Lesbians Are often Left Out when Firms Market to Gays," *Wall Street Journal Interactive* (October 11, 1999).

83. Ellen Byron, "Cognac and a Splash of Controversy," *Wall Street Journal* (April 29, 2004): B5.

84. Stephanie N. Mehta, "Photo Chain Ventures beyond Big Hair," *Wall Street Journal* (May 13, 1996): B1, 2.

85. Dennis W. Rook, "Body Cathexis and Market Segmentation," in *The Psychology of Fashion,* ed. Michael R. Solomon (Lexington, MA: Lexington Books, 1985), 233–241.

86. Catherine Dawson March, "No More Ugly Duckling Feelings," *Globe and Mail* (April 5, 2003): F11.

87. Erin White, "Dove 'Firms' with Zaftig Models: Unilever Brand Launches European Ads Employing Non-Supermodel Bodies," *Wall Street Journal* (April 21, 2004): B3.

88. *The Dove Report: Challenging Beauty,* Unilever 2004, available at *http://www.dove.com/real_beauty/article.asp?id=430*.

89. Geoffrey Cowley, "The Biology of Beauty," *Newsweek* (June 3, 1996): 61–66.

90. Corky Siemaszko, "Depends on the Day: Women's Sex Drive a very Cyclical Thing," *New York Daily News* (June 24, 1999): 3.

91. Lois W. Banner, *American Beauty* (Chicago, IL: University of Chicago Press, 1980). For a philosophical perspective, see Barry Vacker and Wayne R. Key, "Beauty and the Beholder: The Pursuit of Beauty through Commodities," *Psychology & Marketing* 10, 6 (November/December 1993): 471–494.

92. Rune Bjerke and Rosemary Polegato, "Cross-Cultural Meanings of Healthy and Beautiful in Words, Beauty Types, and Products: Implications for International Advertising," *Journal of Promotion Management,* 7 (2001): 117–139. Numbers 1/2.

93. "Report Delivers Skinny on Miss America," *Montgomery Advertiser* (March 22, 2000): 5A.

94. Kathleen Boyes, "The New Grip of Girdles Is Lightened by Lycra," *USA Today* (April 25, 1991): 6D.

95. Stuart Elliott, "Ultrathin Models in Coca-Cola and Calvin Klein Campaigns Draw Fire and a Boycott Call," *New York Times* (April 26, 1994): D18; Cyndee Miller, "'Give Them a Cheeseburger,'" *Marketing News* (June 6, 1994): 1, 2.

96. Donna Nebenzahl, "Ladies Bare All for Research," *Vancouver Sun* (May 20, 2000): B10.

97. Jill Neimark, "The Beefcaking of America," *Psychology Today* (November/December 1994): 32, 11.

98. Richard H. Kolbe and Paul J. Albanese, "Man to Man: A Content Analysis of Sole-Male Images in Male-Audience Magazines," *Journal of Advertising* 25 (Winter 1996) 4: 1–20.

99. Hannah Karp, "Jeans Makers Launch New Styles to Flatter the Male Figure," *Wall Street Journal* (June 25, 2004): B1

100. Grant McCracken, *Big Hair: A Journey into the Transformation of Self* (Toronto, ON: Penguin Books Canada, 1995).

101. Elaine L. Pedersen and Nancy L. Markee, "Fashion Dolls: Communicators of Ideals of Beauty and Fashion" (paper presented at the International Conference on Marketing Meaning, Indianapolis, IN, 1989); Dalma Heyn, "Body Hate," *Ms.* (August 1989): 34; Mary C. Martin and James W. Gentry, "Assessing the Internationalization of Physical Attractiveness Norms," *Proceedings of the American Marketing Association Summer Educators Conference* (Summer 1994): 59–65.

102. Lisa Bannon, "Barbie Is Getting Body Work, and Mattel Says She'll Be 'Rad,'" *Wall Street Journal Interactive Edition* (November 17, 1997).

103. *www.emmesupermodel.com,* accessed December 17, 2002; *www.tonnerdoll.com/emme.htm,* accessed December 17, 2002; Jennifer Barrett, "Must Have, Plus Size," *Newsweek* (August 26, 2002): 60.

104. Jennifer Stoffel, "What's New in Weight Control," *New York Times* (November 26, 1989): F17.

105. Debra A. Zellner, Debra F. Harner, and Robbie I. Adler, "Effects of Eating Abnormalities and Gender on Perceptions of Desirable Body Shape," *Journal of Abnormal Psychology* 98 (February 1989): 93–96.

106. Robin T. Peterson, "Bulimia and Anorexia in an Advertising Context," *Journal of Business Ethics* 6 (1987): 495–504.

107. Jane E. Brody, "Personal Health," *New York Times* (February 22, 1990): B9.

108. Judy Folkenberg, "Bulimia: Not for Women Only," *Psychology Today* (March 1984): 10.

109. Eleanor Grant, "The Exercise Fix: What Happens When Fitness Fanatics Just Can't Say No?" *Psychology Today* 22 (February 1988): 24.

110. Annette C. Hamburger and Holly Hall, "Beauty Quest," *Psychology Today* (May 1988): 28.

111. Emily Yoffe, "Valley of the Silicon Dolls," *Newsweek* (November 26, 1990): 72.

112. Ruth P. Rubinstein, "Color, Circumcision, Tattoos, and Scars," in *The Psychology of Fashion,* ed. Michael R. Solomon (Lexington, MA: Lexington Books, 1985), 243–254; Peter H. Bloch and Marsha L. Richins, "You Look Mahvelous: The Pursuit of Beauty and Marketing Concept," *Psychology & Marketing* 9 (January 1992): 3–16.

113. Sondra Farganis, "Lip Service: The Evolution of Pouting, Pursing, and Painting Lips Red," *Health* (November 1988): 48–51.

114. Michael Gross, "Those Lips, Those Eyebrows; New Face of 1989 (New Look of Fashion Models)," *New York Times Magazine* (February 13, 1989): 24.

115. "White Weight," *Psychology Today* (September/October 1994): 9.

116. Elizabeth Hayt, "Over-40 Rebels with a Cause: Tattoos," *New York Times* (December 22, 2002): sec. 9, 2.

117. Quoted in Wendy Bounds, "Body-Piercing Gets under America's Skin," *Wall Street Journal* (April 4, 1994): B1, 2.

118. Dinitia Smith, "Demonizing Fat in the War on Weight," *New York Times on the Web* (May 1, 2004).

Lisa and Anna, executives in a high-powered Toronto advertising agency, are exchanging ideas about how they are going to spend the big bonus everyone in the firm has been promised for landing an important tele-communications account. They are baffled by their friend Margie in accounting, who has been avidly surfing the net for information about a state-of-the-art home theatre system she plans to put into her condo. What a couch potato! Lisa, who fancies herself a bit of a thrill seeker, plans to blow her bonus on a wild trip to Nanaimo, British Columbia, where a week of outrageous bungee jumping awaits her. She can only imagine the stories she'll bring home—assuming she lives to tell about it, of course, but that uncertainty is half the fun! Anna replies, "Been there, done that! Believe it or not, I'm staying put right here—heading over to the driving range to hit some balls." Seems that Anna's been bitten by the golfing bug ever since she started leafing through *Women's Golf*, a magazine targeted to the growing number of women taking up the sport.

Lisa and Anna are sometimes amazed at how different they are from Margie, who's content to spend her downtime watching old movies or reading books. All three women make about the same salary, and Anna and Margie even went to the same university together. How can their tastes be so different? Oh well, they figure, that's why they make peach-mango and chocolate-chocolate-chip ice cream.

CHAPTER → 6

Personality and Lifestyles

PERSONALITY

Just what makes Lisa and Anna so different from their more sedate friend, Margie? One answer may lie in the concept of **personality**, which refers to a person's unique psychological makeup and how it consistently influences the way a person responds to his or her environment. In recent years the nature of the personality construct has been hotly debated. Many studies have found that people tend not to behave consistently across different situations and that they do not seem to exhibit stable personalities. In fact, some researchers feel that people do not exhibit a consistent personality across different situations; they argue that this is merely a convenient way to think about other people.

This argument is a bit hard to accept intuitively, possibly because we tend to see others in a limited range of situations, and so, to us, most people do act consistently. On the other hand, each of us knows that we are not all that consistent; we may be wild and crazy at times and the model of respectability at others. Although certainly not all psychologists have abandoned the idea of personality, many now recognize that a person's underlying characteristics are but one part of the puzzle and that situational factors often play a very large role in determining behaviour.[1] Still, some aspects of personality continue to be included in marketing strategies. These dimensions are usually employed in concert with a person's choices of leisure activities, political outlook, aesthetic tastes, and other individual factors to segment consumers in terms of *lifestyles*, a process we'll focus on more fully in this chapter.

Many approaches to understanding the complex concept of personality can be traced to psychological theorists who began to develop these perspectives in the early part of the century. These perspectives were qualitative, in the sense that they were largely based on analysts' interpretations of patients' accounts of dreams, traumatic experiences, and encounters with others.

Consumer Behaviour on the Couch: Freudian Theory

Sigmund Freud developed the idea that much of human behaviour stems from a fundamental conflict between a person's desire to gratify his or her physical needs and the necessity to function as a responsible member of society. This struggle is carried out in the mind among three systems. (Note that these systems do not refer to physical parts of the brain.)

FREUDIAN SYSTEMS

The **id** is entirely oriented toward immediate gratification—that is, it is the "party animal" of the mind. It operates according to the **pleasure principle**: Behaviour is guided by the primary desire to maximize pleasure and avoid pain. The id is selfish and illogical. It directs a person's psychic energy toward pleasurable acts without regard for any consequences.

The **superego** is the counterweight to the id. This system is essentially the person's conscience. It internalizes society's rules (especially as communicated by parents) and works to prevent the id from seeking selfish gratification.

Finally, the **ego** is the system that mediates between the id and the superego. It is, in a way, a referee in the fight between temptation and virtue. The ego tries to balance these two opposing forces according to the reality principle. It finds ways to gratify the id that will be acceptable to the outside world. These conflicts occur on an unconscious level, so the person is not necessarily aware of the underlying reasons for behaviour.

→ This ad focuses on the conflict between the desire for hedonic gratification (represented by the id) versus the need to engage in rational, task-oriented activities (represented by the superego). *United Airlines/WHQ AD.*

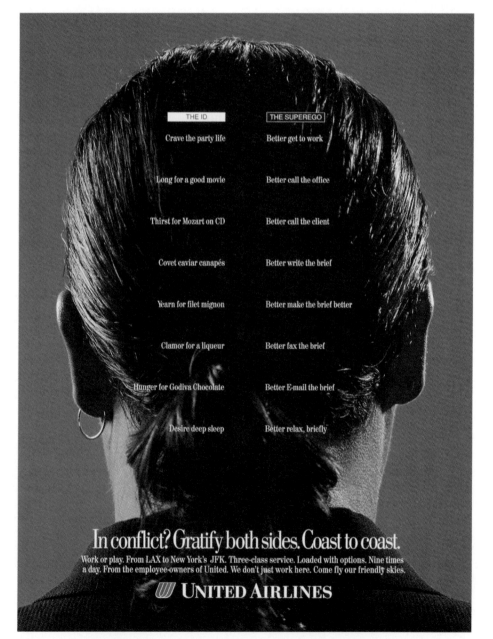

Some of Freud's ideas have also been adapted by consumer researchers. In particular, his work highlights the potential importance of unconscious motives underlying purchases. The implication is that consumers cannot necessarily tell us their true motivations for choosing a product, even if we can devise a sensitive way to ask them directly.

The Freudian perspective also hints at the possibility that the ego relies on the symbolism in products to compromise between the demands of the id and the prohibitions of the superego. The person channels his or her unacceptable desires into acceptable outlets by using products that signify these underlying desires. This is the connection between product symbolism and motivation: The product stands for, or represents, a consumer's true goal, one that is socially unacceptable or unattainable; by acquiring the product, the person is able to experience vicariously the forbidden fruit.

SOMETIMES A CIGAR IS JUST A CIGAR

Most Freudian applications in marketing are related to the sexuality of products. For example, some analysts have speculated that a sports car is a substitute for sexual gratification for many men. Indeed, some men do seem inordinately attached to their cars and may spend many hours lovingly washing and polishing them.

Others focus on male-oriented symbolism—the so-called phallic symbol—that appeals to women. Although Freud himself joked that "sometimes a cigar is just a cigar," many pop applications of Freud's ideas revolve around the use of objects that resemble sex organs (such as cigars, trees, or swords for men, and tunnels for women). This focus stems from Freud's analysis of dreams, which were often interpreted as communicating repressed desires through symbols.

← The seductive synergy between the asparagus curl and the butter curl suggests a natural combination of food flavours and textures.
Photo by Georges Simhoni. Reprinted by permission of the Dairy Farmers of Canada.

Motivational Research

The first attempts to apply Freudian ideas to understanding the deeper meanings of products and advertisements were made in the 1950s, when a perspective known as **motivational research** was developed. This approach is largely based on psychoanalytic (Freudian) interpretations, with a heavy emphasis on unconscious motives. A basic assumption is that socially unacceptable needs are channelled into acceptable outlets.

Motivational research relies on *in-depth interviews* with individual consumers. Instead of asking many consumers a few general questions about product usage and combining these responses with those of many other consumers in a representative statistical sample, this technique uses relatively few consumers but probes deeply into each person's purchase motivations. An in-depth interview might take several hours and is based on the assumption that the respondent cannot immediately articulate his or her latent, or underlying, motives; these can be derived only after meticulous questioning and interpretation on the part of a carefully trained interviewer.

This technique was pioneered by Ernest Dichter, a psychoanalyst who trained in Vienna in the early part of the century. Dichter conducted in-depth interview studies on more than 230 different products, and many of his findings have been incorporated in actual marketing campaigns.[2] For example, Esso (now Exxon) for many years reminded consumers to "Put a tiger in your tank" after Dichter found that people responded well to this powerful animal symbolism containing vaguely suggestive overtones. A summary of major consumption motivations identified using this approach appears in Table 6–1.

Motivational research is attacked for two quite opposite reasons. Some feel it does not work, while others feel it works too well. On the one hand, social critics have reacted much the same way as they have reacted to subliminal perception studies (see Chapter 2). They have attacked this school of thought for giving advertisers the power to manipulate consumers.[3] On the other hand, many consumer researchers feel the research has lacked sufficient rigour and validity, since interpretations are subjective and indirect.[4] Because conclusions are based on the analyst's own judgment and are derived from discussions with a small number of people, some researchers are dubious as to the degree to which these results can be generalized to a large market. In addition, because the original motivational researchers were heavily influenced by orthodox Freudian theory, their interpretations usually carried strong sexual overtones. This emphasis tends to overlook other plausible causes for behaviour.

Motivational research has great appeal to at least some marketers for several reasons, some of which are detailed here:

- *Cost efficiency:* Motivational research tends to be less expensive than large-scale, quantitative surveys because interviewing and data-processing costs are relatively minimal.

- *Providing insights:* The knowledge derived from motivational research can possibly help to develop marketing communications that appeal to deep-seated needs and thus provide a more powerful hook to relate a product to consumers. Even if they are not necessarily valid for all consumers in a target market, these insights can be valuable when used in an exploratory way. For example, the rich imagery that may be associated with a product can be used creatively when developing advertising copy.

- *Intuitive sense:* Some of the findings seem intuitively plausible after the fact. For example, motivational studies concluded that coffee is associated with companionship, that people avoid prunes because they remind them of old age, and that men fondly equate the first car they owned as an adolescent with the onset of their sexual freedom.

TABLE 6–1

MAJOR MOTIVES FOR CONSUMPTION AS IDENTIFIED BY ERNEST DICHTER

Motive	Associated Products
Power–masculinity–virility	Power: Sugary products and large breakfasts (to charge oneself up), bowling, electric trains, hot rods, power tools
	Masculinity–virility: Coffee, red meat, heavy shoes, toy guns, shaving with a razor
Security	Ice cream (to feel like a loved child again), full drawer of neatly ironed shirts, home baking, hospital care
Eroticism	Sweets (to lick), gloves (to be removed by women as a form of undressing), a man lighting a woman's cigarette (to create a tension-filled moment culminating in pressure, then relaxation)
Moral purity–cleanliness	White bread, cotton fabrics (to connote chastity), harsh household cleaning chemicals, bathing, oatmeal (sacrifice, virtue)
Social acceptance	Companionship: Ice cream (to share fun), coffee
	Love and affection: Toys (to express love for children), sugar and honey (to express terms of affection)
	Acceptance: Soap, beauty products
Individuality	Gourmet foods, foreign cars, cigarette holders, vodka, perfume, fountain pens
Status	Scotch, fur coats, luxury cars
Femininity	Cakes and cookies, dolls, silk, tea, household curios (to have a light, decorative, and heavy tactile component)
Reward	Cigarettes, candy, alcohol, ice cream, cookies
Mastery over environment	Kitchen appliances, boats, sporting goods
Disalienation (a desire to feel a connectedness to things)	Home decorating, skiing, morning radio broadcasts (to feel "in touch" with the world)
Magic–mystery	Soups (have healing powers), paints (change the mood of a room), carbonated drinks (magical effervescent property), vodka (romantic history), unwrapping of gifts

Source: Adapted from Jeffrey F. Durgee, "Interpreting Dichter's Interpretations: An Analysis of Consumption Symbolism" in *The Handbook of Consumer Motivations, Marketing and Semiotics: Selected Papers* from the Copenhagen Symposium, eds. Hanne Hartvig-Larsen, David Glen Mick, and Christian Alstead (Copenhagen, 1991).

Other interpretations are hard for some people to swallow, such as the observations that, to a woman, baking a cake symbolizes giving birth, or that men are reluctant to give blood because they feel their vital fluids are being drained. On the other hand, some people do refer to a pregnant woman as "having a bun in the oven," and Pillsbury claims that "nothing says lovin' like something from the oven." Motivational research for the Canadian Blood Services (***www.bloodservices.ca***) did find that men (but not women) tend to overestimate drastically the amount of blood that is taken during a donation. This group counteracted the fear of loss of virility by symbolically equating the act of giving blood with fertilization: "Give the gift of life."

Despite its drawbacks, motivational research continues to be a useful diagnostic tool. Its validity is enhanced, however, when used in conjunction with the other research techniques available to the consumer researcher.

NEO-FREUDIAN THEORIES

Freud's work had a huge influence on subsequent theories of personality. Although Freud opened the door to the realization that explanations for behaviour may lurk beneath the surface, many of his co-workers and students felt that an individual's personality was more influenced by how he or she handled relationships with others. These theorists are often called *neo-Freudian* (meaning following from or being influenced by Freud).

KAREN HORNEY   One of the most prominent neo-Freudians was a psychoanalyst named Karen Horney. She proposed that people can be described as moving toward others (compliant), away from others (detached), or against others (aggressive).[5] Some research indicates that these three types prefer different kinds of products. For example, one study found that compliant people are more likely to gravitate toward name-brand products, that detached types are more likely to be tea drinkers, and that males classified as aggressive prefer brands with a strong masculine orientation (e.g., Old Spice deodorant).[6] Other well-known neo-Freudians include Alfred Adler, who proposed that many actions are motivated by people's desire to overcome feelings of inferiority relative to others, and Harry Stack Sullivan, who focused on how personality evolves to reduce anxiety in social relationships.[7]

CARL JUNG   Carl Jung was also a disciple of Freud (and was being groomed by Freud to be his successor). However, Jung was unable to accept Freud's emphasis on sexual aspects of personality, and this was a contributing factor in the eventual dissolution of their relationship. Jung went on to develop his own method of psychotherapy, which became known as *analytical psychology*. This approach emphasized both the individual's development as a creative person (his or her future) and his or her individual and racial history (his or her past) in the formation of personality.

Jung believed that people are shaped by the cumulative experiences of past generations. A central part of his perspective was an emphasis on what Jung called the *collective unconscious,* which is a storehouse of memories inherited from our ancestral past. For example, Jung would argue that many people are afraid of the dark because their distant ancestors had good reason to exhibit this fear. These shared memories create **archetypes**, or universally shared ideas and behaviour patterns. Archetypes involve themes, such as birth, death, or the devil, that appear frequently in myths, stories, and dreams.

Jung's ideas may seem a bit far-fetched, but advertising messages often do invoke (at least intuitively) archetypes to link products with underlying meanings. For example, some of the archetypes identified by Jung and his followers include the *old wise man* and the *earth mother*.[8] These images appear frequently in marketing messages that use such characters as wizards, revered teachers, or even Mother Nature to convince people of the merits of products. Our culture's current infatuation with stories like Harry Potter and the Lord of the Rings speaks to the power of these images.

Marketing, advertising, and consumer behaviour researchers have long accepted the assertion that some brands have personalities that are, in many ways, quite similar to human personalities. Accurately and adequately *measuring* those personalities has been quite problematic, however. In the early days (some 25 or more years ago), researchers used adjective check-offs and adjective rating scales, and even asked consumers questions like, "If this brand were an animal (or tree, or colour, or flower, or whatever), what kind of animal (or tree, or colour, or flower, or whatever) would it be?" The problem with such approaches is that the results are idiosyncratic to the project at hand and not generalizable across brands or studies. In 2000 the BrandAsset Valuator® (BAV®) group at the Young & Rubicam advertising agency (later known as the Knowledge Group of Young & Rubicam Brands) started measuring brand personality using the BrandAsset® Archetypes model depicted in Figure 6–1. This was done in conjunction with BAV® Brand Health measures.

FIGURE 6–1 BRANDASSET VALUATOR® ARCHETYPES

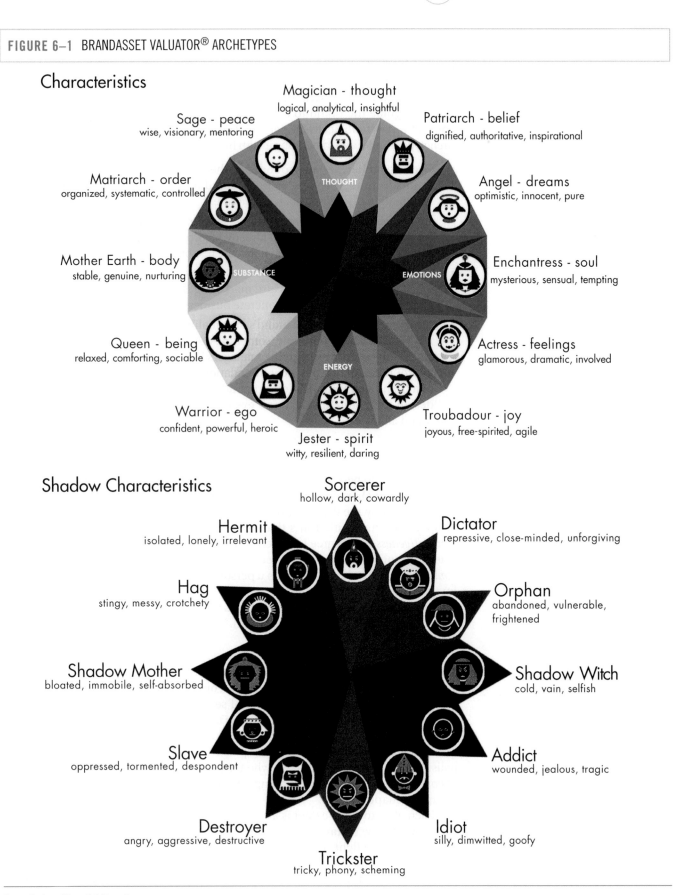

Characteristics

Sage - peace
wise, visionary, mentoring

Magician - thought
logical, analytical, insightful

Patriarch - belief
dignified, authoritative, inspirational

Matriarch - order
organized, systematic, controlled

Angel - dreams
optimistic, innocent, pure

Mother Earth - body
stable, genuine, nurturing

Enchantress - soul
mysterious, sensual, tempting

Queen - being
relaxed, comforting, sociable

Actress - feelings
glamorous, dramatic, involved

Warrior - ego
confident, powerful, heroic

Troubadour - joy
joyous, free-spirited, agile

Jester - spirit
witty, resilient, daring

THOUGHT
SUBSTANCE
EMOTIONS
ENERGY

Shadow Characteristics

Hermit
isolated, lonely, irrelevant

Sorcerer
hollow, dark, cowardly

Dictator
repressive, close-minded, unforgiving

Hag
stingy, messy, crotchety

Orphan
abandoned, vulnerable,
frightened

Shadow Mother
bloated, immobile, self-absorbed

Shadow Witch
cold, vain, selfish

Slave
oppressed, tormented, despondent

Addict
wounded, jealous, tragic

Destroyer
angry, aggressive, destructive

Idiot
silly, dimwitted, goofy

Trickster
tricky, phony, scheming

Source: Courtesy of Young & Rubicam Group.

The model proposes healthy relationships among Archetypes as well as unhealthy ones. Researchers at the agency use the model to identify whether a brand has a sick personality or not. A healthy personality is one in which the Archetypes overwhelm their corresponding Shadows; a sick personality occurs when one or more Shadows prevail. When a brand's shadows dominate, it is necessary to take action to guide the brand to a healthier personality, much like one would try to counsel a psychologically ill person. The advantages of using the BrandAsset® Archetypes model and integrating it with BAV® Brand Health measures are numerous:

- Because Archetypes are grounded in the human psyche across all cultures and points in time, it is easy to understand a brand's personality—often times multinationally—using such a structure.

- Archetypes telegraph instantly to those responsible for brand communication. Indeed, the best of this group already incorporate these notions into how they think of the brand; the model helps the rest of them "catch up."

- Linking measures of BrandAsset® Archetypes to measures of Brand Health provides strong evidence to assure marketing decision makers that the changes recommended will achieve concrete business objectives.

- Measuring the health of a brand's personality can act as an "early warning" signal that a brand is in trouble, sometimes years in advance of marketplace indicators, thus alerting marketing managers in enough time to tweak the brand as appropriate. Archetypes recommendations can (and should) inform all aspects of a brand's communication, from advertising to public relations to package design to in-store displays and even including choosing mutually beneficial brand alliances.[9]

Trait Theory

One approach to personality is to focus on the quantitative measurement of **traits**, or identifiable characteristics that define a person. For example, people can be distinguished by the degree to which they are socially outgoing (the trait of *extroversion*). Some specific traits that are relevant to consumer behaviour include *innovativeness* (the degree to which a person likes to try new things), *materialism* (the amount of emphasis placed on acquiring and owning products), *self-consciousness* (the degree to which a person deliberately monitors and controls the image of the self that is projected to others), and *need for cognition* (the degree to which a person likes to think about things and, by extension, to expend the necessary effort to process brand information).[10]

ARE YOU AN INNIE OR AN OUTIE?

Perhaps the trait dimension most relevant to consumer behaviour is the extent to which a person is motivated to consume in order to please others or to fit in versus consuming to express a unique sense of self without much concern about being accepted by a group. A sociologist named David Reisman first introduced the terms *inner-directed* and *outer-directed* to our culture.[11] This general idea has resurfaced in a variety of ways. As we'll see in Chapter 16, some cultures tend to stress individualism while others reward those who try to fit in. We'll talk more about the power of conformity (the impact of shaping one's behaviour to meet the expectations of a group) in Chapter 11.

Each of us to some extent is a conformist by definition because as members of society we follow certain rules. As a simple example, we each "agree" to stop at a corner when the light turns red. Still, some of us are more concerned about the reactions of others to what we do, while some seem to "march to their own tune." One personality trait we can measure is the *need for uniqueness* (the degree to which a person is motivated to conform to the preferences of others versus standing apart from the crowd).[12]

Net Profit +

As the saying goes, "Birds of a feather flock together." We tend to like people who are like us. New research reveals that the same folk wisdom may apply to our computers. People respond to the personality cues in computer-generated speech just as they would to those of flesh-and-blood individuals. In a recent study, people who were classified as either extroverts or introverts listened to an identical book review read by a computer-synthesized voice designed to sound like either an extrovert or an introvert (quieter, slower). Subjects were more likely to buy the book if the computer's voice matched their own personality.[13]

Some recent research examines consumption differences between individuals who are **idiocentrics** (having an individualist orientation) and those who are **allocentrics** (having a group orientation). Some differences between these two personality types include the following:

- *Contentment:* Idiocentrics scored higher than allocentrics on the statement "I am very satisfied with the way things are going in my life these days." They also are more satisfied with their financial situations.

- *Health consciousness:* Allocentrics are more likely to avoid foods that are high in cholesterol, have a high salt content, have additives in them, or have a high amount of fat.

- *Food preparation:* The kitchen is the favourite room of allocentrics, who spend more time preparing meals than do idiocentrics.

- *Workaholics:* Idiocentrics are more likely to say they work very hard most of the time, and they stay late at work more than do allocentrics.

- *Travel and entertainment:* Idiocentrics are more interested in other cultures and travelling than are allocentrics. They also are more likely to go to movies, art galleries, and museums. Compared to idiocentrics, allocentrics visited the public library and finished reading books with a greater frequency. Allocentrics reported working on craft projects such as needlework and model building. On the other hand, idiocentric individuals were more likely to collect stamps or rocks, work on do-it-yourself projects, and take photos. They also were more likely to play the lottery.[14]

PROBLEMS WITH TRAIT THEORY IN CONSUMER RESEARCH

The notion that consumers buy products that are extensions of their personalities makes intuitive sense. This idea is endorsed by many marketing managers, who try to create brand personalities that will appeal to different types of consumers. However, the use of standard personality-trait measurements to predict product choices has met with mixed success at best. In general, marketing researchers simply have not been able to predict consumers' behaviours on the basis of measured personality traits. A number of explanations have been offered for these equivocal results:[15]

- Many of the scales are not sufficiently valid or reliable; they do not adequately measure what they are supposed to measure, and their results may not be stable over time.

- Personality tests are often developed for specific populations (e.g., people with a mental illness); these tests are then "borrowed" and applied to the general population, where their relevance is questionable.

- The tests often are not administered under the appropriate conditions; they may be given in a classroom or over a kitchen table by people who are not properly trained.

- The researchers often make changes in the instruments to adapt them to their own situations, in the process deleting or adding items and renaming variables. These ad hoc changes dilute the validity of the measures and also reduce researchers' ability to compare results across consumer samples.

- Many trait scales are intended to measure gross, overall tendencies (such as emotional stability or introversion); these results are then used to make predictions about purchases of specific brands.

- In many cases a number of scales are given with no advance thought about how these measures should be related to consumer behaviour. The researchers then use a shotgun approach, following up on anything that happens to look interesting.

Although the use of personality measures by marketing researchers was largely abandoned after many studies failed to yield meaningful results, some researchers have not abandoned the early promise of this line of work. More recent efforts (many in Europe) have been focused on benefiting from past mistakes. These researchers are using more specific measures of personality traits that they have reason to believe are relevant to economic behaviour. They are trying to increase the validity of these measures, primarily by using multiple measures of behaviour rather than by relying on the common practice of trying to predict purchasing responses from a single item on a personality test.

In addition, researchers have toned down their expectations of what personality traits can tell them about consumers. They now recognize that traits are only part of the solution, and personality data must be incorporated with information about people's social and economic conditions in order to be useful.[16] As a result, some more recent research has had better success at relating personality traits to such consumer behaviours as alcohol consumption among young men or shoppers' willingness to try new, healthier food products.[17]

BRAND PERSONALITY

In 1886 a momentous event occurred: The Quaker Oats man first appeared on boxes of hot cereal. Quakers had a reputation in nineteenth-century America for being shrewd but fair, and peddlers sometimes dressed as Quakers for this reason. The cereal company's decision to "borrow" this imagery for its packaging signalled the recognition that purchasers might make the same associations with their product.[18] A **brand personality** is the set of traits people attribute to a product as if it were a person. Many of the most recognizable figures in popular culture are spokescharacters for long-standing brands, such as the Jolly Green Giant. And, like real people, these characters sometimes need a "makeover" to keep them fresh and young-looking. The venerable Mr. Peanut recently got one: After decades of being depicted as a dignified dandy with his monocle and cane (he's based on a 1916 drawing by a Virginia schoolboy), Planters now lets Mr. Peanut show off his moves on the basketball court and the dance floor, and in one spot he even poses as a centrefold.[19]

Our feelings about a brand's personality are an important part of **brand equity**, which refers to the extent to which consumers hold strong, favourable, and unique associations with a brand in memory—and the extent to which they are willing to pay more for the branded version of a product than for a non-branded (generic) version.[20] Building strong brands is good business. If you don't believe it, consider that in a study of 760 *Fortune 1000* companies after the stock market took a nosedive in October of 1997, the 20 strongest corporate brands (e.g., Microsoft and General Electric) actually gained in market value, whereas the 20 weakest lost an average of $1 billion each.[21]

Name recognition has become so valuable that some companies are completely outsourcing production to focus on nurturing the brand. Nike doesn't own any sneaker factories, and Sara Lee sold off many of its bakeries, meat-processing plants, and textile mills to become a "virtual" corporation. Its CEO commented, "Slaughtering hogs and running knitting machines are businesses of yesterday."[22]

So how do people think about brands? Advertisers are keenly interested in this question, and several conduct extensive consumer research to help them understand, before they roll out campaigns, how consumers connect to a brand. For example, DDB Worldwide carries out a global study called "Brand Capital" of 14 000 consumers for this purpose. Leo Burnett's "Brand Stock" project involves 28 000 interviews. WPP Group has "BrandZ" and Young & Rubicam has its Brand-Asset Valuator®. DDB's worldwide brand planning director observes, "We're not marketing just to isolated individuals. We're marketing to society. How I feel about a brand is directly related [to] and affected by how others feel about that brand."

Some personality dimensions that can be used to compare and contrast the perceived characteristics of brands in various product categories include:[23]

- old-fashioned, wholesome, traditional
- surprising, lively, "with it"
- serious, intelligent, efficient
- glamorous, romantic, sexy
- rugged, outdoorsy, tough, athletic

The following memo was written to help an advertising agency figure out how a client should be portrayed in advertising. Based on this description of the "client," can you guess who he is? "He is creative... unpredictable... an imp.... He not only walks and talks, but has the ability to sing, blush, wink, and work with little devices like pointers.... He can also play musical instruments.... His walking motion is characterized as a 'swagger.'... He is made of dough and has mass."[24]

Of course, we all know today that packaging and other physical cues create a "personality" for a product (in this case, the Pillsbury Doughboy!—*www.pillsbury.com*). In addition, the marketing activities undertaken on behalf of the product also can influence inferences about its "personality." Some of these actions are shown in Table 6–2.

Indeed, consumers appear to have little trouble assigning personality qualities to all sorts of inanimate products, from personal-care products to more mundane, functional ones—even kitchen appliances. In research done by Whirlpool, its products were seen as more feminine than competing brands. They were regarded as a modern, family-oriented woman living in the suburbs—attractive but not flashy. In contrast, the company's KitchenAid brand was seen as a modern professional woman who was glamorous and wealthy and enjoyed classical music and the theatre.[25]

The creation and communication of a distinctive *brand personality* is one of the primary ways marketers can make a product stand out from the competition and inspire years of loyalty to it. This process can be understood in terms of **animism**, the practice found in many cultures whereby inanimate objects are given qualities

TABLE 6–2

BRAND BEHAVIOURS AND POSSIBLE PERSONALITY TRAIT INFERENCE

Brand Action	Trait Inference
Brand is repositioned several times or changes its slogan repeatedly.	Flighty, schizophrenic
Brand uses continuing character in its advertising.	Familiar, comfortable
Brand charges a high price and uses exclusive distribution.	Snobbish, sophisticated
Brand is frequently available on a special deal.	Cheap, uncultured
Brand offers many line extensions.	Versatile, adaptable
Brand sponsors show on PBS or uses recycled materials.	Helpful, supportive
Brand features easy-to-use packaging or speaks at consumer's level in advertising.	Warm, approachable
Brand offers seasonal clearance sale.	Planful, practical
Brand offers five-year warranty or free customer hotline.	Reliable, dependable

Source: Adapted from Susan Fournier, "A Consumer-Brand Relationship Framework for Strategic Brand Management," Doctoral Dissertation, Department of Marketing, University of Florida, 1994, Table 2.2, p. 24.

that make them somehow alive. Animism is in some cases a part of a religion: sacred objects, animals, or places are believed to have magical qualities or to contain the spirits of ancestors. In our society these objects may be "worshipped" in the sense that they are believed to impart desirable qualities to the owner, or they may in a sense become so important to a person that they can be viewed as a "friend."

Two types of animism can be identified to describe the extent to which human qualities are attributed to a product:[26]

- Level 1: In the highest order of animism, the object is believed to be possessed by the soul of the being—as is sometimes the case for spokespersons in advertising. This strategy allows the consumer to feel that the spirit of the "celebrity" is available through the brand. In other cases, a brand may be strongly associated with a loved one, alive or deceased. ("My grandmother always served Kraft blueberry jam.")

- Level 2: Objects are *anthropomorphized*—given human characteristics. A cartoon character or mythical creation may be treated as if it were a person, and even assumed to have human feelings. Think about such familiar spokes-characters as the Jolly Green Giant, the Pillsbury Doughboy, or the Michelin Man. Grey Advertising, in research for its client Sprint Business Services, found that when customers were asked to imagine long-distance carriers as animals, they envisioned AT&T as a lion, MCI as a snake, and Sprint as a puma. Grey used these results to position Sprint as a company that could "help you do more business" rather than taking the more aggressive approach of its competitors.[27]

Personality of Positioning

As we saw in Chapter 2, a brand's positioning strategy is a statement about what that brand wants to be in the eyes of its customers—especially relative to the competition. Marketers are used to thinking in these terms, routinely describing their brands and the competition as if they were people. For example, here's how the marketing director for Philips Electronics in Asia sums up the problem he faces in updating his brand so that it will be seen as hip and young by Chinese consumers: "To put it bluntly, we are received well by middle-aged gentlemen.... But a brand like Sony is seen as younger, more arrogant, with a space-age personality."[28]

In a sense, then, a brand personality is also a statement about how the brand is positioned. Understanding this concept is crucial to the success of a marketing strategy, especially if consumers don't see the brand the way its makers intend them to, which means the makers must try to *reposition* the product (i.e., give it a personality makeover). That's the problem now being faced by Volvo, whose cars are renowned for safety but are not exactly seen as exciting or sexy. A safe and solid brand personality makes it hard to sell a racy convertible like the C70 model, so a British ad tries to change that perception with the tag line, "Lust, envy, jealousy. The dangers of a Volvo." Just as with people, however, there's only so far a marketer can go to convince others that a brand's personality has changed. But for the most part consumers don't buy a change in a brand's personality. As one brand consultant observed, "You get the sort of feeling you get when you see your grandparents trying to dance the latest dance. Slightly amused and embarrassed."[29]

LIFESTYLES AND PSYCHOGRAPHICS

Anna and Margie, whom we met at the beginning of this chapter, strongly resemble one another demographically. They were both raised in middle-class households, have similar educational backgrounds, are about the same age, and share the same occupation and income. However, as their leisure choices show, it would be a big mistake to assume that their consumption choices are similar as well. Each of them chooses products, services, and activities that help her define a unique *lifestyle*. This section first explores how marketers approach the issue of lifestyle and then how they apply information about these consumption choices to tailor products and communications to individual lifestyle segments.

Lifestyle: Who We Are, What We Do

In traditional societies consumption options are largely dictated by class, caste, village, or family. In a modern consumer society, however, people are more free to select the set of products, services, and activities that defines them and, in turn, to create a social identity that can be communicated to others. A person's choice of goods and services indeed makes a statement about who that person is and about the types of people with whom that person desires to identify—and even about those he or she wishes to avoid.

Lifestyle refers to a pattern of consumption reflecting a person's choices of how he or she spends time and money. Many of the factors already discussed in this book, such as a person's self-concept, ethnicity, and social class, are used as "raw ingredients" to fashion a unique lifestyle. In an economic sense a person's lifestyle represents the way he or she has elected to allocate income both to different products and services and to specific alternatives within these categories.[30] Other somewhat similar distinctions have been made to describe consumers in terms of their broad patterns of consumption.[31] For example, consumers can be distinguished by their social class, which can be determined by the proportion of expenditures on food, advanced technology, or such information-intensive goods as entertainment and education.

A *lifestyle marketing perspective* recognizes that people sort themselves into groups on the basis of the things they like to do, how they like to spend their leisure time, and how they choose to spend their disposable income.[32] These choices are reflected, for example, in the growing number of niche magazines that cater to specialized interests. In 1998–1999, *WWF Magazine* (World Wrestling Federation) gained 913 000 readers and *4 Wheel & Off Road* gained 749 000, while mainstream *Reader's Digest* lost more than 3 million readers and *People* lost more than 2 million.[33] These choices, in turn, create opportunities for market-segmentation strategies that recognize the potency of a consumer's chosen lifestyle in determining both the types of products purchased and the specific brands more likely to appeal to a designated lifestyle segment.

LIFESTYLES AS GROUP IDENTITIES

The economic approaches are useful in tracking changes in broad societal priorities, but they do not begin to embrace the symbolic nuances that separate lifestyle groups. Lifestyle is more than the allocation of discretionary income. It is a statement about who we are in society and who we are not. Group identities, whether of hobbyists, athletes, or drug users, jell around forms of expressive symbolism. The self-definitions of group members are derived from the common symbol system to which the group is dedicated. Such self-definitions have been described by a number of terms, including *lifestyle, taste public, consumer group, symbolic community,* and *status culture.*[34]

Patterns of consumption based on lifestyles often comprise many ingredients that are shared by others in similar social and economic circumstances. Still, each person also provides a unique "twist" to this pattern that allows him or her to inject some individuality into a chosen lifestyle. For example, a "typical" university student (if there is such a thing) may dress much like his or her friends, hang out in the same places, and like the same foods, yet still indulge in a passion for marathon running, stamp collecting, or community activism that makes him or her a unique person.

And lifestyles are not set in stone. Unlike deep-seated values, people's tastes and preferences evolve over time, so that consumption patterns that were viewed favourably at one point in time may be laughed at (or sneered at) a few years later. If you don't believe that, simply think back to what you, your friends, and your family were wearing, doing, and eating five or ten years ago. Where *did* you find those clothes?

Because people's attitudes regarding physical fitness, social activism, gender roles for men and women, the importance of home life and family, and many other things do change, it is vital for marketers to monitor continually the social landscape to try to anticipate where these changes will lead. Some of the most important lifestyle changes (known as trends) will be discussed later in this chapter.

Products Are the Building Blocks of Lifestyles

Consumers often choose particular products, services, and activities over others because they are associated with a certain lifestyle. For this reason, lifestyle marketing strategies attempt to position a product by fitting it into an existing pattern of consumption.

Because a goal of lifestyle marketing is to allow consumers to pursue their chosen ways of enjoying their lives and expressing their social identities, a key aspect of this strategy is to focus on product usage in desirable social settings (see Chapter 10). The goal of associating a product with a social situation is a long-standing one for advertisers, whether the product is included in a round of golf, a family barbecue, or a night at a glamorous disco surrounded by jet-setters.[35] Thus people, products, and settings are combined to express a certain consumption style, as diagrammed in Figure 6–2. Even Coca-Cola and Pepsi, which have for years produced glitzy ads featuring celebrities like Madonna and Michael Jackson, are refocusing on a lifestyle approach that weaves their drinks into regular—albeit duller—everyday life. To encourage more cola consumption as many consumers instead reach for water and juice, both companies feel the need to demonstrate how their flagship soft drink brands fit into simple situations, like coming home from school or having a barbecue.[36]

The adoption of a lifestyle marketing perspective implies that we must look at *patterns* of behaviour to understand consumers. We can get a clearer picture of how people use products to define lifestyles by examining how they make choices in a variety of product categories. As one study noted, "all goods carry meaning, but none by itself.... The meaning is in the relations between all the goods, just as music is in the relations marked out by the sounds and not in any one note."[37]

Indeed, many products and services do seem to "go together," usually because they tend to be selected by the same types of people. In many cases, products do not seem to "make sense" if unaccompanied by companion products (e.g., fast food and paper plates or a suit and tie) or are incongruous in the presence of others (e.g., a Chippendale chair in a high-tech office). Therefore, an important part of lifestyle marketing is to identify the *set* of products and services that seems to be linked in consumers' minds to a specific lifestyle.

FIGURE 6–2

LINKING PRODUCTS TO LIFESTYLES

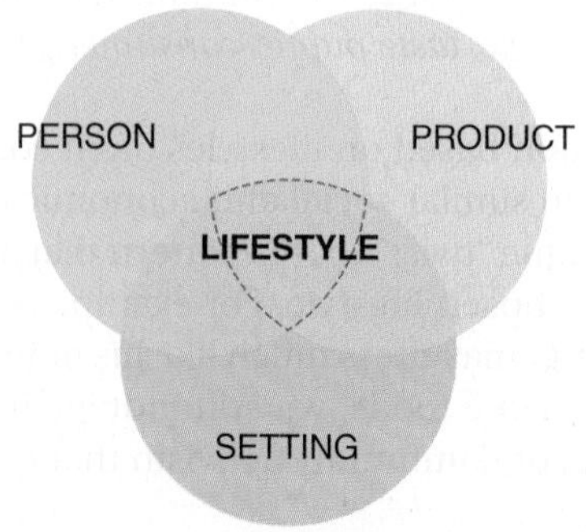

PERSON   PRODUCT

LIFESTYLE

SETTING

And research evidence suggests that even a relatively unattractive product becomes more appealing when evaluated with other, liked products.[38] Marketers who pursue **co-branding strategies** intuitively understand this, as the following examples show:

- The German car maker Porsche is teaming up with Canada's Fairmont Hotels & Resorts chain to appeal to each other's customers. Porsche figures Fairmont's upscale clientele is the perfect market for its recently upgraded Boxster convertible and new Cayenne sport-utility vehicle.[39]

- Unilever will be handing out samples of its new Dove Body Refreshers to women as they enter Bally Total Fitness gyms.[40]

- Nike and Polaroid formed a partnership to promote the I-Zone, an instant pocket camera targeted to teens. Now, buyers of the portable camera can also pick up shoes with a clear pocket that will let them display their photos as they walk.[41]

Product complementarity occurs when the symbolic meanings of different products are related to each other.[42] These sets of products, termed *consumption constellations,* are used by consumers to define, communicate, and perform social roles.[43] For example, the yuppie of the 1980s was defined by such products as a Rolex watch (***www.rolex.com***), BMW automobile, Gucci briefcase, squash racket, fresh pesto, white wine, and Brie. Although people today take pains to avoid being classified as yuppies, this social role had a major influence on defining cultural values and consumption priorities in the 1980s.[44] What consumption constellation might characterize you and your friends today?

Psychographics

In 1998, Cadillac introduced its sport-utility vehicle called the Escalade. Critics scoffed at the bizarre pairing of this old-line luxury brand with a truck, but the vehicle quickly became associated with the hip hop lifestyle. Music artists like Jennifer Lopez, Outkast, and Jay-Z referred to it in songs, and Jermaine Dupri proclaimed "gotta have me an Escalade." Three years later, Cadillac went even further when it rolled out its 5.5-metre Escalade EXT pickup with a sticker price of US$50 000.

Interior designers rely on consumption constellations when choosing items to furnish a room. A decorating style involves integrating products from many different categories—such as appliances, furnishings, knick-knacks, and even artwork—into a unified whole that conveys a certain "look."
Reproduced with the permission of the copyright owner, General Electric Company.

The brand manager for Cadillac describes the target customer for luxury pickups as a slightly earthier version of the SUV buyer. She says that although the two drivers may own $2-million homes next door to each other, the typical luxury SUV driver is about 50, has an MBA, belongs to a golf club, maintains connections with his college friends, and works hard at keeping up with the Joneses. In contrast, the luxury pickup driver is roughly five years younger. He might have inherited his father's construction business, and he's been working since he was 18 years old. He may or may not have attended college, and unlike the SUV driver he is absolutely still connected to his high-school friends.[45]

As this example shows, marketers often find it useful to develop products that appeal to different lifestyle groups. Just knowing a person's income doesn't predict whether he will drive a Cadillac Escalade SUV, an Escalade EXT pickup, or a Cadillac El Dorado sedan. Consumers can share the same demographic characteristics and still be very different people.

For this reason, marketers need a way to "breathe life" into demographic data to really identify, understand, and target consumer segments that will share a set of preferences for their products and services. This chapter discussed some of the important differences in consumers' personalities that play a big role in determining product choices. When personality variables are combined with knowledge of lifestyle preferences, marketers have a powerful lens with which to view consumer segments.

This tool is known as **psychographics**, which involves the "use of psychological, sociological, and anthropological factors...to determine how the market is segmented by the propensity of groups within the market—and their reasons—to make a particular decision about a product, person, ideology, or otherwise hold an attitude or use a medium."[46]

Psychographics can help marketers fine-tune their offerings to meet the needs of different segments. For example, the Best Buy consumer electronics chain recently decided to revamp its stores according to the types of customers they serve. The company identified five prototypical customers:

- "Jill," a busy suburban mom who wants to talk about how electronics can help her family
- "Buzz," a focused, active younger male who is interested in buying (and showing off) the latest gadgets
- "Ray," a family man who likes his technology practical
- "BB4B" (short for Best Buy for Business), a small employer
- "Barry," an affluent professional male who's likely to drop tens of thousands of dollars on a home theatre system and who is an action-movie enthusiast

The chain is trying to identify the two most dominant customer types who patronize each of its outlets and plan accordingly. Store clerks receive hours of training to help them pick out the most likely category in which to pigeonhole a customer. A customer who says his family has a regular "movie night," for example, is labelled as a "Ray" or "Jill" and is steered toward home-theatre equipment. Stores catering to the "Jill" segment will feature play areas for kids. Instead of a booming bass beat, the soundtrack playing in the background will be instrumental or children's music.[47]

It is possible to identify distinct psychographic segments even for mundane products—like soup. A major soup company did this after noticing that different types of people preferred different varieties.[48] To verify their hunches, company researchers interviewed "experts"—waitresses at diners—and asked them questions like, "If the soup of the day is chicken noodle, what kind of person would order that soup?" After getting responses that did indicate differences (e.g., the waitresses reported that chicken noodle fanciers seemed to be most friendly and upbeat, while tomato soup fans often talked about a pet and were likely to read a paperback if eating alone), the company conducted in-depth interviews with self-proclaimed fanatics of each flavour, and then administered a survey to about 1000 North American adults. Table 6–3 summarizes some of their findings.

THE ROOTS OF PSYCHOGRAPHICS

Psychographic research was first developed in the 1960s and 1970s to address the shortcomings of two other types of consumer research: motivational research and quantitative survey research. As discussed earlier, *motivational research,* which involves intensive one-to-one interviews and projective tests, yields a lot of information about a few people. This information, however, is often idiosyncratic and not very useful or reliable. At the other extreme, *quantitative survey research,* or large-scale demographic surveying, yields only a little information about a lot of people. As some researchers observed, "The marketing manager who wanted to know why people ate the competitor's cornflakes was told '32 percent of the respondents said taste, 21 percent said flavour, 15 percent said texture, 10 percent said price, and 22 percent said don't know or no answer.'"[50]

Although consumers can be segmented on the basis of many psychographic variables, all of these variables share the underlying principle of going beyond surface characteristics in order to understand consumers' motivations for purchasing and using products and services.

Demographics allows us to describe *who* buys, but psychographics allows us to understand *why* they do. To illustrate how this approach works, consider a very popular campaign for Molson Export beer that based its commercials on psychographic

TABLE 6–3

LIFESTYLE AND PERSONALITY VARIABLES USED TO DIFFERENTIATE SOUP PREFERENCES

Lifestyle	Personality
Active Lifestyle (Vegetable) • I am outdoorsy • I am physically fit • I am a workaholic • I am socially active	**Mentally Alert (Clam Chowder)** • I am intellectual • I am sophisticated • I am creative • I am detail oriented • I am witty • I am nutrition conscious
Family Spirited (Chicken Noodle) • I am family oriented • I am a churchgoer • I am pretty traditional	**Social (Chili)** • I am fun at parties • I am outgoing • I am not shy • I am spontaneous • I am a trendsetter
Homebody (Tomato) • I enjoy spending time alone • I am a homebody • I am a good cook • I am a pet lover	**Athletic (Cream Soups)** • I am athletic • I am competitive • I am adventurous
Intellectually Stimulated Pastimes (French Onion) • I am a technology whiz • I am a world traveller • I am a book lover	**Carefree (Minestrone)** • I am down-to-earth • I am affectionate • I am fun loving • I am optimistic

Source: Brian Wansink and S. Park, "Accounting for Taste: Prototypes that Predict Preference," *Journal of Database Marketing*, 2000, 308—320, as described in Norman Bradburn, Seymour Sudman and Brian Wansink, *Asking Questions*, 2004: Jossey-Bass, NY.

findings. Research showed that Molson's target customers tended to be like boys who had never grown up, were uncertain about the future, and were intimidated by women's new-found freedom. Accordingly, the ads featured a group of men—"Fred and the boys"—whose get-togethers emphasized male companionship, protection against change, and the idea that the beer "keeps on tasting great."[51]

Conducting a Psychographic Analysis

Some early attempts at lifestyle segmentation "borrowed" standard psychological scales (often used to measure pathology or personality disturbances) and tried to relate scores on these tests to product usage. As might be expected, such efforts were largely disappointing. These tests were never intended to be related to every-day consumption activities and yielded little in the way of explanation for purchase behaviours. The technique is more effective when the variables included are more closely related to actual consumer behaviours. If one wants to understand purchases of household cleaning products, it is better to ask people about their attitudes toward household cleanliness than to test for personality disorders.

Psychographic studies can take several different forms:

- a lifestyle profile that looks for items that differentiate between users and non-users of a product
- a product-specific profile that identifies a target group and then profiles these consumers on product-relevant dimensions
- a study that uses personality traits as descriptors, where some variable, such as concern for the environment, is analyzed to see which personality traits are most likely to be related to it
- a general lifestyle segmentation, where the respondents in a large sample are placed into homogenous groups based on similarities in their overall preferences
- a product-specific segmentation, where questions used in a general approach are tailored to a product category. For example, in a study done specifically for a stomach medicine, an item like "I worry too much" might be rephrased as "I get stomach problems if I worry too much." This allows the researcher to discriminate more finely between users of competing brands[52]

AIOs

Most contemporary psychographic research attempts to group consumers according to some combination of three categories of variables—activities, interests, and opinions—known as **AIOs**. Using data from large samples, marketers create profiles of customers who resemble each other in their activities and patterns of product usage.[53] The dimensions used to assess lifestyles are listed in Table 6–4 on page 176.

To group consumers into common AIO categories, researchers give respondents a long list of statements and ask them to indicate how much they agree with each one. Lifestyle is thus "boiled down" by discovering how people spend their time, what they find interesting and important, and how they view themselves and the world around them, as well as by discovering demographic information.

Typically, the first step in conducting a psychographic analysis is to determine which lifestyle segments are producing the bulk of customers for a particular product. According to a very general rule of thumb used frequently in marketing research, the **20/80 rule**, only 20 percent of a product's users account for 80 percent of the volume of product sold. Researchers attempt to determine who uses the brand and try to isolate heavy, moderate, and light users. They also look for patterns of usage and attitudes toward the product. In many cases, just a few lifestyle segments account for the majority of brand users.[54] Marketers target primarily these heavy users, even though they may constitute a relatively small number of total users.

TABLE 6–4

LIFESTYLE DIMENSIONS

ACTIVITIES	INTERESTS	OPINIONS	DEMOGRAPHICS
Work	Family	Themselves	Age
Hobbies	Home	Social issues	Education
Social events	Job	Politics	Income
Vacation	Community	Business	Occupation
Entertainment	Recreation	Economics	Family size
Club membership	Fashion	Education	Dwelling
Community	Food	Products	Geography
Shopping	Media	Future	City size
Sports	Achievements	Culture	Stage in life cycle

Source: William D. Wells and Douglas J. Tigert, "Activities, Interests, and Opinions," *Journal of Advertising Research* 11 (August 1971): 27–35. ©1971 by The Advertising Research Foundation.

After the heavy users are identified and understood, the brand's relationship to them is considered. Heavy users may have quite different reasons for using the product; they can be further subdivided in terms of the *benefits* they derive from using the product or service. For instance, marketers at the beginning of the walking-shoe craze assumed that purchasers were basically burned-out joggers. Subsequent psychographic research showed that there were actually several different groups of walkers, ranging from those who walk to get to work to those who walk for fun. This realization resulted in shoes aimed at different segments, from Footjoy Joy-Walkers (***www.footjoy.com***) to Nike Healthwalkers.

Uses of Psychographic Segmentation

Psychographic segmentation can be applied in a variety of ways:

- *To define the target market:* This information allows the marketer to go beyond simple demographic or product-usage descriptions (e.g., middle-aged men or frequent users).

- *To create a new view of the market:* Sometimes the marketer creates a strategy with a "typical" customer in mind. This stereotype may not be correct because the actual customer may not match these assumptions. For example, marketers of a facial cream for women were surprised to find their key market was composed of older, widowed women rather than the younger, more sociable women to whom they were pitching their appeals.

- *To position the product:* Psychographic information can allow the marketer to emphasize features of the product that fit in with a person's lifestyle. Products targeted at people whose lifestyle profiles show a high need to be around other people might focus on the product's ability to help meet this social need.

- *To better communicate product attributes:* Psychographic information can offer very useful input to the advertising creative person who must communicate something about the product. The artist or writer obtains a much richer mental image of the target consumer than that obtained through dry statistics, and this insight improves his or her ability to "talk" to that consumer.

- *To develop overall strategy:* Understanding how a product fits, or does not fit, into consumers' lifestyles allows the marketer to identify new product opportunities,

chart media strategies, and create environments most consistent and harmonious with these consumption patterns.

* *To market social and political issues:* Psychographic segmentation can be an important tool in political campaigns and can also be employed to find commonalities among types of consumers who engage in destructive behaviours, such as drug use or excessive gambling.

A psychographic study of men aged 18 to 24 who drink and drive highlights the potential for this perspective to help in the eradication of harmful behaviours. This demographic segment accounts for a disproportionately high share of alcohol-related fatalities. Researchers divided this segment into four groups: "good timers," "well adjusted," "nerds," and "problem kids." They found that one group in particular—good timers—is more likely to believe that it is fun to be drunk, that the chances of a drunk driver having an accident are low, and that drinking increases their appeal to the opposite sex. Since the study showed that this group is also the most likely to drink at rock concerts and parties, is most likely to watch MTV, and tends to listen to rock-oriented radio stations, reaching good timers with a prevention campaign is made easier and more efficient.[55]

Psychographic Segmentation Typologies

Marketers are constantly on the prowl for new insights that will allow them to identify and reach groups of consumers that are united by a common lifestyle. To meet this need, many research companies and advertising agencies have developed their own *segmentation typologies* that divide people into segments. Respondents answer a battery of questions that allow the researchers to cluster them into a set of distinct lifestyle groups. The questions usually include a mixture of AIOs, plus other items relating to their perceptions of specific brands, favourite celebrities, media preferences, and so on. These systems are usually sold to companies that want to learn more about their customers and potential customers.

At least at a superficial level, many of these typologies are fairly similar to one another, in that a typical typology breaks up the population into roughly five to eight segments. Each cluster is given a descriptive name, and a profile of the "typical" member is provided to the client. Unfortunately, it is often difficult to compare or evaluate different typologies, since the methods and data used to devise these systems frequently are *proprietary*—that is, the information is developed and owned by the company, and the company feels that it would not be desirable to release this information to outsiders.

VALS2™

The most well-known and widely used segmentation system is **VALS (Values and Lifestyles)**, developed at what is now SRI International in California. The VALS2 system has been used by well over 200 corporations and advertising agencies in their marketing efforts.

VALS2 divides people into eight groups, according to both psychological characteristics and resources, which include such factors as income, education, energy levels, and eagerness to buy. In the VALS2 structure, groups are arrayed vertically by resources and horizontally by self-orientation, as shown in Figure 6–3. The top group is termed *innovators,* who are successful consumers with many resources. This group is concerned with social issues and is open to change. The next three groups also have sufficient resources but differ in their outlooks on life:[56]

- *Thinkers* are satisfied, reflective, and comfortable. They tend to be practical and value functionality.

- *Achievers* are career-oriented and prefer predictability over risk or self-discovery.

- *Experiencers* are impulsive and young and enjoy offbeat or risky experiences.

FIGURE 6–3

VALS2 SEGMENTATION SYSTEM

Source: SRI International, Menlo Park, CA.

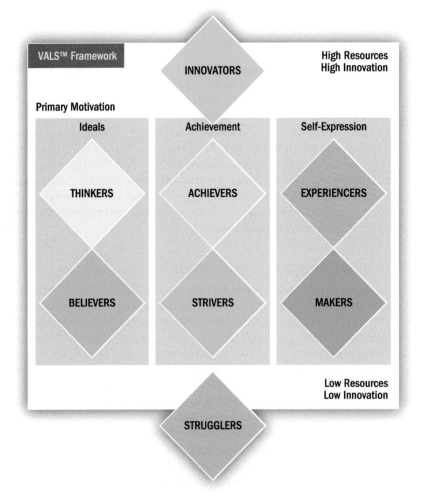

The next three groups have fewer resources:

- *Believers* have strong principles and favour proven brands.

- *Strivers* are like achievers but with fewer resources. They are very concerned about the approval of others.

- *Makers* are action oriented and tend to focus their energies on self-sufficiency. They will often be found working on their cars, canning their own vegetables, or building their own houses.

Finally comes the group with the fewest resources:

- *Strugglers* are at the bottom of the ladder. They are most concerned with meeting the needs of the moment and thus strongly resemble the survivor and sustainer groups they replaced.

The VALS2™ system has been a useful way to understand people like Lisa and Anna. SRI estimates that 12 percent of adults are thrill seekers, who tend to fall into the system's Experiencer category and who are likely to agree with statements such as "I like a lot of excitement in my life" and "I like to try new things." Experiencers like to break the rules and are strongly attracted to extreme sports such as sky surfing or bungee jumping. Not too surprisingly, fully one-third of consumers aged 18 to 34 years belong in this category, so it has attracted the interest of many marketers who are trying to appeal to younger people (more on this in Chapter 15). If you want to see what VALS2 type you would be classified as, go to *www.sric-bi.com*. It will take you about 10 minutes to log on, take the test, and see which category best describes your approach to life. Just omit the zip code question, which is irrelevant for Canadians.

Geodemography

Geodemography refers to analytical techniques that combine data on consumer expenditures and other socio-economic factors with geographic information about the areas in which people live in order to identify consumers who share common consumption patterns. The assumption is that "birds of a feather flock together"—that is, people who have similar needs and tastes also tend to live near one another—so it should be possible to locate pockets of like-minded people who can then be reached more economically by direct mail and other methods.

Geographic information increasingly is being combined with other data to paint an even more complete picture of the Canadian consumer. Several marketing research ventures now employ single-source data, in which information about a person's actual purchasing history is combined with geodemographic data. This method allows marketers to learn even more about the types of marketing strategies that motivate some people—but not others—to respond.

LIFESTYLE TRENDS

Consumer lifestyles are a moving target; society's priorities and preferences are constantly evolving. It is essential for marketers to track these changes and, more important, to try to anticipate them. One "quick and dirty" way to appreciate change is to look at business headings in the *Yellow Pages*. Within the last few years, these categories have been dropped from many telephone directories: livestock, records, mops, and worms. New headings include angels, body piercing, cyber cafés, feng shui, permanent makeup, and aromatherapy.[57]

Of course, many lifestyle trends are rooted in economic and demographic patterns, so understanding these developments usually entails an appreciation of such factors as employment rates, educational attainment, and population growth.

Marketing Opportunity !

Lifestyle malls are popping up across the country as retail developers try to create a back-to-the-country atmosphere. A lifestyle mall, such as the Village at Park Royal Vancouver, relies less on retailers that sell on price (Wal-Mart) and more on restaurants, cafés, and one-location retailers. The big-box stores are located on the outside and in the middle, a main street lifestyle is created with parallel or diagonal parking. This way consumers do not have to make long treks from their car to the stores. What these high-end consumers crave is easy access to retailers, a distinctive destination, and a place to linger, whether over lunch, a latte, or a beer.[58]

→ The service-oriented, engaging atmosphere of Pete's Frootique appeals to consumers who are interested in the pleasure of eating well-prepared food and who are highly involved in food shopping.
Courtesy of Pete's Frootique.

Trend Forecasting: Peering into the Crystal Ball of Consumer Behaviour

If a marketer could see into the future, he or she would obviously have an enormous advantage when developing products and services that will meet the needs of consumers next year, in five years, or in ten years. No one is able to do that yet, but a number of marketing research firms do try very hard to predict social trends. For example, the Lifestyle Monitor, now run by the firm Yankelovich Clancy Shulman, interviews 2500 American adults annually. Advertising agency Backer Spielvogel Bates's Global Scan program divides markets in 18 countries into psychographic segments and charts changes in attitudes. Since 1975 the DDB Needham Worldwide advertising agency has been conducting its Needham Lifestyle Study, an ongoing study of changes in consumer behaviour consisting of a sample of 4000 Americans' answers to a battery of 1000 questions.

Of course, new lifestyle trends constantly are bubbling to the surface. Many of these changes in consumer behaviour are driven by young consumers who are continually redefining what's hot and what's not, as in the list shown in Table 6–5.

These transformations may come from such growing movements as the new hip hop poets and performance artists who express their alienation from mainstream culture at open-mike nights in poets' cafés. Or perhaps the "technorganics" who believe in a minimalist lifestyle, but who embrace new technologies and spend their time in chat rooms sharing their philosophy of the future, will lead the way. Right now, it's anyone's bet. But savvy marketers understand that the only thing they can count on is that lifestyles will continue to change.

TABLE 6–5

AN EXAMPLE OF AN IN LIST FOR 2004

IN	OUT
Live people answering a company's phone line	Press 1; Press 2; Press 3; Press 4. Enter your 15 digit personal number
Chicken soup	Pizza
Public relations	TV advertising
Wine	Wine coolers
Community living	Retirement homes
Fresh food	Preservatives
Water	Colas
Payroll cards	Paycheques

CHAPTER SUMMARY

A CONSUMER'S PERSONALITY INFLUENCES THE WAY HE OR SHE RESPONDS TO MARKETING STIMULI, BUT EFFORTS TO USE THIS INFORMATION IN MARKETING CONTEXTS HAVE MET WITH MIXED RESULTS.

- The concept of personality refers to a person's unique psychological makeup and how it consistently influences the way a person responds to his or her environment. Marketing strategies based on personality differences have met with mixed success, partly because of the way these differences in personality traits have been measured and applied to consumption contexts. Some approaches have attempted to understand underlying differences in small samples of consumers by employing techniques based on Freudian psychology and variations of this perspective, whereas others have tried to assess these dimensions more objectively using large samples and sophisticated quantitative techniques.

KNOWLEDGE OF CONSUMERS' LIFESTYLES IS KEY TO MANY MARKETING STRATEGIES.

- A consumer's lifestyle refers to the ways he or she chooses to spend time and money and how his or her values and tastes are reflected by consumption choices. Lifestyle research is useful for tracking societal consumption preferences and also for positioning specific products and services to different segments. Marketers segment by lifestyle differences, often by grouping consumers in terms of their AIOs (activities, interests, and opinions).

PSYCHOGRAPHICS GO BEYOND SIMPLE DEMOGRAPHICS IN HELPING MARKETERS UNDERSTAND AND REACH DIFFERENT CONSUMER SEGMENTS.

- Psychographic techniques attempt to classify consumers in terms of psychological, subjective variables in addition to observable characteristics (demographics). A variety of systems, such as VALS2, have been developed to identify consumer "types" and to differentiate them in terms of their brand or product preferences, media usage, leisure-time activities, and attitudes toward such broad issues as politics and religion.

IDENTIFYING PATTERNS OF CONSUMPTION CAN BE SUPERIOR TO KNOWLEDGE OF INDIVIDUAL PURCHASES WHEN CRAFTING A LIFESTYLE MARKETING STRATEGY.

- Interrelated sets of products and activities are associated with social roles to form consumption constellations. People often purchase a product or service because it is associated with a constellation that, in turn, is linked to a lifestyle they find desirable. A set of techniques called geodemography analyzes consumption patterns using geographical and demographic data, and identifies clusters of consumers who exhibit similar psychographic characteristics.

KEY TERMS

20/80 rule   p. 175

AIOs   p. 175

Allocentrics   p. 165

Animism   p. 167

Archetype   p. 162

Brand equity   p. 166

Brand personality   p. 166

Co-branding strategies   p. 171

Ego   p. 158

Geodemography   p. 179

Id   p. 158

Idiocentrics   p. 165

Lifestyle   p. 169

Motivational research   p. 160

Personality   p. 157

Pleasure principle   p. 158

Product complementarity   p. 172

Psychographics   p. 173

Superego   p. 158

Traits   p. 164

VALS2™   p. 178

REVIEW QUESTIONS

1. Describe the id, ego, and superego and tell how they work together according to Freudian theory.
2. What is motivational research? Give an example of a marketing study that used this approach.
3. Describe three personality traits relevant to marketers.
4. List three problems with applying trait theory to marketing contexts.
5. Define a brand personality and give two examples.
6. How does lifestyle differ from income?
7. What is the basic philosophy behind a lifestyle marketing strategy?
8. Define psychographics, and describe three ways marketers can use it.
9. What are three specific kinds of AIOs?

CONSUMER BEHAVIOUR CHALLENGE

Discuss

1. What consumption constellation might characterize you and your friends today?
2. Geodemographic techniques assume that people who live in the same neighbourhood have other things in common as well. Why do they make this assumption, and how accurate is it?
3. Single-source data systems give marketers access to a wide range of information about a consumer, just by knowing his or her address. Do you believe this "knowledge power" presents any ethical problems with regard to consumers' privacy? Should the government regulate access to such information? Should consumers have the right to limit access to these data?
4. Should organizations or individuals be allowed to create websites that advocate potentially harmful practices? Why or why not?

Experiential Exercises

5. Construct a brand personality inventory for three different brands within a product category. Ask a small number of consumers to rate each brand on about 10 different personality dimensions. What differences can you identify? Do these "personalities" relate to the advertising and packaging strategies used to differentiate these products?

6. Compile a set of recent ads that attempt to link consumption of a product with a specific lifestyle. How is this goal usually accomplished?
7. Psychographic analyses can be used to market politicians. Conduct research on the marketing strategies used in a recent major election. How were voters segmented in terms of values? Can you find evidence that communications strategies were guided by this information?
8. Construct separate advertising executions for a cosmetics product targeted to the Belonger, Achiever, Experiencer, and Maker VALS2 types. How would the basic appeal differ for each group?
9. Using media targeted to the group, construct a consumption constellation for the social role of university students. What set of products, activities, and interests tend to appear in advertisements depicting "typical" university students? How realistic is this constellation?
10. Extreme sports. Day trading. Chat rooms. Vegetarianism. Can you predict what will be "hot" in the near future? Identify a lifestyle trend that is just surfacing in your universe. Describe this trend in detail, and justify your prediction. What specific styles and/or products are part of this trend?

CBC ⬤ VIDEO VIGNETTE

CONCEPTS AT WORK FOR BRAND PERSONALITY

There are very few Canadians whose lifestyles do not require the support of a motor vehicle—or two. However, vehicles are rarely chosen solely for the transportation function they provide. In fact, most buyers of motor vehicles ascribe attributes to their vehicle purchases that add up to a personality. This tendency among consumers is reinforced by car manufacturers that design features which exude specific traits that provide an advantageous market position. One such manufacturer is DaimlerChrysler.

Ralph Gilles is a Canadian with a passion for cars and a top car designer employed with DaimlerChrysler. His first success was a sedan model called the Chrysler 300. He then revitalized a station wagon called the Magnum. Gilles has a talent for designing "cool" features into cars that are recognized as dimensions of the cars' personalities. His ability to bring a brand to life attracts potential buyers and makes competitors nervous. As each redesigned model meets with market success, another challenge is presented for a personality makeover. Is there a limit to Gilles golden touch? Can he make a minivan sexy?

Questions

1. What role does brand personality play in building brand equity?
2. What role does brand personality play in the positioning of a brand?
3. Describe the brand personality of the Chrysler 300 and the Magnum.
4. Are there limits on the extent to which personalities can be designed for brands?

Resource: "Motown Hit," *Venture #942*, CBC Air Date: March 20, 2005.

NOTES

1. See J. Aronoff and J.P. Wilson, *Personality in the Social Process* (Hillsdale, NJ: Erlbaum, 1985); Walter Mischel, *Personality and Assessment* (New York, NY: Wiley, 1968).

2. Ernest Dichter, *A Strategy of Desire* (Garden City, NY: Doubleday, 1960); Dichter, *The Handbook of Consumer Motivations* (New York, NY: McGraw-Hill, 1964); Jeffrey J. Durgee, "Interpreting Dichter's Interpretations: An Analysis of Consumption Symbolism in *The Handbook of Consumer Motivations*" (unpublished manuscript, Rensselaer Polytechnic Institute, Troy, NY, 1989); Pierre Martineau, *Motivation in Advertising* (New York, NY: McGraw-Hill, 1957).

3. Vance Packard, *The Hidden Persuaders* (New York, NY: D. McKay, 1957).

4. Harold Kassarjian, "Personality and Consumer Behavior: A Review," *Journal of Marketing Research* 8 (November 1971): 409–418.

5. Karen Horney, *Neurosis and Human Growth* (New York, NY: Norton, 1950).

6. Joel B. Cohen, "An Interpersonal Orientation to the Study of Consumer Behavior," *Journal of Marketing Research* 6 (August 1967): 270–278; Pradeep K. Tyagi, "Validation of the CAD Instrument: A Replication," in *Advances in Consumer Research* 10, eds. Richard P. Bagozzi and Alice M. Tybout (Ann Arbor, MI: Association for Consumer Research, 1983), 112–114.

7. For a comprehensive review of classic perspectives on personality theory, see Calvin S. Hall and Gardner Lindzey, *Theories of Personality*, 2nd ed. (New York, NY: John Wiley & Sons, Inc., 1970).

8. Cf. Carl G. Jung, "The Archetypes and the Collective Unconscious," in *Collected Works*, eds. H. Read, M. Fordham, and G. Adler (Princeton, NJ: Princeton University Press, 1959), vol. 9, pt. 1.

9. This material was contributed by Rebecca H. Holman, Senior Vice President and Director, Consumer Knowledge Structures, The Knowledge Group, Young & Rubicam Brands, July 2005.

10. Linda L. Price and Nancy Ridgway, "Development of a Scale to Measure Innovativeness," in *Advances in Consumer Research* 10, eds. Richard P. Bagozzi and Alice M. Tybout (Ann Arbor, MI: Association for Consumer Research, 1983), 679–684; Russell W. Belk, "Three Scales to Measure Constructs Related to Materialism: Reliability, Validity, and Relationships to Measures of Happiness," in *Advances in Consumer Research* 11, ed. Thomas C. Kinnear (Ann Arbor, MI: Association for Consumer Research, 1984), 291; Mark Snyder, "Self-Monitoring Processes," in *Advances in Experimental Social Psychology*, ed. Leonard Berkowitz (New York, NY: Academic Press, 1979), 851–928; Gordon R. Foxall and Ronald E. Goldsmith, "Personality and Consumer Research: Another Look," *Journal of the Market Research Society* 30, 2 (1988): 111–125; Ronald E. Goldsmith and Charles F. Hofacker, "Measuring Consumer Innovativeness," *Journal of the Academy of Marketing Science* 19, 3 (1991): 209–221; Curtis P. Haugtvedt, Richard E. Petty, and John T. Cacioppo, "Need for Cognition and Advertising: Understanding the Role of Personality Variables in Consumer Behavior," *Journal of Consumer Psychology* 1, 3 (1992): 239–260.

11. David Reisman, *The Lonely Crowd: A Study of the Changing American Character* (New Haven: Yale University Press, 1969).

12. Kelly Tepper Tian, William O. Bearden, and Gary L. Hunter, "Consumers' Need for Uniqueness: Scale Development and Validation," *Journal of Consumer Research* 28 (June 2001): 50–66.

13. Bennett Courtney, "Robotic Voices Designed to Manipulate," *Psychology Today* (January/February 2002): 20.

14. Mohan J. Dutta-Bergman and William D. Wells, "The Values and Lifestyles of Idiocentrics and Allocentrics in an Individualist Culture: A Descriptive Approach," *Journal of Consumer Psychology* 12, 3 (2002): 231–242.

15. Jacob Jacoby, *Personality and Consumer Behavior: How Not to Find Relationships*, Purdue Papers in Consumer Psychology, 102 (Lafayette, IN: Purdue University, 1969); Harold H. Kassarjian and Mary Jane Sheffet, "Personality and Consumer Behavior: An Update," in *Perspectives in Consumer Behavior*, 4th ed., eds. Harold H. Kassarjian and Thomas S. Robertson (Glenview, IL: Scott, Foresman and Company, 1991), 291–353; John Lastovicka and Erich Joachimsthaler, "Improving the Detection of Personality Behavior Relationships in Consumer Research," *Journal of Consumer Research* 14 (March 1988): 583–587. For an approach that ties the notion of personality more directly to marketing issues, see Jennifer L. Aaker, "Measuring Brand Personality" (unpublished manuscript, Stanford University, September 1994).

16. Cf. Girish N. Punj and David W. Stewart, "An Interaction Framework of Consumer Decision Making," *Journal of Consumer Research* 10 (September 1983): 181–196.

17. J.F. Allsopp, "The Distribution of On-Licence Beer and Cider Consumption and Its Personality Determinants among Young Men," *European Journal of Marketing* 20, 3 (1986): 44–62; Foxall and Goldsmith, "Personality and Consumer Research: Another Look."

18. Thomas Hine, "Why We Buy: The Silent Persuasion of Boxes, Bottles, Cans, and Tubes," *Worth* (May 1995): 78–83.

19. Stuart Elliott, "Thoroughly Modern Mr. Peanut," *New York Times on the Web* (March 19, 2004).

20. Kevin L. Keller, "Conceptualization, Measuring, and Managing Customer-Based Brand Equity," *Journal of Marketing* 57 (January 1993): 1–22.

21. Linda Keslar, "What's in a Name?" *Individual Investor* (April 1999): 101–102.

22. Rebecca Piirto Heath, "The Once and Future King," *Marketing Tools* (March 1998): 38–43.

23. Jennifer L. Aaker, "Dimensions of Brand Personality," *Journal of Marketing Research* 34, 3 (August 1997): 347–356.

24. Quoted in Bradley Johnson, "They All Have Half-Baked Ideas," *Advertising Age* (May 12, 1997): 8.

25. Tim Triplett, "Brand Personality must Be Managed or It will Assume a Life of Its Own," *Marketing News* (May 9, 1994): 9.

26. Susan Fournier, "A Consumer-Brand Relationship Framework for Strategic Brand Management," Doctoral Dissertation, Department of Marketing, University of Florida, 1994.

27. Rebecca Piirto Heath, "The Frontiers of Psychographics," *American Demographics* (July 1996): 38–43.

28. Quoted in Gabriel Kahn, "Philips Blitzes Asian Market as It Strives to Become Hip," *Wall Street Journal Online* (August 1, 2002).

29. Erin White, "Volvo Sheds Safe Image for New, Dangerous Ads," *Wall Street Journal Online* (June 14, 2002).

30. Benjamin D. Zablocki and Rosabeth Moss Kanter, "The Differentiation of Life-Styles," *Annual Review of Sociology* (1976): 269–297.

31. Mary Twe Douglas and Baron C. Isherwood, *The World of Goods* (New York, NY: Basic Books, 1979).

32. Zablocki and Kanter, "The Differentiation of Life-Styles."

33. "The Niche's the Thing," *American Demographics* (February 2000): 22.

34. Richard A. Peterson, "Revitalizing the Culture Concept," *Annual Review of Sociology* 5 (1979): 137–166.

35. William Leiss, Stephen Kline, and Sut Jhally, *Social Communication in Advertising* (Toronto, ON: Methuen, 1986).

36. Brian Steinberg and Chad Terhune, "Cola Rivals' Over-the-Top Ads Yield to Down-to-Earth Spots. Coke Showcases Celebrities in Pedestrian Situations; Pepsi Stresses Daily Grind," *Wall Street Journal Interactive Edition* (November 7, 2003).

37. Douglas and Isherwood, *The World of Goods*, 72–73.

38. Christopher K. Hsee and France Leclerc, "Will Products Look more Attractive when Presented Separately or Together?" *Journal of Consumer Research* 25 (September 1998): 175–186.

39. Christina Binkley, "Fairmont and Porsche Team Up in Luxury Cross-Marketing Deal," *Wall Street Journal Online* (October 8, 2002).

40. Karen J. Banyan, "Bally, Unilever and Free Product Add Up to a Sampling Campaign," *New York Times on the Web* (April 23, 2002).

41. Cara Beardi, "Photo Op: Nike, Polaroid Pair Up for Footwear Line," *Advertising Age* (April 2, 2001): 8.

42. Michael R. Solomon, "The Role of Products as Social Stimuli: A Symbolic Interactionism Perspective," *Journal of Consumer Research* 10 (December 1983): 319–329.

43. Michael R. Solomon and Henry Assael, "The Forest or the Trees?: A Gestalt Approach to Symbolic Consumption," in *Marketing and Semiotics: New Directions in the Study of Signs for Sale,* ed. Jean Umiker-Sebeok (Berlin: Mouton de Gruyter, 1988) 189–218; Michael R. Solomon, "Mapping Product Constellations: A Social Categorization Approach to Symbolic Consumption," *Psychology & Marketing* 5, 3 (1988): 233–258. See also Stephen C. Cosmas, "Life Styles and Consumption Patterns," *Journal of Consumer Research* 8, 4 (March 1982): 453–455.

44. Russell W. Belk, "Yuppies as Arbiters of the Emerging Consumption Style," in *Advances in Consumer Research* 13, ed. Richard J. Lutz (Provo, UT: Association for Consumer Research, 1986): 514–519.

45. Danny Hakim, "Cadillac, Too Shifting Focus to Trucks," *New York Times on the Web* (December 21, 2001).

46. See Lewis Alpert and Ronald Gatty, "Product Positioning by Behavioral Life Styles," *Journal of Marketing* 33 (April 1969): 65–69; Emanuel H. Demby, "Psychographics Revisited: The Birth of a Technique," *Marketing News* (January 2, 1989): 21; William D. Wells, "Backward Segmentation," in *Insights into Consumer Behavior,* ed. Johan Arndt (Boston, MA: Allyn & Bacon, 1968), 85–100.

47. Gary McWilliams, "Analyzing Customers, Best Buy Decides Not All Are Welcome. Retailer Aims to Outsmart Dogged Bargain-Hunters, and Coddle Big Spenders Looking for 'Barrys' and 'Jills,'" *Wall Street Journal* (November 8, 2004): A1; Joshua Freed, "Best Buy Stores Adapting to Help Customers They Serve," *Montgomery Advertiser* (May 23, 2004): 31.

48. Brian Wansink and S. Park, "Accounting for Taste: Prototypes that Predict Preference," *Journal of Database Marketing* (2000): 308–320, as described in *Asking Questions*, eds. Norman Bradburn, Seymour Sudman, and Brian Wansink (New York: Jossey-Bass, 2004).

49. Seth Stevenson, "How to Beat Nike," *New York Times on the Web* (January 5, 2003).

50. William D. Wells and Douglas J. Tigert, "Activities, Interests, and Opinions," *Journal of Advertising Research* 11 (August 1971): 27.

51. Ian Pearson, "Social Studies: Psychographics in Advertising," *Canadian Business* (December 1985): 67.

52. Rebecca Piirto Heath, "Psychographics: Q'est-ce que c'est?" *Marketing Tools* (November/December 1995): 73, 6.

53. Alfred S. Boote, "Psychographics: Mind over Matter," *American Demographics* (April 1980): 26–29; William D. Wells, "Psychographics: A Critical Review," *Journal of Marketing Research* 12 (May 1975): 196–213.

54. Joseph T. Plummer, "The Concept and Application of Life Style Segmentation," *Journal of Marketing* 38 (January 1974): 33–37.

55. John L. Lastovicka et al., "A Lifestyle Typology to Model Young Male Drinking and Driving," *Journal of Consumer Research* 14 (September 1987): 257–263.

56. Martha Farnsworth Riche, "VALS 2," *American Demographics* (July 1989): 25.

57. "Let Your Fingers Do the Trend Forecasting," *Time* (June 1, 1998): 24.

58. Eve Lazarus, "Main Street Malls," *Marketing Magazine* (April 3, 2006): 181–182.

It's Saturday night, and Babak, Felix, and Joshua are out on the town. When the bartender comes to take their drink orders, Babak immediately orders his standard: a dry Grey Goose martini, straight up, with a twist. Babak takes his vodka seriously. He's tried them all, and nothing will do but Grey Goose.

Felix, on the other hand, is indecisive. He doesn't drink often, and he can't really tell one concoction from another. Finally he says, "Oh, I don't care. I guess a Heineken will be fine."

Joshua shrugs and says, "Looks like it's going to be Coke for me. I'm the designated driver tonight." Dave the bartender is impressed. "Now that's a nice change for you guys. I guess all the publicity about drunk driving finally got to you." Joshua replies, "Hey, things are different these days! People know they can't party without facing the consequences."

When the drinks are served, Babak and Felix settle back and enjoy their beverages. Joshua eyes their glasses as he munches some popcorn and drinks his Coke. *These two owe me big time*, he thinks, anticipating next Saturday night.

CHAPTER → 7

Attitudes

THE POWER OF ATTITUDES

The term *attitude* is widely used in popular culture. You might be asked, "What is your attitude toward abortion?" A parent might scold, "Young man, I don't like your attitude." Some bars even euphemistically refer to happy hour as "an attitude adjustment period."

For our purposes, an **attitude** is a lasting, general evaluation of people (including oneself), objects, or issues.[1] Anything toward which a person has an attitude, whether it is tangible, such as a brand of vodka, or intangible, such as drunk driving, is called an **attitude object (A_o)**. An attitude is *lasting* because it tends to endure over time. It is *general* because it applies to more than a momentary event, like hearing a loud noise (though you might over time develop a negative attitude toward all loud noises). Consumers have attitudes toward very product-specific behaviours (like using Crest toothpaste rather than Colgate), as well as toward more general consumption-related behaviours (how often they should brush their teeth). Attitudes help to determine whom a person chooses to date, what music he or she listens to, whether he or she will recycle or discard aluminum cans, and whether he or she chooses to become a consumer researcher for a living.

This chapter will consider the contents of an attitude, how attitudes are formed, and how they can be measured, and will review some of the surprisingly complex relationships between attitudes and behaviour. In the next chapter we'll take a closer look at how attitudes can be changed—certainly an issue of prime importance to marketers.

The Functions of Attitudes

The **functional theory of attitudes** was initially developed by psychologist Daniel Katz to explain how attitudes facilitate social behaviour.[2] According to this pragmatic approach, attitudes exist *because* they serve some function for the person; that is, they are determined by a person's motives. Consumers who expect that they will need to deal with similar information at a future time will be more likely to start forming attitudes in anticipation of this event.[3]

Two people can each have the same attitude toward some object for very different reasons. As a result, it can be helpful for a marketer to know *why* an attitude is held before attempting to change it. The following are attitude functions as identified by Katz:

- *Utilitarian function:* The utilitarian function is related to the basic principles of reward and punishment. We develop some of our attitudes toward products simply on the basis of whether these products provide pleasure or pain. If a person likes the taste of a cheeseburger, that person will develop a positive attitude toward cheeseburgers. Ads that stress straightforward product benefits (e.g., you should drink Diet Coke "just for the taste of it") appeal to the utilitarian function.

- *Value-expressive function:* Attitudes that perform a value-expressive function express the consumer's central values or self-concept. A person forms a product attitude not because of its objective benefits, but because of what the product says about him or her as a person ("What sort of man reads *Playboy*?"). Value-expressive attitudes are highly relevant to lifestyle analyses, where consumers cultivate a cluster of activities, interests, and opinions to express a particular social identity.

- *Ego-defensive function:* Attitudes that are formed to protect the person, either from external threats or internal feelings, perform an ego-defensive function. Products that promise to help a man project a "macho" image (such as Marlboro cigarettes) may be appealing to his insecurities about his masculinity. Another example of this function is deodorant campaigns that stress the dire, embarrassing consequences of being caught with underarm odour in public.

- *Knowledge function:* Some attitudes are formed as the result of a need for order, structure, or meaning. This need is often present when a person is in an ambiguous situation or is confronted with a new product ("Bayer wants you to know about pain relievers").

An attitude can serve more than one function, but in many cases a particular one will be dominant. By identifying the dominant function a product serves for consumers (what *benefits* it provides), marketers can emphasize these benefits in their communications and packaging. Ads relevant to the function prompt more favourable thoughts about what is being marketed and can result in a heightened preference for both the ad and the product.

The importance of an attitude object may differ quite a bit for different people. Understanding the attitude's importance to an individual and to others who share similar characteristics can be useful to marketers who are trying to devise strategies that will appeal to different customer segments. A study of football game attendance illustrates that varying levels of commitment result in different fan "profiles."[4] The study identified three distinct clusters of fans:[5]

- One cluster consisted of the real diehard fans who were highly committed to their team and who displayed an enduring love of the game. To reach these fans, the researchers recommend that sports marketers should focus on providing them with greater sports knowledge and relate their attendance to their personal goals and values.

- A second cluster reflected attitudes based on the unique, self-expressive experience provided by the game. They enjoy the stimulation of cheering for a team and the drama of the competition itself. They are more likely to be "brand switchers" who are fair-weather fans, shifting allegiances when the home team no longer provides the thrills they need. This segment can be appealed to by publicizing aspects of the visiting teams, such as advertising the appearance of stars who are likely to give the fans a game they will remember.

- A third cluster were looking for camaraderie above all. These consumers attend games primarily to take part in small group activities such as pre- or post-game parties that accompanied the event. Marketers could appeal to this cluster by providing improved peripheral benefits, such as making it easier for groups to meet at the stadium, improving parking, and offering multiple-unit pricing.

The ABC Model of Attitudes and Hierarchies of Effects

Most researchers agree that an attitude has three components: affect, behaviour, and cognition. **Affect** refers to the way a consumer *feels* about an attitude object. **Behaviour** involves the person's intentions to do something with regard to an attitude object (but, as will be discussed at a later point, an intention does not always result in an actual behaviour). **Cognition** refers to the *beliefs* a consumer has about an attitude object. These three components of an attitude can be remembered as the *ABC model of attitudes*.

This model emphasizes the interrelationships among knowing, feeling, and doing. Consumers' attitudes toward a product cannot be determined simply by identifying their beliefs about it. For example, a researcher may find that shoppers "know" a particular camcorder has an 8:1 power zoom lens, auto-focus, and a flying erase head, but such findings do not indicate whether they feel these attributes are good, bad, or irrelevant, or whether they would actually buy the camcorder.

HIERARCHIES OF EFFECTS

Although all three components of an attitude are important, their relative importance will vary depending upon a consumer's level of motivation with regard to the attitude object. The differences in drink choices among the three friends at the bar illustrate how these elements can be combined in different ways to create attitudes. Attitude researchers have developed the concept of a **hierarchy of effects** to explain the relative impact of the three components. Each hierarchy specifies that a fixed sequence of steps occurs en route to an attitude. Three different hierarchies are summarized in Figure 7–1.

THE HIGH-INVOLVEMENT HIERARCHY

Babak's choice of a favourite drink closely resembles the process by which most attitudes have been assumed to be constructed. A consumer approaches a product decision as a problem-solving process. First, he or she forms beliefs about a product by accumulating knowledge (beliefs) regarding relevant attributes. Next, the consumer evaluates these beliefs and forms a feeling about the product (affect). Over time, Babak integrated information about alternative vodka brands and formed a preference for one kind. Finally, based on this evaluation, the consumer engages in a relevant behaviour, such as buying the product.

This careful choice process often results in the type of brand loyalty displayed by Babak. The consumer "bonds" with the product over time and is not easily persuaded to experiment with other brands. The standard learning hierarchy assumes

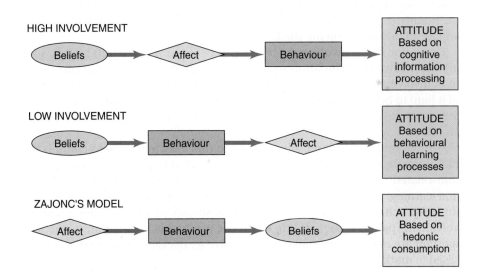

FIGURE 7–1

THREE HIERARCHIES OF EFFECTS

HIGH INVOLVEMENT

Beliefs → Affect → Behaviour → ATTITUDE Based on cognitive information processing

LOW INVOLVEMENT

Beliefs → Behaviour → Affect → ATTITUDE Based on behavioural learning processes

ZAJONC'S MODEL

Affect → Behaviour → Beliefs → ATTITUDE Based on hedonic consumption

→ This advertisement encourages a positive attitude toward safe sex.
Elevator Strategy Advertising and Design and British Columbia Centre for Disease Control

that a consumer is highly involved in making a purchase decision.[6] The person is motivated to seek out a lot of information, carefully weigh alternatives, and come to a thoughtful decision.

THE LOW-INVOLVEMENT HIERARCHY

In sharp contrast to Babak, Felix's interest in the attitude object (a particular brand of alcoholic beverage) is at best lukewarm. He has collected only a minimal amount of information before acting and has an emotional response only after consuming the beverage. Felix is typical of a consumer who forms an attitude via the *low-involvement hierarchy of effects*. In this sequence, the consumer initially does not have a strong preference for one brand over another; he or she instead acts on the basis of limited knowledge and then forms an evaluation only after the fact.[7] The attitude is likely to come about through behavioural learning, where the consumer's choice is reinforced by good or bad experiences with the product after purchase.

The possibility that consumers simply don't care enough about many decisions to carefully assemble a set of product beliefs and then evaluate them is important, because it implies that all the concern about influencing beliefs and carefully communicating information about product attributes may be largely wasted. Consumers aren't necessarily going to pay attention anyway; they are more likely to respond to simple stimulus-response connections when making purchase decisions. For example, a consumer choosing among paper towels might remember that "Bounty is the quicker picker-upper" rather than bothering systematically to compare all the brands on the shelf.

The notion of low involvement on the part of consumers is a bitter pill for some marketers to swallow. Who wants to admit that what they market is not very important or involving? A brand manager for, say, a brand of bubble gum or cat food may find it hard to believe that consumers don't put that much thought into purchasing a product or spend many of their waking (and perhaps sleeping) hours thinking about it.

For marketers, the ironic silver lining to this low-involvement cloud is that under these conditions consumers are not motivated to process a lot of complex brand-related information. Instead, they will be swayed by principles of behavioural learning, such as the simple responses caused by conditioned brand names, point-of-purchase displays, and so on. This results in what we might call the involvement paradox: the *less* important the product is to consumers, the *more* important are many of the marketing stimuli (e.g., packages, jingles) that must be devised to market it.

ZAJONC'S MODEL OF HEDONIC CONSUMPTION

Researchers in recent years have begun to stress the significance of emotional response as a central aspect of an attitude. According to the *experiential hierarchy of effects,* consumers act on the basis of their emotional reactions. This perspective highlights the idea that attitudes can be strongly influenced by product attributes irrelevant to the actual product quality, such as package design and colour, and by consumers' reactions toward accompanying stimuli, such as advertising and even the brand name. As discussed in Chapter 4, resulting attitudes will be affected by consumers' hedonic motivations, such as how the product makes them feel or how much fun it will provide.

Even the emotions expressed by the communicator have an impact. A smile is infectious; in a process termed *emotional contagion,* messages delivered by happy people enhance our attitude toward the product.[8] Numerous studies indicate that the mood a person is in when exposed to a marketing message influences how the ad is processed, the likelihood that the information presented will be remembered, and how the person will feel about the advertised item and related products in the future.[9]

One important debate about the experiential hierarchy concerns the *independence* of cognition and affect. On the one hand, the *cognitive-affective model* argues that an affective judgment is but the last step in a series of cognitive processes. Earlier steps include the sensory registration of stimuli and the retrieval of meaningful information from memory to categorize these stimuli.[10]

On the other hand, the *independence hypothesis* takes the position that affect and cognition involve two separate, partially independent systems; affective responses do not always require prior cognitions.[11] A number-one song on the *Billboard* "Top 40" may possess the same attributes as many other songs (dominant bass guitar, raspy vocals, persistent downbeat), but beliefs about these attributes cannot explain why one song becomes a classic while another sharing the same characteristics winds up in the bargain bin at the local music store. The independence hypothesis does not *eliminate* the role of cognition in experience; it simply balances this traditional, rational emphasis on calculated decision making by paying more attention to the impact of aesthetic, subjective experience. This type of holistic processing is more likely to occur when the product is perceived as primarily expressive or when it delivers sensory pleasure rather than utilitarian benefits.[12]

Product Attitudes Don't Tell the Whole Story

Marketers who are concerned with understanding consumers' attitudes have to contend with an even more complex issue: In decision-making situations, people form attitudes toward objects other than the product itself that can influence their ultimate selections. One additional factor to consider is *attitudes toward the act of buying* in general. As we'll see later in this chapter, sometimes people are reluctant, embarrassed, or just plain too lazy to expend the effort to obtain a desired product or service.

ATTITUDE TOWARD THE ADVERTISEMENT

In addition, consumers' reactions to a product, over and above their feelings about the product itself, are influenced by their evaluations of its advertising. Our evaluation of a product can be determined solely by our appraisal of how it's depicted in marketing communications; that is, we don't hesitate to form attitudes toward products we've never even seen in person, much less used.

One special type of attitude object, then, is the marketing message itself. The **attitude toward the advertisement (A_{ad})** is defined as a predisposition to respond in a favourable or unfavourable manner to a particular advertising stimulus during a particular exposure occasion. Determinants of A_{ad} include the viewer's attitude toward the advertiser, evaluations of the ad execution itself, the

Net Profit

The recognition that emotional responses play a key role in product attitudes has sparked renewed interest in developing high-tech approaches to measuring and manipulating emotional responses. Traditionally, these reactions have been measured in terms of physiological arousal, but the problem with this approach is that it is hard to interpret the results because arousal can be either positive or negative.[13] Several companies are marketing more finely tuned alternatives that track specific responses.

IBM developed a new gadget called the emotion mouse (*www.almaden.ibm.com/cs/blueeyes*). It tracks the user's skin temperature, heart rate, and even very tiny hand movements, along with the electrical conductivity of the skin, which changes with moisture. The computer tries to determine the emotional state of the user in this new field of affective computing. The computer might be able to adjust its interface to reduce frustration, sense when an employee may be burning out, automatically boost computer-game action, or search automatically for television shows based on a user's personal feelings of what is funny. These devices are likely to find their way into other objects, such as car steering wheels that could sense when a driver is getting drowsy, and key chains that tell police if the user seems unusually frightened. Teachers offering lectures over the internet may be able to judge the reactions of their faceless students or even replay parts of lectures where students' minds had wandered.

mood evoked by the ad, and the degree to which the ad affects viewers' arousal levels.[14] A viewer's feelings about the context in which an ad appears can also influence brand attitudes. For example, attitudes about an ad and the brand depicted will be influenced if the consumer sees the ad while watching a favourite TV program.[15] The effects demonstrated by A_{ad} emphasize the importance of an ad's entertainment value in the purchase process.[16] If consumers are not able to view an ad again, both belief in and attitude confidence about that ad rapidly diminish. This research supports marketer's efforts to pulse or frequently repeat advertisements in the media.[17]

ADS HAVE FEELINGS TOO

The feelings generated by advertising have the capacity to directly affect brand attitudes. Commercials can evoke a wide range of emotional responses, from disgust to happiness. These feelings can be influenced both by the way the ad is done (the specific advertising *execution*) and by the consumer's reactions to the advertiser's motives. For example, many advertisers who are trying to craft messages for adolescents and young adults are encountering problems because this age group, having grown up in a "marketing society," tend to be sceptical about attempts to get them to buy things.[18] These reactions can, in turn, influence memory for advertising content.[19] At least three emotional dimensions have been identified in commercials: pleasure, arousal, and intimidation.[20] Specific types of feelings that can be generated by an ad include the following:[21]

- *upbeat feelings*—amused, delighted, playful
- *warm feelings*—affectionate, contemplative, hopeful
- *negative feelings*—critical, defiant, offended

FORMING ATTITUDES

We all have lots of attitudes, and we don't usually question how we got them. Certainly a person isn't born with the conviction that, say, Pepsi is better than Coke, or that heavy-metal music liberates the soul. Where do these attitudes come from?

An attitude can form in several different ways, depending upon the particular hierarchy of effects in operation. It can occur because of *classical conditioning,*

→ This ad for EggStro'dnaire, an egg substitute, illustrates that ads are capable of communicating negative feelings.
Courtesy of Food Service Division, Sandoz Nutrition, Minneapolis, MN 55416.

wherein an attitude object, such as the Pepsi name, is repeatedly paired with a catchy jingle ("You're in the Pepsi Generation …"). Or it can be formed through *instrumental conditioning,* in which consumption of the attitude object is reinforced (e.g., "Pepsi quenches one's thirst"). Or the learning of an attitude can be the outcome of a very complex cognitive process. For example, a teenager may come to model the behaviour of friends and media figures who drink Pepsi because she believes that this act will allow her to fit in with the desirable images of the Pepsi Generation.

Not All Attitudes Are Created Equal

It is important to distinguish among types of attitudes, since not all are formed the same way.[23] For example, a highly brand-loyal consumer like Babak, the Grey Goose drinker, has an enduring, deeply held positive attitude toward an attitude object, and this involvement will be difficult to weaken. On the other hand, another consumer like Felix, the occasional beer drinker, may be less brand loyal; he may have a mildly positive attitude toward a product but be quite willing to abandon it when something better comes along. This section will consider the differences between strongly and weakly held attitudes and briefly review some of the major theoretical perspectives that have been developed to explain how attitudes form and relate to one another in the minds of consumers.

Levels of Commitment to an Attitude

Consumers vary in their *commitment* to an attitude. The degree of commitment is related to their level of involvement with the attitude object, as follows.[24]

- *Compliance:* At the lowest level of involvement, compliance, an attitude is formed because it helps gain rewards or avoid punishments from others. This attitude is very superficial; it is likely to change when the person's behaviour is no longer monitored by others or when another option becomes available. A person may drink Pepsi because this brand is sold in the cafeteria and it is too much trouble to go elsewhere for a Coca-Cola.

- *Identification:* A process of identification occurs when attitudes are formed so that the consumer will then feel similar to another person or group. Advertising that depicts the social consequences of choosing some products over others is relying on the tendency of consumers to imitate the behaviour of desirable models.

- *Internalization:* At a high level of involvement, deep-seated attitudes are internalized and become part of the person's value system. These attitudes are very difficult to change because they are so important to the individual. For example, many consumers had strong attitudes toward Coca-Cola and reacted quite negatively when the company attempted to switch to the New Coke formula. This allegiance to Coke was obviously more than a minor preference for these people; the brand had become intertwined with their social identities, taking on nostalgic properties.

The Consistency Principle

Have you ever heard someone say, "Pepsi is my favourite soft drink. It tastes terrible," or "I love my husband. He's the biggest idiot I've ever met"? Probably you have not heard these statements too often because these beliefs or evaluations are not consistent with one another. According to the **principle of cognitive consistency**, consumers value *harmony* among their thoughts, feelings, and behaviours, and they are motivated to maintain uniformity among these elements. This desire means that, if necessary, consumers will *change* their thoughts, feelings,

→ This ad for *Woman's Day* attempts to counter the role consistency plays in shaping attitudes: Consumers often distort information so that it fits with what they already know or believe.
Courtesy of Woman's Day (Hachette Magazines Inc.).

or behaviours to make them consistent with their other experiences. The consistency principle is an important reminder that attitudes are not formed in a vacuum. A significant determinant of the way an attitude object will be evaluated is how it fits with other, related attitudes already held by the consumer.

COGNITIVE DISSONANCE AND HARMONY AMONG ATTITUDES

The **theory of cognitive dissonance** states that, when a person is confronted with inconsistencies among attitudes or behaviours, he or she will take some action to resolve this "dissonance," perhaps by changing an attitude or modifying behaviour.[25] The theory also has other important ramifications for attitudes, since people often are confronted by situations in which there is some conflict between their attitudes and behaviours.[26]

The theory proposes that people are *motivated* to reduce the negative feelings caused by dissonance by making things fit with one another. The theory focuses on situations where two *cognitive elements* are inconsistent with one another.

A cognitive element can be something people believe about themselves, behaviours they perform, or observations about their surroundings. For example, the two cognitive elements "I know smoking cigarettes causes cancer" and "I smoke cigarettes" are *dissonant* with one another. This psychological inconsistency creates a feeling of discomfort that the smoker is motivated to reduce. The magnitude of dissonance depends upon both the importance and the number of dissonant elements.[27] In other words, the pressure to reduce dissonance is more likely to be observed in high-involvement situations, in which the elements are more important to the individual.

Dissonance reduction can occur by either eliminating, adding, or changing elements. For example, the person could stop smoking (eliminate) or remember great-aunt Sophie, who smoked until the day she died at age 90 (add).

Dissonance theory can help to explain why evaluations of a product tend to increase *after* it has been purchased (i.e., postpurchase dissonance). The cognitive element "I made a stupid decision" is dissonant with the element "I am not a stupid person," so people tend to find even more reasons to like something after it becomes theirs.

A field study performed at a horse race demonstrates postpurchase dissonance. Bettors evaluated their chosen horses more highly and were more confident of their success *after* they had placed a bet than before. Since the bettor is financially committed to the choice, he or she reduces dissonance by increasing the attractiveness of the chosen alternative relative to the unchosen ones.[28] One implication of this phenomenon is that consumers actively seek support for their purchase decisions, so marketers should supply them with additional reinforcement in order to build positive brand attitudes.

SELF-PERCEPTION THEORY

Do attitudes necessarily change following behaviour because people are motivated to feel good about their decisions? **Self-perception theory** provides an alternative explanation of dissonance effects.[29] It assumes that people use observations of their own behaviour to determine what their attitudes are, just as we assume that we know the attitudes of others by watching what they do. The theory states that we maintain consistency by *inferring* that we must have a positive attitude toward an object if we have bought or consumed it (assuming that we freely made this choice). Thus, Babak might say to himself, "I guess I must like this brand of vodka; I seem to order it a lot."

Self-perception theory is relevant to the *low-involvement hierarchy,* since it involves situations in which behaviours are initially performed in the absence of a strong internal attitude. After the fact, the cognitive and affective components of attitude fall into line. Thus, buying a product out of habit may result in a positive attitude toward it *after the fact*—namely, why would I buy it if I didn't like it?

Self-perception theory helps to explain the effectiveness of a sales strategy called the **foot-in-the-door technique**, which is based on the observation that a consumer is more likely to comply with a request if he or she has first agreed to comply with a smaller request.[30] The name for this technique comes from the practice of door-to-door selling, wherein a salesperson was taught to plant his or her foot in a door so that the prospect could not slam it shut. A good salesperson knows that he or she is more likely to get an order if the customer can be persuaded to open the door and talk. By agreeing to do so, the customer has established a willingness to listen to the salesperson. Placing an order is consistent with this self-perception. This technique is especially useful for inducing consumers to answer surveys or to donate money to charity. Such factors as the time lag between the first and second requests, the similarity between the two requests, and whether the same person makes both requests have been found to influence the effectiveness of this technique.[31]

Other variations on this strategy include the *low-ball technique,* in which a person is asked for a small favour and is informed after agreeing to it that it will be very costly; or the *door-in-the-face technique,* in which a person is first asked to do something extreme (a request that is usually refused) and then is asked to do something smaller. In each of these cases, people tend to go along with the smaller request, possibly because they feel guilty about denying the larger one.[32]

SOCIAL JUDGMENT THEORY

Social judgment theory also assumes that people assimilate new information about attitude objects in the light of what they already know or feel.[33] The initial attitude acts as a *frame of reference,* and new information is categorized in terms of this existing standard. Just as our decision that a box is heavy depends in part on other boxes we have lifted, we develop a subjective standard when making judgments about attitude objects.

One important aspect of the theory is the notion that people differ in terms of the information they will find acceptable or unacceptable. They form **latitudes of acceptance and rejection** around an attitude standard. Ideas that fall within a latitude will be favourably received, while those falling outside this zone will not. Since Joshua had a favourable attitude toward the use of designated drivers, he is likely to be receptive to communications urging him to play this role before heading out for an evening on the town. If he were opposed to this practice, these messages would probably not be considered.

Messages that fall within the latitude of acceptance tend to be seen as *more* consistent with our own position than they actually are. This process is called an *assimilation effect.* On the other hand, messages falling in the latitude of rejection tend to be seen as even *farther* from our own position than they actually are, resulting in a *contrast effect.*[34]

As a person becomes more involved with an attitude object, his or her latitude of acceptance gets smaller; in other words, the consumer accepts fewer ideas that are removed from his or her own position and tends to oppose even mildly divergent positions. This tendency is evident in ads that appeal to discriminating buyers, which claim that knowledgeable people will reject anything but the very best (e.g., "Choosy mothers choose Jif"). On the other hand, relatively uninvolved consumers will consider a wider range of alternatives. They are less likely to be brand loyal and more likely to be brand switchers.[35]

BALANCE THEORY

Balance theory considers relations among elements a person might perceive as belonging together.[36] This perspective involves relations (always from the perceiver's subjective point of view) among three elements, so the resulting attitude structures are called *triads*. Each triad contains (1) a person and his or her perceptions of (2) an attitude object and (3) some other person or object.

These perceptions can be either positive or negative. More importantly, people *alter* these perceptions to make relations among them consistent. The theory specifies that people desire relations among elements in a triad to be harmonious, or *balanced.* If they are not, a state of tension will result until somehow perceptions are changed and balance is restored.

Elements can be perceived as going together in one of two ways. They can have either a *unit relation,* where one element is seen as somehow belonging to or being a part of the other (something like a belief), or a *sentiment relation,* where the two elements are linked because one has expressed a preference (or dislike) for the other. A dating couple might be seen as having a positive sentiment relation. Upon getting married, they will have a positive unit relation. The process of divorce is an attempt to sever a unit relation.

To see how balance theory might work, consider the following scenario:

- Monica would like to date Jerry, who is in her consumer behaviour class. In balance theory terms, Monica has a positive sentiment relation with Jerry.

- One day Jerry shows up in class wearing an earring. Jerry has a positive unit relation with the earring. It belongs to him and is literally a part of him.

- Monica does not like men who wear earrings. She has a negative sentiment relation with men's earrings.

According to balance theory, Monica faces an unbalanced triad, and she will experience pressure to restore balance by altering some aspect of the triad, as shown in Figure 7–2. She could, for example, decide that she does not like Jerry after all. Or her liking for Jerry could prompt a change in her attitude toward earrings. She might even try to negate the unit relation between Jerry and the earring by deciding that he must be wearing it only as part of an initiation (thus reducing the free-choice element). Finally, she could choose to "leave the field" by not thinking any more about Jerry and his controversial earring.

Note that although the theory does not specify which of these routes will be taken, it does predict that one or more of Monica's perceptions will probably change in order to achieve balance. Although this distortion is most likely an oversimplified representation of most attitude processes, it helps to explain a number of consumer behaviour phenomena.

MARKETING APPLICATIONS OF BALANCE THEORY Balance theory reminds us that, when perceptions are balanced, attitudes are likely to be stable. On the other hand,

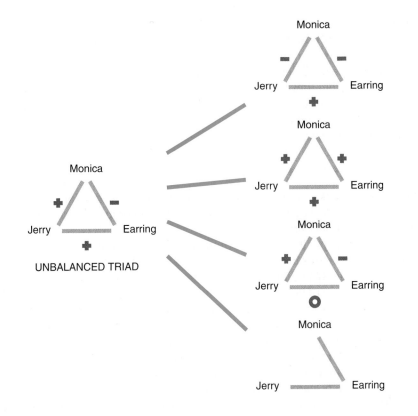

FIGURE 7–2

ALTERNATIVE ROUTES TO
RESTORING BALANCE IN A TRIAD

when inconsistencies are observed, we are more likely to observe changes in attitudes. Balance theory also helps to explain why consumers like to be associated with positively valued objects. Forming a unit relation with a popular product (buying and wearing fashionable clothing or driving a flashy car) may improve one's chances of being included as a positive sentiment relation in other people's triads.

Finally, balance theory is useful in accounting for the widespread use of celebrities to endorse products. In cases where a triad is not fully formed (e.g., one involving perceptions about a new product or one about which the consumer does not yet have a well-defined attitude), the marketer can create a positive sentiment relation between the consumer and the product by depicting a positive unit relation between the product and a well-known personality. In other cases, behaviours are discouraged when admired people argue against them, as is the goal when athletes appear in public-service advertisements against drinking and driving.

This "balancing act" is at the heart of celebrity endorsements, in which it is hoped that the star's popularity will transfer to the product. This strategy will be considered at length in the next chapter. For now, it pays to remember that this creation of a unit relation between product and star can backfire if the public's opinion of the celebrity endorser shifts from positive to negative, as happened when Madonna was associated with a controversial music video involving religion and sex: Pepsi pulled an ad featuring her. The strategy can also cause trouble if the star–product unit relation is questioned, as happened when singer Michael Jackson, who also did promotions for Pepsi, subsequently confessed that he does not drink soft drinks.

ATTITUDE MODELS

A consumer's overall evaluation of a product sometimes accounts for most of his or her attitude toward it. When market researchers want to assess attitudes, it can often be sufficient for them simply to ask consumers, "How do you feel about Labatt Blue?" (see *www.labatt.com*).

However, as we saw earlier, attitudes can be a lot more complex than that. One problem is that a product or service may comprise many *attributes,* or qualities, some of which may be more important than others to particular people. Another problem is that people's decisions to act on their attitudes are affected by other factors, such as whether they feel that buying a product would be met with approval by friends or family. For these reasons, *attitude models* have been developed that try to specify the different elements that might work together to influence people's evaluations of attitude objects.

Multi-Attribute Attitude Models

A simple response does not always tell us everything we need to know about either *why* the consumer feels a certain way toward a product or *what* marketers can do to change the consumer's attitude.

Beliefs about specific brand attributes can be pivotal for a product. Warner-Lambert discovered this in research it did for its Fresh Burst Listerine mouthwash. A research firm paid 37 families to set up cameras in their bathrooms to watch their daily routines. Users of both Fresh Burst and rival Scope said they used mouthwash to make their breath smell good. But Scope users swished the liquid and then spit it out, while Listerine users kept the product in their mouths for a long time. (One user kept it in his mouth until he got in the car and finally spit it out in a sewer a block away!) These findings meant Listerine hadn't shaken its medicine-like image.[37]

For this reason, **multi-attribute attitude models** have been extremely popular among marketing researchers. This type of model assumes that a consumer's attitude (evaluation) of an attitude object (A_o) will depend on the beliefs he or she has about several or many attributes of the object. The use of a multi-attribute model implies that an attitude toward a product or brand can be predicted by identifying these specific beliefs and combining them to derive a measure of the consumer's overall attitude.

We'll describe here how these work, using the example of a consumer evaluating a complex attitude object that should be very familiar to you: a grocery store.

→ This interactive exhibit at the Discovery Museum in Paris is intended to create and explore different attitudes toward food choices.
Courtesy of Rosemary Polegato.

Basic multi-attribute models specify three elements:[38]

1. *Attributes* are characteristics of the A_o. Most models assume that the relevant characteristics can be identified; that is, the researcher can include those attributes that consumers take into consideration when evaluating the A_o. For example, degree of freshness of produce is an attribute of a grocery store.

2. *Beliefs* are cognitions about the specific A_o (usually relative to others similar to it). A belief measure assesses the extent to which the consumer perceives that a brand possesses a particular attribute. For example, a student might have a belief that Sobey's has the freshest produce.

3. *Importance weights* reflect the relative priority of an attribute to the consumer. Although an A_o can be considered on the basis of a number of attributes, some are likely to be more important than others (i.e., they will be given greater weight). And these weights are likely to differ across consumers. In the case of grocery stores, for example, one student might stress low prices while another might assign greater weight to fresh produce.

THE FISHBEIN MODEL

The most influential multi-attribute model is called the *Fishbein model,* named after its primary developer.[39] The model measures three components of attitude:

1. *salient beliefs* people have about an A_o (those beliefs about the object that are considered during evaluation)

2. *object-attribute linkages,* or the probability that a particular object has an important attribute

3. *evaluation* of each of the important attributes

Note, however, that the model makes some assumptions that may not always be warranted. It assumes that we have been able to specify adequately all the relevant attributes that, for example, a student will use in evaluating his or her choice about which university to attend. The model also assumes that he or she will go through the process (formally or informally) of identifying a set of relevant attributes, weighing them and summing them. Although this particular decision is likely to be highly involving, it is still possible that the student's attitude will instead be formed by an overall affective response (a process known as *affect-referral*).

By combining these three elements, a consumer's overall attitude toward an object can be computed. (We'll see later how this basic equation has been modified to increase its accuracy.) The basic formula is:

$$A_{ijk} = \Sigma B_{ijk} I_{ik}$$
where i = attribute
j = brand
k = consumer
I = the importance weight given attribute i by consumer k
B = consumer k's belief regarding the extent to which brand j possesses attribute i
A = a particular consumer k's attitude score for brand j

The overall attitude score (A) is obtained by multiplying a consumer's rating of each attribute for all of the brands considered by the importance rating for that attribute.

To see how this basic multi-attribute model might work, let's suppose we want to predict at which grocery store Narveen is likely to do his weekly shopping. He lives more or less equidistant from three different stores. To decide which one he will go to, he considers the attributes across all three stores and forms an attitude toward each store. We can ask Narveen to assign a rating regarding how well each store performs on each attribute and how important each attribute is to him. An overall attitude score for each store can then be computed by summing scores on each attribute (after weighting each by its relative importance). These hypothetical ratings are shown in Table 7–1.

TABLE 7–1				

THE BASIC MULTI-ATTRIBUTE MODEL: NARVEEN'S GROCERY STORE DECISION

Attribute (i)	Importance (I)	SAFEWAY	Beliefs (B) LOBLAWS	IGA
Low prices	5	2	3	4
Customer loyalty card	3	5	5	1
Free and accessible parking	4	4	3	4
In-store deli	5	5	5	3
Fresh produce	2	3	3	4
Attitude score		**72**	**73**	**62**

Note: These hypothetical ratings are scored from 1 to 5, and higher numbers indicate "better" standing on an attribute.

STRATEGIC APPLICATIONS OF THE MULTI-ATTRIBUTE MODEL

Suppose you were the director of marketing for IGA. How might you use the data from this analysis to improve your image?

CAPITALIZE ON RELATIVE ADVANTAGE   If one's brand is viewed as being superior on a particular attribute, consumers like Narveen need to be convinced that this particular attribute is an important one. For example, although Narveen rates fresh produce highly, he does not believe this attribute is a valued aspect for some grocery stores. As IGA's marketing director, you might emphasize the importance of fruits and vegetables in a healthy balanced diet.

STRENGTHEN PERCEIVED PRODUCT–ATTRIBUTE LINKS   A marketer may discover that consumers do not equate his or her brand with a certain attribute. This problem is commonly addressed by campaigns that stress the product's qualities to consumers (e.g., "new and improved"). Narveen apparently does not think much of IGA's deli. You might develop an information campaign to improve these perceptions (such as "little-known facts about IGA's Deli").

ADD A NEW ATTRIBUTE   Product marketers frequently try to create a position distinct from those of their competitors by adding a product feature. IGA might try to emphasize some unique aspect, such as a fax or internet order system for busy people who do not like to grocery shop.

INFLUENCE COMPETITORS' RATINGS   Finally, you might try to decrease the positivity of competitors. This type of action is the rationale for a strategy of *comparative advertising*. One tactic might be to publish an ad that lists the attributes on which IGA can be favourably compared, as the basis for emphasizing the value obtained for the money spent at IGA (***www.igainc.com***).

USING ATTITUDES TO PREDICT BEHAVIOUR

Although multi-attribute models have been used by consumer researchers for many years, they have been plagued by a major problem: In many cases, knowledge of a person's attitude is *not* a very good predictor of behaviour. In a classic demonstration of "Do as I say, not as I do," many studies have obtained a very low correlation between a person's reported attitude toward something and his or her actual behaviour toward it. Some researchers have been so discouraged that they have questioned whether attitudes are of any use at all in understanding behaviour.[40] This questionable link between attitudes and behaviour can be a big headache for advertisers in that consumers can love a commercial and yet still not buy the product.

The Extended Fishbein Model

The original Fishbein model, which focused on measuring a consumer's attitude toward a product, has been extended in several ways to improve its predictive ability. The newer version is called the **theory of reasoned action**.[41] This model contains several important additions to the original, and although the model is still not perfect, its ability to predict relevant behaviour has been improved.[42] Some of the modifications to this model are considered here.

INTENTIONS VERSUS BEHAVIOUR

Like the motivations discussed in Chapter 4, attitudes have both direction and strength. A person may like or dislike an attitude object with varying degrees of confidence or conviction.[43] It is helpful to distinguish between firmly held attitudes and those that are more superficial, especially since an attitude held with greater conviction makes it more likely that it will be acted upon. One study on environmental issues and marketing activities found, for example, that people who express greater conviction in their feelings regarding environmentally responsible behaviours like recycling show greater consistency between attitudes and behavioural intentions.[44] However, as the old expression goes, "the road to hell is paved with good intentions."

Many factors might interfere with actual behaviour, even if the consumer has sincere intentions. He or she might save up with the intention of buying a stereo system. In the interim, though, any number of things—losing a job, getting mugged on the way to the store, or arriving at the store to find that the desired model is out of stock—could happen. It is not surprising, then, that in some instances past purchase behaviour has been found to be a better predictor of future behaviour than is a consumer's behavioural intention.[45] The theory of reasoned action aims to measure behavioural intentions, recognizing that certain uncontrollable factors inhibit prediction of actual behaviour.

← The likelihood of performing socially desirable behaviours like recycling may be influenced by our subjective norms—the belief that others would approve or disapprove of the behaviour. *Getty Images, Inc.—Photodisc.*

SOCIAL PRESSURE

The theory acknowledges the power of other people in influencing behaviour. Many of our behaviours are not determined in a vacuum. Much as we may hate to admit it, what we think others would *like* us to do may be more crucial than our own individual preferences. Some research approaches try to assess the extent to which people's "public" attitudes and purchase decisions might be different from what they would do if they were in private. For example, one firm uses a technique it calls "engineered theatre." Researchers go to the actual site where a product is being consumed, such as a bar. They arrange for the wrong product to be "mistakenly" served, and then observe the consumer's "naked response" to the brand and his or her reaction to consuming the brand in a social context.[46]

A new element, the *subjective norm* (SN), was thus added to include the effects of what we believe other people think we should do. The value of SN is arrived at by including two other factors: (1) the intensity of a *normative belief* (NB) that others think an action should be taken or not taken, and (2) the *motivation to comply* (MC) with that belief (i.e., the degree to which the consumer takes others' anticipated reactions into account when evaluating a course of action or a purchase).

ATTITUDE TOWARD BUYING

The model now measures **attitude toward the act of buying (A_{act})**, rather than only the attitude toward the product itself. In other words, it focuses on the perceived consequences of a purchase. Knowing how someone feels about buying or using an object turns out to be more valid than merely knowing the consumer's evaluation of the object itself.[47]

To understand this distinction, consider a problem that might arise when measuring attitudes toward condoms. Although a group of college students might have a positive attitude toward condoms, does this necessarily predict that they will buy and use them? A better prediction would be obtained by asking the students how likely they are to buy condoms and use them during sex. Although a person might have a positive A_o toward condoms, A_{act} might be negative because of the embarrassment or the hassle involved in the act of buying.

Obstacles to Predicting Behaviour in the Theory of Reasoned Action

Despite improvements to the Fishbein model, problems arise when it is misapplied. In many cases the model is applied in ways for which it was not intended or where certain assumptions about human behaviour may not be warranted.[48] Other obstacles to predicting behaviour are as follows:

- The model was developed to deal with actual behaviour (e.g., taking a diet pill), not with the outcomes of behaviour (e.g., losing weight) that are instead assessed in some studies.

- Some outcomes are beyond the consumer's control, such as when the purchase requires the co-operation of other people. For instance, consumers might *want* to get a mortgage, but this intention will be worthless if they cannot find a banker to give them one.

- The basic assumption that behaviour is intentional may be invalid in a variety of cases, including those involving impulsive acts, sudden changes in one's situation, novelty-seeking, or even simple repeat buying. One study found that such unexpected events as having guests, changes in the weather, or reading articles about the healthfulness of certain foods exerted a significant effect on actual behaviours.[49]

- Measures of attitude often do not really correspond to the behaviour they are supposed to predict, either in terms of the A_o or when the act will occur. One

Multicultural Dimensions

The theory of reasoned action has been applied primarily in Western settings. Certain assumptions inherent in the model may not necessarily apply to consumers from other cultures. Several of the following cultural roadblocks diminish the universality of the theory of reasoned action:

> The model was developed to predict the performance of any voluntary act. Across cultures, however, many consumer activities, ranging from taking exams and entering military service to receiving an inoculation or choosing a marriage partner, are not necessarily voluntary.

> The relative impact of subjective norms may vary across cultures. For example, Asian cultures tend to value conformity and face-saving, so it is possible that subjective norms involving the anticipated reactions of others to the choice will have an even greater impact on behaviour for many Asian consumers. Indeed, a recent study conducted among voters in Singapore was able to predict voting for political candidates from their voting intentions, which in turn were influenced by such factors as voters' attitudes toward the candidate, attitudes toward the political party, and subjective norms—which in Singapore included an emphasis on harmonious and close ties among members of the society.[52]

> The model measures behavioural intentions and thus presupposes that consumers are actively thinking ahead and planning future behaviours. The intention concept assumes that consumers have a linear time sense (i.e., that they think in terms of past, present, and future). This perspective on time is not held by all cultures.

> A consumer who forms an intention is (implicitly) claiming that he or she is in control of his or her actions. Some cultures (e.g., Muslim) tend to be fatalistic and do not necessarily believe in the concept of free will. Indeed, one study comparing students from the United States, Jordan, and Thailand found evidence for cultural differences in assumptions about fatalism and control over the future.[53]

common problem is a difference in the level of *abstraction* employed. For example, knowing a person's attitude toward sports cars may not predict whether he or she will purchase a Chrysler PT Cruiser. It is very important to match the level of specificity between the attitude and the behavioural intention.

- A similar problem relates to the *time frame* of the attitude measure. In general, the longer the time between the attitude measurement and the behaviour it is supposed to assess, the weaker the relationship will be. For example, predictability would improve markedly by asking consumers about the likelihood of buying a house in the next week as opposed to within the next five years.

- Attitudes formed by direct, personal experience with an A_o are stronger and more predictive of behaviour than those formed indirectly, such as through advertising.[50] According to the *attitude accessibility* perspective, behaviour is a function of the person's immediate perceptions of the A_o in the context of the situation in which it is encountered. An attitude will guide the evaluation of the object, but *only* if it is activated from memory when the object is observed. These findings underscore the importance of strategies that induce trial (by widespread product sampling to encourage the consumer to try the product at home, by taste tests, test drives, etc.) as well as those that maximize exposure to marketing communications.

Trying to Consume

The *theory of trying* states that the criterion of behaviour in the reasoned action model should be replaced with *trying* to reach a goal.[51] This perspective recognizes that additional factors might intervene between intent and performance—both personal and environmental barriers might prevent the individual from attaining the goal. For example, a person who intends to lose weight may have to deal with numerous issues: not believing he or she is capable of slimming down, having a roommate who loves to cook and who leaves tempting goodies lying around the apartment, friends who may be jealous of these attempts to diet and who encourage him or her to pig out, or a genetic predisposition to obesity, in which case cutting down on calories simply will not produce the desired results.

The theory of trying includes several new components that attempt to account for the complex situations in which many factors either help or hurt our chances of turning intentions into actions, as shown in Figure 7–3. These factors include the amount of control the person has over the situation, his or her expectations of success or failure in achieving the goal, social norms related to attaining the goal, and his or her attitude toward the process of trying (i.e., how the action required to attain the goal makes him or her feel, regardless of the outcome). Still other new variables are the frequency and recency of past trying of the behaviour—for example, even if a person does not have specific plans to go on a diet in the next month, the frequency with which he or she has tried to do so in the recent past (and the success—however fleeting—he or she may have experienced) would be the best predictor of future attempts to shed some weight. To predict whether someone would try to lose weight, here are a few sample issues that might be addressed:

- *Past frequency:* How many times in the past year did the person try to lose weight?

- *Recency:* Did he or she try to lose weight in the last week?

- *Beliefs:* Did the person believe he or she would be healthier if he or she lost weight?

- *Evaluations of consequences:* Did the person believe his or her spouse would be happier if he or she succeeded in losing weight? Did this person believe his or her friends would make fun of him or her if he or she tried but failed to lose weight?

- *The process:* Would the diet make him or her uncomfortable or depressed?

- *Expectations of success and failure:* Did this person believe he or she would likely be able to lose weight if he or she tried?

- *Subjective norms toward trying:* Would the people who are important to this person approve of the efforts to lose weight?

FIGURE 7–3   THEORY OF TRYING (TT)

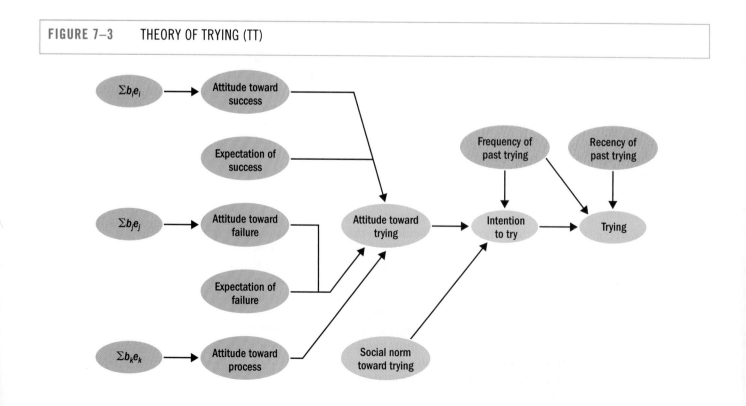

Tracking Attitudes over Time

An attitude survey is like a snapshot taken at a single point in time: It may tell us a lot about a brand's position at that moment, but it does not permit many inferences about progress the brand has made over time or any predictions about possible future changes in consumer attitudes. To accomplish these tasks it is necessary to develop an *attitude-tracking* program. This activity helps to increase the predictability of behaviour by allowing researchers to analyze attitude trends over an extended period of time. It is more like a movie than a snapshot. For example, a longitudinal survey conducted by the Food Marketing Institute of consumers' attitudes toward food content illustrates how priorities can shift in a fairly short time.[54] Concerns about fat and cholesterol content rose dramatically during the 1980s, while nutritional issues, such as interest in sugar content, decreased.

ONGOING TRACKING STUDIES

Attitude tracking involves the administration of an attitude survey at regular intervals. Preferably, the identical methodology is used each time so that results can be compared reliably. Several syndicated services, such as the Gallup Poll or the Yankelovich Monitor, track consumer attitudes over time. Results from a tracking study of ecological attitudes among young people in a set of European countries are shown in Figure 7–4.

This activity can be extremely valuable for many strategic decisions. For example, one financial services firm monitored changes in consumer attitudes toward one-stop banking centres. Although a large number of consumers were warm to the idea when it was first introduced, the number of people who liked the concept did not increase over time despite the millions of dollars invested in advertising to promote the centres. This finding indicated some problems with the way the concept was being presented to consumers, and the company decided to "go back to the drawing board," eventually coming up with a new way to communicate the advantages of this service.

CHANGES TO LOOK FOR OVER TIME

Some of the dimensions that can be included in attitude tracking are the following:

- *Changes in different age groups:* Attitudes tend to change as people age (a *life cycle effect*). In addition, *cohort effects* occur, where members of a particular generation (e.g., yuppies) tend to share certain outlooks. Also, *historical effects* can be observed as large groups of people are affected by profound cultural changes (such as the Great Depression or the democratization of eastern Europe).

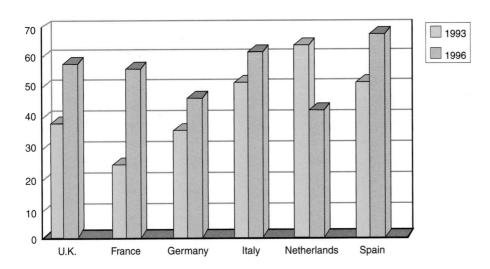

FIGURE 7–4

PERCENTAGE OF 16–24 YEAR OLDS WHO AGREE "WE MUST TAKE RADICAL ACTION TO CUT DOWN ON HOW MUCH WE USE OUR CARS"

Source: The Henley Centre, Frontiers: Planning for Consumer Change in Europe 1996/97.

- *Scenarios about the future:* Consumers are frequently tracked in terms of their future plans, confidence in the economy, and so on. These measures can provide valuable data about future behaviour and yield insights for public policy. For example, people tend to overestimate how much they will earn after retirement, which is potentially a dangerous miscalculation.

- *Identification of change agents:* Social phenomena can change people's attitudes toward basic consumption activities over time, as when consumers' willingness to buy fur products shifts. Or consumers' likelihood of desiring a divorce may be affected by such *facilitators* as changes in the legal system that make this action easier, or by *inhibitors,* such as the prevalence of AIDS and the value of two paycheques in today's economy.[55]

CHAPTER SUMMARY

IT'S IMPORTANT FOR CONSUMER RESEARCHERS TO UNDERSTAND THE NATURE AND POWER OF ATTITUDES.

- An attitude is a predisposition to evaluate an object or product positively or negatively.

ATTITUDES ARE MORE COMPLEX THAN THEY FIRST APPEAR.

- Attitudes are made up of three components: affect, behaviour, and cognition.

WE FORM ATTITUDES IN SEVERAL WAYS.

- Attitude researchers traditionally assumed that attitudes were learned in a fixed sequence, consisting first of the formation of beliefs (cognitions) regarding an attitude object, followed by some evaluation of that object (affect), and then some action (behaviour). Depending upon the consumer's level of involvement and the circumstances, however, attitudes can result from other hierarchies of effects as well. A key to attitude formation is the function the attitude performs for the consumer (e.g., is it utilitarian or ego-defensive?).

CONSUMERS ARE MOTIVATED TO MAINTAIN CONSISTENCY AMONG ALL THE COMPONENTS OF THEIR ATTITUDES, SO THEY MAY ALTER ONE OR MORE PARTS TO REALIZE THIS GOAL.

- One organizing principle of attitude formation is the importance of consistency among attitudinal components; that is, some parts of an attitude may be altered to be in line with others. Such theoretical approaches to attitudes as cognitive dissonance theory and balance theory stress the vital role of the need for consistency.

WE CAN MEASURE ATTITUDES USING SOPHISTICATED MODELS THAT IDENTIFY SPECIFIC COMPONENTS AND COMBINE THEM TO PREDICT WHAT A CONSUMER'S OVERALL ATTITUDE WILL BE.

- The complexity of attitudes is underscored by multi-attribute attitude models, in which sets of beliefs and evaluations are identified and combined to predict an overall attitude. Factors such as subjective norms and the specificity of attitude scales have been integrated into attitude measures to improve predictability.

KEY TERMS

Affect   p. 189

Attitude   p. 187

Attitude object (A_o)   p. 187

Attitude toward the
   act of buying (A_{act})   p. 202

Attitude toward the
   advertisement (A_{ad})   p. 191

Balance theory   p. 196

Behaviour   p. 189

Cognition   p. 189

Foot-in-the-door technique   p. 195

Functional theory of attitudes   p. 187

Hierarchy of effects   p. 189

Latitudes of acceptance and rejection   p. 195

Multi-attribute attitude models   p. 198

Principle of cognitive consistency   p. 193

Self-perception theory   p. 195

Social judgment theory   p. 195

Theory of cognitive dissonance   p. 194

Theory of reasoned action   p. 201

REVIEW QUESTIONS

1. How can an attitude play an ego-defensive function?
2. Describe the ABC model of attitudes.
3. List the three hierarchies of attitudes, and describe the major differences among them.
4. How are emotions (affect) and cognitions (beliefs) related to how attitudes are formed?
5. Other than the direct attitude we might have about a product, what is another type of attitude that might influence whether we buy it?
6. How do levels of commitment to an attitude influence the likelihood it will become part of the way we think about a product in the long term?
7. We sometimes increase our attitude toward a product after we buy it. How does the theory of cognitive dissonance explain this change?
8. What is the foot-in-the-door technique? How does self-perception theory relate to this effect?

9. What are latitudes of acceptance and rejection? How does a consumer's level of involvement with a product affect his latitude of acceptance?
10. According to balance theory, how can we tell if a triad is balanced or unbalanced? How can consumers restore balance to an unbalanced triad?
11. Describe a multi-attribute attitude model, listing its key components.
12. "Do as I say, not as I do." How does this statement relate to attitude models?
13. What is a subjective norm, and how does it influence our attitudes?
14. What are three obstacles to predicting behaviour even if we know a person's attitudes?
15. Describe the theory of reasoned action. Why might it not be equally valuable when it is applied to non-Western cultures?
16. What is the value of attitude tracking? What issues do researchers need to consider when doing this?

CONSUMER BEHAVIOUR CHALLENGE

Discuss

1. Contrast the hierarchies of effects outlined in this chapter. How should marketers' strategic decisions related to the marketing mix change depending on which hierarchy is operative among target consumers?

Experiential Exercises

2. Think of someone who exhibits a behaviour that is inconsistent with his or her attitudes (e.g., attitudes toward cholesterol, drug use, or even buying things to make him or her stand out or attain status). Ask the person to explain the behaviour, and try to identify the way he or she has resolved dissonant elements.

3. Devise an attitude survey for a set of competing automobiles. Identify areas of competitive advantage or disadvantage for each model you incorporate.
4. Construct a multi-attribute model for a set of local restaurants. Based on your findings, suggest how restaurant managers can improve an establishment's image via the strategies described in this chapter.

NOTES

1. Robert A. Baron and Donn Byrne, *Social Psychology: Understanding Human Interaction*, 5th ed. (Boston, MA: Allyn & Bacon, 1987).

2. Daniel Katz, "The Functional Approach to the Study of Attitudes," *Public Opinion Quarterly* 24 (Summer 1960): 163–204; Richard J. Lutz, "Changing Brand Attitudes through Modification of Cognitive Structure," *Journal of Consumer Research* 1 (March 1975): 49–59.

3. Russell H. Fazio, T.M. Lenn, and E.A. Effrein, "Spontaneous Attitude Formation," *Social Cognition* 2 (1984): 214–234.

4. For the original work that focused on the issue of levels of attitudinal commitment, see Herbert Kelman, "Compliance, Identification, and Internalization: Three Processes of Attitude Change," *Journal of Conflict Resolution* 2 (1958): 51–60.

5. Lynn R. Kahle, Kenneth M. Kambara, and Gregory M. Rose, "A Functional Model of Fan Attendance Motivations for College Football," *Sports Marketing Quarterly* V, 4 (1996): 51–60.

6. Michael Ray, "Marketing Communications and the Hierarchy-of-Effects," in *New Models for Mass Communications,* ed. P. Clarke (Beverly Hills, CA: Sage, 1973), 147–176.

7. Herbert Krugman, "The Impact of Television Advertising: Learning Without Involvement," *Public Opinion Quarterly* 29 (Fall 1965): 349–356; Robert Lavidge and Gary Steiner, "A Model for Predictive Measurements of Advertising Effectiveness," *Journal of Marketing* 25 (October 1961): 59–62.

8. Daniel J. Howard and Charles Gengler, "Emotional Contagion Effects on Product Attitudes," *Journal of Consumer Research* 28 (September 2001): 189–201.

9. For some recent studies, see Andrew B. Aylesworth and Scott B. MacKenzie, "Context Is Key: The Effect of Program-Induced Mood on Thoughts about the Ad," *Journal of Advertising* 27 (Summer 1998): 17; Angela Y. Lee and Brian Sternthal, "The Effects of Positive Mood on Memory," *Journal of Consumer Research* 26 (September 1999): 115–128; Michael J. Barone, Paul W. Miniard, and Jean B. Romeo, "The Influence of Positive Mood on Brand Extension Evaluations," *Journal of Consumer Research* 26 (March 2000): 386–401. For a study that compared the effectiveness of emotional appeals across cultures, see Jennifer L. Aaker and Patti Williams, "Empathy versus Pride: The Influence of Emotional Appeals across Cultures," *Journal of Consumer Research* 25 (December 1998): 241–261. For research that relates mood (depression) to acceptance of health-related messages, see Punam Anand Keller, Iassac M. Lipkus, and Barbara K. Rimer, "Depressive Realism and Health Risk Accuracy: The Negative Consequences of Positive Mood," *Journal of Consumer Research* 29 (June 2002): 57–69.

10. Punam Anand, Morris B. Holbrook, and Debra Stephens, "The Formation of Affective Judgments: The Cognitive-Affective Model versus the Independence Hypothesis," *Journal of Consumer Research* 15 (December 1988): 386–391; Richard S. Lazarus, "Thoughts on the Relations between Emotion and Cognition," *American Psychologist* 37, 9 (1982): 1019–1024.

11. Robert B. Zajonc, "Feeling and Thinking: Preferences Need No Inferences," *American Psychologist* 35, 2 (1980): 151–175.

12. Banwari Mittal, "The Role of Affective Choice Mode in the Consumer Purchase of Expressive Products," *Journal of Economic Psychology* 4, 9 (1988): 499–524.

13. Patricia Winters Lauro, "Advertisers Want to Know What People really Think," *New York Times on the Web* (April 13, 2000).

14. Scot Burton and Donald R. Lichtenstein, "The Effect of Ad Claims and Ad Context on Attitude toward the Advertisement," *Journal of Advertising* 17, 1 (1988): 3–11; Karen A. Machleit and R. Dale Wilson, "Emotional Feelings and Attitude toward the Advertisement: The Roles of Brand Familiarity and Repetition," *Journal of Advertising* 17, 3 (1988): 27–35; Scott B. Mackenzie and Richard J. Lutz, "An Empirical Examination of the Structural Antecedents of Attitude toward the Ad in an Advertising Pretesting Context," *Journal of Marketing* 53 (April 1989): 48–65; Scott B. Mackenzie, Richard J. Lutz, and George E. Belch, "The Role of Attitude toward the Ad as a Mediator of Advertising Effectiveness: A Test of Competing Explanations," *Journal of Marketing Research* 23 (May 1986): 130–143; Darrel D. Muehling and Russell N. Laczniak, "Advertising's Immediate and Delayed Influence on Brand Attitudes: Considerations across Message-Involvement Levels," *Journal of Advertising* 17, 4 (1988): 23–34; Mark A. Pavelchak, Meryl P. Gardner, and V. Carter Broach, "Effect of Ad Pacing and Optimal Level of Arousal on Attitude toward the Ad," in *Advances in Consumer Research* 18, eds. Rebecca H. Holman and Michael R. Solomon (Provo, UT: Association for Consumer Research, 1991), 94–99. Some research evidence indicates that a separate attitude is also formed regarding the brand name itself; see George M. Zinkhan and Claude R. Martin, Jr., "New Brand Names and Inferential Beliefs: Some Insights on Naming New Products," *Journal of Business Research* 15 (1987): 157–172.

15. John P. Murry, Jr., John L. Lastovicka, and Surendra N. Singh, "Feeling and Liking Responses to Television Programs: An Examination of Two Explanations for Media-Context Effects," *Journal of Consumer Research* 18 (March 1992): 441–451.

16. Barbara Stern and Judith Lynne Zaichkowsky, "The Impact of Entertaining Advertising on Consumer Responses," *Australian Marketing Researcher* 14 (August 1991): 68–80.

17. Krishnan H. Shanker and Robert E. Smith (1998), "The Relative Endurance of Attitudes, Confidence, and Attitude-Behavior Consistency: The Role of Information Source and Delay," *Journal of Consumer Psychology*, 7, 3, 273–298.

18. For a recent study that examined the impact of scepticism on advertising issues, see David M. Boush, Marian Friestad, and Gregory M. Rose, "Adolescent Skepticism toward TV Advertising and Knowledge of Advertiser Tactics," *Journal of Consumer Research* 21 (June 1994): 165–175.

19. Basil G. Englis, "Consumer Emotional Reactions to Television Advertising and Their Effects on Message Recall," in *Emotion in Advertising: Theoretical and Practical Explorations*, eds. S. Agres, J.A. Edell, and T.M. Dubitsky (Westport, CT: Quorum Books, 1990), 231–254.

20. Morris B. Holbrook and Rajeev Batra, "Assessing the Role of Emotions as Mediators of Consumer Responses to Advertising," *Journal of Consumer Research* 14 (December 1987): 404–420.

21. Marian Burke and Julie Edell, "Ad Reactions over Time: Capturing Changes in the Real World," *Journal of Consumer Research* 13 (June 1986): 114–118.

22. David A. Aaker and Donald E. Bruzzone, "Causes of Irritation in Advertising," *Journal of Marketing* 49 (Spring 1985): 47–57.

23. Kelman, "Compliance, Identification, and Internalization: Three Processes of Attitude Change."

24. Sharon E. Beatty and Lynn R. Kahle, "Alternative Hierarchies of the Attitude-Behavior Relationship: The Impact of Brand Commitment and Habit," *Journal of Academy of Marketing Science* (16, Summer 1998): 110.

25. Leon Festinger, *A Theory of Cognitive Dissonance* (Stanford, CA: Stanford University Press, 1957).

26. Festinger, *A Theory of Cognitive Dissonance*.

27. Chester A. Insko and John Schopler, *Experimental Social Psychology* (New York, NY: Academic Press, 1972).

28. Robert E. Knox and James A. Inkster, "Postdecision Dissonance at Post Time," *Journal of Personality and Social Psychology* 8, 4 (1968): 319–323.

29. Daryl J. Bem, "Self-Perception Theory," in *Advances in Experimental Social Psychology*, ed. Leonard Berkowitz (New York, NY: Academic Press, 1972), 1–62.

30. Jonathan L. Freedman and Scott C. Fraser, "Compliance Without Pressure: The Foot-in-the-Door Technique," *Journal of Personality and Social Psychology* 4 (August 1966): 195–202. For further consideration of possible explanations for this effect, see William DeJong, "An Examination of Self-Perception Mediation of the Foot-in-the-Door Effect," *Journal of Personality and Social Psychology* 37 (December 1979): 221–231; Alice M. Tybout, Brian Sternthal, and Bobby J. Calder, "Information Availability as a Determinant of Multiple-Request Effectiveness," *Journal of Marketing Research* 20 (August 1988): 280–290.

31. David H. Furse, David W. Stewart, and David L. Rados, "Effects of Foot-in-the-Door, Cash Incentives and Follow-ups on Survey Response," *Journal of Marketing Research* 18 (November 1981): 473–478; Carol A. Scott, "The Effects of Trial and Incentives on Repeat Purchase Behavior," *Journal of Marketing Research* 13 (August 1976): 263–269.

32. R.B. Cialdini, J.E. Vincent, S.K. Lewis, J. Catalan, D. Wheeler, and B.L. Darby, "Reciprocal Concessions Procedure for Inducing Compliance: The Door-in-the-Face Effect," *Journal of Personality and Social Psychology* 31 (1975): 200–215.

33. Muzafer Sherif and Carl I. Hovland, *Social Judgment: Assimilation and Contrast Effects in Communication and Attitude Change* (New Haven, CT: Yale University Press, 1961).

34. For a recent treatment, see Joan Meyers-Levy and Brian Sternthal, "A Two-Factor Explanation of Assimilation and Contrast Effects," *Journal of Marketing Research* 30 (August 1993): 359–368.

35. Mark B. Traylor, "Product Involvement and Brand Commitment," *Journal of Advertising Research* (December 1981): 51–56.

36. Fritz Heider, *The Psychology of Interpersonal Relations* (New York: Wiley, 1958).

37. Leslie Kaufman, "Enough Talk," *Newsweek* (August 18, 1997): 48–49.

38. William L. Wilkie, *Consumer Behavior* (New York: Wiley, 1986).

39. Martin Fishbein, "An Investigation of the Relationships between Beliefs about an Object and the Attitude toward that Object," *Human Relations* 16 (1983): 233–240.

40. Allan Wicker, "Attitudes versus Actions: The Relationship of Verbal and Overt Behavioral Responses to Attitude Objects," *Journal of Social Issues* 25 (Autumn 1969): 65.

41. Icek Ajzen and Martin Fishbein, "Attitude-Behavior Relations: A Theoretical Analysis and Review of Empirical Research," *Psychological Bulletin* 84 (September 1977): 888–918.

42. Morris B. Holbrook and William J. Havlena, "Assessing the Real-to-Artificial Generalizability of Multi-Attribute Attitude Models in Tests of New Product Designs," *Journal of Marketing Research* 25 (February 1988): 25–35; Terence A. Shimp and Alican Kavas, "The Theory of Reasoned Action Applied to Coupon Usage," *Journal of Consumer Research* 11 (December 1984): 795–809.

43. R.P. Abelson, "Conviction," *American Psychologist* 43 (1988): 267–275; R.E. Petty and J.A. Krosnick, *Attitude Strength: Antecedents and Consequences* (Mahwah, NJ: Erlbaum, 1995); Ida E. Berger and Linda F. Alwitt, "Attitude Conviction: A Self-Reflective Measure of Attitude Strength," *Journal of Social Behavior and Personality* 11, 3 (1996): 557–572.

44. Berger and Alwitt, "Attitude Conviction ...."

45. Richard P. Bagozzi, Hans Baumgartner, and Youjae Yi, "Coupon Usage and the Theory of Reasoned Action," in *Advances in Consumer Research* 18, eds. Rebecca H. Holman and Michael R. Solomon (Provo, UT: Association for Consumer Research, 1991), 24–27; Edward F. McQuarrie, "An Alternative to Purchase Intentions: The Role of Prior Behavior in Consumer Expenditure on Computers," *Journal of the Market Research Society* 30 (October 1988): 407–437; Arch G. Woodside and William O. Bearden, "Longitudinal Analysis of Consumer Attitude, Intention, and Behavior toward Beer Brand Choice," in *Advances in Consumer Research* 4, ed. William D. Perrault, Jr. (Ann Arbor, MI: Association for Consumer Research, 1977), 349–356.

46. Andy Greenfield, "The Naked Truth (Studying Consumer Behavior)," *Brandweek* 38 (October 13, 1997): 22 (4).

47. Michael J. Ryan and Edward H. Bonfield, "The Fishbein Extended Model and Consumer Behavior," *Journal of Consumer Research* 2 (1975): 118–136.

48. Blair H. Sheppard, Jon Hartwick, and Paul R. Warshaw, "The Theory of Reasoned Action: A Meta-Analysis of Past Research with Recommendations for Modifications and Future Research," *Journal of Consumer Research* 15 (December 1988): 325–343.

49. Kulwant Singh, Siew Meng Leong, Chin Tiong Tan, and Kwei Cheong Wong, "A Theory of Reasoned Action Perspective of Voting Behavior: Model and Empirical Test," *Psychology & Marketing* 12, 1 (January 1995): 37–51.

50. Russell H. Fazio, Martha C. Powell, and Carol J. Williams, "The Role of Attitude Accessibility in the Attitude-to-Behavior Process," *Journal of Consumer Research* 16 (December 1989): 280–288; Robert E. Smith and William R. Swinyard, "Attitude-Behavior Consistency: The Impact of Product Trial versus Advertising," *Journal of Marketing Research* 20 (August 1983): 257–267.

51. Richard P. Bagozzi and Paul R. Warshaw, "Trying to Consume," *Journal of Consumer Research* 17 (September 1990): 127–140.

52. Joseph A. Cote and Patriya S. Tansuhaj, "Culture Bound Assumptions in Behavior Intention Models," in *Advances in Consumer Research* 16, ed. Thom Srull (Provo, UT: Association for Consumer Research, 1989), 105–109.

53. Joseph A. Cote, James McCullough, and Michael Reilly, "Effects of Unexpected Situations on Behavior-Intention Differences: A Garbology Analysis," *Journal of Consumer Research* 12 (September 1985): 188–194.

54. Barbara Presley Noble, "After Years of Deregulation, a New Push to Inform the Public," *New York Times* (October 27, 1991): F5.

55. Matthew Greenwald and John P. Katosh, "How to Track Changes in Attitudes," *American Demographics* (August 1987): 46.

After a hard-fought hockey game, Sean is dying of hunger. The team is off for its post-game dinner at the local Keg Restaurant. Sean is looking forward to the biggest steak on the menu, complete with baked potato smothered in sour cream and green onions. He thinks a man has to eat a lot of protein to keep the muscles in shape and the hunger at bay. And it's a great thing that Alberta beef is being served: it's his favourite. His teammates agree; they wouldn't think of eating anything else but Canadian beef to satisfy their ravenous hunger.

CHAPTER → 8

Attitude Change and Interactive Communications

CHANGING ATTITUDES THROUGH COMMUNICATION

A funny thing happened during the BSE (Bovine Spongiform Encephalopathy) crisis: Canadian beef consumption actually increased. Now that the U.S. border has reopened, beef marketers are poised to grow demand, one meat lover at a time. When the BSE crisis first hit in 2003, Alberta beef producers knew they had only hours to pull together a communications strategy to tell the world that their beef was safe. Years later, rather than having witnessed consumption fall, they've actually seen it rise due mainly to their advertising efforts to build trust in their brand.

Their main message is that their beef is grain fed and not grass fed, and is therefore a superior product that cannot be contaminated by feed.[1]

As consumers, we are constantly bombarded by messages inducing us to change our attitudes. These persuasion attempts can range from logical arguments to graphic pictures, and from intimidation by peers to exhortations by celebrity spokespeople. And communications flow both ways—the consumer may seek out information sources in order to learn more about these options. A person's choice to access marketing messages on his or her own terms is changing the way we think about persuasion attempts.

This chapter will review some of the factors that help to determine the effectiveness of such communication devices. Our focus will be on some basic aspects of communication that specifically help to determine how and if attitudes will be created or modified. This objective relates to **persuasion**, which refers to an active attempt to change attitudes. Persuasion is the central goal of many marketing communications.

We'll learn more about how marketers try to accomplish this throughout the chapter, but for now we can set the stage by listing some basic psychological principles that influence people to change their minds or comply with a request:[2]

- *Reciprocity:* People are more likely to give if they receive. That's why including money in a mail survey questionnaire increases the response rate by an average of 65 percent over the number of responses to mail surveys without monetary incentive.

- *Scarcity:* Items become more attractive when they are less available. In one study that asked people to rate the quality of chocolate chip cookies, participants who only got two cookies liked them better than those who got ten of the same kind of cookie. That helps to explain why we tend to value "limited edition" items.

- *Authority:* We tend to believe an authoritative source much more readily. *The Globe and Mail* carries more weight with respect to public opinion than does *The Toronto Star.* We'll talk more about the importance of who delivers the message later in this chapter.

- *Consistency:* As we saw in the last chapter, people try not to contradict themselves in terms of what they say and do about an issue. In one study, students at an Israeli university who solicited donations to help people with disabilities doubled the amount they normally collected in a neighbourhood by first asking the residents to sign a petition supporting people with disabilities two weeks before asking for donations.

- *Consensus:* We often take into account what others are doing before we decide what to do. We'll talk more about the power of conformity in Chapter 11. This desire to fit in with what others are doing influences our actions; for example, people are more likely to donate to a charity if they first see a list of the names of their neighbours who have already done so.

Decisions, Decisions: Tactical Communications Options

Suppose that a perfume company wants to create an advertising campaign for a new fragrance. As it plans this campaign, it must develop a message that will create desire for the perfume in potential consumers. To craft persuasive messages a number of questions must be answered:

- Who will be depicted as using the scent in an ad? Should it be linked to a glamorous celebrity? a career woman? a rock star? The source of a message helps to determine consumers' acceptance of it, as well as their desire to try the product.

- How should the message be constructed? Should it emphasize the negative consequences of smelling badly? Should it directly compare the fragrance with others already on the market, or maybe present a fantasy where a princess is swept off her feet by a dashing knight after she applies the scent? Product benefits can be expressed in many ways.

- What media should be used to transmit the message? Should it be depicted in a print ad? on television? Should it be sold door-to-door? If a print ad is produced, should it be run in the pages of *Vogue*? *Canadian Living*? *Details*? Sometimes *where* something is said can be as important as *what* is said. Ideally, the attributes of the product should be matched with those of the medium. For example, magazines with high prestige are more effective at communicating messages about overall product image and quality, while specialized, expert magazines do a better job at conveying factual information.[3]

- What characteristics of the target market might influence the ad's acceptance? If targeted users are frustrated in their daily lives, these women might be more receptive to a fantasy appeal. If they don't tend to wear perfume, they may not pay any attention to a traditional perfume ad at all.

The Elements of Communication

Marketers and advertisers have traditionally tried to understand how marketing messages change consumers' attitudes by thinking in terms of the **communications model**, which specifies that a number of elements are necessary for communication to be achieved.

In this model, a *source* must choose and encode a *message* (i.e., initiate the transfer of meaning by choosing appropriate symbolic images that represent this meaning). There are many ways to say something, and the structure of the message has a big effect on how it is perceived. The message must be transmitted via a *medium,* which could be television, radio, magazines, billboards, or even a T-shirt. The message is then decoded by one or more *receivers,* who interpret the symbols in the light of their own experiences. Finally, *feedback* must be received by the source, who uses the reactions of receivers to modify aspects of the message. The communications process is depicted in Figure 8–1.

AN UPDATED VIEW: INTERACTIVE COMMUNICATIONS

Although the traditional communications model is not entirely wrong, it does not tell the whole story—especially in today's dynamic world of interactivity in which consumers have many more choices available to them and greater control over which messages they will choose to process.[4] In fact, a popular strategy known as **permission marketing** is based on the idea that a marketer will be much more successful trying to persuade consumers who have opted into their messages; consumers who "opt out" of listening to the message probably weren't good prospects in the first place.[5] On the other hand, those who say they are interested in learning more are likely to be receptive to marketing communications they have already chosen to see or hear. As the permission marketing concept reminds us, we don't have to just sit there and take it. We have a voice in deciding which messages we choose to see and when—and we exercise that option more and more.

The traditional model was developed in order to understand mass communications, where information is transferred from a producer (source) to many consumers (receivers) at one time—typically via print, television, or radio. This perspective essentially views advertising as the process of transferring information to the buyer before a sale. A message is seen as perishable; it is repeated (perhaps frequently) for a fairly short period of time and then it "vanishes" as a new campaign eventually takes its place.

This model was strongly influenced by a group of theorists known as the Frankfurt School, which dominated mass-communications research for most of the twentieth century. In this view the media exert direct and powerful effects on individuals, and the effects often are used by those in power to brainwash and exploit individuals. The receiver is basically a passive being—a "couch potato" who is simply the receptacle for many messages and who is often duped or persuaded to act based on the information he or she is "fed" by the media.

Uses and Gratifications

Is this an accurate picture of the way we relate to marketing communications? Proponents of **uses and gratifications theory** argue instead that consumers are an

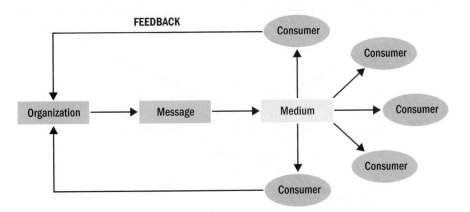

FEEDBACK

FIGURE 8–1

THE TRADITIONAL COMMUNICATIONS MODEL

active, goal-directed audience that draws on mass media as a resource to satisfy needs. Instead of asking what media do for or to people, they ask what people do *with* their media.[6]

The uses and gratifications approach emphasizes that media compete with other sources to satisfy needs and that these needs include diversion and entertainment as well as information. This also means that the line between marketing information and entertainment is continuing to blur—especially as companies are being forced to design more attractive retail outlets, catalogues, and websites in order to induce consumers to stop at them.

Indeed, research interviews with young people in Great Britain find that they rely on advertising for many gratifications, including entertainment (some report that the "adverts" are better than the programs), escapism, play (some report singing along with jingles, others make posters out of magazine ads), and self-affirmation (ads can reinforce their own values or provide role models). It's important to note that this perspective is not arguing that media play a uniformly positive role in our lives, only that recipients are making use of the information in a number of ways.[7] For example, marketing messages have the potential to undermine self-esteem as consumers use the media to establish unrealistic standards for behaviour, attitudes, or even their own appearance. A comment by one study participant illustrates this negative impact. She observes that when she's watching television with her boyfriend, "Really, it makes you think, 'Oh no, what must I be like?' I mean, you're sitting with your boyfriend and he's saying 'Oh, look at her. What a body!'"[8]

Who's in Charge of the Remote?

Whether for good or bad, though, exciting technological and social developments certainly are forcing us to rethink the picture of the passive consumer, as people increasingly are playing a proactive role in communications. In other words, they are to a greater extent becoming partners—rather than potatoes—in the communications process; their input is helping to shape the messages they and others like them receive, and furthermore they may seek out these messages rather than sit home and wait to see them on television or in the paper. This updated approach to interactive communications is illustrated in Figure 8–2.

One of the early signs of this communications revolution was the humble handheld remote control device. As VCRs began to be commonplace in homes, suddenly consumers had more input into what they wanted to watch—and when. No longer were they at the mercy of the television networks to decide when to see their favourite shows, and neither did they necessarily have to forsake a show because it conflicted with another's time slot.

Since that time, of course, our ability to control our media environment has mushroomed. Just ask some of the more than one million people who are now using DVRs (digital video recorders) such as TiVo to watch TV shows whenever they wish—and who are skipping over the commercials.[9] Many people have access to video-on-demand or pay-per-view TV. Home shopping networks encourage us to

FIGURE 8–2

THE INTERACTIVE COMMUNICATION MODEL

Source: Adapted from Donna L. Hoffman and Thomas P. Novak, "Marketing in Hypermedia Computer-Mediated Environments: Conceptual Foundations," *Journal of Marketing* 60, no. 3 (July 1996), Fig. 4.

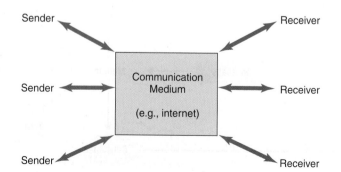

call in and discuss our passion for cubic zirconium live on the air. Caller ID devices and answering machines allow us to decide whether we will accept a phone call during dinnertime and to know the source of the message before picking up the phone. A bit of web surfing allows us to identify kindred spirits around the globe, to request information about products, and even to provide suggestions to product designers and market researchers.

New Message Formats

An array of new ways to transmit information in both text and picture form offers marketers exciting alternatives to traditional advertising on TV, billboards, magazines, and so on.[10]

M-commerce (mobile commerce), where marketers promote their goods and services via wireless devices including cell phones, PDAs, and iPods, is red-hot. In Europe and Asia, consumers already rely on their cell phones to connect them to the world in ways we are only starting to see in North America. Worldwide revenue from mobile information and entertainment will reach $39 billion in 2007. In Asia, tiny cell phone screens have become electronic wallets that buy Cokes from vending machines and devices that dole out McDonald's coupons on the phone screen.

As wireless companies begin to roll out higher-capacity networks, look for commercial messages on *your* phone in the fairly near future. Already, TV companies are using video-enabled cell phones to promote their prime-time lineups by sending teasers of new shows. To promote its Britney Spears cologne, Curious, to teens, Elizabeth Arden mounted a $5-million campaign that began with banner ads on teen internet sites posing questions like, "Do you dare?" Those curious enough to give their phone numbers—27 000 over seven weeks—received a voice message from Britney herself discussing the campaign's TV spot that was running on Viacom's MTV. In only five weeks Curious became the No.1 selling fragrance in North America.

Do you blog? The other media format that's getting a lot of attention is **blogging**, where people post messages to the web in diary form. Blogging started as a grassroots movement where individuals shared their thoughts on a range of topics, from the mundane to the profound. This phenomenon hasn't slowed down yet; people post about 40 000 new blogs every day. New forms of blogging itself continue to develop, such as:

- *Moblogging*: Posting to a blog on the go, from a camera phone or handheld device.
- *Video blogging (vlogging)*: Posting video diaries.
- *Podcasting*: Creating your own radio show that people can listen to either on their computers or iPods. Even Paris Hilton did a podcast to promote her movie *House of Wax*.
- *RSS (Really Simple Syndication)*: People sign up to have updates sent automatically to their computers. Companies like Yahoo! are encouraging this format to keep audiences loyal.
- *Flogs (fake blogs)*: Blogs created by companies to generate buzz.

Levels of Interactive Response

A key to understanding the dynamics of interactive marketing communications is to consider exactly what is meant by a response.[11] The early perspective on communications regarded feedback primarily in terms of behaviour: Did the recipient run out and buy the laundry detergent after being exposed to an ad for it?

However, a variety of other responses are possible as well, including building awareness of the brand, informing us about product features, reminding us to buy a new package when we've run out, and—perhaps most important—building a

Marketing Opportunity !

Consumers who are highly involved with a product and who want to share their opinions with manufacturers are an invaluable (and often free) form of input that can shape marketing decisions in important ways. Consider these recent examples.

The beauty division of the N.P.D. Group, which tracks retail purchases, noticed that a product intended to reduce stretch marks called StriVectin-SD was selling exceptionally well at department-store beauty counters. The firm found that about 75 percent of buyers actually were using it on their faces as a wrinkle fighter. Taking heed of this new use for the product, its manufacturer unveiled a new advertising slogan, "Better than Botox?"

Virtually every component of Jones Soda, from labels to flavours, comes from customers. The company gets suggestions for offbeat flavours (including chocolate fudge and green apple), wacky names (Whoop Ass and MF Grape), and neon colours. Even the "Deep Thoughts" quotes found underneath the bottle caps ("76.4% of all statistics are meaningless") come straight from Jones enthusiasts.

Dannon went to consumers when its reduced-fat Light 'n Fit yogourts were not selling well against rivals. The company emailed 40 000 men and women and asked them to click on a link to help create a new product and get a shot at winning $10 000. They evaluated a series of yogourt containers with different combinations of name, package design, nutritional labelling, and size. By the end of the project, researchers decided that the yogourt should be called Carb Control, come in a red container, be sold in a four-pack of four-ounce cups, and that the label should appeal to dieters by highlighting the claims of "80% less sugar" and "3 grams of carbs."

long-term relationship. Therefore, a transaction is *one* type of response, but forward-thinking marketers realize that customers can interact with them in other valuable ways as well. For this reason it is helpful to distinguish between two basic types of feedback:

- *First-order response*: Direct-marketing vehicles such as catalogues and television infomercials are interactive; if successful they result in an order, which is most definitely a response! So let's think of a product offer that directly yields a transaction as a *first-order response*. In addition to providing revenue, sales data are a valuable source of feedback that allows marketers to gauge the effectiveness of their communications efforts.

- *Second-order response:* However, a marketing communication does not have to result immediately in a purchase to be an important component of interactive marketing. Messages can prompt useful responses from customers, even though these recipients do not necessarily place an order immediately after being exposed to the communication. Customer feedback in response to a marketing message that is not in the form of a transaction is a *second-order response.*

THE SOURCE

Common sense tells us that the same words uttered by different people can have very different effects. Research on *source effects* has been carried out for more than 45 years. By attributing the same message to different sources and measuring the degree of attitude change that occurs after listeners hear it, researchers have found that it is possible to determine what aspects of a communicator will induce attitude change.[12]

Under most conditions, the source of a message can have a big impact on the likelihood the message will be accepted. The choice of a source to maximize attitude change can tap into several dimensions. The source can be chosen because he or she is an expert, attractive, famous, or even a "typical" consumer who is both likeable and trustworthy. Two important source characteristics are *credibility* and *attractiveness.*[13]

How do marketing specialists decide whether to stress either credibility or attractiveness when choosing a message source? There should be a match between the needs of the recipient and the potential rewards offered by the source. When this match occurs, the recipient is more motivated to process the message. People who tend to be sensitive about social acceptance and the opinions of others, for example, are more persuaded by an attractive source, whereas those who are more internally oriented are swayed by a credible, expert source.[14]

The choice may also depend on the type of product. A positive source can help to reduce risk and increase message acceptance overall, but particular types of sources are more effective at reducing different kinds of risk. Experts are effective at changing attitudes toward utilitarian products that have high performance risk, such as vacuums (i.e., they may be complex and not work as expected). Celebrities are more effective when they focus on products such as jewellery and furniture that have high *social risk;* the user of such products is aware of their effect on the impression others have of him or her. Finally, "typical" consumers, who are appealing sources because of their similarity to the recipient, tend to be most effective when providing real-life endorsements for everyday products that are low risk, such as cookies.[15]

Source Credibility

Source credibility refers to the source's perceived expertise, objectivity, or trustworthiness. This characteristic relates to consumers' beliefs that a communicator is competent and willing to provide the necessary information adequately to evaluate competing products. A credible source can be particularly persuasive when the consumer has not yet learned much about a product or formed an opinion of it.[16] The decision to pay an expert or a celebrity to tout a product can be a very costly one, but researchers have concluded that on average the investment is worth it simply because the announcement of an endorsement contract is often used by market analysts to evaluate a firm's potential profitability, thereby affecting its expected return. On average, then, the impact of endorsements on stock returns appears to be so positive that it offsets the cost of hiring the spokesperson.[17]

THE SLEEPER EFFECT

Although, in general, more positive sources tend to increase attitude change, exceptions can occur. Sometimes a source can be obnoxious or disliked and still manage to be effective at getting the product's message across. A case in point is Mr. Whipple, the irritating but well-known character in toilet-paper commercials who, for many years, scolded customers, "Please don't squeeze the Charmin!"

In some instances, the differences in attitude change between positive sources and less positive sources seem to get erased over time. After a while, people appear to "forget" about the negative source and wind up changing their attitudes anyway. This process is known as the **sleeper effect**.[18]

The explanation for the sleeper effect is a subject of debate, as is the more basic question regarding whether and when it really exists. Initially, the *dissociative cue hypothesis* proposed that over time the message and the source become disassociated in the consumer's mind. The message remains on its own in memory, causing a delayed attitude change—the sleeper effect.[19]

A more recent explanation is the *availability-valence hypothesis,* which emphasizes the selectivity of memory owing to limited capacity.[20] If the associations linked to the negative source are less available than those linked to the message information, the residual impact of the message enhances persuasion. Consistent with this view, the sleeper effect has been obtained only when the message was encoded deeply; that is, it had stronger associations in memory than did the source.[21]

BUILDING CREDIBILITY

Credibility can be enhanced if the source's qualifications are perceived as relevant to the product being endorsed. This link can overcome other objections people may have to the endorser or the product. Ronald Biggs, whose claim to fame was taking part in the 1963 Great Train Robbery in the United Kingdom, successfully served as a spokesman in Brazil for a company that makes door locks—a topic about which he is presumably knowledgeable![22] It's important to note that what is credible to one consumer segment may be a turnoff to another. Indeed, rebellious or even deviant celebrities may be attractive to some for just that reason. Tommy Hilfiger cultivated a rebellious, street-smart image by using rapper Snoop Dogg (who was acquitted of murder charges) to help launch his line and rapper Coolio, a former crack addict and thief, as a runway model.[23] Parents may not be thrilled by these message sources—but isn't that the point?

SOURCE BIASES

A consumer's beliefs about a product's attributes can be weakened if the source is perceived to be the victim of bias in presenting information.[24] *Knowledge bias* implies that a source's knowledge about a topic is not accurate. *Reporting bias* occurs where a source has the required knowledge but his or her willingness to convey it accurately is compromised, as when a star tennis player is paid by a racket manufacturer to use its products exclusively. Although his or her credentials might be appropriate, the fact that the expert is perceived as a "hired gun" compromises believability. Of course, it's not always clear that a person has been paid to say he or she loves a product. Microsoft was criticized when the software company offered to pay "travel costs" for professors if they presented papers at conferences and mentioned how Microsoft programs helped them in their work.[25]

Net Profit

Flying in the face of conventional wisdom that says the source of a message is crucial, a popular strategy for online advertising is to disguise the source—or even to make one up. At the hugely successful Subservient Chicken site (*www.subservientchicken.com*), visitors can make a man in a chicken suit obey their whims—and you have to look hard to figure out that Burger King sponsors the site. Alaska Airlines operates a *parody site* at *www.skyhighairlines.com*, and Best Buy, the retail chain, is creating specialty sites tied to particular campaigns, products, and audiences. At one site, Best Buy features the fictional Slothmore Institute (*www.slothmore.com*), which brags of "enabling greatness through sedentary living." At *www.comeclean.com*, visitors are asked to type in confessions, urging, "Start the new year fresh by coming clean." Entered confessions then appear on a hand over a sink, where it is washed away with soap (made by Method, the soap maker that sponsors the site) that you can buy at an online gift shop. Visitors can also peek at previous visitors' anonymous confessions, like this one: "I haven't changed my sheets in about a month or two."[26]

Hype versus Buzz: The Corporate Paradox

Obviously many marketers spend lavishly to create marketing messages that they hope will convince hordes of customers that their products or services are the best. There's the rub—in many cases they may be trying too hard! We can think of this as the **corporate paradox**—the more involved a company appears to be in the dissemination of news about its products, the less credible it becomes.[27] As we'll see in Chapter 11, consumer word of mouth typically is the most convincing kind of message. As Table 8–1 shows, **buzz** is word of mouth that is viewed as authentic and generated by customers. In contrast, **hype** is dismissed as inauthentic—corporate propaganda planted by a company with an axe to grind. So, the challenge to marketers is to get the word out there without looking as though they are working at it.

Some marketers are trying to borrow the veneer of buzz by mounting "stealth" campaigns that seem as if they are untouched by the corporate world. *Buzz building* has become the new mantra at many companies that recognize the power of underground word of mouth.[28] Indeed, a bit of a cottage industry has sprung up as some firms begin to specialize in the corporate shill business by planting comments on websites made to look as if they originated from actual consumers. Consider these recent examples:

- Building on the success of its resurrected Buddy Lee icon, Lee Apparel commissioned 15 websites devoted to the diminutive doll that looked "… horrible, as if fans created them," according to an employee of the company that created the sites. The goal was to make it look as if people were spontaneously turning on to the Buddy Lee phenomenon.[29]

- Dodge's Ram truck made a splash with a website supposedly generated by fans to organize drag races in several cities. The website features amateurishly shot footage of a drag race and contains no reference to the Dodge connection, just a shot of the Ram's grille. Staged drag races were held where, of course, only Ram trucks emerged victorious. Videos of the wins were then posted to the website. Bogus letters were sent to editors of local newspapers protesting the rise in street racing and mentioning the Dodge Ram involvement. Supposedly the guerrilla campaign was so hush-hush even the top brass at the car company was kept in the dark.[30]

- When RCA Records wanted to create a buzz around teen pop singer Christina Aguilera, they hired a team of young people to swarm the web and chat about her on popular teen sites like ***www.alloy.com***, ***www.bolt.com***, and ***www.gurlcom***. Posing as fans, they posted entries, raving about her new material. Just before one of her albums debuted, RCA also hired a direct marketing company to email electronic postcards filled with song snippets and biographical information to 50 000 web addresses.[31] The album quickly went to No. 1 on the charts.

TABLE 8–1

HYPE VERSUS BUZZ

Hype	⟵⟶	Buzz
Advertising		Word of Mouth
Overt		Covert
Corporate		Grassroots
Fake		Authentic
Scepticism		Credibility

As powerful as these tactics are, they have the potential to poison the well in a big way. Web surfers, already sceptical about what they see and hear, may get to the point where they assume every "authentic" site they find is really a corporate front. Until then, however, buzz building online is going strong.

Source Attractiveness

Source attractiveness refers to the source's perceived social value. This quality can emanate from the person's physical appearance, personality, or social status, or from his or her similarity to the receiver (we like to listen to people who are like us). A compelling source has great value, and endorsement deals are constantly in the works. Even dead sources can be attractive: The great grandson of the artist Renoir is putting his famous ancestor's name on bottled water, and the Picasso family licensed their name to the French automaker Citroen.[32]

WHAT IS BEAUTIFUL IS GOOD

Almost everywhere we turn, beautiful people are trying to persuade us to buy or do something. Our society places a very high premium on physical attractiveness, and we tend to assume that people who are good-looking are smarter, cooler, and happier. Such an assumption is called a **halo effect**, which occurs when persons who are rated highly on one dimension are assumed to excel on others as well. The effect can be explained in terms of the consistency principle, discussed in Chapter 7, which states that people are more comfortable when all of their judgments about a person go together. This notion has been termed the "what-is-beautiful-is-good" stereotype.[33]

A physically attractive source tends to facilitate attitude change. His or her degree of attractiveness exerts at least a modest effect on consumers' purchase intentions or product evaluation.[34] How does this happen?

One explanation is that physical attractiveness functions as a cue that facilitates or modifies information processing by directing consumers' attention to relevant marketing stimuli. Some evidence indicates that consumers pay more attention to ads, though not necessarily to the ad copy, that contain attractive models.[35] In other words, an ad with a beautiful person may stand a better chance of getting noticed but not necessarily of being read. Although we may enjoy looking at a beautiful or handsome person, these positive feelings do not necessarily affect product attitudes or purchase intentions.[36]

Beauty can also function as a source of information. The effectiveness of highly attractive spokespeople in ads appears to be largely limited to those situations where the advertised product is overtly related to attractiveness or sexuality.[37] The *social adaptation perspective* assumes that information seen to be instrumental in forming an attitude will be more heavily weighted by the perceiver; we filter out irrelevant information to minimize cognitive effort. Under the right circumstances an endorser's level of attractiveness constitutes a source of information instrumental to the attitude-change process.[38] An attractive spokesperson, for this reason, is more likely to be an effective source when the product is relevant to attractiveness. For example, attractiveness affects attitudes toward ads about perfume or cologne (where attractiveness is relevant) but not toward coffee ads, where attractiveness is not relevant.[39]

STAR POWER: CELEBRITIES AS COMMUNICATIONS SOURCES

Celebrity endorsers don't come cheap, but many advertisers continue to believe in their effectiveness. Tiger Woods is now the richest endorser in sports history, with an estimated income of $62 million per year (not counting the money he makes actually winning golf tournaments!).[40] All kinds of stars are in demand, even when it seems that their "brand personality" isn't consistent with the product being advertised. For example, Victoria's Secret signed none other than Bob Dylan to pitch its "Angels" line of lingerie while models cavort in the background to a

Marketing Pitfall ↘

It's not uncommon for celebrities to pitch products in other countries that they wouldn't want to be associated with back home. For example, Jennifer Aniston has worked as a spokesperson for Heineken beer overseas, but the former *Friends* star restricts the brewer from even posting images of the commercial on the web. At a website called ***www.japander.com***, you can check out a wide range of Hollywood stars who have appeared in Japanese commercials. You can watch George Clooney promote Toyota cars (2001), Harrison Ford sell Kirin beer (mid-1990s), Madonna hawk a rice beverage (1995), and Brad Pitt shill blue jeans (late 1990s).[48]

remixed version of his 1997 song "Love Sick." This from an anti-establishment folk singer who once wrote the lyrics: "Advertising signs that con you/Into thinking you're the one/That can do what's never been done/That can win what's never been won…"[41] Why do stars command this kind of money? One study found that famous faces capture attention and are processed more efficiently by the brain than are "ordinary" faces.[42] Celebrities increase awareness of a firm's advertising and enhance both company image and brand attitudes.[43] A celebrity endorsement strategy can be an effective way to differentiate among similar products. This is especially important when consumers do not perceive many actual differences among competitors, as often occurs when brands are in the mature stage of the product life cycle.

More generally, star power works because celebrities embody *cultural meanings*; they symbolize important categories, such as status and social class (e.g., a "working-class hero" like Drew Carey) or gender (a "ladies' man," such as Leonardo diCaprio). Ideally, the advertiser decides what meanings the product should convey (that is, how it should be positioned in the marketplace) and then chooses a celebrity who has come to evoke a similar meaning. The product's meaning thus moves from the manufacturer to the consumer, using the star as a vehicle.[44]

For celebrity campaigns to be effective, the endorser must have a clear and popular image. In addition, the celebrity's image and that of the product he or she endorses should be similar; this effect is known as the **match-up hypothesis**.[45] Many promotional strategies employing stars fail because the endorser has not been selected very carefully; some marketers just assume that because a person is "famous," he or she will serve as a successful spokesperson.

Celebrities often pitch well-known brands, but sometimes they're also responsible for making the products stars in their own right. Nowhere is this star-making power more pronounced than in the world of hip hop. For example, Busta Rhymes and Diddy almost single-handedly made Courvoisier the "official" drink of the hip hop nation. In a popular video, the two music idols defeat evildoers, get the girls, and toast their triumphs with "yack," hip hop's shorthand for cognac. Courvoisier's U.S. sales skyrocketed, and the drink's brand manager says this is largely because Busta made the drink "the hero of the song." Other luxury products that have benefited from becoming hip hop icons include the Cadillac Escalade, Cristal champagne, Burberry, Prada, and Louis Vuitton.[46]

The images of celebrities can, however, be pretested to increase the probability of consumer acceptance. One widely used technique is the so-called *"Q" rating* (Q stands for quality) developed by a market research company. This rating considers two factors in surveys: consumers' level of familiarity with a name and the number of respondents who indicate that a person, program, or character is a favourite. Although it yields a rather rough measure, the Q rating acknowledges that mere familiarity with a celebrity's name is not sufficient to gauge popularity, since some widely known people are also widely disliked.

The effectiveness of celebrities as communications sources often depends upon their perceived credibility. Consumers may not trust a celebrity's motives for endorsing a product, or they may question the star's competence to evaluate the product's claims critically. This "credibility gap" appears to be widening. In a recent one-year period, for example, the number of consumers who found celebrity advertising "less than credible" jumped to 52 percent. The greatest erosion of confidence came from younger consumers, 64 percent of whom thought that celebrities appeared in ads just for the money.[47] The lack of credibility is aggravated by incidences in which celebrities endorse products that they do not really believe in or in some cases do not use.

NON-HUMAN ENDORSERS

Celebrities can be effective endorsers, but there are drawbacks to using them. As noted previously, their motives may be suspect if they plug products that don't fit their images, or if they come to be seen as never having met a product they didn't like (for a fee). They may be involved in a scandal or upset customers, as when the Milk Processor Education Program suspended "Got Milk?" ads featuring Mary-Kate and Ashley Olsen after Mary-Kate entered a treatment facility for an undisclosed health issue.

For these reasons, some marketers seek alternatives, including cartoon characters and mascots. After all, as the marketing director of a company that manufactures costumed characters for sports teams and businesses points out, "You don't have to worry about your mascot checking into rehab."

Some big companies are trying this approach. As we saw in Chapter 1, Sony Electronics adopted a blue alien character named Plato to sell its Walkman brand. Roots Canada Ltd. employs a "Buddy the Beaver" mascot to promote its outlets. Roots' director of communications observed, "A lot of our stores are in shopping malls. Malls are crowded. People don't pay attention. But it's hard to ignore a seven-foot-tall beaver."[49]

Talking stuffed animals aside, a lot of the real action these days is in the use of virtual models. An **avatar** is the manifestation of a Hindu deity in superhuman or animal form. In the computing world it has come to mean a cyberspace presence represented by a character that you can move around inside a visual, graphical world. Many consumers became more aware of these cybermodels following the recent movie *Simone*, which starred Al Pacino as a washed-up director who creates a virtual actress that the public believes is real. Although a flesh-and-blood woman named Rachel Roberts played the title role, New Line Cinema kept her existence a secret for almost two years as it tried to create a buzz that Simone really was a computer concoction.[50]

Avatars like Simone originated in computer games like The Sims, but now they are starting to appear in online advertising and on e-commerce sites as a mechanism for enhancing the online experience. Rock bands, soft-drink makers, and other big-time marketers are using avatars. Coca-Cola Company recently launched an avatar-populated site for the Hong Kong market where avatars mill around and chat in a Coke-sponsored world. British Telecom also is testing such products as avatar email, which is software that makes the sender's face appear and speak the message aloud.[51]

The creation of avatars for commercial formats is evolving into a cottage industry as demand for compelling figures begins to grow. For example, the German firm NoDNA GmbH (*www.nodna.com*) offers a variety of "virtual stars." These are computer-generated figures that appear as caricatures, "vuppets" (cartoon-type mascots and animals), and "replicants" that are doubles of real people. Its models receive hundreds of love letters and even a few marriage proposals.[52]

One advantage of virtual avatars compared to flesh-and-blood models is that it's possible to change the avatar in real time to suit the needs of the target audience or individual consumer. From an advertising perspective, using avatars is likely to be more cost-effective than hiring a real person. From a personal selling and customer service perspective, they have the ability to handle multiple customers at any one time, they are not geographically limited, and they are operational 24/7, thus freeing up company employees and sales personnel to perform other activities.

The Tangled Web

Men who don't feel like finding a new girlfriend now can buy a virtual one named Vivienne. She appears to be three-dimensional and moves through 18 different settings, including a restaurant, shopping mall, and airport. She can converse on 35 000 topics, from philosophy to movies to sculpture. Software maker Artificial Life Inc. of Hong Kong sells the avatar, who likes to be taken to movies and bars. She loves to be given virtual flowers and chocolates, and she can translate six languages if you travel overseas. She never undresses, although she has some skimpy outfits for the gym, and she is a tease who draws the line at anything beyond blowing kisses. If you marry her in a virtual ceremony, you even end up with a virtual mother-in-law who really does call you in the middle of the night on your cell phone to ask where you are and whether you have been treating her daughter right.[53]

THE MESSAGE

A major study of more than 1000 commercials identified factors that appear to determine whether or not a commercial message will be persuasive. The single most important feature was whether the communication contained a brand-differentiating message.

→ A German firm called NoDNA offers its own stable of cybermodels such as Tyra, who is shown here. *Used with permission of noDNA c/o Vierte Art.*

In other words, did the communication stress a unique attribute or benefit of the product? Other good and bad elements are depicted in Table 8–2.[54]

The characteristics of the commercial message itself help to determine the impact of that message on attitudes. These variables may include how the message is said, as well as what is actually said. Some of the issues facing marketers include the following:

- Should the message be conveyed in words or pictures?
- How concrete or vivid should the arguments and imagery be?
- How often should the message be repeated?
- Should both sides of an argument be presented?
- Should a conclusion be drawn, or should this be left up to the listener?
- Is it effective to explicitly compare a product with that of competitors?
- Should a blatant sexual appeal be used?
- Should the ad be funny?
- Should negative emotions, such as fear, ever be aroused?

| TABLE 8–2 |

POSITIVE AND NEGATIVE EFFECTS OF ELEMENTS IN TELEVISION COMMERCIALS

Positive Effects	Negative Effects
Showing convenience of use	Extensive information on components, ingredients, or nutrition
Showing new product or improved features	
Casting background (i.e., people are incidental to message)	Outdoor setting (message gets lost)
	Large number of on-screen characters
Indirect comparison with other products	Graphic displays
Demonstration of the product in use	
Demonstration of tangible results (e.g., bouncy hair)	
An actor playing the role of an ordinary person	
No principal character (i.e., more time is devoted to the product)	

Source: Adapted from David W. Stewart and David H. Furse, "The Effects of Television Advertising Execution on Recall, Comprehension, and Persuasion," *Psychology & Marketing* 2 (Fall 1985): 135–160. Copyright © 1985 by John Wiley & Sons, Inc. Reprinted by permission.

Sending the Message

The saying "a picture is worth a thousand words" captures the idea that visual stimuli can economically deliver a big impact, especially when the communicator wants to influence the receivers' emotional responses. For this reason, advertisers often place great emphasis on vivid and creative illustrations or photography.[55]

On the other hand, a picture is not always as effective at communicating factual information. Ads that contain the same information, presented in either visual or verbal form, have been found to elicit different reactions. The verbal version affects ratings on the utilitarian aspects of a product, while the visual version affects aesthetic evaluations.[56] Verbal elements are more effective when reinforced by an accompanying picture, especially if the illustration is *framed* (i.e., the message in the picture is strongly related to the copy).[57]

Because it requires more effort to process, a verbal message is most appropriate for high-involvement situations, such as in print contexts where readers are motivated to pay attention to the advertising. Because verbal material decays more rapidly in memory, more frequent exposures are needed to obtain the desired effect. Visual images, in contrast, allow the receiver to *chunk* information at the time of encoding (see Chapter 3 on memory processes). Chunking results in a stronger memory trace, which aids retrieval over time.[58]

Visual elements may affect brand attitudes in one of two ways. First, the consumer may form inferences about the brand and change his or her beliefs because of an illustration's imagery. For example, people who saw an ad for a facial tissue accompanied by a photo of a sunset were more likely to believe that the brand came in attractive colours.

Second, brand attitudes may be affected more directly. A strong positive or negative reaction elicited by the visual elements will influence the consumer's attitude toward the ad (A_{ad}), which will then affect brand attitudes (A_b). This *dual-component model* of brand attitudes is illustrated in Figure 8–3.[59]

VIVIDNESS

Both pictures and words can differ in *vividness*. Powerful descriptions or graphics command attention and are more strongly embedded in memory because they

FIGURE 8–3   EFFECTS OF VISUAL AND VERBAL COMPONENTS OF ADVERTISEMENTS ON BRAND ATTITUDES

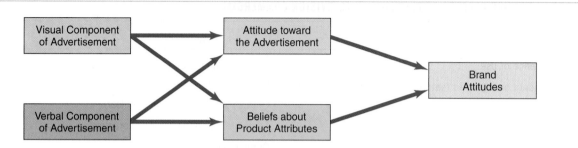

may tend to activate mental imagery, while abstract stimuli inhibit this process.[60] Of course, this effect can cut both ways. Negative information presented in a vivid manner may result in more negative evaluations at a later time.[61]

The concrete discussion of a product attribute in ad copy also influences the importance of that attribute because more attention is drawn to it. For example, the copy for a watch that read, "According to industry sources, three out of every four watch breakdowns are due to water getting into the case" was more effective than the version that read "According to industry sources, many watch breakdowns are due to water getting into the case."[62]

REPETITION

Repetition can be a two-edged sword for marketers. As noted in Chapter 3, multiple exposures to a stimulus are usually required for learning (especially conditioning) to occur. Contrary to the saying "familiarity breeds contempt," people tend to like things that are more familiar to them, even if they were not that keen on them initially.[63] This phenomenon is known as the *mere exposure effect*. Positive effects for advertising repetition are found even in mature product categories; repeating product information has been shown to boost consumers' awareness of the brand, even though nothing new has been said.[64] On the other hand, too much repetition creates *habituation,* wherein the consumer no longer pays attention to the stimulus because of fatigue or boredom. Excessive exposure can cause *advertising wear-out,* which can result in negative reactions to an ad after seeing it too much.[65]

The fine line between familiarity and boredom has been explained by the **two-factor theory,** which proposes that two separate psychological processes are operating when a person is repeatedly exposed to an ad. The positive side of repetition is that it increases familiarity and thus reduces uncertainty about the product. The negative side is that, over time, boredom increases with each exposure. At some point the amount of boredom incurred begins to exceed the amount of uncertainty reduced, resulting in wear-out. This pattern is depicted in Figure 8–4. Its effect is especially pronounced in cases where each exposure is of a fairly long duration (such as a 60-second commercial).[66]

The theory implies that advertisers can overcome this problem by limiting the amount of exposure per repetition (for example, by using 15-second spots). They can also maintain familiarity but alleviate boredom by slightly varying the content of ads over time through campaigns that revolve around a common theme (although each spot may be different). Recipients who are exposed to varied ads about the product absorb more information about product attributes and experience more positive thoughts about the brand than do those exposed repeatedly to the same information. This additional information allows the person to resist attempts to change his or her attitude in the face of a counterattack by a competing brand.[67] For example, H&R Block systematically presents different reasons to use its firm for tax preparation.

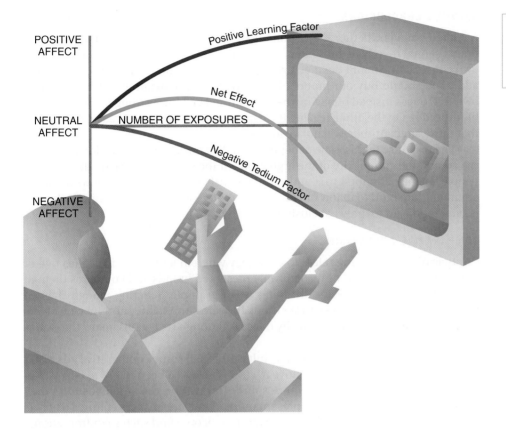

FIGURE 8–4

TWO-FACTOR THEORY AND
ADVERTISING WEAR-OUT

Constructing the Argument

Many marketing messages are similar to debates or trials, in which someone presents arguments and tries to convince the receiver to shift his or her opinion accordingly. The way the argument is presented can thus be very important.

ONE- VERSUS TWO-SIDED ARGUMENTS

Most messages merely present one or more positive attributes about the product or reasons to buy it. These are known as *supportive arguments*. An alternative is to use a *two-sided message,* in which both positive and negative information is presented. Research has indicated that two-sided ads can be quite effective, yet they are not widely used.[68]

Why would a marketer want to devote advertising space to publicizing a product's negative attributes? Under the right circumstances, the use of *refutational arguments,* in which a negative issue is raised and then dismissed, can be quite effective. This approach can increase source credibility by reducing reporting bias. Also, people who are sceptical about the product may be more receptive to a balanced argument as opposed to a "whitewash."[69]

This is not to say that the marketer should go overboard in presenting major problems with the product. In the typical refutational strategy, relatively minor attributes are discussed that may present a problem or fall short when a product is compared with competitors. These drawbacks are then refuted by emphasizing positive, important attributes. Avis got a lot of mileage out of claiming to be only "No. 2," while an ad for Volkswagen woefully described one of its cars as a "lemon" because there was a scratch on the glove-compartment chrome strip.[70]

A two-sided strategy appears to be most effective when the audience is well-educated (and presumably more impressed by a balanced argument).[71] It is also best used when receivers are not already loyal to the product; "preaching to the converted" about possible drawbacks may raise doubts unnecessarily.

DRAWING CONCLUSIONS

A related issue is whether the argument should draw conclusions or whether the points should merely be presented, permitting the consumer to arrive at his or her own conclusion. Should the message say only, "Our brand is superior," or should it add, "You should buy our brand"? On the one hand, consumers who make their own inferences instead of having them spoon-fed will form stronger, more accessible attitudes. On the other, leaving the conclusion ambiguous increases the chance that the desired attitude will not be formed.

The response to this issue depends upon the consumers' motivation to process the ad and the complexity of the arguments. If the message is personally relevant, people will pay attention to it and spontaneously form inferences. However, if the arguments are hard to follow or consumers' motivation to follow them is lacking, it is safer for the ad to draw conclusions.[72]

COMPARATIVE ADVERTISING

Comparative advertising refers to a strategy wherein a message identifies two or more specifically named or recognizably presented brands and compares them in terms of one or more specific attributes.[73] For example, Schering-Plough claimed that "New OcuClear relieves three times longer than Visine," and Bristol-Myers stated that "New Liquid Vanish really does clean tough rust stains below the waterline better than Lysol."

This strategy has yielded mixed results. Although some comparative ads result in desired attitude change, or positive A_{ad}, they have also been found to be lower in believability and may result in more source derogation (i.e., the consumer may doubt the credibility of a biased presentation).[74] Indeed, in some cultures (such as in Asia) comparative advertising is rare because people find such a confrontational approach offensive.

A survey by Leger Marketing asked Canadians whether they felt television advertisements are truthful in their description of products or services being advertised. Only 4 percent of respondents strongly agreed that television ads were truthful, compared with 53 percent who openly distrusted them. What Canadians liked in an ad varied by area, with Quebec residents having quite different preferences from those living in other provinces.[75]

→ Irving Oil emphasizes positive reasons why they are the right choice when it comes to home fuel delivery.
Courtesy of Irving Oil.

Comparative ads do appear to be effective in the case of new products. Here, they are superior in anchoring a new brand closer to a dominant one and in building a clear brand image. However, if the aim is to compare the new brand with the market leader in terms of specific product attributes, merely saying it is as good as or better than the leader is not sufficient. For example, in a study about a fictitious product, the claim "Spring has the same fluoride as Crest" resulted in attitude change for the "product," while the more global statement "Preferred by Europeans in comparison with Crest" did not.[76] And comparative ads are credible only if they don't reach too far by comparing a brand to a competitor that is obviously superior. Not too surprisingly, for example, a survey of new car buyers found TV commercials comparing a Nissan Altima to a Mercedes were not effective.[77]

Types of Message Appeals

The way something is said can be as significant as what is said; the same idea can be encoded in many different ways. It can tug at the heartstrings or scare you, make you laugh, make you cry, or leave you wanting to learn more. In this section we'll review the major alternatives available to communicators who wish to *appeal* to a message recipient.

EMOTIONAL VERSUS RATIONAL APPEALS

The French firm L'Oréal has persuaded millions of women around the world to buy its personal care products by promising them Parisian chic, associating them with its sexy spokeswomen, and touting the self-assured slogan, "Because you're worth it." Now the company is feeling pressure from an unlikely rival. Procter & Gamble is applying the no-nonsense comparative advertising strategy that the company has used for a long time to sell many of its products to cosmetics. After P&G acquired Clairol in 2001, the company better known for Tide detergent and many other household products suddenly became the largest seller of cosmetics in supermarkets and club stores. One P&G promotion for Pantene hair conditioner offered a "10-day challenge," promising hair that was 60 percent healthier, 85 percent shinier, 80 percent less prone to breakage, and 70 percent less frizzy. In another case, after using 60 different methods to measure the size of pores, length of wrinkles, and the colour and size of age spots, P&G researchers used results from one of their tests to proclaim in national ads that Olay Total Effects Night Firming Cream worked better than leading department-store brands (including those made by L'Oréal). Now P&G is trying to penetrate the high-end market, where L'Oréal rules. The head of L'Oréal sneers at this factual approach by arguing that when it comes to selling cosmetics, "you have to both inform, convince but also seduce consumers... and not just ram facts down their throats."[78]

So, which is better: To appeal to the head or to the heart? The answer often depends upon the nature of the product and the type of relationship consumers have with it. This issue was at the core of a fierce debate at Polaroid, a company known for technological innovation rather than "warm and fuzzy" products. Marketers at the photographic products firm argued strenuously that the company needed to develop new, "fun" products to recapture younger consumers. Engineers were antagonistic about this idea; they felt a "toy" camera would cheapen Polaroid's reputation. In this case, the marketers prevailed and convinced the engineers to create a small instant camera with a cheap lens to produce fuzzy thumbnail size photos. The i-Zone Instant Pocket camera was born. In a radical move for the company, the ad campaign is based on the theme "being a little bit bad is good." One execution features a young man who sticks instant pictures on his nipples and then wiggles his chest. Half of the i-Zone's buyers are 13- to 17-year-old girls, and Polaroid reaped revenues of US$270 million for the product in one year.

→ The Canadian Hearing Society uses a rational appeal to build positive attitudes toward deaf, deafened, and hard-of-hearing people.
Courtesy of The Canadian Hearing Society.

Many companies turned to this strategy after realizing that consumers do not find many differences among brands, especially those in well-established, mature categories. Ads for products ranging from cars (Lincoln Mercury) to cards (Hallmark) focus instead on emotional aspects. Mercury's capitalization on emotional attachments to old rock songs succeeded in lowering the median age of its consumers for some models by 10 years.[79]

The precise effects of rational versus emotional appeals are hard to gauge. Though recall of ad contents tends to be better for "thinking" ads than for "feeling" ads, conventional measures of advertising effectiveness (like day-after recall) may not be adequate to assess cumulative effects of emotional ads. These open-ended measures are oriented toward cognitive responses, and feeling ads may be penalized because the reactions are not as easy to articulate.[80]

SEX APPEALS

Under the assumption that "sex sells," many campaigns—for everything from perfumes to automobiles—feature heavy doses of erotic suggestions that range from

FIGURE 8–5

WHAT MAKES A BEER ADVERTISEMENT APPEALING?

Source: Jean-Marc Léger and Dave Scholz, "The Appeal of Beer Ads," *Marketing Magazine* (June 17, 2002): 24. Reprinted with permission of *Marketing Magazine*, Rogers Publishing.

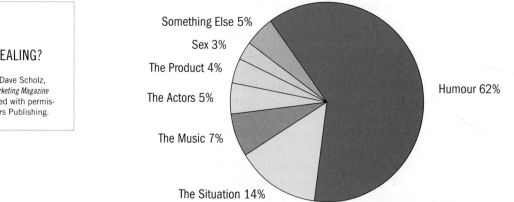

Something Else 5%
Sex 3%
The Product 4%
The Actors 5%
The Music 7%
The Situation 14%
Humour 62%

subtle hints to blatant displays of skin. Perhaps not surprisingly, female nudity in print ads generates negative feelings and tension among female consumers, while men's reactions are more positive.[81] In a case of turnabout being fair play, another study found that males dislike nude males in ads, whereas females responded well to undressed males—but not totally nude ones.[82]

DOES SEX WORK?　Although the use of sex does appear to draw attention to an ad, its use may actually be counterproductive to the marketer. Ironically, a provocative picture can be too effective: It attracts so much attention that it hinders processing and recall of the ad's contents. Sexual appeals appear to be ineffective when used merely as a "trick" to grab attention. They do, however, appear to work when the product is *itself* sexually related. Overall, though, use of a strong sexual appeal is not very well received.[83]

HUMOROUS APPEALS

The use of humour can be tricky, particularly since what is funny to one person may be offensive or incomprehensible to another. Specific cultures may have different senses of humour and also use funny material in diverse ways. For example, commercials in the United Kingdom and Canada are more likely to use puns and satire than those in the United States.[84]

DOES HUMOUR WORK?　Overall, humorous advertisements do get attention. One study found that recognition scores for humorous liquor ads were better than average. However, the verdict is mixed as to whether humour affects recall or product attitudes in a significant way.[85] Humour can be effective when it provides a source of *distraction*. A funny ad inhibits the consumer from counterarguing. This, in turn, increases the likelihood of message acceptance.[86]

Humour is more likely to be effective when the brand is clearly identified and the funny material does not "swamp" the message. This danger is similar to that of beautiful models diverting attention from copy points. Subtle humour is usually better, as is humour that does not make fun of the potential consumer.

Finally, humour should be appropriate to the product's image. An undertaker or a bank might want to avoid humour, while other products adapt to it quite well.

A recent study by two University of McGill researchers found humorous messages can temper ads for threatening situations. For example, people do not want to think too much about disease or other avoidance situations. When the message for these negative scenarios was couched in humour, the advertisements were better received.[87]

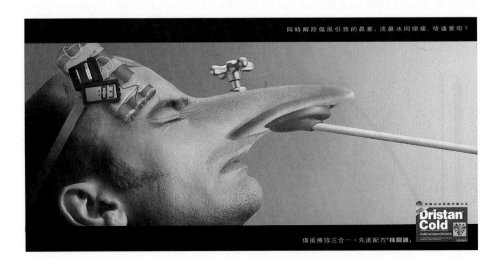

← This humorous ad for Dristan cold medicine, which ran in Hong Kong, reads: "Is this the only way to get rid of a stuffed-up runny nose and the headaches a cold can bring?" Visual humour is often an effective way to get attention and cut through advertising clutter.
Courtesy of Bates Hong Kong, Ltd.

Marketing Pitfall

FEAR APPEALS

Fear appeals highlight the negative consequences that can occur if the consumer fails to change a behaviour or attitude. The arousal of fear is a common tactic for public-policy issues, such as convincing consumers to stop smoking or to drive safely (i.e., to reduce physical risk).

This tactic can also be applied to social-risk issues by appealing to people's anxieties about their careers or love lives. This tactic has been half-jokingly called the "slice-of-death" approach. One increasingly common fear appeal is to prey on people's insecurity about being laid off from their jobs. In a spot for Contac cold medicine, a construction worker wades through a rainstorm. He says that he needed to take Contac in order to get to work that day, adding, "No work, no pay." This ad was developed after interviews with about 800 consumers indicated widespread anxiety about losing their jobs because of illness.[88]

DOES FEAR WORK?   Fear appeals are usually most effective when only a moderate amount of fear is induced. The relationship between fear and attitude change is *nonmonotonic*.[89] As shown in Figure 8–6, this means that increasing levels of fear does not result in increased change; the relationship instead resembles an inverted U-shaped curve. If the threat is too great, the audience tends to deny that it exists as a way of rationalizing the danger.

Fear appeals appear to be most effective when the consumer is already afraid of the problem discussed in the ad. The threats should not be excessive, and a solution to the problem should be presented. (Otherwise, consumers will tune out the ad since they can do nothing to solve the problem.)[90] Fear appeals also work better when source credibility is high.[91]

A study that manipulated subjects' degrees of anxiety about AIDS, for example, found that condom ads were evaluated most positively when a moderate amount of fear was induced. In this context, copy that promoted the use of the condom because "sex is a risky business" (moderate fear) resulted in more attitude change than either a low-fear appeal that emphasized the product's sensitivity or a high-fear appeal that discussed the certainty of death from AIDS.[92] Similarly, scare tactics have not been as effective as hoped in getting teenagers to decrease their use of alcohol or drugs. Teens simply tune out the message or deny its relevance to them.[93] On the other hand, a study of adolescent responses to social threat versus physical threat appeals in drug prevention messages found that social threat is a more effective strategy.[94]

Some of the research on fear appeals may be confusing a threat (the literal content of a message, such as saying "engage only in safe sex or die") with fear (an emotional response to the message). According to this argument, greater fear does result in greater persuasion—but not all threats are equally effective because different people will respond differently to the same threat. Therefore, the strongest threats are not always the most persuasive because they may not have the desired

FIGURE 8–6

THE RELATIONSHIP BETWEEN FEAR AND ATTITUDE CHANGE

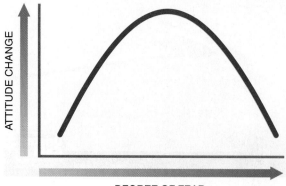

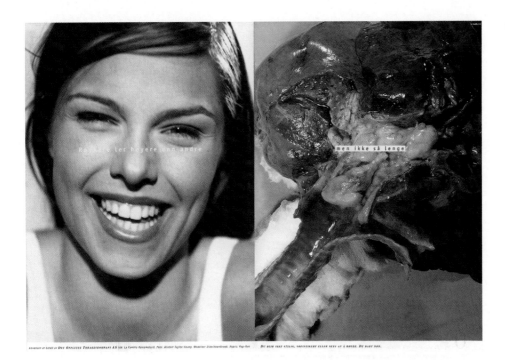

←This Norwegian ad addresses young people's smoking attitudes by arousing strong negative feelings. The ad reads (left panel): "Smokers are more sociable than others." (Right panel): "While it lasts."
Courtesy of Johns Hopkins Center for Communications Programs.

impact on the perceiver. For example, raising the spectre of AIDS is about the strongest threat that can be delivered to sexually active kids—but this tactic is effective only if the kids believe they will get the disease. Since many young people (especially those who live in fairly affluent suburban areas or rural areas) don't believe that "people like them" will be exposed to the AIDS virus, this strong threat may not actually result in a high level of fear.[96] The bottom line is that more precise measures of actual fear responses are needed before definitive conclusions can be drawn about the impact of fear appeals on consumption decisions.

The Message as Art Form: Metaphors Be with You

Marketers may be thought of as storytellers who supply visions of reality similar to those provided by authors, poets, and artists. These communications take the form of stories because the product benefits they describe are intangible and must be given tangible meaning by being expressed in a form that is concrete and visible. Advertising creatives rely (consciously or not) on various literary devices to communicate these meanings. For example, a product or service might be personified by a character such as Mr. Goodwrench, the Jolly Green Giant, or the California Raisins. Many ads take the form of an allegory, wherein a story is told about an abstract trait or concept that has been personified as a person, animal, or vegetable.

A **metaphor** involves the use of an explicit comparison, such as A is B ("Air Canada is your friend in faraway places"). Metaphors allow the marketer to activate meaningful images and apply them to everyday events. In the stock market, "white knights" battle "hostile raiders" using "poison pills," while Tony the Tiger allows us to equate cereal with strength, and the Merrill Lynch bull sends the message that the company is "a breed apart."[97]

Resonance is another type of literary device that is frequently used in advertising. It is a form of presentation that combines a play on words with a relevant picture. Table 8–3 gives some examples of actual ads that rely on the principle of resonance. Although metaphor substitutes one meaning for another by connecting two things that are in some way similar, resonance uses an element that has a double meaning, such as a pun, in which there is a similarity in the sound of a word but a difference in meaning. For example, an ad for a diet

→Participaction uses an attention-getting and humorous play on the metaphor "Healthy as a horse" to promote walking as a regular exercise. *Courtesy of Participaction.*

How Come Nobody Ever Says They're 'Healthy As A Dog?'

One of the many misconceptions about exercise is that everyday activities like walking your best friend does little to improve your health. In fact, nothing could be further from the truth. The daily bound with 'Spot' is great for both of you. And, considering how eager he is to go whenever you are, says a lot about how little it takes to be active and feel good. Just 30 minutes a day, most days of the week, for a whole new leash...er, lease, on life. Of course, if you don't have a dog, there's nothing stopping you from taking yourself for a daily walk. (Leash optional)

Sharing a Healthier Future®

PARTICIPACTION®

strawberry shortcake dessert might bear the copy "berried treasure" so that qualities associated with buried treasure—being rich, hidden, and associated with adventurous pirates—are conveyed for the brand. Because the text departs from expectations, it creates a state of tension or uncertainty in the viewer until he or she figures out the wordplay. Once the consumer "gets it," he or she may prefer the ad over a more straightforward message.[98]

TABLE 8–3

SOME EXAMPLES OF ADVERTISING RESONANCE

Product/Headline	Visual
Embassy Suites: "This Year, We're Unwrapping Suites by the Dozen"	Chocolate kisses with hotel name underneath each kiss
Toyota auto parts: "Our Lifetime Guarantee May Come as a Shock"	Man holding a shock absorber
Bounce fabric softener: "Is There Something Creeping Up Behind You?"	Woman's dress bunched up on her back, caused by static
Pepsi: "This Year, Hit the Beach Topless"	Pepsi bottle cap lying on the sand
ASICS athletic shoes: "We Believe Women Should Be Running the Country"	Woman jogging in a rural setting

Source: Adapted from Edward F. McQuarrie and David Glen Mick, "On Resonance: A Critical Pluralistic Inquiry into Advertising Rhetoric," *Journal of Consumer Research* 19 (September 1992): 182, Table 1. Reprinted with permission of The University of Chicago Press.

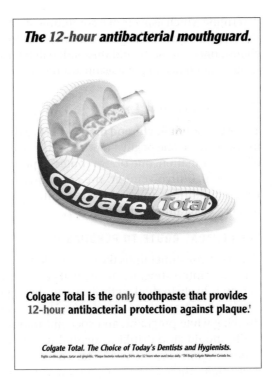

← This Colgate toothpaste ad uses the metaphor of a mouthguard to convey the strength of its antibacterial protection.
Colgate Palmolive Company

FORMS OF STORY PRESENTATION

Just as a story can be told in words or pictures, the way the audience is addressed can also make a difference. Commercials are structured like other art forms, borrowing conventions from literature and art as they communicate their messages.[99]

One important distinction is between a *drama* and a *lecture*.[100] A lecture is like a speech where the source speaks directly to the audience members in an attempt to inform them about a product or persuade them to buy it. Because a lecture clearly implies an attempt at persuasion, the audience will regard it as such. Assuming listeners are motivated to do so, they will weigh the merits of the message along with the credibility of the source. Cognitive responses, such as counterargumentation, will occur. The appeal will be accepted to the extent that it overcomes the consumer's objections and is congruent with his or her beliefs.

In contrast, a drama is similar to a play or movie. While an argument holds the viewer at arm's length, a drama draws the viewer into the action. The characters address the audience only indirectly; they interact with each other about a product or service in an imaginary setting. Dramas attempt to be experiential—to involve the audience emotionally. In *transformational* advertising, the consumer associates the experience of product usage with some subjective sensation. Thus, ads for the Infiniti attempted to transform the "driving experience" into a mystical, spiritual event.

THE SOURCE VERSUS THE MESSAGE: SELL THE STEAK OR THE SIZZLE?

Two major components of the communications model—the source and the message—have been reviewed. Which aspect has the most impact on persuading consumers to change their attitudes? Should marketers worry more about *what* is said or about *how* it's said and *who* says it?

The answer is that it depends. Variations in a consumer's level of involvement, as discussed in Chapter 4, result in the activation of very different cognitive processes when a message is received. Research indicates that this level of involvement will determine which aspects of a communication are processed. The situation appears to resemble that of a traveller who comes to a fork in the road: The traveller can choose only one path, and this path will have a big impact on the factors that will make a difference in persuasion attempts.

The Elaboration Likelihood Model

The **elaboration likelihood model (ELM)** assumes that, once a consumer receives a message, he or she begins to process it.[101] Depending upon the personal relevance of the information, one of two routes to persuasion will be followed. Under conditions of high involvement, the consumer takes the *central route to persuasion*. Under conditions of low involvement, a *peripheral route* is taken instead. This model is diagrammed in Figure 8–7.

THE CENTRAL ROUTE TO PERSUASION

When the consumer finds the information in a persuasive message to be relevant or somehow interesting, he or she will carefully attend to the message content. The person is likely to think actively about the arguments presented and generate *cognitive responses* to these arguments. Upon hearing a radio message warning about drinking while pregnant, an expectant mother might say to herself, "She's right. I really should stop drinking alcohol now that I'm pregnant." Or she might offer *counterarguments*, such as "That's a bunch of baloney. My mother had a cocktail every night when she was pregnant with me, and I turned out fine." If a person generates counterarguments in response to a message, it is less likely that he or she will yield to the message, while the generation of further supporting arguments increases the probability of compliance.[102]

The central route to persuasion is likely to involve the traditional hierarchy of effects, as discussed in Chapter 7. Beliefs are carefully formed and evaluated, and strong attitudes that are then formed will be likely to guide behaviour. The implication is that message factors, such as the quality of arguments presented, will be important in determining attitude change. Prior knowledge about a topic may result in more thoughts about the message and will also increase the number of counterarguments.[103]

FIGURE 8–7   THE ELABORATION LIKELIHOOD MODEL OF PERSUASION

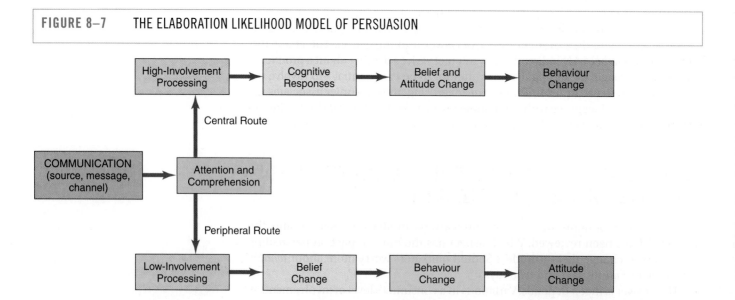

← Source: J. Craig Andrews and Terence A. Shimp, "Effects of Involvement, Argument, Strength, and Source Characteristics on Central and Peripheral Processing in Advertising," Psychology & Marketing 7 (Fall 1990): 195–214.

THE PERIPHERAL ROUTE TO PERSUASION

In contrast, the peripheral route is taken when the person is not motivated to think about the arguments presented. Instead, the consumer is likely to use other cues in deciding on the suitability of the message. These cues might include the product's package, the attractiveness of the source or the context in which the message is presented. Sources of information extraneous to the actual message content are called *peripheral cues* because they surround the actual message.

The peripheral route to persuasion highlights the paradox of low involvement discussed in Chapter 4: When consumers do not care about a product, the stimuli associated with it *increase* in importance. The implication here is that low-involvement products may be purchased chiefly because the marketer has done a good job in designing a "sexy" package, choosing a popular spokesperson, or perhaps just creating a pleasant shopping environment.

Support for the ELM Model

The ELM approach has received a lot of research support.[104] In one typical study, undergraduates were exposed to one of several mock advertisements for Break, a new brand of low-alcohol beer. Using the technique of *thought-listing* or cognitive responses, students were asked to provide their thoughts about the ads, which were later analyzed by the researchers. Two versions of the ads are shown above.[105] Three independent variables crucial to the ELM were manipulated:

1. *Message-processing involvement:* Some subjects were motivated to be highly involved with the ads by being promised a gift of low-alcohol beer for participating in the study and by being told that the brand would soon be available in their area. Subjects who were not promised a gift and who were told that the brand would be introduced in a distant area had low involvement.

2. *Argument strength:* One version of the ad used strong, compelling arguments to drink Break ("Break contains one-half the amount of alcohol of regular beers and therefore has less calories than regular beer …"), while the other listed only weak arguments ("Break is just as good as any other regular beer").

3. *Source characteristics:* Although both ads contained a photo of a couple drinking the beer, their relative social attractiveness was varied by their dress, posture, and non-verbal expressions, and by the background information given about their educational achievements and occupations.

Consistent with the ELM model, high-involvement subjects had more thoughts related to the ad messages than did low-involvement subjects, who devoted more cognitive activity to the sources used in the ad. The attitudes of high-involvement subjects were more likely to be swayed by powerful arguments, while the attitudes of low-involvement subjects were more likely to be influenced by the ad version using attractive sources. The results of this study, paired with those of others, indicate that the relative effectiveness of a strong message and a favourable source depends upon consumers' level of involvement with the product being advertised.

These results underscore the basic idea that highly involved consumers look for the "steak" (strong, rational arguments), while those who are less involved are more affected by the "sizzle" (the colours and images used in packaging, or endorsements by famous people). It is important to remember, however, that the *same* communications variable can be both a central and a peripheral cue, depending upon its relation to the attitude object. The physical attractiveness of a model might serve as a peripheral cue in a car commercial, but her beauty might be a central cue for a product such as shampoo, where the product's benefits are directly tied to enhancing attractiveness.[106]

CHAPTER SUMMARY

CONSUMERS WHO PROCESS MESSAGES ARE NOT NECESSARILY THE PASSIVE RECEIVERS OF INFORMATION MARKETERS ONCE BELIEVED THEM TO BE.

- Persuasion refers to an attempt to change consumers' attitudes. The communications model specifies the elements needed to transmit meaning. These include a source, a message, a medium, a receiver, and feedback.

CONSUMERS' RESPONSES TO A FIRM'S MARKETING MESSAGES DO NOT NECESSARILY HAVE TO TAKE THE FORM OF A PURCHASE TO BE IMPORTANT OR USEFUL TO THE COMPANY.

- The traditional view of communications tends to regard the perceiver as a passive element in the process. Proponents of the uses and gratifications approach instead regard the consumer as an active participant who uses media for a variety of reasons. New developments in interactive communications highlight the need to consider the active roles a consumer might play in obtaining product information and building a relationship with a company. A product-related communication that directly yields a transaction is a first-order response. Customer feedback in response to a marketing message that is not in the form of a transaction is a second-order response. This may take the form of a request for more information about a good, service, or organization, or perhaps receipt of a "wish list" from the customer that specifies the types of product information he or she would like to get in the future.

SEVERAL FACTORS INFLUENCE THE EFFECTIVENESS OF THE SOURCE OF A COMMUNICATION.

- Two important characteristics that determine the effectiveness of a source are its attractiveness and its credibility. Although celebrities often serve these purposes, their credibility is not always as strong as marketers would like.

THE WAY A MESSAGE IS STRUCTURED CAN EXERT A BIG IMPACT ON HOW PERSUASIVE IT WILL BE.

- Some elements of a message that help to determine its effectiveness are whether it is conveyed in words or pictures, whether an emotional or a rational appeal is employed, the frequency with which it is repeated, whether a conclusion is drawn, whether both sides of the argument are presented, and whether the message includes fear, humour, or sexual references. Advertising messages often incorporate elements from art or literature such as drama, lecture, metaphor, and resonance.

CONSUMER VARIABLES HELP TO DETERMINE WHETHER THE NATURE OF THE SOURCE OR THE MESSAGE ITSELF WILL BE RELATIVELY MORE EFFECTIVE IN A PARTICULAR COMMUNICATION.

- The relative influence of the source versus that of the message depends upon the receiver's level of involvement with the communication. The elaboration likelihood model specifies that a less-involved consumer will more likely be swayed by source effects, while a more-involved consumer will more likely attend to and process components of the actual message.

KEY TERMS

Avatar   p. 221

Blogging   p. 215

Buzz   p. 218

Communications model   p. 212

Comparative advertising   p. 226

Corporate paradox   p. 218

Elaboration likelihood model (ELM)   p. 234

Fear appeal   p. 230

Halo effect   p. 219

Hype   p. 218

M-commerce   p. 215

Match-up hypothesis   p. 220

Metaphor   p. 231

Permission marketing   p. 213

Persuasion   p. 211

Resonance   p. 231

Sleeper effect   p. 217

Source attractiveness   p. 219

Source credibility   p. 216

Two-factor theory   p. 224

Uses and gratifications theory   p. 213

REVIEW QUESTIONS

1. List three psychological principles related to persuasion.
2. What is the difference between a first-order response and a second-order response? Give one example of each.
3. Describe the elements of the traditional communications model, and explain how the updated model is different.
4. Compare the perspective on media and attitude change proposed by the Frankfurt School theorists versus those who advocate a uses and gratifications perspective.
5. What are blogs and how can marketers use them?
6. What is source credibility, and what are two factors that influence whether we will perceive a source to be credible?
7. What is the difference between buzz and hype? How does this difference relate to the corporate paradox?
8. What is a halo effect, and why does it happen?

9. What is an avatar, and why might an advertiser choose to use one instead of hiring a celebrity endorser?
10. When should a marketer present a message visually versus verbally?
11. How does the two-factor theory explain the effects of message repetition on attitude change?
12. When is it best to present a two-sided message versus a one-sided message?
13. Do humorous ads work? If so, under what conditions?
14. Should marketers ever try to arouse fear to persuade consumers?
15. Why do marketers use metaphors to craft persuasive messages? Give two examples of this technique.
16. What is the difference between a metaphor and resonance?
17. What is the difference between a lecture and a drama?
18. Describe the elaboration likelihood model, and explain how it is related to the relative importance of what is said versus how it's said.

CONSUMER BEHAVIOUR CHALLENGE

Discuss

1. What are the pros and cons of using rational versus emotional appeals (i.e., trying to persuade consumers by focusing on what they know as opposed to what they feel)? When should marketers use one type or the other?

2. A flog is a fake blog a company posts to build buzz around its brand. Is this ethical?

3. The sleeper effect implies that perhaps we shouldn't worry too much about how positively people evaluate a source. Similarly, there's a saying in public relations that "any publicity is good publicity." Do you agree? Why or why not?

4. Discuss some conditions in which it would be advisable to use a comparative advertising strategy.

5. A marketer must decide whether to incorporate rational or emotional appeals in its communications strategy. Describe conditions that are more favourable to using one or the other.

6. Many companies rely on celebrity endorsers as communications sources to persuade consumers. Especially when targeting younger people, these spokespeople often are "cool" musicians, athletes, or movie stars. In your opinion, who would be the most effective celebrity endorser today, and why? Who would be the least effective? Why?

7. The website for Swiss Legend, a watch brand (*www.wwisslegend. com*), includes a section called "Celebrity Red Room," where there are photographs of famous people sporting the timepieces with their colourful and graphically striking designs. Swiss Legend has found its way to these people despite the fact that it hasn't been around very long, in part because it has been "associated with" events like the Screen Actors Guild (SAG) Awards and the Teen Choice Awards. This means that it has arranged to have its products given away at those events. This practice is called "gifting the talent." The point is not just to get celebrities to wear Swiss Legend watches, which sell in the $150 to $450 price range, but also to leverage the press coverage that focuses on what celebrities wear. The stars have been getting their Swiss Legends by way of Backstage Creations, one of several companies that oversee what has long since become a standard practice at awards shows and other galas. One method of gifting the talent is through "goody bags," a practice now so widely known that goody-bag contents are listed in the celebrity press. Backstage Creations also offers a more elaborate approach, creating an entire backstage environment—or "retreat"—laid out and decorated by a name interior designer and filled with complimentary products.[107] What do you think about the practice of "gifting the talent" to accumulate endorsements? Is this a sound strategy? Is it ethical for celebrities to accept these gifts?

Experiential Exercises

8. A government agency wants to encourage the use of designated drivers by people who have been drinking. What advice could you give the organization about constructing persuasive communications? Discuss some factors that might be important, including the structure of the communications, where they should appear, and who should deliver them. Should fear appeals be used, and if so, how?

9. Why would a marketer consider saying negative things about his or her product? When is this strategy feasible? Can you find examples of it?

10. Collect ads that rely on sex appeal to sell products. How often are benefits of the actual product communicated to the reader?

11. Observe the process of counterargumentation by asking a friend to talk out loud while watching a commercial. Ask him or her to respond to each point in the ad or to write down reactions to the claims made. How much scepticism regarding the claims can you detect?

12. Make a log of all the commercials shown on one network television channel during a two-hour period. Categorize each according to product category and whether they are presented as drama or argument. Describe the types of messages used (e.g., two-sided arguments), and keep track of the types of spokespeople (e.g., TV actors, famous people, animated characters). What can you conclude about the dominant forms of persuasive tactics currently employed by marketers?

13. Collect examples of ads that rely on the use of metaphors or resonance. Do you feel these ads are effective? If you were marketing the products, would you feel more comfortable with ads that use a more straightforward, "hard-sell" approach? Why or why not?

14. Create a list of current celebrities whom you feel typify cultural categories (e.g., clown, mother figure, etc.). What specific brands do you feel each could effectively endorse?

15. Conduct an "avatar hunt" by going to commerce websites, online video game sites, and online communities like The Sims that let people select what they want to look like in cyberspace. What seem to be the dominant figures people are choosing? Are they realistic or fantasy characters? Male or female? What types of avatars do you believe would be most effective for each of these different kinds of websites and why?

CBC ⊕ VIDEO VIGNETTE

CONCEPTS AT WORK FOR ADVERTISING IN CRISIS

Technology is rendering broadcast television irrelevant and is taking advertising for a tail spin! The remote control put the consumer in control of channel hopping and ad zapping. Then the VCR put the consumer in the driver's seat for recording television programs, which delayed or eliminated ad viewing (although with some effort and input of intelligence). Enter the Digital Video Recorder, or DVR, also called the Personal Video Recorder (or PVR). With the push of one button, every time a show is broadcast it is saved to the consumer's hard drive, often without the advertisements. Forrester Research found that early adopters of this technology do 60 percent of their television viewing from their hard drive and skip more than 90 percent of the ads. With overall ad exposure reduced by about one-half, the advertising industry senses an impending crisis.

Television advertising cannot remain as it is and expect to survive as a genre of marketing communication. As the price continues to drop and the market for DVRs grows, the advertising industry will have to adapt to changes in consumer behaviour and the new expectations that clients have for accountability for their advertising expenditures. There is already enough concern among some retailers and television networks to create demand for radical changes in ways to reach target audiences. The days of the 30-second ad and mass media seem to be over. In what ways might the advertising industry be able to meet this challenge? First, start thinking literally and figuratively "outside the box."

Questions

1. Describe the Interactive Communication Model.
2. How does the technology of the DVR change the consumer's exposure to television ads? Be specific.
3. What are some specific strategies and tactics that an advertising agency might use to maintain the consumer's level of exposure to their clients' messages?
4. First, it was the remote control, then the VCR, and now the DVR. What might be the next logical extension of this class of technology? How might it affect the time shift in consumers' viewing habits?

Resources: "Advertising in Crisis," Venture #923, CBC Air Date: October 17, 2004; Pierre Delagrave, "Dawn of the Ad Zapper," Marketing Magazine (February 20, 2006): 20–21.

NOTES

1. Norma Range, "Back in Business," *Marketing Magazine* (August 1/8, 2005): 13–14.
2. Robert B. Cialdini and Kelton V.L. Rhoads, "Human Behavior and the Marketplace," *Marketing Research* (Fall 2001).
3. Gert Assmus, "An Empirical Investigation into the Perception of Vehicle Source Effects," *Journal of Advertising* 7 (Winter 1978): 4–10. For a more thorough discussion of the pros and cons of different media, see Stephen Baker, *Systematic Approach to Advertising Creativity* (New York: McGraw-Hill, 1979).
4. Alladi Venkatesh, Ruby Roy Dholakia, and Nikhilesh Dholakia, "New Visions of Information Technology and Postmodernism: Implications for Advertising and Marketing Communications," in *The Information Superhighway and Private Households: Case Studies of Business Impacts*, eds. Walter Brenner and Lutz Kolbe (Heidelberg: Physical-Verlag, 1966), 319–337; Donna L. Hoffman and Thomas P. Novak, "Marketing in Hypermedia Computer-Mediated Environments: Conceptual Foundations," *Journal of Marketing* 60, 3 (July 1996): 50–68. For an early theoretical discussion of interactivity in communications paradigms, cf. Gratif R. Aubrey Fisher, *Perspectives on Human Communication* (New York: Macmillan, 1978).
5. Seth Godin, *Permission Marketing: Turning Strangers into Friends, and Friends into Customers* (New York: Simon & Schuster, 1999).
6. First proposed by Elihu Katz, "Mass Communication Research and the Study of Popular Culture: An Editorial Note on a Possible Future for this Journal," *Studies in Public Communication* 2 (1959): 1–6. For a more recent discussion on this approach, cf. Stephanie O'Donohoe, "Advertising Uses and Gratifications," *European Journal of Marketing* 28, 8/9 (1994): 52–75.
7. O'Donohoe, "Advertising Uses and Gratifications": 66.
8. Quoted in O'Donohoe, "Advertising Uses and Gratifications": 66.
9. Brad Stone, "The War for Your TV," *Newsweek* (July 29, 2002): 46–47.
10. Geoffrey A. Fowler, "Asia's Mobile Ads," *Wall Street Journal Online Edition* (April 25, 2005); Brooke Barnes, "Coming to Your Cell: Paris Hilton," *Wall Street Journal Online Edition* (March 17, 2005); Alice Z. Cuneo, "Marketers Dial in to Messaging," *Advertising Age* (November 1, 2004): 18; Stephen Baker and Heather Green, "Blogs will Change Your Business," *Business Week* (May 2, 2005): 56 (9).
11. This section is adapted from a discussion in Michael R. Solomon and Elnora W. Stuart, *Marketing: Real People, Real Choices* (Upper Saddle River, NJ: Prentice Hall, 1997).
12. Carl I. Hovland and W. Weiss, "The Influence of Source Credibility on Communication Effectiveness," *Public Opinion Quarterly* 15 (1952): 635–650.

13. Herbert Kelman, "Processes of Opinion Change," *Public Opinion Quarterly* 25 (Spring 1961): 57–78; Susan M. Petroshius and Kenneth E. Crocker, "An Empirical Analysis of Spokesperson Characteristics on Advertisement and Product Evaluations," *Journal of the Academy of Marketing Science* 17 (Summer 1989): 217–226.
14. Kenneth G. DeBono and Richard J. Harnish, "Source Expertise, Source Attractiveness, and the Processing of Persuasive Information: A Functional Approach," *Journal of Personality and Social Psychology* 55, 4 (1988): 541–546.
15. Hershey H. Friedman and Linda Friedman, "Endorser Effectiveness by Product Type," *Journal of Advertising Research* 19, 5 (1979): 63–71. For a recent study that looked at non-target-market effects—the effects of advertising intended for other market segments—see Jennifer L. Aaker, Anne M. Brumbaugh, and Sonya A. Grier, "Non-Target Markets and Viewer Distinctiveness: The Impact of Target Marketing on Advertising Attitudes," *Journal of Consumer Psychology* 9, 3 (2000): 127–140.
16. S. Ratneshwar and Shelly Chaiken, "Comprehension's Role in Persuasion: The Case of Its Moderating Effect on the Persuasive Impact of Source Cues," *Journal of Consumer Research* 18 (June 1991): 52–62.
17. Jagdish Agrawal and Wagner A. Kamakura, "The Economic Worth of Celebrity Endorsers: An Event Study Analysis," *Journal of Marketing* 59 (July 1995): 56–62.
18. Anthony R. Pratkanis et al., "In Search of Reliable Persuasion Effects: III. The Sleeper Effect Is Dead, Long Live the Sleeper Effect," *Journal of Personality and Social Psychology* 54 (1988): 203–218.
19. Herbert C. Kelman and Carl I. Hovland, "Reinstatement of the Communication in Delayed Measurement of Opinion Change," *Journal of Abnormal Psychology* 4, 48 (1953): 327–335.
20. Darlene Hannah and Brian Sternthal, "Detecting and Explaining the Sleeper Effect," *Journal of Consumer Research* 11 (September 1984): 632–642.
21. David Mazursky and Yaacov Schul, "The Effects of Advertisement Encoding on the Failure to Discount Information: Implications for the Sleeper Effect," *Journal of Consumer Research* 15 (June 1988): 24–36. Olaf Schirm, President, NoDNA GmbH, personal internet communication, August 13, 2002.
22. "Robber Makes It Biggs in Ad," *Advertising Age* (May 29, 1989): 26.
23. Robert LaFranco, "MTV Conquers Madison Avenue," *Forbes* (June 3, 1996): 138.
24. Alice H. Eagly, Andy Wood, and Shelly Chaiken, "Causal Inferences about Communicators and Their Effect in Opinion Change," *Journal of Personality and Social Psychology* 36, 4 (1978): 424–435.

25. William Dowell, "Microsoft Offers Tips to Agreeable Academics," *Time* (June 1, 1998): 22.

26. Nat Ives, "Entertaining Web Sites Promote Products Subtly," *New York Times on the Web* (December 22, 2004).

27. This section is based upon a discussion in Michael R. Solomon, *Conquering Consumerspace: Marketing Strategies for a Branded World* (New York: AMACOM, 2003); see also David Lewis and Darren Bridger, *The Soul of the New Consumer: Authenticity—What We Buy and Why in the New Economy* (London: Nicholas Brealey Publishing, 2000).

28. Jeff Neff, "Pressure Points at IPG," *Advertising Age* (December 2001): 4.

29. Eilene Zimmerman, "Catch the Bug," *Sales and Marketing Management*, (February 2001): 78.

30. Becky Ebenkamp, "Guerrilla Marketers of the Year," *Brandweek* (November 13, 2001), 25–32.

31. Wayne Friedman, "Street Marketing Hits the Internet," *Advertising Age* (May 2000): 32; Erin White, "Online Buzz Helps Album Skyrocket to Top of Charts," *Wall Street Journal Interactive Edition* (October 5, 1999).

32. Kruti Trivedi, "Great-Grandson of Artist Renoir Uses His Name for Marketing Blitz," *Wall Street Journal Interactive Edition* (September 2, 1999).

33. Karen K. Dion, "What Is Beautiful Is Good," *Journal of Personality and Social Psychology* 24 (December 1972): 285–290.

34. Michael J. Baker and Gilbert A. Churchill, Jr., "The Impact of Physically Attractive Models on Advertising Evaluations," *Journal of Marketing Research* 14 (November 1977): 538–555; Marjorie J. Caballero and William M. Pride, "Selected Effects of Salesperson Sex and Attractiveness in Direct Mail Advertisements," *Journal of Marketing* 48 (January 1984): 94–100; W. Benoy Joseph, "The Credibility of Physically Attractive Communicators: A Review," *Journal of Advertising* 11, 3 (1982): 15–24; Kahle and Homer, "Physical Attractiveness of the Celebrity Endorser: A Social Adaptation Perspective"; Judson Mills and Eliot Aronson, "Opinion Change as a Function of Communicator's Attractiveness and Desire to Influence," *Journal of Personality and Social Psychology* 1 (1965): 173–177.

35. Leonard N. Reid and Lawrence C. Soley, "Decorative Models and the Readership of Magazine Ads," *Journal of Advertising Research* 23, 2 (1983): 27–32.

36. Marjorie J. Caballero, James R. Lumpkin, and Charles S. Madden, "Using Physical Attractiveness as an Advertising Tool: An Empirical Test of the Attraction Phenomenon," *Journal of Advertising Research* (August/September 1989): 16–22.

37. Baker and Churchill, Jr., "The Impact of Physically Attractive Models on Advertising Evaluations"; George E. Belch, Michael A. Belch, and Angelina Villareal, "Effects of Advertising Communications: Review of Research," in *Research in Marketing* 9 (Greenwich, CT: JAI Press, 1987), 59–117; A.E. Courtney and T.W. Whipple, *Sex Stereotyping in Advertising* (Lexington, MA: Lexington Books, 1983).

38. Kahle and Homer, "Physical Attractiveness of the Celebrity Endorser ...."

39. Baker and Churchill, "The Impact of Physically Attractive Models on Advertising Evaluations."

40. Suzanna Vranica and Sam Walker, "Tiger Woods Switches Watches; Branding Experts Disapprove," *Wall Street Journal Interactive Edition* (October 7, 2002).

41. Brian Steinberg, "Bob Dylan Gets Tangled Up in Pink: Victoria's Secret Campaign Drafts Counterculture Hero; Just Like the Rolling Stones," *Wall Street Journal* (April 2, 2004): B3.

42. Heather Buttle, Jane E. Raymond, and Shai Danziger, "Do Famous Faces Capture Attention?" paper presented at the Association for Consumer Research Conference, Columbus, Ohio (October 1999).

43. Michael A. Kamins, "Celebrity and Noncelebrity Advertising in a Two-Sided Context," *Journal of Advertising Research* 29 (June–July 1989): 34; Joseph M. Kamen, A.C. Azhari, and J.R. Kragh, "What a Spokesman Does for a Sponsor," *Journal of Advertising Research* 15, 2 (1975): 17–24; Lynn Langmeyer and Mary Walker, "A First Step to Identify the Meaning in Celebrity Endorsers," in *Advances in Consumer Research* 18, eds. Rebecca H. Holman and Michael R. Solomon (Provo, UT: Association for Consumer Research, 1991): 364–371.

44. Grant McCracken, "Who Is the Celebrity Endorser? Cultural Foundations of the Endorsement Process," *Journal of Consumer Research* 16, 3 (December 1989): 310–321.

45. Michael A. Kamins, "An Investigation into the 'Match-up' Hypothesis in Celebrity Advertising: When Beauty May Be only Skin Deep," *Journal of Advertising* 19, 1 (1990): 4–13; Kahle and Homer, "Physical Attractiveness of the Celebrity Endorser: A Social Adaptation Perspective."

46. Roberts L. Johnnie, "The Rap of Luxury," *Newsweek* (September 2, 2002): 42–44.

47. Thomas R. King, "Credibility Gap: More Consumers Find Celebrity Ads Unpersuasive," *Wall Street Journal* (July 5, 1989): B5; Haring, "Company Totes Up Popularity Quotients."

48. Erin White, "Found in Translation? Stars Who Make Ads Overseas Recoil at Internet Exposure; Mr. DiCaprio Fights Back," *Wall Street Journal* (September 20, 2004): B1.

49. Quoted in Joel Baglole, "Mascots Are Getting Bigger Role in Corporate Advertising Plans," *Wall Street Journal Online* (April 9, 2002).

50. David Germain, "Simone Leading Lady Is Living and Breathing Model," *New York Times* (August 26, 2002): D1.

51. Christopher Lawton, "Virtual Characters Push Cigarettes in New Vending Machine," *Wall Street Journal*, (August 6, 2002), B1 (2).

52. Tran T.L. Knanh and Regalado Antonio, "Web Sites Bet on Attracting Viewers with Humanlike Presences of Avatars," *Wall Street Journal Interactive Edition* (January 24, 2001).

53. Keith Bradsher, "Sad, Lonely? For a Good Time, Call Vivienne*," *New York Times on the Web* (February 24, 2005).

54. David W. Stewart and David H. Furse, "The Effects of Television Advertising Execution on Recall, Comprehension, and Persuasion," *Psychology & Marketing* 2 (Fall 1985): 135–160.

55. R.C. Grass and W.H. Wallace, "Advertising Communication: Print vs. TV," *Journal of Advertising Research* 14 (1974): 19–23.

56. Elizabeth C. Hirschman and Michael R. Solomon, "Utilitarian, Aesthetic, and Familiarity Responses to Verbal versus Visual Advertisements," in *Advances in Consumer Research* 11, ed. Thomas C. Kinnear (Provo, UT: Association for Consumer Research, 1984), 426–431.

57. Andrew A. Mitchell and Jerry C. Olson, "Are Product Attribute Beliefs the Only Mediator of Advertising Effects on Brand Attitude?" *Journal of Marketing Research* 18, 3 (1981): 318–332.

58. Terry L. Childers and Michael J. Houston, "Conditions for a Picture-Superiority Effect on Consumer Memory," *Journal of Consumer Research* 11 (September 1984): 643–654.

59. Andrew A. Mitchell, "The Effect of Verbal and Visual Components of Advertisements on Brand Attitudes and Attitude toward the Advertisement," *Journal of Consumer Research* 13 (June 1986): 12–24.

60. John R. Rossiter and Larry Percy, "Attitude Change through Visual Imagery in Advertising," *Journal of Advertising Research* 9, 2 (1980): 10–16.

61. Jolita Kiselius and Brian Sternthal, "Examining the Vividness Controversy: An Availability-Valence Interpretation," *Journal of Consumer Research* 12 (March 1986): 418–431.

62. Scott B. Mackenzie, "The Role of Attention in Mediating the Effect of Advertising on Attribute Importance," *Journal of Consumer Research* 13 (September 1986): 174–195.

63. Robert B. Zajonc, "Attitudinal Effects of Mere Exposure," *Journal of Personality and Social Psychology* 8 (1968): 1–29.

64. Giles D'Souza and Ram C. Rao, "Can Repeating an Advertisement more Frequently than the Competition Affect Brand Preference in a Mature Market?" *Journal of Marketing* 59 (April 1995): 32–42.

65. George E. Belch, "The Effects of Television Commercial Repetition on Cognitive Response and Message Acceptance," *Journal of Consumer Research* 9 (June 1982): 56–65; Marian Burke and Julie Edell, "Ad Reactions over Time: Capturing Changes in the Real World," *Journal of Consumer Research* 13 (June 1986): 114–118; Herbert Krugman, "Why Three Exposures May Be Enough," *Journal of Advertising Research* 12 (December 1972): 11–14.

66. Robert F. Bornstein, "Exposure and Affect: Overview and Meta-Analysis of Research, 1968–1987," *Psychological Bulletin* 106, 2 (1989): 265–289; Arno Rethans, John Swasy, and Lawrence Marks, "Effects of Television Commercial Repetition, Receiver Knowledge, and Commercial Length: A Test of the Two-Factor Model," *Journal of Marketing Research* 23 (February 1986): 50–61.

67. Curtis P. Haugtvedt et al., "Advertising Repetition and Variation Strategies: Implications for Understanding Attitude Strength," *Journal of Consumer Research* 21 (June 1994): 176–189.

68. Linda L. Golden and Mark I. Alpert, "Comparative Analysis of the Relative Effectiveness of One- and Two-Sided Communication for Contrasting Products," *Journal of Advertising* 16 (1987); Kamins, "Celebrity and Noncelebrity Advertising in a Two-Sided Context"; Robert B. Settle and Linda L. Golden, "Attribution Theory and Advertiser Credibility," *Journal of Marketing Research* 11 (May 1974): 181–185.

69. See Alan G. Sawyer, "The Effects of Repetition of Refutational and Supportive Advertising Appeals," *Journal of Marketing Research* 10 (February 1973): 23–33;

George J. Szybillo and Richard Heslin, "Resistance to Persuasion: Inoculation Theory in a Marketing Context," *Journal of Marketing Research* 10 (November 1973): 396–403; Ayn E. Crowley and Wayne D. Hoyer, "An Integrative Framework for Understanding Two-Sided Persuasion," *Journal of Consumer Research* 20, 4 (March 1994): 561–574; Cornelia Pechmann, "Predicting When Two-Sided Ads Will be more Effective than One-Sided Ads: The Role of Correlational and Correspondent Inferences," *Journal of Marketing Research* 29 (November 1992): 441–453.

70. Golden and Alpert, "Comparative Analysis of the Relative Effectiveness of One- and Two-Sided Communication for Contrasting Products."

71. G. Belch, M. Belch, and Villareal, "Effects of Advertising Communications ...."

72. Frank R. Kardes, "Spontaneous Inference Processes in Advertising: The Effects of Conclusion Omission and Involvement on Persuasion," *Journal of Consumer Research* 15 (September 1988): 225–233.

73. Cornelia Dröge and Rene Y. Darmon, "Associative Positioning Strategies through Comparative Advertising: Attribute vs. Overall Similarity Approaches," *Journal of Marketing Research* 24 (1987): 377–389; D. Muehling and N. Kangun, "The Multidimensionality of Comparative Advertising: Implications for the FTC," *Journal of Public Policy and Marketing* (1985): 112–128; Beth A. Walker and Helen H. Anderson, "Reconceptualizing Comparative Advertising: A Framework and Theory of Effects," in *Advances in Consumer Research* 18, eds. Rebecca H. Holman and Michael R. Solomon (Provo, UT: Association for Consumer Research, 1991), 342–347; William L. Wilkie and Paul W. Farris, "Comparison Advertising: Problems and Potential," *Journal of Marketing* 39 (October 1975): 7–15; R.G. Wyckham, "Implied Superiority Claims," *Journal of Advertising Research* (February/March 1987): 54–63.

74. Stephen A. Goodwin and Michael Etgar, "An Experimental Investigation of Comparative Advertising: Impact of Message Appeal, Information Load, and Utility of Product Class," *Journal of Marketing Research* 17 (May 1980): 187–202; Gerald J. Gorn and Charles B. Weinberg, "The Impact of Comparative Advertising on Perception and Attitude: Some Positive Findings," *Journal of Consumer Research* 11 (September 1984): 719–727; Terence A. Shimp and David C. Dyer, "The Effects of Comparative Advertising Mediated by Market Position of Sponsoring Brand," *Journal of Advertising* 3 (Summer 1978): 13–19; R. Dale Wilson, "An Empirical Evaluation of Comparative Advertising Messages: Subjects' Responses to Perceptual Dimensions," in *Advances in Consumer Research* 3, ed. B.B. Anderson (Ann Arbor, MI: Association for Consumer Research, 1976), 53–57; Randall L. Rose et al., "When Persuasion Goes Undetected: The Case of Comparative Advertising," *Journal of Marketing Research* 30 (August 1993): 315–330.

75. Jean-Marc Léger and Dave Scholz, "What Canadians Think of TV Ads," *Marketing Magazine* (January 20, 2002), **www.marketingmag.ca**.

76. Dröge and Darmon, "Associative Positioning Strategies through Comparative Advertising ...."

77. Jean Halliday, "Survey: Comparative Ads Can Dent Car's Credibility," *Advertising Age* (May 4, 1998): 26.

78. Quoted in Sarah Ellison and John Carreyrou, "Beauty Battle: Giant L'Oreal Faces Off against Rival P&G," *Wall Street Journal Interactive Edition* (January 9, 2003).

79. Edward F. Cone, "Image and Reality," *Forbes* (December 14, 1987): 226.

80. H. Zielske, "Does Day-After Recall Penalize Feeling Ads?" *Journal of Advertising Research* 22 (1982): 19–22.

81. G. Belch, M. Belch, and Villareal, "Effects of Advertising Communications"; Courtney and Whipple, *Sex Stereotyping in Advertising*; Michael S. LaTour, "Female Nudity in Print Advertising: An Analysis of Gender Differences in Arousal and Ad Response," *Psychology & Marketing* 7, 1 (1990): 65–81; B.G. Yovovich, "Sex in Advertising—The Power and the Perils," *Advertising Age* (May 2, 1983): M4–M5.

82. Penny M. Simpson, Steve Horton, and Gene Brown, "Male Nudity in Advertisements: A Modified Replication and Extension of Gender and Product Effects," *Journal of the Academy of Marketing Science* 24, 3 (1996): 257–262.

83. Michael S. LaTour and Tony L. Henthorne, "Ethical Judgments of Sexual Appeals in Print Advertising," *Journal of Advertising* 23, 3 (September 1994): 81–90.

84. Marc G. Weinberger and Harlan E. Spotts, "Humor in U.S. versus U.K. TV Commercials: A Comparison," *Journal of Advertising* 18, 2 (1989): 39–44.

85. Thomas J. Madden, "Humor in Advertising: An Experimental Analysis" (working paper no. 8327, University of Massachusetts, 1984); Thomas J. Madden and Marc G. Weinberger, "The Effects of Humor on Attention in Magazine Advertising," *Journal of Advertising* 11, 3 (1982): 8–14; Weinberger and Spotts, "Humor in U.S. versus U.K. TV Commercials."

86. David Gardner, "The Distraction Hypothesis in Marketing," *Journal of Advertising Research* 10 (1970): 25–30.

87. Ashesh Mulcherjee and Laurette Dube, "The Use of Humour in Threat-Related Advertising," reported in Danny Kucharsky, "Laughter Really Is the Best Medicine," *Marketing Magazine* (August 5, 2002): 8.

88. Kevin Goldman, "Everybody's Afraid of the Big Bad Boss," *New York Times* (January 12, 1994): B1 (2 pp.).

89. Michael L. Ray and William L. Wilkie, "Fear: The Potential of an Appeal Neglected by Marketing," *Journal of Marketing* 34, 1 (1970): 54–62; Tony L. Henthorne, Michael S. LaTour, and Rajan Nataraajan, "Fear Appeals in Print Advertising: An Analysis of Arousal and Ad Response," *Journal of Advertising* 22, 2 (June 1993): 59–70; Thomas Giese, Dana-Nicoleta Lascu, and Terry M. Weisenberger, "Intended and Unintended Consequences of the Use of Fear and Guilt Appeals in Marketing Communications," *Proceedings of the Southern Marketing Association* (1993): 12.

90. Judith Waldrop, "They're Coming to Take You Away (Fear as a Form of Persuasion)," *American Demographics* (June 15, 1988): 2; John F. Tanner, Jr., James B. Hunt, and David R. Eppright, "The Protection Motivation Model: A Normative Model of Fear Appeals," *Journal of Marketing* 55 (July 1991): 36–45.

91. Brian Sternthal and C. Samuel Craig, "Fear Appeals: Revisited and Revised," *Journal of Consumer Research* 1 (December 1974): 22–34.

92. Ronald Paul Hill, "An Exploration of the Relationship between AIDS-Related Anxiety and the Evaluation of Condom Advertisements," *Journal of Advertising* 17, 4 (1988): 35–42.

93. Randall Rothenberg, "Talking too Tough on Life's Risks?" *New York Times* (February 16, 1990): D1.

94. Denise D. Schoenbachler and Tommy E. Whittler, "Adolescent Processing of Social and Physical Threat Communications," *Journal of Advertising* 25, 4 (Winter 1996): 37–54.

95. Anne M. Lavack, "Fear Appeals in Anti-Smoking TV Commercials 1980–1994" (paper presented at the 1994 Administrative Sciences Association of Canada [ASAC] Conference, Halifax, June 25–28, 1994).

96. "A Drive to Woo Women—and Invigorate Sales," *New York Times* (April 2, 1989).

97. Barbara B. Stern, "Medieval Allegory: Roots of Advertising Strategy for the Mass Market," *Journal of Marketing* 52 (July 1988): 84–94.

98. Edward F. McQuarrie and David Glen Mick, "On Resonance: A Critical Pluralistic Inquiry into Advertising Rhetoric," *Journal of Consumer Research* 19 (September 1992): 180–197.

99. See Linda M. Scott, "The Troupe: Celebrities as Dramatis Personae in Advertisements," in *Advances in Consumer Research* 18, eds. Rebecca H. Holman and Michael R. Solomon (Provo, UT: Association for Consumer Research, 1991), 355–363; Barbara Stern, "Literary Criticism and Consumer Research: Overview and Illustrative Analysis," *Journal of Consumer Research* 16 (1989): 322–334; Judith Williamson, *Decoding Advertisements* (Boston, MA: Marion Boyars, 1978).

100. John Deighton, Daniel Romer, and Josh McQueen, "Using Drama to Persuade," *Journal of Consumer Research* 16 (December 1989): 335–343.

101. Richard E. Petty, John T. Cacioppo, and David Schumann, "Central and Peripheral Routes to Advertising Effectiveness: The Moderating Role of Involvement," *Journal of Consumer Research* 10, 2 (1983): 135–146.

102. Jerry C. Olson, Daniel R. Toy, and Philip A. Dover, "Do Cognitive Responses Mediate the Effects of Advertising Content on Cognitive Structure?" *Journal of Consumer Research* 9, 3 (1982): 245–262.

103. Julie A. Edell and Andrew A. Mitchell, "An Information Processing Approach to Cognitive Responses," in *Research Frontiers in Marketing: Dialogues and Directions*, ed. S.C. Jain (Chicago, IL: American Marketing Association, 1978).

104. See Mary Jo Bitner and Carl Obermiller, "The Elaboration Likelihood Model: Limitations and Extensions in Marketing," in *Advances in Consumer Research* 12, eds. Elizabeth C. Hirschman and Morris B. Holbrook (Provo, UT: Association for Consumer Research, 1985), 420–425; Meryl P. Gardner, "Does Attitude toward the Ad Affect Brand Attitude under a Brand Evaluation Set?" *Journal of Marketing Research* 22 (1985): 192–198; C.W. Park and S.M. Young, "Consumer Response to Television Commercials: The Impact of Involvement and Background Music on Brand Attitude Formation," *Journal of Marketing Research* 23 (1986): 11–24; Petty, Cacioppo, and Schumann, "Central and Peripheral Routes to Advertising Effectiveness ...." For a discussion of how different kinds of involvement interact with the ELM, see Robin A. Higie, Lawrence F. Feick, and Linda L. Price, "The Importance of Peripheral Cues in Attitude Formation for Enduring and Task-Involved Individuals," in *Advances in Consumer Research* 18, eds. Rebecca H. Holman and Michael R. Solomon (Provo, UT: Association for Consumer Research, 1991), 187–193.

105. J. Craig Andrews and Terence A. Shimp, "Effects of Involvement, Argument Strength, and Source Characteristics on Central and Peripheral Processing in Advertising," *Psychology & Marketing* 7 (Fall 1990): 195–214.

106. Richard E. Petty et al., "Affect and Persuasion: A Contemporary Perspective," *American Behavioral Scientist* 31, 3 (1988): 355–371.

107. Rob Walker, "The Gifted Ones," *New York Times* (November 14, 2004).

SECTION 3

Consumers as Decision Makers

This section explores how we make consumption decisions and discusses the many influences exerted by others in this process. Chapter 9 focuses on the basic sequence of steps we undergo when making decisions. Chapter 10 considers how the particular situation we find ourselves in affects these decisions and how we go about evaluating the results of our choices. Chapter 11 provides an overview of group processes and discusses the reasons we are motivated to conform to the expectations of others when we choose and display our purchases. It also considers how some individuals in particular (called "opinion leaders") are likely to influence the consumption behaviour of others in a group. Chapter 12 goes on to discuss the many instances in which our purchase decisions are made in conjunction with others, especially family members.

SECTION OUTLINE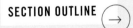

Bill has had it. He can't go on watching his tiny, antiquated TV set. It was bad enough watching scratchy videos on MTV and squinting at *Friends*, but when he couldn't tell the Canucks from the Leafs during an NHL game, he went next door to watch the second period on Mark's high-definition wall unit and realized what he'd been missing. Budget or not, it was time to act.

Where to start looking? The web, naturally. Bill checks out a few comparison-shopping websites, including **www.selectsmart.com** and **www.shoppingspot.com**. After narrowing down his options, he ventures out to scope out a few sets in person. Bill figures he'll get a decent selection and price at one of those new warehouse stores. At Zany Zach's Appliance Emporium he heads straight for the Video Zone, barely noticing the rows of toasters, microwave ovens, and stereos on his way. In minutes he's accosted by a smiling salesman. Even though he could use some help, Bill says he's just browsing. He figures these guys don't know what they're talking about and are just out to make a sale.

Bill examines the features on the 60-inch colour sets. His friend Carol really liked her Prime Wave, and his sister Diane warned him to avoid the Kamashita. He finds a Prime Wave model with a sleep timer, onscreen programming menu, cable-compatible tuner, and remote control, but chooses the less expensive Precision 2000X, with one feature that really catches his fancy: stereo broadcast reception.

Later that day, Bill is happy as he sits in his easy chair, watching Ashanti on MTV. If he's going to be a couch potato, he's going to be one in style.

CHAPTER 9

Individual Decision Making

CONSUMERS AS PROBLEM SOLVERS

A consumer purchase is a response to a problem, which in Bill's case is the perceived need for a new television set. His situation is similar to that encountered by consumers virtually every day of their lives: He realizes that he wants to make a purchase, and he goes through a series of steps in order to make it. These steps can be described as (1) problem recognition, (2) information search, (3) evaluation of alternatives, and (4) product choice. Of course, after the decision is made, the quality of that decision affects the final step in the process, when learning occurs based on how well the choice worked out. This learning process in turn influences the likelihood that the same choice will be made the next time the need for a similar decision occurs. An overview of this decision-making process appears in Figure 9–1 on page 246.

This chapter begins by considering various approaches consumers use when faced with a purchase decision. It then focuses on three of the steps in the decision process: how consumers recognize the problem or need for a product; their search for information about product choices; and the ways in which they evaluate alternatives to arrive at a decision. Chapter 10 considers the actual purchase situation, as well as the person's satisfaction with the decision.

Since some purchase decisions are more important than others, the amount of effort we put into each differs. Sometimes the decision-making process is done almost automatically; we seem to make snap judgments based on very little information. At other times, coming to a purchase decision begins to resemble a full-time job. A person may literally spend days or weeks thinking about an important purchase, such as a new home, even to the point of obsession.

This intensive decision-making process gets even more complicated in today's environment where we have so many options from which to choose. Ironically, for many modern consumers, one of the biggest problems is not having too *few* choices but too *many*. We can think of this profusion of options as **consumer hyperchoice**, a condition where the large number of available options forces us to make repeated choices that may drain psychological energy while decreasing our abilities to make smart decisions.[1]

Perspectives on Decision Making

Traditionally, consumer researchers have approached decision makers from a **rational perspective**. In this view, people calmly and carefully integrate as much

FIGURE 9–1

STAGES IN CONSUMER
DECISION MAKING

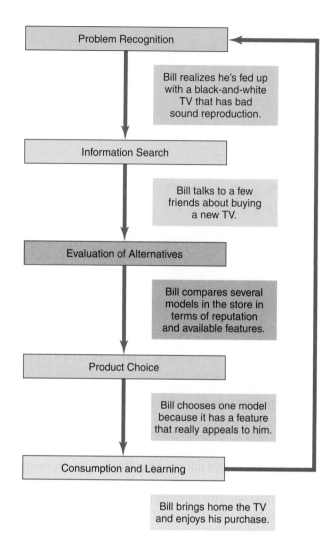

information as possible with what they already know about a product, painstakingly weigh the pluses and minuses of each alternative, and arrive at a satisfactory decision. This process implies that steps in decision making should be carefully studied by marketing managers to understand how information is obtained, how beliefs are formed, and what product-choice criteria are specified by consumers. Products can then be developed that emphasize appropriate attributes, and promotional strategies can be tailored to deliver the types of information most likely to be desired in the most effective formats.[2]

Although the steps in decision making are followed by consumers for some purchases, such a process is not an accurate portrayal of many purchase decisions.[3] Consumers simply do not go through this elaborate sequence for every decision. If they did, their entire lives would be spent making such decisions, leaving them very little time to enjoy the things they eventually decide to buy. Some of our buying behaviours simply don't seem "rational"; they don't serve a logical purpose (e.g., collecting red shoes). Other purchases are made with virtually no advance planning at all (e.g., impulsively grabbing that tempting candy bar from the rack while waiting to pay for groceries). Still other actions actually are contrary to those predicted by rational models. For example, **purchase momentum** occurs when these initial impulses actually increase the likelihood that we will buy even more (instead of less as our needs are satisfied), almost as if we get "revved up" and plunge into a spending spree (think IKEA).[4]

Researchers are now beginning to realize that decision makers actually possess a repertoire of strategies. A consumer evaluates the effort required to make a particular choice, and then he or she chooses a strategy best suited to the level of effort required. This sequence of events is known as *constructive processing*. Rather than using a big club to kill an ant, consumers tailor their degree of cognitive "effort" to the task at hand.[5]

Some decisions are made under conditions of low involvement, as discussed in Chapter 4. In many of these situations, the consumer's decision is a learned response to environmental cues (see Chapter 3), as when a person decides to buy on impulse something that is promoted as a "surprise special" in a store. Concentrating on these types of decisions can be described as the **behavioural influence perspective**. Under these circumstances managers must concentrate on assessing the characteristics of the environment, such as physical surroundings and product placement, that influence members of a target market.[6]

In other cases consumers are highly involved in a decision, but this involvement may not lend itself to the rational approach. For example, the traditional approach is hard-pressed to explain a person's choice of art, music, or even a spouse. In these cases no single quality is the determining factor. Instead, the **experiential perspective** stresses the *gestalt,* or totality, of the product or service. Marketers focus on measuring consumers' affective responses to products or services and develop offerings that elicit appropriate subjective reactions.

Types of Consumer Decisions

One helpful way to characterize the decision-making process is to consider the amount of effort that goes into the decision each time it must be made. Consumer researchers have found it convenient to think in terms of a continuum, which is anchored at one end by **habitual decision making** and at the other by **extended problem solving**. Many decisions fall somewhere in the middle and are characterized by **limited problem solving**. This continuum is presented in Figure 9–2.

EXTENDED PROBLEM SOLVING

Decisions involving extended problem solving correspond most closely to the traditional decision-making perspective. As indicated in Table 9–1, the extended problem-solving process is usually initiated by a motive that is fairly central to the self-concept (see Chapter 5), and the eventual decision is perceived to carry a fair degree of risk. The consumer tries to collect as much information as possible, both from memory (internal search) and from outside sources (external search). Based on the importance of the decision, each product alternative is carefully evaluated. The evaluation is often done by considering the attributes of one brand at a time and seeing how each brand's attributes shape up to some set of desired characteristics.

LIMITED PROBLEM SOLVING

Limited problem solving is usually more straightforward and simple. Buyers are not as motivated to search for information or to evaluate each alternative rigorously. People instead use simple *decision rules* to choose among alternatives. These cognitive shortcuts enable them to fall back on general guidelines instead of having to start from scratch every time a decision is to be made.

FIGURE 9–2   A CONTINUUM OF BUYING DECISION BEHAVIOUR

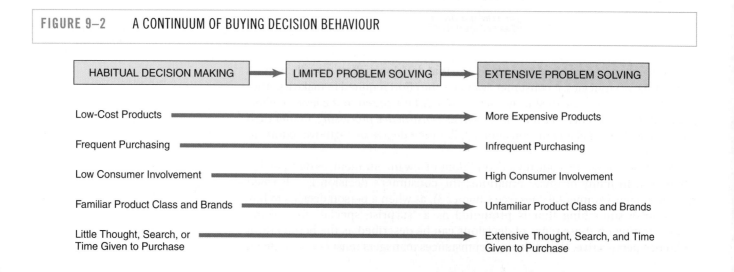

TABLE 9–1

CHARACTERISTICS OF LIMITED VERSUS EXTENDED PROBLEM SOLVING

	Limited Problem Solving	Extended Problem Solving
Motivation	Low risk and involvement	High risk and involvement
Information Search	Little search	Extensive search
	Information processed passively	Information processed actively
	In-store decision likely	Multiple sources consulted prior to store visits
Alternative Evaluation	Weakly held beliefs	Strongly held beliefs
	Only most prominent criteria used	Many criteria used
	Alternatives perceived as basically similar	Significant differences perceived among alternatives
	Non-compensatory strategy used	Compensatory strategy used
Purchase	Limited shopping time; may prefer self-service	Many outlets shopped if needed
	Choice often influenced by store displays	Communication with store personnel often desirable

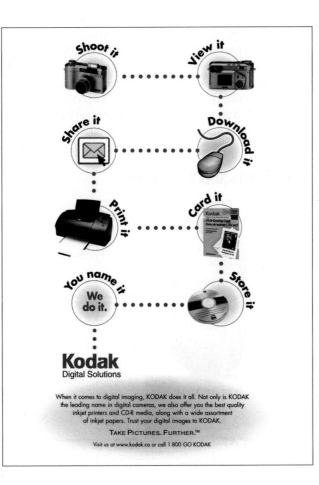

← This Kodak ad sends the message that digital imaging can be simplified by simply (and habitually) going to Kodak for digital solutions.
Courtesy © Kodak Canada Inc.

HABITUAL DECISION MAKING

Both extended and limited problem-solving modes involve some degree of information search and deliberation, varying in the degree to which these activities are undertaken. At the other end of the choice continuum, however, are decisions that are made with little or no conscious effort. Many purchase decisions are so routine that we may not realize we've made them until we look in our shopping carts. Choices characterized by *automaticity* are performed with minimal effort and without conscious control.[7] Although this kind of thoughtless activity may seem dangerous or, at best, stupid, it is actually an efficient way to operate. The development of habitual, repetitive behaviour allows consumers to minimize the time and energy spent on mundane purchase decisions.

On the other hand, habitual decision making poses a problem when a marketer tries to introduce a new way of doing an old task. In this case consumers must be convinced to "unfreeze" their former habits and replace them with new ones—perhaps by using an ATM instead of going to an actual bank teller, or switching to a self-service gas pump instead of being waited on by an attendant at a gas station. Changing consumers' habits is the obstacle now confronting a device called the Personal Valet, a cabinet-size clothes refresher made by Whirlpool that removes odours and wrinkles using a chemical formula developed by Procter & Gamble. For the product to succeed, the two companies must find a way to "unfreeze" the habit of taking one's clothes to the dry cleaner.[8]

PROBLEM RECOGNITION

Problem recognition occurs whenever the consumer sees a significant difference between his or her current state of affairs and some desired or ideal state. The consumer perceives there is a problem to be solved, which may be small or large, simple or complex. A person who unexpectedly runs out of gas on the highway has a problem, as does the person who becomes dissatisfied with the image of his or her car, even though there is nothing mechanically wrong with it. For example, although the quality of Bill's TV had not changed, his standard of comparison had altered, and he was confronted with a need he did not have prior to watching his friend's TV.

Figure 9–3 shows that a problem can arise in one of two ways. As in the case of the person running out of gas, the quality of the consumer's actual state can move

→ This cooperative ad, with a touch of whimsy, focuses on the facts about the nutritional attributes of potatoes.
Courtesy McCain Food (Canada).

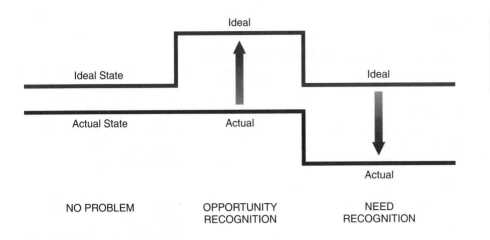

FIGURE 9–3

PROBLEM RECOGNITION: SHIFTS IN ACTUAL OR IDEAL STATES

downward (*need recognition*). On the other hand, as in the case of the person who craves a newer, flashier car, the consumer's ideal state can move upward (*opportunity recognition*). Either way, a gulf occurs between the actual state and the ideal state.[11] In Bill's case, a problem was perceived as a result of opportunity recognition; his ideal state in terms of television reception was altered.

Need recognition can occur in several ways. The quality of the person's actual state can be diminished by simply running out of a product, by buying a product that turns out not to satisfy needs adequately, or by creating new needs (e.g., deciding to buy a house). Opportunity recognition often occurs when a consumer is exposed to different or better-quality products. This shift often occurs because the person's circumstances have somehow changed, as when an individual goes to college or university or gets a new job. As the person's frame of reference shifts, a variety of purchases are made to adapt to the new environment.

Although problem recognition can and does occur naturally, this process is often spurred by marketing efforts. In some cases marketers attempt to create *primary demand,* wherein consumers are encouraged to use a product or service regardless of the brand they choose. Such needs are often encouraged in the early stages of a product's life cycle, as, for example, when microwave ovens were first introduced. *Secondary demand,* in which consumers are prompted to prefer a specific brand over others, can occur only if primary demand already exists. At this point marketers must convince consumers that a problem can best be solved by choosing their brand over others in a category. Many marketing communications are designed to make consumers aware that they have a problem and then (conveniently) provide a solution.

INFORMATION SEARCH

Once a problem has been recognized, consumers need adequate information to resolve it. **Information search** is the process in which the consumer surveys his or her environment for appropriate data to make a reasonable decision. This section will review some of the factors involved in this search.

Types of Search

A consumer may explicitly search the marketplace for specific information after a need has been recognized (a process called *prepurchase search*). On the other hand, many consumers, especially veteran shoppers, enjoy hunting for information and keeping track of developments just for the fun of it (i.e., *browsing*) or because they like to maintain current information for future use. They engage in *ongoing search.*[12] Some differences between these two search modes are described in Table 9–2.

TABLE 9–2

A FRAMEWORK FOR CONSUMER INFORMATION SEARCH

Prepurchase Search	Ongoing Search
Determinants	
Involvement in the purchase	Involvement with the product
Market environment	Market environment
Situational factors	Situational factors
Motives	
Making better purchase decisions	Building a bank of information for future use
	Experiencing fun and pleasure
Outcomes	
Increased product and market knowledge	Increased product and market knowledge leading to
Better purchase decisions	• future buying efficiencies
Increased satisfaction with the purchase outcome	• personal influence
	Increased impulse buying
	Increased satisfaction from search and other outcomes

Source: Peter H. Bloch, Daniel L. Sherrell, and Nancy M. Ridgway, "Consumer Search: An Extended Framework," *Journal of Consumer Research* 13 (June 1986): 120. Reprinted with permission by The University of Chicago Press.

INTERNAL VERSUS EXTERNAL SEARCH

Information sources can be roughly broken down into two kinds: internal and external. As a result of prior experience and simply living in a consumer culture, each of us already has in memory some degree of knowledge about many products. When confronted with a purchase decision, we may engage in *internal search* by scanning our own memory banks to assemble information about different product alternatives (see Chapter 3). Usually, though, even the most market savvy of us need to supplement this knowledge with *external search,* where information is obtained from advertisements, friends, or people-watching.

DELIBERATE VERSUS "ACCIDENTAL" SEARCH

Our existing knowledge of a product may be the result of *directed learning,* wherein on a previous occasion we had already searched for relevant information or experienced some of the alternatives. A parent who bought a birthday cake for one child last month, for example, probably has a good idea of the best kind to buy for another child this month.

Alternatively, we may have acquired information in a more passive manner. Even though a product may not be of interest, exposure to advertising, packaging, and sales promotion activities may result in *incidental learning.* Mere exposure over time to conditioned stimuli and observations of others results in the learning of much material that may not be needed for some time after the fact, if ever. For marketers, this result is actually a benefit of steady, "low-dose" advertising, since product associations are established and maintained until the time they are needed.[13]

In some cases we may be so expert about a product category (or at least believe we are) that no additional search is undertaken. Frequently, however, our own existing state of knowledge is not satisfactory to make an adequate decision, and we must go outside ourselves for more information. The sources we consult for advice vary. They may be impersonal and marketer-dominated sources, such as retailers and catalogues; they may be friends and family members; or they may be unbiased third parties, such as *Consumer Reports* (***www.consumerreports.org***).[14]

The Economics of Information

The traditional decision-making perspective brings the *economics-of-information approach* to the search process; this perspective assumes that consumers will gather as much data as needed to make an informed decision. Consumers form expectations of the value of additional information and continue to search to the extent that the rewards of doing so (the *utility*) exceed the costs. This utilitarian assumption also implies that the most valuable units of information will be collected first; additional pieces will be absorbed only to the extent that they are seen as adding to what is already known.[15] In other words, people will put themselves out to collect as much information as possible as long as the process of gathering it is not too onerous or time consuming.[16] **Variety seeking** can influence a consumer to switch from his or her favourite product to a less pleasurable item. This can even occur before an individual becomes satiated or tired of the favourite product. The explanation of this phenomenon comes from research that supports the idea that consumers are willing to trade enjoyment for variety, and that variety seeking is a choice strategy that occurs as a result of pleasurable memories for a varied sequence.[17]

DO CONSUMERS ALWAYS SEARCH RATIONALLY?

The assumption of rational search cannot always be supported. The amount of external search undertaken for most products is surprisingly small, even when additional information would most likely benefit the consumer. For example, lower-income shoppers, who have more to lose by making a bad purchase, actually search less prior to buying than do more affluent people.[18] Like our friend Bill, some consumers typically visit only one or two stores and rarely seek out unbiased information sources prior to making a purchase decision, especially when little time is available to do so.[19] This pattern is especially prevalent for decisions regarding durables, even when these products represent significant investments. One study of Australian car buyers found that more than one-third of those surveyed had made only two or fewer trips to inspect cars prior to buying one.[20]

This tendency to avoid external search is less prevalent when consumers consider the purchase of symbolic items, such as clothing. In those cases, not surprisingly, people tend to do a fair amount of external search, although most of it involves seeking the opinions of peers.[21] Although the stakes may be lower financially, these self-expressive decisions may be seen as having negative social consequences if the wrong choice is made. The level of perceived risk, a concept to be discussed shortly, is therefore high.

In addition, consumers are often observed to engage in *brand switching*, even if their current brands satisfy their needs. For example, researchers who were studying the beer market for British brewer Bass Export discovered the consumer trend of having a repertoire of two to six favourite brands rather than sticking to only one. This preference for brand switching led them to decide to begin exporting their Tennent's 1885 lager to the United States, positioning the brew as an alternative for young drinkers' usual favourite brands.[22] Sometimes it seems that people just like to try new things—that is, they are interested in variety seeking in which the priority is to vary one's product experiences, perhaps as a form of stimulation to reduce boredom.

Variety seeking is especially likely to occur when people are in a good mood, or when there is relatively little stimulation elsewhere in their environment.[23] In the case of foods and beverages, variety seeking can occur because of a phenomenon known as *sensory-specific satiety*. Put simply, this means the pleasantness of food just eaten drops while the pleasantness of uneaten foods remains unchanged.[24] So even though we have favourites, we still like to sample other possibilities. Ironically,

Marketing Pitfall

Labels provide valuable information about the proper way to use products, but sometimes they can be . . . less than clear. Here are some examples of "interesting" labels:[25]

> On a Conair Pro Style 1600 hair dryer:
  Warning: Do not use in shower. Never use while sleeping.

> Instructions for folding up a portable baby carriage:
  Step 1: Remove baby.

> On a bag of Fritos:
  You could be a winner! No purchase necessary. Details inside.

> On some Swanson frozen dinners:
  Serving suggestion: defrost.

> On Tesco's Tiramisu dessert (printed on bottom of box):
  Do not turn upside down.

> On Marks & Spencer bread pudding:
  Product will be hot after heating.

> On packaging for a Rowenta iron:
  Do not iron clothes on body.

> On Nytol sleeping aid:
  Warning: May cause drowsiness.

consumers actually may switch to less-preferred options for variety's sake even though they enjoy the more familiar option more.[26] On the other hand, when the decision situation is ambiguous, or when there is little information about competing brands, consumers tend to opt for the safe choice by selecting familiar brands and maintaining the status quo.

Figure 9–4 shows the brand attributes consumers consider most important when choosing among alternatives, according to a survey conducted by *Advertising Age*.

BIASES IN THE DECISION-MAKING PROCESS

Consider the following scenario: You've been given a free ticket to an exciting hockey game. At the last minute a sudden snowstorm makes getting to the arena somewhat dangerous. Would you go?

Now, assume the same game and snowstorm, except this time you paid handsomely for the ticket. Would you go?

Analysis of people's responses to this situation and to others illustrates principles of **mental accounting**, where decisions are influenced by the way a problem is posed (called *framing*) and by whether it is put in terms of gains or losses.[27] For example, people are more likely to risk their personal safety in the storm if they paid for the hockey ticket. Only the most diehard fan would fail to recognize that this is an irrational choice, since the risk to the person is the same regardless of whether he or she got a great deal on the ticket. This decision-making bias is called the *sunk-cost fallacy*—having paid for something makes us reluctant to waste it.

→ This Singaporean beer ad reminds us that not all product decisions are made rationally. *Courtesy of La Guillotine Beer.*

May cause drowsiness, dizzy spells, and vomiting. If affected, carry on. It's normal.

La Guillotine Beer 9·1% Proof. Have a nice coma.

FIGURE 9–4   IMPORTANT BRAND ATTRIBUTES

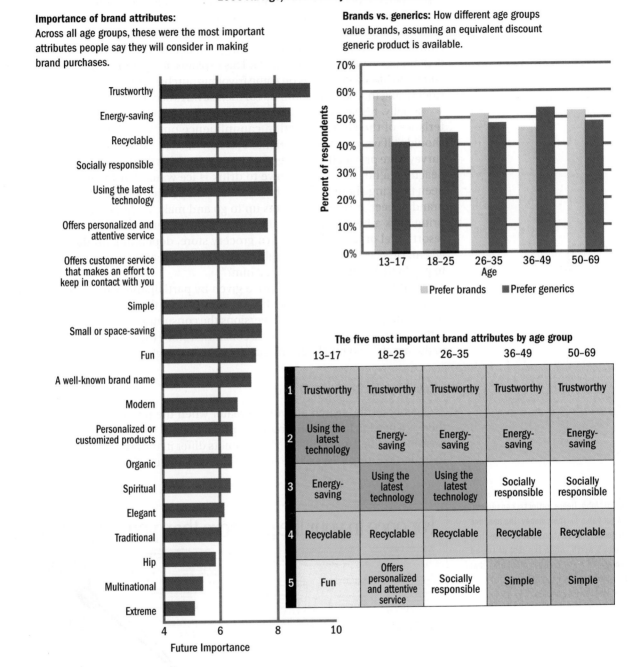

1999 *Ad Age*/ARC Survey: Brand Attributes

Importance of brand attributes: Across all age groups, these were the most important attributes people say they will consider in making brand purchases.

Brands vs. generics: How different age groups value brands, assuming an equivalent discount generic product is available.

Another bias is known as *loss aversion*. People place much more emphasis on loss than they do on gain. For example, for most people losing money is more unpleasant than the pleasure of gaining money. **Prospect theory**, a descriptive model of choice, finds that utility is a function of gains and losses, and risk differs when the consumer faces options involving gains versus those involving losses.[28]

To illustrate this bias, consider the following choices. For each, would you take the safe bet or choose to gamble?

- Option #1: You're given $30 and then offered a chance to flip a coin: heads you win $9, tails you lose $9.

- Option #2: You're given a choice of getting $30 outright or accepting a coin flip that will win you either $39 or $21.

In one study 70 percent of those given option #1 chose to gamble, compared with just 43 percent of those offered option #2. Yet the odds are the same for both options! The difference is that people prefer "playing with the house money"; they are more willing to take risks when they perceive they're using someone else's resources. So, contrary to a rational decision-making perspective, we value money differently depending on where it comes from. This explains, for example, why someone might choose to blow a big bonus on some frivolous purchase, while they would never consider taking that same amount out of their savings account for this purpose.

Finally, research in mental accounting demonstrates that extraneous characteristics of the choice situation can influence our selections, even though they shouldn't if we were totally rational decision makers. For example, participants in a survey were provided with one of two versions of this scenario: "You are lying on the beach on a hot day. All you have to drink is ice water. For the last hour you have been thinking about how much you would enjoy a nice cold bottle of your favourite brand of beer. A companion gets up to go and make a phone call, and he offers to bring back a beer from the only nearby place where beer is sold [either a fancy resort hotel or a small, run-down grocery store, depending on the version you're given]. He says that the beer might be expensive and asks how much you are willing to pay for it. What price do you tell him?"

In this survey the median price given by participants who were in the fancy-resort version was $5.00, while those who were told the grocery-store version were only willing to pay $2.25! In both versions the consumption act is the same, the beer is the same, and no "atmosphere" is consumed since the beer is being brought back to the beach.[29] So much for rational decision making!

How Much Search Occurs?

As a general rule, search activity is greater when the purchase is important, when there is a need to learn more about the purchase, and when the relevant information is easily obtained and utilized.[30] Consumers differ in the amount of search they tend to undertake, regardless of the product category in question. All things being equal,

→This ad for John Deere reflects consumers' desire to get value for their money. The headline plays on people's frustrations about not getting their money's worth, while the rest of the ad underscores the many product attributes that make the lawnmower a good buy.
Courtesy of John Deere & Company.

younger, better-educated people who enjoy the shopping/fact-finding process tend to conduct more information search. Women are more inclined to search than men, as are those who place greater value on style and the image they present.[31]

AMOUNT OF INFORMATION AVAILABLE

Contrary to expected behaviour, more information is not always better for the consumer. We know that consumers have limited capacity in their short-term memory and adjust to their environment by making it more manageable. Therefore, when in choice environments with more information than we can easily process, we truncate the environment to deal efficiently with a subset of it. For example, when shopping for wine or beer, shoppers do not consider all information available, such as bottler, ingredients, price, brand, image, or reputation. Shoppers consider only partial information because there are just too many combinations of all the attributes to take into short-term memory and process effectively.

THE CONSUMER'S PRIOR EXPERTISE

Should prior product knowledge make it more or less likely that a consumer will engage in a search? Product experts and novices use very different procedures during decision making. Novices who know little about a product should be the most motivated to find out more about it; however, experts, who are more familiar with the product category, should be able to better understand the meaning of any new product information they might acquire.

So who searches more? The answer is neither: Search tends to be greatest among those consumers who are *moderately* knowledgeable about the product. There is an inverted U-shaped relationship between knowledge and external search effort, as shown in Figure 9–5. People with very limited expertise may not feel they are capable of searching extensively. In fact, they may not even know where to start. Bill, who did not spend a lot of time researching his purchase, is representative of this situation. He visited one store and looked only at brands with which he was already familiar. In addition, he focused on only a small number of product features.[32]

The *type* of search undertaken by people with varying levels of expertise differs as well. Because experts have a better sense of what information is relevant to the decision, they tend to engage in *selective search*, which means their efforts are more focused and efficient. In contrast, novices are more likely to rely upon the opinions of others and upon "non-functional" attributes, such as brand name and price, to distinguish among alternatives. They may also process information in a "top-down"

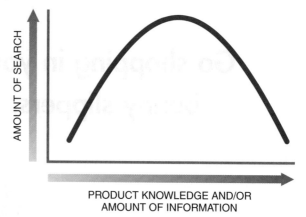

rather than a "bottom-up" manner, focusing less on details than on the big picture. For instance, they may be more impressed by the sheer amount of technical information presented in an ad than by the actual significance of the claims made.[33]

PERCEIVED RISK

As a rule, purchase decisions that involve extensive search also entail some kind of **perceived risk**, or the belief that the product has potentially negative consequences. Perceived risk may be present if the product is expensive or is complex and hard to understand. Alternatively, perceived risk can be a factor when a product choice is visible to others and we run the risk of embarrassment if the wrong choice is made.

Figure 9–6 lists five basic kinds of risk—including both objective factors (such as physical danger) and subjective factors (like social embarrassment)—as well as the products subject to each type of risk. As this figure notes, consumers with greater "risk capital" are less affected by perceived risks associated with the products. For example, a highly self-confident person would be less worried about the social risk inherent in a product, while a more vulnerable, insecure consumer might be reluctant to take a chance on a product that might not be accepted by peers.

EVALUATION OF ALTERNATIVES

Much of the effort that goes into a purchase decision occurs at the stage at which a choice must be made from the available alternatives. After all, modern consumer society abounds with choices. In some cases there may be literally hundreds of different brands (as in beer) or different variations of the same brand (as in shades of lipstick), each screaming for our attention.

Just for fun, ask a female friend to name all the brands of perfume she can think of. The odds are she will reel off three to five names rather quickly and then stop to think awhile before coming up with a few more. It is likely that perfumes in the first set of brands are those with which she is highly familiar, and she probably wears one or more of these. The list may also contain one or two brands that she does not like and would perhaps like to forget. Note also that there are many, many more brands on the market than she named.

If your friend were to go to the store to buy perfume, it is likely that she would consider buying some or most of the brands she listed initially. She might also consider a few more possibilities if these were forcefully brought to her attention while at the store—for example, if she were "ambushed" by an employee who sprays scent samples on shoppers, which is a common occurrence in some department stores.

↓ Seals of approval reduce perceived risk for consumers.
Courtesy of CVMA Pet Food Certification Program.

	BUYERS MOST SENSITIVE TO RISK	PURCHASES MOST SUBJECT TO RISK
MONETARY RISK	Risk capital consists of money and property. Those with relatively little income and wealth are most vulnerable.	High-ticket items that require substantial expenditures are most subject to this form of risk.
FUNCTIONAL RISK	Risk capital consists of alternative means of performing the function or meeting the need. Practical consumers are most sensitive.	Products or services whose purchase and use require the buyer's exclusive commitment and preclude redundancy are most sensitive.
PHYSICAL RISK	Risk capital consists of physical vigour, health, and vitality. Those who are elderly, frail, or in ill health are most vulnerable.	Mechanical or electrical goods (such as vehicles or flammables), drugs and medical treatment, and food and beverages are most sensitive.
SOCIAL RISK	Risk capital consists of self-esteem and self-confidence. Those who are insecure and uncertain are most sensitive.	Socially visible or symbolic goods, such as clothes, jewellery, cars, homes, or sports equipment, are most subject to this form of risk.
PSYCHO-LOGICAL RISK	Risk capital consists of affiliations and status. Those lacking self-respect or attractiveness to peers are most sensitive.	Expensive personal luxuries that may engender guilt; durables; and services whose use demands self-discipline or sacrifice are most sensitive.

FIGURE 9–6

FIVE TYPES OF PERCEIVED RISK

Really, really clean washrooms.
We know that fuel isn't the only reason you stop at Irving. So rest assured you'll find our washrooms clean and comfortable. You'll find everything else you need here too. Fresh coffee and snacks, delicious home-cooked meals served by the friendly staff at our restaurants, and of course, really clean gasoline to get you back on the road. So whether you need to get going or just need to go, make Irving the next stop on your trip.

IRVING

← In this ad, Irving acknowledges one of the attributes that consumers use to decide where they will stop for gas or a bite to eat.
Reprinted with permission from Irving Oil.

Marketing Opportunity !

Is there a "buy button" in your brain? Some corporations are teaming up with neuro-scientists to find out. This work in so-called **neuromarketing** uses a brain-scanning device called *functional magnetic resonance imaging* (or FMRI), a machine that tracks blood flow as people perform mental tasks. Scientists know that specific regions of the brain light up in these scans to show increased blood flow when a person recognizes a face, hears a song, makes a decision, senses deception, and so on. Now they are trying to harness this technology to measure consumers' reactions to movie trailers, choices about automobiles, the appeal of a pretty face, and loyalty to specific brands. DaimlerChrysler took brain scans of men as they looked at photos of cars and confirmed that sports cars activated their reward centres.[34]

Another study that looked at brain scans when people drank competing soft drink brands illustrates how loyalty to a brand can colour our reactions even at a very basic, physiological level. When the researchers monitored brain scans of 67 people who were given a blind taste test of Coca-Cola and Pepsi, each soft drink lit up the brain's reward system. The participants were evenly split as to which drink they preferred—even though three out of four participants *said* they preferred Coke. When told they were drinking "the real thing," as Coke is widely known, the regions of their brains that control memory lit up, drowning out the area that reacts simply to taste cues. In this case, Coke's strong brand identity triumphed over the sensations coming from consumers' taste receptors. If indeed researchers can reliably track consumers' brand preferences by seeing how their brains react, there may be many interesting opportunities for new research techniques that rely on what we (or at least our brains) *do* rather than what we *say*.

Identifying Alternatives

How do we decide which criteria are important, and how do we narrow down product alternatives to an acceptable number and eventually choose one over the others? The answer varies depending on how the consumer decides. A consumer engaged in extended problem solving may carefully evaluate several brands, while someone making a habitual decision may not consider any alternatives to his or her normal brand. And some evidence indicates that more extended processing occurs in situations where negative emotions are aroused by conflicts among the choices available.[35] This is most likely to occur where difficult trade-offs are involved, as when a person must choose between the risk involved in undergoing a bypass operation versus the potential improvement in his or her life if the operation is successful.[36]

The alternatives actively considered during a consumer's choice process are his or her **consideration** or **evoked set**. The evoked set comprises those products already in memory (the retrieval set) plus those prominent in the retail environment. For example, recall that Bill did not know much about the technical aspects of television sets and that he had only a few major brands in memory. Of these, two were acceptable possibilities and one was not. The alternatives that the consumer is aware of but would not consider buying are his or her *inert set,* while those not entering the game at all compose the *inept set.* These categories are depicted in Figure 9–7.

Consumers often consider a surprisingly small number of alternatives in their evoked set. One study combined results from several large-scale investigations of consumers' evoked sets and found that, although there are some marked variations by product category and across countries, the number of products included in these sets is limited. For example, the average size of the evoked set for a U.S. beer consumer was fewer than three, while Canadian consumers typically considered seven brands. In contrast, whereas auto buyers in Norway studied two alternatives, North American consumers on average looked at more than eight models before making a decision.[37]

For obvious reasons, a marketer who finds that her or his brand is not in the evoked set of many consumers in the target market has cause to worry. A product is not likely to be placed in the evoked set after it has previously been considered and rejected. Indeed, a new brand is more likely to be added to the evoked set than is an existing brand that was previously considered but passed over, even after additional positive information is provided for that brand.[38] For marketers, this unwillingness to give a rejected product a second chance underscores the importance of ensuring that it performs well from the time it is introduced.

FIGURE 9–7

IDENTIFYING ALTERNATIVES: GETTING IN THE GAME

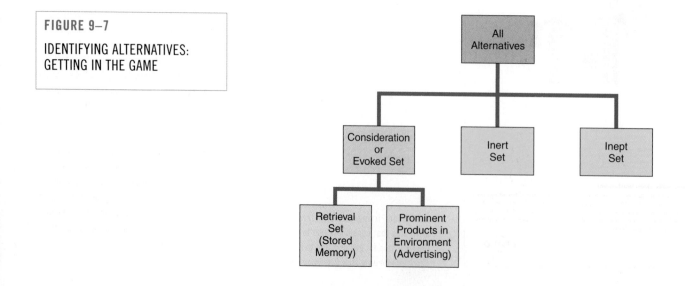

Product Categorization

Remember that, when consumers process product information, they do not do so in a vacuum. Instead, a product stimulus is evaluated in terms of what people already know about the product or things similar to it. A person evaluating a particular 35-mm camera will most likely compare it with other 35-mm cameras rather than with a Polaroid camera, and the consumer would certainly not compare it with a slide projector or a VCR. Since the category in which a product is placed determines the other products it will be compared with, *categorization* is a crucial determinant of how a product is evaluated.

The products in a consumer's evoked set are likely to be those that share some similar features. This process of categorizing products can either help or hurt a product, depending upon what people compare it to. For example, in one survey, about 25 percent of consumers said they would be less likely to buy a product made of hemp if they knew it was derived from the same plant as marijuana (but without any of the latter's effects). When faced with a new product, consumers refer to their already existing knowledge in familiar product categories to form new knowledge.[39]

It is important to understand how this knowledge is represented in a consumer's cognitive structure, which refers to a set of factual knowledge (i.e., beliefs) about products and the way these beliefs are organized in people's minds.[40] These knowledge structures were discussed in Chapter 4. One reason this knowledge is important is that marketers want to ensure that their products are correctly grouped. For example, General Foods brought out a new line of Jell-O flavours such as Cranberry Orange, called Jell-O Gelatin Flavours for Salads. Unfortunately, the company discovered that people would use it only for salad since the name encouraged them to put the product in their "salad" structure rather than in their "dessert" structure. The line had to be dropped.[41]

← An orange marketer like Sunkist hopes that portraying a slice of orange on a lollipop stick will categorize oranges as sweet snacks in the consumer's mind.
Reprinted with permission of Sunkist Growers, Inc. All rights reserved.

Marketing Pitfall

Kimberly-Clark Corp., the maker of well-known paper products including Kleenex and Scott tissues, learned the hard way about the perils of product categorization and consumers' resistance to new categories. The company announced "the most significant category innovation since toilet paper first appeared in roll form in 1890." Even Jay Leno covered the news of the new product: Cottonelle Fresh Rollwipes, a roll of moist wipes in a plastic dispenser that clips onto a regular toilet-paper holder. To quiet sceptics who questioned whether consumers would change their habits so dramatically, Kimberly-Clark unveiled research showing that 63 percent of adults were already in the habit of wetting toilet paper or using a wipe.

Although the company spent more than $100 million to develop the roll and dispenser and even guards the product with more than 30 patents, high hopes for the rollwipes have gone down the toilet. Part of the problem is that the company is dealing with a product most people don't even want to discuss in the first place. Furthermore, its advertising failed to show consumers what the wipes even do. The company's ad agency tried to create a fun image, including TV ads showing shots of people splashing in the water with the slogan, "sometimes wetter is better." A print ad with an extreme close-up of a sumo wrestler's derriere didn't go over much better. To make matters worse, the company didn't design a version in small product sizes, so it couldn't pass out free samples. And the wipes are packaged in a container that is immediately visible in a bathroom—another strike for people already bashful about buying the product.[45]

LEVELS OF CATEGORIZATION

Not only do people group things into categories, but these groupings also occur at different levels of specificity. Typically, a product is represented in a cognitive structure at one of three levels. To understand this idea, consider how someone might respond to the following questions about an ice cream cone: What other products share similar characteristics? Which would be considered as alternatives to eating a cone?

The questions may be more complex than they first appear. At one level a cone is similar to an apple because both could be eaten as a dessert. At another level a cone is similar to a piece of pie since both are eaten for dessert and both are fattening. At still another level a cone is similar to an ice cream sundae; both are eaten for dessert, are made of ice cream, and are fattening.

It is easy to see that the items a person associates with, say, the category "fattening dessert" influence the choices he or she will make for what to eat after dinner. The middle level, known as a *basic level category*, is typically the most useful in classifying products, since items grouped together at this level tend to have a lot in common with each other but still permit a range of alternatives to be considered. The first level, the broader *superordinate category*, is more abstract, while the third, more specific *subordinate category*, often includes individual brands.[42] These three levels are depicted in Figure 9–8. Of course not all items fit equally well into a category. Apple pie is a better example of the subordinate category "pie" than is rhubarb pie, even though both are legitimate kinds of pies. Apple pie is thus more prototypical and would tend to be considered first, especially by category novices. In contrast, pie experts will tend to have knowledge about category examples that are both typical and atypical.[43]

STRATEGIC IMPLICATIONS OF PRODUCT CATEGORIZATION

Product categorization has many strategic implications. The way a product is grouped with others has very important ramifications for determining both its competitors and what criteria will be used to make this choice.

PRODUCT POSITIONING   The success of a *positioning strategy* often hinges on the marketer's ability to convince the consumer that his or her product should be considered within a given category. For example, the orange-juice industry tried to reposition orange juice as a drink that could be enjoyed all day long ("It's not just for breakfast anymore"). On the other hand, soft-drink companies are now attempting to do the opposite by portraying their beverages as suitable for breakfast consumption. They are trying to make their way into consumers' "breakfast drink" category, along with orange juice, grapefruit juice, and coffee. Indeed, this categorization already exists for many consumers in the southern United States, who routinely guzzle a soft drink with their breakfast! Of course, this strategy can backfire, as Pepsi-Cola discovered when it introduced Pepsi A.M. and positioned it as a coffee substitute. The company did such a good job of categorizing the drink as a morning beverage that customers wouldn't drink it at any other time. The product failed.[44]

FIGURE 9–8

LEVELS OF ABSTRACTION IN DESSERT CATEGORIES

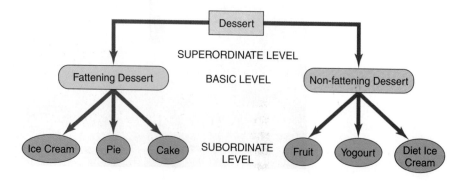

IDENTIFYING COMPETITORS   At the abstract, superordinate level, many different product forms compete for membership. Both bowling and ballet may be considered subcategories of "entertainment" by some people, but many would not necessarily consider the substitution of one of these activities for the other. Products and services that, on the surface, are quite different actually compete with each other at a broad level, often for consumers' discretionary dollars. Although bowling or ballet may not be a likely trade-off for many people, it is feasible, for example, that a symphony might try to lure away ballet season ticket-holders by positioning itself as an equivalent member of the category "cultural event."[46]

Consumers are often faced with choices between non-comparable categories, in which a number of attributes exist that cannot be directly related to one another (the old problem of comparing apples and oranges). The comparison process is easier when consumers can derive an overlapping category that encompasses both items (such as entertainment value or usefulness) and then rate each alternative in terms of that superordinate category.[47]

EXEMPLAR PRODUCTS: RHUBARB VERSUS APPLES, FOR EXAMPLE   If a product is a really good example of a category, it is more familiar to consumers and, as a result, is more easily recognized and recalled.[48] Judgments about category attributes tend to be disproportionately influenced by the characteristics of category exemplars.[49] In a sense, brands that are strongly associated with a category get to "call the shots" by defining the criteria that should be used to evaluate all category members.

Being a bit less than prototypical is not necessarily a bad thing. Products that are moderately unusual within their product category may stimulate more information processing and positive evaluations, since they are neither so familiar that they will be taken for granted nor so discrepant that they will be dismissed.[50] Further, a brand that is strongly discrepant may occupy a unique niche position, while those that are moderately discrepant remain in a differentiated position within the general category.[51]

LOCATING PRODUCTS   Product categorization can also affect consumers' expectations regarding the places they can locate a desired product. If products do not clearly fit into categories (e.g., is a rug furniture?), consumers' ability to find them or make sense of them may be affected. For instance, a frozen dog food that had to be thawed and cooked failed in the market, partly because people could not adapt to the idea of buying dog food in the "frozen foods for people" section.

←This ad for Sunkist lemon juice attempts to establish a new category for the product by repositioning it as a salt substitute.
Courtesy of Sunkist Growers Inc.

Product Choice: Selecting among Alternatives

Once the relevant options from a category have been assembled, a choice must be made among them.[52] Recall that the decision rules that guide choice can range from very simple and quick strategies to complicated processes requiring a lot of attention and cognitive processing. The choice can be influenced by integrating information from such sources as prior experience with the product, information present at the time of purchase, and beliefs about the brands that have been created by advertising.[53]

EVALUATIVE CRITERIA

When Bill was looking at different television sets, he focused on one or two product features and completely ignored several others. He narrowed down his choices by considering only two specific brand names, and from the Prime Wave and Precision models he chose the one that featured stereo capability.

Evaluative criteria are the dimensions used to judge the merits of competing options. In comparing alternative products, Bill could have chosen from among any number of criteria, ranging from very functional attributes (does this TV come with a remote control?) to experiential ones (does this TV's sound reproduction make me imagine I'm in a concert hall?).

Another important point is that criteria on which products differ carry more weight in the decision process. If all brands being considered rate equally well on one attribute (e.g., if all television sets come with remote controls), consumers will have to find other attributes to use in making a choice. Attributes that are actually used to differentiate among choices are **determinant attributes**.

Marketers can play a role in educating consumers about which criteria should be used as determinant attributes. For example, consumer research by Church & Dwight indicated that many consumers view the use of natural ingredients as a determinant attribute. The result was a promotion for a toothpaste made from baking soda, which the company already manufactured for its Arm & Hammer brand.[54] And sometimes the company can even invent a determinant attribute: Pepsi-Cola accomplished this by stamping freshness dates on pop cans. The company spent about $25 million on an advertising and promotional campaign to convince consumers that there's nothing quite as horrible as a stale can of pop—even though it has been estimated that 98 percent of all cans are consumed well before this could

→ Lava soap lays out the options and invites us to choose the solution.
Courtesy of WD-40 Company.

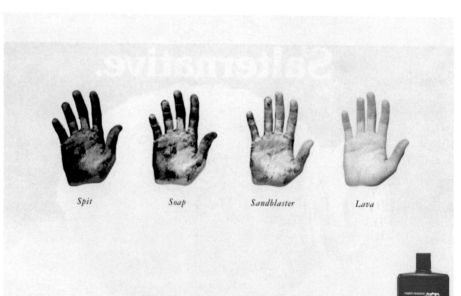

Spit　　Soap　　Sandblaster　　Lava

Hey, your choice.　Lava

be a problem. Six months after introducing the campaign, an independent survey found that 61 percent of respondents felt that freshness dating is an important attribute for a soft drink![55]

The decision about which attributes to use is the result of *procedural learning*, in which a person undergoes a series of cognitive steps before making a choice. These steps include identifying important attributes, remembering whether competing brands differ on those attributes, and so on. In order for a marketer to recommend a new decision criterion effectively, his or her communication should convey three pieces of information:[56]

1. It should point out that there are significant differences among brands on the attribute.

2. It should supply the consumer with a decision-making rule, such as, "*If* [deciding among competing brands], *then* [use the attribute as a criterion]."

3. It should convey a rule that can be easily integrated with the way the person has made this decision in the past. Otherwise the recommendation is likely to be ignored because it requires too much mental work.

Cybermediaries

As anyone who's ever typed a phrase like "home theatres" into a search engine knows, the web delivers enormous amounts of product and retailer information in seconds. In fact, the biggest problem surfers face these days is narrowing down their choices, not beefing them up. With the tremendous number of websites available, and the huge number of people surfing the web each day, how can people organize information and decide where to click? One type of business that is growing to meet this demand is called a **cybermediary**. This is an intermediary that helps to filter and organize online market information so that customers can identify and evaluate alternatives more efficiently.[57] Cybermediaries take different forms.[58]

Directories and *portals* such as Yahoo! or ***www.fashionmall.com*** are general services that tie together a large variety of different sites. *Website evaluators* reduce the risk to consumers by reviewing sites and recommending the best ones. For example, Point Communications selects sites that it designates as the Top 5 Percent of the Web.

Forums, fan clubs, and *user groups* offer product-related discussions to help customers sift through options (more on these in Chapter 11). Other sites like ***www.about.com*** help to narrow alternatives by actually connecting you with human guides who make recommendations. This approach is especially prevalent in the travel industry, where several sites now connect surfers to travel experts (often volunteers who just like to share their expertise about travel), like ***www.bootsnall.com***.

Financial intermediaries authorize payments from buyer to seller. Payment systems include electronic equivalents to writing cheques (Checkfree), paying in cash (Digicash), and sending secure electronic mail authorizing a payment (First Virtual).

Intelligent agents are sophisticated software programs that use *collaborative filtering* technologies to learn from past user behaviour in order to recommend new purchases. For example, when you let ***Amazon.com*** suggest a new book, it's using an intelligent agent to suggest novels based on what you and others like you have bought in the past. This approach was introduced in 1995 (the Stone Age in web time!) by Firefly to make recommendations for taste-based products like music, books, and films.[59] Now, a variety of "shopping bots" are available to act as online purchasing shopping agents, including ***www.mysimon.com*** and ***www.shopping.com***. Collaborative filtering is still in its infancy. In the next few years, expect to see many new web-based methods to simplify the consumer decision-making process. Now, if only someone could come up with an easier way to pay for all the great stuff you find courtesy of shopping bots!

Researchers are working hard to understand how consumers go about finding information online, and in particular how they react to and integrate recommendations they receive from different kinds of online agents into their own product choices. An **electronic recommendation agent** is a software tool that tries to understand a human decision maker's multi-attribute preferences for a product category by asking the user to communicate his or her preferences. Based on that data, the software then recommends a list of alternatives sorted by the degree to which they fit with the person's preferences. Some findings now emerging include the following:[60]

- Consumers who consult recommendation agents select the recommended products twice as often as those who do not.

- The extent to which a consumer has agreed with the agent on past recommendations influences the likelihood that he or she will accept the agent's advice.

- Recommendation agents have a greater impact on decisions when consumers feel the decision is risky (e.g., if the consequences of making a poor decision are high, or if the item is expensive).

- When a recommendation agent asks a consumer about his or her preferences for a particular product attribute, the consumer will weigh that attribute more when making an actual product choice.

- Consumers who are provided with a strong rationale as to why certain attributes are included in the recommendation agent will rely more on the agent's recommendation and engage in less information search than other consumers.

Heuristics: Mental Shortcuts

To simplify decisions, consumers often employ decision rules that allow them to use some dimensions as substitutes for others. For example, Bill relied on certain assumptions as substitutes for a prolonged information search. In particular, he assumed the selection at Zany Zach's would be more than sufficient, so he did not bother to shop at any of Zach's competitors. This assumption served as a shortcut to more extensive information processing.[61] Especially where limited problem solving occurs prior to making a choice, consumers often fall back upon **heuristics**, or mental rules of thumb that lead to a speedy decision. These rules range from the very general ("Higher-priced products are higher-quality products" or "I buy the same brand I bought last time") to the very specific ("I buy Redpath, the brand of sugar my mother always bought").[62]

Sometimes these shortcuts may not be in consumers' best interests. For example, a consumer who personally knows one or two people who have had problems with a particular make of car might assume he or she would have similar trouble with it and thus overlook the model's overall excellent repair record.[63] The influence of such assumptions may be enhanced if the product has an unusual name, which makes it *and* the experiences with it more distinctive.[64]

RELYING ON A PRODUCT SIGNAL

One frequently used shortcut is the tendency to infer hidden dimensions of products from observable attributes. The aspect of the product that is visible acts as a **product signal** of some underlying quality. Such inferences explain why someone trying to sell a used car takes great pains to be sure the car's exterior is clean and shiny: Potential buyers often judge the vehicle's mechanical condition by its appearance, even though this means they may drive away in a shiny, clean clunker.[65]

When product information is incomplete, judgments are often derived from beliefs about *covariation*, or associations among events.[66] For example, a consumer may form an association between product quality and the length of time a manufacturer has been in business. Other signals or attributes believed to coexist with good or bad products include well-known brand names, country of origin, price, and the retail outlets that carry the product.

Unfortunately, consumers tend to be poor estimators of covariation. Their beliefs persist despite evidence to the contrary. Similar to the consistency principle discussed in Chapter 7, people tend to see what they are looking for. They will look for product information that confirms their guesses. In one experiment, consumers sampled four sets of products to determine whether price and quality were related. Those who believed in this relationship prior to the study elected to sample higher-priced products, thus creating a sort of self-fulfilling prophecy.[67]

MARKET BELIEFS: IS IT BETTER IF I HAVE TO PAY MORE FOR IT?

Consumers often form specific beliefs about relationships in the marketplace. These beliefs then become the shortcuts—whether or not they are accurate—that guide their decisions.[68] Our friend Bill's decisions were influenced by his **market beliefs**. Recall, for instance, that he chose to shop at a large "electronics supermarket" because he assumed the selection would be better (though the prices would be lower). A large number of market beliefs have been identified. Some of these are listed in Table 9–3 on page 268. How many do you share?

Do higher prices mean higher quality? The assumption of a *price-quality relationship* is one of the most pervasive market beliefs.[69] Novice consumers may, in fact, consider price as the only relevant product attribute. Experts also consider this information, although in the case of experts price tends to be used for its informational value, especially for products that are known to have wide quality variations in the marketplace (like virgin wool). When this quality level is more standard or strictly regulated (e.g., Harris Tweed sport coats), experts do not weigh price in their decisions. For the most part this belief is justified; you do tend to get what you pay for. However, let the buyer beware: The price-quality relationship is not always justified.[70]

COUNTRY OF ORIGIN AS A HEURISTIC

Modern consumers choose among products made in many countries. Canadians may buy Brazilian shoes, Japanese cars, clothing imported from Taiwan, or microwave ovens built in South Korea. Consumers' reactions to these imports are mixed. In some cases people have come to assume that a product made overseas is of better quality (e.g., cameras or cars), while in other cases the knowledge that a product has been imported tends to lower perceptions of product quality (e.g., apparel).[71] In general, people tend to rate their own country's products more favourably than they do foreign products, and products from industrialized countries are rated better than those from developing countries.

Roper Starch Worldwide interviewed 30 000 customers in 30 countries regarding their feelings about different cultures around the world.[72] The firm categorized people in terms of their attachment to their own culture versus affinity for other cultures. Among the segments identified were the following:

- *Nationalists* (26 percent of the sample): Nationalists feel close to their own culture. Their key personal values include duty, respect for ancestors, status, and social stability. These consumers tend to be somewhat older and are likely to be either female homemakers or blue-collar men.

- *Internationalists* (15 percent of the sample): Internationalists feel close to three or more outside cultures. Their key personal values include open-mindedness, learning, creativity, and freedom. They are more likely to be male, better educated, and upscale.

- *Disengaged* (7 percent of the sample): These people do not feel great attachment to any culture, including their own. They are bored and disenchanted, and tend to be younger and less educated.

TABLE 9–3

COMMON MARKET BELIEFS

Brand	All brands are basically the same.
	Generic products are just name brands sold under a different label at a lower price.
	The best brands are the ones that are purchased the most.
Store	Specialty stores are great places to familiarize yourself with the best brands; but once you figure out what you want, it's cheaper to buy it at a discount outlet.
	A store's character is reflected in its window displays.
	Salespeople in specialty stores are more knowledgeable than other sales personnel.
	Larger stores offer better prices than small stores.
	Locally owned stores give the best service.
	A store that offers a good value on one of its products probably offers good value on all of its items.
	Credit and return policies are most lenient at large department stores.
	Stores that have just opened usually charge attractive prices.
Prices/Discounts/Sales	Sales are typically run to get rid of slow-moving merchandise.
	Stores that are constantly having sales don't really save you money.
	Within a given store, higher prices generally indicate higher quality.
Advertising and Sales Promotion	"Hard-sell" advertising is associated with low-quality products.
	Items tied to "give-aways" are not a good value (even with the freebie).
	Coupons represent real savings for customers because they are not offered by the store.
	When you buy heavily advertised products, you are paying for the label, not for higher quality.
Product/Packaging	Largest-sized containers are almost always cheaper per unit than smaller sizes.
	New products are more expensive when they're first introduced; prices tend to settle down as time goes by.
	When you are not sure what you need in a product, it's a good idea to invest in the extra features, because you'll probably wish you had them later.
	In general, synthetic goods are lower in quality than goods made of natural materials.
	It's advisable to stay away from products when they are new to the market; it usually takes the manufacturer a little time to work the bugs out.

Source: Adapted from Calvin P. Duncan, "Consumer Market Beliefs: A Review of the Literature and an Agenda for Future Research," in *Advances in Consumer Research* 17, ed. Marvin E. Goldberg, Gerald Gorn, and Richard W. Pollay (Provo, UT: Association for Consumer Research, 1990), pp. 729–735.

A product's *country of origin* in some cases is an important piece of information in the decision-making process.[73] Certain items are strongly associated with specific countries, and products from those countries often attempt to benefit from these links. Country-of-origin can function as a **stereotype**—a knowledge structure based on inferences across products. These stereotypes are often biased or inaccurate, but they do play a constructive role in simplifying complex choice situations.[74]

Recent evidence indicates that the consumer's knowledge of a product's country of origin is not necessarily good or bad. Instead it has the effect of stimulating the consumer's interest in the product to a greater degree. The purchaser thinks more extensively about the product and evaluates it more carefully.[75] The origin of the product thus can act as a product attribute that combines with other attributes to influence evaluations.[76] In addition, the consumer's own expertise with the product category moderates the effects of this attribute. When other information is

available, experts tend to ignore country-of-origin information whereas novices continue to rely on it. However, when other information is unavailable or ambiguous, both experts and novices will rely on this attribute to make a decision.[77]

Canada as a country of origin is extremely important for some products, especially bottled water and vitamins. An ad for Jamieson vitamins sold in Japan reads, "This product is imported from Canada, home of forests and lakes."[78] The image that Canada is portraying is clean, pure, and trustworthy. Other research has looked at the profile of Canadians and Canadian products in terms of how these images compare against those of other international competitors.[79]

The tendency to prefer products or people of one's own culture over those from other countries is called **ethnocentrism**. Ethnocentric consumers are likely to feel it is wrong to buy products from other countries, particularly because of the negative effect this may have on the domestic economy. This trait has been measured on the Consumer Ethnocentrism Scale (CETSCALE) that was devised for this purpose. The scale identifies ethnocentric consumers by their extent of agreement with items such as the following:

• Purchasing foreign-made products is un-Canadian.

• Curbs should be put on all imports.

Multicultural Dimensions

French Canadians and English Canadians were asked about their attitudes toward products made in Quebec, Ontario, Great Britain, and France. The French Canadians rated products made in Quebec the best, while English Canadians rated products made in Ontario and Great Britain the highest.[80] These findings suggest that ethnocentricity may influence product evaluation. However, whether they were even aware of where products were made before being asked their opinion is another question altogether.

- Consumers who purchase products made in other countries are responsible for putting their fellow citizens out of work.[81]

Canadian nationalism was stoked by a commercial for Molson Canadian beer called "The Rant" that almost overnight became an unofficial anthem in Canada. A flannel-shirted young Canadian walks onto a stage and calmly begins explaining away Canadian stereotypes: "I'm not a lumberjack or a fur trader. I don't live in an igloo or eat blubber or own a dog sled.... My name is Joe and I ... AM ... CANADIAN!" In the six weeks after the ad started airing, the Molson brand gained almost two points in market share.[82]

Choosing Familiar Brand Names: Loyalty or Habit?

Branding is a marketing strategy that often functions as a heuristic. People form preferences for favourite brands and then may literally never change their mind in the course of their lifetime. A study by the Boston Consulting Group of the market leaders in 30 product categories found that 27 of the brands that were No. 1 in 1930 are still No. 1 today. These brands include such perennial favourites as Ivory soap, Campbell's soup, and Coca-Cola.[83]

Marketers treasure a brand commanding fierce loyalty—and for good reason. Brands that dominate their markets are as much as 50 percent more profitable than their nearest competitors.[84] Small wonder, then, that companies work very hard to cultivate loyalty. When the Disney Channel failed to appear on Teenage Research Unlimited's survey of the 50 coolest teen brands, the company tried to spice up its image to attract a loyal adolescent following. The channel began to play music videos—even if it meant doctoring some of the lyrics to maintain its clean-cut image. For example, the lyrics to "Genie in a Bottle" by Christina Aguilera were changed from "My body's saying let's go" to "My friends are saying let's go"; "I'm a genie in a bottle, baby, you gotta rub me the right way" became "You gotta treat me the right way."[85]

Even musical groups understand the value of catering to their loyal following. For example, touring bands like the New Orleans Cajun rock band the Radiators work with travel agencies to offer packages covering airfare, lodging, and meals to hard-core groupies. Fanatic followers of jam bands like the String Cheese Incident and Phish descend upon hotels in the tradition of the Grateful Dead, who encouraged bootleg recordings of their extended musical sets but prospered by selling concert paraphernalia to hard-core fans.[86]

Consumers' attachments to certain brands, such as Coca-Cola, are so powerful that this loyalty is often considered a positive product attribute in and of itself. Brand equity can actually be quantified in terms of *goodwill*, defined as the difference between the market value and the book value of a brand.

INERTIA: THE FICKLE CONSUMER

Many people tend to buy the same brand just about every time they go to the store. This consistent pattern is often due to inertia, where a brand is bought out of habit merely because less effort is required. If another product comes along that is for some reason easier to buy (e.g., it is cheaper or the original product is out of stock), the consumer will not hesitate to do so. A competitor who is trying to change a buying pattern based on inertia often can do so rather easily, because little resistance to brand switching will be encountered if some reason to switch is apparent.

Since there is little to no underlying commitment to the product, such promotional tools as point-of-purchase displays, extensive couponing, or noticeable price reductions may be sufficient to "unfreeze" a consumer's habitual pattern.

BRAND LOYALTY: A "FRIEND," TRIED AND TRUE

This kind of fickleness will not occur if true **brand loyalty** exists. In contrast to inertia, brand loyalty is a form of repeat-purchasing behaviour reflecting a

Three-peat performance.

Thanks Canada, for making the Honda Civic the best selling car in the country for the 3rd year in a row.

CIVIC Best New Economy Car of the Year
AUTOMOBILE JOURNALISTS ASSOCIATION OF CANADA

CIVIC ★ ★ ★ ★ ★
NHTSA Five-Star Safety Rating

HONDA

www.honda.ca

← This Honda ad emphasizes the high brand loyalty of Honda owners and so portrays the act of choosing a new car as one of simple, habitual decision making.
Courtesy of Honda Canada Inc.

conscious decision to continue buying the same brand. This concept thus refers to a pattern of purchases over time where actual decision making occurs.[87] For brand loyalty to exist, a pattern of repeat purchasing must be accompanied by an underlying positive attitude toward the brand. Brand loyalty may be initiated by customer preference based on objective reasons, but after the brand has been around for a long time and is heavily advertised, it can also create an emotional attachment, either by being incorporated into the consumer's self-image or because it is associated with prior experiences.[88] Purchase decisions based on brand loyalty also become habitual over time, but the underlying commitment to the brand is much stronger.

Compared with the consumer who passively accepts a brand because of inertia, a brand-loyal consumer is actively (sometimes passionately) involved with his or her favourite. Because of the emotional bonds that can be created between brand-loyal consumers and products, "true-blue" users react more vehemently when these products are altered, redesigned, or eliminated.[89] Witness, for example, the national call-in campaigns, boycotts, and other protests when Coca-Cola replaced its tried-and-true formula with New Coke.

Two decades ago, marketers struggled with the problem of *brand parity*, which refers to consumers' beliefs that there are no significant differences among brands. For example, more than one-half of consumers worldwide considered all brands of beer and cigarettes to be about the same, and more than 70 percent believed that all paper towels, soaps, and snack chips are alike.[90] Some analysts even proclaimed the death of brand names, predicting that private label or generic products that offer the same value for less money would kill off the tried-and-true products.

However, these gloomy predictions turned out to be wrong as major brands made a dramatic comeback. In the early part of the twenty-first century, branding is king! Some attribute this renaissance to information overload—with too many alternatives (many of them unfamiliar names) to choose from, people seem to be looking for clear signals of quality. Branded products are in demand today—but sophisticated shoppers are less picky about where they buy them. Old stigmas about shopping in discount stores seem to have largely vanished as consumers figure out that in many cases they can get the same brand-name products at retailers like Costco or Wal-Mart.

Decision Rules

Consumers consider sets of product attributes by using different rules, depending upon the complexity of the decision and its importance to them. As we have seen, in some cases these rules are quite simple: People simply rely on a "shortcut" to make a choice. In other cases, though, more effort and thought are put into carefully weighing alternatives before coming to a decision.

Net Profit

One way to differentiate among decision rules is to divide them into those that are *compensatory* versus those that are *non-compensatory*. Compensatory rules imply that one good attribute can "compensate" for other poorer attributes. This is not the case with non-compensatory rules, where some poor attributes may eliminate the choice despite its strength on other attributes. As an aid in the discussion, the attributes of the television sets that Bill considered are summarized in Table 9–4. Now let's see whether some of these rules result in different brand choices.

NON-COMPENSATORY DECISION RULES

Simple decision rules are **non-compensatory**, and a product with a low standing on one attribute cannot make up for this position by being better on another attribute. In other words, people simply eliminate all options that do not meet some basic standards. A consumer like Bill who uses the decision rule "Only buy well-known brand names," would not consider a new brand, even if it were equal or superior to existing ones. When people are less familiar with a product category or not very motivated to process complex information, they tend to use simple, non-compensatory rules.[91]

THE LEXICOGRAPHIC RULE   When the *lexicographic rule* is used, the brand that is the best on the most important attribute is selected. If two or more brands are seen as being equally good on that attribute, the consumer then compares them using the second most important attribute. This selection process goes on until the tie is broken. In Bill's case, since both the Prime Wave and Precision models were tied on his most important attribute (a 60-inch screen), the Precision model was chosen because of its rating on his second-most-important attribute—its stereo capability.

THE ELIMINATION-BY-ASPECTS RULE   Again, brands are evaluated on the most important attribute under the *elimination-by-aspects rule*. In this case, though, specific cut-offs are imposed. For example, if Bill had been more interested in having a sleep timer on his TV (i.e., if it had a higher importance ranking), he might have stipulated that his choice "must have a sleep timer." Since the Prime Wave model had one and the Precision did not, the Prime Wave would have been chosen.

THE CONJUNCTIVE RULE   While the two former rules involve processing by attribute, the *conjunctive rule* entails processing by brand. As with the elimination-by-aspects procedure, cut-offs are established for each attribute. A brand is chosen if it meets all the cut-offs, while failure to meet any one cut-off means rejection. If none of the brands meets all of the cut-offs, the choice may be delayed, the decision rule may be changed, or the cut-offs themselves may be modified. Note that this rule rates negative data more heavily.

THE DISJUNCTIVE RULE   Here the consumer develops acceptable standards for each attribute. Usually the standards are higher than the shopper's minimum cut-offs for attributes. If a choice alternative exceeds the standard for *any* attribute, it is accepted. Although this strategy may be difficult to envisage, think about a consumer shopping for a new T-shirt or sweater to spruce up his wardrobe. Perhaps the consumer does not know exactly what he will buy before going shopping, but once in the choice environment he will select something that is exceptional in some unique way. The article may be a great new colour, style, or type of fabric that exceeds his standards. When the shopper finds two great sweaters, then he must go to a different decision rule to choose between them.

If Bill had stipulated that all attributes had to be rated as "good" or better, he would not have been able to choose any of the options. He might then have modified his decision rule, conceding that it was not possible to attain these high standards in the price range he was considering. Perhaps Bill would have decided that it wasn't so important to have onscreen programming, in which case he would have again considered the Precision model.

TABLE 9–4					

HYPOTHETICAL ALTERNATIVES FOR A TV SET

			Brand Ratings		
Attribute	Personal Importance* Rating	Ranking	Prime Wave	Precision	Kamashita
Size of screen	5	6	Excellent 5	Excellent 5	Excellent 5
Stereo broadcast capability	4	5	Poor 1	Excellent 5	Good 4
Brand reputation	2	4	Excellent 5	Excellent 5	Poor 1
Onscreen programming	2	3	Excellent 5	Poor 1	Poor 1
Cable-ready capability	4	2	Good 4	Good 4	Good 4
Sleep timer	1	1	Excellent 5	Poor 1	Good 4

*Note that higher numbers denote more importance.

COMPENSATORY DECISION RULES

Unlike non-compensatory decision rules, **compensatory rules** give a product a chance to make up for its shortcomings. Consumers who employ these rules tend to be more involved in the purchase and thus are willing to exert the effort to consider the entire picture in a more exacting way. The willingness to let good and bad product qualities balance out can result in quite different choices. For example, if Bill hadn't been as concerned about having stereo reception, he might have chosen the Prime Wave model using a compensatory rule. But because this brand did not feature this highly ranked attribute, it didn't stand a chance when he used a non-compensatory rule.

Two basic types of compensatory rules have been identified. When using the *simple additive rule,* the consumer merely chooses the alternative with the largest number of positive attributes. This choice is most likely to occur when his or her

← This ad for *The Globe and Mail* (***www.globeandmail. com***) simplifies for the readers the distinction between the writing styles of two newspaper writers.
Courtesy of The Globe and Mail.

ability or motivation to process information is limited. One drawback to this approach for the consumer is that some of these attributes may not be very meaningful or important. An ad containing a long list of product benefits may be persuasive, despite the fact that many of the benefits included are actually standard within the product class and aren't determinant attributes at all.

The more complex version is known as the *weighted additive rule*.[93] When using this rule, the consumer also takes into account the relative importance of positively rated attributes, essentially multiplying brand ratings by importance weights. If this process sounds familiar, it should. The calculation process strongly resembles the multi-attribute attitude model described in Chapter 7.

In the course of the many purchases people make in their lifetime, many different decision rules are used by the same people for different purchases. The recurring decision is when to stop acquiring additional information and commit to the leading alternative. We know that this decision is governed by the costs and benefits of the search process, as weighed by the consumer.[94] There is some attempt to model this question of how much data a consumer should acquire before choice.[95]

CHAPTER SUMMARY

CONSUMER DECISION MAKING IS A CENTRAL PART OF CONSUMER BEHAVIOUR, BUT THE WAYS IN WHICH PEOPLE EVALUATE AND CHOOSE PRODUCTS (AND THE AMOUNT OF THOUGHT THEY PUT INTO THESE CHOICES) VARY WIDELY, DEPENDING ON SUCH DIMENSIONS AS THE DEGREE OF NOVELTY OR RISK RELATED TO THE DECISION.

- Consumers are constantly faced with the need to make decisions about products. Some of these decisions are very important and entail great effort, whereas others are made on a virtually automatic basis. The decision-making task is further complicated by the sheer number of decisions we need to make in a marketplace environment characterized by consumer hyperchoice.

- Perspectives on decision making range from focusing on habits that people develop over time, to novel situations involving a great deal of risk in which consumers must carefully collect and analyze information prior to making a choice. Many of our decisions are highly automated and are made largely by habit. This trend is accelerating as marketers begin to introduce smart products that enable silent commerce, where some purchases are made automatically by the products themselves (e.g., a malfunctioning appliance that contacts the repair department directly).

A DECISION IS ACTUALLY COMPOSED OF A SERIES OF STAGES THAT RESULTS IN THE SELECTION OF ONE PRODUCT OVER COMPETING OPTIONS.

- A typical decision process involves several steps. The first is problem recognition, in which the consumer first realizes that some action must be taken. This realization may be prompted in a variety of ways, ranging from the actual malfunction of a current purchase to a desire for new things based on exposure to different circumstances or advertising that provides a glimpse into what is needed to "live the good life."

- Once the consumer recognizes a problem and sees it as sufficiently important to warrant some action, information search begins. This search may range from simply scanning memory to determine what's been done to resolve the problem in the past, to extensive fieldwork in which the consumer consults a variety of sources to amass as much information as possible. In many cases, people engage in surprisingly little search. Instead, they rely on various mental shortcuts, such as brand names or price, or may even simply imitate others' choices.

- In the evaluation-of-alternatives stage, the product alternatives a person considers comprise his or her evoked set. Members of an evoked set usually share some characteristics; they are categorized similarly. The way people mentally group products influences the alternatives they will consider. They will usually associate some brands more strongly with these categories than others (i.e., they will find them more prototypical).

DECISION MAKING IS NOT ALWAYS RATIONAL.

- Research in the field of behavioural economics illustrates that decision making is not always strictly rational. Principles of mental accounting demonstrate that decisions can be influenced by the way a problem is posed (called framing) and whether it is put in terms of gains or losses.

OUR ACCESS TO ONLINE SOURCES IS CHANGING THE WAY WE DECIDE WHAT TO BUY.

- The World Wide Web has changed the way many consumers search for information. Today, the problem often is weeding out excess detail rather than needing to search for more. Comparative search sites and intelligent agents help to filter and guide the search process. We can rely on cybermediaries such as web portals to sort through massive amounts of information as a way to simplify the decision-making process.

WE OFTEN FALL BACK ON WELL-LEARNED "RULES OF THUMB" TO MAKE DECISIONS.

- Very often we use heuristics, or mental rules of thumb, to simplify decision making. In particular, people develop many market beliefs over time. One of the most common beliefs is that price is positively related to quality. Other heuristics rely on well-known brand names or a product's country of origin as signals of product quality. When a brand is consistently purchased over time, this pattern may be due to true brand loyalty, or simply to inertia because it's the easiest thing to do.

CONSUMERS RELY UPON DIFFERENT DECISION RULES WHEN EVALUATING COMPETING OPTIONS.

- When consumers eventually make a product choice from among alternatives, they can use any one of a number of decision rules. Noncompensatory rules eliminate alternatives that are deficient on any of the criteria the consumers have chosen to use. Compensatory rules, which are more likely to be applied in high-involvement situations, allow decision makers to consider each alternative's good and bad points more carefully to arrive at the overall best choice.

KEY TERMS

Behavioural influence perspective   p. 247

Brand loyalty   p. 270

Compensatory decision rules   p. 273

Consideration set   p. 260

Consumer hyperchoice   p. 245

Cybermediary   p. 265

Determinant attributes   p. 264

Electronic recommendation agent   p. 266

Ethnocentrism   p. 269

Evaluative criteria   p. 264

Evoked set   p. 260

Experiential perspective   p. 248

Extended problem solving   p. 248

Habitual decision making   p. 248

Heuristics   p. 266

Information search   p. 251

Limited problem solving   p. 248

Market beliefs   p. 267

Mental accounting   p. 254

Neuromarketing   p. 259

Non-compensatory decision rules   p. 272

Perceived risk   p. 258

Problem recognition   p. 250

Product signal   p. 266

Prospect theory   p. 255

Purchase momentum   p. 246

Rational perspective   p. 245

Silent commerce   p. 250

Stereotype   p. 268

Variety seeking   p. 253

REVIEW QUESTIONS

1. Why do we say that "mindless" decision making can actually be more efficient?
2. List the steps in the model of rational decision making.
3. What is purchase momentum, and how does it relate (or not) to the model of rational decision making?
4. What is the difference between the behavioural influence and experiential perspectives on decision making? Give an example of the type of purchase that most likely would be explained by each perspective.
5. Name two ways a consumer problem can arise.
6. What is the economics-of-information perspective, and how does it relate to information search?
7. Give an example of the sunk-cost fallacy.
8. What is prospect theory? Does it support the argument that people are rational decision makers?
9. Describe the relationship between a consumer's level of expertise and how much he or she is likely to search for information about a product.

10. List three types of perceived risk, giving an example of each.
11. "Marketers need to be extra sure their product works as promised when they first introduce it." How does this statement relate to what we know about consumers' evoked sets?
12. Describe the difference between a superordinate category, a basic level category, and a subordinate category.
13. What is an example of an exemplar product?
14. List three product attributes that consumers can use as product quality signals and provide an example of each.
15. How does a brand function as a heuristic?
16. Describe the difference between inertia and brand loyalty.
17. What is the difference between a non-compensatory and a compensatory decision rule? Give one example of each.

CONSUMER BEHAVIOUR CHALLENGE

Discuss

1. The chapter argues that in our society having too many choices is a bigger problem than not having enough. Do you agree? Is it possible to have too much of a good thing?

2. Silent commerce has the potential to automate many of our decisions. Do you see any downsides to this trend?

3. How can retailers compete if people believe they can get the same items everywhere?

4. Commercial Alert, a consumer group, is highly critical of neuromarketing, calling it Orwellian. The group's executive director wrote, "What would happen in this country if corporate marketers and political consultants could literally peer inside our brains and chart the neural activity that leads to our selections in the supermarket and voting booth?" "What if they then could trigger this neural activity by various means, so as to modify our behaviour to serve their own ends?"[96] What do you think? Is neuromarketing dangerous?

5. If people are not always rational decision makers, is it worth the effort to study how they make purchasing decisions? What techniques might marketers employ to understand experiential consumption and to translate this knowledge into marketing strategy?

6. Why is it difficult to place a product in a consumer's evoked set after it has already been rejected? What strategies might a marketer use to accomplish this goal?

7. Discuss two different non-compensatory decision rules and highlight the difference(s) between them.

8. How might the use of one rule versus another result in a different product choice?

9. Technology has the potential to make our lives easier by reducing the amount of clutter we need to work through in order to access the information on the internet that really interests us. On the other hand, perhaps intelligent agents limit us by making recommendations based only on what we and others like us have chosen in the past; they reduce the chance that we will stumble on something (e.g., a book on a topic we've never heard of, or a music group that's different from the style we usually listen to). Will the proliferation of "shopping bots" make our lives too predictable by giving us only more of the same? If so, is this a problem?

Experiential Exercises

10. The chapter discusses the expensive failure of the Cottonelle Fresh Rollwipe. If the company hired you as a consultant to revamp this effort, what recommendations would you make to persuade consumers to try such a sensitive product?

11. Find examples of electronic recommendation agents on the web and evaluate them. Are they helpful? What characteristics of the sites are likely to make you buy products you wouldn't have bought on your own?

12. Conduct a poll based on the list of market beliefs you'll find in Table 9-3. Do people agree with these beliefs? How much do they influence their decisions?

13. Pepsi invented freshness dating and managed to persuade consumers that this was an important product attribute. Devise a similar strategy from another product category by coming up with a brand new product attribute. Using the steps in procedural learning as described in this chapter, how would you communicate this attribute to your customers?

14. Define the three levels of product categorization described in this chapter. Diagram these levels for a health club.

15. Choose a friend or parent who grocery shops on a regular basis and keep a log of their purchases of common consumer products during the term. Can you detect any evidence of brand loyalty in any categories based on consistency of purchases? If so, talk to the person about these purchases. Try to determine if his or her choices are based on true brand loyalty or on inertia. What techniques might you use to differentiate between the two?

16. Form a group of three. Pick a product and develop a marketing plan based on each of the three approaches to consumer decision making: rational, experiential, and behavioural influence. What are the major differences in emphasis among the three perspectives? Which is the most likely type of problem-solving activity for the product you have selected? What characteristics of the product make this so?

17. Identify a person who is about to make a major purchase. Ask that person to make a chronological list of all the information sources consulted prior to making a decision. How would you characterize the types of sources he or she is using (i.e., internal versus external, media versus personal, etc.)? Which sources appeared to have the most impact on the person's decision?

18. Perform a survey of country-of-origin stereotypes. Compile a list of five countries and ask people what products they associate with each. What are their evaluations of the products and their likely attributes?

19. The power of a country stereotype can also be demonstrated in another way. Prepare a brief description of a product, including a list of features, and ask people to rate it in terms of quality, likelihood of purchase, and so on. Make several versions of the description, varying only in terms of the country from which the product comes. Do ratings change as a function of the country of origin?

20. Ask a friend to "talk through" the process she used to choose one brand over others during a recent purchase. Based on this description, can you identify the decision rule she most likely employed?

21. Give one of the scenarios described in the section on "biases in decision making" to 10 to 20 people. How do your results compare with those reported in this chapter?

22. Think of a product you recently shopped for online. Describe your search process. How did you become aware that you wanted/needed the product? How did you evaluate alternatives? Did you wind up buying online? Why or why not? What factors would make it more or less likely that you would buy something online versus in a traditional store?

CBC ⬤ VIDEO VIGNETTE

CONCEPTS AT WORK FOR EXTENDED WARRANTIES

Technological advancements have resulted in a continuous flow of a wide range of electronic products into the marketplace. Many of these new products are more complex than their predecessors, but this complexity has not stopped inexperienced consumers of all ages from purchasing them. They are worth the risk in more ways than one. After a period of pondering the features, shopping around, and pocketbook assessment, consumers of large and small electronic products find themselves standing before a cash register ready to take the plunge.

Teenagers, who are avid consumers of stereos, flat-screen televisions, and mini disc players, are a case in point. But wait—at the checkout, there's yet another decision to be made: "Do you want to buy an extended warranty (that is, extra insurance in case something goes wrong and you can't fix it)?"

Indeed, at some store outlets, buyers are strongly encouraged to purchase extended warranties. Many are convinced to pay $20 to $100 more for additional coverage. It's worth it, right? Or is it? The answer seems to depend, at least in part, on which side of the counter you're standing on.

Questions

1. Why do buyers of electronic products often buy extended warranties?
2. What do consumers expect from extended warranties?
3. Do extended warranties protect consumers? Why or why not?
4. How should consumers respond to sales pressure to buy an extended warranty?

Resource: "Extended Warranties," Marketplace #6, CBC Air Date: November 12, 2002.

NOTES

1. David Glen Mick, Susan M. Broniarczyk, and Jonathan Haidt, "Choose, Choose, Choose, Choose, Choose, Choose, Choose: Emerging and Prospective Research on the Deleterious Effects of Living in Consumer Hyperchoice," *Journal of Business Ethics* 52 (2004): 207–211; see also Barry Schwartz, *The Paradox of Choice: Why More Is Less* (Toronto: HarperCollins Canada/Ecco Press, 2005).

2. John C. Mowen, "Beyond Consumer Decision Making," *Journal of Consumer Marketing* 5, 1 (1988): 15–25.

3. Richard W. Olshavsky and Donald H. Granbois, "Consumer Decision Making: Fact or Fiction," *Journal of Consumer Research* 6 (September 1989): 93–100.

4. Ravi Dhar, Joel Huber, and Uzma Khan, "The Shopping Momentum Effect," paper presented at the Association for Consumer Research, Atlanta, October 2002.

5. James R. Bettman, "The Decision Maker Who Came in from the Cold," Presidential Address, in *Advances in Consumer Research* 20, eds. Leigh McAlister and Michael Rothschild (Provo, UT: Association for Consumer Research), 1993, 7–11; John W. Payne, James R. Bettman, and Eric J. Johnson, "Behavioral Decision Research: A Constructive Processing Perspective," *Annual Review of Psychology* 4 (1992): 87–131. For an overview of recent developments in individual-choice models, see Robert J. Meyer and Barbara E. Kahn, "Probabilistic Models of Consumer Choice Behavior," in *Handbook of Consumer Behavior*, eds. Thomas S. Robertson and Harold H. Kassarjian (Englewood Cliffs, NJ: Prentice Hall, 1991): 85–123.

6. Mowen, "Beyond Consumer Decision Making."

7. Joseph W. Alba and J. Wesley Hutchinson, "Dimensions of Consumer Expertise," *Journal of Consumer Research* 13 (March 1988): 411–454.

8. Julian E. Barnes, "Whirlpool Trying to Change Consumer Habits," *New York Times on the Web* (March 16, 2001).

9. Kevin Maney, "Tag It: Tiny Wireless Wonders Improve Convenience," *Montgomery Advertiser* (May 6, 2002): D1.

10. Ibid.

11. Gordon C. Bruner III and Richard J. Pomazal, "Problem Recognition: The Crucial First Stage of the Consumer Decision Process," *Journal of Consumer Marketing* 5, 1 (1988): 53–63.

12. Peter H. Bloch, Daniel L. Sherrell, and Nancy M. Ridgway, "Consumer Search: An Extended Framework," *Journal of Consumer Research* 13 (June 1986): 119–126.

13. Girish Punj, "Presearch Decision Making in Consumer Durable Purchases," *Journal of Consumer Marketing* 4 (Winter 1987): 71–82.

14. H. Beales et al., "Consumer Search and Public Policy," *Journal of Consumer Research* 8 (June 1981): 11–22.

15. Itamar Simonson, Joel Huber, and John Payne, "The Relationship between Prior Brand Knowledge and Information Acquisition Order," *Journal of Consumer Research* 14 (March 1988): 566–578.

16. John R. Hauser, Glen L. Urban, and Bruce D. Weinberg, "How Consumers Allocate Their Time when Searching for Information," *Journal of Marketing Research* 30 (November 1993): 452–466; George J. Stigler, "The Economics of Information," *Journal of Political Economy* 69 (June 1961): 213–225.

17. Rebecca K. Ratner, Barbara E. Kahn, and Daniel Kahneman, "Choosing Less-Preferred Experiences for the Sake of Variety," *Journal of Consumer Research* 26 (June 1999): 1–15.

18. Cathy J. Cobb and Wayne D. Hoyer, "Direct Observation of Search Behavior," *Psychology & Marketing* 2 (Fall 1985): 161–179.

19. Sharon E. Beatty and Scott M. Smith, "External Search Effort: An Investigation across Several Product Categories," *Journal of Consumer Research* 14 (June 1987): 83–95; William L. Moore and Donald R. Lehmann, "Individual Differences in Search Behavior for a Nondurable," *Journal of Consumer Research* 7 (December 1980): 296–307.

20. Geoffrey C. Kiel and Roger A. Layton, "Dimensions of Consumer Information Seeking Behavior," *Journal of Marketing Research* 28 (May 1981): 233–239. See also Narasimhan Srinivasan and Brian T. Ratchford, "An Empirical Test of a Model of External Search for Automobiles," *Journal of Consumer Research* 18 (September 1991): 233–242.

21. David F. Midgley, "Patterns of Interpersonal Information Seeking for the Purchase of a Symbolic Product," *Journal of Marketing Research* 20 (February 1983): 74–83.

22. Cyndee Miller, "Scotland to U.S.: 'This Tennent's for You,'" *Marketing News* (August 29, 1994): 26.

23. Satya Menon and Barbara E. Kahn, "The Impact of Context on Variety Seeking in Product Choices," *Journal of Consumer Research* 22 (December 1995): 285–295; Barbara E. Kahn and Alice M. Isen, "The Influence of Positive Affect on Variety Seeking among Safe, Enjoyable Products," *Journal of Consumer Research* 20 (September 1993): 257–270.

24. J. Jeffreey Inman, "The Role of Sensory-Specific Satiety in Consumer Variety Seeking among Flavors," unpublished manuscript, A.C. Nielsen Center for Marketing Research, University of Wisconsin–Madison (July 1999).

25. Examples provided by Dr. William Cohen, personal communication, October 1999.

26. Ratner, Kahn, and Kahneman, "Choosing Less-Preferred Experiences for the Sake of Variety."

27. Gary Belsky, "Why Smart People Make Major Money Mistakes," *Money* (July 1995): 76 (10 pp.); Richard Thaler and Eric J. Johnson, "Gambling with the House Money or Trying to Break Even: The Effects of Prior Outcomes on Risky Choice," *Management Science* 36 (June 1990): 643–660; Richard Thaler, "Mental Accounting and Consumer Choice," *Marketing Science* 4 (Summer 1985): 199–214.

28. Daniel Kahneman and Amos Tversky, "Prospect Theory: An Analysis of Decision under Risk," *Econometrica* 47 (March 1979): 263–291; Timothy B. Heath, Subimal Chatterjee, and Karen Russo France, "Mental Accounting and Changes in Price: The Frame Dependence of Reference Dependence," *Journal of Consumer Research* 22, 1 (June 1995): 90–97.

29. Quoted in Thaler, "Mental Accounting and Consumer Choice," 206.

30. Girish N. Punj and Richard Staelin, "A Model of Consumer Search Behavior for New Automobiles," *Journal of Consumer Research* 9 (March 1983): 366–380.

31. Cobb and Hoyer, "Direct Observation of Search Behavior"; Moore and Lehmann, "Individual Differences in Search Behavior for a Nondurable"; Punj and Staelin, "A Model of Consumer Search Behavior for New Automobiles."

32. James R. Bettman and C. Whan Park, "Effects of Prior Knowledge and Experience and Phase of the Choice Process on Consumer Decision Processes: A Protocol Analysis," *Journal of Consumer Research* 7 (December 1980): 234–248.

33. Alba and Hutchinson, "Dimensions of Consumer Expertise"; Bettman and Park, "Effects of Prior Knowledge"; Merrie Brucks, "The Effects of Product Class Knowledge on Information Search Behavior," *Journal of Consumer Research* 12 (June 1985): 1–16; Joel E. Urbany, Peter R. Dickson, and William L. Wilkie, "Buyer Uncertainty and Information Search," *Journal of Consumer Research* 16 (September 1989): 208–215.

34. Sandra Blakeslee, "If You Have a 'Buy Button' in Your Brain, What Pushes It?" *New York Times on the Web* (October 19, 2004).

35. Mary Frances Luce, James R. Bettman, and John W. Payne, "Choice Processing in Emotionally Difficult Decisions," *Journal of Experimental Psychology: Learning, Memory, and Cognition* 23 (March 1997): 384–405.

36. Luce, Bettman, and Payne, "Choice Processing in Emotionally Difficult Decisions." Example provided by Prof. James Bettman, personal communication, December 17, 1997.

37. John R. Hauser and Birger Wernerfelt, "An Evaluation Cost Model of Consideration Sets," *Journal of Consumer Research* 16 (March 1990): 393–408.

38. Robert J. Sutton, "Using Empirical Data to Investigate the Likelihood of Brands Being Admitted or Readmitted into an Established Evoked Set," *Journal of the Academy of Marketing Science* 15 (Fall 1987): 82.

39. Cyndee Miller, "Hemp is Latest Buzzword," *Marketing News* (March 17, 1997): 1.

40. Alba and Hutchinson, "Dimensions of Consumer Expertise"; Joel B. Cohen and Kunal Basu, "Alternative Models of Categorization: Toward a Contingent Processing Framework," *Journal of Consumer Research* 13 (March 1987): 455–472.

41. Robert M. McMath, "The Perils of Typecasting," *American Demographics* (February 1997): 60.

42. Eleanor Rosch, "Principles of Categorization," in *Recognition and Categorization*, eds. E. Rosch and B.B. Lloyd (Hillsdale, NJ: Lawrence Erlbaum, 1978).

43. Michael R. Solomon, "Mapping Product Constellations: A Social Categorization Approach to Symbolic Consumption," *Psychology & Marketing* 5, 3 (1988): 233–258.

44. McMath, "The Perils of Typecasting."

45. Emily Nelson, "Moistened Toilet Paper Wipes Out after Launch for Kimberly-Clark," *Wall Street Journal Interactive Edition* (April 15, 2002).

46. Elizabeth C. Hirschman and Michael R. Solomon, "Competition and Cooperation among Culture Production Systems," in *Marketing Theory: Philosophy of Science Perspectives*, eds. Ronald F. Bush and Shelby D. Hunt (Chicago, IL: American Marketing Association, 1982), 269–272.

47. Michael D. Johnson, "The Differential Processing of Product Category and Noncomparable Choice Alternatives," *Journal of Consumer Research* 16 (December 1989): 300–309.

48. Mita Sujan, "Consumer Knowledge: Effects on Evaluation Strategies Mediating Consumer Judgments," *Journal of Consumer Research* 12 (June 1985): 31–46.

49. Rosch, "Principles of Categorization."

50. Joan Meyers-Levy and Alice M. Tybout, "Schema Congruity as a Basis for Product Evaluation," *Journal of Consumer Research* 16 (June 1989): 39–55.

51. Mita Sujan and James R. Bettman, "The Effects of Brand Positioning Strategies on Consumers' Brand and Category Perceptions: Some Insights from Schema Research," *Journal of Marketing Research* 26 (November 1989): 454–467.

52. Cf. William P. Putsis, Jr., and Narasimhan Srinivasan, "Buying or Just Browsing? The Duration of Purchase Deliberation," *Journal of Marketing Research* 31 (August 1994): 393–402.

53. Robert E. Smith, "Integrating Information from Advertising and Trial: Processes and Effects on Consumer Response to Product Information," *Journal of Marketing Research* 30 (May 1993): 204–219.

54. Jack Trout, "Marketing in Tough Times," *Boardroom Reports* 2 (October 1992): 8.

55. Stuart Elliott, "Pepsi-Cola to Stamp Dates for Freshness on Soda Cans," *New York Times* (March 31, 1994); Emily DeNitto, "Pepsi's Gamble Hits Freshness Dating Jackpot," *Advertising Age* (September 19, 1994): 50.

56. Amna Kirmani and Peter Wright, "Procedural Learning, Consumer Decision Making and Marketing Communication," *Marketing Letters* (1992).

57. Michael Porter, *Competitive Advantage* (New York, NY: Fress Press, 1985).

58. Material in this section adapted from Michael R. Solomon and Elnora W. Stuart, *Welcome to Marketing.com: The Brave New World of E-Commerce* (Englewood Cliffs, NJ: Prentice Hall, 2001).

59. Phil Patton, "Buy Here, and We'll Tell You What You Like," *New York Times on the Web* (September 22, 1999).

60. Andrew D. Gershoff, Ashesh Mukherjee, and Anirban Mukhopadhyay, "Consumer Acceptance of Online Agent Advice: Extremity and Positivity Effects," *Journal of Consumer Psychology* 12, no. 1&2 (2003): 161–170; Vanitha Swaminathan, "The Impact of Recommendation Agents on Consumer Evaluation and Choice: The Moderating Role of Category Risk, Product Complexity, and Consumer Knowledge," *Journal of Consumer Psychology* 12, no.1&2 (2003), 93–101; Gerald Haubl and Kyle B. Murray, "Preference Construction and Persistence in Digital Marketplaces: The Role of Electronic Recommendation Agents," *Journal of Consumer Psychology* 13, no. 1&2 (2003): 75–91; Dan Ariely, John G. Lynch, Jr., and Manuel Aparicio IV, "Learning by Collaborative and Individual-Based Recommendation Agents," *Journal of Consumer Psychology* 14, no. 1&2 (2004): 81–95; Sylvain Senecal and Jacques Nantel, "The Influence of Online Product Recommendations on Consumers' Online Choices," *Journal of Retailing* 80, no. 2 (2004): 159–169.

61. Robert A. Baron, *Psychology: The Essential Science* (Boston, MA: Allyn & Bacon, 1989); Valerie S. Folkes, "The Availability Heuristic and Perceived Risk," *Journal of Consumer Research* 15 (June 1989): 13–23; Kahneman and Tversky, "Prospect Theory: An Analysis of Decision under Risk.

62. Wayne D. Hoyer, "An Examination of Consumer Decision Making for a Common Repeat Purchase Product," *Journal of Consumer Research* 11 (December 1984): 822–829; Calvin P. Duncan, "Consumer Market Beliefs: A Review of the Literature and an Agenda for Future Research," in *Advances in Consumer Research* 17, eds. Marvin E. Goldberg, Gerald Gorn, and Richard W. Pollay (Provo, UT: Association for Consumer Research, 1990), 729–735; Frank Alpert, "Consumer Market Beliefs and Their Managerial Implications: An Empirical Examination," *Journal of Consumer Marketing* 10, 2 (1993): 56–70.

63. Michael R. Solomon, Sarah Drenan, and Chester A. Insko, "Popular Induction: When Is Consensus Information Informative?" *Journal of Personality* 49, 2 (1981): 212–224.

64. Folkes, "The Availability Heuristic and Perceived Risk."

65. Beales et al., "Consumer Search and Public Policy."

66. Gary T. Ford and Ruth Ann Smith, "Inferential Beliefs in Consumer Evaluations: An Assessment of Alternative Processing Strategies," *Journal of Consumer Research* 14 (December 1987): 363–371; Deborah Roedder John, Carol A. Scott, and James R. Bettman, "Sampling Data for Covariation Assessment: The Effects of Prior Beliefs on Search Patterns," *Journal of Consumer Research* 13 (June 1986): 38–47; Gary L. Sullivan and Kenneth J. Berger, "An Investigation of the Determinants of Cue Utilization," *Psychology & Marketing* 4 (Spring 1987): 63–74.

67. John, Scott, and Bettman, "Sampling Data for Covariation Assessment ...."

68. Duncan, "Consumer Market Beliefs ...."

69. Chr. Hjorth-Andersen, "Price as a Risk Indicator," *Journal of Consumer Policy* 10 (1987): 267–281.

70. David M. Gardner, "Is There a Generalized Price-Quality Relationship?" *Journal of Marketing Research* 8 (May 1971): 241–243; Kent B. Monroe, "Buyers' Subjective Perceptions of Price," *Journal of Marketing Research* 10 (1973): 70–80.

71. Durairaj Maheswaran, "Country of Origin as a Stereotype: Effects of Consumer Expertise and Attribute Strength on Product Evaluations," *Journal of Consumer Research* 21 (September 1994): 354–365; Ingrid M. Martin and Sevgin Eroglu, "Measuring a Multi-Dimensional Construct: Country Image," *Journal of Business Research* 28 (1993): 191–210; Richard Ettenson, Janet Wagner, and Gary Gaeth, "Evaluating the Effect of Country of Origin and the Made in the U.S.A. Campaign: A Conjoint Approach," *Journal of Retailing* 64 (Spring 1988): 85–100; C. Min Han and Vern Terpstra, "Country-of-Origin Effects for Uni-National & Bi-National Products," *Journal of International Business* 19 (Summer 1988): 235–255; Michelle A. Morganosky and Michelle M. Lazarde, "Foreign-Made Apparel: Influences on Consumers' Perceptions of Brand and Store Quality," *International Journal of Advertising* 6 (Fall 1987): 339–348.

72. Thomas A.W. Miller, "Cultural Affinity, Personal Values Factors in Marketing," *Advertising Age* (August 16, 1999): H22(2).

73. See Richard Jackson Harris et al., "Effects of Foreign Product Names and Country-of-Origin Attributions on Advertisement Evaluations," *Psychology & Marketing* 11, 2 (March/April 1994): 129–145; Terence A. Shimp, Saeed Samiee, and Thomas J. Madden, "Countries and Their Products: A Cognitive Structure Perspective," *Journal of the Academy of Marketing Science* 21, 4 (Fall 1993): 323–330.

74. Maheswaran, "Country of Origin as a Stereotype: Effects of Consumer Expertise and Attribute Strength on Product Evaluations."

75. Sung-Tai Hong and Robert S. Wyer, Jr., "Effects of Country-of-Origin and Product-Attribute Information on Product Evaluation: An Information Processing Perspective," *Journal of Consumer Research* 16 (September 1989): 175–187; Marjorie Wall, John Liefeld, and Louise A. Heslop, "Impact of Country-of-Origin Cues on Consumer Judgments in Multi-Cue Situations: A Covariance Analysis," *Journal of the Academy of Marketing Science* 19, 2 (1991): 105–113.

76. Wai-Kwan Li and Robert S. Wyer Jr., "The Role of Country of Origin in Product Evaluations: Informational and Standard-of-Comparison Effects," *Journal of Consumer Psychology* 3, 2 (1994): 187–212.

77. Maheswaran, "Country of Origin as a Stereotype: Effects of Consumer Expertise and Attribute Strength on Product Evaluations."

78. Barrie McKenna, "Canada's Image Used to Sell Vitamins," *Globe and Mail* (May 6, 1997): B19.

79. Nicholas Papadopoulous, Louise A. Heslop, and Gary Bamossy, "An International Comparative Analysis of Consumer Attitudes toward Canada and Canadian Products," *Canadian Journal of Administrative Sciences* 11 (3): 224–239. See also *Product Country Images: Impact and Role in International Marketing*, eds. Nicholas Papadopoulous and Louise A. Heslop (New York, NY: International Business Press, 1993).

80. Louise Heslop, Nicolas Papadopoulos, and Margie Bourk, "An International and Intercultural Perspective on Subcultural Differences in Product Evaluations," *Canadian Journal of Administrative Sciences*, 15(2) (1998): 113–127.

81. Items excerpted from Terence A. Shimp and Subhash Sharma, "Consumer Ethnocentrism: Construction and Validation of the CETSCALE," *Journal of Marketing Research* 24 (August 1987): 282.

82. Adam Bryant, "Message in a Beer Bottle," *Newsweek* (May 29, 2000): 43.

83. Richard W. Stevenson, "The Brands with Billion-Dollar Names," *New York Times* (October 28, 1988): A1.

84. Ronald Alsop, "Enduring Brands Hold Their Allure by Sticking Close to Their Roots," *Wall Street Journal*, centennial ed. (1989): B4.

85. Bruce Orwall, "Some Hip Hopes: Disney Channel Spices Up its Image for Teenagers," *Wall Street Journal Interactive Edition* (October 13, 1999).

86. Jennifer Ordonez, "Travel Packages that Let Devotees Join Rock Bands on the Road Can Cause Jams," *Wall Street Journal Interactive Edition* (December 11, 2001).

87. Jacob Jacoby and Robert Chestnut, *Brand Loyalty: Measurement and Management* (New York: Wiley, 1978).

88. Anne B. Fisher, "Coke's Brand Loyalty Lesson," *Fortune* (August 5, 1985): 44.

89. Jacoby and Chestnut, *Brand Loyalty*.

90. Ronald Alsop, "Brand Loyalty Is Rarely Blind Loyalty," *Wall Street Journal* (October 19, 1989): B1.

91. C. Whan Park, "The Effect of Individual and Situation-Related Factors on Consumer Selection of Judgmental Models," *Journal of Marketing Research* 13 (May 1976): 144–151.

92. Hope Jensen Schau and Mary C. Gilly, "We Are What We Post: The Presentation of Self in Personal Webspace," *Journal of Consumer Research* (2003); Hope Schau, Temple University, personal communication, March 2003.

93. Joseph W. Alba and Howard Marmorstein, "The Effects of Frequency Knowledge on Consumer Decision Making," *Journal of Consumer Research* 14 (June 1987): 14–25.

94. Gad Saad and J. Edward Russo, "Stopping Criteria and Sequential Choice," *Organizational Behavior and Human Decision Processes* 67, 3 (September 1996): 258–270.

95. Gad Saad, "SMAC: An Interface for Investigating Sequential Multiattribute Choices," *Behavioral Research Methods, Instruments, and Computers* 28, 2 (1996): 259–64.

96. Blakeslee, "If You Have a 'Buy Button' in Your Brain, What Pushes It?"

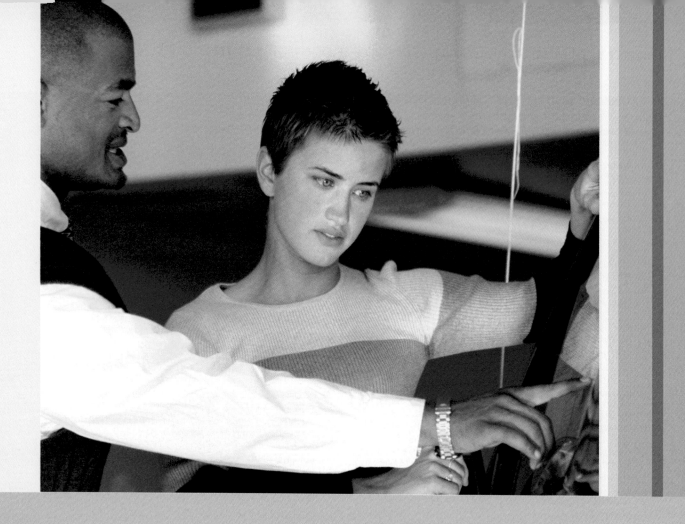

Mark is psyched. The big day has arrived. He's going to buy a car. He's had a bit of time to shop around, and he's had his eye on a silver 2000 Camaro at Russ's Auto-Rama. The sticker says $2999, but Mark figures he can probably get this baby for $2000. He hopes to convince the salesperson to take his offer, especially since he can pay the full amount today. He's also done his homework on the web. First he found out the wholesale value of similar used Camaros from the Kelley Blue Book (*www.kbb.com*), and then he scouted out some cars for sale in his area at *www.autobytel.com*. So Mark figures he's coming in loaded for bear—he's going to show these guys they're not dealing with some rube.

At the Auto-Rama, big signs proclaim that today is Russ's Auto-Rama Rip Us Off Day! This is better than Mark expected. Maybe he can get the Camaro for less than he had planned. He is surprised when a salesperson named Melanie comes over. He expected to deal with a middle-aged man in a loud sports coat—a stereotype he has about used-car salespeople—but this is more good luck: He figures he won't have to be so tough when dealing with a woman his own age.

Melanie laughs at his $1800 offer and says if she takes such a low bid to her boss she'll lose her job. Her enthusiasm for the car convinces him all the more that he has to have it. When he finally writes a cheque for $2700, he's exhausted! In any case Mark figures he'll get his money back when he sells the car in a few years, and he did get the car for less than the sticker price. That web surfing really paid off! He's a tougher negotiator than he thought.

CHAPTER 10

Buying and Disposing

INTRODUCTION

Many consumers dread the act of buying a car. In fact, a survey by Yankelovich Partners Inc. found that buying a car is the most anxiety-provoking and least satisfying of any retail experience.[1] But change is in the wind as the car showroom is being transformed. Car shoppers are logging on to internet buying services, calling auto brokers who negotiate for them, buying cars at warehouse clubs, and visiting giant auto malls where they can comparison shop.

Mark's experience in buying a car illustrates some of the concepts to be discussed in this chapter. Making a purchase is often not a simple, routine matter of going to a store and quickly picking out something. As illustrated in Figure 10–1, a consumer's choices are affected by many personal factors, such as his or her mood, whether there is time pressure to make the purchase, and the particular situation or context in which the product is needed. In some situations, such as the purchase of a car or home, the salesperson or realtor plays a pivotal role in the final selection. And today people are using the web to arm themselves with product and price information before they even enter a dealership or a store, which puts added pressure on retailers to deliver the value consumers expect. But the sale doesn't end at the time of purchase.

A lot of important consumer activity occurs *after* a product has been purchased and brought home. After using a product, the consumer must decide whether he or she is satisfied with it. The satisfaction process is especially important to a savvy marketer who realizes that the key to success is not selling a product one time, but rather forging a relationship with the consumer so that he or she will continue to buy the products in the future. Finally, just as Mark thought about the resale value of his car, we must also consider how consumers go about disposing of products and how secondary markets (such as used-car dealers) often play a pivotal role in product acquisition. This chapter considers many issues related to purchase and postpurchase phenomena.

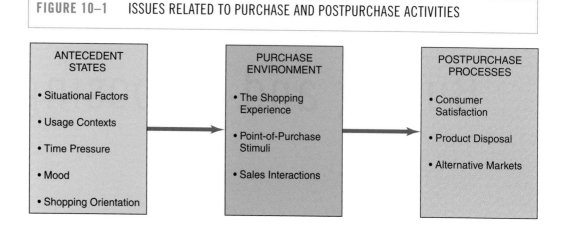

FIGURE 10–1 ISSUES RELATED TO PURCHASE AND POSTPURCHASE ACTIVITIES

SITUATIONAL EFFECTS ON CONSUMER BEHAVIOUR

A *consumption situation* is defined by factors over and above characteristics of the person and the product. Situational effects can be behavioural (e.g., entertaining friends) or perceptual (being depressed or feeling pressed for time).[2] Common sense tells us that people tailor their purchases to specific occasions and that the way they feel at a specific point in time affects what they feel like buying or doing.

Smart marketers understand these patterns and tailor their efforts to coincide with situations where people are most prone to buy. For example, book clubs tend to invest heavily in promotional campaigns in June, since many people are thinking about stocking up on "beach books" to read during the summer.[3]

Our moods change radically even during the day, so at different times we might be more or less interested in what a marketer has to offer. A recent study used a technique called the *Day Reconstruction Method* to track these changes. More than 900 working women kept a diary of everything they did during the day, from reading the paper in the morning to falling asleep in front of the TV at night. The next day they relived each diary entry and rated how they felt at the time (annoyed, happy, etc.). Overall, researchers found that the study participants woke up a little grumpy but soon entered a state of mild pleasure that increased by degrees through the day, punctuated by occasional bouts of anxiety, frustration, and anger. Not surprisingly, the subjects were least happy when they were doing activities like housework and commuting to work, while they rated sex, socializing with friends, and relaxing as most enjoyable. Contrary to prior findings, however, the women reported being happier when watching television than when shopping or talking on the phone, and they ranked taking care of children below cooking and not far above housework. The good news: overall people seem to be pretty happy, and ratings don't appear to be influenced very much by factors like household income or job security. The two factors that most upset daily moods were a poor night's sleep and tight work deadlines.[4]

In addition to the functional relationship between products and usage situations, though, another reason to take environmental circumstances seriously is that the role a person plays at any time is partly determined by his or her *situational self-image,* where he or she basically asks, "Who am I right now?"[5] (See Chapter 5.) Someone trying to impress his date by playing the role of "man about town" may spend more lavishly, ordering champagne instead of beer and buying flowers—purchases he would never consider when he is hanging around with his friends, slurping beer, and playing the role of "one of the boys." As this discussion

Net Profit

Technology is allowing marketers to fine-tune their messages to the consumption situation in exciting new ways. McDonald's is testing a digital signage system that can automatically update its menu boards as environmental conditions change. If this system is successful, in the morning customers will be greeted with animated photos of steaming hash browns and Egg McMuffins that will abruptly change to photos of fries, Big Macs, and ice-cold soft drinks at 10 o'clock a.m., when breakfast service is over. Enter the restaurant in a snowstorm, and those images of soft drinks will be replaced by hot cups of coffee.[6]

Even the technology of highway billboards will change, as sensors on billboards will be able to detect which radio stations most drivers are listening to as they pass by. This information can then be matched to the demographic profiles of the people who listen to these stations, and the billboards will display an advertisement targeted to that profile. For example, if a sensor detects that the majority of drivers at a certain time are listening to a radio station known to have an affluent audience, the board itself can select and display an ad for a luxury product or service, such as a deluxe car stereo system or a home renovation service.[7]

demonstrates, knowledge of what consumers are doing at the time a product is consumed can improve predictions of product and brand choice.[8]

By systematically identifying important usage situations, marketers can develop market segmentation strategies to position products that will meet the specific needs arising from these situations. Many product categories are amenable to this form of segmentation. For example, consumers' furniture choices are often tailored to specific settings. We prefer different styles for a city apartment, a beach house, or an executive suite. Similarly, motorcycles can be distinguished in terms of what riders use them for, including commuting, riding them as dirt bikes, or using them on a farm or for highway travel.[9]

Coach, the maker of luxury leather goods, decided to overhaul its marketing strategy to convince women that they need more than just one bag for everyday use and another for dressy occasions. Now, they're helping women to update their wardrobes by offering them weekend bags, evening bags, backpacks, satchels, clutches, totes, briefcases, diaper bags, coin purses, duffels, and a mini handbag that doubles as a bag-within-a-bag called a wristlet. The company even makes new bags to fill what it calls "usage voids"—activities that range from weekend getaways to trips to the grocery store. Coach introduced its Hamptons Weekend collection by displaying bags stuffed with beach towels and colourful flip-flops. Have bag, will travel![10]

Physical and Social Surroundings

A consumer's physical and social environment can make a big difference in motives for product usage and also affect how the product is evaluated. Important cues include the person's physical surroundings as well as the number and type of other consumers also present in that situation. Dimensions of the physical environment, such as décor, smells, and temperature, can significantly influence consumption (one study found that pumping in certain odours in a Las Vegas casino actually increased the amount of money patrons fed into slot machines!).[11] We'll take a closer look at some of these factors a bit later in this chapter when considering strategic issues related to store design.

In addition to physical cues, though, many of a consumer's purchase decisions are significantly affected by current groups or social settings. In some cases, the sheer presence or absence of other patrons ("co-consumers") in a setting can function as a product attribute, such as when an exclusive resort or boutique promises to provide privacy to privileged customers. At other times, the presence of others can have positive value. A sparsely attended ball game or an empty bar can be depressing sights.

The presence of large numbers of people in a consumer environment increases arousal levels, so that a consumer's subjective experience of a setting tends to be more intense. This polarization, however, can be both positive and negative. Although the presence of other people creates a state of arousal, the consumer's actual experience depends upon his or her *interpretation* of this arousal. It is important to distinguish between *density* and *crowding* for this reason. The former term refers to the actual number of people occupying a space, while the psychological state of crowding exists only if a negative affective state occurs as a result of this density.[12] For example, 100 students packed into a classroom designed for 75 may be unpleasant for all concerned, but the same number of people jammed together at a party occupying a room of the same size might just make for a great party.

In addition, the *type* of consumers who patronize a store or service can serve as an attribute. We may infer something about a store by examining its customers. For this reason some restaurants require men to wear jackets for dinner (and supply them if they don't), and bouncers of some "hot" nightspots hand-pick patrons based on whether they have the right "look" for the club. To paraphrase the comedian Groucho Marx, "I would never join a club that would have me for a member."

All-star coach.

Tuesday night book club.

World's best babysitter.

Number one neighbour.

'tis the reason.

Every Pot of Gold® Truffle features a luscious centre, making each an exquisite celebration of its own.
One of 11 Pot of Gold® collections.

© Hershey Canada Inc.

↑ Pot of Gold® offers a collection of chocolates suitable for many consumer situations.
© Hershey Canada Inc.

Temporal Factors

Time is one of consumers' most limiting resources. We talk about "making time" or "spending time," and we are frequently reminded that "time is money." Our perspectives on time can affect many stages of decision making and consumption, such as when needs are stimulated, the amount of information search we undertake, and so on. Common sense tells us that more careful information search and deliberation occurs when we have the luxury of taking our time. A meticulous shopper who would normally price an item at three different stores before buying it might be found running through the mall at five o'clock on Christmas Eve, furiously scooping up anything left on the shelf that might serve as a last-minute gift.

ECONOMIC TIME

Time is an economic variable; it is a resource that must be divided among activities.[13] Consumers try to maximize satisfaction by allocating time to the appropriate combination of tasks. Of course, people's allocation decisions differ; we all know people who seem to play all the time and others who are workaholics. An individual's priorities determine his or her *timestyle*.[14]

Many consumers believe they are more pressed for time than ever before. This feeling, called **time poverty**, may, however, be due more to perception than to fact. People may just have more options for spending their time and feel pressured by the weight of all these choices. The average working day at the turn of the century was 10 hours (six days a week), and women did 27 hours of housework per week, compared with less than 5 hours weekly now. Of course, one reason for this difference is that men are sharing these burdens more.[15] Still, about a third of consumers report always feeling rushed—up from 25 percent of the population in 1964.[16]

This sense of time poverty has made consumers very responsive to marketing innovations that allow them to save time. For example, rush-hour commuters in Hong Kong no longer need to stand in line to buy subway tokens. Instead, a scanner automatically reads an Octopus card and automatically deducts the fare from their accounts. The card doesn't even require direct contact to be read correctly; a woman can just pass her entire handbag over the scanner, and then race to catch the train.[17]

→ Time—that is, taking the time to produce a high-quality product—is woven into this detailed description of the values, atmosphere, and pace of a PEI dairy farm.
Courtesy of Amalgamated Dairies Limited.

With the increase in time poverty, researchers are also noting a rise in *poly-chronic activity,* wherein consumers do more than one thing at a time.[18] One area where this type of activity is especially prevalent is eating. Consumers often do not allocate a specific time to dining but instead eat on the run. In a recent poll, 64 percent of respondents said they usually do something else while eating. As one food industry executive commented, "We've moved beyond grazing and into gulping."[19]

The food industry is racing to meet consumers' desires to eat on the run. Here are a few on-the-go products that you may see at a grocery store in the near future:

- General Mills is turning its Yoplait yogourt into a meal with Nouriche, a non-fat yogourt smoothie fortified with 20 vitamins and minerals. A television commercial proclaims, "No time for a meal? Nouriche yourself."

- Kraft Foods is launching Nabisco Go-Paks, featuring mini versions of its cookies and crackers, similar to the Frito-Lay Go Snacks already on the market.

- A wider variety of foods in squeezable tubes is the next big thing: Watch out for Hershey's Portable Pudding in tubes as well as Jolly Rancher Gel Snacks.[20]

PSYCHOLOGICAL TIME

"Time flies when you're having fun," but other situations seem to last forever (like some classes, perhaps?). Our experience of time is subjective and is influenced by our immediate priorities and needs. The fluidity of time is important for marketers to understand, because we're more likely to be in a consuming mood at certain times than others. In fact, we can identify time categories in terms of when people are likely to be receptive to marketing messages:[21]

- *Flow time:* As we saw in Chapter 4, in a flow state we become so absorbed in an activity we notice nothing else. Not a good time to be hitting people with ads.

- *Occasion time:* This includes special moments when something monumental occurs, such as a birth or an important job interview. Ads clearly relevant to the situation will be given our undivided attention.

- *Deadline time:* Any time when we're working against the clock is the worst time to try to catch our attention.

- *Leisure time:* During downtime, we are more likely to notice ads and perhaps try new things.

- *Time to kill:* This is when we're waiting for something to happen, like catching a plane or sitting in a waiting room. This is bonus time, where we feel we have the luxury to focus on extraneous things. As a result, we're more receptive to commercial messages, even for products we don't normally use.

A recent study examined how the timestyles of a group of women influenced their consumption choices.[22] The researchers identified four dimensions of time: 1) the *social dimension,* which refers to individuals' categorization of time as either "time for me" or "time with/for others"; 2) the *temporal orientation dimension,* which depicts the relative significance individuals attach to past, present, or future; 3) the *planning orientation dimension,* which alludes to different time-management styles varying on a continuum from analytic to spontaneous; and 4) the *poly-chromic orientation dimension,* which distinguishes between people who prefer to do one thing at a time from those who have multitasking timestyles. After interviewing and observing these women, the researchers identified a set of five metaphors that they say capture the participants' perspective on time:

- *Time is a pressure cooker:* Women who personify this metaphor are usually analytic in their planning, other-oriented, and monochronic in their timestyles. They treat shopping in a methodical manner and often feel under pressure and in conflict.

Multicultural Dimensions

To most Western consumers time is a neatly compartmentalized thing: We wake up in the morning, go to school or work, come home, eat dinner, go out, go to sleep, wake up, and do it all over again. This perspective is called linear sep-arable time; events proceed in an orderly sequence and different times are well defined ("There's a time and a place for everything"). There is a clear sense of past, present, and future. Many activities are performed as the means to some end that will occur later, as when people "save for a rainy day."

This conception of time is not universal. Large cultural differences exist in terms of people's time perspectives.[23] Some cultures run on procedural time and ignore the clock completely. People decide to do something "when the time is right." Alternatively, in *circular* or *cyclic* time, people are governed by natural cycles, such as the regular occurrence of the seasons (a per-spective found in many Latin cultures). To these consumers the notion of the future does not make sense, because that time will be much like the present. Since the concept of future value does not exist, these consumers often prefer to buy an inferior product that is available now rather than wait for a better one that may be available later. Also, it is hard to convince people who function on circular time to buy insurance or save for the future when they do not endorse this concept.

A social scientist compared the pace of life in 31 cities around the world as part of a study on timestyles. He and his assistants timed how long it takes pedestrians to walk 60 feet (18 m) and postal clerks to sell a stamp.[24] Based on these responses, he claims that the fastest and slowest countries are as follows:

Fastest countries: (1) Switzerland, (2) Ireland, (3) Germany, (4) Japan, (5) Italy.

Slowest countries: (31) Mexico, (30) Indonesia, (29) Brazil, (28) El Salvador, (27) Syria.

- *Time is a map*: Women who exemplify this metaphor are usually analytic planners, and have a future temporal orientation and a polychronic timestyle. They often engage in extensive information search and in comparison shopping.

- *Time is a mirror*: Women in this group are also analytic planners and have a polychromic orientation. However, they have a past temporal orientation. Due to their risk averseness in time use, these women are usually loyal to products and services they know and trust. They prefer convenience-oriented products.

- *Time is a river*: Women whose timestyles can be described by this metaphor are usually spontaneous in their planning orientation and have a present focus. They go on unplanned, short, and frequent shopping trips undertaken on impulse.

- *Time is a feast*: These women are analytic planners who have a present temporal orientation. They view time as something to be consumed in the pursuit of sensory pleasure and gratification; hence, they are motivated by hedonic and variety-seeking desires in their consumption behaviour, which explains why they prefer fresh and novel ingredients when they buy food.

Our experience of time is largely a result of our culture, because different societies have varying perspectives on this experience. To most Western consumers, time is a neatly compartmentalized thing: We wake up in the morning, go to school or work, come home, eat dinner, go out, go to sleep, wake up, and do it all over again. We call this perspective *linear separable time;* events proceed in an orderly sequence, and different times are well-defined, as exemplified by the phrase "There's a time and a place for everything." There is a clear sense of past, present, and future. Many activities are performed as the means to some end that will occur later, as when people "save for a rainy day."

The psychological dimension of time, or how it is experienced, is an important factor in **queuing theory**, the mathematical study of waiting lines. A consumer's experience of waiting can radically influence his or her perceptions of service quality. Although we assume that something must be pretty good if we have to wait for it, the negative feelings aroused by long waits can quickly turn customers off.[25]

Marketers have adopted a variety of "tricks" to minimize psychological waiting time. These techniques range from altering customers' perceptions of a line's length to providing distractions that divert attention away from waiting. Here are some of these techniques:[26]

- Airline passengers often complain of the time they must wait to claim their baggage. In one airport passengers had to walk for one minute from the plane to the baggage carousel and then wait seven minutes for their luggage. When the layout was changed so that the walk to the carousel took six minutes and bags arrived two minutes after that, complaints were almost entirely eliminated.

- Anticipating complaints about the wait for elevators, most hotels install mirrors near the elevator banks. Even though installing mirrors does not reduce the actual waiting time, people naturally tend to check their appearance, making the wait seem shorter.

- Air Canada has ATM-like machines that allow people to print their own boarding passes and luggage tags. Alaska Airlines allows people to print boarding passes from their home computers to save time.[27]

- Restaurant chains are scrambling to put the *fast* back into fast food, especially for drive-through lanes, which now account for 65 percent of revenues. In a study that ranked the speed of 25 fast-food chains, cars spent an average of 203.6 seconds from the menu board to departure. Wendy's was clocked the fastest at 150.3 seconds. To speed things up and eliminate spills, McDonald's created a salad that comes in a container to fit into car cup holders. Arby's is working on a "high viscosity" version of its special sauce that's less likely to spill. Burger King is testing "see-thru" bags so customers can quickly check their orders before speeding off.[28]

Antecedent States: If It Feels Good, Buy It . . .

A person's mood or physiological condition at the time of purchase can have a big impact on what is bought and can also affect how products are evaluated.[29] One reason is that behaviour is directed toward certain goal states, as was discussed in Chapter 4. People spend more in the grocery store if they have not eaten for a while, because food is a priority at that time.

A consumer's mood can have a big impact on purchase decisions. For example, stress can impair information-processing and problem-solving abilities.[30] Two dimensions determine whether a shopper will react positively or negatively to a store environment. These are *pleasure* and *arousal*. A person can enjoy or not enjoy a situation, and he or she can feel stimulated or not. As Figure 10–2 indicates, different combinations of pleasure and arousal levels result in a variety of emotional states. For example, an arousing situation can be either distressing or exciting, depending on whether the context is positive or negative (e.g., a street riot versus a street festival, such as Mardi Gras). Maintaining an "up" feeling in a pleasant context is one factor behind the success of theme parks like Disney World (*www.disneyworld.com*), which try to provide consistent doses of carefully calculated stimulation to patrons.[31]

A specific mood is some combination of these two factors. The state of happiness, for instance, is high in pleasantness and moderate in arousal, while elation would be high on both dimensions.[32] In general, a mood state (either positive or negative) biases judgments of products and services in that direction.[33] Put simply, consumers like things better when they are in a good mood. (This explains the popularity of the business lunch!) Moods can be affected by store design, the weather, or other factors specific to the consumer. In addition, music and television programming can affect mood, which has important consequences for commercials.[34] When consumers hear happy music or watch happy programs, they have more positive reactions to commercials and products, especially when the marketing appeals are aimed at arousing emotional reactions.[35] When in positive moods, consumers process ads with less elaboration. They pay less attention to specifics of the messages and rely more on heuristic processing (see Chapter 9).[36]

Shopping: A Job or an Adventure?

People often shop even though they do not necessarily intend to buy anything at all; others have to be dragged to a mall. Shopping is a way to acquire needed products and services, but social motives for shopping also are important. Thus, shopping is an activity that can be performed for either utilitarian (functional or

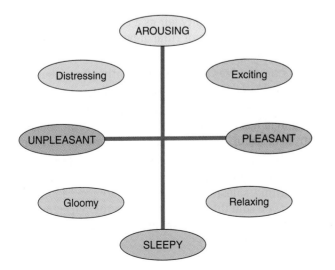

FIGURE 10–2

DIMENSIONS OF EMOTIONAL STATES

→ Yorkdale Shopping Centre sends the message that it has stores for many kinds of shoppers.
Reprinted by permission of Yorkdale Shopping Centre.

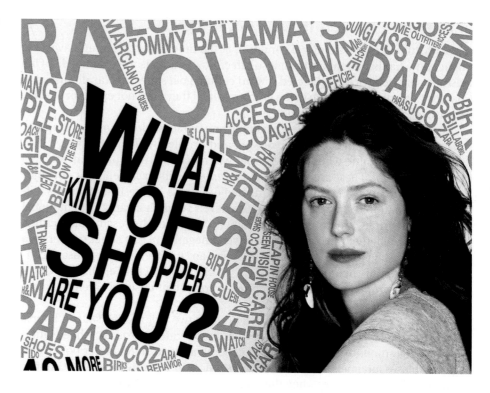

tangible) or hedonic (pleasurable or intangible) reasons.[37] Indeed, some researchers suggest that most women "shop to love" while most men "shop to win." In this view, women find emotional fulfillment in the act of buying, while men seek to demonstrate their expertise or ability to procure status items.[38] Obviously, there are many exceptions to this viewpoint, but nonetheless it's clear that the reasons for shopping are more complex than may appear on the surface.

REASONS FOR SHOPPING

These different motives are illustrated by scale items used by researchers to assess people's underlying reasons for shopping. One item that measures hedonic value is the statement, "During the trip, I felt the excitement of the hunt." When that type of sentiment is compared with a functionally related statement, such as "I accomplished just what I wanted to on this shopping trip," the contrast between these two dimensions is clear.[39] Hedonic shopping motives can include the following:[40]

- *Social experiences*: The shopping centre or department store has replaced the traditional town square or county fair as a community gathering place. Many people (especially in suburban or rural areas) may have no place else to go to spend their leisure time.

- *Sharing of common interests*: Stores frequently offer specialized goods that allow people with shared interests to communicate.

- *Interpersonal attraction*: Shopping centres are natural places to congregate. The shopping mall has become a central hangout for teenagers. It also represents a controlled, secure environment for other groups, such as seniors.

- *Instant status*: As every salesperson knows, some people savour the experience of being waited on, even though they may not necessarily buy anything. One men's clothing salesman offered this advice: "Remember their size, remember what you sold them last time. Make them feel important! If you can make people feel important, they are going to come back. Everybody likes to feel important!"[41]

- *The thrill of the chase*: Some people pride themselves on their knowledge of the marketplace. Unlike Mark, they may relish the process of haggling and bargaining, viewing it almost as a sport.

Which way is it? Do people hate to shop or love it? It depends. Consumers can be segmented in terms of their **shopping orientation**, or general attitudes about shopping. These orientations may vary depending on the particular product categories and store types considered. Mark hates to shop for a car, but he may love to browse in record stores. Several shopping types have been identified:[42]

- *economic consumer*—a rational, goal-oriented shopper who is primarily interested in maximizing the value of his or her money
- *personalized consumer*—a shopper who tends to form strong attachments to store personnel ("I shop where they know my name.")
- *ethical consumer*—a shopper who likes to help out the underdog and will support locally owned stores against big chains
- *apathetic consumer*—one who does not like to shop and sees it as a necessary but unpleasant chore
- *recreational shopper*—a person who views shopping as a fun social activity (a preferred way to spend leisure time)

E-commerce: Clicks versus Bricks

As more and more websites pop up to sell everything from refrigerator magnets to Mack trucks, marketers are hotly debating how this new format will affect how they conduct business.[43] In particular, many are losing sleep wondering whether e-commerce is destined to replace traditional retailing, work in concert with it, or perhaps even fade away to become another fad your kids will laugh about someday.

For marketers, the growth of online commerce is a sword that cuts both ways: On the one hand, they can reach customers around the world even if they're physically located 150 kilometres from nowhere. On the other hand, their competition now comes not only from the store across the street, but also from thousands of websites spanning the globe. A second problem is that offering products directly to consumers has the potential to cut out the intermediary—the loyal store-based retailers who carry the firm's products and sell them at a marked-up price.[44] The "clicks versus bricks" dilemma is raging in the marketing world.

What makes e-commerce sites successful? According to a survey by N.P.D. Online, 75 percent of online shoppers surveyed said that good customer service would make them shop at the site again.[45] And many successful e-tailers are learning that using technology to provide extra value for customers is attracting and keeping customers. For example, Eddie Bauer (***www.eddiebauer.com***) offers customers a virtual dressing room. The Cover Girl makeup site (***www.covergirl.com***) allows a woman to find colours that match her skin and hair type and design a total look that's right for her lifestyle. Soon MTV viewers will be able to use their remote controls to purchase the CDs that go with the music videos they are watching.

However, all is not perfect in the virtual world; e-commerce does have its limitations. Security is one important concern. We hear horror stories of consumers whose credit card numbers and other identity information have been stolen. Although an individual's financial liability in most theft cases is limited to $50, the damage to one's credit rating can last for years. Some shady companies are making money by prying and then selling personal information to others—one company promotes itself as "an amazing new tool that allows you to find out EVERYTHING you ever wanted to know about your friends, family, neighbours, employees and even your boss!"[46] Pretty scary. Almost daily we hear of hackers getting into a business's or even a government's website and causing havoc. Businesses risk the loss of trade secrets and other proprietary information. Many must spend significant amounts to maintain security and to conduct regular audits to ensure the integrity of their sites.

Other limitations of e-commerce relate to the actual shopping experience. Although it may be satisfactory to buy a computer or a book on the internet, buying clothing and other items where touching the item or trying it on is essential may be less attractive. Even though most companies have very liberal return policies, consumers can still get stuck with large delivery and return shipping charges for items that don't fit or simply aren't the right colour.

It's clear that traditional shopping isn't dead quite yet, but bricks-and-mortar retailers do need to work harder to give shoppers something they can't get (yet, anyway) in the virtual world: a stimulating or pleasant environment in which to browse. Now let's consider how they're doing that.

Retailing as Theatre

The competition for customers is becoming even more intense as non-store alternatives, from websites and print catalogues to TV shopping networks and home shopping parties, continue to multiply. With all of these shopping alternatives available, how can a traditional store compete? Shopping malls have tried to gain the loyalty of shoppers by appealing to their social motives, as well as by providing access to desired goods. More than half of all retail purchases (excluding automobiles and gasoline) are made in a mall.[47] Malls are becoming giant entertainment centres, almost to the point where their traditional retail occupants seem like an afterthought. It is now typical to find such features as carousels, miniature golf, or batting cages in a suburban mall. As one retailing executive put it, "Malls are becoming the new mini-amusement parks."[48]

The quest to entertain means that many stores are going all out to create imaginative environments that transport shoppers to fantasy worlds or provide other kinds of stimulation. This strategy is called **retail theming**. Innovative merchants today use four basic kinds of themes:

- *Landscape themes* rely upon associations with images of nature, the earth, animals, and the physical body. Bass Pro Shops, for example, creates a simulated outdoor environment including pools stocked with fish.

- *Marketscape themes* build upon associations with human-made places. An example is The Venetian hotel in Las Vegas that lavishly recreates parts of the Italian city.

- *Cyberspace themes* are built around images of information and communications technology. eBay's retail interface instills a sense of community among its vendors and traders.

- *Mindscape themes* draw upon abstract ideas and concepts, introspection, and fantasy, and often possess spiritual overtones. At the Seibu store in Tokyo, shoppers enter as neophytes at the first level. As they progress through the physical levels of the store, each level has a different theme that connotes an increased level of "consciousness" until they emerge at the summit as "completed" shoppers.[49]

Store Image

With so many stores competing for customers, how do consumers pick one over another? Like products, stores may be thought of as having "personalities." Some stores have very clearly defined images (either good or bad). Others tend to blend into the crowd; they may not have anything distinctive about them and may be overlooked for this reason. This personality, or **store image**, comprises many different factors. Store features, coupled with such consumer characteristics as shopping

← The FedEx makeover: before and after.
Project Photography: Ronnie Levitan, RSA. Project Designer: Development Design Group, Inc. U.S.

orientation, help to predict which shopping outlets people will prefer.[51] Some of the important dimensions of a store's profile are location, merchandise suitability, and the knowledge and congeniality of the sales staff.[52]

Store image can be a crucial part of the shopping experience for all kinds of products and services. Today, even automobile dealers are ramping up their efforts to craft a distinctive retail presence, realizing that customers like Mark can make inferences about a dealership from its physical appearance. Hummer's new showrooms include exposed concrete, metal rafters, and helicopter-like ceiling fans. With arched roofs and 20-foot-high front windows that lean outward, the newly designed Audi dealerships look a little like airport hangars. They are intended to replicate the company's 20-year-old plant in Germany, where customers often go to pick up new cars as they roll off the line.[53]

The features of a store profile typically work together to create an overall impression. When shoppers think about stores, they may not say, "Well, that place is fairly good in terms of convenience, the salespeople are acceptable, and services are good." They are more likely to say, "That place gives me the creeps," or "I always enjoy shopping there." Consumers evaluate stores in terms of both their specific attributes *and* a global evaluation, or *gestalt* (see Chapter 2).[54] This overall feeling may have more to do with such intangibles as interior design and the types of people in the store than with such aspects as return policies or credit availability. As a result, some stores are likely to be consistently in consumers' evoked sets, while others will never be considered.[55]

A recent makeover of FedEx retail outlets illustrates the crucial role that design can play in communicating a desirable store image. As shown in Figure 10–3, consumer research conducted by Ziba Design for FedEx indicated that, compared to its main competitors, the firm's brand personality was more innovative, leading edge, and outgoing—but this impression was certainly not reinforced by its cluttered storefront locations where customers go to drop off packages for delivery. The designers used colours and shapes associated with the brand personality to make over the stores.

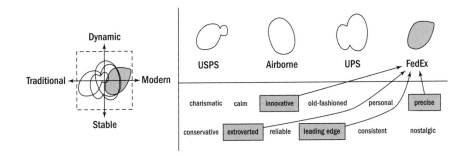

FIGURE 10–3

FEDEX BRAND IMAGE

ATMOSPHERICS

Because a store's image is now recognized to be a very important aspect of the retailing mix, attention is increasingly paid to **atmospherics**, or the "conscious designing of space and its various dimensions to evoke certain effects in buyers."[56]

These dimensions include colours, scents, and sounds. For example, stores done in red tend to make people tense, while a blue décor imparts a calmer feeling.[57] As was noted in Chapter 2, some preliminary evidence indicates that smells (olfactory cues) also can influence evaluations of a store's environment.[58]

A store's atmosphere in turn affects purchasing behaviour. One recent study reported that the extent of pleasure reported by shoppers five minutes after entering a store was predictive of the amount of time spent in the store as well as the level of spending there.[59]

To boost the entertainment value of shopping (and to lure online shoppers back to bricks-and-mortar stores), some retailers are developing activity stores that let consumers participate in the production of the products or services being sold there:

- The Build-A-Bear Workshop chain provides customers with a selection of empty bear bodies that are then stuffed, fluffed, and dressed in costumes ranging from bridal veils to baseball gloves. Customers use an in-store computer to print each bear's "birth certificate" and special wish.

- At a chain of stores called Club Libby Lu, which caters to preteen girls, customers enter a fantasyland environment where girls can dress as princesses and mix their own fragrances.

- Viking Range Corp. has combined its kitchen appliances with cooking lessons through two chains called Viking Home Chef and the Viking Culinary Academy, which together have almost a dozen stores. These stores have built-in classrooms offering lessons in a full spectrum of cuisine, from gingerbread houses to Indian. Products in the store change to match the lessons.[60]

Many elements of store design can be cleverly controlled to attract customers and produce desired effects on consumers. Light colours impart a feeling of spaciousness and serenity, and signs in bright colours create excitement. In one subtle but effective application, fashion designer Norma Kamali replaced fluorescent lights with pink ones in department-store dressing rooms. The light had the effect of flattering the face and banishing wrinkles, making female customers more willing to try on (and buy) the company's bathing suits.[61] Wal-Mart found that sales were higher in areas of a prototype store lit in natural daylight compared with the more typical artificial light.[63] One study found that brighter in-store lighting influenced people to examine and handle more merchandise.[64]

In addition to visual stimuli, all sorts of cues can influence behaviours.[65] Patrons of country-and-western bars drink more when the jukebox music is slower. According to a researcher, "Hard drinkers prefer listening to slower paced, wailing, lonesome, self-pitying music…."[66] Similarly, music can affect eating habits. A study found that diners who listened to loud, fast music ate more food. In contrast, those who listened to Mozart or Brahms ate less and more slowly. The researchers concluded that diners who choose soothing music at mealtimes can increase weight loss by at least five pounds (2.3 kg) a month![67]

In-Store Decision Making

Despite all their efforts to "presell" consumers through advertising, marketers increasingly are recognizing the significant degree to which many purchases are influenced by the store environment. It has been estimated that about two out of every three supermarket purchases are decided in the aisles. The proportion of unplanned purchases is even higher for some product categories. It is estimated that 85 percent of candy and gum, almost 70 percent of cosmetics, and 75 percent of oral-hygiene purchases are unplanned.[68] And people with lists are just as likely to make spontaneous purchases as those without them.[69]

Marketers are scrambling to engineer purchasing environments in order to increase the likelihood that their products will be available to consumers at the exact time they make a decision. This strategy even applies to drinking behaviour: Diageo, the world's largest liquor company, discovered that 60 percent of bar customers don't know what they will drink until seconds before they place their orders. To make it more likely that the customer's order will include Smirnoff vodka, Johnnie Walker scotch, or one of its other brands, Diageo launched its Drinks Invigoration Team to increase what it calls its "share of throat." The Dublin-based team experiments with bar "environments," bottle-display techniques, and how to match drinks to customers' moods. For example, company researchers discovered that images of bubbles stimulate the desire for spirits, so the company is developing bubble machines to put in the back of bars. Diageo has even categorized bars into types and is identifying the types of drinkers—and the drinks they prefer—who frequent each type of bar. These include "style bars," where cutting-edge patrons like to sip fancy fresh-fruit martinis, and "buzz bars," where the clientele is receptive to a drink made of Smirnoff and energy brew Red Bull.[70]

SPONTANEOUS SHOPPING

When a shopper is prompted to buy something while in the store, one of two different processes may be at work. *Unplanned buying* may occur when a person unfamiliar with a store's layout is under some time pressure. Or a person may be reminded to buy something by seeing it on a store shelf. About one-third of unplanned buying has been attributed to the recognition of new needs while within the store.[71]

In contrast, **impulse buying** occurs when the person experiences a sudden urge that he or she cannot resist. The tendency to buy spontaneously is most likely to result in a purchase when the consumer believes that acting on impulse is appropriate, such as when purchasing a gift for a sick friend or picking up the tab for a meal.[72] To cater to these urges, so-called *impulse items,* such as candy and gum, are conveniently placed near the checkout. Similarly, many supermarkets have installed wider aisles to encourage browsing, and the widest tend to contain products with the highest margin. Items with low markup that are purchased regularly tend to be stacked high in narrower aisles, to allow shoppers to speed through.[73]

A more recent high-tech tool has been added to encourage impulse buying. A device called the Portable Shopper is a personal scanning gun that allows customers to ring up their own purchases as they shop. The gun initially was developed for Albert Hejin, the Netherlands' largest grocery chain, to move customers through the store more quickly. It's now in use in more than 150 grocery chains worldwide.[74]

Shoppers can be categorized in terms of how much advance planning they do. *Planners* tend to know what products and specific brands they will buy beforehand; *partial planners* know they need certain products but do not decide on specific brands until they are in the store; and *impulse purchasers* do no advance planning whatsoever.[75]

POINT-OF-PURCHASE STIMULI

It has been estimated that impulse purchases increase by 10 percent when appropriate displays are used. A **point-of-purchase stimulus (POP)** can be an elaborate product display or demonstration, a coupon-dispensing machine, or someone giving out free samples of a new cookie in the grocery aisle. Some of the more dramatic POP displays have included the following:[76]

- *Timex* (**www.timex.com**): A still-ticking watch sits in the bottom of a filled aquarium.
- *Kellogg's Corn Flakes*: A button with a picture of Cornelius the Rooster is placed within the reach of children near the Corn Flakes display. When a child presses the button, he or she hears the rooster "cock-a-doodle-do."
- *Elizabeth Arden*: The company introduced "Elizabeth," a computer and video makeover system that allows customers to test out their images with different shades of makeup without having actually to apply the products first.
- *HMV*: A music sampler allows customers to hear CDs before buying them and to custom-design their own recordings by mixing and matching singles from assorted artists.
- *Trifari*: This company offers paper "punch-out" versions of its jewellery so that customers can try on the pieces at home.
- *Charmin*: Building on the familiar "Please don't squeeze the Charmin" theme, the company deploys the Charmin Squeeze Squad. Employees hide behind stacks of the toilet tissue and jump out and blow horns at any "squeezers" they catch in the aisles.

The Salesperson

One of the most important in-store factors is the salesperson, who attempts to influence the buying behaviour of the customer.[77] This influence can be understood in terms of **exchange theory**, which stresses that every interaction involves an exchange of value; each participant gives something to the other and hopes to receive something in return.[78]

What "value" does the customer look for in a sales interaction? There are a variety of resources a salesperson might offer. He or she might offer expertise about the product to make the shopper's choice easier. Alternatively, the customer may be reassured because the salesperson is an admired or likeable person whose tastes are similar to the customer's own and who is therefore seen as someone to be trusted.[79] In fact, a long stream of research attests to the impact of a salesperson's appearance on sales effectiveness. In sales, as in much of life, attractive people appear to hold the upper hand.[80] In addition, it's not unusual for service personnel and customers to form fairly warm personal relationships; these have been termed *commercial* friendships. (Think of all those patient bartenders who double as therapists for many people!) Researchers have found that commercial friendships are similar to other friendships in that they can involve affection, intimacy, social support, loyalty, and reciprocal gift giving. They also work to support marketing objectives such as satisfaction, loyalty, and positive word of mouth.[81]

A buyer/seller situation is like many other dyadic encounters (those within two-person groups): It is a relationship where some agreement must be reached about the role of each participant. In other words, a process of *identity negotiation* occurs.[83] For example, if Melanie immediately establishes herself as an all-knowing expert (and if Mark accepts this position), she is likely to have more influence over him through the course of the relationship. Some of the factors that help to determine a salesperson's role (and relative effectiveness) are his or her age, appearance, educational level, and motivation to sell.[84]

In addition, more effective salespeople usually know their customers' traits and preferences better than do ineffective salespeople, since this knowledge allows them to adapt their approach to meet the needs of specific customers.[85] The ability to be adaptable is especially vital when customers and salespeople differ in terms of their *interaction styles*.[86] Consumers, for example, vary in the degree of assertiveness they bring to interactions. At one extreme, non-assertive people believe that complaining is not socially acceptable and may be intimidated in sales situations. Assertive people are more likely to stand up for themselves in firm but non-threatening ways, while aggressives may resort to rudeness and threats if they do not get their way.[87]

POSTPURCHASE SATISFACTION

Consumer satisfaction/dissatisfaction (CS/D) is determined by the overall feelings, or attitude, a person has about a product after it has been purchased. Consumers are engaged in a constant process of evaluating the things they buy as these products are integrated into their daily consumption activities.[88]

Despite evidence that customer satisfaction is steadily declining in many industries, good marketers are constantly on the lookout for sources of dissatisfaction so that they can improve.[89] For example, when United Airlines' advertising agency set out to identify specific aspects of air travel that were causing problems, they gave frequent flyers crayons and a map showing different stages in a long-distance trip and asked them to fill in colours: hot hues to symbolize

areas causing stress and anger, cool for parts of the trip associated with satisfaction and calm feelings. Although jet cabins tended to be filled in with a serene aqua colour, lo and behold, ticket counters were coloured orange and terminal waiting areas were fire-engine red. This research led the airline to focus more on overall operations instead of just inflight experiences, and the "United Rising" campaign was born.[90]

Perceptions of Product Quality

Just what do consumers look for in products? That's easy: They want quality and value. Especially because of foreign competition, claims of product quality have become strategically crucial to maintaining a competitive advantage.[91] Consumers use a number of cues to infer quality, including brand name, price, and even their own estimates of how much money has been put into a new product's advertising campaign.[92] These cues and others, such as product warranties and follow-up letters from the company, are often used by consumers to relieve perceived risk and assure themselves that they have made smart purchase decisions.[93]

Although everyone wants quality, it is not clear exactly what quality means. Certainly, many manufacturers claim to provide it. The Ford Motor Company ad shown on the next page emphasizes "Quality is Job 1." Similar claims that have been made at one time or another by various car manufacturers include the following:[94]

- Lincoln-Mercury: "the highest quality cars of any major American car company"
- Chrysler: "quality engineered to be the best"
- GMC trucks: "quality built yet economical"
- Oldsmobile: "fulfilling the quality needs of American drivers"
- Audi: "quality backed by our outstanding new warranty"

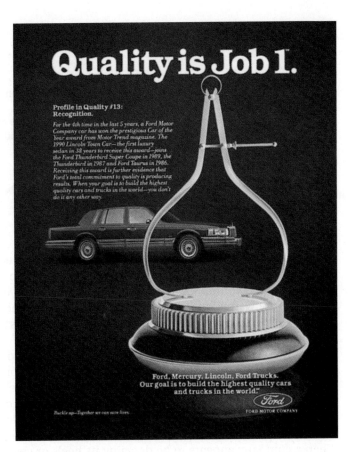

Quality Is What We Expect It to Be

In the book *Zen and the Art of Motorcycle Maintenance,* a cult hero of college students in an earlier generation literally went crazy trying to figure out the meaning of quality.[95] Marketers appear to use the word *quality* as a catch-all for "good." Because of its wide and imprecise usage, the attribute of "quality" threatens to become a meaningless claim. If everyone has it, what good is it?

To muddy the waters a bit more, satisfaction or dissatisfaction is more than a reaction to the actual performance quality of a product or service; it is influenced by prior expectations regarding the level of quality. According to the expectancy disconfirmation model, consumers form beliefs about product performance based upon prior experience with the product and/or upon communications about the product that imply a certain level of quality.[96] When something performs the way we thought it would, we may not think much about it. If, on the other hand, something fails to live up to expectations, a negative affect may result. And if performance happens to exceed our expectations, we are satisfied and pleased.

To understand this perspective, think about different types of restaurants. People expect to be provided with sparkling clear glassware at fancy restaurants, and they might become upset if they discover grimy glasses. On the other hand, we may not be surprised to find fingerprints on our beer mugs at a local greasy spoon; we may even shrug it off because it contributes to the "charm" of the place. An important lesson emerges for marketers from this perspective: Don't overpromise.[97]

This perspective underscores the importance of *managing expectations.* Customer dissatisfaction usually is due to expectations that exceed the company's ability to deliver. Figure 10–4 illustrates the alternative strategies a firm can choose in these situations. When confronted with unrealistic expectations about what it can do, the firm can either accommodate these demands by improving the range or quality of products it offers, attempt to alter the expectations, or perhaps even

FIGURE 10–4 MANAGING QUALITY EXPECTATIONS

FIGURE 10–4 MANAGING QUALITY EXPECTATIONS

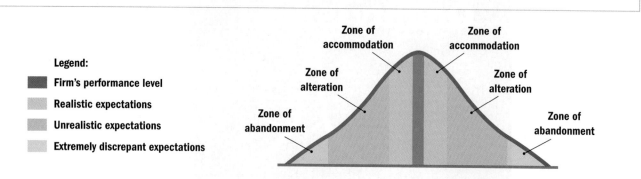

Legend:

- **Firm's performance level**
- **Realistic expectations**
- **Unrealistic expectations**
- **Extremely discrepant expectations**

choose to abandon the customer if it is not feasible to meet his or her needs.[98] Consumers' expectations can be altered, for example, when waiters tell patrons in advance that the portion size they have ordered will not be very big, or when new-car buyers are warned of strange smells they will experience during the break-in period. A firm also can *underpromise*, as when Xerox inflates the time it will take for a service rep to visit.

The power of claims of quality is most evident when a company's product fails. Here, consumers' expectations are dashed and dissatisfaction results. In these situations, marketers must immediately take steps to reassure customers. When the company confronts the problem truthfully, consumers are often willing to forgive and forget, as was the case with Chrysler (disconnecting odometers on executives' cars and reselling them as new) and Perrier (traces of benzene found in the water). When a company appears to be dragging its heels or covering up, on the other

→ This ad personalizes how the wide assortment of Quality Street chocolates will bring satisfaction to those who come together for holiday celebrations and visits.

Nestle Confectionary.

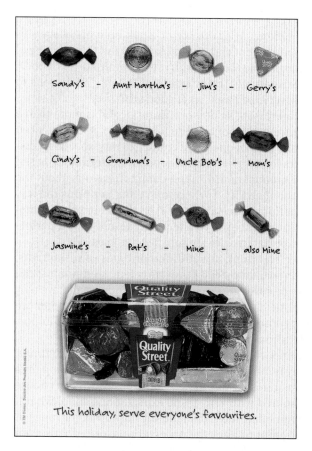

hand, consumer resentment will grow, as occurred during Union Carbide's chemical disaster in India, the massive Alaskan oil spill caused by the tanker *Exxon Valdez*, and recent corporate scandals, such as the collapse of Enron.

Acting on Dissatisfaction

If a person is not happy with a product or service, what can be done? Essentially, a consumer has three different courses of action available (note that more than one can be taken):[99]

1. *Voice response*: The consumer can appeal directly to the retailer for redress (e.g., a refund).

2. *Private response*: The consumer can express dissatisfaction about the store or product to friends and/or can boycott the store. As will be discussed in Chapter 11, negative word of mouth (WOM) can be very damaging to a store's reputation.

3. *Third-party response*: The consumer can take legal action against the merchant, register a complaint with the Better Business Bureau, or write a letter to a newspaper.

In one study, business majors wrote complaint letters to companies. Those who were sent a free sample in response indicated their image of the company significantly improved, while those who received only a letter of apology also changed their evaluations of the company. However, students who got no response reported an even more negative image than before, indicating that some form of response is better than none.[100]

A number of factors influence which response route is eventually taken. The consumer may, in general, be an assertive person or a meek one. Action is more likely to be taken for expensive products, such as household durables, cars, and clothing, than for inexpensive products.[101]

In addition, consumers who are satisfied with a store are more likely to complain; they take the time to complain because they feel connected to the store. Older people are more likely to complain and are much more likely to believe the store will actually resolve the problem. Shoppers who get their problems resolved feel even *better* about the store than if nothing went wrong.[102] On the other hand, if the consumer does not believe that the store will respond well to a complaint, the person will be more likely to simply switch than fight.[103] Ironically, marketers should actually *encourage* consumers to complain to them: People are more likely to spread the word to their friends about unresolved negative experiences than they are to boast about positive occurrences.[104]

Total Quality Management: Going to the Gemba

Many analysts who study consumer satisfaction or who are trying to design new products or services to increase customer satisfaction recognize that it is crucial to understand how people actually interact with their environments in order to identify potential problems. These investigations typically are done in focus groups, where a small group of consumers try a new item at a company's facility while being observed by company personnel. However, some researchers advocate a more up-close and personal approach that allows them to watch people in the actual environment where the item is consumed.

The Japanese approach to *total quality management* (*TQM*), which is a complex set of management and engineering procedures aimed at reducing errors and increasing quality, has influenced this perspective. To help attain this objective, researchers can "go to the gemba." The **gemba** means the one true source of information. According to this Japanese philosophy, it's essential to send marketers and designers to the precise place where the product or service is being used rather than ask consumers to interact with it in a simulated environment. Figure 10–5

The Tangled Web

Many dissatisfied customers and disgruntled former employees have been inspired to create their own websites just to share their tales of woe with others. For example, a website that provided a forum for people to complain about the Dunkin' Donuts chain got to be so popular the company bought it in order to control the bad press it was getting. A customer initially created the site to express his outrage over the fact that he was unable to get skim milk for his coffee.[105]

The web has become a very efficient staging ground for mass demonstrations. Political activists protesting corporate policies are able to mobilize large numbers of consumers by touting their causes online. Some websites, like *www.fightback.com*, maintained by consumer activist David Horowitz, focus on a range of consumerism issues, while others like *www.mcspotlight.org* chronicle the ostensible misdeeds of a specific company like McDonald's. Indeed, although the lifespans of these types of websites are often brief, there are, at any point in time, a surprising number of existing webpages devoted to trashing specific companies, such as *www.walmartsucks.com* and *www.starbucked.com*.

FIGURE 10–5

GOING TO THE GEMBA

Source: Used with permission of the Quality Function Deployment Institute.

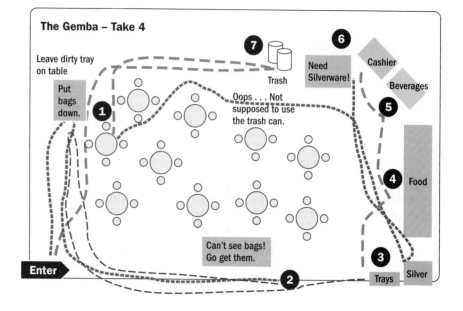

illustrates this idea in practice. Host Foods, which operates food concessions in major airports, sent a team to the gemba—in this case, an airport cafeteria—to identify problem areas. Employees watched as customers chose (or didn't) to enter the facility, then followed them as they inspected the menu, procured silverware, paid, and then found a table. The findings were crucial to Host's redesign of the facility to make it more accessible. For example, the team hadn't realized the problem caused by having to put down luggage to enter the food line and not being able to keep an eye on valuables during the process.[106]

PRODUCT DISPOSAL

Because people often do form strong attachments to products, the decision to dispose of something may be a painful one. One function performed by possessions is to serve as anchors for our identities: Our past lives on in our things.[107] This attachment is exemplified by the Japanese, who ritually "retire" worn-out sewing needles, chopsticks, and computer chips by burning them as thanks for good service.[108]

Although some people have more trouble than others in discarding things, even a "pack rat" does not keep everything. Consumers must often dispose of things, either because they have fulfilled their designated functions or possibly because they no longer fit with consumers' views of themselves. Concern about the environment coupled with a need for convenience has made ease of product disposal a key attribute in categories from razors to diapers.

Disposal Options

When a consumer decides that a product is no longer of use, several choices are available. The person can (1) keep the item, (2) temporarily dispose of it, or (3) permanently dispose of it. In many cases a new product is acquired even though the old one still functions. Some reasons for this replacement include a desire for new features, a change in the person's environment (e.g., a refrigerator is the wrong colour for a freshly painted kitchen), or a change in the person's role or self-image.[109] Figure 10–6 provides an overview of consumers' disposal options.

The issue of product disposal is doubly vital because of its enormous public policy implications. We live in a throw-away society, which creates problems for the environment and also results in a great deal of unfortunate waste. In a recent

← The Salvation Army provides a disposal option to consumers—give it away!
Courtesy of the Governing Council of the Salvation Army.

FIGURE 10–6   CONSUMERS' DISPOSAL OPTIONS

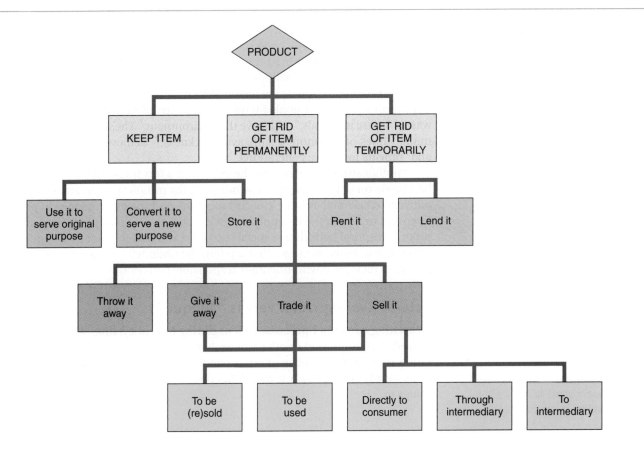

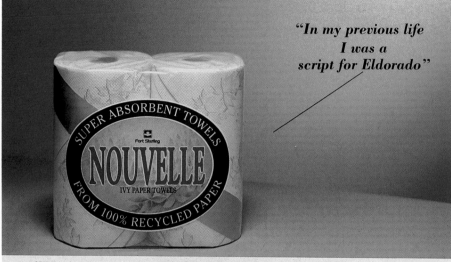

"In my previous life I was a script for Eldorado"

SUPER ABSORBENT TOWELS

Fort Sterling

NOUVELLE

IVY PAPER TOWELS

FROM 100% RECYCLED PAPER

SUPERIOR PAPER TOWELS FROM RECYCLED PAPER

Marketing Pitfall ↘

As if disposing of other kinds of waste was not bad enough, one consequence of our infatuation with new technology is figuring out what to do with the stuff that quickly becomes obsolete. Now even discarded cell phones are becoming a problem as customers rapidly switch among mobile services and upgrade to new models. One popular solution seems to be to ship unwanted electronic waste such as old computer monitors and circuit boards to developing countries. As much as 50 percent to 80 percent of electronics waste collected for recycling in North America is placed on container ships and sent to China, India, Pakistan, or other developing countries, where it is reused or recycled under largely unregulated conditions. Recycling industries in these places often use young children to handle cathode ray tubes filled with lead and other toxic substances. The European Union is so concerned about the problem that it is moving toward requiring manufacturers to take cradle-to-grave responsibility for their products.[116]

survey, 15 percent of adults admitted they are pack rats and another 64 percent said they are selective savers. In contrast, 20 percent said they throw out as much garbage as they can. The consumers most likely to save things are older people and single households.[110] Training consumers to recycle has become a priority in many countries. Japan recycles about 40 percent of its garbage, and this relatively high rate of compliance is partly due to the social value the Japanese place on recycling. Citizens are encouraged by garbage trucks that periodically rumble through the streets playing classical music or children's songs.[111]

Companies continue to search for ways to use resources more efficiently, often at the prompting of activist consumer groups. McDonald's restaurants bowed to pressure by eliminating the use of styrofoam packages, and its outlets in Europe are experimenting with edible breakfast platters made of maize.[112]

A recent study examined the relevant goals consumers have in recycling. It used a means-end chain analysis of the type described in Chapter 4 to identify how specific instrumental goals are linked to more abstract terminal values. The most important lower-order goals identified were "avoid filling up landfills," "reduce waste," "reuse materials," and "save the environment." These were linked to the terminal values of "promote health/avoid sickness," "achieve life-sustaining ends," and "provide for future generations."

Another study reported that the perceived effort involved in recycling was the best predictor of whether people would go to the trouble; this pragmatic dimension outweighed general attitudes toward recycling and the environment in predicting intention to recycle.[113] By applying such techniques to study recycling and other product disposal behaviours, social marketers will find it easier to design advertising copy and other messages that tap into the underlying values that will motivate people to increase environmentally responsible behaviour.[114]

Lateral Cycling: Junk versus "Junque"

Interesting consumer processes occur during **lateral cycling**, where already purchased objects are sold to others or exchanged. Many purchases are second-hand rather than new. The reuse of other people's things is so important in our throwaway society because, as one researcher put it, "there is no longer an 'away' to throw things to."[115]

Flea markets, garage sales, classified advertisements, bartering for services, hand-me-downs, and the black market all represent important alternative marketing systems that operate in addition to the formal marketplace. These outlets provide consumers with opportunities to buy and sell items related to popular cultural events and people to which they have long-term attachments. For example, demand for rock 'n' roll memorabilia about icons like the Beatles or Buddy Holly remains strong. A buyer recently paid $850 000 for a guitar that formerly belonged to the Grateful Dead's Jerry Garcia.[117]

How do we bring ourselves to part with these "precious" items? Some researchers recently examined the ways consumers practise **divestment rituals**, where they take steps to gradually distance themselves from things they treasure so that they can sell them or give them away (more on rituals in Chapter 16). As they observed people preparing to sell their items at garage sales, the researchers identified the following rituals:

- *iconic transfer ritual*—taking pictures and videos of objects before selling them
- *transition-place ritual*—putting items in an out-of-the-way location, such as a garage or attic, before disposing of them
- *ritual cleansing*—washing, ironing, and/or meticulously wrapping the item[118]

The internet has revolutionized the lateral cycling process, as millions of people flock to eBay to buy and sell their "treasures." This phenomenally successful online auction site started as a trading post for Beanie Babies and other collectibles. Now two-thirds of the site's sales are for practical goods. eBay expects to sell $2 billion worth of used cars and $1 billion worth of computers a year. eBay also offers event tickets, food, industrial equipment, and real estate.[119]

Despite its success, there's sometimes a bittersweet quality to eBay. Some of the sellers are listing computers, fancy cars, jewellery, and other luxury items because they desperately need the money. As one vendor explained when he described the classic convertible he wanted to sell, "I am out of money and need to pay my rent, so my toys have to be sold." The site witnessed a particularly strong surge in these kinds of messages following 9/11 when many people got laid off in the wake of a sluggish economy. In the words of an accountant who lost his job, "Things were bad before, and then they got really bad after the bombings. Everything completely dried up." Noting that he used to sell merchandise on eBay as a hobby but was then forced to sell some of his own possessions, including his BMW and his wife's jewellery, he commented, "If it weren't for eBay, I'm not sure what I'd be doing. We definitely would not be able to pay the bills."[120]

Although traditional marketers have not paid much attention to used-product sellers, factors such as concern about the environment, demands for quality, and cost and fashion consciousness are conspiring to make these "secondary" markets more important.[121] Other growth areas in lateral cycling include student markets for used computers and textbooks, and ski swaps, where millions of dollars' worth of used ski equipment is exchanged.

A new generation of second-hand-store owners is developing markets for everything from used office equipment to cast-off kitchen sinks. Many are non-profit ventures started with government funding. Habitat for Humanity has "ReStores" across Canada (***www.habitat.ca***). They accept and recycle household items such as appliances, cupboards, doors, windows, etc. Anyone doing renovations can buy these used items and support the organization at the same time. These efforts remind us that recycling is actually the last step in the familiar mantra of the environmental movement: reduce, reuse, recycle. Only if no use can be found for an item should it be shredded and made into something else.[122]

CHAPTER SUMMARY

THE OUTCOME OF AN ACTUAL TRANSACTION IS INFLUENCED BY MANY FACTORS OVER AND ABOVE THE QUALITIES OF THE PRODUCT OR SERVICE. FACTORS OPERATING AT THE TIME OF PURCHASE CAN DRAMATICALLY INFLUENCE THE CONSUMER DECISION-MAKING PROCESS.

- The act of purchase can be affected by many factors. These include the consumer's antecedent state (his or her mood, time pressure, or disposition toward shopping). Time is an important resource that often determines how much effort and search will go into a decision. Mood can be affected by the degree of pleasure and arousal present in a store environment.

- The usage context of a product can be a basis for segmentation. Consumers look for different product attributes depending upon the uses to which they intend to put their purchases. The presence or absence of other people—and the types of people they are—can also affect a consumer's decisions.

- The shopping experience is a pivotal part of the purchase decision. In many cases retailing is like theatre; that is, the consumer's evaluation of stores and products may depend upon the type of "performance" he or she witnesses. This evaluation can be influenced by the actors (salespeople), the setting (the store environment), and the props (store displays). A store image, like a brand personality, is determined by a number of factors, such as perceived convenience, sophistication, knowledgeability of salespeople, and so on. With increasing competition from non-store alternatives, the creation of a positive shopping experience has never been more important. Online shopping is growing in importance, and this new way to acquire products has both good (e.g., convenience) and bad (e.g., security) aspects.

IN ADDITION TO WHAT SHOPPERS ALREADY KNOW OR BELIEVE ABOUT A PRODUCT, INFORMATION PROVIDED IN THE STORE OR A WEBSITE CAN STRONGLY INFLUENCE THEIR PURCHASE DECISIONS.

- Because many purchase decisions are not made until the time the consumer is actually in the store, point-of-purchase (POP) stimuli are very important sales tools. These include product samples, elaborate package displays, place-based media, and in-store promotional materials, such as "shelf talkers." POP stimuli are particularly useful in stimulating impulse buying, where a consumer yields to a sudden urge for a product.

A SALESPERSON CAN BE THE CRUCIAL LINK BETWEEN INTEREST IN A PRODUCT AND ITS ACTUAL PURCHASE.

- The consumer's encounter with a salesperson is a complex and important process. The outcome can be affected by such factors as the salesperson's similarity to the customer and his or her perceived credibility.

MARKETERS NEED TO BE CONCERNED ABOUT A CONSUMER'S EVALUATIONS OF A PRODUCT AFTER THE PERSON BUYS IT AS WELL AS BEFORE.

- Consumer satisfaction is determined by the person's overall feeling toward the product after purchase. Many factors influence perceptions of product quality, including price, brand name, and product performance. Satisfaction is often determined by the degree to which a product's performance is consistent with the consumer's prior expectations of how well it will function.

GETTING RID OF PRODUCTS WHEN THEY ARE NO LONGER NEEDED OR WANTED IS A MAJOR CONCERN BOTH TO MARKETERS AND TO PUBLIC POLICY MAKERS.

- Product disposal is an increasingly important problem. Recycling is one option that will continue to be stressed as consumers' environmental awareness grows. Products may also be introduced by consumers into secondary markets during a process of lateral cycling, which occurs when objects are sold second-hand, fenced, or bartered.

KEY TERMS

Atmospherics   p. 292

Consumer satisfaction/dissatisfaction
   (CS/D)   p. 295

Divestment rituals   p. 303

Exchange theory   p. 294

Gemba   p. 299

Impulse buying   p. 293

Lateral cycling   p. 302

Point-of-purchase (POP) stimuli   p. 294

Queuing theory   p. 286

Retail theming   p. 290

Shopping orientation   p. 289

Store image   p. 290

Time poverty   p. 284

REVIEW QUESTIONS

1. What is the situational self-image? Give an example of this phenomenon.
2. Describe the difference between density and crowding. Why is this difference relevant in purchase environments?
3. What is time poverty, and how can it influence our purchase decisions?
4. What are the two dimensions that determine whether we will react positively or negatively to a purchase environment?
5. List three separate motivations for shopping, giving an example of each.
6. What are some important pros and cons of e-commerce?
7. List three factors that help to determine store image.
8. What is the difference between unplanned buying and impulse buying?
9. What is a commercial friendship? Provide an example.
10. How do consumers' prior expectations about product quality influence their satisfaction with the product after they buy it?
11. List three actions consumers can take if they are dissatisfied with a purchase.
12. What is the underground economy?

CONSUMER BEHAVIOUR CHALLENGE

Discuss

1. Is the customer always right? Why or why not?
2. Discuss some of the motivations for shopping described in this chapter. How might a retailer adjust its strategy to accommodate these motivations?
3. What are some of the positive and negative aspects of requiring employees who interact with customers to wear some kind of uniform, or of mandating a dress code in the office?
4. Think about exceptionally good and bad salespeople you have encountered in the past. What qualities seem to differentiate them?
5. Discuss the concept of timestyle. Based on your own experiences, how might consumers be segmented in terms of their timestyles?
6. Compare and contrast different cultures' conceptions of time. What are some of the implications for marketing strategy within each of these frameworks?
7. The movement away from a disposable consumer society toward one that emphasizes creative recycling creates many opportunities for marketers. Can you identify some?
8. The Hooters restaurant chain is known for its attractive female waitresses. Should a retailer have the right to recruit employees who are consistent with its image, even if this means excluding certain types of people (e.g. non-Caucasians or men) from the sales floor?
9. The mall of the future will most likely be less about purchasing products than about exploring them in a physical setting. This means that retail environments will have to become places that can build brand image rather than simply sell products. What are some strategies stores can use to enhance the emotional/sensory experiences of their customers?
10. The store environment is heating up as more and more companies put their promotional dollars into point-of-purchase efforts. Shoppers are now often confronted by DVDs at the checkout counter, computer monitors attached to their shopping carts, and so on. We're increasingly exposed to ads in nonshopping environments. Do you feel that these innovations are overly intrusive? At what point might shoppers "rebel" and demand some peace and quiet while shopping? Do you see any market potential in the future for stores that countermarket by promising a hands-off shopping environment?
11. Court cases in recent years have attempted to prohibit special interest groups from distributing literature in shopping malls. Mall managements claim that these centres are private property. On the other hand, these groups argue that the mall is the modern-day version of the town square and as such is a public forum. What is the current status of the mall as a public forum? Do you agree with this concept?

Experiential Exercises

12. Conduct naturalistic observation at a local mall. Sit in a central location and observe the activities of mall employees and patrons. Keep a log of the nonretailing activities you observe (e.g., special performances, exhibits, socializing, etc.). Do these activities enhance or detract from business conducted at the mall? As malls become more like high-tech game rooms, how valid is the criticism that shopping areas are encouraging more loitering by teenage boys, who don't spend a lot in stores and simply scare away other customers?
13. Select three competing clothing stores in your area and conduct a store image study for each. Ask a group of consumers to rate each store on a set of attributes, and plot these ratings on the same graph. Based on your findings, are there any areas of competitive advantage or disadvantage you could bring to the attention of store management?
14. What applications of queuing theory can you find employed among local services? Interview consumers who are waiting in lines to determine how this experience affects their satisfaction with the service.
15. New interactive tools are being introduced that allow surfers on sites such as *www.landsend.com* to view apparel product selections on virtual models in full, 360-degree rotational view. In some cases the viewer can modify the models' bodies, faces, skin colouring, and hairstyles. In others, the consumer can project his or her *own* likeness into the space by scanning a photo into a "makeover" program. Visit *www.landsend.com* or another site that offers a personalized mannequin. Surf around. Try on some clothes. How was your experience? How helpful was the mannequin? When you shop for clothes online,

would you rather see how they look on a body with dimensions the same as yours, or on a different body? What advice can you give website designers who are trying to personalize these shopping environments by creating life-like models to guide you through the site?

16. Interview people who are selling items at a flea market or garage sale. Ask them to identify some items to which they have a strong attachment. Then, see if you can prompt them to describe one or more divestment rituals they went through as they prepared to offer these items for sale.

17. Identify three people who own an electric coffeemaker and then "go to the gemba" by observing them as they actually prepare coffee in the appliance at home. Based on these experiences, what recommendations might you make to the designer of a new coffeemaker model that would improve customers' experience with the product?

NOTES

1. Keith Naughton, "Revolution in the Showroom," *Business Week* (February 19, 1996): 70 (8 pp.).

2. Pradeep Kakkar and Richard J. Lutz, "Situational Influence on Consumer Behavior: A Review," in *Perspectives in Consumer Behavior*, 3rd ed., eds. Harold H. Kassarjian and Thomas S. Robertson (Glenview, IL: Scott, Foresman and Company, 1981), 204–214.

3. Shelly Reese, "Every Product Has a Season," *American Demographics* (December 1995): 17–18.

4. Benedict Carey, "TV Time, Unlike Child Care, Ranks High in Mood Study," *New York Times on the Web* (December 3, 2004).

5. Carolyn Turner Schenk and Rebecca H. Holman, "A Sociological Approach to Brand Choice: The Concept of Situational Self-Image," in *Advances in Consumer Research* 7, ed. Jerry C. Olson (Ann Arbor, MI: Association for Consumer Research, 1980), 610–614.

6. Kenneth Hein, "Was That a Big Mac or a McNugget? The Latest in Technology," *Brandweek* (February 25, 2002): 21.

7. Matt Richtel, "New Billboards Sample Radios as Cars Go By, Then Adjust," *New York Times on the Web* (December 27, 2002).

8. Russell W. Belk, "An Exploratory Assessment of Situational Effects in Buyer Behavior," *Journal of Marketing Research* 11 (May 1974): 156–163; U.N. Umesh and Joseph A. Cote, "Influence of Situational Variables on Brand-Choice Models," *Journal of Business Research* 16, 2 (1988): 91–99. See also J. Wesley Hutchinson and Joseph W. Alba, "Ignoring Irrevelant Information: Situational Determinants of Consumer Learning," *Journal of Consumer Research* 18 (December 1991): 325–345.

9. Peter R. Dickson, "Person-Situation: Segmentation's Missing Link," *Journal of Marketing* 46 (Fall 1982): 56–64.

10. Ellen Byron, "How Coach Won a Rich Purse by Inventing New Uses for Bags: What Was a Semiannual Buy Is now a Regular Ritual; Wristlets, Clutches, Totes Fresh Competition from Gap," *Wall Street Journal on the Web* (November 17, 2004): A1.

11. Alan R. Hirsch, "Effects of Ambient Odors on Slot-Machine Usage in a Las Vegas Casino," *Psychology & Marketing* 12, 7 (October 1995): 585–594.

12. Daniel Stokols, "On the Distinction between Density and Crowding: Some Implications for Future Research," *Psychological Review* 79 (1972): 275–277.

13. Carol Felker Kaufman, Paul M. Lane, and Jay D. Lindquist, "Exploring More than 24 Hours a Day: A Preliminary Investigation of Polychronic Time Use," *Journal of Consumer Research* 18 (December 1991): 392–401.

14. Laurence P. Feldman and Jacob Hornik, "The Use of Time: An Integrated Conceptual Model," *Journal of Consumer Research* 7 (March 1981): 407–419. See also Michelle M. Bergadaà, "The Role of Time in the Action of the Consumer," *Journal of Consumer Research* 17 (December 1990): 289–302.

15. Robert J. Samuelson, "Rediscovering the Rat Race," *Newsweek* (May 15, 1989): 57.

16. John P. Robinson, "Time Squeeze," *Advertising Age* (February 1990): 30–33.

17. "Plugged In: Hong Kong Embraces the Octopus Card," *New York Times on the Web* (June 8, 2002).

18. Kaufman, Lane, and Lindquist, "Exploring More than 24 Hours a Day: A Preliminary Investigation of Polychronic Time Use."

19. Quoted in Kleiman, "Fast Food? It just Isn't Fast enough Anymore," *New York Times* (December 6, 1989): A1.

20. Stephanie Thompson, "'To Go' Becoming the Way to Go," *Advertising Age* (13 May 2002): 73.

21. David Lewis and Darren Bridger, *The Soul of the New Consumer: Authenticity— What We Buy and Why in the New Economy* (London: Nicholas Brealey Publishing, 2000).

22. June Cotte, S. Ratneshwar, and David Glen Mick, "The Times of Their Lives: Phenomenological and Metaphorical Characteristics of Consumer Timestyles," *Journal of Consumer Research* 31 (September 2004): 333–345.

23. Robert J. Graham, "The Role of Perception of Time in Consumer Research," *Journal of Consumer Research* 7 (March 1981): 335–342.

24. Alan Zarembo, *Newsweek* (June 30, 1997); based on research reported in Robert Levine, *A Geography of Time: The Temporal Misadventures of a Social Psychologist, or How Every Culture Keeps Time just a Little Bit Differently* (New York: Basic Books, 1997).

25. Cf. Shirley Taylor, "Waiting for Service: The Relationship between Delays and Evaluations of Service," *Journal of Marketing* 58 (April 1994): 56–69.

26. David H. Maister, "The Psychology of Waiting Lines," in *The Service Encounter: Managing Employee/Customer Interaction in Service Businesses*, eds. John A. Czepiel, Michael R. Solomon, and Carol F. Surprenant (Lexington, MA: Lexington Books, 1985), pp. 113–124.

27. David Leonhardt, "Airlines Using Technology in a Push for Shorter Lines," *New York Times on the Web* (May 8, 2000).

28. Jennifer Ordonez, "An Efficiency Drive: Fast-Food Lanes, Equipped with Timers, Get even Faster," *Wall Street Journal Interactive Edition* (May 18, 2000).

29. Laurette Dube and Bernd H. Schmitt, "The Processing of Emotional and Cognitive Aspects of Product Usage in Satisfaction Judgments," in *Advances in Consumer Research* 18, eds. Rebecca H. Holman and Michael R. Solomon (Provo, UT: Association for Consumer Research, 1991), 52–56; Lalita A. Manrai and Meryl P. Gardner, "The Influence of Affect on Attributions for Product Failure," in *Advances in Consumer Research* 18, 249–254.

30. Kevin G. Celuch and Linda S. Showers, "It's Time to Stress *Stress*: The Stress-Purchase/Consumption Relationship," in *Advances in Consumer Research* 18, 284–289; Lawrence R. Lepisto, J. Kathleen Stuenkel, and Linda K. Anglin, "Stress: An Ignored Situational Influence," in *Advances in Consumer Research* 18, 296–302.

31. See Eben Shapiro, "Need a Little Fantasy? A Bevy of New Companies Can Help," *New York Times* (March 10, 1991): F4.

32. John D. Mayer and Yvonne N. Gaschke, "The Experience and Meta-Experience of Mood," *Journal of Personality and Social Psychology* 55 (July 1988): 102–111.

33. Meryl Paula Gardner, "Mood States and Consumer Behavior: A Critical Review," *Journal of Consumer Research* 12 (December 1985): 281–300; Scott Dawson, Peter H. Bloch, and Nancy M. Ridgway, "Shopping Motives, Emotional States, and Retail Outcomes," *Journal of Retailing* 66 (Winter 1990): 408–427; Patricia A. Knowles, Stephen J. Grove, and W. Jeffrey Burroughs, "An Experimental Examination of Mood States on Retrieval and Evaluation of Advertisement and Brand Information," *Journal of the Academy of Marketing Science* 21 (April 1993); Paul W. Miniard, Sunil Bhatla, and Deepak Sirdeskmukh, "Mood as a Determinant of Postconsumption Product Evaluations: Mood Effects and Their Dependency on the Affective Intensity of the Consumption Experience," *Journal of Consumer Psychology* 1, 2 (1992): 173–195; Mary T. Curren and Katrin R. Harich, "Consumers' Mood States: The Mitigating Influence of Personal Relevance on Product Evaluations," *Psychology & Marketing* 11, 2 (March/April 1994): 91–107; Gerald J. Gorn, Marvin E. Rosenberg,

and Kunal Basu, "Mood, Awareness, and Product Evaluation," *Journal of Consumer Psychology* 2, 3 (1993): 237–256.

34. Gordon C. Bruner, "Music, Mood, and Marketing," *Journal of Marketing* 54 (October 1990): 94–104; Basil G. Englis, "Music Television and Its Influences on Consumers, Consumer Culture, and the Transmission of Consumption Messages," in *Advances in Consumer Research* 18.

35. Marvin E. Goldberg and Gerald J. Gorn, "Happy and Sad TV Programs: How They Affect Reactions to Commercials," *Journal of Consumer Research* 14 (December 1987): 387–403; Gorn, Rosenberg, and Basu, "Mood, Awareness, and Product Evaluation"; Curren and Harich, "Consumers' Mood States ...."

36. Rajeev Batra and Douglas M. Stayman, "The Role of Mood in Advertising Effectiveness," *Journal of Consumer Research* 17 (September 1990): 203.

37. For a scale that was devised to assess these dimensions of the shopping experience, see Barry J. Babin, William R. Darden, and Mitch Griffin, "Work and/or Fun: Measuring Hedonic and Utilitarian Shopping Value," *Journal of Consumer Research* 20 (March 1994): 644–656.

38. Cele Otnes and Mary Ann McGrath, "Perceptions and Realities of Male Shopping Behavior," *Journal of Retailing* 77 (Spring 2001): 111–137.

39. Babin, Darden, and Griffin, "Work and/or Fun ...."

40. Edward M. Tauber, "Why Do People Shop?" *Journal of Marketing* 36 (October 1972): 47–48.

41. Quoted in Robert C. Prus, *Making Sales: Influence as Interpersonal Accomplishment* (Newbury Park, CA: Sage Library of Social Research, Sage Publications, Inc., 1989), p. 225.

42. Gregory P. Stone, "City Shoppers and Urban Identification: Observations on the Social Psychology of City Life," *American Journal of Sociology* 60 (1954): 36–45; Danny Bellenger and Pradeep K. Korgaonkar, "Profiling the Recreational Shopper," *Journal of Retailing* 56, 3 (1980): 77–92.

43. Some material in this section was adapted from Michael R. Solomon and Elnora W. Stuart, *Welcome to Marketing.Com: The Brave New World of E-Commerce* (Englewood Cliffs, NJ: Prentice Hall, 2001).

44. Rebecca K. Ratner, Barbara E. Kahn, and Daniel Kahneman, "Choosing Less-Preferred Experiences for the Sake of Variety," *Journal of Consumer Research* 26 (June 1999): 1–15.

45. Jennifer Gilbert, "Customer Service Crucial to Online Buyers," *Advertising Age* (September 13, 1999): 52.

46. Quoted in Timothy L. O'Brien, "Aided by Internet, Identity Theft Soars," *New York Times on the Web* (April 3, 2000).

47. For a recent study of consumer shopping patterns in a mall that views the mall as an ecological habitat, see Peter N. Bloch, Nancy M. Ridgway, and Scott A. Dawson, "The Shopping Mall as Consumer Habitat," *Journal of Retailing* 70, 1 (1994): 23–42.

48. Quoted in Jacquelyn Bivins, "Fun and Mall Games," *Stores* (August 1989): 35.

49. Millie Creighton, "The Seed of Creative Lifestyle Shopping: Wrapping Consumerism in Japanese Store Layouts," in *Servicescapes: The Concept of Place in Contemporary Markets*, ed. John F. Sherry Jr. (Lincolnwood, IL: NTC Business Books, 1998): 199–228.

50. Kathleen Martin, "Froot Flavoured," *Marketing Magazine* (April 3, 2006): 13–14.

51. Susan Spiggle and Murphy A. Sewall, "A Choice Sets Model of Retail Selection," *Journal of Marketing* 51 (April 1987): 97–111; William R. Darden and Barry J. Babin, "The Role of Emotions in Expanding the Concept of Retail Personality," *Stores* 76, 4 (April 1994): RR7–8.

52. Most measures of store image are quite similar to other attitude measures, as discussed in Chapter 5. For an excellent bibliography of store-image studies, see Mary R. Zimmer and Linda L. Golden, "Impressions of Retail Stores: A Content Analysis of Consumer Images," *Journal of Retailing* 64 (Fall 1988): 265–293.

53. David Wethe, "Car Dealerships Face the Great Homogenization," *New York Times on the Web* (January 11, 2004).

54. Zimmer and Golden, "Impressions of Retail Stores."

55. Spiggle and Sewall, "A Choice Sets Model of Retail Selection."

56. Philip Kotler, "Atmospherics as a Marketing Tool," *Journal of Retailing* (Winter 1973/74): 10–43. For a review of more recent research, see J. Duncan Herrington, "An Integrative Path Model of the Effects of Retail Environments on Shopper Behavior," *Marketing: Toward the Twenty-First Century*, ed. Robert L. King (Richmond, VA: Southern Marketing Association, 1991), pp. 58–62.

57. Joseph A. Bellizzi and Robert E. Hite, "Environmental Color, Consumer Feelings, and Purchase Likelihood," *Psychology & Marketing* 9, 5 (September/October 1992): 347–363.

58. For a study that assessed olfaction in a controlled, simulated store environment, see Eric R. Spangenberg, Ayn E. Crowley, and Pamela W. Henderson, "Improving the Store Environment: Do Olfactory Cues Affect Evaluations and Behaviors?" *Journal of Marketing* 60 (April 1996): 67–80.

59. Robert J. Donovan et al., "Store Atmosphere and Purchasing Behavior," *Journal of Retailing* 70, 3 (1994): 283–294.

60. Alice Z. Cuneo, "Malls Seek Boost with 'Activity' Stores," *Advertising Age* (July 21, 2003): 6.

61. Deborah Blumenthal, "Scenic Design for In-Store Try-Ons," *New York Times* (April 9, 1988).

62. Julie Flaherty, "Ambient Music Has Moved to Record Store Shelves," *New York Times on the Web* (July 4, 2001).

63. John Pierson, "If Sun Shines In, Workers Work Better, Buyers Buy More," *Wall Street Journal* (November 20, 1995): B1 (2 pp.).

64. Charles S. Areni and David Kim, "The Influence of In-Store Lighting on Consumers' Examination of Merchandise in a Wine Store," *International Journal of Research in Marketing* 11, 2 (March 1994): 117–125.

65. Judy I. Alpert and Mark I. Alpert, "Music Influences on Mood and Purchase Intentions," *Psychology & Marketing* 7 (Summer 1990): 109–134.

66. Quoted in "Slow Music Makes Fast Drinkers," *Psychology Today* (March 1989): 18.

67. Brad Edmondson, "Pass the Meat Loaf," *American Demographics* (January 1989): 19.

68. Marianne Meyer, "Attention Shoppers!" *Marketing and Media Decisions* 23 (May 1988): 67.

69. Jennifer Lach, "Meet You in Aisle Three," *American Demographics* (April 1999): 41.

70. Beck Ernest, "Diageo Attempts to Reinvent the Bar in an Effort to Increase Spirits Sales," *Wall Street Journal* (February 23, 2001).

71. Easwar S. Iyer, "Unplanned Purchasing: Knowledge of Shopping Environment and Time Pressure," *Journal of Retailing* 65 (Spring 1989): 40–57; C. Whan Park, Easwar S. Iyer, and Daniel C. Smith, "The Effects of Situational Factors on In-Store Grocery Shopping," *Journal of Consumer Research* 15 (March 1989): 422–433.

72. Dennis W. Rook and Robert J. Fisher, "Normative Influences on Impulsive Buying Behavior," *Journal of Consumer Research* 22 (December 1995): 305–313; Francis Piron, "Defining Impulse Purchasing," in *Advances in Consumer Research* 18, 509–514; Dennis W. Rook, "The Buying Impulse," *Journal of Consumer Research* 14 (September 1987): 189–199.

73. Michael Wahl, "Eye POPping Persuasion," *Marketing Insights* (June 1989): 130.

74. "Zipping Down the Aisles," *New York Times Magazine* (April 6, 1997).

75. Cathy J. Cobb and Wayne D. Hoyer, "Planned versus Impulse Purchase Behavior," *Journal of Retailing* 62 (Winter 1986): 384–409; Easwar S. Iyer and Sucheta S. Ahlawat, "Deviations from a Shopping Plan: When and Why Do Consumers Not Buy as Planned," in *Advances in Consumer Research* 14, eds. Melanie Wallendorf and Paul Anderson (Provo, UT: Association for Consumer Research, 1987), 246–249.

76. Bernice Kanner, "Trolling in the Aisles," *New York* (January 16, 1989): 12; Michael Janofsky, "Using Crowing Roosters and Ringing Business Cards to Tap a Boom in Point-of-Purchase Displays," *New York Times* (March 21, 1994): D9.

77. See Robert B. Cialdini, *Influence: Science and Practice,* 2nd ed. (Glenview, IL: Scott, Foresman and Company, 1988).

78. Richard P. Bagozzi, "Marketing as Exchange," *Journal of Marketing* 39 (October 1975): 32–39; Peter M. Blau, *Exchange and Power in Social Life* (New York, NY: Wiley, 1964); Marjorie Caballero and Alan J. Resnik, "The Attraction Paradigm in Dyadic Exchange," *Psychology & Marketing* 3, 1 (1986): 17–34; George C. Homans, "Social Behavior as Exchange," *American Journal of Sociology* 63 (1958): 597–606; Paul H. Schurr and Julie L. Ozanne, "Influences on Exchange Processes: Buyers' Preconceptions of a Seller's Trustworthiness and Bargaining Toughness," *Journal of Consumer Research* 11 (March 1985): 939–953; Arch G. Woodside and J.W. Davenport, "The Effect of Salesman Similarity and Expertise on Consumer Purchasing Behavior," *Journal of Marketing Research* 8 (1974): 433–436.

79. Paul Busch and David T. Wilson, "An Experimental Analysis of a Salesman's Expert and Referent Bases of Social Power in the Buyer-Seller Dyad," *Journal of Marketing Research* 13 (February 1976): 3–11; John E. Swan et al., "Measuring Dimensions of Purchaser Trust of Industrial Salespeople," *Journal of Personal Selling and Sales Management* 8 (May 1988): 1.

80. For a study in this area, see Peter H. Reingen and Jerome B. Kernan, "Social Perception and Interpersonal Influence: Some Consequences of the Physical Attractiveness Stereotype in a Personal Selling Setting," *Journal of Consumer Psychology* 2, 1 (1993): 25–38.

81. Linda L. Price and Eric J. Arnould, "Commercial Friendships: Service Provider-Client Relationships in Context," *Journal of Marketing* 63 (October 1999): 38–56.

82. Sally Beatty, "Bank of America Places Ads in ATMs to Offset Expenses," *Wall Street Journal Interactive Edition* (July 25, 2002); David L. Margulus, "Going to the A.T.M. for More than a Fistful of Twenties," *New York Times on the Web* (January 17, 2002).

83. Mary Jo Bitner, Bernard H. Booms, and Mary Stansfield Tetreault, "The Service Encounter: Diagnosing Favorable and Unfavorable Incidents," *Journal of Marketing* 54 (January 1990): 7–84; Robert C. Prus, *Making Sales* (Newbury Park, CA: Sage Publications, Inc., 1989); Arch G. Woodside and James L. Taylor, "Identity Negotiations in Buyer-Seller Interactions," in *Advances in Consumer Research* 12, eds. Elizabeth C. Hirschman and Morris B. Holbrook (Provo, UT: Association for Consumer Research, 1985), 443–449.

84. Gilbert A. Churchill, Jr., et al., "The Determinants of Salesperson Performance: A Meta-Analysis," *Journal of Marketing Research* 22 (May 1985): 103–118.

85. Siew Meng Leong, Paul S. Busch, and Deborah Roedder John, "Knowledge Bases and Salesperson Effectiveness: A Script-Theoretic Analysis," *Journal of Marketing Research* 26 (May 1989): 164; Harish Sujan, Mita Sujan, and James R. Bettman, "Knowledge Structure Differences between More Effective and Less Effective Salespeople," *Journal of Marketing Research* 25 (February 1988): 81–86; Robert Saxe and Barton Weitz, "The SOCCO Scale: A Measure of the Customer Orientation of Salespeople," *Journal of Marketing Research* 19 (August 1982): 343–351; David M. Szymanski, "Determinants of Selling Effectiveness: The Importance of Declarative Knowledge to the Personal Selling Concept," *Journal of Marketing* 52 (January 1988): 64–77; Barton A. Weitz, "Effectiveness in Sales Interactions: A Contingency Framework," *Journal of Marketing* 45 (Winter 1981): 85–103.

86. Jagdish M. Sheth, "Buyer-Seller Interaction: A Conceptual Framework," in *Advances in Consumer Research* (Cincinnati, OH: Association for Consumer Research, 1976), 382–386; Kaylene C. Williams and Rosann L. Spiro, "Communication Style in the Salesperson-Customer Dyad," *Journal of Marketing Research* 22 (November 1985): 434–442.

87. Marsha L. Richins, "An Analysis of Consumer Interaction Styles in the Marketplace," *Journal of Consumer Research* 10 (June 1983): 73–82.

88. Rama Jayanti and Anita Jackson, "Service Satisfaction: Investigation of Three Models," in *Advances in Consumer Research* 18, 603–610; David K. Tse, Franco M. Nicosia, and Peter C. Wilton, "Consumer Satisfaction as a Process," *Psychology & Marketing* 7 (Fall 1990): 177–193.

89. Constance L. Hayes, "Service Takes a Holiday," *New York Times* (December 23, 1998): C1(2).

90. Leslie Kaufman, "Enough Talk," *Newsweek* (August 18, 1997): 48–49.

91. Robert Jacobson and David A. Aaker, "The Strategic Role of Product Quality," *Journal of Marketing* 51 (October 1987): 31–44. For a recent review of issues regarding the measurement of service quality, see J. Joseph Cronin, Jr. and Steven A. Taylor, "Measuring Service Quality: A Re-examination and Extension," *Journal of Marketing* 56 (July 1992): 55–68.

92. Anna Kirmani and Peter Wright, "Money Talks: Perceived Advertising Expense and Expected Product Quality," *Journal of Consumer Research* 16 (December 1989): 344–53; Donald R. Lichtenstein and Scot Burton, "The Relationship between Perceived and Objective Price-Quality," *Journal of Marketing Research* 26 (November 1989): 429–443; Akshay R. Rao and Kent B. Monroe, "The Effect of Price, Brand Name, and Store Name on Buyers' Perceptions of Product Quality: An Integrative Review," *Journal of Marketing Research* 26 (August 1989): 351–357.

93. Shelby Hunt, "Post-Transactional Communication and Dissonance Reduction," *Journal of Marketing* 34 (January 1970): 46–51; Daniel E. Innis and H. Rao Unnava, "The Usefulness of Product Warranties for Reputable and New Brands," in *Advances in Consumer Research* 18, 317–322; Terence A. Shimp and William O. Bearden, "Warranty and Other Extrinsic Cue Effects on Consumers' Risk Perceptions," *Journal of Consumer Research* 9 (June 1982): 38–46.

94. Morris B. Holbrook and Kim P. Corfman, "Quality and Value in the Consumption Experience: Phaedrus Rides Again," in *Perceived Quality: How Consumers View Stores and Merchandise,* eds. Jacob Jacoby and Jerry C. Olson (Lexington, MA: Lexington Books, 1985), pp. 31–58.

95. Ibid.; Robert M. Pirsig, *Zen and the Art of Motorcycle Maintenance: An Inquiry into Values* (New York, NY: Bantam Books, 1974).

96. Gilbert A. Churchill, Jr., and Carol F. Surprenant, "An Investigation into the Determinants of Customer Satisfaction," *Journal of Marketing Research* 19 (November 1983): 491–504; John E. Swan and I. Frederick Trawick, "Disconfirmation of Expectations and Satisfaction with a Retail Service," *Journal of Retailing* 57 (Fall 1981): 49–67; Peter C. Wilton and David K. Tse, "Models of Consumer Satisfaction Formation: An Extension," *Journal of Marketing Research* 25 (May 1988): 204–212. For a discussion of what may occur when customers evaluate a new service for which comparison standards do not yet exist, see Ann L. McGill and Dawn Iacobucci, "The Role of Post-Experience Comparison Standards in the Evaluation of Unfamiliar Services," in *Advances in Consumer Research* 19, eds. John F. Sherry, Jr. and Brian Sternthal (Provo, UT: Association for Consumer Research, 1992), 570–578; William Boulding et al., "A Dynamic Process Model of Service Quality: From Expectations to Behavioral Intentions," *Journal of Marketing Research* 30 (February 1993): 7–27.

97. John W. Gamble, "The Expectations Paradox: The More You Offer Customer, Closer You Are to Failure," *Marketing News* (March 14, 1988): 38.

98. Jagdish N. Sheth and Banwari Mittal, "A Framework for Managing Customer Expectations," *Journal of Market Focused Management* 1 (1996): 137–158.

99. Mary C. Gilly and Betsy D. Gelb, "Post-Purchase Consumer Processes and the Complaining Consumer," *Journal of Consumer Research* 9 (December 1982): 323–228; Diane Halstead and Cornelia Dröge, "Consumer Attitudes toward Complaining and the Prediction of Multiple Complaint Responses," in *Advances in Consumer Research* 18, 210–216; Jagdip Singh, "Consumer Complaint Intentions and Behavior: Definitional and Taxonomical Issues," *Journal of Marketing* 52 (January 1988): 93–107.

100. Gary L. Clark, Peter F. Kaminski, and David R. Rink, "Consumer Complaints: Advice on How Companies Should Respond Based on an Empirical Study," *Journal of Services Marketing* 6, 1 (Winter 1992): 41–50.

101. Alan Andreasen and Arthur Best, "Consumers Complain—Does Business Respond?" *Harvard Business Review* 55 (July/August 1977): 93–101.

102. Tibbett L. Speer, "They Complain because They Care," *American Demographics* (May 1996): 13–14.

103. Ingrid Martin, "Expert-Novice Differences in Complaint Scripts," in *Advances in Consumer Research* 18, 225–231; Marsha L. Richins, "A Multivariate Analysis of Responses to Dissatisfaction," *Journal of the Academy of Marketing Science* 15 (Fall 1987): 24–31.

104. John A. Schibrowsky and Richard S. Lapidus, "Gaining a Competitive Advantage by Analyzing Aggregate Complaints," *Journal of Consumer Marketing* 11, 1 (1994): 15–26.

105. "Dunkin' Donuts Buys Out Critical Web Site," *New York Times on the Web* (August 27, 1999).

106. Material adapted from a presentation by Glenn H. Mazur, QFD Institute, 2002.

107. Russell W. Belk, "The Role of Possessions in Constructing and Maintaining a Sense of Past," in *Advances in Consumer Research* 17, eds. Marvin E. Goldberg, Gerald Gorn, and Richard W. Pollay (Provo, UT: Association for Consumer Research, 1989), 669–676.

108. David E. Sanger, "For a Job Well Done, Japanese Enshrine the Chip," *New York Times* (December 11, 1990): A4.

109. Jacob Jacoby, Carol K. Berning, and Thomas F. Dietvorst, "What About Disposition?" *Journal of Marketing* 41 (April 1977): 22–28.

110. Jennifer Lach, "Welcome to the Hoard Fest," *American Demographics* (April 2000): 8–9.

111. Mike Tharp, "Tchaikovsky and Toilet Paper," *U.S. News & World Report* (December 1987): 62; B. Van Voorst, "The Recycling Bottleneck," *Time* (September 14, 1992): 52–54; Richard P. Bagozzi and Pratibha A. Dabholkar, "Consumer Recycling Goals and Their Effect on Decisions to Recycle: A Means-End Chain Analysis," *Psychology & Marketing* 11, 4 (July/August 1994): 313–340.

112. "Finally, Something at McDonald's You Can Actually Eat," *Utne Reader* (May–June 1997): 12.

113. Debra J. Dahab, James W. Gentry, and Wanru Su, "New Ways to Reach Non-Recyclers: An Extension of the Model of Reasoned Action to Recycling Behaviors," in *Advances in Consumer Research* 22, eds. Frank R. Kardes and Mita Sujan (Provo, UT: Association for Consumer Research, 1995), 251–256.

114. Bagozzi and Dabholkar, "Consumer Recycling Goals and Their Effect on Decisions to Recycle...." See also L.J. Shrum, Tina M. Lowrey, and John A. McCarty, "Recycling as a Marketing Problem: A Framework for Strategy Development," *Psychology & Marketing* 11, 4 (July/August 1994): 393–416; Dahab, Gentry, and Su, "New Ways to Reach Non-Recyclers ...."

115. John F. Sherry, Jr., "A Sociocultural Analysis of a Midwestern American Flea Market," *Journal of Consumer Research* 17 (June 1990): 13–30.

116. John Markoff, "Technology's Toxic Trash Is Sent to Poor Nations," *New York Times on the Web* (February 25, 2002); "Recycling Phones to Charities, Not Landfills," *New York Times on the Web* (October 26, 2002).

117. Alex Markels, "Collectors Shake, Rattle and Watch Those Bankrolls," *New York Times on the Web* (October 13, 2002).

118. John L. Lastovicka and Karen V. Fernandez, "Three Paths to Disposition: The Movement of Meaningful Possessions to Strangers," *Journal of Consumer Research* 31 (March 2005): 813–823.

119. Saul Hansell, "Meg Whitman and eBay, Net Survivors," *New York Times on the Web* (May 5, 2002).

120. Quoted in Stephanie Stoughton, "Unemployed Americans Turn to E-Bay to Make Money," *The Boston Globe* (October 16, 2001).

121. Allan J. Magrath, "If Used Product Sellers Ever Get Organized, Watch Out," *Marketing News* (June 25, 1990): 9; Kevin McCrohan and James D. Smith, "Consumer Participation in the Informal Economy," *Journal of the Academy of Marketing Science* 15 (Winter 1990): 62.

122. "New Kind of Store Getting More Use Out of Used Goods," *Montgomery Advertiser* (December 12, 1996): 7A.

Carlo leads a secret life. During the week he is a straight-laced stock analyst for a major investment firm. But come Friday evening, it's off with the Harry Rosen suit and on with the black leather, as he trades in his BMW for his treasured Harley-Davidson motorcycle. A dedicated member of HOG (Harley Owners Group), Carlo belongs to the faction of Harley riders known as "RUBs" (rich urban bikers). Everyone in his group wears expensive leather vests with Harley insignia and owns a customized "Low Rider."

Carlo finally got a new Harley belt buckle after he ordered it from the Genuine Harley-Davidson Roadstore at *www.harley-davidson.com*. (As he surfed around the site, he realized the lengths to which some of his fellow enthusiasts go to make sure others know they are HOG riders.) He had to restrain himself from buying more Harley stuff; there were vests, eyewear, belts, jewellery, even housewares ("home is the road") for sale. He settled for a set of Harley salt-and-pepper shakers for his buddy's new townhouse. Carlo has spent a lot on his bike and on outfitting himself to be like the rest of the group. But it's worth it. He feels a real brotherhood with his fellow RUBs. The group rides together in two-column formation to bike rallies—events that sometimes attract 300 000 cycle enthusiasts. What a sense of power he feels when they're all cruising together!

Of course, an added benefit is the business networking he's been able to accomplish during his weekend jaunts with his fellow professionals—who also wait for the weekend to "ride on the wild side."[1] Sometimes sharing a secret can pay off in more ways than one!

CHAPTER 11

Group Influence and Opinion Leadership

REFERENCE GROUPS

Humans are social animals. We all belong to groups, try to please others, and take cues about how to behave by observing the actions of those around us. In fact, our desire to "fit in" or to identify with desirable individuals or groups is the primary motivation for many of our purchases and activities. We will often go to great lengths to please the members of a group whose acceptance we covet.[2] Carlo's biker group is an important part of his identity, and this membership influences many of his buying decisions. He has spent many thousands of dollars on parts and accessories since acquiring his identity as a RUB. He and his fellow riders are united by their consumption choices to the extent that total strangers feel an immediate bond with each other when they meet. The publisher of *American Iron*, an industry magazine, observed, "You don't buy a Harley because it's a superior bike; you buy a Harley to be a part of a family."[3]

Carlo doesn't model himself after just *any* biker. Only the people with whom he really identifies can exert that kind of influence on him. For example, his group doesn't have much to do with outlaw clubs, which primarily comprise blue-collar riders sporting Harley tattoos. The members of his group also have only polite contact with "Ma-and-Pa" bikers whose bikes are the epitome of comfort, featuring such niceties as radios, heated handgrips, and floorboards. Essentially, only the RUBs compose Carlo's *reference group*.

A **reference group** is "an actual or imaginary individual or group conceived of as having significant relevance upon an individual's evaluations, aspirations, or behavior."[4] Reference groups influence consumers in three ways. These influences—*informational*, *utilitarian*, and *value-expressive*—are described in Table 11–1 on page 312.

This chapter focuses on how other people, whether fellow bikers, co-workers, friends, family, or just casual acquaintances, influence our purchase decisions. It considers how our preferences are shaped by our group memberships, by our desire to please or be accepted by others, or by the actions of famous people whom we've never even met. Finally, it explores why some people are more influential than others in affecting consumers' product preferences and how marketers go about finding those people and enlisting their support in the persuasion process.

TABLE 11–1

THREE FORMS OF REFERENCE GROUP INFLUENCE

Informational Influence	The individual seeks information about various brands from an association of professionals or an independent group of experts.
	The individual seeks information from those who work with the product in a profession.
	The individual seeks brand-related knowledge and experience (such as how Brand A's performance compares with Brand B's) from those friends, neighbours, relatives, or work associates who have reliable information about the brands.
	The brand the individual selects is influenced by observing a seal of approval from an independent testing agency (such as Good Housekeeping).
	The individual's observation of what experts do (such as observing the type of car that police drive or the brand of television that repair people buy) influences his or her choice of a brand.
Utilitarian Influence	So that he or she satisfies the expectations of fellow work associates, the individual's decision to purchase a particular brand is influenced by their preferences.
	The individual's decision to purchase a particular brand is influenced by the preferences of people with whom he or she has social interaction.
	The individual's decision to purchase a particular brand is influenced by the preferences of family members.
	The desire to satisfy the expectations of others has an impact on the individual's brand choice.
Value-Expressive Influence	The individual feels that the purchase or use of a particular brand will enhance the image others have of him or her.
	The individual feels that those who purchase or use a particular brand possess the characteristics that he or she would like to have.
	The individual sometimes feels that it would be nice to be like the type of person that advertisements show using a particular brand.
	The individual feels that the people who purchase a particular brand are admired or respected by others.
	The individual feels that the purchase of a particular brand would help show others what he or she is or would like to be (such as an athlete, successful business person, good parent, etc.).

Source: Adapted from C. Whan Park and V. Parker Lessig, "Students and Housewives: Differences in Susceptibility to Reference Group Influence," *Journal of Consumer Research* 4 (September 1977): 102. Reprinted with permission of The University of Chicago Press.

Types of Reference Groups

Although two or more people are normally required to form a group, the term *reference group* is often used a bit more loosely to describe *any* external influence that provides social cues.[5] The referent may be a cultural figure and have an impact on many people, or it may be a person or group whose influence is confined to the consumer's immediate environment (e.g., Carlo's biker club). Reference groups that affect consumption can include parents, fellow motorcycle enthusiasts, the Liberal Party, the Toronto Raptors, or bands like the Barenaked Ladies.

Obviously, some groups and individuals exert a greater influence than others and for a broader range of consumption decisions. For example, our parents may play a pivotal role in forming our values related to many important issues, such as attitudes about marriage or where to go to university. This type of influence is **normative influence**; that is, the reference group helps to set and enforce fundamental standards of conduct. In contrast, a Harley-Davidson club might exert **comparative influence**, where decisions about specific brands or activities are affected.[6]

← Ownership of a Harley is not limited to men; women want to operate their own bikes rather than piggyback.
Courtesy of Harley-Davidson Canada.

FORMAL VERSUS INFORMAL GROUPS

A reference group can take the form of a large, formal organization that has a recognized structure, complete with a charter, regular meeting times, and officers. Or it can be small and informal, such as a group of friends or students living in a dormitory. Marketers tend to be more successful at influencing formal groups because they are more easily identifiable and accessible.

However, as a rule it is small, informal groups that exert a more powerful influence on individual consumers. These groups tend to be more involved in individuals' day-to-day lives and to be more important to them because the groups are high in normative influence. Larger, formal groups tend to be more product or activity specific and thus are high in comparative influence.

BRAND COMMUNITIES AND TRIBES

Before the popular Xbox game Halo 2 was released, the company put up a website to explain the storyline. But there was a catch: The story was written from the point of view of the Covenant (the aliens in the game who are preparing to attack Earth)—in *their* language. Within 48 hours, avid gamers around the world worked together by sharing information in gaming chat rooms to crack the code and translate the text. More than 1.5 million people pre-ordered the game before its release.[7]

Some marketing researchers are embracing a new perspective on reference groups as they identify groups built around shared allegiance to a product or activity. A **brand community** is a set of consumers who share a set of social relationships based upon usage or interest in a product. Unlike other kinds of communities, these members typically don't live near each other—except when they may meet for brief periods at organized events called *brandfests*, such as those sponsored by Jeep, Saturn, or Harley-Davidson. These brandfests help owners to "bond" with fellow enthusiasts and strengthen their identification with the product as well as with others who share their passion.

Researchers find that people who participate in these events feel more positive about the products as a result, and this enhances brand loyalty. They are more forgiving than others of product failures or lapses in service quality and less likely to switch brands even if they learn that competing products are as good or better. Furthermore, these community members become emotionally involved in the company's welfare, and they often serve as brand missionaries by carrying its marketing message to others.[8]

The notion of a **consumer tribe** is similar, because this refers to a group of people who share a lifestyle and who can identify with each other because of a shared allegiance to an activity or a product. Although these tribes are often unstable and short-lived, at least for a time members identify with others through shared emotions, moral beliefs, styles of life, and of course the products they jointly consume as part of their tribal affiliation. The challenge of **tribal marketing** is to link one's product to the needs of a group as a whole. Many tribes devoted to activities like skateboarding or basketball are youth-oriented. We'll talk more about these in Chapter 15.[9]

MEMBERSHIP VERSUS ASPIRATIONAL REFERENCE GROUPS

Although some reference groups consist of people the consumer actually knows, others comprise people the consumer can either identify with or admire. Not surprisingly, many marketing efforts that specifically adopt a reference-group appeal concentrate on highly visible, widely admired figures (such as well-known athletes or performers). **Aspirational reference groups** comprise idealized figures, such as successful business people, athletes, or performers. One study that included business students who aspired to the "executive" role found a strong relationship between products the students associated with their *ideal selves* (see Chapter 5) and those products they assumed would be owned or used by executives.[10]

Since people tend to compare themselves with others who are similar, they often are swayed by knowing how people like them conduct their lives. For this reason many promotional strategies include "ordinary" people whose consumption activities provide informational social influence.

The likelihood that people will become part of a consumer's identificational reference group is affected by several factors, including the following:

- *Propinquity:* As physical distance between people decreases and opportunities for interaction increase, relationships are more likely to form. Physical nearness is called *propinquity.* An early study on friendship patterns in a housing complex showed this factor's strong effects: Residents were much more likely to be friends with the people next door than with those who lived only two doors away. And people who lived next to a staircase had more friends than those at the ends of a hall (presumably they were more likely to "bump into" people using the stairs).[11] Physical structure has a lot to do with whom we get to know and how popular we are.

- *Mere exposure:* We come to like persons or things simply as a result of seeing them more often, which is known as the *mere exposure phenomenon.*[12] Greater frequency of contact, even if unintentional, may help to determine a person's set of local referents. The same effect holds when evaluating works of art or political candidates.[13]

- *Group cohesiveness:* The degree to which members of a group are attracted to each other and value their group membership is called *cohesiveness.* As the

→ Dewar's has successfully used non-celebrities as endorsers in its "Profiles" campaign, which is now being adapted for other countries, as this Spanish ad illustrates.
Courtesy of Schenley Industries.

value of the group to the individual increases, so too does the likelihood that the group will guide consumption decisions. Smaller groups tend to be more cohesive, because it is more difficult to relate to larger groups of people. By the same token, groups often try to restrict membership to a select few, which increases the value of membership to those who are admitted. Exclusivity of membership is a benefit often touted by credit-card companies, book clubs, and so on, even though the actual membership base might be fairly large.

POSITIVE VERSUS NEGATIVE REFERENCE GROUPS

Reference groups may exert either a positive or a negative influence on consumption behaviours. In most cases, consumers model their behaviour to be consistent with what they think the group expects of them. In some cases, though, a consumer may try to distance him or herself from other people or groups that function as *avoidance groups.* He or she may carefully study the dress or mannerisms of a disliked group (e.g., "nerds," "druggies," or "preppies") and scrupulously avoid buying anything that might identify him or her with that group. Rebellious adolescents often resent parental influence and may deliberately do the opposite of what their parents would like as a way of making a statement about their independence.

The motivation to distance ourselves from a negative reference group can be as or more powerful than the desire to please a positive group.[14] That's why advertisements occasionally show an undesirable person using a competitor's product to subtly make the point that the target of the message can avoid winding up like *that* kind person by staying away from that product. As a once-popular book reminded us, "Real men *don't* eat quiche!"[15] Today, others have adapted this avoidance group appeal to point out the ways we define ourselves by not consuming some products or services. For example, a T-shirt for sale on a computer-oriented website proudly proclaims, "Real Men Don't Click Help."

When Reference Groups Are Important

Reference group influences are not equally powerful for all types of products and consumption activities. For example, products that are not very complex, that are low in perceived risk, and that can be tried prior to purchase are less susceptible to personal influence.[16] In addition, the specific impact of reference groups may vary. At times they may determine the use of certain products rather than others (e.g., owning or not owning a computer, or eating junk food versus health food), while at other times they may have specific effects on brand decisions within a product category (wearing Levi's jeans versus Diesel jeans, or drinking Molson rather than Labatt).

Two dimensions that influence the degree to which reference groups are important are whether the purchase is to be consumed publicly or privately and whether it is a luxury or a necessity. As a rule, reference group effects are more robust for purchases that are (1) luxuries (such as sailboats) rather than necessities, since products purchased with discretionary income are subject to individual tastes and preferences, and necessities do not offer this range of choice; and (2) items that are socially conspicuous or visible to others (like living-room furniture or clothing), since consumers are not swayed as much by the opinions of others if their purchases will never be observed by anyone but themselves.[17] The relative effects of reference group influences on some specific product classes are shown in Figure 11–1.

The Power of Reference Groups

Why are reference groups so persuasive? The answer lies in the potential power they wield over us.

Social power refers to "the capacity to alter the actions of others."[18] To the degree that you are able to make someone else do something, whether he or she does it willingly or not, you have power over that person. The following classification

FIGURE 11–1 RELATIVE REFERENCE GROUP INFLUENCE ON PURCHASE DECISIONS

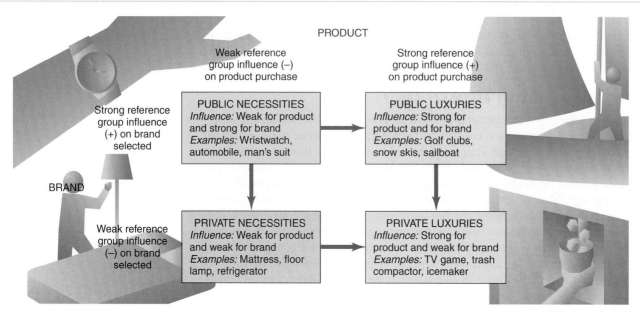

Adapted from William O. Bearden and Michael J. Etzel, "Reference Group Influence on Product and Brand Purchase Decisions," *Journal of Consumer Research* (September 1982): 185. Reprinted with permission by The University of Chicago Press.

of *power bases* can help us to distinguish among the reasons a person can exert power over another, the degree to which the influence is allowed voluntarily, and whether this influence will continue to have an effect in the absence of the power source.[19]

REFERENT POWER

If a person admires the qualities of an individual or a group, he or she will try to imitate those qualities by copying the referent's behaviours (e.g., choice of clothing, cars, and leisure activities) as a guide to forming consumption preferences, just as Carlo's preferences are affected by his fellow bikers. Prominent people in all walks of life can affect people's consumption behaviours by virtue of product endorsements. Referent power is important to many marketing strategies because consumers voluntarily change behaviours to please or identify with a referent.

INFORMATION POWER

A person can have information power simply because he or she knows something others would like to know. Editors of trade publications such as *Wish* often possess power because of their ability to compile and disseminate information that can make or break individual designers or companies. People with information power are able to influence consumer opinion by virtue of their (assumed) access to the "truth."

LEGITIMATE POWER

Sometimes people are granted power by virtue of social agreements, such as that given to police officers and professors. The legitimate power conferred by a uniform is recognized in many consumer contexts, including teaching hospitals, where medical students don white coats to enhance their aura of authority with patients.[20] This form of power may be "borrowed" by marketers to influence consumers. For example, an ad featuring a model wearing a white doctor's coat can add an aura of legitimacy or authority to the presentation of the product.

EXPERT POWER

Expert power is derived from possessing a specific knowledge or skill. Consumers are often influenced by experts who are assumed to be able to evaluate products in an objective, informed way. The power of celebrity experts can be measured by their visibility on talk shows, lecture circuits, and so on. Prominent economists can receive between $5000 and $20 000 for a speech, depending on their level of perceived expertise. One analysis of economist superstars noted the following requirements for success:[21]

- affiliation with an elite university, think-tank, or investment house
- authorship of a slim, easy-to-read book that yields a vision of the future

David Foot, author of *Boom, Bust & Echo*, has these traits and is currently racking up the consulting dollars, in addition to his university salary and book royalties. The need to provide evidence of expert power creates other marketing opportunities, ranging from the provision of certificates and diplomas to coaching for licensing exams.

REWARD POWER

When a person or group has the means to provide positive reinforcement (see Chapter 3), that entity will have power over a consumer to the extent that this reinforcement is valued or desired. The reward may be tangible, as occurs when an employee is given a raise. Or the reward may be intangible: Social approval or acceptance is often what is exchanged in return for moulding one's behaviour to a group or buying the products expected of group members. The Everlast ad shown below humorously acknowledges others' power to reward us for "correct" product choices.

COERCIVE POWER

Although coercive power is often effective in the short term, it does not tend to produce permanent attitudinal or behavioural change. Surveillance of some sort is usually required to make people do something they do not wish to do. Fortunately, coercive power is rarely employed in marketing situations. However, elements of this power base are evident in fear appeals, in intimidation in personal selling, and in some campaigns that emphasize the negative consequences that might occur if people do not use a product.

← This ad for Everlast (*www.everlast.com*) pokes fun at the power of peer groups to reward people for wearing the right clothes.
Courtesy of Goldsmith/Jeffrey, Inc., N.Y.

CONFORMITY

The early bohemians who lived in Paris around 1830 made a point of behaving, well, differently from others. One flamboyant figure of the time became famous for walking a lobster on a leash through the gardens of the Royal Palace. His friends drank wine from human skulls, cut their beards in strange shapes, and slept in tents on the floors of their garrets.[22]

Although in every age there certainly are those who "march to their own drummer," most people tend to follow society's expectations regarding how they should act and look (with a little improvisation here and there, of course).

Conformity refers to a change in beliefs or actions as a reaction to real or imagined group pressure. In order for a society to function, its members develop **norms**, or informal rules, that govern behaviour. If such a system of agreements did not evolve, chaos would result. Imagine the confusion if a simple norm such as stopping for a red traffic light did not exist. Although norms change slowly over time, there is general agreement within a society about which ones should be obeyed, and we adjust our way of thinking to conform to these norms.

We conform in many small ways every day—even though we don't always realize it. Unspoken rules govern many aspects of consumption. In addition to norms regarding appropriate use of clothing and other personal items, we conform to rules that include gift-giving (we expect birthday presents from loved ones and get upset if they do not materialize), gender roles (men often are expected to pick up the check on a first date), and personal hygiene (we are expected to shower regularly to avoid offending others).

Factors Influencing Likelihood of Conformity

Conformity is not an automatic process, and many factors contribute to the likelihood that consumers will pattern their behaviour after others.[23] Among the factors that affect the likelihood of conformity are the following:

- *Cultural pressures:* Different cultures encourage conformity to a greater or lesser degree. Japanese society is characterized by the dominance of collective well-being and group loyalty over individuals' needs.

- *Fear of deviance*: The individual may have reason to believe that the group will apply *sanctions* to punish behaviour that differs from the group's. It is not unusual to observe adolescents shunning a peer who is "different," or a corporation passing over a person for promotion because he or she is not a "team player."

- *Commitment*: The more a person is dedicated to a group and values membership in it, the more motivated he or she will be to follow the dictates of the group. Rock groupies and followers of television evangelists may do anything that is asked of them, and terrorists are willing to die for the good of their causes. According to the *principle of least interest*, the person or group that is least committed to staying in a relationship has the most power, because that party won't be susceptible to threatened rejection.[24]

- *Group unanimity, size, and expertise*: As groups gain in power, compliance increases. It is often harder to resist the demands of a large number of people than those of just a few, and this difficulty is compounded when the group members are perceived as knowing what they are talking about.

- *Susceptibility to interpersonal influence:* This trait refers to an individual's need to identify or to enhance his or her image in the opinion of significant others. This enhancement process often is accompanied by the acquisition of products the person believes will impress his or her audience and by the tendency to learn about products by observing how others use them.[25] Consumers who

are low on this trait have been called *role-relaxed*; they tend to be older and affluent and to have high self-confidence. Based on research identifying role-relaxed consumers, Subaru created a communications strategy to reach these people. In one commercial a man is heard saying, "I want a car … Don't tell me about wood panelling, about winning the respect of my neighbours. They're my neighbours. They're not my heroes…."

Social Comparison

Informational social influence implies that sometimes we look to the behaviour of others to provide a yardstick about reality. **Social comparison theory** occurs as a way to increase the stability of one's self-evaluation, especially when physical evidence is unavailable.[26] Social comparison even applies to choices for which there is no objectively correct answer. Such stylistic decisions as tastes in music and art are assumed to be a matter of individual choice, yet people often believe that some types are "better" or more "correct" than others.[27] If you have ever been responsible for choosing the music to play at a party, you can probably appreciate the social pressure involved in choosing the right "mix."

Although people often like to compare their judgments and actions with those of others, they tend to be selective about precisely whom they will use as benchmarks. Similarity between the consumer and others used for social comparison boosts confidence that the information is accurate and relevant (though we may find it more threatening to be outperformed by someone similar to ourselves).[28] We tend to value the views of obviously dissimilar others only when we are reasonably certain of our own.[29]

In general, people tend to choose a *co-oriented peer,* or a person of equivalent standing, when undergoing social comparison. For example, a study of adult cosmetics users found that women were more likely to seek information about product choices from similar friends in order to reduce uncertainty and to trust the judgments of similar others.[30] The same effects have been found for evaluations of products as diverse as men's suits and coffee.[31]

TACTICAL REQUESTS

How do we increase the likelihood that a person will conform to our wishes? The way a request for compliance is phrased or structured can make a difference. One well-known sales tactic (introduced in Chapter 7) is known as the *foot-in-the-door technique,* wherein the consumer is first asked a small request and then is hit up for something bigger.[32] This term is adapted from door-to-door selling. Experienced salespeople know that they are much more likely to make a sale if they first convince a customer to let them in the house to deliver a sales pitch. Once the person has agreed to this small request, it is more difficult to refuse a larger one, since the consumer has legitimized the salesperson's presence by entering into a dialogue. He or she is no longer a threatening stranger at the door.

Other variations on this strategy include the *low-ball technique,* in which a person is asked for a small favour and is informed, after agreeing to it, that it will be very costly; or the *door-in-the-face technique,* wherein a person is first asked to do something extreme (a request that is usually refused) and then is asked to do something smaller. People tend to go along with the smaller request, possibly because they feel guilty about denying the larger one.[33]

GROUP EFFECTS ON INDIVIDUAL BEHAVIOUR

With more people in a group, it becomes less likely that any one member will be singled out for attention. People in larger groups or those in situations wherein they are unlikely to be identified tend to focus less attention on themselves, so normal restraints on behaviour are reduced. You may have observed that people sometimes behave more wildly at costume parties or on Halloween night than they do normally. This phenomenon is known as **deindividuation**, in which individual identities get submerged within a group.

There is some evidence that decisions made by groups differ from those that would be made by each individual. In many cases group members show a greater willingness to consider riskier alternatives following group discussion than they would if each member made his or her own decision with no discussion. This change is known as the **risky shift**.[34]

Several explanations have been advanced to explain this increased riskiness. One possibility is that, as more people are involved in a decision, each individual is less accountable for the outcome, so *diffusion of responsibility* occurs.[35] Another explanation is termed the *value hypothesis.* In this case, riskiness is a culturally valued characteristic, and social pressures operate on individuals to conform to attributes valued by society.[36]

Evidence for the risky shift is mixed. A more general effect appears to be that group discussion tends to increase **decision polarization**. Whichever direction the group members were leaning in before discussion began—toward a risky choice or a conservative one—becomes even more extreme after discussion. Group discussions regarding product purchases tend to create a risky shift for low-risk items, but they yield even more conservative group decisions for high-risk products.[37]

Even shopping behaviour changes when people do it in groups. For example, people who shop with at least one other person tend to make more unplanned purchases, to buy more, and cover more areas of a store, than those who go alone.[38] These effects are due to both normative and informational social influence. Group members may be convinced to buy something to gain the approval of the others, or they may simply be exposed to more products and stores by pooling information with the group. For these reasons retailers would be well advised to encourage group shopping activities.

Social loafing refers to the fact that people do not devote as much effort to a task when their contribution is part of a larger group effort.[39] Wait staff are painfully aware of social loafing: People who eat in groups tend to tip less per person than those who eat alone.[40] For this reason, many restaurants automatically tack on a fixed gratuity for groups of six or more.

Home shopping parties, as epitomized by the Tupperware party, capitalize on group pressures to boost sales.[41] A company representative makes a sales presentation to a group of people who have gathered in the home of a friend or acquaintance. This format is effective because of informational social influence:

Participants model the behaviour of others who can provide them with information about how to use certain products, especially because the home party is likely to be attended by a relatively homogenous group (e.g., neighbourhood homemakers) that serves as a valuable benchmark. Normative social influence also operates because actions are publicly observed. Pressures to conform may be particularly intense and may escalate as more and more group members begin to "cave in" (this process is sometimes termed the *bandwagon effect*).

In addition, deindividuation and/or the risky shift may be activated: As consumers get caught up in the group, they may find themselves willing to try new products they would not normally consider. These same dynamics underlie the latest wrinkle on the Tupperware home selling technique: the Botox party. The craze for Botox injections that paralyze facial nerves to reduce wrinkles (for three to six months anyway) is being fuelled by gatherings where dermatologists or plastic surgeons redefine the definition of house calls. For patients, mixing cocktail hour with cosmetic injections takes some of the anxiety out of the procedure. Egged on by the others at the party, as many as 10 patients can be dewrinkled in an hour. An advertising executive who worked on the Botox marketing strategy explained that the appeal of the membership reference group is more effective than the traditional route of using a celebrity spokesperson to tout the injections in advertising: "We think it's more persuasive to think of your next-door neighbour using it."[42] The only hitch is that after you get the injections, your face is so rigid that your friends can't tell whether you're smiling.

Resisting Conformity

Many people pride themselves on their independence, unique style, or ability to resist the best efforts of salespeople and advertisers to sell products to them.[43] Indeed, individuality should be encouraged by the marketing system: Innovation creates change and demand for new products and styles. It is important to distinguish between *independence* and *anticonformity,* in which defiance of the group is the actual object of behaviour.[44] Some people will go out of their way *not* to buy whatever happens to be in at the moment. Indeed, they may spend a lot of time and

← This ad invites the would-be buyer to stand out and be unique by buying this age-old whisky, rather than trendier liquors and new market entrants.
Courtesy of The Glenlivit.

→ This ad for Ford audio systems targets non-conformists by depicting a "loner" who prefers wide open spaces to groups of people.
Courtesy of Ford Motor Company.

effort to ensure that they will not be caught in style. This behaviour is a bit of a paradox, since in order to be vigilant about not doing what is expected, one must always be aware of what is expected. In contrast, truly independent people are oblivious to what is expected; like the "loner" in the Ford audio systems ad above, they "march to their own drummers."

People have a deep-seated need to preserve freedom of choice. When they are threatened with a loss of this freedom, they try to overcome this loss. This negative emotional state is termed **reactance**.[45] For example, efforts to censor books, television shows, or rock music because some people find the content objectionable may result in an *increased* desire for these products by the public.[46] Similarly, extremely overbearing promotions that tell consumers they must or should use a product may wind up losing more customers in the long run—even those who were already loyal to the advertised brand!

WORD-OF-MOUTH COMMUNICATION

A 200-year-old breath mint called Altoids is all the rage these days, even though the manufacturer did virtually no advertising for most of the brand's history. How did this happen? The revival began when the mint began to attract a devoted following among smokers and coffee drinkers who hung out in the blossoming Seattle club scene during the 1980s. Until 1993, when manufacturer Callard & Bowser was bought by Kraft (***www.kraft.com***), the product was bought only by those "in the know." At that point, the brand's marketing manager persuaded this bigger company to hire advertising agency Leo Burnett to develop a modest promotional effort. The agency decided to publicize the candy by using subway posters sporting retro imagery and other "low-tech" media to avoid making the product seem mainstream; that would turn off the original audience.[47] As the product was shared among young people, its popularity mushroomed.

As the Altoids success story illustrates, a lot of product information is conveyed by individuals to other individuals on an informal basis. **Word-of-mouth communication (WOM)** is product information transmitted by individuals to individuals.

Because we get the word from people we know, WOM tends to be more reliable and trustworthy than recommendations we get through more formal marketing channels. And, unlike advertising, WOM often is backed up by social pressure to conform with these recommendations.[48] Ironically, despite all of the money pumped into creating lavish advertisements, WOM is far more powerful: It's estimated to influence two-thirds of all consumer goods sales.[49]

If you think carefully about the content of your own conversations in the course of a normal day, you will probably agree that much of what you discuss with friends, family members, or co-workers is product related. Whether you compliment someone on her dress and ask her where she bought it, recommend a new restaurant to a friend, or complain to your neighbour about the shoddy treatment you got at the bank, you are engaging in word-of-mouth communication. Recall, for example, that many of Carlo's biker purchases are directly initiated by comments and suggestions from his fellow RUBs.

Marketers have been aware of the power of WOM for many years, but recently they've been more aggressive about trying to promote and control it instead of sitting back and hoping people will like their products enough to talk about them.

Communications theorists began in the 1950s to challenge the assumption that advertising is the primary determinant of purchases. It is now generally accepted that advertising is more effective at reinforcing existing product preferences than at creating new ones.[50] Studies in both industrial and consumer-purchase settings underscore the idea that although information from impersonal sources is important for creating brand awareness, word of mouth is relied upon in the later stages of evaluation and adoption.[51] The more positive information a consumer gets about a product from peers, the more likely it is that he or she will adopt the product.[52] The influence of others' opinions is at times even more powerful than one's own perceptions. In one study of furniture choices, consumers' estimates of how much their friends would like the furniture were better predictors of purchase than were their own evaluations of it.[53]

Reality Check ✓

The strategy of *viral marketing* gets customers to sell a product to other customers on behalf of the company. That often means convincing your friends to climb on the bandwagon, and sometimes you get a cut if they wind up buying something.[54] Some might argue that means you're selling out your friends (or at least selling to your friends) in exchange for a piece of the action. Others might say you're just sharing the wealth with those you care about. Have you been involved in viral marketing by passing along names of your friends or sending them to a website such as *www.hotmail.com*? If so, what happened? How do you feel about this practice?

> I can recall recommending website services such as hotmail and MSN messenger among others. I've also spread the word about food products, clothing, and even car models. I believe that it is most people's nature to recommend a good or service that has proven to be satisfactory and useful for that person.

Even though I've never done this for profit, I think I would do it if what I'm "selling" really stands for what is being promoted. Otherwise, I would consider it almost a non-ethical practice, or at least uncomfortable when it comes to mixing friends and business.

Constanza Montes Larranaga,
Universidad de Chile, Chile

> Honestly, I think it is a huge hassle. I don't think it is a bad idea from the company's standpoint, but I don't know of many people who actually enjoy participating in this process.

Fant Walker, University of Mississippi, USA

> The one time I intentionally participated in viral marketing was through *www.physique.com*. Their hair care products are ones I particularly like. However, they are pretty expensive. Their website offers a coupon good for one free, full-sized product if you send an email to seven friends, recommending the product. After you enter their addresses, your name is inserted in what appears to be a personal message raving about the product's benefits. Were my friends gullible and easily duped people, perhaps I would have felt bad. However, knowing my friends delete most emails before they even read them . . . I was not concerned.

Concetta Rini, The College of William and Mary, USA

The Tangled Web

In addition, consumers may find their own reasons to push a brand that takes the manufacturer by surprise: That's what happened in the United States with Mountain Dew, whose popularity among younger consumers can be traced to the "buzz" about the soda's high caffeine content. As an advertising executive explained, "The caffeine thing was not in any of Mountain Dew's television ads. This drink is hot by word-of-mouth."[55] Mountain Dew sold in Canada, however, does not contain any caffeine.

FACTORS ENCOURAGING WOM

WOM is especially powerful when the consumer is relatively unfamiliar with the product category. Such a situation would be expected in the case of new products (e.g., medications to prevent hair loss) or those that are technologically complex (e.g., CD players). As one example, the strongest predictor of a person's intention to buy a residential solar water-heating system was found to be the number of solar-heating users the person knows.[56]

Product-related conversations can be motivated by a number of factors:[57]

- A person might be highly involved with a type of product or activity and take pleasure in talking about it. Computer hackers, avid birdwatchers, and "fashion plates" seem to share the ability to steer conversations toward their particular interests.

- A person might be knowledgeable about a product and use conversations as a way to let others know it. Thus, word-of-mouth communication sometimes enhances the ego of the individual who wants to impress others with his or her expertise.

- A person might initiate such a discussion out of a genuine concern for someone else. We often are motivated to ensure that people we care about buy what is good for them, do not waste their money, and so on.

Negative WOM

Word of mouth is a two-edged sword that can cut both ways for marketers. Informal discussions among consumers can make or break a product or store. And **negative word of mouth** is weighted *more* heavily by consumers than are positive comments.

According to one study, 90 percent of unhappy customers will not do business with a company again. Each of these people is likely to share a grievance with at least nine other people, and 13 percent of these disgruntled customers will go on to tell more than 30 people of their negative experience.[58] Especially when making a decision about trying a product innovation, the consumer is more likely to pay attention to negative information than positive information and to relate news of this experience to others.[59] Negative WOM has been shown to reduce the credibility of a firm's advertising and to influence consumers' attitudes toward a product as well as their intention to buy it.[60]

Negative WOM is even easier to spread online. Many dissatisfied customers and disgruntled former employees have been "inspired" to create websites just to share their tales of woe with others. For example, a website for people to complain about the Dunkin' Donuts chain got to be so popular the company bought it in order to control the bad press it was getting. It grew from a complaint of the original owner that he could not get skim milk for his coffee.[61]

RUMOURS: DISTORTION IN THE WORD-OF-MOUTH PROCESS

In the 1930s "professional rumour mongers" were hired to organize word-of-mouth campaigns to promote clients' products and criticize those of competitors.[62] More recently, Bio Business International, a small Canadian company that markets 100 percent cotton nonchlorine-bleached tampons under the name Terra Femme, encouraged women to spread a message that tampons made by its American competitors contain dioxin. There is very little evidence to support the claim that these products are dangerous, but as a result of this rumour, Procter & Gamble received thousands of complaints about its feminine hygiene products.[64] A rumour, even if it has no basis in fact, can be a very dangerous thing. As information is transmitted among consumers, it tends to change. The resulting message usually does not at all resemble the original.

Social scientists who study rumours have examined the process by which information gets distorted. The British psychologist Frederic Bartlett used the method of *serial reproduction* to examine this phenomenon. As in the game of "Telephone," a subject is asked to reproduce a stimulus, such as a drawing or a story. Another subject is given this reproduction and asked to copy that, and so on. This technique is shown in Figure 11–2. Bartlett found that distortions almost inevitably follow a pattern. They tend to change from ambiguous forms to more conventional ones as subjects try to make them consistent with pre-existing schemas. This process, known as *assimilation,* is characterized by *levelling,* wherein details are omitted to simplify the structure, or *sharpening,* wherein prominent details are accentuated.

Cutting-Edge WOM Strategies

As marketers increasingly recognize the power of WOM to make or break a new product, they are coming up with new ways to get consumers to help them sell. Let's review three successful strategies.

VIRTUAL COMMUNITIES

In ancient times (that is, before the web was widely accessible), most membership reference groups consisted of people who had face-to-face contact. Now it's possible to

Original Drawing

FIGURE 11–2

THE TRANSMISSION OF MISINFORMATION

Source: Kenneth J. Gergen and Mary Gergen, *Social Psychology* (New York: Harcourt Brace Jovanovich, 1981), p. 365, Fig. 10–3; adapted from F.C. Bartlett, *Remembering* (Cambridge: Cambridge University Press, 1932).

share interests with people whom you've never met—and probably never will. Consider the case of Widespread Panic. The band has never had a music video on MTV or cracked the Billboard Top 200, but it's one of the top 40 touring bands in the U.S. How did it get to be so successful? Simple—the group built a virtual community of fans and opened itself up to them. It enlisted listeners to help promote the group in exchange for free tickets and backstage passes. Then it went virtual: The band lets fans send messages to its recording studio, and hard-core followers can find out vital information like what band members ate for lunch via regular updates on their website.[65]

A **virtual community of consumption** is a collection of people whose online interactions are based upon shared enthusiasm for and knowledge of a specific consumption activity. These anonymous groups grow up around an incredibly diverse set of interests—everything from Barbie dolls to fine wine. However, members remain anonymous because they only interact with each other in cyberspace. Virtual communities come in many different forms:[66]

- *Multi-user dungeons (MUD):* Originally, these were environments where players of fantasy games met. Now they refer to any computer-generated environment where people socially interact through the structured format of role and game playing. Online gaming is catching on in a big way: Sony Online Entertainment's games website, The Station (***www.station.com***), has more than 12 million registered users, while Microsoft's Gaming Zone (***www.zone. com***) boasts a membership of 29 million.[67]

- *Rooms, rings, and lists:* These include internet relay chat (IRC), otherwise known as *chat rooms. Rings* are organizations of related home pages, and *lists* are groups of people on a single mailing list who share information.

- *Boards:* These are online communities organized around interest-specific electronic bulletin boards. Active members read and post messages sorted by date and subject. There are boards devoted to musical groups, movies, wine, cigars, cars, comic strips, and even fast-food restaurants.

Net Profit +

The emergence of gaming as an online, shared experience opens new vistas to marketers. Consider this: Toyota's digital racing game called "Tundra Madness" attracts 8000 consumers who spend an average of eight minutes on the site daily. The company's research showed that the campaign raised brand awareness by 28 percent and intent to purchase by 5 percent. Heartened by the success of this experiment, Toyota launched more games to promote other models. To target first-time car buyers, the company created the "Matrix Video Mixer" game, which it promoted through sites like ***www.rollingstone.com***, ***www.getmusic.com***, and ***www.launch.com***. The effort was tied to a Gravity Games sponsorship and an in-theatre commercial campaign. About three in ten registered users forwarded videos created through the game to their friends via email; 65 percent of those emails were opened.[68]

The secret behind the appeal of this format is the huge chunks of time people spend immersed in these games. The average online player logs 17 hours per week, and firms like Sony, Microsoft, and Sega are building their own virtual worlds to get a piece of the action. As one game company executive put it, "This is not a genre of game but a break-through new medium. It provides a completely new social, collaborative shared experience. We're basically in the Internet community business."[69]

Sony Online's "EverQuest" is among the most successful of the new breed of Massively Multiplayer Online Role-Player Games that allow people to live shadow lives. More than 430 000 registered players worldwide belong to "guilds" in a never-ending journey to slay monsters and earn points. "EverQuest" combines the stunning graphics of advanced gaming with the social scene of a chat room. As with "The Sims," a player can create a character as a virtual alter ego, which may be a wise elf or a backstabbing rogue. Some players sell powerful characters on eBay for $1000 or more.

The game is also the centre of an active social scene. Players can "travel" in groups of six. In many cases they settle into a regular group and spend two to three hours each night online with the same people.[70] They may also mingle offline; Fan Faires attract several thousand people who often dress as their game characters.[71] The average "EverQuest" subscriber spends about 20 hours a week living in this virtual world. Some view it as a possible addiction; EverCrack is a popular nickname for the game. One factor that makes it hard to kick the habit may be peer pressure: logging off may hurt a guild's chances of advancing in the game, even if just one player logs off.[72]

- *Blogs:* The newest and fastest growing form of online community is the **weblog**, or **blog**. These online personal journals are building an avid following among internet users who like to dash off a few random thoughts, post them on a website, and read similar musings by others. Although these sites are similar to webpages offered by *GeoCities.com* and other free services, they employ a different technology that lets people upload a few sentences without going through the process of updating a website built with conventional homepage software. For example, one site (*www.livejournal.com*) has signed up 690 000 registered users in four years and is adding another 1100 every day. Bloggers can fire off thoughts on a whim, click a button, and quickly have them appear on a site. Weblogs frequently look like online diaries, with brief musings about the days' events and perhaps a link or two of interest. A new blogger puts in his or her two cents every 40 seconds, so this burgeoning **blogosphere** (the name given to the universe of active weblogs) is a force to be reckoned with.

How do people get drawn into consumption communities? Internet users tend to progress from asocial information gathering ("lurkers" are surfers who like to watch but don't participate) to increasingly affiliative social activities. At first they will merely browse the site, but later they may well be drawn into active participation.

The intensity of identification with a virtual community depends on two factors. The first is that the more central the activity is to a person's self-concept, the more likely he or she will be to pursue an active membership in a community. The second is that the intensity of the social relationships the person forms with other members of the virtual community helps to determine the extent of his or her involvement. As Figure 11–3 shows, combining these two factors creates four distinct member types.

Devotees and insiders are the most important targets for marketers who wish to leverage communities for promotional purposes because they are the heavy users of virtual communities. And by reinforcing usage, the community may upgrade tourists and minglers to insiders and devotees.[73] But marketers have only scratched the surface of this intriguing new virtual world.

GUERRILLA MARKETING

Lyor Cohen, former CEO of the Def Jam hip hop label and now with Warner Music Group, built his business using street marketing tactics. To promote hip hop albums, Def Jam and other labels start building a buzz months before a release, leaking advance copies to deejays who put together "mix tapes" to sell on the street. If the kids seem to like a song, *street teams* then push it to club deejays. As the official release date nears, these groups of fans start slapping up posters around the inner city. They plaster telephone poles, sides of buildings, and car windshields with promotions announcing the release of new albums.[74]

These streetwise strategies started in the mid 1970s, when pioneering deejays like Kool DJ Herc and Afrika Bambaataa promoted their parties through graffiti-style flyers. This type of grassroots effort epitomizes **guerrilla marketing**, promotional strategies that use unconventional locations and intensive word-of-mouth

---

1. *Tourists* lack strong social ties to the group and maintain only a passing interest in the activity. 2. *Minglers* maintain strong social ties, but are not very interested in the central consumption activity. 3. *Devotees* express strong interest in the activity, but have few social attachments to the group. 4. *Insiders* exhibit both strong social ties and strong interest in the activity.	**FIGURE 11–3** VIRTUAL COMMUNITIES

The Tangled Web

Virtual consumption communities hold great promise, but there is also great potential for abuse if members can't trust that other visitors are behaving ethically. Many hard-core community members are sensitive to interference from companies and react negatively when they suspect that another member may in fact be a shill of a marketer who wants to influence evaluations of products on the site. One of the reasons for the success of the eBay auction site is that buyers rate the quality and trustworthiness of sellers, so potential bidders can get a pretty good idea of who they're dealing with before participating. In some cases even this system has fallen flat as unscrupulous people find ways to violate the bond of trust.

More generally, e-commerce sites know that consumers give more weight to the opinions of real people, so they are finding ways to let these opinions be included on their websites. This trend of posting customer reviews was started by **Amazon.com** way back in 1995. Now sellers of computers and other high-priced products post customer reviews.[82] A great idea—but in a highly publicized lawsuit, Amazon was accused of charging publishers to post positive reviews on the site. The company had to offer refunds for all books it recommended, and now Amazon tells customers when a publisher has paid for a prominent display on its site.[83] Similarly, some online investment forums have had to hire patrols to keep an eye out for stock promoters who have been hired by companies to create a buzz about their stocks.

campaigns to push products. As Ice Cube observed, "Even though I'm an established artist, I still like to leak my music to a kid on the street and let him duplicate it for his homies before it hits radio."[75]

Today, big companies are buying into guerrilla marketing strategies big time, as the following examples show:

- Procter & Gamble started a business unit called Tremor to spread the word about its products among young people. Tremor has recruited almost 300 000 kids between the ages of 13 and 19 to deliver endorsements in school cafeterias, at sleepovers, and by cell phone and email. These kids are being tapped to talk up just about everything, from movies and music (such as new releases by artists like Lenny Kravitz and Coldplay) to milk and motor oil—and they do it for free. Tremor looks for kids with a wide social circle and a gift of the gab. To register, kids fill out a questionnaire that asks them, among other things, to report how many friends, family members, and acquaintances they communicate with every day. ("Tremorites" have an average of 170 names on their buddy lists; a typical teen has 30). P&G rewards the kids for their help by sending them exclusive music mixes and other trinkets, like shampoo and cheap watches.[76]

- A growing number of marketers are experimenting with using human beings as *brand ambassadors* who pop up in eye-catching outfits to announce a new brand or service at places where the brand or service is consumed. Dewar's is training a squad of men in the Scotch brand's lore and traditions so they can play the role of the "Dewar Highlander," roaming bars and restaurants and teaching patrons and bartenders how to enjoy whisky and mix cocktails with Dewar's.[77]

VIRAL MARKETING

Many students are big fans of Hotmail, a free email service. But there's no such thing as a free lunch: Hotmail inserts a small ad on every message sent, making each user a salesperson. The company had five million subscribers in its first year and continues to grow exponentially.[78] **Viral marketing** refers to the strategy of getting customers to sell a product on behalf of the company that creates it. This approach is particularly well-suited to the web, since emails circulate so easily. According to a study by Jupiter Communications, only 24 percent of consumers say they learn about new websites in magazine or newspaper ads. Instead, they rely on friends and family for new site recommendations, so viral marketing is their main source of information about new sites. The chief executive of *www.gazooba.com*, a company that creates viral marketing promotions, observed that "the return mail address of a friend is a brand that you trust."[79] Here are some other examples of viral marketing at work:

- Viral marketing for motor oil? Pretty slick. WD-40 quadrupled visitors to its fan club's website by offering 1000 AM/FM radios in the shape of oil cans to individuals who signed up 10 other members.[80]

- To promote its new Pocket Paks oral breath care strips, Listerine created a "Germinator" game on the brand's website. Players are encouraged to email their scores to friends to goad them into playing as well.[81]

Social Networking

Social networking websites let members post information about themselves and make contact with others who share similar interests and opinions, or with those who want to make business contacts. People who register on sites like MySpace and Friendster can set up a homepage with photos, a profile, and links to others in their social networks. Users can browse for friends, dates, partners for activities, and contacts of all kinds, and can invite them to join the users' personal networks as "friends." These sites range from the fun to the serious:

- Facebook (***www.facebook.com***) was started by five Harvard students and is now the most popular way to either network or waste time for a million college students at around 300 colleges in the United States. Students sign up from their campus email addresses (only school networks are accepted) and are able to visit the listing of everyone who is signed up at their school, with thumbnail links (just name and picture) to students at all the other colleges. In addition to listing their favourite movies, books, music, and so on, they can also submit lists of friends as they form groups based on common interests. These groups cover the waterfront; they include such pressing issues as "People Against Popped Collars" (the preppy look of rolling up the collar of your knit shirt), "Future Trophy Wives of America," and even a group called "People Against Groups."[84]

- At Ryze (***www.ryze.com***), registrants set up personal webpages to communicate with current and prospective business contacts. A typical page might include photos and graphics, along with a resumé-like description of business and academic achievements, before going into personal hobbies and other non-business topics. Users can build a network of "friends of friends" by visiting pages of acquaintances and asking permission to include their names on a list there.[85]

- Procter & Gamble promoted its Secret Sparkle deodorant using music stars' personal profiles on a social networking website. The MySpace homepage (***www.myspace.com***) features a profile of the singer Hilary Duff accompanied by logos for Secret Sparkle, an extension of the Secret brand. Consumers who view the profile can try to win an iPod in the "Secret 'Discover the Secret Strength of Today's Hottest Rising Music Stars' Sweepstakes," and sign up for more information on Secret Sparkle, other Procter & Gamble products, or Ms. Duff.[86]

OPINION LEADERSHIP

Although consumers get information from personal sources, they do not tend to ask just *anyone* for advice about purchases. If you decide to buy a new stereo, you will most likely seek advice from a friend who knows a lot about sound systems. This friend may own a sophisticated system or may subscribe to specialized magazines, such as *Stereo Review,* and spend free time browsing through electronics stores. On the other hand, you may have another friend who has a reputation for being stylish and who spends free time reading *Gentlemen's Quarterly* and shopping at trendy boutiques. Although you might not bring up your stereo problem with this friend, this may be the person you take with you to shop for a new fall wardrobe.

The Nature of Opinion Leadership

Everyone knows people who are knowledgeable about products and whose advice is taken seriously by others. These individuals are **opinion leaders**. An opinion leader is a person who is frequently able to influence others' attitudes or behaviours.[87]

Opinion leaders are valuable information sources for a number of reasons:

1. They are technically competent and thus are convincing because they possess expert power.[88]

2. They have prescreened, evaluated, and synthesized product information in an unbiased way, so they possess knowledge power.[89] Unlike commercial endorsers, opinion leaders do not actually represent the interests of one company. They are more credible because they have no "axe to grind."

→ This ad for MTV (***www.mtv.com***) focuses on the importance of young opinion leaders in shaping their friends' preferences.
Courtesy of Viacom International.

BUY THIS 24-YEAR-OLD
AND GET ALL HIS FRIENDS
ABSOLUTELY FREE.

3. They tend to be socially active and highly interconnected in their communities.[90] They are likely to hold office in community groups and clubs and to be active outside the home. As a result, opinion leaders often have legitimate power by virtue of their social standing.

4. They tend to be similar to the consumer in terms of their values and beliefs, so they possess referent power. Note that although opinion leaders are set apart by their interest or expertise in a product category, they are more convincing to the extent that they are *homophilous* rather than *heterophilous. Homophily* refers to the degree to which two individuals are similar in terms of education, social status, and beliefs.[91] Effective opinion leaders tend to be slightly higher than those they influence in terms of status and educational attainment, but not so high as to be in a different social class.

5. Opinion leaders often are among the first to buy new products, so they absorb much of the risk. This experience reduces uncertainty for others who are not as courageous. And although company-sponsored communications tend to focus exclusively on the positive aspects of a product, this hands-on experience makes opinion leaders more likely to impart both positive and negative information about product performance.

THE EXTENT OF AN OPINION LEADER'S INFLUENCE

When marketers and social scientists initially developed the concept of the opinion leader, it was assumed that certain influential people in a community would exert an overall impact on group members' attitudes. Later work, however, began to question the assumption that there is such a thing as a *generalized opinion leader*—somebody whose recommendations are sought for all types of purchases. Very few people are capable of being expert in a number of fields. Sociologists distinguish between those who are *monomorphic,* or experts in a limited field, and those who are *polymorphic,* or experts in several fields.[92] Even the opinion leaders who are polymorphic tend to concentrate on one broad domain, such as electronics or fashion.

Research on opinion leadership generally indicates that although opinion leaders do exist for multiple product categories, expertise tends to overlap across similar categories. It is rare to find a generalized opinion leader. An opinion leader for home appliances is likely to serve a similar function for home cleaners, but not for cosmetics. In contrast, a *fashion opinion leader,* whose primary influence is on clothing choices, may also be consulted for recommendations on cosmetics purchases, but not necessarily on microwave ovens.[93]

TYPES OF OPINION LEADERS

Early conceptions of the role of the opinion leader also assumed a static process: The opinion leader absorbs information from the mass media and in turn transmits these data to opinion receivers. This view has turned out to be overly simplified; it confuses the functions of several different types of consumers.

Opinion leaders may or may not be purchasers of the products they recommend. As we will see in Chapter 17, early purchasers are known as *innovators*. Opinion leaders who are also early purchasers have been termed *innovative communicators*. One study identified a number of characteristics of college men who were innovative communicators for fashion products. These men were among the first to buy new fashions, and their fashion opinions were incorporated by other students in their own clothing decisions. Other characteristics of these men included the following:[94]

- They were socially active.
- They were appearance-conscious and narcissistic (i.e., they were quite fond of themselves and self-centred).
- They were involved in rock culture.
- They were heavy magazine readers, including *Playboy* and *Sports Illustrated*.
- They were likely to own more clothing, and a broader range of styles, than other students.
- Their intellectual interests were relatively limited.

Opinion leaders also are likely to be *opinion seekers*. They are generally more involved in a product category and actively search for information. As a result, they are more likely to talk about products with others and to solicit others' opinions as well. Contrary to the static view of opinion leadership, most product-related conversation does not take place in a "lecture" format, wherein one person does all the talking. A lot of product-related conversation is prompted by the situation and occurs in the context of a casual interaction rather than as formal instruction.[95] One study, which found that opinion seeking is especially high for food products, revealed that two-thirds of opinion seekers also view themselves as opinion leaders.[96] This updated view of interpersonal product communication is contrasted with the traditional view in Figure 11–4.

Consumers who are expert in a product category may not actively communicate with others, while other consumers may have a more general interest in being

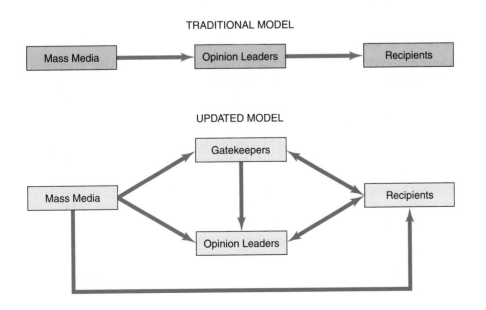

TRADITIONAL MODEL

Mass Media → Opinion Leaders → Recipients

UPDATED MODEL

Gatekeepers

Mass Media

Recipients

Opinion Leaders

FIGURE 11–4

PERSPECTIVES ON THE COMMUNICATIONS PROCESS

Net Profit +

involved in product discussions. A consumer category called the **market maven** has been proposed to describe people who are actively involved in transmitting marketplace information of all types. Market mavens are not necessarily interested in certain products and may not necessarily be early purchasers of products. They come closer to the function of a generalized opinion leader because they tend to have a solid overall knowledge of how and where to procure products.[97] The following scale items, to which respondents indicate how much they agree or disagree, have been used to identify market mavens:

1. I like introducing new brands and products to my friends.
2. I like helping people by providing them with information about many kinds of products.
3. People ask me for information about products, places to shop, or sales.
4. If someone asked me where to get the best buy on several types of products, I could tell him or her where to shop.
5. My friends think of me as a good source of information when it comes to new products or sales.[98]

Think about a person who has information about a variety of products and likes to share this information with others. This person knows about new products, sales, stores, and so on, but does not necessarily feel he or she is an expert on one particular product. How well would you say this description fits you?

In addition to everyday consumers who are influential in affecting others' purchase decisions, a class of marketing intermediary called the **surrogate consumer** is an active player in many categories. A surrogate consumer is a person who is hired to provide input into purchase decisions. Unlike the opinion leader or market maven, the surrogate is usually compensated for this involvement.

Interior decorators, stockbrokers, professional shoppers, or college consultants can all be thought of as surrogate consumers. Whether or not they actually make the purchase on behalf of the consumer, surrogates' recommendations can be enormously influential. The consumer in essence relinquishes control over several or all decision-making functions, such as information search, evaluation of alternatives, or the actual purchase. For example, a client may commission an interior decorator to redo her house, while a broker may be entrusted to make crucial buy/sell decisions on behalf of investors. The involvement of surrogates in a wide range of purchase decisions tends to be overlooked by many marketers, who may be mistargeting their communications to end-consumers instead of to the surrogates who are actually sifting through product information.[99]

Identifying Opinion Leaders

Because opinion leaders are so central to consumer decision making, marketers are quite interested in identifying influential people for a product category. In fact, many ads are intended to reach these influentials rather than the average consumer, especially if the ads contain a lot of technical information. For example, CBS sent a CD-ROM to 10 000 critics, affiliates, advertising agencies, and others it had identified as "influencers" in order to plug the network's prime-time shows.[100]

Unfortunately, since most opinion leaders are everyday consumers and are not formally included in marketing efforts, they are harder to find. A celebrity or an influential industry executive is, by definition, easy to locate. He or she has national or at least regional visibility or may be listed in published directories. In contrast, most opinion leaders tend to operate at the local level and may influence five to ten consumers rather than an entire market segment. In some cases, companies have been known to identify influentials and involve them directly in their marketing efforts, hoping to create a "ripple effect" as these consumers sing the company's praises to their friends. To promote the film *Crouching Tiger, Hidden Dragon,* the producers enlisted a core group of celebrities ranging from rapper Ghostface Killah to feminist author Naomi Wolf to attend early screenings, hoping they would fan out and create a sort of party-circuit dialogue about the film. Similarly, the Walt Disney Company set up screenings for orchestra leaders, music teacher associations, and music instrument makers to stimulate expert WOM about the movie *Mr. Holland's Opus* in which actor Richard Dreyfuss plays a music teacher.[102] And many department stores, for example, have "fashion panels," usually comprising adolescent girls, who provide input into fashion trends, participate in fashion shows, and so on.

Because of the difficulties involved in identifying specific opinion leaders in a large market, most attempts to do so instead focus on exploratory studies in which the characteristics of representative opinion leaders can be identified and then generalized to the larger market. This knowledge helps marketers target their product-related information to appropriate settings and media. One attempt to identify financial opinion leaders found that these consumers were more likely to be involved in managing their own finances and tended to use a computer to do so. They also were more likely to follow their investments on a daily basis and to read books and watch television shows devoted to financial issues.[103]

THE SELF-DESIGNATING METHOD

The most commonly used technique to identify opinion leaders is simply to ask individual consumers whether they consider themselves to be opinion leaders. This is called the *self-designating method.*

Although respondents who report a greater degree of interest in a product category are more likely to be opinion leaders, the results of surveys intended to identify self-designated opinion leaders must be viewed with some scepticism. Some people have a tendency to inflate their own importance and influence, while others who really are influential might not admit to this quality.[104] Just because we transmit advice about products does not mean other people *take* that advice. For someone to be considered a bona fide opinion leader, his or her advice must actually be heard and heeded by opinion seekers.

An alternative to self-designation is to select certain group members (*key informants*) who are then asked to identify opinion leaders. The success of this approach hinges on locating those who have accurate knowledge of the group and on minimizing their response biases (e.g., the tendency to inflate one's own influence on the choices of others).

Although the self-designating method is not as reliable as a more systematic analysis (where individual claims of influence can be verified by asking others whether the person is really influential), it does have the advantage of being easy to administer to a large group of potential opinion leaders. In some cases not all members of a community are surveyed. An updated version of the original measurement scale developed for self-designation of opinion leaders is shown in Figure 11–5.[105]

SOCIOMETRY

The popular play and movie *Six Degrees of Separation* is based on the basic premise that everyone on the planet indirectly knows everyone else—or at least knows people who know them. Indeed, it is estimated that the average person has 1500 acquaintances and that any two people in the world could be connected by five to six intermediaries.[106]

Sociometric methods, which trace communication patterns among group members, allow researchers to systematically map out interactions that take place among group members. People who tend to be sources of product-related information can be identified by asking group members whom they go to for product information. Although this method is the most precise, it is very hard and expensive to implement, since it involves very close study of interaction patterns in small groups. For this reason, sociometric techniques are best applied in closed, self-contained social settings, such as hospitals, prisons, and army bases, where members are largely isolated from other social networks.

FIGURE 11–5 A REVISED AND UPDATED VERSION OF THE OPINION LEADERSHIP SCALE

Please rate yourself on the following scales relating to your interactions with friends and neighbours regarding _____.

1. In general, do you talk to your friends and neighbours about _____:
   very often   never
       5   4   3   2   1

2. When you talk to your friends and neighbours about _____ do you:
   give a great deal of information   give very little information
       5   4   3   2   1

3. During the past six months, how many people have you told about a new _____?
   told a number of people   told no one
       5   4   3   2   1

4. Compared with your circle of friends, how likely are you to be asked about new _____?
   very likely to be asked   not at all likely to be asked
       5   4   3   2   1

5. In discussion of new _____, which of the following happens most?
   you tell your friends about _____   your friends tell you about _____
       5   4   3   2   1

6. Overall, in all of your discussions with friends and neighbours, are you:
   often used as a source of advice   not used as a source of advice
       5   4   3   2   1

Source: Adapted from Terry L. Childers, "Assessment of the Psychometric Properties of an Opinion Leadership Scale," *Journal of Marketing Research* 23 (May 1986): 184–188; Leisa Reinecke Flynn, Ronald E. Goldsmith, and Jacqueline K. Eastman, "The King and Summers Opinion Leadership Scale: Revision and Refinement," *Journal of Business Research* 31 (1994): 55–64.

Many professionals and services marketers depend primarily upon word of mouth to generate business. In many cases consumers recommend a service provider to a friend or co-worker, and in other cases other business people make recommendations to their customers. Only 0.2 percent of respondents in one study reported choosing physicians based on advertising; advice from family and friends was the most widely used criterion.[107]

Sociometric analyses can be used to better understand *referral behaviour* and to locate strengths and weaknesses in terms of how one's reputation is communicated through a community. *Network analysis* focuses on communication in social systems; it considers the relations among people in a *referral network* and measures the *tie strength* among them. Tie strength refers to the nature of the bond between people. It can range from strong primary (e.g., your spouse) to weak secondary (an acquaintance you rarely see). A strong tie relationship may be thought of as a primary reference group, in which interactions are frequent and important to the individual.

Although strong ties are important, weak ties can perform a *bridging function*. This type of connection allows a consumer access between subgroups. For example, you might have a regular group of friends who serve as a primary reference group (strong ties). If you have an interest in tennis, say, one of these friends might introduce you to a group of people who play on the tennis team. As a result you gain access to their valuable expertise through this bridging function. This referral process demonstrates the strength of weak ties.

CHAPTER SUMMARY

CONSUMERS DON'T MAKE PURCHASE DECISIONS IN A VACUUM. THEY ARE OFTEN HEAVILY INFLUENCED BY OTHERS WHOSE OPINIONS AND PRODUCT CHOICES EXERT VARIOUS KINDS OF POWER OVER THEM.

- Consumers belong to or admire many different groups and are often influenced in their purchase decisions by a desire to be accepted by others. Individuals or groups whose opinions or behaviour are particularly important are called reference groups. Both formal and informal groups influence an individual's purchase decisions, although the impact of reference group influence is affected by such factors as the conspicuousness of the product and the relevance of the reference group for a particular purchase.

- Individuals hold influence in a group to the extent that they possess social power; types of social power include information power, referent power, legitimate power, expert power, reward power, and coercive power.

CONSUMERS OFTEN SEEK OUT OTHERS WHO SHARE SIMILAR INTERESTS IN PRODUCTS OR SERVICES.

- Brand communities unite consumers who share a common passion for a particular product. Brandfests, organized by companies to encourage this kind of community, can build brand loyalty and reinforce group membership.

WE MAY BE MOTIVATED TO BUY OR USE PRODUCTS IN ORDER TO BE CONSISTENT WITH WHAT OTHER PEOPLE DO.

- We conform to the desires of others for two basic reasons. Some people model their behaviour after others because they take that behaviour as evidence of the correct way to act; these people are conforming because of informational social influence. Other people conform to satisfy others' expectations, or to be accepted by the group; these individuals are affected by normative social influence. Group members often do things they would not do as individuals because their identities become merged with the group; they become deindividuated.

THE THINGS THAT OTHER CONSUMERS TELL US ABOUT PRODUCTS (BOTH GOOD AND BAD) ARE OFTEN MORE INFLUENTIAL THAN THE ADVERTISING WE ARE EXPOSED TO ABOUT THOSE PRODUCTS.

- Much of what we know about products is learned through word-of-mouth communication (WOM) rather than formal advertising. Product-related information tends to be exchanged in casual conversations. Guerrilla marketing strategies try to accelerate the WOM process by enlisting consumers to help spread the word.

- Although WOM often is helpful for making consumers aware of products, it can also hurt companies when damaging product rumours or negative WOM occurs.

ONLINE TECHNOLOGIES ARE ACCELERATING THE IMPACT OF WORD-OF-MOUTH COMMUNICATION.

- The web has greatly amplified consumers' abilities to be exposed to numerous reference groups. Virtual consumption communities are composed of people who are united by a common bond—enthusiasm about or knowledge of a specific product or service. Emerging marketing strategies try to leverage the potential of the web to spread information from consumer to consumer extremely quickly. Some companies use viral marketing techniques to enlist individuals to tout products, services, websites, etc. to others. Blogging allows consumers to easily post their thoughts about products for others to see.

CERTAIN PEOPLE ARE PARTICULARLY LIKELY TO INFLUENCE OTHERS' PRODUCT CHOICES.

- Opinion leaders who are knowledgeable about a product and whose opinions are highly regarded tend to influence others' choices. Specific opinion leaders are somewhat hard to identify, but marketers who know their general characteristics can try to target them in their media and promotional strategies. Other influencers include market mavens, who have a general interest in marketplace activities, and surrogate consumers, who are compensated for their advice about purchases.

KEY TERMS

Aspirational reference group   p. 314

Blog (weblog)   p. 327

Blogosphere   p. 327

Brand community   p. 313

Comparative influence   p. 312

Conformity   p. 318

Consumer tribe   p. 314

Decision polarization   p. 320

Deindividuation   p. 320

E-fluentials   p. 332

Guerrilla marketing   p. 327

Home shopping parties   p. 320

Market maven   p. 332

Negative word of mouth   p. 324

Normative influence   p. 312

Norms   p. 318

Opinion leaders   p. 329

Reactance   p. 322

REVIEW QUESTIONS

1. Name two dimensions that influence whether reference groups have an impact on an individual's purchase decisions.
2. List three types of social power, giving an example of each.
3. Which groups tend to be more powerful influences on behaviour: large formal groups or small informal groups? Why?
4. What is a brand community, and why is it of interest to marketers?
5. Explain the difference between a membership and an aspirational reference group, giving an example of each.
6. Name one factor that makes it more likely that a person will become part of a consumer's membership reference group.
7. Define deindividuation and give an example of this effect.
8. What is the risky shift, and how does it relate to going shopping with friends?
9. What is the difference between normative and informational social influence?
10. Define conformity and give three examples of it. Name three reasons why people conform.
11. How does the principle of least interest relate to your success in a romantic relationship?
12. What is social comparison? What type of person do we usually choose to compare ourselves to?

13. What is the difference between independence and anticonformity?
14. Define reactance and give an example.
15. What is word of mouth, and why is it more powerful than advertising?
16. Which is more powerful: positive or negative word of mouth? Why?
17. Describe some ways in which marketers are using the internet to encourage positive WOM.
18. What is viral marketing? Guerrilla marketing? Give an example of each.
19. What is an opinion leader? Give three reasons why opinion leaders are powerful influences on consumers' opinions. What are some characteristics of this type of person?
20. Is there such a thing as a generalized opinion leader? Why or why not?
21. What is the relationship between an opinion leader and an opinion seeker?
22. What is the difference between a market maven and a surrogate consumer?
23. How can marketers use opinion leaders to help them promote their products or services?
24. What are sociometric techniques? Under what conditions does it make sense to use them?

CONSUMER BEHAVIOUR CHALLENGE

Discuss

1. The chapter describes four types of virtual community members. Which type are you?
2. The average internet user in North America spends three hours a day online, with much of that time devoted to work and more than half of it to communications. Researchers report that the internet has displaced television watching and a range of other activities. Internet users watch television for one hour and 42 minutes per day, compared with the national average of two hours. One study reported increasing physical isolation among internet users; the study created a controversy and drew angry complaints from some users who insisted that the time they spent online did not detract from their social relationships. However, the researchers said they have now gathered further evidence showing that internet use has lowered the amount of time people spend socializing with friends—and even sleeping. According to the study, an hour of time spent using the internet reduces face-to-face contact with friends, co-workers, and family by 23.5 minutes, lowers the amount of time spent watching television by 10 minutes, and shortens sleep by 8.5 minutes per day.[108] What's your perspective on this issue? Does the increasing use of the internet have positive or negative implications for interpersonal relationships in our society?

3. The Word of Mouth Marketing Association recently announced a new set of rules and guidelines for word-of-mouth advertising. The trade group maintains that marketers must make sure that people who talk up products or services disclose whom they are working for. They also must use real consumers, not actors, who discuss what they really believe about a product.[109] What do you think about "stealth" campaigns like this? Should marketers be required to disclose their true intentions when they try to initiate positive word of mouth?

4. The adoption of a certain brand of shoe or apparel by athletes can be a powerful influence on students and other fans. Should high-school and university coaches be paid to determine what brand of athletic equipment their players will wear?

5. The strategy of viral marketing gets customers to sell a product to other customers on behalf of the company. That often means convincing your friends to climb on the bandwagon, and sometimes you get a

cut if they wind up buying something.[110] Some might argue that means you're selling out your friends (or at least selling to your friends) in exchange for a piece of the action. Others might say you're just sharing the wealth with those you care about. Have you been involved in viral marketing by passing along names of your friends or sending them to a website such as *www.hotmail.com*? If so, what happened? How do you feel about this practice?

6. Are home shopping parties that put pressure on friends and neighbours to buy merchandise ethical?

Experiential Exercises

7. The power of unspoken social norms often becomes obvious only when these norms are violated. To witness this result firsthand, try one of the following: Stand facing the back wall in an elevator; serve dessert before the main course; offer to pay cash for dinner at a friend's home; or tell someone not to have a nice day.

8. Identify fashion opinion leaders on your campus. Do they fit the profile discussed in this chapter?

9. See if you can demonstrate the risky shift. Get a group of friends together and ask each to privately rate the likelihood on a scale from one to seven that they would try a controversial new product (e.g., a credit card that works with a chip implanted in a person's wrist). Then ask the group to discuss the product and rate the idea again. If the average rating changes from the first one, you've just observed a risky shift.

10. Trace a referral pattern for a particular service provider (such as a hairstylist) by tracking how clients came to choose that individual. See if you can identify opinion leaders who are responsible for referring several clients to the business person. How might the service provider take advantage of this process to grow his or her business?

CBC ⊕ VIDEO VIGNETTE

CONCEPTS AT WORK FOR BUZZ MARKETING

Matthew George, a "product seeder" for Adidas, watches intently while the Huskies of George Brown College play the Mountaineers of Mohawk College. He's looking for a basketball trendsetter to become the walking ad for the $160 T-Mac shoe, named after Tracy McGrady, who is a professional basketball star. Through this process, Adidas hopes to get others talking about the new shoe—that is, to create a "buzz" about it.

Some marketers are convinced that buzz marketing is worth a try. In an environment of fragmented markets, distracted consumers, and rampant ad zapping, relying on word-of-mouth strategies makes sense. It puts new products into the hands of potential consumers. It is a way to get products out in the open and into social networks at events—such as basketball games, parties, and concerts—where the potential market can see others similar to itself experiencing the latest market offering.

Recent research shows that two-thirds of all consumer goods sales are now directly influenced by word of mouth and that buzz marketing costs one-tenth of the price of traditional advertising campaigns. It can also help some companies connect with hard-to-reach consumers, such as urban teenagers.

Matchstick Productions, a Canadian company, has built its business on instigating positive word of mouth in Vancouver, Montreal, and Toronto for products as diverse as shoes, breath mints, gin, and perfume. However, not everyone is so enthusiastic. Critics of buzz marketing claim that it is a commercial approach that is under the consumer's radar, that it is underhanded and manipulative, and that it promotes materialism.

Questions

1. How does buzz marketing influence the diffusion of innovations or fashion fads?
2. What is the process for instigating buzz marketing?
3. In what product categories has buzz marketing been used? Why does buzz marketing seem appropriate for these product categories?
4. What are the criticisms of buzz marketing? How do marketers address these criticisms?

Resources: "Buzz Marketing," *Marketplace #17, CBC Air Date: March 27, 2002; Hollie Shaw, "Grassroots and Growing," Financial Post, May 20, 2006: FP3.*

NOTES

1. Details adapted from John W. Schouten and James H. McAlexander, "Market Impact of a Consumption Subculture: The Harley-Davidson Mystique," in *Proceedings of the 1992 European Conference of the Association for Consumer Research*, eds. Fred van Raaij and Gary Bamossy (Amsterdam, 1992).

2. Joel B. Cohen and Ellen Golden, "Informational Social Influence and Product Evaluation," *Journal of Applied Psychology* 56 (February 1972): 54–59; Robert E. Burnkrant and Alain Cousineau, "Informational and Normative Social Influence in Buyer Behavior," *Journal of Consumer Research* 2 (December 1975): 206–215; Peter H. Reingen, "Test of a List Procedure for Inducing Compliance with a Request to Donate Money," *Journal of Applied Psychology* 67 (1982): 110–118; William O. Bearden, Randall L. Rose, and Jesse E. Teel, "Correlates of Conformity in the Consumption of Illicit Drugs and Alcohol," *Journal of Business Research* 30, 1 (May 1994): 25–31.

3. Quoted in Dyan Machan, "Is the Hog Going Soft?" *Forbes* (March 10, 1997): 114–119, p. 117.

4. C. Whan Park and V. Parker Lessig, "Students and Housewives: Differences in Susceptibility to Reference Group Influence," *Journal of Consumer Research* 4 (September 1977): 102–110.

5. Kenneth J. Gergen and Mary Gergen, *Social Psychology* (New York: Harcourt Brace Jovanovich, 1981).

6. Harold H. Kelley, "Two Functions of Reference Groups," in *Basic Studies in Social Psychology*, eds. Harold Proshansky and Bernard Siedenberg (New York, NY: Holt, Rinehart and Winston, 1965), pp. 210–214. For a recent empirical application in the area of teen apparel shopping, see Oswald A. Mascarenhas and Mary A. Higby,

"Peer, Parent, and Media Influences in Teen Apparel Shopping," *Journal of the Academy of Marketing Science* 21, 1 (Winter 1993): 53–58.

7. Kris Oser, "Microsoft's Halo 2 Soars on Viral Push," *Advertising Age* (October 25, 2004): 46.

8. James H. McAlexander, John W. Schouten, and Harold F. Koenig, "Building Brand Community," *Journal of Marketing* 66 (January 2002): 38–54; Albert Muniz and Thomas O'Guinn, "Brand Community," *Journal of Consumer Research* (March 2001): 412–432.

9. Veronique Cova and Bernard Cova, "Tribal Aspects of Postmodern Consumption Research: The Case of French In-Line Roller Skaters," *Journal of Consumer Behavior* 1 (June 2001): 67–76.

10. A. Benton Cocanougher and Grady D. Bruce, "Socially Distant Reference Groups and Consumer Aspirations," *Journal of Marketing Research* 8 (August 1971): 79–81; James E. Stafford, "Effects of Group Influences on Consumer Brand Preferences," *Journal of Marketing Research* 3 (February 1966): 68–75.

11. L. Festinger, S. Schachter, and K. Back, *Social Pressures in Informal Groups: A Study of Human Factors in Housing* (New York, NY: Harper and Row, 1950).

12. R.B. Zajonc, H.M. Markus, and W. Wilson, "Exposure Effects and Associative Learning," *Journal of Experimental Social Psychology* 10 (1974): 248–263.

13. D.J. Stang, "Methodological Factors in Mere Exposure Research," *Psychological Bulletin* 81 (1974): 1014–1025; R.B. Zajonc et al., "Exposure, Satiation and Stimulus Discriminability," *Journal of Personality and Social Psychology* 21 (1972): 270–280.

14. Basil G. Englis and Michael R. Solomon, "To Be and Not to Be: Reference Group Stereotyping and *The Clustering of America*," *Journal of Advertising* 24 (Spring 1995): 13–28; Michael R. Solomon and Basil G. Englis, "I Am Not, Therefore I Am: The Role of Anti-Consumption in the Process of Self-Definition," Special Session at the Association for Consumer Research meetings, October 1996, Tucson, Arizona.

15. Bruce Feirstein, *Real Men Don't Eat Quiche* (New York: Pocket Books, 1982); **www.auntiefashions.com**, accessed December 31, 2002.

16. Jeffrey D. Ford and Elwood A. Ellis, "A Re-examination of Group Influence on Member Brand Preference," *Journal of Marketing Research* 17 (February 1980): 125–132; Thomas S. Robertson, *Innovative Behavior and Communication* (New York: Holt, Rinehart and Winston, 1980), ch. 8.

17. William O. Bearden and Michael J. Etzel, "Reference Group Influence on Product and Brand Purchase Decisions," *Journal of Consumer Research* 9, 2 (1982): 183–194.

18. Gergen and Gergen, *Social Psychology*, p. 312.

19. J.R.P. French, Jr. and B. Raven, "The Bases of Social Power," in *Studies in Social Power*, ed. D. Cartwright (Ann Arbor, MI: Institute for Social Research, 1959), pp. 150–167.

20. Michael R. Solomon, "Packaging the Service Provider," *Service Industries Journal* 5 (March 1985): 64–72.

21. Augustin Hedberg, "Lights! Camera! Economists! (celebrity economists)," *Money* (October 1987): 118.

22. Luc Sante, "Be Different! (Like Everyone Else!)," *New York Times Magazine* [online] (October 17, 1999).

23. For an attempt to measure individual differences in proclivity to conformity, see William O. Bearden, Richard G. Netemeyer, and Jesse E. Teel, "Measurement of Consumer Susceptibility to Interpersonal Influence," *Journal of Consumer Research* 15 (March 1989): 473–481.

24. John W. Thibaut and Harold H. Kelley, *The Social Psychology of Groups* (New York: John Wiley, 1959); W.W. Waller and R. Hill, *The Family, a Dynamic Interpretation* (New York: Dryden, 1951).

25. William O. Bearden, Richard G. Netemeyer, and Jesse E. Teel, "Measurement of Consumer Susceptibility to Interpersonal Influence," *Journal of Consumer Research* 9, 3 (1989): 183–194; Lynn R. Kahle, "Observations: Role-Relaxed Consumers: A Trend of the Nineties," *Journal of Advertising Research* (March/April 1995): 66–71; Lynn R. Kahle and Aviv Shoham, "Observations: Role-Relaxed Consumers: Empirical Evidence," *Journal of Advertising Research* 35, 3 (May/June 1995): 59–62.

26. Leon Festinger, "A Theory of Social Comparison Processes," *Human Relations* 7 (May 1954): 117–140.

27. Chester A. Insko et al., "Conformity as a Function of the Consistency of Positive Self-Evaluation with Being Liked and Being Right," *Journal of Experimental Social Psychology* 19 (1983): 341–358.

28. Abraham Tesser, Murray Millar, and Janet Moore, "Some Affective Consequences of Social Comparison and Reflection Processes: The Pain and Pleasure of Being Close," *Journal of Personality and Social Psychology* 54, 1 (1988): 49–61.

29. L. Wheeler et al., "Factors Determining the Choice of a Comparison Other," *Journal of Experimental Social Psychology* 5 (1969): 219–232.

30. George P. Moschis, "Social Comparison and Informal Group Influence," *Journal of Marketing Research* 13 (August 1976): 237–244.

31. Burnkrant and Cousineau, "Informational and Normative Social Influence in Buyer Behavior"; M. Venkatesan, "Experimental Study of Consumer Behavior Conformity and Independence," *Journal of Marketing Research* 3 (November 1966): 384–387.

32. J.L. Freedman and S. Fraser, "Compliance Without Pressure: The Foot-in-the-Door Technique," *Journal of Personality and Social Psychology* 4 (1966): 195–202.

33. R.B. Cialdini et al., "Reciprocal Concessions Procedure for Inducing Compliance: The Door-in-the-Face Effect," *Journal of Personality and Social Psychology* 31 (1975): 200–215.

34. Nathan Kogan and Michael A. Wallach, "Risky Shift Phenomenon in Small Decision-Making Groups: A Test of the Information Exchange Hypothesis," *Journal of Experimental Social Psychology* 3 (January 1967): 75–84; Nathan Kogan and Michael A. Wallach, *Risk Taking* (New York: Holt, Rinehart and Winston, 1964); Arch G. Woodside and M. Wayne DeLozier, "Effects of Word-of-Mouth Advertising on Consumer Risk Taking," *Journal of Advertising* (Fall 1976): 12–19.

35. Kogan and Wallach, *Risk Taking*.

36. Roger Brown, *Social Psychology* (New York, NY: Free Press, 1965).

37. David L. Johnson and I.R. Andrews, "Risky Shift Phenomenon Tested with Consumer Product Stimuli," *Journal of Personality and Social Psychology* 20 (1971): 382–385. See also Vithala R. Rao and Joel H. Steckel, "A Polarization Model for Describing Group Preferences," *Journal of Consumer Research* 18 (June 1991): 108–118.

38. Donald H. Granbois, "Improving the Study of Customer In-Store Behavior," *Journal of Marketing* 32 (October 1968): 28–32.

39. B. Latane, K. Williams, and S. Harkins, "Many Hands Make Light the Work: The Causes and Consequences of Social Loafing," *Journal of Personality and Social Psychology* 37 (1979): 822–832.

40. S. Freeman et al., "Diffusion of Responsibility and Restaurant Tipping: Cheaper by the Bunch," *Personality and Social Psychology Bulletin* 1 (1978): 584–587.

41. Len Strazewski, "Tupperware Locks in New Strategy," *Advertising Age* (February 8, 1988): 30.

42. Quoted in Melanie Wells, "Smooth Operator," *Forbes* (May 13, 2002): 167–168.

43. Gergen and Gergen, *Social Psychology*.

44. L.J. Strickland, S. Messick, and D.N. Jackson, "Conformity, Anticonformity and Independence: Their Dimensionality and Generality," *Journal of Personality and Social Psychology* 16 (1970): 494–507.

45. Jack W. Brehm, *A Theory of Psychological Reactance* (New York: Academic Press, 1966).

46. R.D. Ashmore, V. Ramchandra, and R. Jones, "Censorship as an Attitude Change Induction" (paper presented at meetings of Eastern Psychological Association, New York, 1971); R.A. Wicklund and J. Brehm, *Perspectives on Cognitive Dissonance* (Hillsdale, NJ: Lawrence Erlbaum, 1976).

47. Pat Wechsler, "A Curiously Strong Campaign," *Business Week* (April 21, 1997): 134.

48. Johan Arndt, "Role of Product-Related Conversations in the Diffusion of a New Product," *Journal of Marketing Research* 4 (August 1967): 291–295.

49. John Gaffney, "Enterprise Marketing: The Cool Kids Are Doing It. Should You?" *Asiaweek* (November 23, 2001): 1.

50. Elihu Katz and Paul F. Lazarsfeld, *Personal Influence* (Glencoe, IL: Free Press, 1955).

51. John A. Martilla, "Word-of-Mouth Communication in the Industrial Adoption Process," *Journal of Marketing Research* 8 (March 1971): 173–178. See also Marsha L. Richins, "Negative Word-of-Mouth by Dissatisfied Consumers: A Pilot Study," *Journal of Marketing* 47 (Winter 1983): 68–78.

52. Arndt, "Role of Product-Related Conversations in the Diffusion of a New Product."

53. James H. Myers and Thomas S. Robertson, "Dimensions of Opinion Leadership," *Journal of Marketing Research* 9 (February 1972): 41–46.

54. Thomas E. Weber, "Viral Marketing: Web's Newest Ploy May Make You an Unpopular Friend," *Wall Street Journal Interactive Edition* (September 13, 1999).

55. Quoted in Ellen Neuborne, "Generation Y," *Business Week* (February 15, 1999): 80(7).

56. Dorothy Leonard-Barton, "Experts as Negative Opinion Leaders in the Diffusion of a Technological Innovation," *Journal of Consumer Research* 11 (March 1985): 914–926.

57. James F. Engel, Robert J. Kegerreis, and Roger D. Blackwell, "Word of Mouth Communication by the Innovator," *Journal of Marketing* 33 (July 1969): 15–19.

58. Chip Walker, "Word of Mouth," *American Demographics* (July 1995): 38–44.

59. Richard J. Lutz, "Changing Brand Attitudes through Modification of Cognitive Structure," *Journal of Consumer Research* 1 (March 1975): 49–59. For some suggested remedies to bad publicity, see Mitch Griffin, Barry J. Babin, and Jill S. Attaway, "An Empirical Investigation of the Impact of Negative Public Publicity on Consumer Attitudes and Intentions," in *Advances in Consumer Research* 18, eds. Rebecca H. Holman and Michael R. Solomon (Provo, UT: Association for Consumer Research, 1991), 334–341; Alice M. Tybout, Bobby J. Calder, and Brian Sternthal, "Using Information Processing Theory to Design Marketing Strategies," *Journal of Marketing Research* 18 (1981): 73–79.

60. Robert E. Smith and Christine A. Vogt, "The Effects of Integrating Advertising and Negative Word-of-Mouth Communications on Message Processing and Response," *Journal of Consumer Psychology* 4, 2 (1995): 133–151; Paula Fitzgerald Bone, "Word-of-Mouth Effects on Short-Term and Long-Term Product Judgments," *Journal of Business Research* 32 (1995): 213–223.

61. "Dunkin' Donuts Buys Out Critical Web Site," *New York Times on the Web* (August 27, 1999).

62. Charles W. King and John O. Summers, "Overlap of Opinion Leadership across Consumer Product Categories," *Journal of Marketing Research* 7 (February 1970): 43–50.

63. Nat Ives, "Marketing's Flip Side: The 'Determined Detractor,'" *New York Times on the Web* (December 27, 2004).

64. Michael Fumento, "Tampon Terrorism," *Forbes* (May 17, 1999): 170(2).

65. Greg Jaffe, "No MTV for Widespread Panic, Just Loads of Worshipful Fans," *Wall Street Journal Interactive Edition* (February 17, 1999).

66. This typology is adapted from material presented in Robert V. Kozinets, "E-Tribalized Marketing: The Strategic Implications of Virtual Communities of Consumption," *European Management Journal* 17, 3 (June 1999): 252–264.

67. Hassan Fattah and Pamela Paul, "Gaming Gets Serious," *American Demographics* (May 2002): 39–43.

68. Fattah and Paul, "Gaming Gets Serious."

69. Quoted in Marc Gunther, "The Newest Addiction," *Fortune* (August 2, 1999): 123.

70. Tom Weber, "Net's Hottest Game Brings People Closer," *Wall Street Journal Interactive Edition* (March 20, 2000).

71. David Kushner, "Where Warriors and Ogres Lock Arms Instead of Swords," *New York Times on the Web* (August 9, 2002).

72. Martha Irvine, "Mother Blames Internet Game for Son's Suicide," *Montgomery Advertiser* (May 26, 2002): 6(A).

73. Robert V. Kozinets, "E-Tribalized Marketing . . . ."

74. Sonia Murray, "Street Marketing Does the Trick," *Advertising Age* (March 20, 2000): s12.

75. Quoted in "Taking to the Streets," *Newsweek* (November 2, 1998): 70–73.

76. Melanie Wells, "Wabbing," *Forbes* (February 2, 2004): 84–88; Jeff Leeds, "The Next Hit Song? Ask P&G," *New York Times on the Web* (November 8, 2004).

77. Kate Fitzgerald, "Branding Face to Face," *Advertising Age* (October 21, 2002): 47.

78. Jared Sandberg, "The Friendly Virus," *Newsweek* (April 12, 1999): 65–66.

79. Karen J. Bannan, "Marketers Try Infecting the Internet," *New York Times on the Web* (March 22, 2000).

80. "Sitelab's Execution of Viral Marketing Campaign for WD-40 Helps Net Nearly 40,000 Fans," *Business Wire* (January 14, 2002): 279.

81. Jeff Neff, "Pressure points at IPG," *Advertising Age* (December 2001): 4.

82. Bob Tedeschi, "Online Retailers Find that Customer Reviews Build Loyalty," *New York Times on the Web* (September 6, 1999).

83. "Bookseller Offers Refunds for Advertised Books," *Opelika-Auburn News* (February 11, 1999): A11.

84. Peter Applebome, "On Campus, Hanging Out by Logging On," *New York Times on the Web* (December 1, 2004).

85. Bob Tedeschi, "Social Networks: Will Users Pay to Get Friends?" *New York Times on the Web* (February 9, 2004).

86. Nat Ives, "Pitch to Online Crowd Mixes Pop Stars and Personals," *New York Times on the Web* (December 3, 2004).

87. Everett M. Rogers, *Diffusion of Innovations,* 3rd ed. (New York: Free Press, 1983).

88. Leonard-Barton, "Experts as Negative Opinion Leaders"; Rogers, *Diffusion of Innovations.*

89. Herbert Menzel, "Interpersonal and Unplanned Communications: Indispensable or Obsolete?" in *Biomedical Innovation* (Cambridge, MA: MIT Press, 1981), pp. 155–163.

90. Meera P. Venkatraman, "Opinion Leaders, Adopters, and Communicative Adopters: A Role Analysis," *Psychology & Marketing* 6 (Spring 1989): 51–68.

91. Rogers, *Diffusion of Innovations.*

92. Robert Merton, *Social Theory and Social Structure* (Glencoe, IL: Free Press, 1957).

93. King and Summers, "Overlap of Opinion Leadership across Consumer Product Categories." See also Ronald E. Goldsmith, Jeanne R. Heitmeyer, and Jon B. Freiden, "Social Values and Fashion Leadership," *Clothing and Textiles Research Journal* 10 (Fall 1991): 37–45; J.O. Summers, "Identity of Women's Clothing Fashion Opinion Leaders," *Journal of Marketing Research* 7 (1970): 178–185.

94. Steven A. Baumgarten, "The Innovative Communicator in the Diffusion Process," *Journal of Marketing Research* 12 (February 1975): 12–18.

95. Russell W. Belk, "Occurrence of Word-of-Mouth Buyer Behavior as a Function of Situation and Advertising Stimuli," in *Combined Proceedings of the American Marketing Association,* series no. 33, ed. Fred C. Allvine (Chicago, IL: American Marketing Association, 1971), pp. 419–422.

96. Lawrence F. Feick, Linda L. Price, and Robin A. Higie, "People Who Use People: The Other Side of Opinion Leadership," in *Advances in Consumer Research* 13, ed. Richard J. Lutz (Provo, UT: Association for Consumer Research, 1986), 301–305.

97. For discussion of the market-maven construct, see Lawrence F. Feick and Linda L. Price, "The Market Maven," *Managing* (July 1985): 10. Although it is possible to identify market mavens within a study population using this type of scale, to date no clear demographic profile that characterizes this type has been identified.

98. Lawrence Feick and Linda Price, "The Market Maven: A Diffuser of Marketplace Information," *Journal of Marketing* 51 (January 1987): 83–87.

99. Michael R. Solomon, "The Missing Link: Surrogate Consumers in the Marketing Chain," *Journal of Marketing* 50 (October 1986): 208–218.

100. "CBS Extends Its High-Tech Reach: CD-ROM Goes to 'Influencers,'" *PROMO: The International Magazine for Promotion Marketing* (October 1994): 59.

101. Burson-Marsteller, "The e-fluentials: 2000," Burson Marsteller. Retrieved April 23, 2002 from "The E-fluentials: 2000," [online magazine] [cited 23 April 2002] Burson Marsteller, available from ***http://bm.com***; S. Khodarahmi, "Pass It On," [online magazine] [cited 26 April 2002] DotCEO; available from ***www.dotceo.com***; Seana Mulcahy, "Selling to E-Fluentials," [online magazine] [cited 27 April 2002] *ClickZ Today,* 3 January 2002; available from ***www.e-fluentials.com/news***.

102. John Lippman, "Sony's Word-of-Mouth Campaign Creates Buzz for 'Crouching Tiger,'" *Wall Street Journal* (January 11, 2001).

103. Barbara B. Stern and Stephen J. Gould, "The Consumer as Financial Opinion Leader," *Journal of Retail Banking* 10 (Summer 1988): 43–52.

104. William R. Darden and Fred D. Reynolds, "Predicting Opinion Leadership for Men's Apparel Fashions," *Journal of Marketing Research* 1 (August 1972), 324–328. A modified version of the opinion leadership scale with improved reliability and validity can be found in Terry L. Childers, "Assessment of the Psychometric Properties of an Opinion Leadership Scale," *Journal of Marketing Research* 23 (May 1986): 184–188.

105. Several studies have provided updates on the content and validity of the original King and Summers scale. The scale presented here reflects two changes from the original scale: (1) the response format has been changed to a uniform five-point format; and (2) one of the original items has been dropped because of low reliability. See Childers, "Assessment of the Psychometric Properties of an Opinion Leadership Scale"; Ronald E. Goldsmith and Rene Desborde, "A Validity Study of a Measure of Opinion Leadership," *Journal of Business Research* 22 (1991): 11–19; Leisa Reinecke Flynn, Ronald E. Goldsmith, and Jacqueline K. Eastman, "The King and Summers Opinion Leadership Scale: Revision and Refinement," *Journal of Business Research* 31 (1994): 55–64.

106. Dan Seligman, "Me and Monica," *Forbes* (March 23, 1998): 76(2).

107. "Referrals Top Ads as Influence on Patients' Doctor Selections," *Marketing News* (January 30, 1987): 22.

108. John Markoff, "Internet Use Said to Cut into TV Viewing and Socializing," *New York Times on the Web* (December 30, 2004).

109. Suzanne Vranica, "Getting Buzz Marketers to Fess Up," *Wall Street Journal Interactive Edition* (February 9, 2005): B9.

110. Weber, "Viral Marketing: Web's Newest Ploy May Make You an Unpopular Friend."

Tuesday is grocery day, and P.J. is accompanying his mom, Tina. He doesn't usually go along, and he thinks she would rather go alone. She spends less and gets home faster without him, she says. But he's going today anyway, partly to be sure she picks cool stuff for his tenth birthday party. The Smiley tablecloth and cupcakes were OK last year, but this year he's lobbying heavily for cool food (like yummy Cheestrings) and Harry Potter decorations for his Wizard Party. His mom already reserved the latest Harry Potter DVD.

First they get the family's regular shopping out of the way. Tina gets exasperated as P.J. and his sister argue over the best food to get for their new puppy. Finally they move on to the next aisle, where Tina throws two cans of tuna into the cart. She moves on, but from behind her she hears P.J. say, "Whoa! Just chill here, Mom! You're not going to buy that brand, are you? Don't you know they use nets to catch tuna—nets that kill hundreds of innocent dolphins every year!" This was news to Tina. Getting over her irritation at being told how to shop by a kid who can't even clean up his room, she realizes that P.J. is making sense.

As she puts the cans back on the shelf, she smiles and reminds herself that her two children have been very helpful in steering her away from all kinds of products that could harm the environment or the family's health. "Now, where did I see those Harry Potter Magic Puzzles?"

CHAPTER 12

Family
Decision Making

FAMILY DECISION MAKING

P.J.'s influence on his mother's choice of an environmentally safe product illustrates that many consumer decisions are made jointly and that children influence family decisions. The individual decision-making process described in detail in Chapter 9 is, in many cases, overly simplistic. In fact, more than one person may be involved in any stage of the problem-solving sequence, from initial problem recognition and information search to evaluation of alternatives and choice of products. To further complicate matters, these decisions often involve two or more people who may not have the same level of investment in the outcome, the same tastes and preferences, or the same consumption priorities. For example, the decision to get a pet is often made jointly by family members. The children may be instrumental in persuading their reluctant parents to get a dog or a cat, while the parents may be responsible for the information search to determine what kind to get or where to get it. Then the entire family may be involved in actually selecting the puppy or kitten that will soon become another family member.

This chapter examines issues related to *family decision making,* where more than one person is involved in the purchasing process for products or services that may be used by multiple consumers. Specifically, we'll consider how members of a family negotiate among themselves and how important changes in family structure are affecting this process. The chapter concludes by focusing on how children learn to be consumers.

THE FAMILY

It is not unusual to read in newspapers and magazines about the "death of the family unit." Although it is true that the proportion of people living in a traditional family structure, consisting of a married couple with children, has declined (to 41 percent of all Canadian families in the 2001 census), many other types of families are growing in number rapidly. Indeed, some experts argue that, as traditional family living arrangements have waned, people are placing even greater emphasis on the roles of siblings, close friends, and other relatives in providing companionship and social support.[1] Some people are even joining "intentional families"; these are groups of unrelated people who meet regularly for meals and who spend holidays together.[2] Indeed, for some people the act of meeting together to consume

homemade food plays a central role in defining family; it is a symbolic way to separate a family unit from other social groups by allowing the cook(s) to personalize the meal and express affection via the effort that went into preparing the feast.[3]

As part of the design for the labels of their specialty coffee roasts, the owners of Caffe Artigiano, a coffeehouse chain in British Columbia, selected 16 photographs from their family albums to convey the message that they are a family-owned business. Employees are also considered part of the family.[4]

Defining the Modern Family

The **extended family** was once the most common family unit. It consists of three generations living together and often includes grandparents, aunts, uncles, and cousins. As evidenced by television families of the 1950s, the **nuclear family**—a mother and a father and one or more children (perhaps with a sheepdog thrown in for good measure)—became the model family unit over time. Although people may continue to conjure up an image of the typical family based on old shows, demographic data show that this image of the family is no longer a realistic picture.

JUST WHAT IS A HOUSEHOLD?

When it conducts the national census every five years, Statistics Canada regards any occupied housing unit as a household, regardless of the relationships among the people living there. A **census family**, as defined by Statistics Canada, is a household that contains at least one family (a husband and wife, married or living common-law, or a lone-parent of any marital status, with or without children who have never married living at home).[5] As of 2006, a couple living common-law may be of the opposite or same sex. Although Statistics Canada and other survey firms compile a massive amount of data on family households, certain categories are of particular interest to marketers.

There's no doubt that the way we think of family is evolving. Well over 1.6 million Canadians were divorced in 2005, and about 16 percent of families are lone-parent.[6] Divorces and separations are an accepted part of our culture, and marital breakups are an ever-present theme in popular books, music, and movies.[7] These changes in consumers' family structure often represent opportunities for marketers as purchasing patterns change and people make new choices about products and

www.cows.ca

Cows
Prince Edward Island

PEI's Ice Cream!
Original design T's, sweats and souvenirs!
Free catalogue 1 800 565 2697

← Decisions about family vacations are complex and involve the input of family members with diverse needs. This ad by Cow's suggests that it has something that will appeal to all family members.
Courtesy of Cow's.

brands.[8] For example, a Canadian entrepreneur created DivorceX, a digital imaging service that removes ex-spouses from family pictures![9] *Divorce Magazine* (***www.divorcemag.com***) targets this segment and offers wide-ranging advice on its website. And the theme is showing up in ads for products, such as cars and muscle pain relievers.[10]

Ironically, although many people proclaim that the traditional family is dead, it appears to be making a bit of a comeback among young couples. About 35 percent of Canadian mothers stay at home. However, the trend of taking time off from work to raise small children is concentrated among the best-educated and highest-achieving women. Staying at home appeals to those who have the luxury to do it. People in this age group consider balancing home and work their biggest challenge, and they also see it as a higher priority than earning a mega-income or an impressive title.[11]

AGE OF THE FAMILY

Most Canadians younger than 24 years have never been married or in a common-law relationship. The vast majority of 35 to 74 year olds are in these relationships. However, as might be expected as a result of the baby boom effect, the 35–44 age group has the greatest number of marriages and common-law relationships.[12] An important reason for these trends is that people are waiting longer to get married; according to Statistics Canada, the average age of first marriages is now 32 for women and 34 for men.[13] This trend has implications for businesses ranging from catering to cutlery. For example, because couples tend to marry later and many already have acquired basic household items, the trend is toward giving non-traditional items as wedding gifts, such as home electronics and computers.[14]

Marketing Opportunity !

Coca-Cola Co. executives in the U.K. realized that many of their hard-core consumers don't live in traditional families. The company's research found that a majority of British households were either childless couples or single people, many of them sharing a home with a roommate due to rising housing costs. To meet this need, the company introduced a "share size" bottle (1.25 litres) to make it easier for two roommates to share their soft drinks in the same way a traditional family would share a larger bottle. A clever advertising campaign depicts people sharing various products. One poster shows a young man and woman wearing a huge, stretched pair of underwear, while another features two middle-aged men sharing a slimy-looking toupee. The ads read, "New share size Coke. For those who like to share."[15]

→ Motorola (*www.motorola.com*) recognizes the new, mobile lifestyles of many modern families. The company has positioned its paging products to meet the needs of on-the-go parents. *Courtesy of Motorola Paging Products Group.*

FAMILY SIZE

In 1971, the average Canadian family was close to 4.0 people, but in 1997 that number slipped to 3.0 people, where it has remained.[16] Family size is dependent on factors such as educational level, the availability of birth control, and religion.[17] The **total fertility rate (TFR)** is based on the number of births per woman aged 15 to 49 years. Marketers keep a close eye on the population's birth rate to gauge how the pattern of births will affect demand for products in the future. The fertility rate increased dramatically in the late 1950s and early 1960s, the period of the so-called baby boomers. It declined in the 1970s and began to climb again in the 1980s as baby boomers began to have their own children in a "baby boomlet," and then fell again. In 2003, the TFR was 1.5, significantly below the replacement rate of 2.1 needed to maintain a stable Canadian population.[18]

Worldwide, surveys show that almost all women want smaller families today. This trend is a problem for European countries whose fertility rates have plummeted over the last decades. Ironically, although populations are booming in some developing parts of the world, industrialized countries face future crises because there will be relatively fewer young people to support their elders. For population levels to remain constant, this rate needs to be 2.0, so that the two children can replace their parents. That's not happening in places like Spain, Sweden, Germany, and Greece, where the fertility rate is 1.4 or lower. In contrast, the United States has a 2.0 rate, which demographers attribute to greater immigration.

Some countries are considering a variety of measures to encourage people to have more children. For example, Spain is weighing the options of cheaper utility bills for large families, assistance for young couples trying to afford homes, and the creation of hundreds of thousands of new preschools and nursery schools. The Italian government provides mothers with nearly full salary compensation for about a half-year of maternity leave, but women are stubbornly refusing to have more kids.[19]

NON-TRADITIONAL FAMILY STRUCTURES

As mentioned earlier, Statistics Canada regards any occupied housing unit as a household, regardless of the relationships among people living there. Thus, one person living alone, three roommates, or two lovers (whether straight or gay) constitutes a household. Less traditional households increased rapidly in the 1990s. For example, one-person households accounted for more than one-quarter of all households in 2001,[20] providing opportunities for new products to be developed, such as Pommery's POP Champagne, sold in single servings, which is a hit in Canada as well as in England, France, and Hong Kong.[21] Nearly 20 percent of all children live in lone-parent families,[22] about 19 percent of which were headed by men in 2001.[23] Same-sex households are increasingly common; as a result, more marketers are targeting them as a family unit; **www.gayweddings.com** and **www.twobrides.com** offer wedding decorations and gifts.[24] And companies that make products such as baby food and children's clothing are starting to advertise in *And Baby*, a gay parenting magazine.[25]

Many people share a living arrangement called *POSSLQ*, which stands for Persons of Opposite Sex Sharing Living Quarters. These changes are part of a broader shift toward non-family and child-free households.[26] Child-free couples are an attractive market segment for some companies (obviously not for others like Gerber Baby Food). Two-income couples without children tend to be better educated than two-income couples with children; for example, the child-free are more likely to have professional or managerial occupations.[27]

WHO'S LIVING AT HOME?

Although traditional families are shrinking, ironically in other cases the traditional extended family is very much a reality. Many adults care for their own parents as well as for their children. Some label middle-aged people "the sandwich generation" because they must attend to those above and below them in age.

In addition to dealing with live-in parents, many adults are surprised to find that their children are living with them longer or are moving back in.[28] As an Argentinean jeans ad asks, "If you are over 20 and still live with your parents, this is wrong. Isn't it high time you started looking for an apartment for them?" Demographers call these returnees **boomerang kids**. In 2001, 57 percent of young adults aged 20 to 24 lived at home (up from 41 percent in 1981); boomerang kids represented 24 percent of this group.[29]

Canadian young men are far more likely than young women to live with their parents.[30] Almost half of unmarried men in their twenties live at home, while just over one-third of unmarried women of that age range do.[31] Young adults who do leave the nest to live by themselves are relatively unlikely to return, whereas those

←Folger's Coffee has addressed an important need by allowing single people to brew one cup of coffee at a time.
Courtesy of Procter & Gamble.

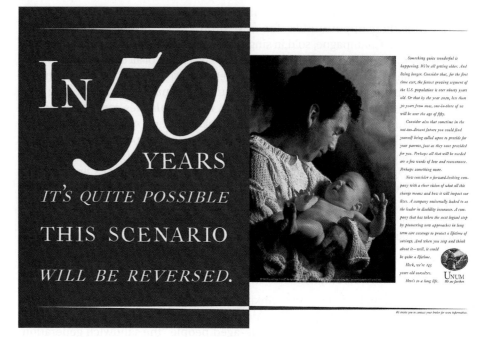

who move in with roommates are more likely to come back. And young people who move in with a romantic partner are more likely than average to end up back home if the relationship fails![41] If this trend continues, it will affect a variety of markets because boomerang kids spend less on housing and staples and more on discretionary purchases, such as entertainment.

The Family Life Cycle

A family's needs and expenditures are affected by factors such as the number of people (children and adults) in the family, their ages, and whether one, two, or more adults are employed outside the home. Two important factors that determine how a couple spends time and money are (1) whether they have children and (2) whether the woman works outside the home. Families with working mothers, for example, must often make allowances for expenses such as daycare, a work wardrobe for the woman, and home-cleaning services.

Recognizing that family needs and expenditures change over time, marketers apply the **family life cycle (FLC)** concept to segment households. The FLC combines trends in income and family composition with the changes in demands placed upon this income. As we age, our preferences and needs for products and activities tend to change. Households headed by 20-somethings spend less than average on most products and services because their households are small and their incomes are low. Income levels tend to rise (at least until retirement), so that people can afford more over time. Older consumers spend more per capita on luxury items such as gourmet foods and upscale home furnishings.[42] In addition, many purchases that must be made at an early age do not have to be repeated very often. For example, we tend to accumulate durable goods, such as large appliances, and replace them only as necessary.

A life-cycle approach to the study of the family assumes that pivotal events alter role relationships and trigger new stages of life that alter our priorities. These events include couples moving in together, the birth of a first child, the departure of the last child from the house, the death of a spouse, retirement of the principal wage earner, and possibly divorce.[43] As people move through these life stages we observe significant changes in expenditures in leisure, food, durables, and services, even after the figures have been adjusted to reflect changes in income.[44]

He left me. Good riddance.

He never picked up his socks. He thought I was

his mother. He didn't make me laugh anymore.

He's gone. Who cares... I kept the sofa.

280 KING STREET EAST, TORONTO 416.361.0331 | 4404 BLVD ST. LAURENT, MONTREAL 514.845.8285

← This ad reflects the growing acceptance of divorce as a non-traditional family structure.
Courtesy of Montauk.

← IKEA made history by daring to create what is believed to be the first mainstream TV ad to feature a gay relationship.
*Courtesy of IKEA US, Inc. **www.ikea.ca***

FLC MODELS

This focus on longitudinal changes in priorities is particularly valuable in predicting demand for specific product categories over time. For example, the money spent by a couple with no children on dining out and on vacations will probably be diverted for quite different purchases after the birth of a child. Ironically, although the entertainment industry focuses on winning the hearts and wallets of young consumers, it's mature consumers who have become North America's true party animals. Canadians under 35 years of age represent 25 percent of the population and 22 percent of expenditures on entertainment (just over $22 500 per capita); those older than 55 represent one-third of the population and 25 percent of entertainment expenditures (almost $33 000 per capita).[45]

Researchers have proposed a number of models to describe family life-cycle stages, but their usefulness has been limited because, in many cases, they have failed to take into account important social trends, such as the changing role of women, the acceleration of alternative lifestyles, child-free and delayed-child marriages, and single-parent households. Baby showers, for example, may be considered as a rite of passage to motherhood, fatherhood, or parenthood, depending on the gender ideologies and work orientation of one or both parents.[46]

Four variables are necessary to describe these trends adequately: (1) the age of the adult head of household, (2) marital status, (3) the presence or absence of children in the home, and (4) the children's ages. In addition, our definition of marital status (at least for analysis purposes) must be relaxed to include any couple living together in a long-term relationship. Thus, although roommates might not be considered "married," a man and woman who have established a household would be, as would two homosexual men who have a similar understanding.

When these changes are considered, this approach allows us to identify a set of categories that include many more types of family situations.[47] Figure 12–1 shows that these categories divide consumers into groups in terms of age, whether there is

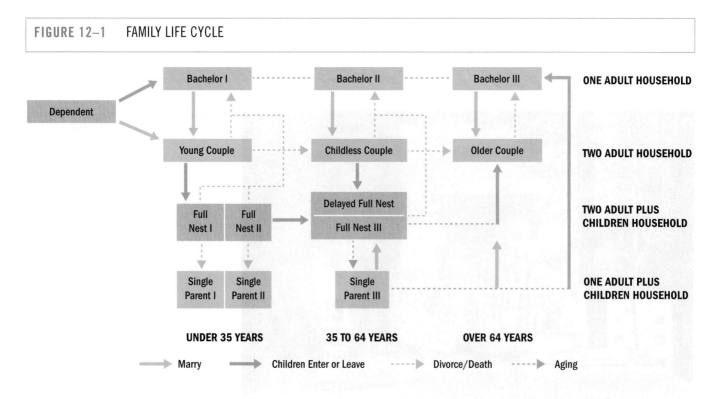

FIGURE 12–1   FAMILY LIFE CYCLE

Source: Robert E. Wilkes, "Household Life-cycle Stages, Transitions, and Product Expenditures," *Journal of Consumer Research* 22 (June 1995): 29. Published by The University of Chicago Press. Used with permission.

more than one adult present, and whether there are children at home. For example, it makes a distinction between the consumption needs of people in the Full Nest I category (in which the youngest child is younger than six), the Full Nest II category (in which the youngest child is older than six), the Full Nest III category (in which the youngest child is older than six and the parents are middle-aged), and the Delayed Full Nest (in which the parents are middle-aged but the youngest child is younger than six).

Life Cycle Effects on Buying

Consumers classified into these FLC stages show marked differences in consumption patterns.[48] Young bachelors and newlyweds have the most "modern" gender-role attitudes and are more likely to engage in exercise; to go out to bars, concerts, movies, and restaurants; to go out dancing; and to drink alcohol. Perhaps reflecting the bounty of wedding gifts, newlyweds are the most likely to own appliances, such as toaster ovens and electric coffee grinders. This tendency also explains why IKEA hosted a Toronto wedding in its store for a couple whose names were drawn from entries made at a special website.[49] Couples with children generally have higher expenses, such as for food and utility bills. Raising a Canadian child to age 18 cost almost $164 500 for a boy and $1000 less for a girl in 2001.[50] Families with young children are more likely to consume health foods, such as fruit, juice, and yogourt, while those made up of single parents and older children buy more junk foods. The dollar value of homes, cars, and other durables is lowest for bachelors and single parents, but it increases as people go through the full-nest and childless-couple stages. Readership for magazines such as *Canadian Family* and *Today's Parent* and visits to parenting websites like ***www.kaboose.ca*** and ***www.sweetmama.ca*** is highest among households with young children.[51] Babysitter and daycare usage is, of course, highest among single-parent and full-nest households, while home-maintenance services (e.g., lawnmowing) are most likely to be employed by older couples and bachelors.

An overall understanding of how the FLC can be applied can help marketers identify more clearly their target markets. Heinz Canada, for example, successfully changed its target from teenagers to families with children with an ad featuring a young boy feeding a french fry to a duck that eats the fry only after the duck has dipped it in ketchup.[52] Resorts targeting the family market, such as Keltic Lodge on Cape Breton Island, offer amenities such as baby-proofed rooms, hangouts for teenagers, and healthy children's food.[53] Now let's review how these different households make all these decisions in the first place.

FAMILY DECISION MAKING

The decision process within a household unit is a collective process. Certain matters are put on the table for discussion, different members may have different priorities and agendas, and there may be power struggles. In just about every living situation, whether a conventional family, students sharing a house or apartment, or some other non-traditional arrangement, group members seem to take on different roles.

Household Decisions

It is important for marketers to understand household decision-making dynamics. For example, when Chevrolet wanted to win back drivers with its new Venture minivan, the company sent teams of anthropologists to observe families in their natural habitats. Conventional wisdom says that minivan buyers are practical; they care about affordability, lots of features, and plenty of room. But these researchers

Net Profit

Seventy-seven percent of engaged couples use the internet when making wedding plans, The top three items they research online are cakes, dresses, and bridal bouquets. The top three purchases are favours, attendant gifts, and reply cards. Wherever you live, Jackie Howell can even help you plan your wedding from St. John's, Newfoundland! Her website, ***www.virtuallyhitched.com***, provides a lighthearted and highly personalized approach to making all the large and small decisions for the big day. Colourful cartoons and easily navigated pages serve thousands of future brides and grooms around the globe. Supplier partners include Wal-Mart, Wedding Star, and Canadian Tire. Top designers also advertise on the site.[54]

discovered a different story: People see the vehicles as part of the family. When consumers were asked to identify the best metaphor for a minivan, many picked a photo of a hang-glider because it represents freedom and families on the go. The advertising slogan for the Venture became "Let's go."[55]

Families make two basic types of decisions.[56] In a **consensual purchase decision** the group agrees on the desired purchase, differing only in terms of how it will be achieved. In these circumstances the family will most likely engage in problem solving and consider alternatives until the means for satisfying the group's goal is found. For example, a household considering adding a dog to the family, but that is concerned about who will take care of it, might decide to get a dog and draw up a chart assigning individuals to specific duties.

Unfortunately, life is not always so easy. In an **accommodative purchase decision**, group members have different preferences or priorities and cannot agree on a purchase that will satisfy the minimum expectations of all involved. It is here that bargaining, coercion, compromise, and the wielding of power are all likely to be used to achieve the primary goal of agreement on what to buy and who gets to use it. Family decisions, such as those related to the purchase and use of a family computer, often are characterized by an accommodative rather than a consensual decision. Some Canadians use computers for work they bring home and have to jockey with other family members for time on it. The computer industry geared up to sell multiple computers to solve these problems, but for many families less expensive forms of diplomacy are required.[57]

Conflict occurs when there is not complete correspondence in family members' needs and preferences. Although money is the most common source of conflict between partners, television choices come in a close second![58] And IKEA admits that 60 percent of couples argue while shopping in their stores. In general, decisions will involve conflict among family members to the extent that they are

Reality Check

University students living away from home can be thought of as having a substitute "family." Whether you live with your parents, with a spouse, or with other students, how are decisions made in your university residence "family?" Give a specific example of a decision that had to be made and the roles that were played.

> Everything we buy in our house is split 50:50 so one person making all the ultimate decisions is not going to be popular.... For example, whoever is in the bathroom when the toilet roll runs out obviously recognizes the need that now exists. This can be any unfortunate soul! The next person to go down to the shop is told to buy some more. Now the purchaser does not want to spend money on toilet roll when they could be spending it on food and drink. So, they usually have a quick glance, find the cheapest alternative and throw it into their basket. That is the extent of the search. It is a heuristic—buy the cheapest brand of toilet roll. There is no postpurchase evaluation unless somebody notices that it is

of particularly poor quality and so, next time, the second cheapest toilet roll is bought. Heuristics are very common amongst college residences. They make life easy for everyone.

Pamela Gillen, Dublin City University, Ireland

> A specific instance would be when my roommate and I decided whether or not we should get cable at our apartment. I was the information gatherer; I contacted the cable company to ask about rates, I looked into Bell ExpressVu, and I looked at the option of buying rabbit ears for the TV. My roommate's role was mainly that of being an influencer. She felt she didn't have the money to pay for cable or ExpressVu and, since we both had the position of buyer, her opinion heavily impacted the final decision. In the end, we chose rabbit ears for the TV.

Kari Groundwater, Mount Allison University, Canada

> A non-verbal rapport exists between my roommate and myself, that is, we each do our fair share. However,

when it comes time for the purchase of luxury items, such as television and/or stereo equipment, computer enhancements, etc., because my roommate has the financial resources to support the decision, the decision is primarily based upon his discretion. However, he does seek some of my input because he's considerate of the space that we share.

Eric Jude Guacena, Virginia Commonwealth University, USA

> Household decisions are often made by the core group by reference to common heuristics, and coercive power is used to impress these decisions on other members of the group, even those that were not party to the decision-making process. This differs from parental power, which is based on legitimate and reward power.

James Beattie, University of Exeter, England

somehow important or novel and/or if individuals have strong opinions about good and bad alternatives. The degree to which these factors generate conflict determines the type of decision the family will make.[59] Some specific factors determining the degree of conflict in family decision making include the following:[60]

- *Interpersonal need* (a person's level of investment in the group): A teenager may care more about what his or her family buys for the house than will a university student who is temporarily living on campus.

- *Product involvement and utility* (the degree to which the product in question will be used or will satisfy a need): A family member who is an avid coffee-drinker will obviously be more interested in the purchase of a new coffeemaker to replace a malfunctioning one than a similar expenditure for some other item.

- *Responsibility* (for procurement, maintenance, payment, and so on): People are more likely to have disagreements about a decision if it entails long-term consequences and commitments. A family decision about getting a dog may involve conflict regarding who will be responsible for walking it and feeding it.

- *Power* (the degree to which one family member exerts influence over the others in making decisions): In traditional families, the husband tends to have more power than the wife, who in turn has more than the oldest child, and so on. In family decisions, conflict can arise when one person continually uses the power he or she has within the group to satisfy his or her priorities. For example, if P.J. believed that his life would end if he could not have a Harry Potter birthday party, he might be more willing to resort to extreme tactics to influence his parents, perhaps by throwing a tantrum or refusing to participate in family chores.

DECISION ROLES

A number of specific roles are played by family members when a collective decision must be made. Depending on the nature of the decision, some or all of the family members may be involved, and one person may play any number (or even all) of these roles. These roles include:[61]

- *Initiator*—the family member who brings up the idea or need.

- *Information gatherer*—the family member who gathers information on a product or service.

- *Gatekeeper*—the family member who conducts the information search and controls the flow of information available to the group.

- *Influencer*—the family member who tries to sway the outcome of the decision; Some family members may be more motivated to get involved, and family members also differ in terms of the amount of power they have to convince others of their choice.

- *Decision maker*—the family member who holds the singular or joint power to determine whether or not to buy a product or service.

- *Buyer*—the family member who actually makes the purchase. The buyer may or may not actually use the product. This person may pay for the item, actually procure it, or both.

- *Preparer*—the family member who processes the product or directs the service into a form that can be consumed by other family members.

- *User*—the family member who ultimately uses the product or service.

- *Maintainer*—the family member responsible for the maintenance and upkeep of a product or service.

- *Disposer*—the family member who discards or discontinues the use of a product or service.

→Family members play a variety of roles in many activities, such as hiking trips.
© *The Procter & Gamble Company. Used by permission.*

IVORY.
Pure
Natural
For families

As a proud sponsor of the Trans Canada Trail, Ivory is linking Canadian families all across our great nation.

Help Ivory make it happen.

Gender Roles and Decision-Making Responsibilities

Who is responsible for making purchase decisions in the family? When one family member chooses a product, this is called an **autonomic decision**. In traditional households, for example, men often have sole responsibility for selecting a car, whereas decorating choices fall to women. **Syncratic decisions**, such as choosing a vacation destination, are made jointly. According to a study conducted by Roper Starch Worldwide, wives tend to have more say when buying groceries, children's toys, clothes, and medicines.

Syncratic decisions are common for cars, vacations, homes, appliances, furniture, home electronics, interior design, and long-distance phone services. As the couple's education increases, more decisions are likely to be made together.[62] Roper sees signs of a shift in marital decision making toward more compromise and turn-taking. For example, wives tend to win out in arguments about how the house is kept, while husbands get control of the remote.[63] In any case, spouses typically exert significant influence on decision making—even after one of them has died. An Irish study found that many widows claim to sense the continued presence of their dead husbands and to conduct "conversations" with them about household matters![64] Comments from married women who participated in focus groups conducted for *Redbook* magazine illustrate some of the dynamics of autonomic versus syncratic decision making:

- We just got our steps done and that was a big project. The contractor would talk (to my husband) and not talk to me. And I said, "Excuse me, I'm here, too."

- We are looking for a house now, and we're making decisions on which side of town we want and what size house we want, and it's a together decision. That's never how my mother did it.

- My husband did not want a van, because we have just one child, but I said, "I want a van. And it's not because everyone else has a van. I want comfort." He wanted a convertible. And we got a van.[65]

IDENTIFYING THE DECISION MAKER

Figuring out who makes buying decisions is an important issue for marketers because this information tells them who to target and whether or not they need to reach both spouses to influence a decision. For example, when marketing research in the 1980s indicated that women were playing a larger role in household purchasing decisions, lawnmower manufacturers began to emphasize the rotary mower over other power mowers. Rotary mowers, which conceal the cutting blades and engine, were often depicted being used by young women and smiling grandmothers to downplay fears of injuries.[66]

Researchers have paid special attention to which spouse plays the role of the **family financial officer (FFO)**, the individual who keeps track of the family's bills and decides how any surplus funds will be spent. Among newlyweds this role tends to be played jointly, and then, over time, one spouse or the other tends to take over these responsibilities.[67] As shown in Table 12–1, dual-earner couples in Canada differ in how they handle their respective incomes. The majority pool their income, but about 20 percent of husbands and 30 percent of wives keep their income separate.[68] Interestingly, husbands are perceived as the experts—that is, more knowledgeable—in the area of RRSPs by both themselves and their wives, and play a fairly significant role in most stages of wives' decision making regarding their RRSPs.[69] However, a recent survey by LeoShe found that women are increasingly acting as money managers.[70]

In traditional families (and especially those with low educational levels), women are primarily responsible for family financial management—that is, the man makes it and the woman spends it.[71] Each spouse "specializes" in certain activities.[72] The pattern is different among families in which spouses adhere to more modern gender-role norms. These couples believe that there should be more shared participation in family-maintenance activities. In these cases, husbands assume more responsibility for laundering, housecleaning, grocery shopping, parenting, and so

TABLE 12–1

HOW CANADIAN DUAL-EARNER COUPLES HANDLE THEIR INCOME

How Income Is Handled	Husbands	Wives
Separate—I handle all my income and keep it separate	18.9%	30.3%
Combined—I handle part of my income and give rest to partner or put in common pool	17.2%	16.2%
Pooled—all my income goes into common pool	58.1%	52.0%
My partner handles all my income	5.7%	1.5%

Source: Adapted from Judith Madill and Frances Woolley, unpublished preliminary findings of the Study of Financial Management and Decision Making in Canadian Households, 1997. Used with permission.

on, while the wife shares in traditionally "male" tasks, such as home maintenance and garbage removal.[76]

Decision-making responsibilities continue to evolve, especially as women continue to work outside the home and have less time to do the duties traditionally assigned to them. These working mothers often struggle with what one researcher has called the "juggling lifestyle," a frenzied, guilt-ridden compromise between conflicting cultural ideals of motherhood and professionalism.[77] Some Canadian families have worked out solutions that allow fathers to devote more time (or full time) to children and household concerns.[78]

Crown Diamond, a paint company, targets men who want to "take the pain out of painting,"[79] while Nissan Quest minivans are targeted at working moms with the tag line, "Moms have changed. Shouldn't minivans?"[80] Statistics Canada's website (*www.statscan.ca*) has a link that outlines the average time spent on a wide range of household and family activities by men and women. Overall, the degree to which a couple adheres to traditional gender-role norms determines how much their allocation of responsibilities, including consumer decision making, will fall along traditional lines.

Four factors appear to determine the degree to which decisions will be made jointly or by one or the other spouse:[81]

1. *Gender-role stereotypes*: Couples who believe in traditional gender-role stereotypes tend to make individual decisions for gender-typed products (i.e., those considered to be "masculine" or "feminine").

2. *Spousal resources:* The spouse who contributes more resources to the family has the greater influence. Interestingly, though, a recent study found that in households where wives earn more than their husbands, the women did not gain domestic power.[82]

3. *Experience:* Couples who have gained experience as a decision-making unit make individual decisions more frequently than those with less experience.

4. *Socio-economic status:* Middle-class families make more joint decisions than do either higher- or lower-class families.

With many women now working outside the home, men are participating more in housekeeping activities, as shown in Table 12–2. Among married Canadian couples it was found that about one-third of the husbands did the family food shopping by themselves and at similar times during the week. However, among those same couples, nearly 80 percent of the wives versus about 25 percent of the husbands had sole responsibility for getting the family food shopping done according to expectations.[83] The spouses used similar strategies for time management, store loyalty, and in-store shopping but were different in some important tactical areas. Husbands saw budgeting as a distinct activity, while wives saw it as related to organizing and using a shopping list. Wives were also more likely to be drawn to other stores in search of bargains and to place more importance on in-store service and product availability.[84] On the other hand, there is evidence that men enjoy cooking. Kitchenware shops across Canada report that half their customers are men.[85]

A study of married Canadian couples showed that working wives (career-oriented and income-oriented) have a convenience-based, pragmatic orientation toward food shopping compared with at-home wives; they are interested in accessibility, availability, and one-stop shopping. More surprisingly, the income-oriented wives were found to differ from the career-oriented wives; income-oriented wives were most likely to share the responsibility for food shopping with their husbands and to be flexible in the arrangements.[86] And if they need additional support they can always visit a "meal assembly centre," where they can assemble family meals from prepared ingredients. These centres include Dinner Works in Vancouver, Dashing Dishes in Calgary, Supper Works in Toronto, and What's for Supper? in Halifax.[87]

TABLE 12–2

CONSUMER BEHAVIOUR OF FAMILY SEGMENTS BASED ON WORK ORIENTATION OF SPOUSES

	Dual Career	Dual Income	Traditional
Grocery Shopping			
Who does it?	Whoever enjoys it	Wife usually	Wife
How often?	Once a week or once a month	Once a week or once a month	Once a week
When?	No specific day	Same day	Same day
Store loyalty	No	Yes	Yes
Household Conveniences			
Dishwasher and microwave oven	Yes	No	No
Freezer	For bulk purchases, extra cooking	For bulk purchases	For garden harvest
Attitude toward conveniences	Appreciate time saved	To save money	To save money
Child Care			
Discipline	Both spouses	Wife, husband supportive	Wife, husband laissez-faire
Preparation for school	Both spouses	Wife	Wife
Family Vacation			
Who decides?	Both spouses and children	Both spouses	Both spouses
Who goes?	Family, sometimes separate holiday for children	Family	Family
Arrangements	Both spouses	Wife	Wife
Criteria	Culture	Family and friends visiting	Family visits
Transportation	Fly, some driving	Drive	Drive
Places	Europe, North America	North America	Canada
Household Durables			
Who decides?	Both spouses	Both spouses	Wife
Who buys?	Both spouses	Wife, sometimes with husband	Wife
Criteria	Time saving, style, price not a factor, very little shopping around, quality stores	Price major factor, comparison shopping, mid-quality stores	Price major factor, comparison shopping, mid-bargain stores
Lifestyle	Integration of career and family life by both spouses. Affluence allows for conveniences that make both family and individual leisure-time pursuits possible.	Both spouses focus on the family, although the wife usually tends to household and child-care concerns. Both spouses work to provide needs of family.	The wife's domain is the home, the husband's domain is work. Range of individual and family activities is influenced by specialized roles and the earning power of the husband's job.

Source: Adapted from James W. Hanson and Rosemary Polegato, "Identifying Dual Career, Dual Income and Traditional Family Segments," in *Marketing* 4, ed. James D. Forbes (Montreal: Administrative Sciences Association of Canada, 1983), pp. 30–38.

Despite recent changes in decision-making responsibilities, women still are primarily responsible for the continuation of the family's **kin-network system**: They perform rituals intended to maintain ties among family members, both immediate and extended. This function includes activities such as coordinating visits among relatives, calling and writing family members, sending greeting cards, making social engagements, and elder care.[89] This organizing role means that women often make important decisions about their families' leisure activities and are more likely to decide with whom their families will socialize.

HEURISTICS IN JOINT DECISION MAKING

The **synoptic ideal** calls for the husband and wife to take a common view and act as joint decision makers. According to this ideal, they would very thoughtfully weigh alternatives, assign one another well-defined roles, and calmly make mutually beneficial consumer decisions. The couple would act rationally and analytically and would use as much information as possible to maximize joint utility. In reality, however, spousal decision making is often characterized by the use of influence or methods that are likely to reduce conflict. A couple "reaches" rather than "makes" a decision. This process has been described as "muddling through."[90]

One common technique for simplifying the decision-making process is the use of *heuristics* (see Chapter 9). Some decision-making patterns observed frequently when a couple makes decisions in buying a new house illustrate the use of heuristics:

- The couple's common preferences are based upon salient, objective dimensions rather than more subtle, hard-to-define cues. For example, a couple may easily agree on the number of bedrooms they need in the new home but will have difficulty achieving a common view of how the home should look.

- The couple agrees on a system of task specialization, in which each is responsible for certain duties or decision areas and does not interfere in the other's "turf." For many couples these assignments are likely to be influenced by their perceived gender roles. For example, the wife may scout out houses in advance that meet the couple's requirements, while the husband determines whether the couple can obtain a mortgage.

- Concessions are based on the intensity of each spouse's preferences. One spouse will yield to the influence of the other in many cases simply because his or her level of preference for a certain attribute is not particularly intense, whereas in other situations he or she will be willing to exert effort to obtain a favourable decision.[91] In cases where intense preferences for different attributes exist, rather than attempt to influence each other, spouses will "trade off" a less-intense preference for a more strongly felt one. For example, a husband who is somewhat indifferent about kitchen design may defer to his wife but expect that, in turn, he will be allowed to design his own garage workshop.

CHILDREN AS DECISION MAKERS: CONSUMERS-IN-TRAINING

It's hard to find an adult in Helsinki (home to the Finnish company Nokia) who doesn't have a cell phone; 92 percent of the city's households have at least one, if not several. But although cell phones have been an accepted part of daily life for grown-ups and teenagers for more than a decade, the latest boom in cell phone use is occurring among young children. Many of them get their first phone at around age seven, when they start to engage in activities, such as soccer practice, where their parents aren't present.

Now there's an expanding market for accessories, such as phone covers decorated with pictures of Donald Duck or Star Wars characters, even though Finland has very strict laws about how products can be pitched to children. Because they are forbidden to market directly to children, companies try to convince their parents that the phones are an essential child-rearing tool in a society where most parents work. They argue that "mobile parenting" lets mom and dad keep track of their children by telephone rather than in person, and in return Finnish children get a head start on using an adult product.[92]

The Finns are not the only ones who bend over backward to please their kids with loads of "stuff." Anyone who has had the "delightful" experience of grocery shopping with children in tow knows that children often have a say (sometimes a loud, whiny one) in what their parents buy. It has been estimated that children between the ages of 4 and 12 collectively spend, or influence their parents to spend, billions of dollars a year.[93] Indeed, children make up three distinct markets:[94]

1. *Primary market:* Children spend a lot on their own wants and needs. Many receive allowances. The rest of their earning power comes from money earned for doing household chores and from gifts from relatives. They buy food, beverages, toys, apparel, movies, and games.[95]

2. *Influence market:* **Parental yielding** occurs when a parental decision maker is influenced by a child's request and "surrenders." This is a key driver of product selections because about 90 percent of requests to a parent are by brand name.[96] Indeed, research conducted by Corus Entertainment indicated that children in Canada have memorized between 300 and 400 brand names by the time they are 10 years old and that they influence about $20 million in household spending. Parents respond favourably to 75 percent of their children's requests.[97] In a recent study, Youth Culture found that 60 percent of back-to-school purchases were made by parents, but 70 percent of teens went along on the shopping trip to try to ensure they got what they wanted.[98]

The likelihood that yielding will occur depends partly upon the dynamics within a particular family. As we all know, parental styles range from permissive to strict, and they also vary in terms of the amount of responsibility children are given to make decisions.[102] One study documented the strategies that kids use to request purchases. Although most children simply asked for things, some other common tactics included saying they had seen the product on television, saying that a sibling or friend had the product, or bargaining by offering to do chores. Other actions were less innocuous; they included directly placing the object in the cart and continuous pleading—often a "persuasive" behaviour.[103] In addition, the amount of influence children have over consumption is culturally determined. Children who live in individualistic cultures, like those in Canada and the United States, have more direct influence, while children in collective cultures like the Japanese get their way more indirectly.[104]

3. *Future market:* Children have a way of growing up to be adults (eventually), and savvy marketers try to lock in brand loyalty at an early age. That explains why Kodak is working so hard to encourage children to become photographers. Currently, a small percentage of 5- to 12-year-old children own cameras, and they shoot an average of just one roll of film a year. The company produces ads that portray photography as a cool pursuit and as a form of rebellion. Some cameras are packaged with an envelope so that the film can be mailed directly for processing so parents can't see the photos. Another example is the cling vinyl Magic Mirror used by Colgate-Palmolive Canada to build a long-term brand relationship with young children. This media vehicle appealed to children (and their parents) because it helped to make brushing a positive experience.[105]

Indeed, many of the allegiances we form to products as children do stay with us as we age. This tendency is especially pronounced in Japan, where the culture encourages adults to act like children. The Japanese are obsessed with "cute" images and products that may strike some North Americans as a bit, well, juvenile. Nippon Airways spent about $1.5 million (Canadian) in licensing fees and paint to decorate the exterior of three of its 747s with seven-metre high images of pocket monsters from Pokémon. Cute characters abound in Japan, including the image of Miffy the bunny on Asahi Bank ATM cards and Hello Kitty charm bags at Shinto shrines. When a Japanese baseball player hits a home run, he is awarded a stuffed animal. Some explain this obsession by noting that the Japanese miss childhood because adulthood in Japan is so demanding and there is such pressure to conform.[106]

Consumer Socialization

We've seen that children are responsible for a lot of marketplace activity, but how do they know what they like and want? Children do not spring from the womb with consumer skills already in memory. **Consumer socialization** is the process "by which young people acquire skills, knowledge and attitudes relevant to their functioning in the marketplace."[107] Where does this knowledge come from? Friends and teachers certainly participate in the process. For instance, children talk to one another about consumer products, and this tendency increases with age.[108] Especially for young children, though, the two primary socialization sources are the family and television.

INFLUENCE OF PARENTS

Parents' influences in consumer socialization are both direct and indirect. (See, for example, ***www.canadianparents.com***.) They deliberately try to instill their own values about consumption in their children ("You're going to learn the value of a dollar"). Parents also determine the degree to which their children will be exposed to other information sources, such as television, salespeople, and peers.[109] Cultural expectations regarding the involvement of children in purchase decisions influence when and how parents socialize their children as consumers. For example, parents in traditional cultures, such as Greece and India, have later developmental time-tables for consumer-related skills and understanding advertising practices than do American and Australian parents.[110]

Grown-ups serve as significant models for observational learning (see Chapter 3). Children learn about consumption by watching their parents' behaviour and imitating it. Marketers encourage this practice by packaging adult products in child versions. In addition, many retailers are trying to attract parents by offering environments where children and grown-ups can feel at home. Home Depot conducts weekly workshops for children. Starbucks coffee shops have built children's play areas to encourage moms to gather there and drink coffee.[111] This "passing down" of product preferences helps to create brand loyalty; researchers have found evidence of intergenerational influence when they have studied the product choices of mothers and their daughters.[112]

The process of consumer socialization begins with infants, who accompany their parents to stores where they are initially exposed to marketing stimuli. Within the first two years, children begin to make requests for desired objects. As they learn to walk, they also begin to make their own selections when they are in stores. By around the age of five, most children are making purchases with the help of parents and grandparents, and by eight most are making independent purchases and have become full-fledged consumers.[113] Gentle guidance and high parental trust and expectations in giving an allowance or pocket money seem to lead to more knowledgeable 8- to 10-year-old consumers.[114] The sequence of steps involved in turning kids into consumers is summarized in Figure 12–2.

Parents characterized by certain styles have been found to socialize their children differently.[115] For example, "authoritarian parents" who are hostile, restrictive, and emotionally uninvolved do not have warm relationships with their children, are active in filtering the types of media to which their children are exposed, and tend to have negative views about advertising. "Neglecting parents" also do not have warm relationships, but they are more detached from their children and do not exercise much control over what their children do. In contrast, "indulgent parents" communicate more with their children about consumption-related matters and are less restrictive. They believe that children should be allowed to learn about the marketplace without much intervention.

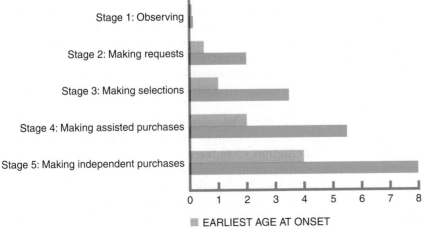

A CONSUMER IS BORN

Children start accompanying parents to the marketplace as early as one month old and begin to make independent purchases as early as four years old.

- Stage 1: Observing
- Stage 2: Making requests
- Stage 3: Making selections
- Stage 4: Making assisted purchases
- Stage 5: Making independent purchases

■ EARLIEST AGE AT ONSET
■ MEDIAN AGE AT ONSET

FIGURE 12–2

FIVE STAGES OF CONSUMER DEVELOPMENT BY EARLIEST AGE AT ONSET AND MEDIAN AGE AT ONSET

Source: Adapted from McNeal and Yeh, *American Demographics* (June 1993): 36. Reprinted by permission of American Demographics, Inc.

Advertising's influence over us begins at a very early age. As we've seen, many marketers start to push their products on children to encourage them to build a habit early on. One recent, controversial exception occurred in France, where a McDonald's ad placed in the magazine *Femme Actuelle* actually encouraged parents to limit children's visits to its outlets by proclaiming, "There is no reason to eat excessive amounts of junk food, nor go more than once a week to McDonald's." A spokesman for McDonald's in the United States said the U.S. company did not agree with the views expressed in the ad.[117] This anti-consumption message is certainly a notable exception to the barrage of messages aimed at children, especially on television. An interesting twist is McDonald's two-minute workout television spots for children, which air on Teletoon and YTV. The tag line is: "It's what I eat and what I do...I'm lovin' it." Images of fries, burgers, and the Golden Arches are absent.[118]

In 2001, Canadian children aged 2 to 17 watched an average of 14 to 15 hours of television per week.[119] As a result, they are constantly bombarded with messages about consumption, contained both in commercials and in the shows themselves. Because the media teaches people about a culture's values and myths, the more a child is exposed to television, whether the show is *The Osbournes*, *Da Vinci's Inquest*, or *Barney*, the more he or she will accept the images depicted there as real.[120] A British TV show called *Teletubbies* targets viewers from three months to two years old. The show has become an international obsession, attracting viewers from more than 20 countries every weekday morning. A Teletubbies record even sold enough copies to make it to the number one spot on the British charts.[121]

In addition to seeing the large volume of programming targeted directly at children, children are also exposed to idealized images of what it is like to be an adult. Because children over the age of six do about a quarter of their television viewing during prime time, they are affected by programs and commercials targeted at adults.[122] Interestingly, Corus Entertainment found a marked increase in Canadian parents co-viewing television shows with their children. Programs included *SpongeBob SquarePants* and YTV's weekend movie block.[123]

Gender-Role Socialization

Children pick up on the concept of gender identity (see Chapter 5) at an earlier age than was previously believed—perhaps as young as age one or two. By the age of three most children categorize driving a truck as masculine and cooking and cleaning as feminine.[124] Even cartoon characters who are portrayed as helpless are most likely to wear frilly or ruffled dresses.[125] Toy companies perpetuate these stereotypes by promoting gender-linked toys with commercials that reinforce gender-role expectations through their casting, emotional tone, and copy.[126]

One function of children's play is to rehearse for adulthood. Children act out different roles they might assume later in life and learn about the expectations others have of them. The toy industry provides the props children use to perform these roles.[127] Depending on which side of the debate you're on, these toys either reflect or teach children about what society expects of males versus females. Preschool boys and girls do not exhibit many differences in toy preferences, but after the age of five they part company: Girls tend to stick with dolls, while boys gravitate toward "action figures" and high-tech diversions.

Industry critics charge that this is because the toy industry is dominated by males, while toy-company executives counter that they are simply responding to the natural preferences of children.[128] Indeed, after two decades of working to avoid boy-versus-girl stereotypes, many companies seem to have decided that differences are inevitable. Lego is usually identified as a product for boys, but it now has a CLIKITS line for girls. Toys R Us unveiled a new store design after interviewing 10 000 customers, and the chain now has separate sections called Girls World and Boys World.[129] Boys tend to be more interested in battle and competition, while girls

---

The Tangled Web

Canadian children are increasingly choosing their computers over their televisions, but TV is still an important medium for reaching them. Many kids move back and forth between the two media; YTV research found that 40 percent of tweens watch TV while surfing the internet. Their studies also show that tweens spend progressively more time on the internet as they get older:

- 9 and 10 year olds: three hours per week
- 11 and 12 year olds: five hours per week
- 13 and 14 year olds: eight hours per week

A 2003/2004 study by Nielsen Media Research found that children aged 2 to 11 watched television 17.3 hours per week (up from 14.2 hours in 1997/1998); viewers in the 12 to 17 age group watched 16.8 hours per week (up from 15.8 in 1997/1998). With television still an important medium among children, many programs and sites are linked together through branded games, contests, and even content.

According to YTV and Youthography, respectively, 29 percent of children download movies or TV shows, and 63 percent play online games. One popular site is *www.neopets.com*, which has more than 30 million members around the world who spend an average of six hours per month creating, raising, and playing games with virtual pets. Games at *www.family.ca* are also very popular, with 800 000 unique visits per month.

Websites for younger children, such as *www.treehouse.ca*, also have areas for parents. Research shows that 36 percent of users are parents surfing with their children; 26 percent are parents surfing alone; and 38 percent are children surfing alone. The children's area of the site is ad-free, but the parents' area advertises events, books, and some household products.

Older children love to interact with friends and meet new friends online, so ensuring safety through monitoring continues to be a concern. A 2005 study showed that 60 percent of tweens use instant messaging (IM) regularly, and 40 percent consider IM their favourite online activity. Ninety-five percent of Canadian IM users use IM Canada.[130]

are more interested in creativity and relationships. This is what experts refer to as "male and female play patterns." Because children in daycare are exposed to other children earlier than in the past, these patterns are being observed in younger children than used to be the case.[131]

Recognizing the powerful role toys play in consumer socialization, doll manufacturers are creating characters they hope will teach little girls about the real world. Recently, a group of California entrepreneurs brought out a line of dolls called Smartees. These characters include Ashley the attorney, Emily the entrepreneur, and Destiny the doctor. A paperback tells each doll's story and includes a sample resumé for a person who might have that job in real life. Not to be outdone, Barbie's recent rebirth as a career woman illustrates how a firm can take concerns about socialization to heart.[132] Now a Working Woman Barbie is on the market as the result of a partnership between Mattel and *Working Woman* magazine. She comes with a miniature play computer and cell phone, as well as a CD-ROM with information about understanding finances.[133]

Some companies have tried to level the playing field by doing research to understand differences in how boys and girls play.[134] Games like "Tetris," "Myst," and "Where in the World Is Carmen Sandiego?" appeal equally to girls and boys. These games are essentially non-violent and include puzzles, quizzes, and intriguing narrative.[135]

Cognitive Development

The ability of children to make mature, "adult" consumer decisions obviously increases with age (not that grown-ups always make mature decisions!). Marketers can segment children by age in terms of their **stage of cognitive development**, or ability to comprehend concepts of increasing complexity. The foremost proponent of the idea that children pass through distinct stages of cognitive development was the Swiss psychologist Jean Piaget, who believed that each stage is characterized by a certain cognitive structure the child uses to handle information.[136] In one classic demonstration of cognitive development, Piaget poured the contents of a short, squat glass of lemonade into a taller, thinner glass. Five year olds, who still believed that the shape of the glass determined the amount of its contents, thought this glass held more liquid than the first glass. They are in what Piaget termed a *pre-operational stage of development*. In contrast, six year olds tended to be unsure, but seven year olds knew the amount of lemonade had not changed.

Many developmental specialists no longer believe that children necessarily pass through these fixed stages at the same time. An alternative approach regards children as differing in *information processing capability*, or ability to store and retrieve information from memory (see Chapter 3). The following three groupings have been identified by this approach:[137]

1. *Limited:* Below the age of 6 years, children do not employ storage-and-retrieval strategies.

2. *Cued:* Children between the ages of 6 and 12 years employ these strategies, but only when prompted.

3. *Strategic:* Children 12 years and older spontaneously employ storage-and-retrieval strategies.

This sequence of development underscores the notion that children do not think like adults and cannot be expected to use information in the same way. It also reminds us that they do not necessarily form the same conclusions as adults when presented with product information. For example, children are not as likely to realize that something they see on television is not "real," and as a result they are more vulnerable to persuasive messages.

There is evidence that indicates that very young children are able to learn consumption-related information surprisingly well.[138] Recent research underscores the idea that children's understanding of brand names evolve as they age. Children learn to relate to brand names at an early age, recognizing brand names in stores, developing preferences for certain brands over others, and requesting branded items by name. However, when it comes to kids, brand names function as simple perceptual cues, identifying a familiar object with particular features. Conceptual brand meanings, which specify the non-observable abstract features of the product, enter into the picture in middle childhood (around age eight); children incorporate them into their thinking and judgments a few years later. By the time children reach 12 years of age, they are able to think about brands on a conceptual or symbolic level, and are also likely to incorporate these meanings into many types of brand-related judgments.[139]

Marketing Research and Children

Despite their buying power, relatively little real data on children's preferences or influences on spending patterns are available. Compared with adults, they are difficult subjects for market researchers. They tend to be undependable reporters of their own behaviour, they have poor recall, and they often do not understand abstract questions.[140] This problem is compounded in Europe, where some countries restrict marketers' ability to interview children. Still, market research can pay off, and many companies, as well as a number of specialized firms, have been successful in researching some aspects of this segment.[141]

PRODUCT TESTING

A particularly helpful type of research with children is product testing. Young subjects can provide a valuable perspective on what products will succeed with other children. These insights are obtained either by watching children play with toys or by involving them in focus groups. The Fisher-Price Company maintains a nursery known as the Playlab. Children are chosen from a waiting list of 4000 to play with new toys while staff members watch from behind a one-way mirror.[142] Heinz Canada recently held a nationwide contest for kids to create new ketchup bottle labels and received thousands of entries,[143] and McCain's relied on information

THERE'S NO SUBSTITUTE FOR THE ZOO.

Get your annual pass at calgaryzoo.ab.ca. **calgaryzoo**

← This poster for the Calgary Zoo appeals to children as well as adults.
Courtesy of the Calgary Zoo.

from focus groups with 6 to 12 years olds to come up with the names and characters for Zwak, their juice-box fruit beverage.[145]

MESSAGE COMPREHENSION

Because children differ in their ability to process product-related information, many serious ethical issues are raised when advertisers try to appeal directly to them.[146] Children's advocacy groups argue that children under the age of seven years did not understand the persuasive intent of commercials, and younger children could not readily distinguish between a commercial and programming.[147]

Children's cognitive defences are not yet sufficiently developed to filter out commercial appeals, so, in a sense, altering their brand preferences may be likened to "shooting fish in a barrel," as one critic put it.[148] Although some ads include a disclaimer, which is a disclosure intended to clarify a potentially misleading or deceptive statement, the evidence suggests that young children do not adequately understand disclaimers.[149] Nonetheless, the new American model seems to view the child consumer, referred to as the "kid customer," not as someone to be sheltered from the market, but as someone who should engage in its pleasures.[150]

Advertising to Children: An Ethical Minefield

It has been suggested that children should be better educated as to how advertising works and encouraged to question what they see on television, perhaps through public-service advertising.[151] However, there is some controversy about who should provide that education. Of some help is *Street Cents*, a children's version of *Marketplace*; media education in schools and communities; and *Media Madness: An Insider's Guide to Media,* published by Kids Can Press.[152]

In addition, the Canadian Advertising Foundation's Broadcast Code for Advertising to Children provides industry guidelines in areas such as product claims (is it clear how the toy actually looks and works?); sales pressure techniques (do they urge the child to ask parents to buy the product?); endorsements by program characters; scheduling (no more than eight minutes per hour of children's programming); safety; and social values.

Canadians are not alone in their concern about children's advertising. In Europe regulations are confusing, because each country still has different rules. For example, the Netherlands bars ads for sweets before eight o'clock p.m., the ads cannot feature children under age 14, and a toothbrush must appear on the screen for at least part of the commercial. Spain and Germany ban ads for war toys.[153] In Denmark and the United States, there is also a call for rules to govern marketing operations on the internet when children are the target.[154]

CHAPTER SUMMARY

MARKETERS OFTEN NEED TO UNDERSTAND CONSUMERS' BEHAVIOUR RATHER THAN CONSUMER BEHAVIOUR, BECAUSE IN MANY CASES MORE THAN ONE PERSON IS INVOLVED IN DECIDING WHAT TO BUY.

- Many purchasing decisions are made by more than one person. Family or household decision making occurs whenever two or more people are involved in evaluating, selecting, or using a product or service. In families, several different roles may be played during the decision-making process. These roles include initiator, information gatherer, gatekeeper (one who controls the flow of information within the group), influencer, decision maker, buyer, preparer, user, maintainer, and disposer.

MANY IMPORTANT DEMOGRAPHIC DIMENSIONS OF A POPULATION RELATE TO FAMILY AND HOUSEHOLD STRUCTURE.

- Demographics are statistics that measure a population's characteristics. Some of the most important of these relate to family structure—for example, the total fertility rate, the marriage rate, and the divorce rate. A household is an occupied housing unit.

OUR TRADITIONAL NOTIONS ABOUT FAMILIES OFTEN ARE OUTDATED.

- The number and type of Canadian households are changing in many ways, including delays in getting married and having children, and differences in the

composition of family households, which increasingly are headed by a single parent. New perspectives on the family life cycle, which focus on how people's needs change as they move through different stages in their lives, are forcing marketers to consider more seriously consumer segments such as homosexuals, divorcees, and childless couples when they develop targeting strategies.

MEMBERS OF A FAMILY UNIT PLAY DIFFERENT ROLES AND HAVE DIFFERENT AMOUNTS OF INFLUENCE WHEN MAKING PURCHASE DECISIONS.

- Families must be understood in terms of their decision-making dynamics. Spouses in particular have different priorities and exert varying amounts of influence in terms of effort and power. Children are also increasingly influential during a widening range of purchase decisions.

CHILDREN LEARN OVER TIME WHAT AND HOW TO CONSUME.

- Children undergo a process of socialization whereby they learn how to be consumers. Parents and friends instill some of this knowledge, but a lot of it comes from exposure to mass media and advertising. Because children are, in some cases, easily persuaded, the ethical aspects of marketing to them are hotly debated among consumers, academics, and marketing practitioners.

KEY TERMS

Accommodative purchase decision   p. 350

Autonomic decisions   p. 352

Boomerang kids   p. 345

Census family   p. 342

Consensual purchase decision   p. 350

Consumer socialization   p. 358

Extended family   p. 342

Family financial officer (FFO)   p. 353

Family life cycle (FLC)   p. 346

Kin-network system   p. 356

Nuclear family   p. 342

Parental yielding   p. 357

Stage of cognitive development   p. 361

Syncratic decisions   p. 352

Synoptic ideal   p. 356

Total fertility rate (TFR)   p. 344

REVIEW QUESTIONS

1. What is a nuclear family, and how is it different from an extended family?

2. How is a nation's total fertility rate (TFR) calculated? What TFR is required to ensure that population size does not decline?

3. Who are the boomerang kids?

4. What is the FLC, and why is it important to marketers?

5. List some variables we must consider when trying to understand different stages in the FLC.

6. What is the difference between a consensual and an accommodative purchase decision? What are some factors that help to determine how much conflict the family will experience when making a decision?

7. List at least four roles taken by family members in family decision making.

8. Summarize the difference between an autonomic and a syncratic decision.

9. What are some differences between "traditional" and "modern" couples in terms of how they allocate household responsibilities?

10. What factors help to determine if decisions will be made jointly or by one spouse or the other?

11. What is a kin-network system?

12. Describe a heuristic that a couple might use when making a decision, and provide an example.

13. What are three reasons why children are an important segment to marketers?

14. What is consumer socialization? Who are some important players in this process? How do toys contribute?

15. Discuss stages of cognitive development and how these relate to the comprehension of marketing messages.

16. Why is it difficult to conduct marketing research with children?

CONSUMER BEHAVIOUR CHALLENGE

Discuss

1. Is the family unit dead? Please explain your answer.

2. Discuss the pros and cons of the childless movement. Are followers of this philosophy selfish?

3. Are marketers robbing kids of their childhood?

4. Do you think market research should be performed on children? Give the reasons for your answer.

5. What do you think of the practice of companies and survey firms collecting public data (e.g., from marriage licences, birth records, and even death announcements) to compile targeted mailing lists? State your opinion from both a consumer's and a marketer's perspective.

6. Marketers have been criticized for donating products and services to educational institutions in exchange for free promotion. Is this a fair exchange in your opinion, or should corporations be prohibited from attempting to influence youngsters in school?

7. For each of these five product categories—groceries, cars, vacations, furniture, and appliances—describe the way in which you believe a married couple's choices would be affected if they had children.

8. In identifying and targeting newly divorced couples, do you think marketers are exploiting these couples' situations? Are there instances when you think marketers may actually be helpful to them? Support your answers with examples.

Experiential Exercises

9. Arrange to interview two married couples, one younger and one older. Prepare a response form listing five product categories—groceries, furniture, appliances, vacations, and cars—and ask each spouse to indicate, without consulting the other, whether purchases in each category are made by joint or unilateral decisions, and to indicate whether the unilateral decisions are made by the husband or the wife. Compare each couple's responses for agreement between husbands and wives relative to who makes the decisions and compare both couples' overall responses for differences relative to the number of joint versus unilateral decisions. Report your findings and conclusions.

10. Collect ads for three different product categories in which the family is targeted. Find another set of ads for different brands of the same items in which the family is not featured. Prepare a report on the

effectiveness of the approaches. Which specific categories would most likely benefit from a family emphasis?

11. Observe the interactions between parents and children in the cereal section of a local grocery store. Prepare a report on the number of children who expressed preferences, how they expressed their preferences, and how parents responded, including the number who purchased the child's choice.

12. Watch three hours of children's programming on commercial television stations and evaluate the marketing techniques used in the commercials in terms of the ethical issues raised in the final section of this chapter. Report your findings and conclusions.

13. Select a product category and, using the life cycle stages given in the chapter, list the variables that will affect consumers' purchase decisions for the product in each stage of the cycle.

14. Consider three important changes in modern family structure. For each, find an example of a marketer who has attempted to be conscious of this change as reflected in product communications, retailing innovations, or other aspects of the marketing mix. If possible, find examples of marketers who have failed to keep up with these developments.

CBC ⏚ VIDEO VIGNETTE

CONCEPTS AT WORK FOR ADVERTISING TO CHILDREN

Children are socialized as citizens and consumers by influences in their environment ranging from their parents to the media. As early as the 1970s, parents began voicing their concerns about how advertising, especially television advertising, creates problems for them as parents and for society in general. This activism has been salved, in part, by the establishment of the Broadcast Code for Advertising to Children and the Canadian Toy Testing Council. However, concerns persist and flare up when parents, educators, and other professionals who are interested in the media's effects on children hear about books, conferences, and industry activities related to selling products to children.

Questions

1. How do children learn to be consumers? How large is the children's market in Canada?

2. What exactly are parents' concerns about advertising aimed at children?

3. How effective is the Canadian Toy Testing Council and the Broadcast Code for Advertising to Children (under 12 years old)?

4. Do media literacy programs address parents' concerns about the effect of advertising on children?

Resource: "Kids' Advertising," *Marketplace #5,* CBC Air Date: November 14, 2001.

NOTES

1. "Census Families in Private Households by Family Structure and Presence of Children, by Province and Territory (2001 Census)," Statistics Canada's website, *www40.statcan.ca/l01/cst01/famil54a.htm?sdi=family*, accessed May 26, 2006. Robert Boutilier, "Diversity in Family Structures," *American Demographics Marketing Tools* (1993): 4–6; W. Bradford Fay, "Families in the 1990s: Universal Values, Uncommon Experiences," *Marketing Research: A Magazine of Management & Applications* 5, 1 (Winter 1993): 47.

2. Ellen Graham, "Craving Closer Ties, Strangers Come Together as Family," *Wall Street Journal* (March 4, 1996): B1 (2 pp.).

3. Risto Moisio, Eric J. Arnould, and Linda L. Price, "Between Mothers and Markets: Constructing Family Identity through Homemade Food," *Journal of Consumer Culture* 4, no. 3 (2004): 361–384.

4. Eve Lazarus, "Family Brew," *Marketing Magazine* (October 24, 2005): 8.

5. "Concept: Census Family," Statistics Canada's website, *www.statcan.ca/english/concepts/definitions/cen-family.htm*, accessed May 26, 2006.

6. "Population by Marital Status and Sex," Statistics Canada's website, *www40.statcan. ca/l01/cst01/famil01.htm*, accessed May 26, 2006; Darren Yourk, "Canadian Family Portrait Changing," *Globe and Mail* (October 22, 2003), accessed at *globeandmail.com*.

7. "Study Finds Why Marriage Is on the Decline," *Jet* 96 (July 26, 1999): 16–19.

8. Alan R. Andreasen, "Life Status Changes and Changes in Consumer Preferences and Satisfaction," *Journal of Consumer Research* 11 (December 1984): 784–94; James H. McAlexander, John W. Schouten, and Scott D. Roberts, "Consumer Behavior and Divorce," *Research in Consumer Behavior* 6 (1993): 153–184.

9. Wendy Bounds, "An Easy Way to Get an Ex Out of the Picture—and No Lawyer!" *Wall Street Journal* (June 16, 1994): B1.

10. Laura Metcalf, "Divorce, Advertising Style," *Marketing Magazine* (February 16, 1998): 9.

11. Terry Poulton, "The Paradox of the Working Mom," *Strategy Magazine* (October 20, 2003): 19; "Mommy Is Really Home from Work," *Business Week* (November 25, 2002): 101–102.

12. *Profiling Canada's Families III* (Ottawa: The Vanier Institute of the Family, 2004), p. 125.

13. "Marriages," *The Daily* (November 20, 2003), Statistics Canada's website, *www.statcan.ca/Daily/English/031120/d031120c.htm*, accessed May 26, 2006.

14. Cyndee Miller, "'Til Death Do They Part," *Marketing News* (March 27, 1995): 1–2.

15. Erin White and Betsy McKay, "Coke's New Twist: A Bottle for Two," *Wall Street Journal* (May 17, 2002): B2.

16. "Census Families, Number and Average Size," Statistics Canada's website, *www40.statcan.ca/l01/cst01/famil40a.htm*, accessed May 26, 2006.

17. Karen Hardee-Cleaveland, "Is Eight Enough?" *American Demographics* (June 1989): 60.

18. "Births," *The Daily* (July 12, 2005), Statistics Canada's website, *www.statcan.ca/Daily/English/050712/d050712a.htm*, accessed May 26, 2006.

19. Frank Bruni, "Persistent Drop in Fertility Reshapes Europe's Future," *New York Times on the Web* (December 26, 2002).

20. "Household size, provinces and territories," Statistics Canada's website, *www.statcan.ca/english/Pgdb/famil53a.htm*, accessed October 28, 2003.

21. Leah McLaren, "New Year's for One, Please," *Globe and Mail* (December 30, 2000): R3.

22. Percentage calculation based on *Canada's Families: They Count*, (Ottawa: The Vanier Institute of the Family, 1996).

23. Joe Woodard, "Love and Marriage Isn't for Faint of Heart: Young Adults Find Comfort Under Parents' Roof," *Calgary Herald* (September 28, 2003): A4

24. Ronald Alsop, "Businesses Market to Gay Couples as Same Sex Households Increase," *Wall Street Journal Interactive Edition* (August 8, 2002).

25. Alsop, "Businesses Market to Gay Couples as Same Sex Households Increase."

26. Brad Edmondson, "Inside the New Household Projections," *The Number News* (July 1996).

27. P. Paul, "Childless by Choice," *American Demographics* (November 2001): 45–48, 50.

28. Thomas Exter, "Disappearing Act," *American Demographics* (January 1989): 78. See also Keren-Ami Johnson and Scott D. Roberts, "Incompletely-Launched and Returning Young Adults: Social Change, Consumption, and Family Environment," in *Enhancing Knowledge Development in Marketing*, eds. Robert P. Leone and V. Kumar (Chicago, IL: American Marketing Association, 1992), pp. 249–254; John Burnett and Denise Smart, "Returning Young Adults: Implications for Marketers," *Psychology & Marketing* 11, 3 (May/June 1994): 253–269.

29. Martin Turcotte, "Parents with Adult Children Living at Home," *Canadian Social Trends* (Spring 2006): 1–10,*www.statcan.ca/english/studies/11-008/feature/11-008-XIE20050049124.pdf*, accessed May 26, 2006.

30. Dawn McCarthy, "Young Adults Flock Back to Nest in Record Numbers," *Globe and Mail* (March 12, 1999): A3.

31. Woodard, "Love and Marriage Isn't for Faint of Heart: Young Adults Find Comfort Under Parents' Roof."

32. Ipsos-Reid Survey, *Paws & Claws* (March 2001), *www.spca.com*, accessed May 26, 2006; Survey by Leger Marketing across Canada (March 2001), *www.spca.com*, accessed May 26, 2006.

33. "Going to the Dogs," Spectrum Section of *Globe and Mail* (November 2002).

34. Rebecca Gardyn, "Animal Magnetism," *American Demographics* (May 2002): 31–37.

35. See Russell W. Belk, "Metaphoric Relationships with Pets," *Society and Animals* 4, no. 2 (1996): 121–146.

36. Youssef M. Ibrahim, "French Love for Animals: Too Fervent?" *New York Times* (February 2, 1990): A5.

37. "Going to the Dogs."

38. Michelle Halpern, "Heavy Petting," *Marketing Magazine* (March 21/28, 2005): 14–16.

39. Lisa Murphy, "Pets Are People Too," *Marketing Magazine* (April 4, 2005): 16, 18.

40. Halpern, "Heavy Petting"; David Brown, "Canine Campaign," *Marketing Magazine* (November 2, 2005): 4.

41. Marcia Mogelonsky, "The Rocky Road to Adulthood," *American Demographics* (May 1996): 26.

42. Brad Edmondson, "Do the Math," *American Demographics* (October 1999): 50–56.

43. Mary C. Gilly and Ben M. Enis, "Recycling the Family Life Cycle: A Proposal for Redefinition," in Andrew A. Mitchell, ed., *Advances in Consumer Research* 9 (Ann Arbor, MI: Association for Consumer Research, 1982): 271–276.

44. Charles M. Schaninger and William D. Danko, "A Conceptual and Empirical Comparison of Alternative Household Life Cycle Models," *Journal of Consumer Research* 19 (March 1993): 580–594; Robert E. Wilkes, "Household Life-Cycle Stages, Transitions, and Product Expenditures," *Journal of Consumer Research* 22 (June 1995): 27–42.

45. Niel Tseng, "Expenditures on Entertainment," *Consumer Expenditure Survey Anthology* (2003): 73–78,*www.bls.gov/cex/anthology/csxanth10.pdf*, accessed May 26, 2006.

46. Eileen Fischer and Brenda Gainer, "Baby Showers: A Rite of Passage," in *Advances in Consumer Research* 20, eds. Leigh McAlister and Michael L. Rothschild (Provo, UT: Association for Consumer Research, 1993), 320–324.

47. These categories are an adapted version of an FLC model proposed by Gilly and Enis (1982). Based upon a recent empirical comparison of several competing models, Schaninger and Danko found that this framework outperformed others, especially in terms of its treatment of non-conventional households, though they recommend several improvements to this model as well. See Mary C. Gilly and Ben M. Enis, "Recycling the Family Life Cycle: A Proposal for Redefinition," in *Advances in Consumer Research* 9, ed. Andrew A. Mitchell (Ann Arbor, MI: Association for Consumer Research, 1982), 271–276; Charles M. Schaninger and William P. Danko, "A Conceptual and Empirical Comparison of Alternate Household Life Cycle Markets," *Journal of Consumer Research* 19 (March 1993): 580–594; Scott D. Roberts, Patricia K. Voli, and Keren-Ami Johnson, "Beyond the Family Life Cycle: An Inventory of Variables for Defining the Family as a Consumption Unit," in *Developments in Marketing Science* 15, ed. Victoria L. Crittenden (Coral Gables, FL: Academy of Marketing Science, 1992), 71–75.

48. Yong Liu and Daniel S. Putler, "Household Life-Cycle Theory: An Empirical Examination of 'Received Wisdom,'" Working paper (1999) (University of British Columbia).

50. "Ikea Gets into Wedding Biz," *Marketing Magazine* (July 28/August 4, 2003): 9.

50. "Family Facts," The Vanier Institute of the Family, *www.vifamily.ca/library/facts/facts.html*, accessed May 26, 2006.

51. David Chilton, "Families Feud," *Marketing Magazine* (February 6, 2006): 7.

52. "Families Target of Heinz 'Duck,' " *Marketing Magazine* (May 20, 2002): Cover.

53. "Keltic Lodge Makes List of Family-Friendly Resorts," *The Chronicle-Herald* (October 8, 2005): D3.

54. Susan Bradley, "Here Comes the Bride," *Halifax Chronicle-Herald* (June 3, 2006): F2; Paula Adamski, "Here Comes the Digital Bride," *Atlantic Progress* (May 2006): 17, 19.

55. Jennifer Lach, "Intelligence Agents," *American Demographics* (March 1999): 52–60.

56. Harry L. Davis, "Decision Making within the Household," *Journal of Consumer Research* 2 (March 1972): 241–260; Michael B. Menasco and David J. Curry, "Utility and Choice: An Empirical Study of Wife/Husband Decision Making," *Journal of Consumer Research* 16 (June 1989): 87–97. For a recent review, see Conway Lackman and John M. Lanasa, "Family Decision-Making Theory: An Overview and Assessment," *Psychology & Marketing* 10, 2 (March/April 1993): 81–94.

57. Neal Templin, "The PC Wars: Who Gets to Use the Family Computer?" *Wall Street Journal* (October 5, 1995): B1 (2 pp.).

58. Shannon Dortch, "Money and Marital Discord," *American Demographics* (October 1994): 11 (3 pp.); Jessica Johnson, "Walking Down the Aisle: How Shopping Tests Your Relationship," *Globe and Mail* (April 12, 2003): L1.

59. For research on factors affecting how much influence adolescents exert in family decision making, see Ellen Foxman, Patriya Tansuhaj and Karin M. Ekstrom, "Family Members' Perceptions of Adolescents' Influence in Family Decision Making," *Journal of Consumer Research* 15, 4 (March 1989): 482–491; Sharon E. Beatty and Salil Talpade, "Adolescent Influence in Family Decision Making: A Replication with Extension," *Journal of Consumer Research* 21, 2 (September 1994): 332–341.

60. Daniel Seymour and Greg Lessne, "Spousal Conflict Arousal: Scale Development," *Journal of Consumer Research* 11 (December 1984): 810–821.

61. This list of roles is adapted from Fred E. Webster and Yoram Wind, *Organizational Buying Behavior* (New York, NY: Prentice Hall, 1972) and expanded in J. Paul Peter, Jerry C. Olson and Jerry A. Rosenblatt, *Understanding Consumer Behavior* (Toronto, ON: Times Mirror Professional Publishing, 1996), p. 359; John C. Mowen, *Consumer Behavior* (Englewood Cliffs, NJ: Prentice Hall, 1995), p. 658; Gail Tom, *Applications in Consumer Behavior: Readings and Exercises* (Englewood Cliffs, NJ: Prentice Hall, 1984), p. 106; and Gurprit S. Kindra, Michel Laroche, and Thomas E. Muller, *The Canadian Perspective: Consumer Behavior* (Scarborough, ON: Nelson Canada, 1994), p. 465.

62. Diane Crispell, "Dual-Earner Diversity," *American Demographics* (July 1995): 32–37.

63. "Marriage: The Art of Compromise," *American Demographics* (February 1998): 41.

64. Darach Turley, "Dialogue with the Departed," *European Advances in Consumer Research* 2 (1995): 10–13.

65. "Wives and Money," *American Demographics* (December 1997): 34.

66. Thomas Hine, *Populuxe* (New York: Alfred A. Knopf, 1986).

67. Robert Boutilier, "Targeting Families: Marketing to and through the New Family," *American Demographics* (1993).

68. Judith Madill and Frances Woolley, Unpublished preliminary findings of Study of Financial Management and Decision Making in Canadian Households, 1997.

69. Judith Madill and Frances Woolley, "The Purchase of RRSPs in Canadian Households: Husband–Wife Decision Making," abstract in *Marketing* 18, ed. Herbert MacKenzie (Administrative Sciences Association of Canada, 1997), p. 187.

70. Paul-Mark Rendon, "Queens of the Castle," *Marketing Magazine* (June 27, 2005): 4.

71. Dennis L. Rosen and Donald H. Granbois, "Determinants of Role Structure in Family Financial Management," *Journal of Consumer Research* 10 (September 1983): 253–258.

72. Robert F. Bales, *Interaction Process Analysis: A Method for the Study of Small Groups* (Reading, MA: Addison-Wesley, 1950).

73. Rebecca Harris, "We Love Our Stoves," *Marketing Magazine* (August 1/8, 2005): 4.

74. Mike Miner, "A Room of His Own," *Globe and Mail* (April 8, 2006): L8.

75. Eve Lazarus, "Mrs. Fix-it," *Marketing Magazine* (November 28, 2005): 6; Canadian Press, "Renos Still Hot," *Marketing Magazine* (April 25, 2005): 10.

76. Alma S. Baron, "Working Parents: Shifting Traditional Roles," *Business* 37 (January/March 1987): 36; William J. Qualls, "Household Decision Behavior: The Impact of Husbands' and Wives' Sex Role Orientation," *Journal of Consumer Research* 14 (September 1987): 264–279; Charles M. Schaninger and W. Christian Buss, "The Relationship of Sex-Role Norms to Household Task Allocation," *Psychology & Marketing* 2 (Summer 1985): 93–104; John Gray, "Domesticity, Diapers and Dad," *Globe and Mail* (June 15, 1996): D1, D2.

77. Craig J. Thompson, "Caring Consumers: Gendered Consumption Meanings and the Juggling Lifestyle," *Journal of Consumer Research* 22 (March 1996): 388–407.

78. Gayle MacDonald, "Sugar Mommies," *Globe and Mail* (May 13, 2000): R1, R4.

79. Alain Ouellet, "Prescription for Painting," *Marketing Magazine* (September 29, 2003): 15.

80. Terry Poulton, "The Paradox of the Working Mom," *Strategy Magazine* (October 20, 2003): 19.

81. Gary L. Sullivan and P.J. O'Connor, "The Family Purchase Decision Process: A Cross-Cultural Review and Framework for Research," *Southwest Journal of Business & Economics* (Fall 1988): 43; Marilyn Lavin, "Husband-Dominant, Wife-Dominant, Joint," *Journal of Consumer Marketing* 10, 3 (1993): 33–42.

82. Suraj Commuri and James W. Gentry, "Resource Allocation in Households with Women as Chief Wage Earners," *Journal of Consumer Research* 13 (September 2005): 185–195.

83. Rosemary Polegato, "The Role of Family Members in Food Shopping: Implications for Retailers and Manufacturers," *Journal of Food Products Marketing* 2, 1 (1994): 3–15.

84. Rosemary Polegato and Judith L. Zaichkowsky, "Family Food Shopping Strategies: Strategies Used by Husbands and Wives," *Journal of Consumer Affairs* 28, 2 (Winter 1994): 278–299.

85. Susan Kelman, "No Man's Land," *Report on Business Magazine* (August 1990): 52–57.

86. Rosemary Polegato and Judith L. Zaichkowsky, "Food Shopping Profiles of Career-Oriented, Income-Oriented, and At-Home Wives," *Journal of Consumer Research* 33, 1 (Summer 1999): 110–133.

87. Karen von Hahn, "Meal Assembly," *Globe and Mail* (April 15, 2006): L3; Holly Fraughton, "What's for Supper?" *Halifax Chronicle-Herald* (June 3, 2006): D1, D12.

88. Paul Brent, "The Family Guy," *Marketing Magazine* (May 1, 2006): 17–19.

89. Micaela DiLeonardo, "The Female World of Cards and Holidays: Women, Families, and the Work of Kinship," *Signs* 12 (Spring 1942): 440–53; Dorothy Lipovenko, "Women Bear Brunt of Elder-Care," *Globe and Mail* (March 27, 1997): A1, A7.

90. C. Whan Park, "Joint Decisions in Home Purchasing: A Muddling-through Process," *Journal of Consumer Research* 9 (September 1982): 151–162. See also William J. Qualls and Françoise Jaffe, "Measuring Conflict in Household Decision Behavior: Read My Lips and Read My Mind," in *Advances in Consumer Research* 19, eds. John F. Sherry, Jr., and Brian Sternthal (Provo, UT: Association for Consumer Research, 1992), 522–531.

91. Kim P. Corfman and Donald R. Lehmann, "Models of Cooperative Group Decision-Making and Relative Influence: An Experimental Investigation of Family Purchase Decisions," *Journal of Consumer Research* 14 (June 1987): 1–13.

92. Sarah Lyall, "Jacks? Dolls? Yo-Yos? No, They Want Cellphones," *New York Times on the Web* (October 24, 2002).

93. Sharen Kindel, "They May Be Small, but They Spend Big," *Adweek* (February 10, 1992): 38.

94. James U. McNeal, "Tapping the Three Kids' Markets," *American Demographics* (April 1998): 3, 737–741.

95. Harris Curtis, "Making Kids Street Smart," *Newsweek* (September 16, 2002): 10.

96. Stephanie Thompson, "Mrs. Butterworth's Changes Her Target," *Advertising Age* (December 20, 1999): 44.

97. Chris Powell, "Under the Influence," *Marketing Magazine* (February 16, 2004): 9–10.

98. Andea Zoe Aster, "New Marketing Lessons for Back to School," *Marketing Magazine* (August 11/18, 2003): 20–21.

99. Claudia Penteado, "Coke Taps Maternal Instinct with New Latin American Ads," *Advertising Age International* (January 1997): 15.

100. Quoted in Miriam Jordan, "India's Medicine Men Market an Array of Contraceptives," *Wall Street Journal Interactive Edition* (September 21, 1999).

101. Louise Lee, "Ad Agencies in Asia Hit a Nerve, Showing Men Doing Housework," *Wall Street Journal Interactive Edition* (August 14, 1998).

102. Les Carlson, Ann Walsh, Russell N. Laczniak, and Sanford Grossbart, "Family Communication Patterns and Marketplace Motivations, Attitudes, and Behaviours of Children and Mothers," *Journal of Consumer Affairs* 28, 1 (Summer 1994): 25–53; see also Roy L. Moore and George P. Moschis, "The Role of Family Communication in Consumer Learning," *Journal of Communication* 31 (Autumn 1981): 42–51.

103. Leslie Isler, Edward T. Popper, and Scott Ward, "Children's Purchase Requests and Parental Responses: Results from a Diary Study," *Journal of Advertising Research* 27 (October/November 1987): 28–39.

104. Gregory M. Rose, "Consumer Socialization, Parental Style, and Development Timetables in the United States and Japan," *Journal of Marketing* 63, 3 (1999): 105–119.

105. Patrick Casey, "Reflective Marketing," *Marketing Magazine* (April 18, 2005): 24–25.

106. Mary Roach, "Cute Inc.," *Wired* (December 1999): 330–343.

107. Scott Ward, "Consumer Socialization," in *Perspectives in Consumer Behavior*, eds. Harold H. Kassarjian and Thomas S. Robertson (Glenville, IL: Scott, Foresman and Company, 1980), p. 380.

108. Thomas Lipscomb, "Indicators of Materialism in Children's Free Speech: Age and Gender Comparisons," *Journal of Consumer Marketing* (Fall 1988): 41–46.

109. George P. Moschis, "The Role of Family Communication in Consumer Socialization of Children and Adolescents," *Journal of Consumer Research* 11 (March 1985): 898–913.

110. Gregory M. Rose, Vassilis Dalakas, and Fredric Kropp, "A Five-Nation Study of Developmental Timetables, Reciprocal Communication and Consumer Socialization," *Journal of Business Research* 55 (2002): 943–949.

111. Bruce Horovitz, "Targeting the Kindermarket," *USA Today* (March 3, 2000): B1(2).

112. Elizabeth S. Moore, William L. Wilkie, and Richard J. Lutz, "Passing the Torch: Intergenerational Influences as a Source of Brand Equity," *Journal of Marketing* 66 (April 2002): 17–37.

113. James U. McNeal and Chyon-Hwa Yeh, "Born to Shop," *American Demographics* (June 1993): 34–39.

114. Patricia Pliner et al., "Children's Consumer Behavior in a Store with Unattractive Merchandise: The 'Caveat Emptorium,'" *Journal of Economic Psychology* 15 (1994): 449–65.

115. See Les Carlson, Sanford Grossbart, and J. Kathleen Stuenkel, "The Role of Parental Socialization Types on Differential Family Communication Patterns Regarding Consumption," *Journal of Consumer Psychology* 1, 1 (1992): 31–52.

116. "Kraft Halts Production of Roadkill Candy," *New York Times on the Web* (February 26, 2005).

117. Marian Burros, "McDonald's France Puts Its Mouth Where Its Money Is," *New York Times on the Web* (October 30, 2002).

118. Gail Powell, "Salad, Fries and Exercise," *Marketing Magazine* (July 27, 2005): 6.

119. "Television Viewing," *The Daily* (March 31, 2005), Statistics Canada's website, *www.statcan.ca/Daily/English/031121/d031121a.htm*, accessed May 26, 2006.

120. See Patricia M. Greenfield et al., "The Program-Length Commercial: A Study of the Effects of Television/Toy Tie-Ins on Imaginative Play," *Psychology & Marketing* 7 (Winter 1990): 237–256, for a study on the effects of commercial programming on creative play.

121. Marina Baker, "Teletubbies Say 'Eh Oh. ... It's War!'" *Independent* (March 6, 2000): 7; "A Trojan Horse for Advertisers," *Business Week* (April 3, 2000): 10.

122. Gerald J. Gorn and Renee Florsheim, "The Effects of Commercials for Adult Products on Children," *Journal of Consumer Research* 11 (March 1985): 962–967. For a study that assessed the impact of violent commercials on children, see V. Kanti Prasad and Lois J. Smith, "Television Commercials in Violent Programming: An Experimental Evaluation of Their Effects on Children," *Journal of the Academy of Marketing Science* 22, 4 (1994): 340–351.

123. Powell, "Under the Influence."

124. Glenn Collins, "New Studies on Girl Toys and Boy Toys," *New York Times* (February 13, 1984): D1.

125. Susan B. Kaiser, "Clothing and the Social Organization of Gender Perception: A Developmental Approach," *Clothing and Textiles Research Journal* 7 (Winter 1989): 46–56.

126. D.W. Rajecki et al., "Gender Casting in Television Toy Advertisements: Distributions, Message Content Analysis, and Evaluations," *Journal of Consumer Psychology* 2, 3 (1993): 307–327.

127. Lori Schwartz and William Markham, "Sex Stereotyping in Children's Toy Advertisements," *Sex Roles* 12 (January 1985): 157–70.

128. Joseph Pereira, "Oh Boy! In Toyland, You Get more if You're Male," *Wall Street Journal* (September 23, 1994): B1 (2 pp.); Joseph Pereira, "Girls' Favorite Playthings: Dolls, Dolls, and Dolls," *Wall Street Journal* (September 23, 1994): B1 (2 pp.).

129. Lisa Bannon, "More Kids' Marketers Pitch Number of Single-Sex Products," *Wall Street Journal Interactive Edition* (February 14, 2000).

130. Michelle Halpern, "Child's Play," *Marketing Magazine* (August 29/September 5, 2005): 19–20.

131. Bannon, "More Kids' Marketers Pitch Number of Single-Sex Products."

132. Constance L. Hays, "A Role Model's Clothes: Barbie Goes Professional," *New York Times on the Web* (April 1, 2000).

133. Hays, "A Role Model's Clothes: Barbie Goes Professional."

134. Laura A. Peracchio, "How Do Young Children Learn to Be Consumers? A Script-Processing Approach," *Journal of Consumer Research* 18 (March 1992): 425–440; Laura A. Peracchio, "Young Children's Processing of a Televised Narrative: Is a Picture Really Worth a Thousand Words?" *Journal of Consumer Research* 20, 2 (September 1993): 281–293. See also M. Carole Macklin, "The Effects of an Advertising Retrieval Cue on Young Children's Memory and Brand Evaluations," *Psychology & Marketing* 11, 3 (May/June 1994): 291–311.

135. Jasmine Miller, "This Is What Little Girls Are Made of?" *Canadian Business (Technology)* (Summer 1997): 52–56.

136. Jean Piaget, "The Child and Modern Physics," *Scientific American* 196, 3 (1957): 46–51. See also Kenneth D. Bahn, "How and When Do Brand Perceptions and Preferences First Form? A Cognitive Developmental Investigation," *Journal of Consumer Research* 13 (December 1986): 382–393.

137. Deborah L. Roedder, "Age Differences in Children's Responses to Television Advertising: An Information-Processing Approach," *Journal of Consumer Research* 8 (September 1981): 144–153. See also Deborah Roedder John and Ramnath Lakshmi-Ratan, "Age Differences in Children's Choice Behavior: The Impact of Available Alternatives," *Journal of Marketing Research* 29 (May 1992): 216–226; Jennifer Gregan-Paxton and Deborah Roedder John, "Are Young Children Adaptive Decision Makers? A Study of Age Differences in Information Search Behavior," *Journal of Consumer Research* 21 (March 1995): 567–580; Jennifer Gregan-Paxton and Deborah Roedder John, "The Emergence of Adaptive Decision Making in Children," *Journal of Consumer Research* 24 (June 1997): 43–56.

138. Peracchio, "How Do Young Children Learn to Be Consumers? A Script-Processing Approach"; Peracchio, "Young Children's Processing of a Televised Narrative: Is a Picture Really Worth a Thousand Words?"; see also Macklin, "The Effects of an Advertising Retrieval Cue on Young Children's Memory and Brand Evaluations."

139. Gwen Bachmannn Achenreiner and Deborah Roedder John, "The Meaning of Brand Names to Children: A Developmental Investigation," *Journal of Consumer Psychology* 13, no. 3 (2003): 205–219.

140. Janet Simons, "Youth Marketing: Children's Clothes Follow the Latest Fashion," *Advertising Age* (February 14, 1985): 16.

141. Stipp, "Children as Consumers." See Laura A. Peracchio, "Designing Research to Reveal the Young Child's Emerging Competence," *Psychology & Marketing* 7 (Winter 1990): 257–276, for details regarding the design of research on children.

142. Laura Shapiro, "Where Little Boys Can Play with Nail Polish," *Newsweek* (May 28, 1990): 62.

143. Matt Murray, "Marketers Want Kids' Help and Their Parents' Loyalty," *Wall Street Journal Interactive Edition* (May 6, 1997).

144. Paula Lyon Andruss, "'Dora' Translates Well," *Marketing News* (October 13, 2003): 8.

145. Rebecca Harris, "Zwak Attack," *Marketing Magazine* (June 5, 2005): 4.

146. Gary Armstrong and Merrie Brucks, "Dealing with Children's Advertising: Public Policy Issues and Alternatives," *Journal of Public Policy and Marketing* 7 (1988): 98–113.

147. Bonnie Reece, "Children and Shopping: Some Public Policy Questions," *Journal of Public Policy and Marketing* (1986): 185–194.

148. Reece, "Children and Shopping: Some Public Policy Questions."

149. Mary Ann Stutts and Garland G. Hunnicutt, "Can Young Children Understand Disclaimers in Television Commercials?" *Journal of Advertising* 16 (Winter 1987): 41–46.

150. Daniel Cook, University of Illinois, personal communication December 2002 and "Contradictions and Conundrums of the Child Consumer: The Emergent Centrality of an Enigma in the 1990s" (paper presented at the Association for Consumer Research, October 2002).

151. Merrie Brucks, Gary M. Armstrong, and Marvin E. Goldberg, "Children's Use of Cognitive Defenses against Television Advertising: A Cognitive Response Approach," *Journal of Consumer Research* 14 (March 1988): 471–482.

152. "Child's Play," *Marketing Magazine* (April 25, 2005): 7.

153. Edmund L. Andrews, "F.C.C. Limits Ads on TV Shows Aimed at Children," *New York Times* (April 10, 1991): D6; Laurel Wentz, "Playing by the Same Rules: Harmonization of Children's Ads Sought via Self-Regulation," *Advertising Age* (December 2, 1991): S–2.

154. See, for example, reports in *Consumer News & Reviews* (American Council on Consumer Interests, July–August 1997): "Denmark Internet Deception": 2 and "On-line Marketing to Young Consumers": 3.

SECTION → 4

Consumers and Subcultures

The chapters in this section consider some of the social and subcultural influences that help to determine who we are, with an emphasis on the subcultures that help to define each of our unique identities. Chapter 13 focuses on factors that define social class and on how membership in a social class exerts a strong pull on what we buy with the money we make. This chapter also considers more broadly how the economic conditions of a society at any point in time affect purchase decisions. Chapter 14 discusses the ways in which our ethnic and regional affinities and our national identification help to stamp our social identities. Chapter 15 examines how the bonds we share with others who were born at roughly the same time unite us.

SECTION OUTLINE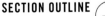

Finally, the big day has come! Victor is going to meet Marilyn's parents. Victor had been doing contracting work at the securities firm where Marilyn works, and it was love at first sight. Vic attended the "School of Hard Knocks" on the streets of Toronto, and Marilyn was fresh out of Havergal College—but they knew they could work things out despite their vastly different backgrounds. Marilyn's been hinting that the Caldwells (her family) have money, but Vic isn't intimidated. He knows guys from his neighbourhood who wheeled and dealed their way into six figures; he can handle one more big shot in a silk suit, flashing a roll of bills, and showing off his expensive modern furniture with mirrors and gadgets everywhere you look.

When they arrive in Rosedale, Victor looks for a Rolls-Royce in the driveway but sees only a beat-up Jeep Cherokee—which, he decides, must belong to a servant. Inside, Vic is surprised by how simply the house is decorated and how shabby it seems. The hall has a faded oriental rug, and all the furniture looks really old. In fact, there doesn't seem to be a new stick of furniture anywhere, just a lot of antiques.

Vic is even more surprised when he meets Mr. Caldwell. He half expected Marilyn's father to be wearing a tuxedo and holding a large brandy snifter, like the people he's seen in the movies. In fact, Vic had put on his best Italian suit and wore his large cubic zirconium "pinky ring" so this guy would know he had some money too. When Marilyn's father emerges in a rumpled cardigan and tennis sneakers, Victor realizes he's definitely not one of those guys from the old neighbourhood.

CHAPTER 13

Income and Social Class

CONSUMER SPENDING AND ECONOMIC BEHAVIOUR

As Victor's eye-opening experience at the Caldwells suggests, there are many ways to spend money, and a wide gulf exists between those who have it and those who do not. Perhaps an equally wide one exists between those who have had it for a long time and those who "made it the hard way"—by earning it! This chapter begins by considering briefly how general economic conditions affect the way consumers allocate their money. Then, reflecting the adage "the rich are different," it will explore how people who occupy different positions in society consume in very different ways.

Whether a skilled worker like Victor or a child of privilege like Marilyn, a person's social class has a profound impact on what he or she does with money and on how consumption choices reflect the person's "place" in society. As this chapter illustrates, these choices play another role as well. The specific products and services we buy are often intended to make sure *other* people know what our social standing is—or what we would like it to be. Products are frequently bought and displayed as markers of social class; they are valued as *status symbols*. This is especially true in large, modern societies where behaviour and reputation can no longer be counted on to convey one's position in a community.

INCOME PATTERNS

Many Canadians would probably say that they don't make enough money, but in reality the average Canadian's standard of living continues to improve. Average family income increased from about $42 900 in 1970 (in 2000 dollars) to $54 725 in 2000.[1] Between 1990 and 2000, the average annual income for Canadian wage earners increased from $35 143 to $46 656 (an increase of 30.8 percent); from $161 460 to $185 070 for the top 10 percent (up 14.6 percent); and from $10 260 to $10 341 (less than 1 percent) for the bottom 10 percent.[2] The large, upward income shifts are linked to two key factors: a shift in women's roles and increases in educational attainment.[3]

→Luxury items like diamond engagement rings are valued as status symbols the world over, as this Brazilian ad for a jeweller reminds us.
Courtesy of Natan and F. Nazca, Saatchi & Saatchi.

Woman's Work

One reason for this increase in income is that there has been a larger proportion of people of working age participating in the labour force. Mothers with preschool children are the fastest growing segment of working people. Furthermore, many of their jobs are in high-paying occupations, such as medicine and architecture, which used to be dominated by men. Although women are still a minority in most professional occupations, their ranks continue to swell. Among about 24 percent of Canadian couples, it is the wives' paycheques that are propelling the couples up the income ladder. Nearly 30 percent of wives in dual-earner couples without children earn more than their spouses.[4]

Yes, it Pays to Go to School

Another factor that determines who gets a bigger piece of the pie is education. Although paying for university often entails great sacrifice, it still pays off in the long run. In 2001, just over 50 percent of Canadians had some postsecondary education; about 25 percent had some university education, while just over 15 percent had a university degree. Nearly 202 000 Canadians earned baccalaureate or first professional degrees in 2003.[5] In 2000, the average earnings for university graduates was about $61 000, compared to about $43 000 for those at all education levels.[6] In 1999, Canadian households in which the highest income earner had a university certificate or bachelor's degree had 80 percent more net worth than those in which the highest earner was a high school graduate.[7] So, hang in there!

To Spend or Not to Spend: That Is the Question

Consumer demand for goods and services depends on *both* the ability to buy and the willingness to buy. Although demand for necessities tends to be stable over time, other expenditures can be postponed or eliminated if people don't feel that now is a good time to spend money.[8] For example, a person may decide to "make do" with a current clunker for another year rather than buy a new car right away.

Discretionary income is the money available to a household over and above that required for a comfortable standard of living. As might be expected, discretionary income increases as overall income goes up and as debt and tax burdens are relieved. People aged 35 to 55 years, whose incomes are at a peak, account for roughly half of this amount. As the population ages and income levels rise, the typical household is changing the way it spends its money. The most noticeable change is that a much larger share of the budget is spent on shelter and transportation, and less on food and apparel. These shifts are due to factors such as an increase in the prevalence of home ownership and in the need for working wives to pay commuting and employment costs. On a more cheerful note, households are spending more now on entertainment, reading, and education than in the past.

Consumers' spending decisions reverberate around the world, as the interest in goods and services and the ability to purchase them among the citizens of one country affects the fortunes of people in other lands. As the economies of developing countries in Asia and Latin America grow, millions of new consumers are

←Education is strongly linked to a higher standard of living. People who earn a university degree are likely to earn much more during their lives than those who do not.
Digital Vision/Getty Images, Inc. — Liaison.

acquiring the creature comforts that people in North America and Europe have come to expect. Sometimes goods that Western consumers regard as basic necessities take on added significance as discretionary fashion items for people in other countries. For example, companies like Whirlpool typically offer refrigerators in a wide range of colours in Asian countries, because people are more likely to display these appliances in their living rooms.[9]

In the wake of 9/11, many consumers are experiencing doubts about their individual and collective futures and are anxious about holding on to what they have. Of course, not everyone has the same attitudes about money and its importance. A consumer's anxieties about money are not necessarily related to how much he or she actually has; acquiring and managing money is more a state of mind than of wallet. For example, we all know people who are "tightwads" with their money and others whose cash seems to burn a hole in their wallets until they part with it. In recent years being frugal has become a passion for some people, who consider it a point of honour not to pay more than they have to for anything. The invitation of the Norfolk Hotel, located near Fredericton, New Brunswick, to "spend the night, not a fortune" is likely to calm the anxieties of the frugal vacation traveller. On the other hand, the more than 53 million credit cards in circulation among Canadian adults allows them to forget they're actually spending money. Debt, which in the past used to be associated with indulgent shopping behaviour, has become a "normal" feature of society.[10]

Money has a variety of complex psychological meanings; it can be equated with success or failure, social acceptability, security, love, or freedom.[11] Michael Adams in his book *Better Happy Than Rich?* examines attitudes of Canadians toward money and the meaning of life. Segmenting by social values and age (discussed in Chapter 15), he concludes that generally those with more money report higher levels of happiness than those with less money. However, it is not money per se or the buying power that money supports that Canadians value, but the freedom (i.e., personal autonomy) that money affords. Of course, there are happy people who have very little money and well-off people who are miserable. To find out how you compare to other Canadians, visit ***www.environics.net***.[12]

Consumer Confidence

The field of **behavioural economics**, or economic psychology, is concerned with the "human" side of economic decisions. Beginning with the pioneering work of psychologist George Katona, this discipline studies how consumers' motives and their expectations about the future affect their current spending, and how these individual decisions add up to affect a society's economic well-being.[13]

Consumers' beliefs about what the future holds are an indicator of **consumer confidence**, which reflects the extent to which people are optimistic or pessimistic about the future health of the economy and how they will fare down the road. These beliefs influence how much money consumers will pump into the economy when making discretionary purchases.

Many businesses take forecasts about anticipated spending very seriously, and periodic surveys attempt to "take the pulse" of the Canadian consumer. The Conference Board of Canada conducts a survey of consumer confidence, as does the Angus Reid Group. Types of questions posed to consumers in these surveys include:[14]

- Would you say that you and your family are better off or worse off financially than a year ago?

- Will you be better off or worse off a year from now?

- Do you plan to buy a car in the next year?

When people are pessimistic about their prospects and about the state of the economy, they tend to cut back their spending and take on less debt. On the other

TURN YOUR **BUNGALOW** INTO A **CHATEAU.**

← This ad for a home improvement program suggests that you can turn your home into a chateau, implying a kind of social mobility through house renovation.

hand, when they are optimistic about the future, they tend to reduce the amount they save, take on more debt, and buy discretionary items. Thus, the overall savings rate is influenced by (1) consumers' pessimism or optimism about their personal circumstances (e.g., fear of being laid off versus a sudden increase in personal wealth due to an inheritance), (2) national and world events (e.g., the election of a new prime minister or an international crisis), and (3) cultural differences in attitudes toward saving.[15]

SOCIAL CLASS

All societies can be divided roughly into the "haves" and the "have-nots" (though sometimes "having" is a question of degree). As Victor's encounter with the Caldwells suggests, a consumer's standing in society, or **social class**, is determined by a complex set of variables, including income, family background, and occupation.

The place a person occupies in the social structure is an important determinant not just of *how much* money is spent but also *how* it is spent. Victor is surprised that the Caldwells, who clearly have a lot of money, do not seem to flaunt it. This understated way of living is a hallmark of so-called old money; people who have had it for a long time don't need to prove they've got it. In contrast, consumers who are relative newcomers to affluence might allocate the same amount of money very differently.

A Universal Pecking Order

In many animal species a social organization is developed whereby the most assertive or aggressive animals exert control over the others and have the first pick of food, living space, and mating partners. Chickens, for example, develop a clearly defined dominance-submission hierarchy. Within this hierarchy, each hen has a position in which she is submissive to all the hens above her and dominates all the ones below her (hence, the origin of the term *pecking order*).[16]

People are not much different. They also develop a pecking order whereby they are ranked in terms of their relative standing in society. This standing determines their access to resources such as education, housing, and consumer goods. People try to improve their ranking by moving up in the social order whenever possible. This desire to improve our lot in life, and often to let others know that we have done so, is at the core of many marketing strategies.

Net Profit +

Many high-end merchants hesitate to sell their wares on the web. One reason for their reluctance is the importance of exclusivity. If just anyone can buy a luxury item, they fear the snob appeal of the brand name might lose some of its cachet. On the other hand, the average web user is a high income earner, so a few high-end retailers are dipping a toe into the waters of e-commerce. Some luxury sites, such as *www.eluxury.com*, serve as portals for a number of upscale retailers. *www.eluxury.com* is so high-end that it refuses to carry a brand like Coach leather because those products are too low-end! This site provides services for its well-heeled clientele, including a calendar of society events.[17] As the old saying goes, if you have to ask how much it costs, you can't afford it!

Social Class Affects Access to Resources

Just as marketers try to carve society into groups for segmentation purposes, sociologists have developed ways to describe meaningful divisions of society in terms of people's relative social and economic resources. Some of these divisions involve political power, whereas others revolve around purely economic distinctions. Karl Marx, the nineteenth-century economic theorist, felt that position in a society was determined by a person's relationship to the *means of production*. Some people (the haves) control resources, and they use the labour of others to preserve their privileged positions. The have-nots lack control and depend on their own labour for survival, so these people have the most to gain by changing the system. Distinctions among people that entitle some to more than others are perpetuated by those who will benefit by doing so.[18] The German sociologist Max Weber showed that the rankings people develop are not one-dimensional. Some rankings involve prestige or "social honour" (he called these *status groups*), some focus on power (or *party*), and some revolve around wealth and property (*class*).[19]

Social Class Affects Tastes and Lifestyles

The term *social class* is used now more generally to describe the overall rank of people in a society. People who are grouped within the same social class are approximately equal in terms of their social standing in the community. They work in roughly similar occupations, and they tend to have similar lifestyles by virtue of their income levels and common tastes. These people tend to socialize with one another and share many ideas and values regarding the way life should be lived.[20] Indeed, "birds of a feather do flock together." We tend to marry people similar in social class to ourselves, a tendency sociologists call **homogamy** or "assortative mating."[21]

Social class is as much a state of being as it is of having. As Victor saw, class is also a question of what a person *does* with money and how that person defines his or her role in society. Although people may not like the idea that some members of society are better off or "different" from others, most consumers do acknowledge the existence of different classes and the effect of class membership on consumption. As one wealthy woman observed when asked to define social class:

> I would suppose social class means where you went to school and how far. Your intelligence. Where you live…Where you send your children to school. The hobbies you have. Skiing, for example, is higher than the snowmobile…It can't be [just] money, because nobody ever knows that about you for sure.[22]

Social Stratification

In school, it always seems that some kids get all the breaks. They have access to many resources, such as special privileges, fancy cars, large allowances, or dates with other popular classmates. At work, some people are put on the fast track and are promoted to high-prestige jobs, given higher salaries, and perhaps perks such as a parking space, a large office, or the keys to the executive washroom.

In virtually every context, some people seem to be ranked higher than others. Patterns of social arrangements evolve whereby some members get more resources than others by virtue of their relative standing, power, or control in the group.[23] The phenomenon of **social stratification** refers to this creation of artificial divisions in a society and can be defined as "those processes in a social system by which scarce and valuable resources are distributed unequally to status positions that become more or less permanently ranked in terms of the share of valuable resources each receives."[24]

ACHIEVED VERSUS ASCRIBED STATUS

Think back to groups to which you've belonged. You'll probably agree that in many instances some members seem to get more than their fair share of goodies, while other individuals are not so lucky. Some of these resources may have gone to people who earned them through hard work or diligent study. This allocation is due to *achieved status*. Adrienne Stringer, founder of Molly Maid Home Care Services, once quipped that, "Every hair in my mink coat represents a toilet I've cleaned."[25] Other rewards may have been obtained because the person was lucky enough to be born with "a silver spoon in her mouth." Such good fortune reflects *ascribed status.*

Whether rewards go to "the best and the brightest" or to someone who happens to be related to the boss, allocations are rarely equal within a social group. Most groups exhibit a structure, or **status hierarchy**, in which some members are somehow better off than others. They may have more authority or power, or they are simply better liked or respected.

CLASS STRUCTURE IN CANADA

Canada supposedly does not have a rigid, objectively defined class system. Nevertheless, Canada has tended to maintain a stable class structure in terms of income distribution. Unlike other countries, however, what *does* change is the groups (ethnic, racial, and religious) that have occupied different positions within this structure at different times.[26] The most influential and perhaps earliest attempt to describe Canadian class structure was proposed by Bernard Blishen, a sociologist, in 1958. Blishen constructed an occupational class scale incorporating assumptions about the educational, income, and prestige levels attached to each occupation. The index was improved through further work with various researchers, and the final version recognizes gender differences affecting occupational and social status.[27]

Among consumer researchers in the United States, an alternative view of social class is that proposed by Richard P. Coleman, who built on the work of earlier researchers, notably W. Lloyd Warner.[28] Their classifications imply (in ascending order) some judgment of desirability in terms of access to resources such as money, education, and luxury goods. Coleman's view of American class structure, shown in Figure 13–1, can also be applied to the Canadian context.

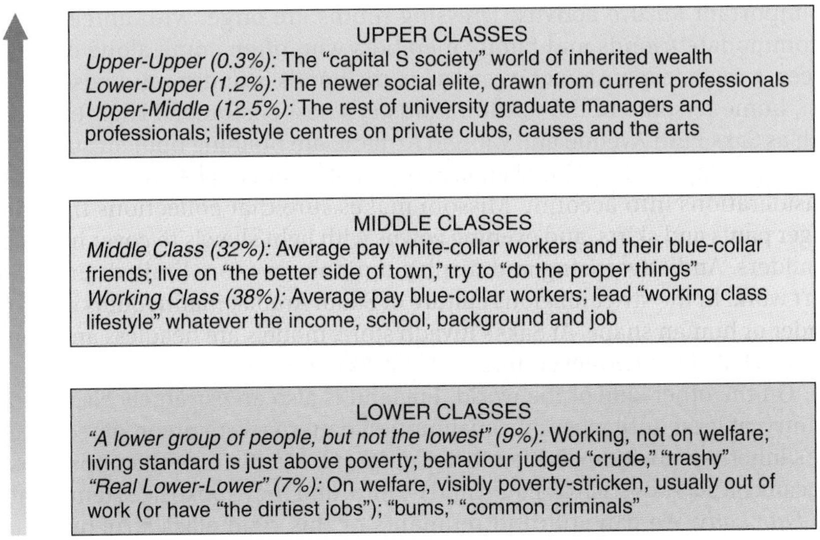

INCOME

UPPER CLASSES
Upper-Upper (0.3%): The "capital S society" world of inherited wealth
Lower-Upper (1.2%): The newer social elite, drawn from current professionals
Upper-Middle (12.5%): The rest of university graduate managers and professionals; lifestyle centres on private clubs, causes and the arts

MIDDLE CLASSES
Middle Class (32%): Average pay white-collar workers and their blue-collar friends; live on "the better side of town," try to "do the proper things"
Working Class (38%): Average pay blue-collar workers; lead "working class lifestyle" whatever the income, school, background and job

LOWER CLASSES
"A lower group of people, but not the lowest" (9%): Working, not on welfare; living standard is just above poverty; behaviour judged "crude," "trashy"
"Real Lower-Lower" (7%): On welfare, visibly poverty-stricken, usually out of work (or have "the dirtiest jobs"); "bums," "common criminals"

FIGURE 13–1

A CONTEMPORARY VIEW OF THE AMERICAN CLASS STRUCTURE

Source: Richard P. Coleman, "The Continuing Significance of Social Class to Marketing," *Journal of Consumer Research* 10 (December 1983): 265–280. Reprinted with permission of The University of Chicago Press.

CLASS STRUCTURE AROUND THE WORLD

Every society has some type of hierarchical class structure, which determines people's access to products and services. The Chinese are a great example; an economic boom is rapidly creating a middle class of about 130 million people that is projected to grow to more than 400 million in 10 years. During the Cultural Revolution, Mao's Red Guards seized upon even the smallest possessions—a pocket watch or silk scarf—as evidence of "bourgeois consciousness." Change came rapidly in the early 1990s, after Mao's successor Deng Xiaoping uttered the phrase that quickly became the credo of the new China: "To get rich is glorious." Because costs are low, a family with an annual income below the North American poverty line can enjoy middle-class comforts, including stylish clothes, Chinese-made colour televisions, DVD players, and cell phones.[29] Wealthier Chinese entrepreneurs can indulge in Cuban Cohiba cigars that sell for $25 each, a quarter of the average Chinese labourer's monthly wage.

The rise of the Chinese middle class has been especially profitable for Nike, named China's "coolest brand" in a recent survey. Nike shoes have become a symbol of success, and the company is opening an average of 1.5 new stores every day there. Nike worked for a long time to attain this status; it started by outfitting top Chinese athletes and sponsoring all the teams in China's new pro basketball league in 1995. Still, becoming a fashion icon (and persuading consumers to spend twice the average monthly salary for a pair of shoes) was no mean feat in a country that wasn't exactly sports-crazy. So Nike affiliated with the NBA (which had begun televising games in China), bringing players like Michael Jordan for visits. Slowly but surely, in-the-know Chinese came to call sneakers "Nai-ke." In 2001, Nike coined a new phrase for its Chinese marketing campaign: "Hip Hoop."[30]

Japan is a highly status-conscious society where upscale designer labels are quite popular, even though the economy is not very healthy now. The Japanese love affair with top brands started in the 1970s when the local economy was booming and many Japanese could buy Western luxury accessories for the first time. Some analysts say Japan's long slump may be fostering a psychological need to splurge on small luxuries, giving consumers the illusion of wealth and allowing them to forget their anxieties about the future. One group largely responsible for fueling Japan's luxury-goods spending is single, working women (about three-quarters of Japanese women aged 25 to 29 are employed outside the home). Often, these single women save money by living with their parents, leaving themselves with cash on hand to spend on clothes, accessories, and vacations.[31]

Shopping also is a major pastime for many Arab women. In contrast to the Japanese, few of them work, so searching for the latest in Western luxury brands is an important leisure activity. Dressing rooms are large, with antechambers to accommodate friends and family members who often come along on shopping sprees. A major expansion of Western luxury brands is underway across the Middle East, home to some of the fashion industry's best customers. High-end retailers, such as Saks Fifth Avenue and Giorgio Armani, are building opulent stores to cater to this growing market. However, fashion retailers must take cultural and religious considerations into account. Missoni makes sure that collections there include longer pants and skirts, and evening gowns with light shawls to cover heads or bare shoulders. And advertising and display options are more limited: Erotic images don't work. In the strict religious culture of Saudi Arabia, mannequins can't reveal a gender or human shape. At Saks's Riyadh store, models are headless and don't have fingers. Half of the two-level store is off-limits to men.[32]

On the other side of the world, England is also an extremely class-conscious country; at least until recently, consumption patterns were preordained in terms of one's inherited position and family background. Members of the upper class were educated at schools such as Eaton and Oxford, and they spoke like Henry Higgins in *My Fair Lady*. We can still find remnants of this rigid class structure: "Hooray Henrys" (wealthy young men) play polo at Windsor, and hereditary peers still dominate the House of Lords.

However, the dominance of inherited wealth appears to be fading in Britain's traditionally aristocratic society. According to a survey, 86 of the 200 wealthiest people in England made their money the old-fashioned way: They earned it. Even the sanctity of the royal family, which epitomizes the aristocracy, has been diluted through tabloid exposure and the antics of younger family members who have been transformed into celebrities more like rock stars than royalty. As one observer put it, "the royal family has gone down-market...to the point that it sometimes resembles soap opera as much as grand opera."[33]

Now some big marketers such as Unilever and Groupe Danone have set their sights on a previously overlooked, more lower-class group called **chavs**. The British use this term widely; it refers to young, lower-class men and women who mix flashy brands and accessories from big names like Burberry with track suits. Their style icons include soccer star David Beckham and his wife, Victoria—formerly Posh Spice of the Spice Girls pop group. Despite their (alleged) tackiness, chavs are attractive to marketers because they have a lot of disposable income to spend on fashion, food, and gadgets. France's Danone, which makes HP Sauce, a condiment the British have poured over bacon sandwiches and fries for a century, launched a series of ads playing up to the chav culture. One features a brawl over the sauce at a wedding buffet; another includes soccer players' glammy wives mingling cattily at a party.[34]

THE RISE OF MASS CLASS

Although social class still matters, it's getting more difficult to clearly link certain brands or stores with a specific class; changes in the marketplace make it more difficult for the casual observer to accurately place a consumer in a certain class based only on the products he or she buys. That's because a lot of "affordable luxuries" now are within reach of many consumers who could not have managed to acquire them in the past. The driver of this global change is income distribution. In many countries, traditionally there has been a huge gulf between the rich and the poor—you were either one or the other. Today, rising incomes in many economically developing countries, such as South Korea and China, coupled with decreasing prices for quality consumer goods and services are leveling the playing field so that there are many more opportunities for people making modest incomes to get a taste of the good life.

This change is fueling demand for mass-consumed products that still offer some degree of panache or style. Think about the success of companies such as Nokia, H&M, Zara, ING, DELL Computers, Gap, Nike, EasyJet, and L'Oréal. They cater to a consumer segment that analysts have labelled the **mass class**, which includes the hundreds of millions of global consumers who now enjoy a level of purchasing power that enables them to afford high-quality products—except for big-ticket items like university educations, housing, or luxury cars. The mass-class market, for example, has spawned several versions of affordable cars: Latin Americans have their Volkswagen Beetle (affectionately called 'el huevito, the little egg), Indian consumers have their Maruti 800 (selling for as little as $5720CAD), and emerging economies such as Brazil, Argentina, India, China, and Turkey have the Fiat Palio, the company's "world car." Today the Fiat Palio is marketed in 40 countries.[35]

Social Mobility

To what degree do people tend to change their social classes? In some societies, such as India, social class is very difficult to change, but in Canada change is possible. **Social mobility** refers to the "passage of individuals from one social class to another"[36]

This passage can be upward, downward, or horizontal. *Horizontal mobility* refers to movement from one position to another that is roughly equivalent in social status—for instance, becoming a nurse instead of an elementary school teacher. *Downward mobility* is, of course, not very desirable, but this pattern is unfortunately quite evident in recent years as displaced workers have been forced to go on social assistance or have joined the ranks of the homeless. A conservative estimate is that 25 000 Torontonians and 15 000 Montrealers are homeless on any given day.[37]

Despite this discouraging trend, demographics decree that there must be *upward mobility* in our society. The middle and upper classes reproduce less (i.e., have fewer children per family) than the lower classes (an effect known as *differential fertility*), and they tend to restrict family size below replacement level (i.e., often having only one child). Therefore, so the reasoning goes, positions of higher status over time must be filled by those of lower status.[38] Overall, though, the offspring of blue-collar consumers tend also to be blue-collar, while the offspring of white-collar consumers tend to wind up as white-collar.[39] People tend to improve their positions over time, but these increases are not usually dramatic enough to catapult them from one social class to another.

Components of Social Class

When we think about a person's social class, there are a number of pieces of information we may consider. Two major ones are occupation and income. A third important factor is educational attainment, which is related strongly to income and occupation.

OCCUPATIONAL PRESTIGE

In a system in which (like it or not) a consumer is defined to a great extent by what he or she does for a living, *occupational prestige* is one way to evaluate the "worth" of people. Hierarchies of occupational prestige tend to be quite stable over time, and they tend also to be similar in different societies. Similarities in occupational prestige have been found in countries as diverse as Brazil, Ghana, Guam, Japan, and Turkey.[40]

A typical ranking includes a variety of professional and business occupations at the top (e.g., chief executive officer of a large corporation, physician, and university professor), while those jobs hovering near the bottom include shoe shiner, ditch-digger, and garbage collector. Because a person's occupation tends to be linked strongly to his or her use of leisure time, allocation of family resources, political orientation, and so on, this variable is often considered to be the single best indicator of social class.

→Occupational prestige is a major component of social status. This ad for Imagewear demonstrates ways to professionalize the image of skilled workers. For example, the caption under the first image reads: "Sure beats a plaid shirt and old jeans."

Courtesy of Mark's Work Wearhouse.

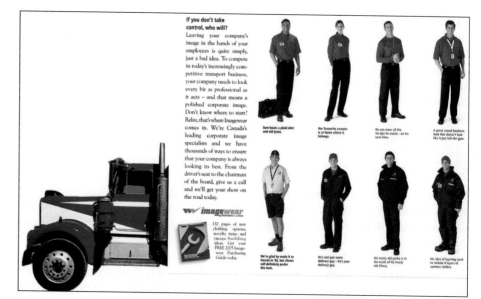

INCOME

The distribution of wealth is of great interest to social scientists and to marketers because it determines which groups have the greatest buying power and market potential. Wealth is by no means distributed evenly across the classes. In 1999, the top 10 percent of Canadian households controlled 45 percent of the net worth accumulated by individuals and families.[41] However, as we have seen, income per se is often not a very good indicator of social class, because the way money is spent is more telling than how much is spent. Still, people need money to allow them to obtain the goods and services they need to express their tastes, so obviously income is still very important. Canadian consumers are getting both wealthier and older, and these changes will continue to influence consumption preferences.

THE RELATIONSHIP BETWEEN INCOME AND SOCIAL CLASS

Although consumers tend to equate money with class, the precise relationship between other aspects of social class and income is not clear and has been the subject of debate among social scientists.[42] The two are by no means synonymous, which is why many people with a lot of money try to use it to upgrade their social class.

One problem is that, even if a family increases household income by adding wage earners, each additional job is likely to be of lower status. For example, a spouse who gets a part-time job is not as likely to get one that is of equal or greater status than the primary wage-earner's full-time job. In addition, the extra money earned is often not pooled toward the common good of the family. Instead, the individual uses it for his or her own personal spending. More money does not then result in increased status or changes in consumption patterns because it tends to be devoted to buying more of the usual products rather than to upgrading to higher-status products.[43]

The following general conclusions can be made regarding the relative value of indicators of social class (i.e., place of residence, occupation, cultural interests, etc.) versus income in predicting consumer choices of products that are purchased for functional reasons rather than primarily for symbolic reasons (e.g., to convey a desired impression to others):

- Social class appears to be a better predictor of purchases that have symbolic aspects but low-to-moderate prices (e.g., cosmetics and liquor).

- Income is a better predictor of major expenditures that do not have status or symbolic aspects (e.g., major appliances).

- Both social class and income data are needed to predict purchases of expensive, symbolic products (e.g., cars and homes).

Measuring Social Class

Because social class is a complex concept that depends on a number of factors, it is not surprising that it is difficult to measure. Early measures included the Index of Status Characteristics and the Index of Social Position developed by Hollingshead.[44] These indices used various combinations of individual characteristics (e.g., income and type of housing) to arrive at a label of class standing. Blishen's Socio-economic Index for Occupations in Canada may be used when occupation is the most appropriate variable to use to collect information on socio-economic status.[45] An alternative is to adapt Coleman's approach, shown in Figure 13–2, which explicitly includes four variables: education, occupational prestige, area of residence, and family income.

PROBLEMS WITH MEASURES OF SOCIAL CLASS

Marketing researchers were among the first to propose that people from different social classes can be distinguished from each other in important ways. Some of these class distinctions still exist, but others have changed.[46] Unfortunately, many of these measures are badly dated and are not as valid today for a variety of reasons.[47]

One reason is that most measures of social class were designed to accommodate the traditional nuclear family, with a male wage earner in the middle of his career and a female full-time homemaker. Such measures have trouble accounting for two-income families, young singles living alone, or households headed by women, which are prevalent in today's society (see Chapter 12).

Another problem with measuring social class is the increasing anonymity of our society. Earlier studies relied on the *reputational method*, in which extensive interviewing was done within a community to determine the reputations and backgrounds of individuals. This information, coupled with the tracing of interaction patterns among people, provided a very comprehensive view of social standing within a community. However, this approach is virtually impossible to implement in most communities today. One compromise is to interview individuals to obtain demographic data and to combine these data with the subjective impressions of the interviewer regarding the person's possessions and standard of living.

An example of this approach appears in Figure 13–2. Note that the accuracy of this questionnaire relies largely on the interviewer's judgment, especially regarding the quality of the respondent's neighbourhood. These impressions are in danger of being biased by the interviewer's own circumstances, which may affect his or her standard of comparison. Furthermore, the characteristics are described by highly subjective and relative terms: "inner city" and "excellent" are not objective measures. These potential problems highlight the need for adequate training of interviewers, as well as for some attempt to cross-validate such data, possibly by employing multiple judges to rate the same area.

One problem with assigning people to a social class is that they may not be equal in their standing with respect to all of the relevant dimensions. A person

---

FIGURE 13-2   EXAMPLE OF A COMPUTERIZED STATUS INDEX

Interviewer circles code numbers (for the computer) which in his/her judgment best fit the respondent and family. Interviewer asks for detail on occupation, then makes rating. Interviewer often asks the respondent to describe neighbourhood in own words. Interviewer asks respondent to specify income—a card is presented to the respondent showing the eight brackets—and records R's response. If interviewer feels this is over-statement or under-statement, a "better judgment" estimate should be given, along with explanation.

	Respondent	Respondent's Spouse
EDUCATION:		
Grammar school (8 yrs or less)	−1	−1
Some high school (9 to 11 yrs)	−2 R's Age	−2 Spouse's Age
Graduated high school (12 yrs)	−3	−3
Some post high school (business, nursing, technical, 1 yr college)	−4	−4
Two, three years of university—possibly Associate of Arts degree	−5	−5
Graduated four-year university (B.A./B.S.)	−7	−7
Master's or five-year professional degree	−8	−8
Ph.D. or six/seven-year professional degree	−9	−9

OCCUPATION PRESTIGE LEVEL OF HOUSEHOLD HEAD: Interviewer's judgment of how head of household rates in occupational status.

(Respondent's description—asks for previous occupation if retired, or if R. is widow, asks husband's: _____)

Chronically unemployed—"day" labourers, unskilled; on welfare	−0
Steadily employed but in marginal semi-skilled jobs; custodians, minimum-pay factory help, service workers (gas attendants, etc.)	−1
Average-skill assembly-line workers, bus and truck drivers, police and firefighters, route delivery people, carpenters, brickmasons	−2
Skilled crafts people (electricians), small contractors, factory supervisors, low-pay salesclerks, office workers, postal employees	−3
Owners of very small firms (2–4 employees), technicians, salespeople, office workers, civil servants with average level salaries	−4
Middle management, teachers, social workers, lesser professionals	−5
Lesser corporate officials, owners of middle-sized businesses (10–20 employees), moderate-success professionals (dentists, engineers, etc.)	−7
Top corporate executives, "big successes" in the professional world (leading doctors and lawyers), "rich" business owners	−9

AREA OF RESIDENCE: Interviewer's impressions of the immediate neighbourhood in terms of its reputation in the eyes of the community.

Inner city area: people on relief, common labourers	−1
Strictly working class: not slummy but some very poor housing	−2
Predominantly blue-collar with some office workers	−3
Predominantly white-collar with some well-paid blue-collar workers	−4
Better white-collar area: not many executives, but hardly any blue-collar either	−5
Excellent area: professionals and well-paid managers	−7
"Wealthy" or "society"-type neighbourhood	−9

TOTAL SCORE _____

TOTAL FAMILY INCOME PER YEAR:

Under $9000	−1	$60 000 to $69 999	−7
$10 000 to $19 999	−2	$70 000 to $79 999	−8
$20 000 to $29 999	−3	$80 000 to $89 999	−9
$30 000 to $39 999	−4	$90 000 and over	−10
$40 000 to $49 999	−5	$1 000 000 and over	−11
$50 000 to $59 999	−6		

Estimated Status _____

Source: Adapted from Richard P. Coleman, "The Continuing Significance of Social Class to Marketing," *Journal of Consumer Research* 10 (December 1983): 265–280. Reprinted with permission of The University of Chicago Press.

might come from a low-status ethnic group but have a high-status job, whereas another may live in a fancy part of town but not have finished high school. The concept of **status crystallization** was developed to assess the impact of inconsistency on the self-concept and on social behaviour.[48] The logic behind this idea is that because the rewards from each part of such an "unbalanced" person's life would be variable and unpredictable, stress would result. People who exhibit such inconsistencies tend to be more receptive to social change than are those whose identities are rooted more firmly.

Marketing
Pitfall

A related problem occurs when a person's social-class standing creates expectations that are not met. Some people find themselves in the not unhappy position of making more money than is expected of those in their social class. This situation is known as an *overprivileged* condition, and is usually defined as one where an individual earns an income that is at least 25 percent to 30 percent greater than the median for one's class.[49] In contrast, *underprivileged* consumers, who earn at least 15 percent less than the median, must often allocate a big chunk of their income toward maintaining the impression that they occupy a certain status.

The traditional assumption is that husbands define a family's social class while wives must live it; women achieve their social status from their husbands.[50] Indeed, evidence indicates that physically attractive women tend to "marry up" in social class to a greater extent than attractive men do. Women trade the resource of sexual appeal, which historically was one of the few assets they were allowed to possess, for the economic resources of men.[51]

The accuracy of this assumption in today's world must be questioned. Many women now contribute equally to the family's well-being and work in positions of comparable or even greater status than their spouses. Employed women tend to average both their own and their husband's respective positions when estimating their own subjective status.[52] Nevertheless, a prospective spouse's social class is often an important "product attribute" when evaluating alternatives in the interpersonal marketplace (as Victor and Marilyn were to find out).

PROBLEMS WITH SOCIAL CLASS SEGMENTATION: A SUMMARY

Social class remains an important way to categorize consumers. Many marketing strategies do target different social classes. However, marketers have failed to use social class information as effectively as they could for the following reasons:

- They have ignored status inconsistency.
- They have ignored intergenerational mobility.
- They have ignored subjective social class (i.e., the class a consumer identifies with rather than the one to which he or she objectively belongs).
- They have ignored consumers' aspirations to change their class standing.
- They have ignored the social status of working wives.

HOW SOCIAL CLASS AFFECTS PURCHASE DECISIONS

Consumers perceive different products and stores as appropriate for certain social classes.[53] Working-class consumers tend to evaluate products in more utilitarian terms, such as sturdiness or comfort, rather than in terms of style or fashionability. They are less likely to experiment with new products or styles, such as modern furniture or coloured appliances.[54] In contrast, more affluent people living in the suburbs tend to be concerned about appearance and body image, so they are more avid consumers of diet foods and drinks compared with people in more downscale small towns. These differences mean that marketers can use social-class standing to segment markets for soft drinks and other similar products.[55]

Class Differences in World View

A major social-class difference involves the *world view* of consumers. The world of the working class (i.e., the lower-middle class) is more intimate and constricted. For example, working-class men are likely to name local sports figures as heroes and are less likely to take long vacation trips to out-of-the-way places.[56] Immediate needs, such as a new refrigerator or television set, tend to dictate buying behaviour

Whatever your customers love to do for fun, Libbey refreshes them along the way. Libbey offers glasses to fit any lifestyle and specific taste.□You can satisfy your customers' preferences and reflect your store's distinctiveness, too.□Contact your Libbey representative today for a personal viewing. We will come out to see you with so many choices, we know it will be very refreshing indeed.   **Libbey**

"Peach cooler, please."   "Gimme a brew."

←This ad for Libbey Glass (*www.libbey.com*) implies that there are social-class differences in leisure activities and preferred beverages.
Courtesy of Libbey Glass Inc.

for these consumers, whereas the higher classes tend to focus more on long-term goals, such as saving for university tuition or retirement.[58] Four out of ten Canadian professionals contribute to Registered Retirement Savings Plans, and internet usage skews very heavily to upper-income earners.[59]

Working-class consumers depend heavily on relatives for emotional support and tend to orient themselves in terms of the community rather than the world at large. They are more likely to be conservative and family-oriented. Maintaining the appearance of one's home and property is a priority, regardless of the size of the house.

Although they would like to have more in the way of material goods, working-class people do not necessarily envy those who rank above them in social standing.[60] The maintenance of a high-status lifestyle is sometimes not seen as worth the effort. As one blue-collar consumer commented: "Life is very hectic for those people. There are more breakdowns and alcoholism. It must be very hard to sustain the status, the clothes, the parties that are expected. I don't think I'd want to take their place."[61]

This person may be right. Although good things appear to go hand in hand with higher status and wealth, the picture is not that clear. The social scientist Emile Durkheim observed that suicide rates are much higher among the wealthy; he wrote in 1897, "The possessors of most comfort suffer most."[62] Durkheim's wisdom may still be accurate today. Many well-off consumers seem to be stressed or unhappy despite or even due to their wealth, a condition sometimes termed *affluenza*.[63]

Taste Cultures, Codes, and Cultural Capital

A *taste culture* differentiates people in terms of their aesthetic and intellectual preferences. This concept helps to illuminate the important yet sometimes subtle distinctions in consumption choices among the social classes. For example, a comprehensive analysis of social-class differences using data from 675 000 households suggests that differences in consumption patterns for mass-marketed products have largely disappeared between the upper and upper-middle classes and between the middle and working classes. However, strong differences still emerge in terms of *how* consumers spend their discretionary income and leisure time. Upper- and upper-middle-class people are more likely to visit museums and attend live theatre; middle-class consumers are more likely to go camping and fishing. The

Marketing Opportunity !

About one-third of Canada's 1.5 million working-class youth (aged 18 to 25 years) are actually "gold-collar apirationalists," according to a study by Synovate. They buy products such as fashions, premium alcohol, and cell phones to define who they are. They will buy $230 skin creams, $500 handbags, $300 sunglasses, and expensive coffees.

How can these young earners of less than $30 000 per year afford these high-end purchases? Most live at home, do not have student-loan debt (unlike their university counterparts), and are not saving to buy a home (unlike blue-collar youth); in other words, they have very high discretionary income. Premium products with celebrity endorsements are very appealing to this gold-collar class.[64]

Music: Up and under.

Announcer: Maurice Carter has a subscription to the Toronto Symphony Orchestra. This does not make sense. Because Maurice does not press his underwear. His is not a medieval language enthusiast. Nor does he own a "Queen's Visit to Canada" commmemorative plate collection. As it happens, Maurice is a 31-year-old physiotherapist with eight percent body fat, two cell phones, and three girlfriends. This didn't sound like the boring, uptight TSO subscriber we'd envisioned. So we called Wanda, Cheryl, and Regan and found out two things: Maurice loves Beethoven. And he'd better watch his no-good, hound-dog, three-timin' butt. The Toronto Symphony Orchestra. Subscribe now at ***www.tso.ca***. You'd be surprised who goes to the TSO.

upper class is more likely to listen to all-news programs, while the middle classes are more likely to tune in to country music.[65]

Although analyses based on distinguishing taste cultures have met with criticism because of the implicit value judgments involved, they are valuable because they recognize the existence of groupings based on shared tastes in literature, art, and home decoration. In one of the classic studies of social differences in taste, researchers catalogued homeowners' possessions while asking more typical questions about income and occupation. Specific "clusters" of furnishings and decorative items that seemed to appear together with some regularity were identified. These clusters appeared to depend upon the consumer's social status. For example, religious objects, artificial flowers, and still lifes tended to be found together in relatively lower-status living rooms, while a cluster containing abstract paintings, sculptures, and modern furniture was more likely to appear in a higher-status home.[66]

Another approach to social class focuses on differences in the types of *codes* (the ways in which meanings are expressed and interpreted by consumers) used within different social strata. Discovery of these codes is valuable to marketers because this knowledge allows them to communicate to markets using concepts and terms most likely to be understood and appreciated by specific consumers. For example, a life insurance ad targeted at a lower-class person might depict in simple, straightforward terms a hard-working family man who feels good immediately after purchasing a policy. A more upscale appeal might depict a more affluent older couple surrounded by photos of their children and grandchildren, and contain extensive copy emphasizing the satisfaction that comes from planning for the future and highlighting the benefits of a whole-life insurance policy.

The nature of these codes varies among social classes: Restricted codes are dominant among the working class, whereas elaborated codes tend to be used by the middle and upper classes. **Restricted codes** focus on the content of objects, not on relationships among objects. **Elaborated codes**, in contrast, are more complex and depend upon a more sophisticated world view. These code differences extend to the way consumers approach basic concepts such as time, social relationships, and objects. Table 13–1 summarizes differences between these two types.

Clearly, not all taste cultures are created equal. The upper classes have access to resources that enable them to perpetuate their privileged position in society. A French theorist named Pierre Bourdieu wrote at length about the process by which people compete for resources, or *capital*. Bourdieu did large-scale surveys to track people's wealth and to relate this "economic capital" to patterns of taste in entertainment and the arts. He concluded that "taste" is a status-marking force or **habitus** that causes consumption preferences to cluster together. Analyses of American consumers largely confirm these relationships; for example, higher-

TABLE 13-1

EFFECTS OF RESTRICTED VERSUS ELABORATED CODES

	Restricted Codes	Elaborated Codes
General characteristics	Emphasize description and contents of objects	Emphasize analysis and inter-relationships between objects, i.e., hierarchical organization and instrumental connections
	Have implicit meanings (context-dependent)	Have explicit meanings
Language	Use few qualifiers: i.e., few adjectives or adverbs	Have language rich in personal, individual qualifiers
	Use concrete, descriptive, tangible symbolism	Use large vocabulary, complex conceptual hierarchy
Social relationships	Stress attributes of individuals over formal roles	Stress formal role structure, instrumental relationships
Time	Focus on present; have only general notion of future	Focus on instrumental relationship between present activities and future rewards
Physical space	Locate rooms, spaces in context of other rooms and places, e.g., "front room," "corner store"	Identify rooms, spaces in terms of usage; formal ordering of spaces: e.g., "dining room," "financial district"
Implications for marketers	Stress inherent product quality, contents (or trustworthiness, goodness of "real-type"), spokesperson	Stress differences, advantages vis-à-vis other products in terms of some autonomous evaluation criteria
	Stress implicit fit of product with total lifestyle	Stress product's instrumental ties to distant benefits
	Use simple adjectives, descriptors	Use complex adjectives, descriptors

Source: Adapted from Jeffrey F. Durgee, "How Consumer Sub-Cultures Code Reality: A Look at some Code Types," in *Advances in Consumer Research* 13, ed. Richard J. Lutz (Provo, UT: Association for Consumer Research, 1986), p. 332.

income people are more likely than the average consumer to attend the theatre, while lower-income people are more likely to attend a wrestling match.[67]

Capital takes on forms other than just money. In addition to *economic capital* (financial resources), Bourdieu pointed to *social capital* (organizational affiliations and networks). The importance of access to social capital is demonstrated by the legions of aspiring professionals who in recent years have taken up golf because so much business is conducted on the greens.

Bourdieu also reminds us of the consequences of **cultural capital**, a set of distinctive and socially rare tastes and practices—knowledge of "refined" behaviour that admits a person into the realm of the upper class.[68] The elites in a society collect a set of skills that enable them to hold positions of power and authority, and they pass these on to their children (think etiquette lessons). These resources gain in value because access to them is restricted. Much as we hate to admit it, the rich *are* different.

Targeting the Poor

About 13 percent of Canadian families and about 10 percent of Canadian children live below the poverty line.[69] Still, although poor people obviously have less to spend than rich ones, they have the same basic needs as everyone else. Low-income families purchase staples, such as milk, orange juice, and tea, at the same rates as average-income families. Minimum-wage-level households spend a greater-than-average share of income on out-of-pocket costs for housing and food eaten at home.[70] Unfortunately, these resources are harder to obtain due to the reluctance of many businesses to locate in lower-income areas. On average, residents of poor neighbourhoods must travel more than two miles (three kilometres) to have the same access to supermarkets, large drug stores, and banks as do residents of more affluent areas.[71]

In developing countries such as India, China, and the Philippines, single-serve packages of consumer goods such as shampoo, tea, aspirin, condiments, cookies, and matches, priced at about a penny a piece, are good sellers for both global and local firms. In fact, in India 60 percent of shampoo sales are single-serve packets.[72]

Targeting the Affluent

We live in a time when one can purchase a Pink Splendor Barbie, complete with crystal jewellery and a bouffant gown sewn with 24-karat threads.[73] To dress a "living doll," Victoria's Secret offers its Million Dollar Miracle Bra, with more than 100 carats of real diamonds![74] Even the way we pay for these lavish items can become a statement about wealth—especially if you're one of the only 5000 people American Express has invited to hold its black Centurion credit card. The mysterious card is blank except for a black-on-black pattern. To be deemed worthy of having the card, a shopper has to charge more than $150 000 per year and pay an annual fee of $2500.

Many marketers try to target affluent, upscale markets. This practice often makes sense because these consumers obviously have the resources to spend on costly products (often with higher profit margins). However, it is a mistake to assume that everyone with a high income should be placed in the same market segment. As noted earlier, social class involves more than absolute income; it is also a way of life, and affluent consumers' interests and spending priorities are significantly affected by factors such as where they got their money, how they got it, and how long they have had it.[75]

Interestingly, many affluent people don't consider themselves to be rich. One tendency noticed by many researchers is that they indulge in luxury goods while pinching pennies on everyday items—buying shoes at upscale stores and deodorant at Wal-Mart, for example.[76] Nevertheless, Canadian businesses, such as Birk's and Bernard Callebaut, cater successfully to consumers seeking premium or luxury products. And Winners, with more than 170 Canadian and 200 international stores, makes designer labels and luxurious items accessible to the middle-market consumer. Other marketers are creating entry-level products at lower price points and are using merchandise approaches that offer luxury at every price point.[77]

SRI Consulting Business Intelligence (the research firm that developed VALS2™ as discussed in Chapter 6) divides consumers into three groups based on their attitudes toward luxury:

1. *Luxury is functional:* These consumers buy things that will last and have enduring value. They conduct extensive prepurchase research and make logical decisions rather than emotional or impulsive choices.

2. *Luxury is a reward:* These consumers tend to be younger than the first group but older than the third group. They often use luxury goods to say, "I've made it." The desire to be successful and to demonstrate their success to others motivates these consumers to purchase conspicuous luxury items, such as high-end automobiles and homes in exclusive communities.

3. *Luxury is indulgence:* This group is the smallest of the three and tends to include younger consumers and slightly more males than the other two groups. To these consumers, the purpose of owning luxury items is to be extremely lavish and self-indulgent. This group is willing to pay a premium for goods that

express their individuality and make others take notice. These consumers have a more emotional approach to luxury spending and are more likely than the other two groups to make impulse purchases.[81] Indulgent consumers are probably good candidates for the microchips being implanted in the upper left arms of big-spending patrons at the Baja Beach Club in Barcelona; the chips allow them EZ-pass-like entry to the club's ultra-exclusive VIP lounge. Once there, they can pay for their drinks by merely flexing their triceps before a handheld electronic reader.[82]

OLD MONEY

"Old money" (e.g., the Bronfmans, Westons, Killams, McCains, etc.) live primarily on inherited money. Merely having wealth is not sufficient to achieve social prominence in these circles. Money must be accompanied by a family history of public service and philanthropy, which is often manifested in tangible markers (e.g., Ivey Business School or Zwicker's Gallery) that enable these donors to achieve a kind of immortality.[83] Old-money consumers tend to make distinctions among themselves in terms of ancestry and lineage rather than wealth.[84] Old-money people (like the Caldwells) are secure in their status. In a sense, they have been trained their whole lives to be rich.

THE NOUVEAUX RICHES

Today there are many people—including high-profile billionaires such as Bill Gates, Galen Weston, and Richard Branson—who can be thought of as "the working wealthy."[85] The myth where a person goes from "rags to riches" through hard work and a bit of luck is still a powerful force. Canada's most affluent workers (who make up 10 percent of the labour force) credit hard work, education, and intelligence for their financial success; however, only 20 percent of them consider themselves highly skilled at managing their money.[86]

Although many people do in fact become "self-made millionaires," they often encounter a problem (although not the worst problem one could think of!) after they become wealthy and change their social status. Consumers who have achieved extreme wealth and have relatively recently become members of upper social classes are known as the *nouveaux riches,* a term that some people use in a derogatory manner to describe newcomers to the world of wealth.

Alas, many *nouveaux riches* are plagued by *status anxiety.* They monitor the cultural environment to ensure that they are doing the "right" thing, wearing the "right" clothes, being seen at the "right" places, using the "right" caterer, and so on.[87] Flamboyant consumption can thus be viewed as a form of symbolic self-completion, where the excessive display of symbols thought to denote "class" is used to make up for an internal lack of assurance about the "correct" way to behave.[88] In major Chinese cities like Shanghai, for example, some people have taken to wearing pajamas in public as a way to flaunt their new-found wealth. As one consumer explained, "Only people in cities can afford clothes like this. In farming villages, they still have to wear old work clothes to bed."[89]

Advertising directed toward this group often plays on these insecurities by emphasizing the importance of "looking the part." Clever merchandising supplies these consumers with the props to masquerade as old-money people. For example, some princes and princesses of Canada's New Economy dream big when it comes to expressing themselves in housing. Architects and designers have seen everything: Pools on rooftops. Aquariums filled with Japanese koi, mounted in a front-hall ceiling. Kitchens with walk-in freezers. Wine cellars with tasting rooms. Bathrooms with waterfalls.[90]

Upscale retailing areas, such as Robson Street in Vancouver, Hazelton Lanes in Toronto, and Historic Properties in Halifax, are targeted at this segment. Montreal's Westmount Square is one of Canada's largest multifaceted shopping and entertainment centres for upscale consumers. (For an interesting example of

Marketing Opportunity

According to the 2004 World Wealth Report, the number of millionaires worldwide rose to 7.7 million in 2003. Taddingtone Consulting claims that there are 350 000 Canadian millionaires who can be profiled into three groups: 290 000 massmillionaires, with $1 million to $5 million; 43 000 pentamillionaires, with $5 million to $10 million; and 17 000 decamillionaires, with more than $10 million. Just over 40 percent of them live in Ontario, while another 40 percent are divided evenly between British Columbia and Quebec. They enjoy at least two of the following leisure activities: golf, skiing, boating, tennis, running, and fishing. These discriminating shoppers appreciate exclusivity and optimal customer service.[91]

Opera is another leisure pursuit of the affluent. Canada's 647 000 opera fans tend to be female (57 percent), older (40 percent are over 50), well-read (32 percent are heavy magazine readers), and well-educated (they are twice as likely as the average Canadian to be university graduates). They also like to cycle (33 percent), ice skate (24 percent), golf (23 percent), play tennis and downhill ski (21 percent for each), and garden and entertain at home (50 percent for each).[92]

→ Hazelton Lanes in Toronto is a mecca for the nouveaux riches (***www.hazeltonlanes.com***).
Courtesy of Hazelton Lanes and Bensiman • Byrne • DMB&B.

Don't forget to **separate** the crystal from the **glass** on blue box day.

Fifty-five Avenue Road, two blocks north of Bloor.
Truly unique houseware items you won't find anywhere else.
Reduce, reuse, and if necessary, replace.

Hazelton Lanes

The best will always suffice.

internet marketing for malls, see ***www.torontomalls.com***.) Interestingly, Harley-Davidson, which improved its quality and its dealerships in recent years, is doing a thriving business with rich urban bikers (RUBs) across Canada.[93]

STATUS SYMBOLS

People have a deep-seated tendency to evaluate themselves, their professional accomplishments, and their material well-being relative to others. The popular phrase "keeping up with the Joneses" (in Japan it's "keeping up with the Satos") refers to the comparison between people's standard of living and that of their neighbours.

Often it's not enough to have wealth or fame—what matters is that you have more of it than others. A major motivation for the purchase and display of products

is not to enjoy them, but rather to let others know that we can afford them. In other words, these products function as **status symbols**. The popular bumper-sticker slogan, "He who dies with the most toys wins," summarizes the desire to accumulate these "badges of achievement." Status seeking is a significant source of the motivation (see Chapter 4) to procure appropriate products and services that the user hopes will let others know that he or she has "made it."

The particular products that count as status symbols vary, of course, across cultures and locales. For example, owning a private helicopter is a must for well-to-do Brazilians, who are dogged by traffic snarls and kidnappers.[94] In China, children are status symbols (partly because couples are strongly discouraged from having more than one baby). Parents want to show off their pampered child and are eager to surround their "little emperors" with luxury goods. Chinese families spend one-third to one-half of their disposable income on their children.[95]

Conspicuous Consumption

The social analyst Thorstein Veblen first discussed the motivation to consume for the sake of consuming at the turn of the twentieth century. Veblen felt that a major role of products was **invidious distinction**—to inspire envy in others through the display of wealth or power.

Veblen coined the term **conspicuous consumption** to refer to people's desire to provide prominent, visible evidence of their ability to afford luxury goods. His work was motivated by the excesses of his time. Veblen wrote in the era of the American Robber Barons, when the likes of J.P. Morgan and William Vanderbilt were building massive financial empires and flaunting their wealth by throwing lavish parties. Some of these events of excess became legendary, as described in this account:

> There were tales, repeated in the newspapers, of dinners on horseback; of banquets for pet dogs; of hundred-dollar bills folded into guests' dinner napkins; of a hostess who attracted attention by seating a chimpanzee at her table; of centerpieces in which lightly clad living maidens swam in glass tanks, or emerged from huge pies; of parties at which cigars were ceremoniously lighted with flaming banknotes of large denominations.[96]

Sounds as if they really lived it up back in the old days, right? Well, perhaps the more things change, the more they stay the same. The recent wave of corporate scandals involving companies like Enron, WorldCom, and Tyco infuriated many consumers as they discovered that some top executives were living it up even as other employees of the same company were being laid off. One account of a US$1 million birthday party thrown by the chief executive of Tyco for his wife sounds eerily familiar to the shindigs thrown by those old Robber Barons: The party reportedly had a gladiator theme and included an ice sculpture of Michelangelo's David with vodka streaming from his penis into crystal glasses. The company also furnished the executive's New York apartment with "essentials," such as a US$6000 shower curtain, a US$2200 gilt wastebasket, and a US$17 100 "traveling toilet box."[97]

THE TROPHY WIFE

This phenomenon of conspicuous consumption was, for Veblen, most evident among what he termed the *leisure class,* people for whom productive work is taboo. In Marxist terms this reflects a desire to link oneself to ownership or control of the means of production, rather than to the production itself. Any evidence that one actually has to labour for a living is to be shunned, as suggested by the term the "idle rich."

This analysis also included wives: Veblen criticized the "decorative" role women were often forced to play as they were showered with expensive clothes,

Marketing Opportunity !

The quest for status influences both kids and adults, though the symbols we choose to pursue vary as we age. However, the cell phone is emerging as a new status symbol that cuts across age groups.

Young people view a cell phone as a necessity, not a luxury. It's their primary means of staying connected with others. But a cell phone is not just a means of communication. It is an accessory, a fashion statement, an instant messenger, a toy, and a social prop. It is a symbol of independence second only to the car, and many teenagers say it's an extension of their personality. Phone manufacturers are scrambling to provide what kids want. The companies have their sights set on young people for good reason: The market has plenty of room for growth. Firms such as Wildseed offer customizable faceplates to let users express their unique identity.

Adults aren't immune to the status appeal of a cell phone, and some research suggests that men are especially susceptible to its lure. Researchers at the University of Liverpool in the U.K. were inspired to investigate this phenomenon after reading newspaper accounts about night clubs in South America that began requiring patrons to check their cell phones at the door. The clubs' managers soon discovered that a huge percentage of the phones were fake.

To see how people were really using their phones as social props, the researchers observed patrons at an upscale pub frequented by lawyers, entrepreneurs, and other single professionals. They discovered that men had a markedly different relationship with their cell phones than did women. The female customers generally kept their phones in their purses and retrieved them only as needed, but the men would take their phones out of their jacket pockets or briefcases upon sitting down and place them on the bar counter or table for all to see.

The authors of this study propose that men use their mobile phones as peacocks use their plumage or male bullfrogs use their croaks—to advertise their status to available mates. They noted that the amount of time the men spent toying with and displaying their phones increased significantly as the number of men relative to women increased—just as male peacocks fan open their feathers more vigorously as the number of competing suitors increases.[98]

And even the phone numbers assigned to cell phones appear to function as status symbols for some. Numbers ending in "00" or "000" are hot and in demand even though (or because?) most phone companies charge extra to assign them.[99] That's status calling!

pretentious homes, and a life of leisure as a way to advertise the wealth of their husbands—this type of woman was a sort of "walking billboard." Fashions, such as high heels, tight corsets, billowing trains on dresses, and elaborate hairstyles all conspired to ensure that wealthy women could barely move without assistance, much less perform manual labour. Similarly, the Chinese practice of foot binding severely handicapped women, who had to be carried from place to place.

Veblen was inspired by anthropological studies of the Kwakiutl Indians, who lived in the Pacific Northwest. At a ceremonial feast called a potlatch, the host showed off his wealth and gave extravagant presents to the guests. The more he gave away, the better he looked to the others. Sometimes the host would use an even more radical strategy to flaunt his wealth: He would publicly destroy some of his property to demonstrate how much he had.

Tribe members also used this ritual as a social weapon. Because guests were expected to reciprocate, a poorer rival could be humiliated by inviting him to a lavish potlatch. The need to give away as much as the host, even though he could not afford it, could essentially force the hapless guest into bankruptcy. If this practice sounds "primitive," think for a moment about many modern weddings. Parents commonly invest huge sums of money to throw a lavish party and compete with others for the distinction of giving their daughter the "best" or most extravagant wedding, even if they have to dip into their retirement savings to do it.

Like the potlatch ritual, the desire to convince others that we have a surplus of resources creates the need for evidence of this abundance. Accordingly, priority is

Reality Check ✓

Status symbols are products that are valued because they show others how much money or prestige a person has, such as expensive cars. Do you believe that your peer group values status symbols? Why or why not? If yes, what are the products that you think are regarded as status symbols now for consumers your age?

> Frequently status symbols…reflect a shared preference for lifestyle choices. For example, participants in extreme sports, such as mountain biking, often use their sporting gear as casual clothing, reflecting their choice of activities in their everyday attire. Hence, my peer group does still value status symbols, although they are likely to be different for different groups….However, some items continue to carry connotations across several groups. The most obvious are our cars. Functionality isn't enough. We need to look cool.

Satish Magan Ranchod, University of Auckland, New Zealand

> By the time Chileans turn eighteen, their parents try to buy them the best new car in the market, so they can show their economic status.

Constanza Montes Larranaga, Universidad de Chile, Chile

> I feel that young adults today place a strong value on products that symbolize status. Group membership at university is a major concern for most students…. Products that symbolize status to my peer group are usually on a smaller scale compared to expensive cars or houses, and include brand name clothing and accessories, such as "The Gap" shirts and pants and Mountain Equipment Co-op jackets and school bags…Also, cell phones symbolize a strong sense of status today among university students. By purchasing these types of products, students feel they establish a sense of style that helps them feel part of a particular group.

Kate Graham, Mount Allison University, Canada

> I think that the products related to my peer group are mobile phones (Star Tack), certain types of clothing (such as Zara, Calvin Klein), shoes (Timberland boots, Clarks …) and fragrances (CK One, Hugo Boss…).

Astrid Spielrein, ASSAS University Paris II, France

→ In a twist on conspicuous consumption, this ad for Halston jackets appeals to people who want to avoid the blatant display of status symbols. *Courtesy of Halston for Men Tailored Clothing.*

CONSPICUOUS SUBTLETY

One of the special fabrics that distinguishes Halston as being fashion conscious yet impeccably sensible clothing is Country Silk." Loomed in Scotland along the river Tweed this exclusive fabric is a unique blending of high quality wool and the best of silk.

Great weight, great feel, great looks and the perfect update of a classic sport coat by none other than Halston.

THE ONE LABEL YOU DON'T HAVE TO SEE TO KNOW IT'S THERE.

HALSTON
FOR MEN
1290 AVENUE OF THE AMERICAS, NEW YORK, N.Y 10104 (212) 581 · 8510

FINE FABRICS WOVEN IN SCOTLAND

given to consumption activities that use up as many resources as possible in non-constructive pursuits. This *conspicuous waste*, in turn, shows others that we have the assets to spare. Veblen noted that "we are told of certain Polynesian chiefs, who, under the stress of good form, preferred to starve rather than carry their food to their mouths with their own hands."[100]

PARODY DISPLAY

As the competition to accumulate status symbols escalates, sometimes the best tactic is to switch gears and go in reverse. One way to do this is to deliberately *avoid* status symbols—that is, to seek status by mocking it. This sophisticated form of conspicuous consumption has been termed **parody display**.[101] Popular examples of parody display are frayed edges on denim skirts, unbuttoned cuffs on shirts, and "utility" vehicles, such as Jeeps, purchased by the upper classes (like the Caldwells). Thus, "true" status is shown by the adoption of product symbolism that is deliberately not fashionable.

CHAPTER SUMMARY

OUR DECISIONS ABOUT WHETHER TO SPEND OUR MONEY ARE INFLUENCED BY BOTH PERSONAL AND SOCIAL CONDITIONS.

- The field of behavioural economics considers how consumers decide what to do with their money. In particular, discretionary expenditures are made only when people are able and willing to spend money on items above and beyond their basic needs. Consumer confidence—the state of mind consumers have about their own personal situations, as well as their feelings about their overall economic prospects—helps to determine whether they will purchase goods and services, take on debt, or save their money.

WE CAN GROUP CONSUMERS INTO SOCIAL CLASSES THAT SAY A LOT ABOUT AN INDIVIDUAL'S STANDING IN SOCIETY.

- A consumer's social class refers to his or her standing in society. It is determined by a number of factors, including education, occupation, and income.
- Virtually all groups make distinctions among members in terms of relative superiority, power, and access to valued resources. This social stratification creates a status hierarchy, in which some goods are preferred over others and are used to categorize their owners' social class.

- Although income is an important indicator of social class, the relationship is far from perfect because social class is also determined by factors such as place of residence, cultural interests, and world view.

CONSUMER BEHAVIOUR OFTEN IS AFFECTED BY A PERSON'S DESIRE TO MAKE A STATEMENT ABOUT HIS OR HER SOCIAL CLASS, OR ABOUT THE CLASS TO WHICH HE OR SHE WOULD LIKE TO BELONG.

- Purchase decisions are sometimes influenced by the desire to "buy up" to a higher social class or to engage in the process of conspicuous consumption, wherein one's status is flaunted by the deliberate and non-constructive use of valuable resources. This spending pattern is characteristic of the *nouveaux riches*, whose relatively recent acquisition of income, rather than ancestry or breeding, is responsible for their increased social mobility.
- Products often are used as status symbols to communicate real or desired social class. Parody display occurs when consumers seek status by deliberately avoiding fashionable products.

KEY TERMS

Behavioural economics   p. 376

Chavs   p. 381

Conspicuous consumption   p. 393

Consumer confidence   p. 376

Cultural capital   p. 389

Discretionary income   p. 375

Elaborated codes   p. 388

Habitus   p. 388

Homogamy   p. 378

Mass class   p. 381

Invidious distinction   p. 393

Parody display   p. 397

Restricted codes   p. 388

Social class   p. 377

Social mobility   p. 381

Social stratification   p. 378

Status crystallization   p. 385

Status hierarchy   p. 379

Status symbols   p. 393

REVIEW QUESTIONS

1. How have women contributed to the overall rise in income in our society?
2. Define discretionary income.
3. How does consumer confidence influence consumer behaviour?
4. What is a pecking order?
5. What is social class? Is it different from income? If so, how?
6. What is the difference between achieved and ascribed status?
7. What is a chav?
8. Describe what is meant by the term "mass class" and explain what is causing this phenomenon.
9. Define social mobility and the different forms it can take.
10. What one variable is the best indicator of social class? What are some other important indicators?
11. Why does earning more money often not result in a corresponding change in social class?
12. What are some of the problems associated with efforts to measure social class?
13. Define status crystallization and give an example.
14. How does the world view of blue-collar and white-collar consumers tend to differ?
15. What is a taste culture?
16. Describe the difference between a restricted and an elaborated code, giving an example of each.
17. What is cultural capital, and why is an etiquette class a way to accumulate it?
18. How would you differentiate between consumers who are "old money" versus "*nouveaux riches*?"
19. What is conspicuous consumption? Give a current example.
20. What is a current example of parody display?

CONSUMER BEHAVIOUR CHALLENGE

Discuss

1. Sears and (to a lesser degree) The Bay have made concerted efforts in recent years to upgrade their images and appeal to higher-class consumers. How successful have these efforts been? Do you believe this strategy is wise?
2. What are some of the obstacles to measuring social class in today's society? Discuss some ways to get around these obstacles.
3. Do you believe "affluenza" is a problem among Canadians your age? Why or why not?
4. What consumption differences might you expect to observe between a family characterized as underprivileged and one whose income is average for its social class?
5. How do *you* assign people to social classes, or do you at all? What consumption cues (e.g., clothing, speech, cars, etc.) do you use to determine social standing?
6. Thorstein Veblen argued that women were often used as vehicles to display their husbands' wealth. Is this argument still valid today?
7. Given present environmental conditions and dwindling resources, what is the future of "conspicuous waste"? Can the desire to impress others with affluence ever be eliminated? If not, can it take on another form?

8. This chapter observes that some marketers are finding "greener pastures" by targeting low-income people. How ethical is it to single out consumers who cannot afford to waste their precious resources on discretionary items? Under what circumstances should this segmentation strategy be encouraged or discouraged?

Experiential Exercises

9. Using the status index presented in Figure 13–2, compute a social-class score for people you know, including their parents if possible. Ask several friends (preferably from different places) to compile similar information for people they know. How closely do your answers compare? If you find differences, how can you explain them?
10. Compile a list of occupations, and ask a sample of students in a variety of majors (both business and non-business) to rank the prestige of these jobs. Can you detect any differences in these rankings as a function of students' majors?
11. Compile a collection of ads that depict consumers of different social classes. What generalizations can you make about the reality of these ads and about the media in which they appear?

CBC 🔴 VIDEO VIGNETTE

CONCEPTS AT WORK FOR LUXURY PRODUCTS

There is a retail sector that is beginning to ride the trend toward luxury sales. Consumers are buying luxury goods to show that they can afford to buy them, to reward themselves for achieving a lifetime milestone, or just to celebrate taking a business through a tough economic phase. In Canada, these goods include BMWs, Harry Rosen suits, and jewellery from Chez de Versailles in Toronto. Customers are willing to pay $2600 for a suit, $12 000 for a pen, or a mere $2.2 million for a wristwatch.

Canada has no luxury index, but the movement of high-quality goods seems to be a definite trend. What's more, there is even evidence of repeat sales and brand loyalty. Sales of this sometimes inconspicuous merchandise

are characterized by the presence of a high level of service. The challenge for marketers interested in serving this segment is to understand the consumer characteristics behind these individuals' willingness to reward themselves with luxury purchases.

Questions

1. How do luxury goods differ from other goods? Provide some examples.
2. Describe the consumer who buys luxury goods.
3. Why are luxury goods recession-proof?
4. What is the relationship between social class and income?

Resource: "Luxury Sells," *Venture #578*, Air Date: February 18, 1996.

NOTES

1. Roger Sauvé, *The Current State of Canadian Family Finances 2002 Report* (Ottawa: The Vanier Institute of the Family, 2000).
2. Andrew Willis and Gayle MacDonald, "The Gap between Rich and Rich," *Globe and Mail* (July 5, 2003): F4–F5.
3. Adapted from Fabian Linden, *Consumer Affluence: The Next Wave* (New York, NY: The Conference Board, Inc., 1994).
4. *Canada's Families: They Count* (Ottawa: The Vanier Institute of the Family, 1996). "Canadian Gender Trends in Education and Work: Gender and Labour Market Experiences - Labour Force Participation Rate, December 1999," Human Resources and Social Development Canada's website,*www11.hrsdc.gc.ca/en/cs/sp/hrsdc/arb/publications/research/1999-002380/page08.shtml*, accessed May 29, 2006.
5. Canada E Book, Statistics Canada's website, *http://142.206.72.67/02/02c/02c_007_e.htm#t01*, accessed October 26, 2003. "Population 15 Years and Over by Highest Level of Schooling," Statistics Canada's website,*www40.statcan.ca/l01/cst01/educ43a.htm*, accessed May 29, 2006.
6. "Earnings Groups, Full-Year, Full-Time Workers, Total Level of Schooling for Both Sexes," Statistics Canada's website, *www12.statcan.ca/english/census01/products/highlight/Earnings/Page.cfm?Lang=E&Geo=PR&View=1b&Code=0&Table=4a&StartRec=1&Sort=2&B1+Both&B2=Total*, accessed May 29, 2006.
7. Roger Sauvé, *The Dreams and the Reality—Assets, Debts and Net Worth of Canadian Households* (Ottawa: The Vanier Institute of the Family), p. 27; "University Degrees, Diplomas and Certificates Granted by Sex," Statistics Canada's website,*www.40.statcan.ca/l01/cst01/educ51a.htm?sdi=degrees%20granted*, accessed May 29, 2006.
8. Christopher D. Carroll, "How Does Future Income Affect Current Consumption?" *Quarterly Journal of Economics* 109, 1 (February 1994): 111–147.
9. Rahul Jacob, "The Big Rise," *Fortune* (May 30, 1994): 86.
10. Nora Underwood, "The High Life," *Report on Business Magazine* (January 2000): 67–69; Steve Brearton, "Why We Buy," *Report on Business Magazine* (January 2000): 70–71. "Taking a Closer Look; Credit Cards, May 2005," Canadian Bankers Association's website,*www.cba.ca/en/viewDocument.asp?fl=6&sl=111&tl=&docid=246&pg=1*, accessed May 29, 2006.
11. José F. Medina, Joel Saegert, and Alicia Gresham, "Comparison of Mexican-American and Anglo-American Attitudes toward Money," *Journal of Consumer Affairs* 30, 1 (1996): 124–145.
12. Michael Adams, *Better Happy Than Rich? Canadians, Money and the Meaning of Life* (Toronto, ON: Penguin Books Canada Ltd., 2000).
13. Fred van Raaij, "Economic Psychology," *Journal of Economic Psychology* 1 (1981): 1–24.
14. Richard T. Curtin, "Indicators of Consumer Behavior: The University of Michigan Surveys of Consumers," *Public Opinion Quarterly* (1982): 340–352.
15. George Katona, "Consumer Saving Patterns," *Journal of Consumer Research* 1 (June 1974): 1–12.
16. Floyd L. Ruch and Philip G. Zimbardo, *Psychology and Life,* 8th ed. (Glenview, IL: Scott Foresman and Company, 1971).
17. Leslie Kaufman, "Deluxe Dilemma: To Sell Globally or Sell Haughtily?" *New York Times on the Web* (September 22, 1999).
18. Jonathan H. Turner, *Sociology: Studying the Human System,* 2nd ed. (Santa Monica, CA: Goodyear, 1981).
19. Turner, *Sociology: Studying the Human System,* 2nd ed.
20. Richard P. Coleman, "The Continuing Significance of Social Class to Marketing," *Journal of Consumer Research* 10 (December 1983): 265–280; Turner, *Sociology: Studying the Human System,* 2nd ed.
21. Gardyn Rebecca, "The Mating Game," *American Demographics* (July/August 2002): 33–34.
22. Quoted by Richard P. Coleman and Lee Rainwater, *Standing in America: New Dimensions of Class* (New York, NY: Basic Books, 1978), p. 89.
23. Coleman and Rainwater, *Standing in America.*
24. Turner, *Sociology.*
25. "quoththemaven," *Report on Business Magazine* (March 2000): 22.
26. James Fallows, "A Talent for Disorder (Class Structure)," *U.S. News & World Report* (February 1, 1988): 83.
27. Bernard R. Blishen, William A. Carrol, and Catherine Moore, "The 1981 Socio-economic Index for Occupations in Canada," *Canadian Review of Sociology and Anthropology* 24, 4 (1987): 465–488.
28. Coleman, "The Continuing Significance of Social Class to Marketing"; W. Lloyd Warner with Paul S. Lunt, *The Social Life of a Modern Community* (New Haven, CT: Yale University Press, 1941).
29. J. David Lynch, "Emerging Middle Class Reshaping China," *USA Today* (November 12, 2002): 13A.
30. Russell Flannery, "Long Live the $25 Cigar," *Forbes* (December 27, 2004): 51; Clay Chandler, "China Deluxe," *Fortune* (July 26, 2004): 149–156; Matthew Forney, "How Nike Figured Out China," *Time* (November 2004): A10–A14; Lynch, "Emerging Middle Class Reshaping China."
31. Sebastian Moffett, "The Japanese Paradox Pinched by Economic Slump, Women Buy more Handbags from Vuitton, Prada, Hermes," *Wall Street Journal Interactive Edition* (September 23, 2003).
32. Cecilie Rohwedder, "Design Houses Build Stores, Pamper Demanding Shoppers in Fashion-Industry Hot Spot," *Wall Street Journal Interactive Edition* (January 23, 2004).
33. Robin Knight, "Just You Move Over, 'Enry 'Iggins: A New Regard for Profits and Talent Cracks Britain's Old Class System," *U.S. News & World Report* 106 (April 24, 1989): 40.

34. Robert Guy Matthews, "Bawdy British Ads Target Hot Youth," *Wall Street Journal* (April 20, 2005): B9.

35. Jennifer Steinhauer, "When the Joneses Wear Jeans," *New York Times on the Web* (May 29, 2005); Paul F. Nunes, Brian A. Johnson, and R. Timothy S. Breene, "Moneyed Masses," *Harvard Business Review* (July-August 2004): 94–104; *Trend Update: Massclusivity* report form Reinier Evers & *www.trendwatching.com*, accessed at Zyman Institute of Brand Science, Emory University, at *www.zibs.com*, February 24, 2005.

36. Turner, *Sociology*, p. 260.

37. "The Visible Invisible People: Thousands of Canadians Are Homeless, Yet We Have Few Ideas about How Many There Are and How to Help Improve Their Lives," in *Canada and the World Backgrounder* 60, 2 (November 1994): 26–27. See also Ronald Paul Hill and Mark Stamey, "The Homeless in America: An Examination of Possessions and Consumption Behaviors," *Journal of Consumer Research* 17 (December 1990): 303–321.

38. Joseph Kahl, *The American Class Structure* (New York: Holt, Rinehart and Winston, 1961).

39. Leonard Beeghley, *Social Stratification in America: A Critical Analysis of Theory and Research* (Santa Monica, CA: Goodyear, 1978).

40. Coleman and Rainwater, *Standing in America*, p. 220.

41. Roger Sauvé, *The Dreams and the Reality ...*, p. 3.

42. See Coleman, "The Continuing Significance of Social Class to Marketing"; Charles M. Schaninger, "Social Class versus Income Revisited: An Empirical Investigation," *Journal of Marketing Research* 18 (May 1981): 192–208.

43. Coleman, "The Continuing Significance of Social Class to Marketing."

44. August B. Hollingshead and Fredrick C. Redlich, *Social Class and Mental Illness: A Community Study* (New York, NY: John Wiley, 1958).

45. Blishen, Carrol, and Moore, "The 1981 Socio-economic Index for Occupations in Canada."

46. Donald W. Hendon, Emelda L. Williams, and Douglas E. Huffman, "Social Class System Revisited," *Journal of Business Research* 17 (November 1988): 259.

47. Coleman, "The Continuing Significance of Social Class to Marketing."

48. Gerhard E. Lenski, "Status Crystallization: A Non-Vertical Dimension of Social Status," *American Sociological Review* 19 (August 1954): 405–412.

49. Richard P. Coleman, "The Significance of Social Stratification in Selling," in *Marketing: A Maturing Discipline, Proceedings of the American Marketing Association 43rd National Conference*, ed. Martin L. Bell (Chicago, IL: American Marketing Association, 1960), pp. 171–184.

50. E. Barth and W. Watson, "Questionable Assumptions in the Theory of Social Stratification," *Pacific Sociological Review* 7 (Spring 1964): 10–16.

51. Zick Rubin, "Do American Women Marry Up?" *American Sociological Review* 33 (1968): 750–760.

52. K.U. Ritter and L.L. Hargens, "Occupational Positions and Class Identifications of Married Working Women: A Test of the Asymmetry Hypothesis," *American Journal of Sociology* 80 (January 1975): 934–948.

53. J. Michael Munson and W. Austin Spivey, "Product and Brand-User Stereotypes among Social Classes: Implications for Advertising Strategy," *Journal of Advertising Research* 21 (August 1981): 37–45.

54. Stuart U. Rich and Subhash C. Jain, "Social Class and Life Cycle as Predictors of Shopping Behavior," *Journal of Marketing Research* 5 (February 1968): 41–49.

55. Thomas W. Osborn, "Analytic Techniques for Opportunity Marketing," *Marketing Communications* (September 1987): 49–63.

56. Coleman, "The Continuing Significance of Social Class to Marketing."

57. Rebecca Harris, "No Money Down," *Marketing Magazine* (August 1/8, 2005): 4; Wills and McDonald, "The Gap Between Rich and Rich."

58. Jeffrey F. Durgee, "How Consumer Sub-Cultures Code Reality: A Look at some Code Types," in *Advances in Consumer Research* 13, ed. Richard J. Lutz (Provo, UT: Association for Consumer Research, 1986), 332–337.

59. "A Marketing Profile of RRSP Contributors," *Marketing Magazine* (September 9, 1996): 21; "A Marketing Profile of Internet Users," *Marketing Magazine* (February 24, 1997): 31.

60. David Halle, *America's Working Man: Work, Home, and Politics among Blue-Collar Owners* (Chicago: The University of Chicago Press, 1984); David Montgomery, "America's Working Man," *Monthly Review* (1985): 1.

61. Quoted in Coleman and Rainwater, *Standing in America*, p. 139.

62. Durkheim, quoted in Roger Brown, *Social Psychology* (New York, NY: Free Press, 1965).

63. Kit R. Roane, "Affluenza Strikes Kids," *U.S. News & World Report* (March 20, 2000): 55.

64. Chris Daniels, "The Other Working Class," *Marketing Magazine* (May 9, 2005): 5.

65. Eugene Sivadas, George Mathew, and David J. Curry, "A Preliminary Examination of the Continuing Significance of Social Class to Marketing: A Geodemographic Replication," *Journal of Consumer Marketing* 41, 6 (1997): 463–479.

66. Edward O. Laumann and James S. House, "Living Room Styles and Social Attributes: The Patterning of Material Artifacts in a Modern Urban Community," *Sociology and Social Research* 54 (April 1970): 321–342. See also Stephen S. Bell, Morris B. Holbrook, and Michael R. Solomon, "Combining Esthetic and Social Value to Explain Preferences for Product Styles with the Incorporation of Personality and Ensemble Effects," *Journal of Social Behavior and Personality* (1991): 243–274.

67. Morris B. Holbrook, Michael J. Weiss, and John Habich, "Class-Related Distinctions in American Cultural Tastes," *Empirical Studies of the Arts* 22, no. 1 (2004): 91–115.

68. Pierre Bourdieu, *Distinction: A Social Critique of the Judgment of Taste* (Cambridge: Cambridge University Press, 1984); see also Douglas B. Holt, "Does Cultural Capital Structure American Consumption?" *Journal of Consumer Research* 1, 25 (June 1998): 1–25.

69. *Profiling Canada's Families III* (Ottawa: The Vanier Institute of the Family, 2004): 104, 105.

70. Laumann and House, "Living Room Styles and Social Attributes." See also Bell, Holbrook, and Solomon, "Combining Esthetic and Social Value to Explain Preferences for Product Styles."

71. Linda F. Alwitt and Thomas D. Donley, "Retail Stores in Poor Urban Neighborhoods," *Journal of Consumer Affairs* 31, 1 (1997): 108–127.

72. C.K. Prahalad, "Why Selling to the Poor Makes Good Business," *Fortune* (November 15, 2004): 70, 72.

73. Cyndee Miller, "New Line of Barbie Dolls Targets Big, Rich Kids," *Marketing News* (June 17, 1996): 6.

74. Cyndee Miller, "Baubles Are Back," *Marketing News* (April 14, 1997): 1 (2 pp.).

75. "Reading the Buyer's Mind," *U.S. News & World Report* (March 16, 1987): 59.

76. Shelly Reese, "The Many Faces of Affluence," *Marketing Tools* (November/December 1997): 44–48.

77. Kristen Vinakmens, "Luxury for Everyone," *Strategy Magazine* (June 30, 2003): Cover, 6. Winners' website, *www.winners.ca/en/about.asp*, accessed May 29, 2006.

78. Lisa R. Szykman and Ronald Paul Hill, "A Consumer-Behavior Investigation of a Prison Economy," *Research in Consumer Behavior* 6 (1993): 231–260.

79. T. Bettina Cornwell and Terrance G. Gabel, "Out of Sight, Out of Mind: An Exploratory Examination of Institutionalization and Consumption," *Journal of Public Policy & Marketing* 15, 2 (Fall 1996): 278–295.

80. D. James, "B2-4B Spells Profits," *Marketing News* (November 5, 2001): 1.

81. Rebecca Gardyn, "Oh, the Good Life," *American Demographics* (November 2002): 34.

82. Roger Parloff, "For VIPs, This Implant Is a Must," *Fortune* (May 17, 2004): 44.

83. Elizabeth C. Hirschman, "Secular Immortality and the American Ideology of Affluence," *Journal of Consumer Research* 17 (June 1990): 31–42.

84. Coleman and Rainwater, *Standing in America*, p. 150.

85. Kerry A. Dolan, "The World's Working Rich," *Forbes* (July 3, 2000): 162.

86. "Lifeskills of the Rich and Famous," *Marketing Magazine* (October 23, 1995): 38; Willis and MacDonald, "The Gap between Rich and Rich."

87. Jason DeParle, "Spy Anxiety: The Smart Magazine that Makes Smart People Nervous about Their Standing," *Washingtonian Monthly* (February 1989): 10.

88. For a more recent examination of retailing issues related to the need for status, see Jacqueline Kilsheimer Eastman, Leisa Reinecke Flynn, and Ronald E. Goldsmith, "Shopping for Status: The Retail Managerial Implications," *Association of Marketing Theory and Practice* (Spring 1994): 125–130.

89. Quoted in Fackler Martin, "Pajamas: Not Just for Sleep Anymore," *Opelika-Auburn News* (September 13, 2002): 7A.

90. Gayle MacDonald, "Home Vast Home," *Globe and Mail* (August 12, 2000): R1, R6.

91. Laura Pratt, "How to Market to Millionaires," *Marketing Magazine* (May 9, 2005): 12–13.

92. "The Secret Lives of Opera Fans," *Marketing Magazine* (June 13, 2005): 6.

93. John Heinzl, "Harley Rides Roaring Comeback," *Globe and Mail* (April 2, 1998): B15.

94. Seth Lubove, "Copter Crazy," *Forbes* (May 13, 2002): 50.

95. "Western Companies Compete to Win Business of Chinese Babies," *Wall Street Journal Interactive Edition* (May 15, 1998).

96. John Brooks, *Showing Off in America* (Boston, MA: Little, Brown, 1981): 13.

97. Keith Naughton, "The Perk Wars," *Newsweek* (September 30, 2002): 42–46.

98. Angier Natalie, "Cell Phone or Pheromone? New Props for Mating Game," *New York Times on the Web* (November 7, 2000).

99. Quoted in Shell Branch, "To Some, You're Simply a Zero Without 0's in Your Cell Number," *Wall Street Journal Interactive Edition* (August 28, 2002).

100. Thorstein Veblen, *The Theory of the Leisure Class* (1899; reprint, New York: New American Library, 1953), p. 45.

101. Brooks, *Showing Off in America*.

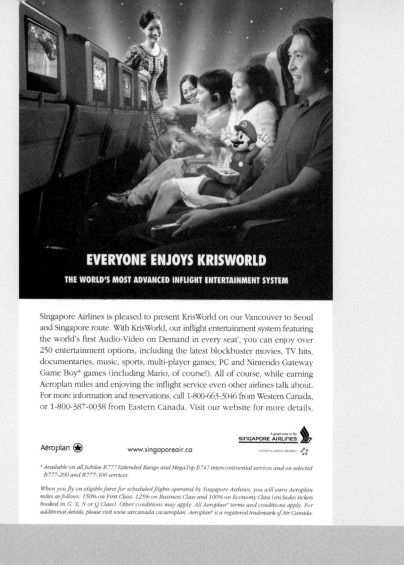
Ming-Ming, waking up early on Saturday, braces for a long day. As usual, her mother expects her to shop and then help prepare food for tonight's family gathering. Her brother Ho-Chiu would never be asked to do the grocery shopping or help in the kitchen. These are women's jobs.

Family gatherings make work, and Ming-Ming wishes her mother would use prepared foods, especially on a Saturday when she has errands of her own. But no! Her mother insists on preparing her food from scratch to ensure that the meals she serves are of the highest quality.

Ming-Ming watches television while getting dressed, then heads to the corner grocer to buy the *Sing Tao Daily*. There are several Chinese newspapers published in her area, and she likes to pick up new ones occasionally. Then Ming-Ming buys the groceries; the list is full of imported brand names, so she finishes quickly. With luck, she'll have a few minutes to go to the mall to see if she can find the cool jacket that was featured in this month's issue of *Jasmine* magazine. Then she'll go back home to chop, peel, and stir for the rest of the afternoon.

Ming-Ming smiles. Vancouver is a great place, and what could be better than spending a lively, fun evening with family—parents, grandparents, brothers, aunts, uncle, her father's business partner and his son, her great-grandmother...

CHAPTER 14

Canadian Identity and Subcultures

SUBCULTURES AND CONSUMER IDENTITY

Yes, Ming-Ming lives in Vancouver, not Beijing, and is an Asian Canadian who has much in common with members of other ethnic groups who live in Canada. They observe the same national holidays, their expenditures are affected by the country's economic health, and they may join together in rooting for the Canadian Olympic team. Nonetheless, although Canadian citizenship provides the raw material for some consumption decisions, other decisions are profoundly affected by enormous variations in the social fabric of Canada.

Consumers' lifestyles are affected by group memberships *within* society at large. These groups are known as **subcultures**, whose members share beliefs and common experiences that set them apart from others. Every consumer belongs to many subcultures. These memberships can be based on similarities in age, race, ethnic background, or place of residence. Ming-Ming's Asian-Canadian heritage exerts a huge influence on her everyday experiences and consumption preferences. Other groups can form around a strong shared identification with an activity or art form; these are called **microcultures**. A good example is the microculture that automobile hobbyists call "tuners." These are single men in their late teens and early twenties, usually in Latino or Asian communities, who share a passion for fast cars but who also indulge in high-tech upgrades and specialized car parts. This microculture got its start when guys would engage in illegal street racing late at night in New York City and Los Angeles. Now, several magazines including *Import Tuner* and *Sport Compact Car* have sprung up, and major companies like Pioneer are courting these high-tech hotrodders.[1]

Whether "tuners," "dead heads," "skinheads," or retirees touring the Maritimes in Winnebagos, each microculture exhibits its own unique set of norms, vocabulary, and product insignias (such as the skulls and roses that signify the Grateful Dead subculture). These microcultures can even gel around fictional characters and events, and they often play a key role in defining the extended self (see Chapter 5). Many devotees of *Star Trek*, for example, immerse themselves in a make-believe world of starships, phasers, and Vulcan mind melds. Our subcultures and microcultures typically command fierce loyalty. "Trekkies" are notorious for their devotion to the cause.[2] *Star Trek* is a merchandising empire that continues to beam up millions of dollars in revenues. Needless to say, it's not alone in this regard. Numerous other microcultures are out there, thriving on their collective worship of mythical and not-so-mythical worlds and characters, ranging from Phish to Hello Kitty.

Net Profit ✛

King for a day? Sure, the internet allows people to form their own microcultures—but how about your own nation? Numerous "micronations" exist in cyberspace, some complete with their own monarchs and constitutions. Here's a sampler of these cybermicrocultures:

- *www.talossa.com*: The "King of Talossa" lives with his father and sister near the University of Wisconsin–Milwaukee campus. At age 14 (more than 20 years ago), he proclaimed his bedroom a sovereign nation.

The name of the country comes from a Finnish word meaning "inside the house." The roughly 60 citizens of Talossa have a body of law, four political parties, an online journal, local holidays, and even a flag. They also have their own language and maintain a dictionary with 28 000 entries.

- *www.new-utopia.com*: This micronation proposes to build a chain of islands in international waters and sells citizenship bonds over the web for $1500.

The country's founder goes by the name of "Prince Lazarus Long." But buyer beware: Due to the bond sales, the Prince does not have the best of diplomatic relations with the Securities Exchange Commission in the United Sates.

Want to start your own micronation? Visit *www.geocities.com/micronations/* for instructions![6]

This chapter begins with general concepts related to ethnicity and consumer behaviour and an overview of the ethnic diversity of the Canadian population. It continues with a look at French Canadians as an ethnic group with a long-standing presence in Canada. Chinese Canadians and the relatively recent wave of Hong Kong immigrants provide an example of acculturation processes as they relate to consumer behaviour. (Although this chapter addresses only two ethnic subcultures, the omission of other groups should not be taken to mean that they are not of interest or importance. Canada is a mosaic of hundreds of diverse and interesting subcultures.) The analysis then proceeds to a regional level. The chapter concludes with an examination of how the Canadian identity is manifested in consumer behaviour.

ETHNIC SUBCULTURES

Ethnic identity is often a significant component of a consumer's self-concept. An **ethnic subculture** consists of a self-perpetuating group of consumers who are held together by common cultural or genetic ties and can be identified both by its members and by others as a distinguishable category.[3]

In some countries, such as Japan, ethnicity is almost synonymous with the dominant culture, because most citizens claim the same homogeneous cultural ties (although Japan has sizeable minority populations, most notably people of Korean ancestry). In a heterogeneous society like Canada, many different cultures are represented, and some consumers may expend great effort to keep their subcultural identifications from being submerged into the mainstream of the dominant society.

Insights into the definition of ethnicity can be gained from a comprehensive study of the issues related to the measurement of English- and French-Canadian ethnicity that was conducted by a group of researchers at Concordia University. In addition to a self-identification measure, ethnic identity was measured by language use in various social communication settings, religious beliefs, social interaction, upbringing/background, and spouse's ethnic identity. The study suggests that the best measure is language use and the weakest measure is religion. However, language may not be the most salient dimension of a particular subcultural group; for example, Jewish ethnicity may be better defined by religious beliefs. The situation is complicated further when one considers that the 2001 census showed that 300 000 Montrealers are bilingual, speak both English and French at home, and consume media in both languages.[4] Thus, at this time, self-identification may be the measure that transcends various ethnicities.[5]

Marketers cannot ignore the growth in the stunning diversity of cultures that is reshaping mainstream society. Often, it makes good business sense to cater to these segments by (literally) speaking their language when promoting products and services. Some Canadian companies have had ethnic marketing programs up and running for a few years. For example, BC Tel and Bell Canada target the more than 850 000 Chinese Canadians who live in British Columbia and Ontario with a Chinese long-distance calling card.[7] As one director of multicultural marketing observed, "Marketing today is part anthropology."[8] Ford targets Asian Canadians with its new Lincoln luxury sports sedan to convince them that it is a luxury car manufacturer. (Traditionally, affluent Asians have favoured well-known car brands, such as BMWs, Mercedes, and other import cars.) Ad campaigns are produced in both Mandarin and Cantonese. Ford also sponsors Chinese New Year Festivals and provides Chinese brochures at the company's website.[9] Chinese Canadians aspire to build a life in Canada, something Ford Canada has been able to speak to directly with its "Practical Lifestyle" campaign.[10]

ETHNICITY AND MARKETING STRATEGIES

Although some people may feel uncomfortable with the notion that people's ethnic differences should be explicitly taken into account when formulating marketing strategies, the reality is that these subcultural memberships are frequently paramount in shaping people's needs and wants. Dimensions of ethnicity that are important to marketers include heritage, life and consumer experiences, and religion and beliefs. Membership in ethnic groups is often predictive of such consumer variables as level and type of media exposure, food preferences, the wearing of distinctive apparel, political behaviour, leisure activities, and willingness to try new products.[11]

The way marketing messages should be structured depends on subcultural differences in how people communicate. IKEA, for example, devised a versatile tag line in Hinglish (a mix of Hindi and English): "Yeh Kea [done this], Who Kea [done that], Fit Hai [it fits]."[12] Furthermore, research evidence indicates that members of minority groups are more likely to find an advertising spokesperson from their own group to be trustworthy, and this enhanced credibility in turn translates into more positive brand attitudes.[13] The Race Relations Advisory Council on Advertising (Canadian Advertising Foundation) provides Canadian marketers with guidelines for successful marketing to ethnic consumers. Diversity studies are being conducted by many Canadian companies to aid in understanding consumers and in recruiting marketers with ethnic insights.[14]

Sociologists distinguish between **high-context cultures** and **low-context cultures**. In a high-context culture, group members tend to be tight-knit, and they are likely to infer meanings that go beyond the spoken word. Symbols and gestures, rather than words, carry much of the weight of the message. Compared with Anglos, many minority cultures are high-context and have strong oral traditions, so their members will be more sensitive to nuances in advertisements that go beyond the message copy.[15]

Canadian advertisers are targeting ethnic consumers in two ways: by fostering inclusiveness through putting more individuals from visible minorities into mainstream advertising, and by "speaking" to specific ethnic groups in their mother tongue.[16] BC Hydro spends about 10 percent of its total marketing budget on ad campaigns in Chinese, Italian, Aboriginal, and Jewish media, as well as using mainstream vehicles. A message is "transcreated"—adapted to work in another language—or run in English in ethnic media.[17]

There are more than 400 ethnic media outlets in Canada, including 14 full-service radio stations, 60 mainstream radio stations with ethnic programming, 150 ethnic newspapers (reaching 40 cultures), 5 ethnic specialty and pay-TV services, and 44 digital specialty services.[18] Both television and radio broadcast multicultural programming. CFMT in Ontario offers programs in 15 languages, in addition to English.[19] Other ethnic media include *eyetalian,* with a readership of one million

Marketing Opportunity

A wide range of Canadian organizations now provide a wide variety of ethnic market offerings:

> Frito-Lay introduced wasabi and curry-flavoured potato chips and promotes its regular and Stax chips on Chinese-language television.[20]

> IKEA participates in Diwali and Idd festivals and has appropriate items on sale at the time of these events.[21]

> Telus targets the Punjabi market, which is brand sensitive, brand loyal, family-oriented, and tech-savvy, with images of hummingbirds and rainbow-coloured fish to promote its home networking service on multicultural television channels.[22]

> The City of Vancouver labels envelopes with "Important information. Please have this translated" in eight languages.

> Poutine, a mélange of french fries, fresh cheese curds, and gravy, is moving from fast-food chains to upscale "poutine au fois gras" versions at restaurants in Montreal, such as Au Pied du Cochon and The Globe, and in Toronto at Bouchon.

> Hispanic Communications recently launched a thrice-weekly newspaper called *Correo Canadiense* to reach the growing—and youthful—Spanish market in Toronto.

> The long-running (since 1969) Oktoberfest in Kitchener-Waterloo successfully broadened its appeal beyond mostly young people to attracting families to its German celebration.

> Italpasta reached the African-Canadian market through a 30-second folklore-style ad sent directly to subscribers of *Black Habits*, an online newsletter.[23]

> Loblaw's format for its ethnic market is Fortino's.

> Honest Ed's, a discount retail outlet that serves recently arrived immigrants and ethnic minority Canadians, now has a legal clinic.[24]

The bagel immigrated to the New World in the nineteenth century when the Jews of Central Europe crossed the Atlantic. However, the bagel is no longer just an ethnic food; it has moved into the mainstream and can be found almost anywhere in North America. While doughnut and muffin sales have declined, bagel sales have increased. Bagels are available in supermarkets and at fast-food outlets, such as Tim Hortons and McDonald's. Flavours include blueberry, poppy seed, raisin, and sun-dried tomato. The bagel appeals to the health-conscious, as well as those who just like its taste and convenience.

Recently, Canada started bringing bagels to the rest of the world. Maple Leaf Foods International exports container loads of frozen bagels to Japan, Korea, Mexico, and Germany. However, purists can still buy bagels 24 hours a day at St-Viateur Bagel Shop in Montreal, where the dough is kneaded by hand and the baking is done in a wood oven.[35]

well-educated second-generation Canadians,[25] *Telatino,* for Spanish-speaking audiences, and Black Entertainment Television. Helpful directories include the *Canadian Italian Business Directory,* the *Chinese Yellow Pages,* the *Jewish Pages Directory,* and the *Black Pages Canada Directory.*

In a study by the Canadian Advertising Foundation, 46 percent of members of visible minorities said they were more likely to buy a product if the ad included a visible minority. However, one study with students of English- and French-Canadian backgrounds found that ethnic brand names lowered recall. Interpretation of the findings suggested that perhaps ethnic (e.g., Spanish, Black, Scottish) brand names have salience only with consumers who identify with a particular ethnicity and that care needs to be taken not to alienate consumers of other ethnicities who may also be in the target market.[26]

Canadian marketers need to be cautious about when to segment markets by ethnicity, especially when more than 80 percent of Canadians with a home language other than English or French watch prime-time television just like every other Canadian. In other words, marketers need to consider that being multicultural in Canada is becoming mainstream and that ethnicity needs to be brought into mainstream ads,[27] as the following examples indicate:

- A study of South Asian, Italian, Portuguese, and Chinese consumers in Toronto found that these ethnic markets do more than three-quarters of their grocery shopping in supermarkets, not in local ethnic food shops. They spend more than the average Toronto household on prepackaged breakfast cereals.
- Italian and Chinese consumers spend about $580 million a year at supermarkets and $50 million on cleaning supplies.
- Branchless bank ING Direct playfully flaunts its Dutch heritage to appeal to the entire Canadian population.[28]

Products that are marketed with an ethnic appeal are not necessarily intended for consumption only by those in the ethnic subculture from which they originate. **De-ethnicitization** refers to the process whereby a product formerly associated with a specific ethnic group is detached from its roots and marketed to other subcultures. This process is illustrated by the case of bagels, a bread product formerly associated with Jewish culture and now mass marketed. Canada's consumption of olive oil, a staple of Mediterranean cooking for centuries, has more than doubled since the late 1980s, and curry flavours of Indian cuisines are enjoyed widely.[29] Many supermarkets carry coconut milk, basmati, and ginger root. In 2003, Canadians spent almost $36 million on Mexican dinner kits (a 10 percent increase in one year); $16 million on Mexican seasonings (a 6 percent increase): and $91 million on ramen (another 6 percent increase).[30] Thus, ethnic food is not only widely accessible, it is increasingly embedded into our lives.[31] De-ethnicitization can also be seen in the hip hop aesthetic, which is well entrenched with inner-city teens, suburban youth, and even those over 40 who grew up with its influence.[32]

Ethnic Groups in Canada

Table 14–1 shows that the two largest ethnic groups in Canada (by single origin) are British (about 9 percent) and French (about 4 percent), which expand to about 50 percent and 16 percent, respectively, when considered with at least one other origin and no overlap with each other.[33] Table 14–2 on page 408 shows that ethnic groups are generally concentrated geographically, providing an opportunity for target marketing in a country with a widely dispersed population. In addition to Canada's two official languages, Chinese, Italian, German, and Ukrainian are the most dominant mother tongues.[34] As mentioned previously, the French-Canadian and Chinese-Canadian markets will be given separate consideration in this chapter. Other ethnic markets can also be studied using the approaches and analyses used to interpret consumer behaviour in these two markets. However, one other market deserves some attention.

TABLE 14–1

ETHNIC ORIGINS OF THE CANADIAN POPULATION (2001 CENSUS)

Ethnic Origins[1]	Number	Percent (%)
Total Canadian population	29 639 035	100.0
Total single origins	18 307 545	61.8
Total multiple origins	11 331 490	38.2
Canadian alone	6 748 135	22.8
Canadian alone or with some other origin	11 682 680	39.4
Aboriginal alone	528 015	1.8
Aboriginal with some other origin	1 308 735	4.4
North American Indian	1 000 890	3.4
Métis	307 845	1.0
British alone (includes English, Scottish, Irish, and Welsh)	2 612 070	8.8
British alone or with some other origin	14 309 110	48.3
French alone	1 060 760	3.6
French alone or with some other origin	4 668 410	15.8
Total Responses		
German	2 742 765	9.3
Italian	1 270 370	4.3
Chinese	1 094 700	3.7
Ukrainian	1 071 060	3.6
Dutch	923 310	3.1
Polish	817 085	2.8
East Indian	713 330	2.4
Norwegian	363 760	1.2
Portuguese	357 690	1.2
Jewish	348 605	1.2
Russian	337 960	1.1
Filipino	327 550	1.1
Swedish	282 760	1.0
Hungarian	267 255	0.9
American	250 005	0.8
Greek	215 105	0.7
Spanish	213 105	0.7
Jamaican	211 720	0.7
Danish	170 780	0.6
Vietnamese	151 410	0.5

Source: Adapted from Statistics Canada's website, *www12.statcan.ca/english/census01/products/highlight/ETO/Table1.cfm?Lang=E&T=501&GV=1&GID=0*, accessed October 29, 2003.

[1]Ethnic origin refers to the ethnic or cultural group(s) to which the respondent's ancestors belong. An ancestor is usually more distant than a grandparent.

TABLE 14–2

DOMINANT MOTHER TONGUE[1] BY PROVINCE AND TERRITORY (SINGLE RESPONSE—ENGLISH OR FRENCH, BILINGUAL—ENGLISH AND FRENCH, AND SIGNIFICANT OTHER LANGUAGES, OF AT LEAST 1 PERCENT OF THE POPULATION), CENSUS 2001.

Province/Territory (population)	English Only (%)	French Only (%)	English and French (%)	Other (%)
Newfoundland (508 075)	98.4	0.4	0.1	1.1
Nova Scotia (897 570)	93.0	3.8	0.3	3.0
Prince Edward Island (133 385)	93.9	4.3	0.3	1.5
New Brunswick (719 710)	64.7	32.9	0.7	1.7
Quebec (7 125 580)	8.0	81.2	0.8	10.0 Italian 1.8 Arabic 1.1
Ontario (11 285 550)	71.6	4.4	0.4	23.7 Chinese (3.6) Italian (2.6) German (1.4) Portuguese (1.4)
Manitoba (1 103 700)	75.8	4.2	0.3	19.9 German (5.3) Ukrainian (2.4) Portuguese (1.4)
Saskatchewan (963 150)	85.7	1.9	0.2	12.2 German (3.4) Cree (2.4) Ukrainian (2.0)
Alberta (2 941 150)	81.8	2.0	0.2	16.0 Chinese (2.7) German (2.7) Ukrainian (1.2)
British Columbia (3 868 875)	74.1	1.5	0.2	24.3 Chinese (2.7) Punjabi (3.2) German (2.2)
Northwest Territories (37 105)	78.1	2.6	0.2	19.0 Inuktitut (2.1)
Yukon Territory (28 525)	87.1	3.1	0.3	9.5
Nunavut (26 665)	27.6	1.5	0.1	70.8 Inuktitut 69.8
Canada (29 639 035)	59.3	22.7	0.4	17.6 Chinese (2.9) Italian (1.6) German (1.5)

Source: Adapted from Statistics Canada's website, *www.statcan.ca/english/Pgdb/demo18a.htm*, accessed October 29, 2003.

[1]First language learned at home in childhood and still understood.

←Street signs in many languages, such as this one in Ukrainian and English, acknowledge the diverse ethnic profile of Canadians.
Courtesy of Judith Zaichkowsky

Canadians of Aboriginal origin number just over one million.[36] They dominate the population of the Northwest Territories and Nunavut. Sixty-five percent of the Aboriginal population is under 35 years old.[37] Little is known about their consumer behaviour in a scientific sense. However, work is being done to adapt the 631 characters in 19 Aboriginal languages and 5 dialects so that communication by computer is possible.[38] Aboriginal Media Services has four newspapers and an Edmonton radio station (CFWE), and it represents about 70 additional Native publications across Canada through which advertisers—Native and otherwise—can reach one of Canada's founding peoples.[39] Aboriginals are responsive to advertising that connects to their values.[40] The Bank of Montreal, TD Canada Trust, and CIBC have attracted Indian and Métis people to their services by building relationships (through activities such as fishing with Native elders, taking Polaroid identification photographs, offering cheques with images by young Native artists, and advertising in Native people's media (such as *Windspeaker* and *Aboriginal Voices*).[41] Aboriginal companies, such as Dinawo Sportswear and Casuals (a brand and specialized clothing retail outlet), are becoming successful, too. Grey Owl Marketing, based in Prince Albert, Saskatchewan, exports about $3 million in wild rice products to health-conscious consumers across North America and Europe.[42]

THE EFFECT OF IMMIGRATION ON CANADIAN DIVERSITY

Statistics Canada estimates that the population of Canada, numbering just over 32 million in 2005, may grow to as many as 37 million by the year 2021. Much of this growth will be accounted for by members of non-white ethnic groups, and a substantial proportion will result from the immigration of people from other countries as opposed to citizens who are born in Canada.[43] Indeed, Canada accepts one million immigrants and refugees every four years, by far the largest per capita rate of immigration in the world.[44] In 2001, 5.4 million Canadians (more than 18 percent of the population) were immigrants—that is, not born in Canada.[45] In all, the 2001 census counted more than 12 million Canadians who are 15 years or older and of single ethnic or mixed ethnic origins other than British or French.[46] The expectation is that by 2017, the year Canada celebrates its 150th birthday, one in five Canadians will be a visible minority.[47]

The three groups that account for much of Canada's growth from immigration are Chinese Canadians, East Indian Canadians, and Polish Canadians. These

Multicultural Dimensions

Ethnic restaurants are a fast-growing segment of the food industry, whether in the United States, Canada, Europe, or Japan.[55] Such restaurants are a part of the internationalization of lifestyles, in which consumers reach out for new experiences. Chinese is the most frequently served ethnic cuisine and is followed closely by Mexican and Italian. Many other cuisines are underrepresented or not represented at all, and this fact may hint at opportunities for entrepreneurs who wish to carve out distinctive niches.

Europeans are also becoming huge fans of ethnic food. Food producers are rapidly adding international dishes to their product lines to keep pace with demand. Unilever NV's Pronto frozen foods include choices such as Indonesian "Bami Goreng" and Indian "Madras Curry." Nestlé added a "Taste of Asia" line to its Findus brand. European consumers also are beginning to show interest in spicier foods, and they are influenced by the healthy image of Far Eastern cuisine. Tex-Mex dishes and beers are also catching fire in Europe, particularly in Britain and Scandinavia.

three groups, along with German Canadians, Italian Canadians, Ukranian Canadians, and Dutch Canadians, make up Canada's largest ethnic groups outside of English and French Canadians. Eighty percent of these consumers live in Vancouver, Toronto, and Montreal.[48] Toronto is the most ethnically diverse city in the world, with more than 49 percent of its population foreign-born (although nearly 70 percent speak English at home[49]). Almost 20 percent of Calgarians and Montrealers, a quarter of Canadians in Southern Ontario, and 40 percent of Vancouverites are first-generation immigrant Canadians. Australia is the only country more ethnically diverse than Canada.[50] And ethnic diversity is expected to increase, affecting not only demand in ethnic markets but also the nature of overall demand. According to a global survey conducted by Leger Marketing with Gallup researchers, 74 percent of Canadians consider immigration to be good for their country; the world average is 43 percent.[51]

New arrivals are best addressed, or marketed to, in their native languages. They tend to cluster together geographically, which makes them easy to reach. The local community is the primary source for information and advice, so word of mouth is especially important (see Chapter 11). Advertising themes that seem to be effective among recent immigrants are based on messages of comfort, familiarity, and appropriateness of language (in response to feelings of fear and insecurity on coming to a new country). Due to the forces of integration, English works well with first-generation Canadians.[52]

IS ETHNICITY A MOVING TARGET?

Although ethnic marketing is in vogue in many firms, the process of actually defining and targeting members of a distinct ethnic group is not always so easy. In the last decade there has been a continuing decline in the proportion of Canadians of British and French origin due to increasing immigration of other Europeans, Asians, and other non-Europeans, stemming from various economic and political events throughout the world. In addition, ethnic intermarriage has blurred ethnic boundaries, particularly, but not solely, among first- and second-generation Canadians. More than 11 million Canadians reported multiple ethnic origins in the 2001 census.[53] Thus, it has become increasingly difficult for marketing researchers and Statistics Canada to classify Canadians into neat ethnic categories, and comparisons across time must be done with special attention to how ethnicity is operationalized for data collection.[54]

The steady increase in the number of mixed marriages is, however, creating opportunities for some marketers who wish to meet the needs of children raised in multicultural families. Because many children are exposed to others from diverse cultural backgrounds, some marketing executives feel that their attitudes will be quite different from those of their parents. Encounters with diverse cultural traditions create the need for products and services that allow consumers to celebrate multiple heritages, including international festivals, language classes, camps with ethnic themes, and travel products and services. Also, celebrations of the arrival, settlement, trials, and successes of the first immigrants to Canada create marketing opportunities as their descendants participate in events that identify the roots of their heritage.

Ethnic Stereotypes

Many subcultures have powerful stereotypes associated with them. Members of a subgroup are assumed to possess certain traits, even though these assumptions are often erroneous. The same trait can be cast either positively or negatively, depending upon the communicator's intentions and biases. For example, the Scottish stereotype in Canada is largely positive, so the supposed frugality of this ethnic group is viewed favourably. Scottish imagery has been used by the 3M Company to denote value (Scotch tape). However, invoking the Scottish "personality" might carry quite different connotations to consumers in Britain or Ireland. Thus, one person's "thrifty" is another's "stingy." In addition, ethnic symbolism has been used in the past by marketers as a shorthand to connote certain product attributes. The images employed were often crude and unflattering.

The Impact of Religion

An Angus Reid poll showed that religion plays an important part in the life of nearly 60 percent of Canadians, three-quarters of whom reported themselves as Christians in the 2001 census, although less than one-quarter attend church weekly.[56] In general, religion is closely associated with ethnicity, social class, and geographic regions. In Canada (as in the United States), WASP (White Anglo-Saxon Protestant) values have been a dominant force.

It seems fair to claim that spirituality is in fashion. For example, we've witnessed an explosion of religion and spirituality in popular culture, including the box-office success of Mel Gibson's movie *The Passion of the Christ* and the tremendous popularity and controversy surrounding the book *The Da Vinci Code*.[57] American Greetings Corporation introduced a Rainbows of Faith line of religious cards, and Hallmark Cards Inc. has a similar Morning Light line.[58] An engaging application of religious sentiment is Michelin's recent ad depicting Bibendum (a.k.a. the Michelin Man) making snow angels (on the next page). The ad reinforces Michelin's safety image by suggesting that Bib is your guardian angel during winter driving.[59] In a different light, so to speak, when the Quebec Major Junior Hockey League awarded a franchise to St. John's, Newfoundland, they called their team "Fog Devils" to capture the elusive element of danger (fog) and the team's tenacity (devil). "Fog devil" is a mariner's term for a strong, swirling patch of fog that surfaces on the ocean without warning. The team's name inspired marketing creativity through merchandising, the creation of the mascot (Scorch), and taglines for marketing communications (e.g., "Get in the thick of it!").[60]

Marketing Pitfall

What are the dominant religions worldwide? The Barna Research Group estimates that there are 2 billion Christians, 1.2 billion Muslims, 900 million Hindus, 315 million Buddhists, and 15 million Jews. A category it terms "primal indigenous" makes up another 190 million. In addition, there are 750 000 practising Scientologists and 700 000 Rastafarians. Thus, religious sensibilities vary around the world, and big trouble can result if marketers violate taboo subjects in other cultures. Here are some recent examples:

> A Lipton ad won the prestigious Gold Lion award in Cannes, but the company had to decline the honour in the face of objections. The ad mocked the Catholic Church by showing a man standing in the communion line with a bowl of onion dip in his hand.

> A poster for Britain's *Drop the Dead Donkey* TV show included a representation of the Turin Shroud with a

donkey's head and the tag line, "Resurrected: The Donkey Has Risen Again." Complainants stated that the poster was particularly offensive because it was run just before the Easter period.[61]

> The Catholic Archdiocese of Montreal won a Grand Coq d'Or (best of show) for the newspaper ad it published shortly after the 9/11 disaster. The "Tours Jumelles" (Twin Towers) were depicted by two columns of "type" within which the text of the Lord's Prayer was repeated. On the other hand, the Archdiocese of Vancouver found itself surrounded by controversy when it withdrew funding from a long-standing partnership with Vancity Credit Union for a popular junior banking program. The funding was withdrawn a year after Vancity launched a campaign in the mainstream press that targeted gays and lesbians with the tag line, "I want to bank with people who value all partnerships."[62]

> Restaurants must adapt to local customs in the Middle East where rules about the mixing of the sexes and the consumption of alcohol are quite strict. McDonald's in Saudi Arabia offers separate dining areas for single men and for women and children. Booths must have screens because women can't be seen eating meat.[63]

> An ad for Levi's jeans produced in London shows a young man buying condoms from a pharmacist and hiding them in the small side pocket of his jeans. When he goes to pick up his date, he discovers that her father is the same pharmacist. The commercial was a hit in the United Kingdom, but in a strongly Catholic country like Italy or Spain it was not appreciated.[64]

The quest for spiritual meaning is influencing mainstream churches. They are evolving with the times, and many are adopting a marketing orientation appropriate for non-profit organizations, especially in the areas of fundraising and community-based activities. Books, religion-oriented merchandise (e.g., apparel), framed art, inspirational gifts, and music are sold. Worship is being redesigned to fit into busy lives. Saturday services, for example, give people flexibility on weekends. Ironically, despite this renewed interest in faith, the number of adults who attend religious services is slipping. However, to avoid large, empty places of worship, attendees have come up with some creative solutions. The Cedars, a place of worship for those who belong to the United Church and Jewish faiths, for example, demonstrates successful co-existence of religious symbolism that was developed by extensive consultation with both groups of worshippers. Some symbols are shared, while others are specific to one group; through the use of movable partitions, each group has a space that is considered suitably sacred. Incidentally, the word "cedar" connotes outreach to Christians and refuge to Jews.[65]

Marketing scholars have not studied religion extensively, possibly because it is seen as a taboo subject.[66] However, the little evidence that has been accumulated indicates that religious affiliation has the potential to be a valuable predictor of consumer behaviour.[67] Religion may exert a particularly significant impact on consumer variables, such as personality, attitudes toward sexuality, birth rates, household formation, income, and political attitudes. In some cases, dietary or dress requirements create demand for certain products, and these items then may gain in popularity among other groups. Although church leaders can encourage consumption, they can more importantly discourage it—sometimes with powerful effects. The Disney Corporation discovered how effective these movements could be when the Southern Baptist Convention in the United States voted to persuade all its members to boycott its operations.[68]

FRENCH CANADIANS

French Canadians are a significant subculture and account for about 16 percent of the Canadian population based on ethnic origin.[69] They form the second-largest ethnic market in Canada, comprising about 80 percent of the Quebec population and a third of the New Brunswick (Acadian) population, and they account for a significant number of residents in Ontario, Manitoba, Saskatchewan, Alberta, and the Northwest Territories. In other words, the French-Canadian market provides the advantage of geographic concentration. The market is even larger when extended to include Canadians of French-with-other origins. On a day-to-day basis, 60 percent of Canadians speak English at home and 23 percent speak French.[70]

Marketing Opportunity !

Halal meat is in demand. Canadian Muslims number 580 000 among 5.5 million in North America and more than 1 billion worldwide. M.G.I. in Kitchener, Ontario, specializes in halal butchering, the only acceptable way for devout Muslims to slaughter animals. Acceptable meats, according to Islamic law, are beef, mutton, and poultry.

M.G.I. was the first to sell halal beef to Canadian Muslims through mainstream supermarkets, as well as specialty butcher shops. Non-Muslim Canadians are also expected to be an important segment due to the careful portioning and packaging of M.G.I.'s products. The private company also exports halal beef to Muslims from Egypt to Indonesia, and to non-Muslim consumers in Japan (beef tongues and tripe), Mexico (cow's lips), and the United States (scalps).[71]

→This guide brings the choices in Quebec cuisine to the forefront. The high-involvement visual draws the reader to the question: "What are we going to eat?"
Amen Agency in Montreal (Nicolas Massey, Karl Robichaud). For clients: Communications Voir Inc. (Michael Fortin, Sylvie Chaumette)

Understanding the French-Canadian Identity

The work of French-Canadian researchers Bruce Mallen and Jacques Bouchard on the nature of the French-Canadian identity has been interpreted for the English-Canadian market.[72] These approaches are informative and practical from a marketing perspective, as the French-Canadian market (at least in Quebec) strives to maintain its identity.[73]

Mallen details the sensate, conservative, and non-price cognitive traits. The sensate trait speaks to the importance of all senses in French-Canadian consumers, as well as their appreciation of aesthetics, fashion consciousness, and social hedonism. He suggests that the conservative trait relates to low risk-taking, the emphasis on family, and the strong brand loyalty of these consumers. Finally, the third trait is thought to result in accepting high price points (within reason) if a product or service meets the criteria of the first two traits.

Bouchard provided an in-depth analysis of six historical and cultural roots of French Canadians: rural, minority, North American, Catholic, Latin, and French. Six responsive keys are associated with each of these six roots. For example, the six keys for the Latin root are joie de vivre, love of children, a need to be seen, artistic talent, sentimentality, and instinctiveness. In a 2004 review of Bouchard's schema, which is more than 30 years after the schema was developed, Eric Blais concluded that even with all the changes in Quebec, the 36 keys remain relevant. *Plus ca change, plus c'est pareil.* (The more things change, the more they stay the same.)[74] Thus, an understanding of these roots could be helpful to marketers and advertising agencies as a sort of cultural psychographic profile.

French-Canadian Consumption Patterns

Most of what is known about the French-Canadian market comes not from theoretical links to their identity (or structural theory) but from descriptive comparisons with English Canadians or segments *within* the French-Canadian market. Although

French-Canadian consumers do differ in some ways from English Canadians, the French-Canadian market is not as identity-based or as homogeneous as many marketers seem to believe.

One study of English Canadian, French Canadian, and French young adults found that fun and enjoyment in life/excitement was equal across all three cultures (a big surprise!), and that English and French Canadians valued security and warm relationships with others. Of the 14 values studied, there were only two on which the English and French Canadians differed; French Canadians put more emphasis on being well respected and less on intellectual and cultural activities than the English Canadians. In terms of nearly 60 lifestyle and consumption habits, very few differences were found between the English and French Canadians when demographics, social class, and economic philosophies were controlled for.[75]

On the other hand, Hostess Frito-Lay developed two successful flavours for the Quebec market: Épices Mexicaines and Fromage Piquant Doritos.[76] Local heroes, such as Jacques Villeneuve, create demand for race-car entertainment among young and old Quebecers. Jean Coutu continues to dominate the drugstore market, and Cirque du Soleil (***www.cirquedusoleil.com***) attracts local as well as national and international audiences.

French Canadians and the Media

Since the 1995 Quebec referendum, some marketers have changed their advertising approaches because they think certain words and connotations have become taboo.[77] In 1994, for example, the maple leaf was removed from the label of Labatt Blue sold in Quebec.[78] On the other hand, Mountain Equipment Co-op, founded in Vancouver, works hard to position its brand as part of Quebec's cultural environment. Membership growth has been bolstered by kayaking events in Quebec City, the introduction of a visual dictionary of MEC products (*Le Petit MEC*), and other media activities that convey a respectful approach to cultural and linguistic differences.[79]

Creative execution designed specifically for the Quebec market has been found to have more impact in terms of characteristics such as originality and credibility than adaptations or translations from English Canadian or American ads.[80] Creative ideas that are likely to work well in Quebec tap into the joie de vivre factor; they also appeal to the senses and emotions and leverage French Quebec talent.[81] Appropriate advertising imagery for Quebec includes shots of the nuclear family, women, and active seniors; visually powerful images (such as close-ups that fill the frame); and Latin or European flair and humour.[82] Let's look at a few examples of these guidelines in practice.

The Quebec preference for instant gratification means that Quebecers are attracted by coupons and dream vacations, but are less impressed by loyalty programs than other Canadians (53- versus 64-percent participation). Even the Aeroplan Miles program, which is popular with nearly 60 percent of other Canadian households, has only 40-percent participation from Quebec households. However, Les Ailes de la Mode has pioneered combining rebates with collecting data about their customers through customer relationship management (CRM). Shoppers Drug Mart (Pharmaprix in Quebec) has also had some success with this approach.[83]

Quebec's three-hour (six o'clock to nine o'clock) morning television show "Salut, Bonjour!" is part of many Quebecers' morning ritual and is the most successful in Canada with a market penetration of well over 60 percent. In many ways the show's success seems to stem from its appeal to unique aspects of Quebec's culture: It is a show for the whole family. The pace is leisurely with longer segments than other shows. It reflects Quebec society in its presentation of arts and entertainment, and it has created stars out of its long-standing hosts.[84] In an interesting twist, a milk campaign entitled "Deux c'est mieux" (conveyed visually by the two-finger peace sign) brought acclaim to the then-unknown Quebec musician Paul

Marketing Opportunity !

Researchers at three Montreal universities studied the pro-environmental knowledge, feelings, and behaviour of French and English Canadians.

French Canadians, compared to English Canadians, were found:

> to be more knowledgeable and concerned about ecological issues

> to perceive that environmentally friendly behaviour is important

> to believe that most corporations are environmentally responsible

> to consider environmental issues more frequently when making a purchase

English Canadians, compared to French Canadians, were found:

> to be more likely to recycle

> to be more willing to pay a premium price for environmentally friendly products

The French-Canadian market seems to require more emphasis on moving positive attitudes and behaviour toward environmentally friendly actions, while the English-Canadian market appears to need messages that link their actions with an awareness of environmental issues, so that their environmentally friendly behaviours are likely to be sustained or expanded.[85]

Perhaps it was the understanding of how French Canadians relate to the environment that led to the very successful launch of reusable plastic bags by the Metro grocery chain in Quebec. An estimated 750 000 of the machine-washable and recyclable bags went quickly into circulation. The company used point-of-sale ads and circulars, as well as a radio ad voiced by Guylaine Tremblay (of *Annie et ses hommes*); it advised that doing something for the planet makes sense and costs only a dollar. The graphic on the blue bags features a leaf with a raindrop.[86]

Maco, who not only provided the music to accompany the ads, but increased milk consumption as well.[87]

Familiprix, a drugstore chain in Quebec, continues to enjoy its pop-cult status and a Grand Coq d'Or (best of show) in its category for its humorous campaign designed around a strange pharmacist who waves his arms and exclaims, "Ah! Ha! Familiprix," whenever hapless individuals are struck by accidents or sickness.[88] The same sense of humour is evident in Familiprix's English ads: Their banner is pasted over some of the letters that spell out a particular ailment, turning the word into something positive. In one example, the logo intervenes to turn "I have fungus" into "I have fun."[89]

Finally, let's consider a few examples of market-specific and adaptive marketing strategies. Moosehead brewery entered the Quebec market in 2002 with unique advertising, because the Quebec beer drinker is very different from the typical English-Canadian beer drinker: English Canadians usually drink beer to get from point A to point B, while Quebecers drink beer to enjoy life. McDonald's and Krispy Kreme also use Quebec-specific advertising, and so does Tourism New Brunswick. Its 2002 campaign boasting warm waters, lots of activities, and a pet lobster helped to attract 50 percent more Quebec tourists during 2002. (Twenty-two percent of New Brunswick's two million visitors are from Quebec.) Nissan "went for the nose" with an ad in *La presse* for its 350Z coupe clearout event. The French headline read, "When it's new, you can smell it," and the copy line suggested that, if you had a nose for good deals, this was the time to take advantage. Both messages were reinforced by a perfume strip in the magazine that released wafts of the unique scent of a new car with a leather interior.[90] However, some companies, such as Zellers and Clarica, have found that adaptations of English market advertising are effective because the selling proposition and the messages are the same for both markets.[91]

CHINESE CANADIANS

At just over one million, Chinese Canadians are the fastest-growing minority group in Canada. They make up one-quarter of Canada's visible minorities.[92] Marketers are just recognizing their potential as a unique market segment. This subculture is attractive to marketers because Asian Canadians typically are hard-working and many have above-average incomes. Chinese Canadians have the highest incomes of all visible minorities.[93] As one indication, readers of the nationally distributed *Ming Pao Daily* have an average family income in excess of $57 000, 60 percent are homeowners, and 65 percent have a university education.[94]

The Chinese-Canadian market, however, is far from homogeneous. The attitudes and behaviour of these consumers are influenced by age, education, gender, household composition, knowledge of English, length of time in Canada, reason for immigration, working status prior to and after immigration, family size, geographic location, and marital and financial status.[95] Recent studies by Angus Reid and DSC Research in Vancouver found that Chinese Canadians whose mother tongue was Cantonese or Mandarin were younger and slightly less wealthy than the average Canadian. They were more likely to be married, tended toward large traditional families, were more likely to be owners of homes and consumer electronics, and played more lotteries and consumed less alcohol than Vancouverites in general.[96]

Reaching the Chinese Canadian Consumer

Despite the potential, Asian Canadians are hard to market to because they actually comprise subgroups that are culturally diverse and speak many different languages and dialects. The term *Asian* refers to 20 ethnic groups, with Chinese being the largest.[97] Chinese Canadians still compose less than 5 percent of the population, so mass-marketing techniques often are not viable to reach them.[98]

However, opportunities do exist. For example, realtors who do business in areas with a high concentration of Asian-Canadian buyers are learning to adapt to their desire for a house that offers a good *feng shui* environment (*feng shui* literally means "the wind and the water").

The *Sing Tao Daily* has been a newspaper for Chinese Canadians for about 20 years. British Columbia has 12 Chinese media outlets—two each of television and radio stations, and eight newspapers and magazines.[100] However, some attempts to translate advertising messages and concepts into Asian media have backfired. Other advertisements have overlooked the complex differences among Asian subcultures, and some have unknowingly been insensitive to cultural practices. The use of the colour red and Chinese characters, the careful use of numbers, and the delivery of high-quality service are all appreciated by Asian consumers.[101] The Vancouver Grizzlies' club name was translated to mean "strong and powerful bear" in Cantonese and Mandarin, rather than the original "grey bear," which suggested a weak image.[102]

Level of Acculturation

Acculturation refers to the process of movement and adaptation to one country's cultural environment by a person from another country.[103] This factor is especially important when considering the Chinese market, because the degree to which these consumers are integrated into the Canadian way of life varies widely. Table 14–3 shows an attempt to segment Hong Kong immigrants in terms of their degree of acculturation. Interestingly, the respondents identified their ethnicity on a five-point scale, ranging from Hong Kong Chinese to Canadian Chinese.[104]

TABLE 14–3

MAU'S 14-ITEM ACCULTURATION INDEX

Item	Measure of Item
Self-defined ethnic identity	5-point scale: 1 = Hong Kong Chinese to 5 = Canadian Chinese
Proportion of time watching English TV	Percentage of time (0–100%)
Proportion of time listening to English radio	Percentage of time (0–100%)
Proportion of time reading English newspapers	Percentage of time (0–100%)
Proportion of time reading English magazines	Percentage of time (0–100%)
Use of English at work/school	Percentage of time (0–100%)
Use of English during shopping	Percentage of time (0–100%)
Use of English among friends	Percentage of time (0–100%)
Proud of Chinese origin	5-point scale: 1 = strongly disagree to 5 = strongly agree
Appreciate Chinese traditional values	5-point scale: 1 = strongly disagree to 5 = strongly agree
Importance of celebrating Chinese New Year	5-point scale: 1 = strongly disagree to 5 = strongly agree
Importance of children learning Chinese	5-point scale: 1 = strongly disagree to 5 = strongly agree
Importance of teaching traditional values	5-point scale: 1 = strongly disagree to 5 = strongly agree
Cronbach's alpha on 14 items	0.79

Source: Adapted from Rosanna W.S. Mau, "The Impact of Acculturation on Decision Making: The Case of Hong Kong Immigrants in Vancouver," unpublished Master of Business Administration thesis, Simon Fraser University, 1997.

Marketing Opportunity !

Some companies have accumulated valuable experience that is reflected in their success in serving the Chinese-Canadian market. Here are a few examples of success stories; the first few provide guidance to the development of effective tailor-made, creative communication strategies:

> Immigrants from Hong Kong speak Cantonese; those from Taiwan and China speak Mandarin. Thus, these consumers read different newspapers and watch different Chinese television channels.

> Symbols that express life or prosperity are well received and so are colours such as red and gold, tigers, dragons, and lucky numbers.

> Chinese Canadians desire respect through seeing their faces in both Chinese-language and mainstream ads.

> Chinese Canadians have similar media habits and the best-developed media infrastructure among Canada's ethnic groups.

> Chinese consumers are brand conscious; brands give a sense of confidence and security to new immigrants.

> Fido entered the Chinese-Canadian wireless telecommunications market with "Fi Dat," which means "speedy" and has the same phonetic sound as the Chinese word for "prosperity." The company was the first Canadian Global System for Mobile communications (GSM) mobile carrier. However, because GSM was the dominant system in Asia, it allowed Chinese Canadians to take their "world phones" back and forth to Canada for business and pleasure.

> Chinese Canadians are early adopters of technology and have high usage rates. As part of Telus Mobility's strategy to serve the highest-value clients, they targeted teenagers and university students with cult Cantonese cartoon celebrities: McMug and McDull. Telus has also supported Chinese charities by raising money through a silent auction for the vanity telephone number 888-8888. (The number eight is considered lucky by the Chinese.)[107]

> The Rona Home and Garden Warehouse in East Vancouver markets successfully to the Asian community in an ever-expanding trading area around the city by using Chinese banners along with English ones, hiring staff that can handle 27 different languages and dialects, displaying as many products as possible, ordering products that are specific to the needs of the Asian community such as high-end range hoods for wok cooking, and celebrating Chinese New Year.

> The Toronto Symphony Orchestra entices a Chinese audience (which has a predisposition to enjoy classical music) to fill its seats by speaking their language in newspapers, radio, brochures, and website communication vehicles; by providing incentives and giveaways; and by appealing to their interest in their children's academic and extracurricular development.[108]

> Best Foods introduced trilingual labelling for its Mazola oil and distributes it to Chinese grocery stores.

Immigrants from Hong Kong represent two extremes. Annual immigration from Hong Kong has ranged from fewer than 1000 in 1957 through almost 15 000 in 1973 to more than 100 000 between 1991 and 1996. (Immigration virtually stopped in 1997).[105] Early immigrants worked hard for many years to establish themselves and are now entrenched in the Canadian political and economic establishment. On the other hand, thousands of recent immigrants are trying to adapt to their new environment. These consumers may need to learn entirely new product categories. The implication for marketers is that these consumers must be taught about a product before they can be convinced to buy one brand over another.

The nature of the transition process is affected by many factors, as shown in Figure 14–1. Individual differences, such as whether the person speaks English, influence how rocky the adjustment will be. The person's contact with **acculturation agents**—people and institutions that teach the ways of a culture—are also crucial. Some of these agents are aligned with the *culture of origin*. These include family, friends, the church, local businesses, and first-language media that keep the consumer in touch with his or her country of origin. For example, the affluent Asian immigrant population is creating demand for ballads known as "Mandarin pop" and music idols. Chinese record companies are using the web to build a bigger following overseas. For example, *www.rockacola.com* is one of the largest Chinese music labels in Taiwan and Hong Kong, and another site called *www.yesasia.com* gets 1.68 million visits a month.[106] Other agents are associated with the *culture of immigration* (in this case, Canada) and help the consumer to learn how to navigate in the new environment. These include schools and English-language media.

Partly due to ESL (English as a second language) programs in Lower Mainland schools in British Columbia, many Hong Kong Chinese will enter their adult lives as English-speaking, culturally integrated Chinese Canadians. They are expected to

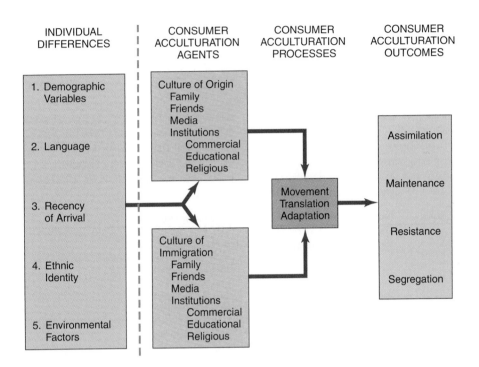

INDIVIDUAL DIFFERENCES — CONSUMER ACCULTURATION AGENTS — CONSUMER ACCULTURATION PROCESSES — CONSUMER ACCULTURATION OUTCOMES

FIGURE 14–1

A MODEL OF CONSUMER ACCULTURATION

Source: Lisa Peñaloza, "Atravesando Fronteras/ Border Crossings: A Critical Ethnographic Exploration of the Consumer Acculturation of Mexican Immigrants," *Journal of Consumer Research* (June 1994): 32–54.

have some values in common with their parents (e.g., to work hard, do postsecondary studies, and seek remunerative careers) but also some values picked up in Canada. The speed with which they adopt Canadian ways depends on their age, the age of their parents, where they were born, where they now live, their personal reactions to change, the attitudes of both children and parents, and their commitment to Canada.[109]

As immigrants adapt to their new surroundings, several processes come into play. *Movement* refers to the factors motivating people to uproot themselves physically from one location and go to another. Upon arrival, immigrants encounter a need for *translation*. This means attempting to master a set of rules for operating in the new environment, whether learning how to decipher a different currency or figuring out the social meanings of unfamiliar clothing styles. This cultural learning leads to a process of *adaptation*, where new consumption patterns are formed.

During the process of acculturation, many immigrants undergo *assimilation*, during which they adopt products that are identified with the mainstream culture. At the same time there is an attempt at *maintenance* of practices associated with the culture of origin. Immigrants stay in touch with their country of birth; for example, many from Hong Kong continue to eat Chinese foods and read Chinese newspapers. Interestingly, a recent study by Canadian researchers suggests that maintenance strategies associated with ethnic identity may, in fact, coexist with the move toward acculturation to mainstream culture.[110] Nevertheless, their continued identification with the culture of origin may cause *resistance*, as they resent the pressure to submerge their cultural identities and take on new roles. Finally, immigrants (voluntarily or not) tend to exhibit *segregation*: They are likely to live and shop in places that are physically separated from mainstream consumers.

In the book *Customers from Afar*, consultant Raymond Ng suggests five phases of adjustment for teenage and adult immigrants:

1. *The honeymoon:* The immigrant marvels at the wonders of the new environment.

2. *Culture shock:* The reality of the situation sets in.

3. *Superficial adjustment:* The immigrant forays into the new culture and manages day-to-day life.

Multicultural Dimensions

One million Chinese Canadians spent nearly $30 billion on consumer goods in 2005.[115] Expenditures concentrated on homes (often large), furnishings, cars (often high-end brands), their children's education, high-tech gadgets, travel (often to their home countries), and gifts. Chinese tend to be brand loyal and family- and community-oriented; they find ads rooted in status, family closeness, and prosperity appealing.[116] Although Chinese consumers are generally well off, recent immigrants from mainland China have lower incomes, while second- and third-generation Chinese, as well as immigrants from Hong Kong and Taiwan, tend to be more affluent. One schema which recognizes that Chinese consumers are not one homogeneous market is that proposed by Manifold Data Mining, which created eight demographic and psychographic profiles of Chinese immigrants based on their living and spending habits.[117]

Segment	Population/% of Chinese Households/Location	Household Income/Occupation	Living and Spending Habits
Top Gun Metro – Owners of New Castles	25 800 (6% of hhlds); Toronto, Vancouver, Calgary, Ottawa	$142 000 Managers, business owners, professionals	Prefer new homes Multiple family hhlds Smoke, eat, drink, eat out, travel, and entertain well above average
Ethnic Cruisers – Chinese Technocrats	61 000 (14% of hhlds); British Columbia and Ontario	$95 000 Management, sales, service occupations (university educated)	Young families Some multiple-family hhlds; Active in real estate Involved in sports, health clubs, social clubs, and investing
Buy Me a New Home – Chinese Home Builders	93 000 (22% of hhlds); Toronto and Vancouver	$76 000	House worth $450 000 Struggle to maintain hhld Six or more persons per hhld
High Trades – Chinese Tradesmen	27 000 (6% of hhlds); Toronto	$59 000 Trades	Rent Thrifty, use public transit Busy, multiple-family hhlds
Comfortable Apartment Dwellers – Chinese Enjoying the Freedom	65 000 (15% of hhlds); Toronto and Vancouver	$50 000 Seniors and young professionals in social sciences, arts and culture, and processing and manufacturing industries	Have time, disposable income, and leisure interests
The New Canadians – Arrived from China	70 000 (16% of hhlds); Toronto, Vancouver, Calgary	Blue-collar jobs below education levels	25 to 34 years old Children under 6 years Establishing life and careers
Empty Nesters – Devoted Grannies	11 600 (2.7% of hhlds); Toronto, Vancouver, Calgary, Edmonton, Ottawa	$60 000 Retirement or near retirement	House worth $298 000 Live in older homes/apartments/condominiums Focus on grandchildren—child care, camps, tuition
Up the Ladder – Fix Me Any Home	33 500 (7.7% of hhlds); Toronto, Vancouver, Calgary, Montreal	$59 000 Dynamic careers	House worth $250 000 Young, middle-class families Child-care expenses Mortgage

4. *Stress and depression:* The immigrant disparages aspects of the new life: lack of high-paying job opportunities, taxes, cold and wet weather. Intergenerational conflicts arise, often over the career choices of children.

5. *Integration:* The immigrant moves through society with a degree of ease comparable to that of the native-born.[111]

For example, it would be a mistake to assume that members of the second generation of visible minorities are the same as their parents. In fact, many of them have dual cultural identities: two sets of values, two languages, two wardrobes (especially women), two sets of celebrities and music, two kinds of humour, and two lives—one at home and one "out there" in the mainstream.[112] Chinese Canadian Mina Shum (director) and Korean Canadian Sandra Oh (lead actress) document the tensions between generations in the award-winning movie *Double Happiness.*[113] *The Communicator,* launched in the Markam, Ontario, area in late 1996, was the first bilingual Chinese/English community newspaper. One of its objectives is to bridge cultural gaps.[114]

Interestingly, some young Chinese Canadians are attached to the rapidly developing Chinese popular culture as a kind of Global Teen view akin to the Eurokids.

Although their parents like to hear messages of comfort and security in advertising, these young people want to hear messages of acceptance from the cultural mainstream.[118] *Jade*, an English magazine for young Chinese Canadians, focuses on fashion, cars, and entertainment with an Asian flavour.[119]

The acculturation of Hong Kong immigrant consumers may be understood in terms of the **progressive learning model**. This perspective assumes that people gradually learn a new culture as they increasingly come in contact with it. Thus, we would expect the consumer behaviour of immigrants to be a mixture of practices taken from their original culture and those of the new culture, or **host culture**.[120] Research evidence has generally supported this pattern when factors such as shopping orientation, the importance placed on various product attributes, media preference, and brand loyalty are examined.[121] When the intensity of ethnic identification is taken into account, consumers who retain a strong ethnic identification differ from their more assimilated counterparts.[122]

Leaving one's culture and family to go to a new place creates many new needs as well as anxieties about fitting into a new environment. Recent immigrants encounter a strange culture and have often left family members behind. Word of mouth is very important in developing customer loyalty among Chinese Canadians of all ages, because the Chinese community is very interactive.[123] Canadian marketers can offer a feeling of belonging to Canadian society by including Asian models in catalogues and advertising.[124]

Overall, these processes and examples illustrate that ethnicity is a fluid concept, and the boundaries of a subculture are constantly being recreated. An *ethnic pluralism* perspective argues that ethnic groups differ from the mainstream in varying degrees and that adaptation to the larger society occurs selectively. Research evidence refutes the idea that assimilation necessarily involves losing identification with the person's original ethnic group. One study found, for example, that many French Canadians show a high level of acculturation, yet still retain a strong ethnic affiliation. The best indicator of ethnic assimilation, these researchers argue, is the extent to which members of an ethnic group have social interactions with members of other groups in comparison to their own.[125]

REGIONAL SUBCULTURES

Citizens of Canada share the same national identity, but the regions of Canada differ in weather patterns, concentration and growth of their populations, age composition, ethnic mix, resources, customs, and the availability of some diversions over others, all of which affect regional lifestyles and product and service preferences. Maritimers, for example, are noted in the tea industry for preferring the Red Rose brand. However, it is probably fair to say that regional segments get far less attention from Canadian marketers than other bases of segmentation, and the contrasts often focus on the major urban centres in each region. Nevertheless, this section explores some of the potential for regional segmentation.

The four regions of Canada are usually identified as Atlantic Canada (or the East Coast), Quebec, Ontario, and the west. Sometimes the Maritime provinces are defined as a region, and sometimes British Columbia is distinguished from the Prairie provinces. The northern territories are sometimes combined with the west, but with the opening of the privately funded Northwest Territories Communication Centre, the stage is set for a more distinctive designation.[126] The most appropriate regional segmentation approach depends on the purpose for making the distinctions and whether the distinctions provide marketing leverage.

If you've travelled to or lived in other parts of the country, you may have experienced the weird feeling of being slightly "out of sync" with your environment. The people may speak the same language, yet you may have difficulty understanding some things they say. Brands and store names may be confusing; some may be

Regional Dimensions

Established in 1984, Fog Forest Gallery (*www.fog-forestgallery.ca*) represents professional visual artists and craftspeople of the Atlantic region. Paintings, handmade prints, sculpture, and fine crafts are featured in frequently changing exhibitions. Art workshops, a visiting artists series, and a custom framing service are also offered within a friendly environment.

The name Fog Forest is taken from an article that first appeared in *Canadian Geographic* magazine. Mike Rosen, an interpreter with Parks Canada, described the area surrounding the Bay of Fundy as a fog forest. The climate, along with the additional moisture created by the fog, encourages very special plants to flourish. Even in this difficult and challenging environment, these beautiful and rare plants thrive.

Fog Forest Gallery, owned and operated by Janet Crawford, displays the special works created by fine artists and craftspeople who, like the plants in the fog forest, give the Atlantic region a distinctive and enduring quality. The Gallery represents Atlantic artists such as Tom Forrestall, Susan Paterson, Don Pentz, Anna Syperek, Lynn Wigginton, Thaddeus Holownia, and Shawn O'Hagan, to name a few.

→ Magazines Canada uses a hint of regionalism to
build loyalty to Canadian publications.
Courtesy of Magazines Canada.

familiar and some not. And some familiar items may masquerade under different names. One person's hero is another's grinder is another's submarine sandwich is another's hoagie.

Marketers need to identify products by names that are understood in regional markets. The following illustrates the potential for product-specific misnomers as identified by Dr. Charles Boberg, a linguistics professor at McGill University:

- Most Canadians watch television while sitting on a couch, except on the Prairies where they sit on a chesterfield.
- Most Canadians get water from a faucet, except on the Prairies where it comes from a tap.
- Montrealers drink soft drinks; other Canadians drink pop.
- British Columbian and Atlantic Canadian children play on a teeter-totter; Montreal kids play on a see-saw.
- Students in Atlantic Canada use scribblers and book bags, while Vancouver kids use notebooks and backpacks.
- Eavestroughs keep the rain off the roof in Ontario, but in other parts of Canada gutters do the trick.
- Fitness enthusiasts in British Columbia and on the Prairies wear runners, Central Canadians wear running shoes, and Atlantic Canadians wear sneakers.[127]

NADbank (Newspaper Audience Databank Inc.) found that on average Canadians spend about three-quarters of an hour with their newspaper on weekdays; Quebecers spend the most time with their papers; and Atlantic Canadians increased their reading time by 10 minutes. NADbank also found that Vancouverites are more likely to have investments than Torontonians and Montrealers. Department store shoppers in the Maritimes are more likely to patronize Sears, while British Columbians prefer The Bay.[128] Loblaw's format for

Atlantic Canada is the Atlantic Superstore, and for Western Canada it's the Real Canadian Superstore.[129]

Regional identification based on ethnic overtones is tied to some consumer preferences and purchases and is perhaps most evident in the entertainment area. Celtic music in its various forms is synonymous with the Atlantic Canadian culture,[130] and Acadian music and cuisine are also associated with the Maritimes. The long-running Festival of the Midnight Sun, the Calgary Stampede, the Natal Day Festival, and the Pacific National Exhibition all bespeak of the attraction to locals and tourists of regional symbols and lifestyles. Frito-Lay Canada plays on a number of regional associations with its Tastes of Canada program: Wild Stampede BBQ, PEI Loaded Baked Potato, Cape Breton Sea Salt and Pepper, and Whistler Cool Dill.[131]

Some regions also have unique symbols that provide communication value for marketers. Inuit art styles are associated with British Columbia and the North, as is the polar bear. The Sasquatch is used to promote Kokanee beer in British Columbia, and Bon-Homme provides the theme for a winter carnival in Quebec City.[132] Air Canada hopes to leverage consumers' association of the petroleum industry with Alberta by creating the Oil Express Pass for frequent flyers between Fort McMurray and various locations in Canada and the United States. Coolers are very popular in Ontario, while Quebec is a beer and wine market, and British Colombia leans strongly toward cider.[133] Regional print media, outside of newspapers, include *Up-here: Life in Canada's North, Western Living, Atlantic Progress, Saltscapes,* and *Beautiful British Columbia.*

Cuisine and food preferences also have regional connections. Cipaille and poutine are associated with Quebec—poutine is now exported to Paris;[134] salmon with British Columbia; beef with Alberta; Oka cheese with Quebec; bakeapple with

Net Profit +

Quebecers, compared to other Canadians, are more likely to use the internet for accessing government services (48.4 percent versus 42.7 percent), for downloading or streaming music (36.8 percent versus 23.5 percent), and for chatting and meeting people (27.3 percent versus 15.0 percent). The rest of Canada outstrips Quebecers for research and information gathering (93.6 percent versus 87.4 percent), emailing (94.2 percent versus 89.5 percent), online banking and investing (46.2 percent versus 40.8 percent), and shopping (31.6 percent versus 15.3 percent).[135]

Newfoundland; scallops with Digby, Nova Scotia. New Brunswick has the highest consumption of sliced white bread per capita, while Alberta leads the rest of the country in bubble-gum sales. More cornflakes are sold on the Prairies, more pop in Newfoundland and Labrador, and more linguini in Toronto. Quebecers are the lowest consumers of frozen french fries.[136] Montreal is the undisputed bagel capital of Canada, while consumption of lobster is most easily enjoyed in Atlantic Canada. Regional differences have also been found in the way common foods are consumed in the various regions, as shown in Table 14–4.

THE CANADIAN IDENTITY

As one journalist so aptly put it, "With its ten provinces, [three] territories, two official languages, three bordering oceans, eight mountain ranges, 970 610 square kilometres of land and water, six time zones and over 28.8 million residents, there's no denying Canada is one very big and unique country. A wonderful mélange of cultures, styles, seasons, landscapes, beliefs, backgrounds, and economies, it's a country built on the very diversities that bring it all together."[137] Among Interbrand Corp's 2006 survey of almost 29 000 respondents across 35 countries, Canada ranked third behind the U.K. and Switzerland; it scored very high on governance and tourism.[138]

The last half of the twentieth century saw a major shift in where Canadians live. Largely through the widespread availability of automobiles, consumers have migrated, and urban areas have grown dramatically. Recently, people have been pushing out even farther beyond cities to rural areas. However, about 80 percent of Canadians were urban dwellers in 2001. Interestingly, the growth in rural areas

TABLE 14–4

REGIONAL COMPARISON OF FOOD HABITS

Region	Attitudes	Food Themes and Favourite Sweets and Snacks	Pantry Products
Atlantic Canada	More laid-back about nutrition	Fewer meatless meals; plenty of hearty suppers (steak, corn, carrots); home-baked desserts, chocolate	Instant mashed potatoes, chocolate products, corn starch, icing, molasses, peanut butter
Quebec	Take food seriously; stay at table longer (50 minutes); try new recipe for main dish at least once a week (creative); more nutrition-conscious	Potato chips; cookies	Soda crackers, melba toast, raisins, dried fruit
Ontario	Believe cooking is creative and they are excellent cooks	Ready-to-eat convenience in meal components	Macaroni and cheese, ready-to-eat foods, package mixes for brownies and other squares, canned pasta
Prairies	Enjoy cooking, but fewer love to cook than in any other region	Convenience (speed); eat out to save time	Individual, ready-made frozen entrées; quick and easy cold cuts; packaged cake mix, dessert topping mix, canned baked beans, canned pie filling
British Columbia	Simple wholesome approach; dislike after-meal clean-up and housework	Sweet between-meals snacks	Oatmeal, cocoa, honey, nuts, herbal teas

Source: Based on a study of 1600 Canadians sponsored by the Food and Consumer Products Manufacturers of Canada, *Chatelaine* (French and English publications) and *Modern Woman*, published in "The Plate of the Nation," Chatelaine (November 1997): 38–47.

since 1971 occurred east of Ontario. About 60 percent of the population of PEI lives in rural areas. Canadian marketers play on the rural theme, and the lure of the wild and the hinterland, by offering products and services such as the Country Palette line of home furnishings and accessories (the Bombay Company), Laker beer (Lakeport Brewing Corporation), Skidoos and Sea-Doos (both manufactured by Bombardier Inc.), Sawmill Creek wine, Canvasback ale (named by Calgary's Big Rock Brewery after the "king of the ducks"), ORCA-FM (the world's first all-whale radio station), and muskox burgers.[139] The United Farmers of Alberta retained their focus on rural values and rural life when they re-branded for the twenty-first century,[140] and the Ottawa Rural Tourism Council launched the successful Ottawa Countryside Adventures.[141] The mini-chain Farm Boy found its niche in farm-fresh, perishable, healthy foods.[142]

Many Canadians dedicated the latter part of the twentieth century to protecting Canadian culture—not surprising for a relatively young country among the world's industrialized nations. Interestingly, a 1995 poll showed that 75 percent of Quebecers and 93 percent of the rest of Canadians feel proud when they see the Canadian flag or hear the national anthem.[143] Following the Quebec referendum of 1995 and the presentation of various political platforms, debating the concept of what Canada is as a country seems to have stirred manifestations of patriotism, interspersed with some feelings of unrest. Canada Day celebrations continue to draw participation from communities across the nation; for example, interest in the Canadian flag and its meaning seem to be increasing. In his book *Ideas of the North: A Guide to Canadian Arts and Culture,* Tom Henighan draws attention to a now-critical mass of Canadian cultural activity.[144] Further, in the 2001 census, almost seven million respondents identified their ethnic origin as "Canadian" and another four million reported being "Canadian with another origin."[145]

The uniquely Canadian dimension of our geography is preserved by our national parks (e.g., Kluane, Jasper, Grasslands, Riding Mountain, Georgian Bay, Forillon, Fundy, and Cape Breton Highlands). In fact, marketers find opportunities in the parks located in many cities, towns, and villages throughout Canada. Parks are places connected to many situational purchases—for example, wedding photos, food for picnics, and equipment for photography and wildlife enthusiasts—and are a major point of interest to tourists.

An interesting and potentially useful way to define Canadians is through their value system. Michael Adams, in his book *Sex in the Snow,* suggests that there are a dozen social value "tribes" in Canada that are defined partly by age groupings:

- *The Elders*: Rational Traditionalists, Extroverted Traditionalists, or Cosmopolitan Modernists.
- *The Boomers*: Disengaged Darwinists, Autonomous Rebels, Anxious Communitarians, or Connected Enthusiasts.
- *The GenXers*: Aimless Dependents, Thrill-Seeking Materialists, Autonomous Postmaterialists, Social Hedonists, or New Aquarians. (Security-Seeking Ascetics emerged as a new tribe in the late 1990s.)

Because Adams describes the motivators, values, icons, and words each group lives by, there is potential to extend the descriptions to include likely purchase behaviour. For example, because the New Aquarians seek experiences, value ecologism, and believe everything is interconnected,[146] they likely have an interest in ecotourism, vacation packages, travel, and international cuisine. However, regardless of their social value "tribe," 75 percent of Canadians across all income brackets, age groups, and regions believe that we have a large responsibility to donate to charitable organizations.[147]

A study of the influence of **country of origin** on consumer behaviour suggests that Canadians appear to have trouble identifying Canadian-made products. Labelling, such as "Think Canadian" and "Canada—Buy Into It," might be one way

→ This ad personifies the first line in this section on the Canadian identity.
Nature Conservancy of Canada.

Marketing Opportunity !

Jost Vineyards is in many ways a quintessential example of special marketing opportunities unique to Atlantic Canada. It is the most eastern Estate Winery operating in North America. Established in 1970 by a German immigrant family with 300 years of history in wine making, the winery is located to take advantage of the long frost-free summers of a unique microclimate on the Malagash Peninsula in Nova Scotia. The award-winning winery, which does 50 percent of its sales on its premises, also offers tours, a deli bar, a licensed patio deck, U-Barbecue, wine tasting, and an artisan's cooperative.

Other Atlantic Canadian wines born out of opportunities based on unique advantages in growing conditions—and creativity—include:

> Domaine de Grand Pre in Nova Scotia
> Rodrigues Winery, which makes Wild Cloudberry (bakeapple) wine and Wild Blueberry Wine, in Newfoundland and Labrador
> Rossignol Estate Wines in Prince Edward Island
> Chez Les Maury Vignoble St-Edouard (with Winegarden Estates) and Bourgeois Farms, which grows cherries, pears, and apples, in New Brunswick[148]

Marketing Pitfall

Canadians get bombarded by an average of 4000 promotional or advertising messages per day. Leger Marketing, in a pan-Canadian survey of more than 1500 people about television advertising, found that 80 percent of Canadians think that there is too much television advertising and that it is increasing. When you add in advertising on billboards, at the doctor's office, inside and outside of taxis, and the bathrooms at restaurants, most Canadians feel it is a bit much. Nevertheless, nearly half of Canadians watch television commercials some of the time, even though they are sceptical about how truthful the ads are. About 40 percent ignore the ads by reading a newspaper or book, and another 40 percent simply flip channels. Less than 5 percent turn the television off, however, and over half said they bought something because they saw it on TV. (They were likely to be middle-aged and in the upper brackets of education and income.) Ads that resonate well with Canadians are humorous, thematic, and consistent.[153] Canadians believe that the most effective ads are short (less than 30 seconds), show the product at the beginning of the ad, and run once during a television program.[154]

→ This ad ties food that tastes good to the diversity in cuisine that is available through farmers' markets across Canada.

Print ad for CanadianFarmersMarket is supplied by Farm Credit Canada. Photography by Greg Huszar.

Canadian Dimensions

We are what we eat—and drink—as the following comparisons between the annual Canadian and American beverage consumption illustrate:

> Canadians drink fewer soft drinks per person than Americans do (113 litres versus 187 litres).

> More Canadian than American soft drinks do not contain caffeine. Mountain Dew for the American market is caffeinated, for example, while Canadian Mountain Dew does not contain caffeine.

> Canadians drink more than twice as much tea per person as Americans do (70 litres versus 30 litres).

> Both Canadians and Americans consume about 100 litres of coffee per person.[155]

to serve consumers more effectively. Rather than focusing just on patriotic appeals, however, highlighting the already positive perceptions about factors such as reliability, performance, and service would enhance the reputation of Canadian-made products by fostering positive associations through classical conditioning mechanisms.[149] The EcoLogo is one example of a labelling program that has high recognition.

Consumer purchases in all provinces and territories of Canada are influenced by the changing seasons. Home Hardware, a Canadian company, has a private label for driveway sealer, a product that prevents and solves driveway problems associated with the severity of Canadian winters. Winter brings demand for products and services such as winter clothing, snow shovels, toboggans, Skidoos, firewood, winter tires, ski wear, windshield scrapers, skates, more electricity, snow removal services, and *Hockey Night in Canada*. Decks, patios (usually in backyards), and porches are Canadian icons of summer that are sometimes overlooked. These are gathering places for friends and families and are tied to some very specialized purchase behaviour (e.g., for barbecues, games, party supplies, maintenance tools, and gardening supplies), as well as consumption areas for food, beverages, and clothing. The cottage or bungalow provides a similar setting for Canadian consumers on a larger scale.

Satire, particularly of a political nature, has been called a national sport.[150] *This Hour Has 22 Minutes*, *Made in Canada*, and *Royal Canadian Air Farce* attract audiences of more than a million. Comedy troupes continue to develop and evolve. Toronto's Second City and Yuk Yuk's encourage Canadian comedy, and Montreal's Just for Laughs Festival is also a success. In 2003, Canada's first all-comedy station was launched in Saint John, New Brunswick. As well, Canadian comedians and musicians are now established internationally.[151]

Sometimes Canadian symbols are more apparent within the context of another culture. Canadian fur coats, for example, are sold in Russia, China, South Korea, Japan, and the United States.[152] Aurias diamonds (**www.aurias.com**) added a fifth

FIGURE 14-2

CANADIAN, EH? FAST FACTS ABOUT US

- Almost one-quarter of Canadians recall Bell Canada's sponsorship of the 2006 Olympics with its two beavers, Frank and Gordon (*Leger Marketing*)

- Vintage Canadian: Mary Maxim sweaters. The Barenaked Ladies donned them for their recent holiday album (*Globe and Mail*)

- Criteria for loyalty to a company: High-quality products/services, customer service, treatment of employees, value for money, and environmental practices (*Decima Research*)

- On cars: Across all regions, 34 percent of Canadians view their cars as expressions of their personal identity; 62 percent view them as purely utilitarian, compared to 54 percent and 40 percent, respectively, for Americans (*Michael Adams*)

- On eating well: In 2004, Canadians ate 67 kg of cereal products, 14 kg of poultry, 63 L of milk, 38 kg of fresh fruit, and 75 kg of vegetables (*Statistics Canada*)

- A good read: 71 percent of Canadians read community newspapers (*Canadian Community Newspapers*)

- Canadian youth are more liberal, more pragmatic, and more nationalistic consumers compared to American youth (*Youthography*)

- E-shoppers: In 2004, 3.5 million adult Canadians bought at least one gift for the holidays online; the average amount spent was $228 (*Ipsos Reid*)

- Top brands: Tim Hortons, President's Choice, WestJet, Canadian Tire, and Loblaws (*The Strategic Counsel and Spencer Francey Peters*)

- Social responsibility: TransFair Canada licenses the use of the Fair Trade Certified Logo; in 2003, retail sales totalled almost $20 million (*R. Harris, Marketing Magazine, December 2004*).

- Kraft Foods Canada–specific brands: Nabob, Shreddies, Delissio pizza, and Peak Freans

Want more fast facts on Canadians? Take a look at "What Canadians Think 'About Almost Everything,'" which is based on more than 500 polls conducted by Ipsos-Reid. Visit **www. canada.gc.ca**.

vancouver 2010

TM/MC

↘ It is hoped that the innukshuk symbol on the logo for the 2010 Olympics will symbolize Canada both at home and around the world.
Vancouver 2010

Net Profit

In 2000, PricewaterhouseCoopers commissioned a Consumer Technology Study to examine how Canadians 18 years and older used the internet. Canadians had the highest at-home use of the internet in the world. Interestingly, just under 60 percent of Canadians (versus 85 percent of Americans) used normal telephone lines to get connected; 30 percent used broadband (cable and ISDN). One-quarter of Canadians spent fewer than 3 hours per week online, while another quarter spent 3 to 10 hours per week online.

Ipsos-Reid found that Canadians spent $4 billion shopping online in 2001 (up from $3 billion in 2000); $1.6 billion was spent over the holiday season. The rate of abandonment of e-shopping carts seems to be reduced by careful execution of online couponing, direct marketing to first-time buyers through email, and online demonstrations of how to place an order. E-tailers must consider how to reach users in a non-intrusive manner; however, in a Strategy/Decima poll, one in five Canadians—mostly those who are either young or middle-aged but earning high incomes—reported that they use ad-blocking software, and another 58 percent said they would use it if it were available and they knew how to use it.[156]

"C" (Canadian) to the other four "Cs" of the world's diamonds (clarity, cut, colour, and carat). In 1993 Canada's oldest independent brewery, Moosehead, became the first Canadian beer to be mass-distributed through the Scandinavian government-controlled liquor board. The Swedish campaign was successfully based on a road sign with the silhouette of a moose and traditional images of the Canadian Rockies: majestic mountains, crystal-clear lakes, and deep blue skies. Like Canada, Sweden has the wilderness, the moose, and the same core values.[157] (Incidentally, "moose" is the most common word in Canadian place names.)

Although the small size of the Canadian market creates challenges for publishers and other media, various target markets can be reached. In fact, 50 percent of newsstand and subscription sales in Canada come from Canadian magazines.[158] Men's magazines include *Menz* and *harry*; French-language magazines include *L'expresse, Les affaires,* and *L'actualité*; women's magazines include *Chatelaine* (English and French), *Modern Woman, Canadian Living, Flare,* and *Fashion*; business magazines include *Maclean's, The Financial Post Magazine, Profit: The Magazine for Canadian Entrepreneurs, Scarlett, Canadian Business,* and *Report on Business Magazine*; children's magazines include *Chickadee* and *Owl* (and its French version, *Hibou*); lifestyle and special interest magazines include *Canadian Geographic, MoneySense, Harrowsmith Country Life, Canadian Home Workshop, Outdoor Canada, House & Home, Peace Magazine, Santé,* and *Canadian Gardening.* (Magazines Canada has a complete list at *www.cmpa.ca.*) CBC radio and television and Radio-Canada provide national coverage in the adult and family market, while YTV is the only national youth channel.

Canadian Dimensions

The ingenuity of Canadian manufacturers, artists, and retailers helps them to serve customers in competitive markets both at home and abroad.

> Rocky Mountain Bicycles (*www.bikes.com*), which operates independently under the Procycle Group, is Canada's first mountain-bike company. Founder Grayson Bain thinks that being Canadian is an advantage because the products are perceived as rugged and reliable. The company is located in Delta, British Columbia.[159]

> Tilley Endurables (*www.tilley.com*) sells travel and adventure clothing to the world.

> The familiar Canadian maple leaf is used successfully in a variety of contexts: Honda ran a "Civic Nation" campaign depicting the maple leaf between two bumpers. Kellogg's emblazoned its Corn Flakes with a red maple leaf to introduce its voluntary compliance with Canada's new nutritional labelling regulations. Molson's Joe Canadian sported a maple leaf when he did "The Rant." And Maple Leaf Foods is establishing its company name at the same time it is branding the poultry category with its humorous Prime Naturally chicken ads.[160]

> Stanfield's outdoor advertising combined scenes from nature with quotes by famous Canadians—

and a touch of Canadian humour. One execution showed a canoe with underwear dangling over the side, with a quote by Pierre Berton: "A Canadian is somebody who knows how to make love in a canoe."[161]

> The Ford Motor Co. incorporated hockey (and Wayne Gretzky) into a successful campaign with the tag line, "Built for Life in Canada."[162]

> On the electronic front, sites like the Great Canadian Restaurant Survey (*www.restaurant.ca*) allow for dining preferences in terms of location, cuisine, price range, features (opening hours, parking, and wheelchair access), and rating of value and service.

> *Due South,* a television series starring Canadian Paul Gross as a member of the Royal Canadian Mounted Police, is now popular as an export to countries such as the United Kingdom.

> Zeller's describes itself as "Truly Canadian," and Canadian Tire's (*www.canadiantire.ca*) company name speaks for itself, as does Sears Canada's (*www.sears.ca*).

> Canadian authors include Alice Munro, Michael Ondaatje, Ann-Marie MacDonald, Robert Munsch, Paulette Bourgeois, Margaret Atwood, Pierre Berton, Stuart McLean, Carol Shields, W. O. Mitchell, and Mordecai Richler.

> Successful Canadian musicians include Susan Aglukark, Diana Krall, Jann Arden, Joni Mitchell, Bryan Adams, Alanis Morissette, Céline Dion, Leonard Cohen, Bruce Cockburn, Anne Murray, kd lang, and Deborah Cox, as well as numerous bands, such as Sloan, the Odds, Great Big Sea, Spirit of the West, the Moffatts, the Tragically Hip, Blue Rodeo, Crash Test Dummies, Barenaked Ladies, Wide Mouth Mason, Arcade Fire, Billy Talent, Rascalz, and Jale. Successful Canadian musicians for children include Raffi, Fred Penner, Eric Nagler, Judy and David, Martha Johnson, and Sharon, Lois, and Bram. Musical instruments of note are Casavant organs and Sabien percussion instruments.

> Mail order services for Canadiana include catalogues for the International Native Arts Festival, Canadian Geographic, Jacaranda Tree, Images of Canada, and Decoratives and Tools for Canadian Gardeners, as well as Craft Connoisseur: A Catalogue of Fine Canadian Crafts, and Mountain Equipment Co-op (*www.mec.ca*).

> "For Better or For Worse," by cartoonist Lynn Johnston, depicts the lifestyle of Canadian families and is enjoyed by Canadians and by fans in other countries.[163]

CHAPTER SUMMARY

CONSUMERS' MEMBERSHIPS IN SUBCULTURES OFTEN PLAY A BIG ROLE IN GUIDING THEIR CONSUMPTION BEHAVIOURS. ADDITIONAL INFLUENCES COME FROM IDENTIFYING WITH MICROCULTURES THAT REFLECT A SHARED INTEREST IN SOME ORGANIZATION OR ACTIVITY.

- Consumers identify with many groups that share common characteristics and identities. These large groups that exist within a society are subcultures, and membership in them often gives marketers clues about individuals' consumption decisions. A large component of a person's identity is often determined by his or her ethnic origins, religious background, and regional roots.
- The three largest ethnic subcultures in Canada are English, French, and Chinese Canadians, but consumers with many diverse backgrounds are considered by marketers as well.
- The growing number of people who claim multi-ethnic backgrounds is beginning to blur the traditional distinctions drawn among these subcultures.
- Care must be taken not to rely on inaccurate (and sometimes offensive) ethnic stereotypes.

RELIGION AND SPIRITUALITY ARE INCREASINGLY BEING USED TO MARKET PRODUCTS.

- Although the impact of religious identification on consumer behaviour is not clear, some differences among religious subcultures do emerge. The quest for spirituality is influencing demand in some product categories including books, music, and movies.
- The sensibilities of believers must be considered carefully when marketers use religious symbolism to appeal to members of different denominations.

FRENCH CANADIANS AND CHINESE CANADIANS ARE TWO OF THE LARGEST ETHNIC SUBCULTURES IN CANADA.

- Both French Canadians and Chinese Canadians tend to be extremely family-oriented, and they are receptive to advertising that understands their heritage and reinforces traditional family values.
- Chinese Canadians are beginning to be courted actively by marketers. The size of this group is increasing rapidly, and in the coming years they will dominate some major markets.
- Key issues for reaching the Asian-Canadian market are consumers' degree of acculturation into mainstream Canadian society and the recognition of important cultural differences among Asian subgroups.

MARKETING PROGRAMS BASED ON REGIONAL SUBCULTURES AND THE CANADIAN IDENTITY ARE BEGINNING TO EMERGE.

KEY TERMS

Acculturation   p. 417

Acculturation agents   p. 418

Country of origin   p. 425

De-ethnicitization   p. 406

Ethnic subculture   p. 404

High-context culture   p. 405

Host culture   p. 421

Low-context culture   p. 405

Microculture   p. 403

Progressive learning model   p. 421

Subculture   p. 403

REVIEW QUESTIONS

1. What is a subculture? How does it differ from a microculture?
2. What is the difference between a high-context culture and a low-context culture? What is an example of this difference?
3. Why is it difficult to identify consumers in terms of their ethnic-subculture membership?
4. What is de-ethnicitization? Give an example.
5. Why are French-Canadian consumers attractive to marketers?
6. What is acculturation? How does it differ from enculturation?
7. Who are acculturation agents? Give two examples.
8. Describe the processes involved when a person assimilates into a new host culture.
9. Why are Asian Canadians an attractive market segment? Why can they be difficult for marketers to reach?
10. How can we compare consumers' allegiance to some products as a form of religious observance?
11. How do religious subcultures affect consumption decisions?

CONSUMER BEHAVIOUR CHALLENGE

Discuss

1. Some industry experts believe that it's acceptable to appropriate symbols from another culture, even if the buyer does not know their original meaning. They argue that even in the host society there is often disagreement about these meanings. What do you think?

2. Should members of a religious group adapt marketing techniques that manufacturers customarily use to increase market share for their products? Why or why not?

3. R.J. Reynolds's controversial plan to test-market a cigarette to Black consumers raised numerous ethical issues about segmenting subcultures. Does a company have the right to exploit a subculture's special characteristics, especially to increase sales of a harmful product like cigarettes? What about the argument that successful businesses design products to meet the needs and tastes of their target markets?

4. Products can function as socialization agents for ethnic groups. What examples can you find that serve this important function? What special problems do these create for marketers?

5. Describe the progressive learning model, and discuss why this phenomenon is important when marketing to subcultures.

6. What are the anticipated effects of immigration patterns on marketing activities in Canada in the next decade?

7. How do regional and national identification affect consumer behaviour?

Experiential Exercises

8. Identify any current examples of marketing stimuli that depend upon an ethnic stereotype to communicate a message. How effective are these appeals?

9. To understand the power of ethnic stereotypes, conduct your own poll. For a set of ethnic groups, ask people to anonymously provide, using the technique of free association, attributes (including personality traits and products) most likely to characterize each group. How much agreement did you obtain among people? Compare the associations for an ethnic group held by actual members of that group with those of non-members.

10. Locate one or more consumers (perhaps family members) who have emigrated from their country of origin. Interview them about how they adapted to their host culture. In particular, what changes did they make in their consumption practices over time?

CBC ⬤ VIDEO VIGNETTE

CONCEPTS AT WORK WITH LIVING COLOUR

In the 2001 census, more than 14 000 British Columbians identified themselves as having "multiple visible minority status." Visible minorities, which have become the "visible majority," have transformed the economic, social, and cultural life of Vancouver. One of the manifestations of this transformation is the prevalence of interracial couples in this city relative to Toronto and Montreal. Second-generation Canadians living in one of the most ethnically diverse cities in the world are, of course, very accustomed to multiculturalism. But they are not alone in their multicultural influence. In a recent study, just under 40 percent of Vancouverites reported that ethnicity was important or very important to them, a much higher figure than in either Montreal or Toronto.

Insights into this "fusion culture" can be gleaned from conversations with soon-to-be married young adults, newlyweds, and young couples. The collective experience of mixing cultures in the various areas of their lives has resulted in moving ethnic culture into the mainstream. These individuals are not secured to their ethnicity in the same way their parents and grandparents are. The ease with which Vancouverites navigate within any

one of a set of diverse cultures challenges existing models of multi-ethnic society. Further, it is the driving force behind the search for people with mixed ethnicity for advertising. Is this integration and blending of cultures the future model of Canada and the rest of the world?

Questions

1. What is the process by which the ethnicity of Canada's immigrants becomes mainstream? What are the most influential factors in this process?

2. Describe the development of the ethnic profile of the City of Vancouver.

3. What significance does the integration and blending of ethnic cultures have for consumer behaviour and marketing?

4. Will the fusion culture that has developed in Vancouver also develop in Montreal and Toronto? Explain your answer.

Resources: "Living With Colour," The National, CBC Air Date: December 7, 2004; Krysten Casumpang, "Mixed Messages," Pacific Rim 2006, pp. 33–35.

Teen Values, Conflicts, and Desires

As anyone who has been there knows, the process of puberty and adolescence can be both the best of times and the worst of times. Many exciting changes happen as individuals leave the role of child and prepare to assume the role of adult. These changes create a lot of uncertainty about the self, and the need to belong and to find a unique identity as a person becomes extremely important. At this age, choices of activities, friends, and "looks" are often crucial to social acceptance. Teens actively search for cues from their peers and from advertising for the "right" way to look and behave. Advertising geared to teens is typically action-oriented and depicts a group of "in" teens using the product.

Consumers in this age subculture have a number of needs, including experimentation, belonging, independence, responsibility, and approval from others. Product usage is a significant medium through which to express these needs. For example, many kids view smoking cigarettes as a status activity due to the numerous movies they've seen that glorify this practice. In one study, Grade 9 students watched original movie footage with either smoking scenes or control footage with the smoking edited out. Sure enough, when the young viewers saw the actors smoking, these images enhanced their perceptions of smokers' social stature and increased their own intent to smoke. (The good news: when kids were shown an antismoking advertisement before the film, the effects of this advertisement cancelled out.)[18]

Teenagers in every culture grapple with fundamental developmental issues as they make the transition from child to adult. Teenagers throughout history have had to cope with insecurity, parental authority, and peer pressure. Teenage Research Unlimited says that today the five most important issues for teens are AIDS, race relations, child abuse, abortion, and the environment. Today's teens often have to cope with additional family responsibilities as well, especially if they live in non-traditional families where they must help with shopping, cooking, and housework. It's hard work being a teen in the modern world.[19] Research by the Saatchi & Saatchi advertising agency identified four themes of conflict that are common to all teens:

1. *Autonomy versus belonging:* Teens need to acquire independence, so they try to break away from their families. On the other hand, they need to attach themselves to a support structure, such as peers, to avoid being alone.

2. *Rebellion versus conformity:* Teens need to rebel against social standards of appearance and behaviour, yet they still need to fit in and be accepted by others. A Canadian company called Rad Cosmetics Ltd. targets this dimension of teenage culture.

3. *Idealism versus pragmatism:* Teens tend to view adults as hypocrites, while they see themselves as sincere. They have to reconcile their view of how the world *should* be with the realities they perceive around them.

4. *Narcissism versus intimacy:* Teens are often obsessed with their own appearances and needs. On the other hand, they also feel the desire to connect with others on a meaningful level.[20]

Although teens have the "rep" of always questioning authority, it's also important to keep in mind that one person's rebellion is another's disobedience; there are strong cultural differences when it comes to the desirability of revolting against the establishment. Teen rebellion is a new phenomenon in Japan, a country known for rigid conformity and constant pressure to achieve. Now, more and more Japanese teenagers seem to be making up for lost time. The dropout rate among junior and senior high-school students increased by 20 percent in a two-year period. More than 50 percent of girls have had intercourse by their senior year of high school.[21]

Elsewhere in Asia, however, things are different: Many Asian teens don't necessarily value rebellion against a middle class that they are just now starting to join. An MTV executive commented, "Asian youth lead double lives, almost. On the one hand, they've got their earrings, belly-button rings, and ponytails, but on the other hand, they're completely conformist." In Singapore, Coca-Cola discovered that teen-oriented ads it had used successfully elsewhere, such as a shirtless guy bodysurfing at a rock concert or recklessly riding a grocery cart down a store aisle, just didn't make it with local kids who thought the ads were too unruly. One 18-year-old Singaporean's reactions to a scene showing kids head-banging sums up this feeling: "They look like they're on drugs constantly. And if they're on drugs, then how can they be performing at school?"

In some cases, advertisers have to walk a fine line: For example, an ad for Bajaj Auto, India's largest scooter and motorcycle maker, features an Indian boy and his Caucasian girlfriend cruising around on a bike. This is a provocative image in a country where most marriages are still arranged in line with strict caste codes. But then the couple arrives at a temple, and the boy respectfully covers the girl's head with a shawl to show there are limits to pushing the envelope.[22]

Marketing to Gen Y

Canadian teenagers spend about $6 billion annually, so naturally marketers are very interested in appealing to them. About one in ten Canadians (2.8 million) is aged 13 to 19. By 2011 there will be about 4.1 young Canadians between the ages of 10 and 19.[23] Collectively, teens earn more than $4 billion. Nearly 80 percent of those aged 18 to 19, and 40 percent of those aged 15 to 17, earn annually an average of about $5600 and $3000, respectively. Their purchasing power from about $500 per month of disposable income does not go unnoticed by manufacturers and retailers of clothing, sports equipment, fast food, electronic equipment, and entertainment.[24]

In 2002, 20 Vic Management, a Canadian property manager that specializes in shopping centres, sponsored 1000 interviews with teens at seven of its malls from Halifax to Burnaby. Some of their findings about Canadian teens follow:

- Twenty-five percent spend less than $25 per week; more than 50 percent spend $25 to $100 per week; 17 percent spend more than $100 per week.
- Fifty percent get their spending money from part-time jobs taking up 6 to 20 hours per week; 33 percent from parents on request; 14 percent from a weekly allowance.
- Two-thirds use debit cards.
- Fifty-five percent own a cell phone.
- Teens named more than 50 "favourite" denim jeans brands.
- Forty percent rent 4 to 9 movies per week; one-third go to the movies more than 4 times per month.
- Eighty percent download music from the internet monthly.
- Fifty-one percent eat breakfast at home; 25 percent prefer water as their morning beverage.
- Forty-two percent spend 5 to 8 hours per week on sports and physical activities.
- Thirty-eight percent volunteer outside of school hours.
- Eighty percent recycle.[25]

Although the spending power of North American teens is well known, lately European companies are also appreciating the vast economic clout of the young. Euroteens also have plenty of cash to spend; a survey of Germans aged 16 to 18 by *Yomag.net*, an online magazine for European teens, found that 60 percent had a job and 92 percent received an allowance, with a significant number having both. Another *Yomag.net* survey of teens from other European countries showed that they received a monthly allowance of about 36.74 euros ($61.16).[26] Indeed, the potential of the global youth market is massive due to the huge proportion of people in many countries who are very young. For example, consider that nearly 19 percent of Canadians are 14 years old or younger. Compare this percentage to the corresponding percentages in some other countries:[27]

Argentina	27%
Brazil	29%
China	25%
India	33%
Iran	33%
Malaysia	35%
Philippines	37%
United States	21%

Gen Yers are much less brand loyal than previous generations and are more accepting of generic labels. One survey reported that 18 to 24 year olds are more likely than other consumers to buy a product on the spur of the moment and to change brands if the mood strikes. Only one in five looks for a particular brand.

They are most likely to throw away their home answering machines and to "cut the cord" on wired phones, relying entirely on cell phones and voice mail. They're jugglers who place high value on being both footloose and connected. The advertising agency Saatchi & Saatchi labels this new kind of lifestyle **connexity**. To help

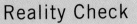

Reality Check

What advice would you give to a marketer who wants to appeal to Gen Y? What are major dos and don'ts? Can you provide some examples of specific marketing attempts targeted at Gen Y that work or don't work?

> Marketing campaigns that encourage self-expression are likely to be successful depicting characters that young people can relate to. To illustrate this point, I will briefly describe a recent advert for Nokia mobile phones that seemed to have won favour amongst youth: A young man seeks to gain the attention of an attractive girl. He does so by asking a friend to keep a close monitor on her lifestyle and movements, which the friend communicates to him by phone. Before too long the young man has quit smoking, begun to mimic her movements by following her jogging, started buying organic and vegetarian produce and reading poetry, all with the aim of impressing and winning her affection. Although this is a very comical and classical depiction of the "boy-chases-girl" scenario, it manages to capture the real and common subtleties of teenagehood, which most of us are able to identify with. I am convinced that being able to identify such a scenario and relating it to a particular product (such as the mobile phone) is the key to marketing success.

Nicole Schragger,
Edinburgh University, Scotland

Gen Yers feel connected with one another, companies like Apple and Philips developed miniature devices such as the iPod and MP3 Key Ring, which store music and images for kids on the run—and then can be plugged directly into a USB port for up- and downloading. When Toyota was developing its youth-oriented Scion model, its researchers learned that echo boomers practically live in their cars; one-quarter of Gen Yers, for example, keep a full change of clothes in their vehicles. So Toyota's designers made the Scion resemble a home on wheels: It has fully reclining front seats so drivers can nap between classes and a 15-volt outlet so they can plug in their computer.[28]

TWEENS

Marketers use the term **tweens** to describe the 2.4 million children aged 9 to 14[29] who are "between" childhood and adolescence and exhibit characteristics of both age groups. As one tween commented, "When we're alone we get weird and crazy and still act like kids. But in public we act cool, like teenagers." This age group drove the success of movies like *Titanic* and boy groups like 'N Sync.[30] They've definitely got marketers' attention.

YTV (*www.ytv.com*), whose viewers are principally tweens, is one of the main sources of information on the tweens market. Tweens' discretionary income comes from gifts for birthdays and holidays, regular allowances, back-to-school money, occasional jobs (babysitting and snow shovelling), and generally indulgent parents. YTV found that 90 percent have influence over the purchase of their own clothes and shoes, and 80 percent get a say in the games, toys, snack food, and restaurants the family chooses. They think school is cool, aspire to being "real" teenagers, are brand-conscious, media-savvy, techno-literate information gatherers; although they have been exposed to their parents' nostalgia for boomer pop culture, they are very much a unique market force unto themselves.[31]

Tweens in Canada control $1.7 billion dollars in consumer spending; worldwide, members of this age group control $197 billion. They like to purchase new brands and styles in clothes and shoes. Their spending power comes from "as needed" parental supplements to their allowance. Tweens influence another $20 billion in purchases for family durables, such as computers, software, audio equipment, and car accessories. Nine out of ten live in homes with working computers; eight out of ten log on to the internet at least once a week, as it is a social hub.[32] About 43 percent of tweens report that they read more than three magazines each month, most of them American celebrity and entertainment magazines.[33] Toys such as the Bratz Rock Angelz dolls are making a brand impression. Bratz is extending into categories such as magazines and a cartoon television show, as well as teaming up with events like the MuchMusic Video Awards, where the dolls were given to celebrities. Bratz's 30 percent market share in Canada is nipping at the heels of Barbie's 58 percent share.[34]

As sophisticated as these consumers might sound, in-depth interviews with 13- and 14-year-old girls in the United States indicate that tween consumers think they can improve their competence as shoppers. Areas for improvement include controlling impulse purchases, making independent and confident choices, dealing with salespeople, and managing their money. On the other hand, they are knowledgable about different stores, brands, and shopping routines.[35]

SPEAKING TO TEENS IN THEIR OWN LANGUAGE

Because modern teens were raised on television and tend to be so much more "savvy" than previous generations, marketers must tread lightly when they try to reach them. In particular, the messages must be seen as authentic and not condescending. As one researcher observed: "They have a B.S. alarm that goes off quick and fast…. They walk in and usually make up their minds very quickly about whether it's phat or not phat, and whether they want it or don't want it. They know a lot of advertising is based on lies and hype"[36] due to the inclusion of media education in high-school curricula.

Interestingly, Reactorz Research found that Canadian teens were able to identify the brand or genre of brands associated with particular advertisements. The researcher also found that a significant segment of the teen clothing market is actively "anti-brand" and shops at second-hand and discount stores, such as Value Village, Winners, Zellers, and Wal-Mart. But two other segments also exist: the "comfort" group, who buy Gap, Old Navy, West 49, and even Vokal and JLo, and the "high-fashion" group, who wear Parasuco, Guess, Buffalo, and Mavi. Clearly, teens' opinion of the advertising doesn't affect their opinion of the clothes![37]

So what are the rules of engagement when it comes to young consumers?[38]

Rule 1: Don't talk down. Younger consumers want to feel they are drawing their own conclusions about products. In the words of one teen: "I don't like it when someone tells me what to do. Those drugs and sex commercials preach. What do they know? Also, I don't like it when they show a big party and say come on and fit in with this product. That's not how it works."

Rule 2: Don't try to be what you're not. Stay true to your brand image. Youth value straight talk. Firms that back up what they say impress them.

Rule 3: Entertain them. Make it interactive and keep the sell short. Gen Y likes to find brands in unexpected places. The prospect of catching appealing ads is part of the reason they're watching that TV show in the first place. If they want to learn more, they'll check out your website.

Rule 4: Show that you know what they're going through, but keep it light. In a commercial for Hershey's Ice Breakers mints, the brand's product benefit is tied to a guy's stress at approaching a strange girl at a club. "I'm wearing my lucky boxers," he reassures himself. "Don't trip. Don't drool. Relax. How's my breath?"

Youth Tribes

Consumer tribes are emerging, and this phenomenon is most pronounced among young consumers. The essence of tribal consumption is that these products and services reinforce the notion of belonging, regardless of the commitment level of the individual. Whether the tribal member is deeply committed or is just an amateur, each person attains a sense of belonging, embracing the trappings and rituals of the tribe.[39] The tribal idea is picking up speed among marketers. Mattel is introducing a line of My Scene dolls, including a more approachable and multicultural Barbie aimed at older girls. As a Mattel executive explains, "They really pick up on this notion [that] there are various tribes girls want to belong to."[40]

In-line roller skaters in France are a great example of the tribal phenomenon at work. There are about two million in-line skaters in France today, divided equally by gender. This group has its "in groups" and "out groups" within the tribe, but all are connected by their shared skating experience. These urban skaters hold national gatherings in Paris that attract as many as 15 000 people, many of whom belong to associations such as Rollers et Coquillages and Paris Roller. Specialized websites for members of the skating tribe let them chat and exchange information. Small tribal divisions exist (e.g., fitness skaters versus stunt skaters), but all identify with the skating tribe.

Tribal gatherings provide manufacturers with an opportunity to strengthen the group bond by offering accessories, such as shoes, key chains, belts and hats, backpacks, sunglasses, T-shirts, and other goodies that reinforce membership. Although many brands of skates are available, including K2, Razors, Oxygen, Tecnica, and Nike, the original Rollerblade product retains cult status within the tribe. Companies like Tatoo, the pager arm of France Telecom, build on tribal bonds with in-line skaters by sponsoring Tatoo Roller Skating in Paris and similar events around the country. The tribe can subscribe to specialized magazines, such as *Crazy Roller*, *Urban*, and *Roller Saga*, which include informational articles and celebrity spots.

Marketing Opportunity !

Some major corporations are figuring out the value of teaming with very dissimilar players to develop youth-based products. Nike and Polaroid formed a partnership that lets teens personalize their sneakers by inserting pictures they take with the i-Zone camera directly into the shoes.[41] Toyota created a special marketing unit called Genesis Group just to reach young adults. Genesis launched its first campaign to support Toyota's new crop of youth-oriented models like the Echo.[42] The company is teaming up with fashionable surfwear maker Roxy to create a surf-friendly version of its Echo sedan for the young female market, complete with water-resistant, neoprene-covered seats, a Yakima roof rack, and wet-gear storage bins.[43]

The tribal phenomenon is perhaps most pronounced in Japan, where teenagers invent, adopt, and discard fads with lightning speed. Teenage girls in Japan exhibit what science-fiction writer William Gibson (who invented the term *cyberspace*) calls "techno-cultural suppleness"—a willingness to grab something new and use it for their own ends—matched by no other group on earth. According to one estimate, cell phones sit in the purses and pockets of about 95 percent of all Japanese teenage girls. Unlike North American phones, these devices are connected constantly to the internet and plug these girls into a massive network.[44]

Researching the Youth Market

Bill Bishop, managing director of Cossette Communication's Alias Urban Marketing, recommends frequent research to measure changes in trends among youth: "Their values are very consistent, [but] it's the expression of values that change."[45] Research and media firms are coming up with innovative ways to tap the desires of teens, many of whom don't respond well to traditional survey techniques. Pizza Hut invites teens into its boardroom to have lunch with company executives and to share their opinions about the perfect pie.[46] Some research companies give teens video cameras and ask them to record a "typical" day at school—along with play-by-play commentary to help interpret what's going on. Procter & Gamble goes to the web to learn what kids are thinking. The company built two teen community websites to identify emerging trends. One of them, *www.tremor.com*, recruits teen members and rewards them with merchandise for spreading the word about products.[47] Firms such as look-look employ **coolhunters**—kids in major markets like New York, Los Angeles, and London who roam the streets to report back on cutting-edge trends.[48]

This research is all about defining what is cool to teens—the Holy Grail of youth marketing. One study asked young people in the United States and the Netherlands to write essays about what is "cool" and "uncool."[49] The researchers found that being cool has several meanings, though there are a lot of similarities between the two cultures when youth use this term. Some of the common dimensions include having charisma, being in control, and being a bit aloof. And many of the respondents agreed that being cool is a moving target: The harder you try to be cool, the more uncool you are! Youth Culture Group, a Canadian company that concentrates exclusively on teenagers, tracks the attitudes of cool teens, or Early Style Adopters, with their Trendscan. Cool teens risk their reputation and dollars in purchasing mainstream or cool clothing brands and are most likely to influence their peers.[50]

Marketers view teens as "consumers in training" because brand loyalty is often developed during this age. A teenager who is committed to a brand may continue to purchase it for many years to come. Such loyalty creates a barrier to entry for other brands that were not chosen during these pivotal years. Thus, advertisers sometimes try to "lock in" consumers to certain brands so that in the future they will buy these brands more or less automatically. As one teen-magazine ad director observed, "We ... always say it's easier to start a habit than stop it."[51]

Teens also exert a big influence on the purchase decisions of their parents (see Chapter 12).[52] In addition to providing "helpful" advice to parents, teens are increasingly *buying* products on behalf of the family. The majority of mothers are now employed outside the home and have less time to shop for the family. This fundamental change in family structure has altered the way marketers must view teenaged consumers. Although teens are still a good market for discretionary items, in recent years their spending on "basics," such as groceries, is even larger than for nonessentials. Marketers are beginning to respond to these changes. Dairy Queen Canada is repositioning itself to attract teenagers to its hamburgers and other fast-food fare.[53]

Canadian publishers and telecasters recently developed an interest in the teen market. Many towns and cities now provide more complete coverage of high-school sports, for example. Canadian teen magazines include *La magazine jeunesse*, and *Pop Life* (*Info Pop* is the French version), published by Pepsi-Cola. *Ego*, published by McDonald's since 1996, is targeted at French-speaking teens in New Brunswick and Quebec.[54] YTV is a channel devoted to programming for Canadian youth. The Breakfast Zone remains one of its most popular segments.

Big (Wo)Man on Campus: We're Talking to You!

Advertisers spend millions each year to influence the purchases of university students, who buy billions of dollars' worth of products annually. Food service on Canadian campuses is a $250-million-a-year industry, attracting fast-food providers like Pizza Hut, Taco Bell, and Tim Hortons, as well as catering companies like Sodhexo-Marriott, Versa, and Beaver Foods.[55] After paying for books, board, and tuition, the average student has hundreds of dollars per month to spend, so this interest is not surprising. As one marketing executive observed, "This is the time of life when they're willing to try new products.... This is the time to get them in your franchise."[56] The university market is also attractive to many companies because these novice consumers are away from home for the first time, so they have yet to form unshakeable brand loyalty to products, such as cleaning supplies.

Nevertheless, university students pose a special challenge for marketers because they are hard to reach via conventional media, such as newspapers. Of course, online advertising is very effective: Virtually all university students go online at least a few times each week, and 90 percent do so daily.[57] In addition, enterprises like *www.mtv.com* are blossoming because they reach students where they live and play.[58]

Other strategies to reach students include the widespread distribution of sampler boxes containing a variety of personal-care products in student centres and

Net Profit

Teens use products to express their identities, to explore the world and their new-found freedoms in it, and also to rebel against the authority of their parents and other socializing agents. A thriving internet subculture has developed among many teens to serve this purpose. The net is the preferred method of communication for many young people because its anonymity makes it easier to talk to people of the opposite sex or of different ethnic and racial groups.[59] The web also provides a forum for experimentation that appeals to teens grappling with identity issues. Researchers report that teens value privacy when surfing the web because they view it as a way to express their individuality.[60]

Indeed, many teens are using the web to experiment with different identities. More than half have more than one screen name or email address. Almost one-quarter of this multi-monikered group keep at least one name secret so they can go online without being recognized by friends. And 24 percent of teens who use email, instant messaging (IM), or chat rooms pretend to be someone else.[61]

Popular cyber hangouts for Canadian teens include Friendster, Nexopia, and CHUM's Habbo Hotel. Brands such as Dentyne Ice, Nintendo, Doritos, Alesse, West 49, Oh Henry, Sony, and Pizza Hut connect to these teen social networks through contests, blogging, and dynamic product placement, and by providing features that enable teens to order products.[62]

Many are into portable media, such as cell phones, iPods, and PSPs. It's been estimated that more than half of teens have portable players. The interactivity and targetability of these media are encouraging marketers to reach the youth market with customized approaches, often with shortcode campaigns. Some marketers are leading the way with forays into m-couponing, mobisodes, podvertising, ringtone and game sponsorship, and other innovative online marketing approaches.[63]

→A growing number of marketers are capitalizing on the ritual of Spring Break to reach university and college students.
© *John Henley/CORBIS/MAGMA.*

Marketing Pitfall

Youthography conducts surveys of Canadian high-school and university students to understand students' views of marketing in their educational milieus. Interestingly, high-school students viewed marketing activities in schools less favourably in 2002 than in 2001. Further, the data suggest that students who had mixed feelings about marketing activities in 2001 may have decided that they don't like it at all:

> 26.4 percent (versus 17.1 percent in 2001) do not want any marketing in their schools.

> 9.6 percent (versus 11.1 percent in 2001) said it is perfectly fine.

> 64.0 percent (versus 71.8 percent in 2001) said it is acceptable as long as there are special circumstances, or the company is giving back.

Max Valiquette, president of Youthography, recommends that marketers need to think about school first (as institutions of education and socialization) and marketing second; long-term brand equity will come only if companies are perceived as genuinely helping students.[67]

residences and the use of posters (termed *wall media*). In addition, a growing number of marketers are capitalizing on the ritual of Spring Break or Reading Week to reach university students; it is estimated that about 40 percent of students now make the annual trek to points south. Beach promotions used to be dominated by suntan lotion and beer companies, but now firms such as Chanel, Hershey, Chevrolet, Procter & Gamble, and Columbia Pictures join them.[64]

BABY BUSTERS: GENERATION X

The cohort of consumers in their twenties consists of 6.0 million Canadians who will be a powerful force through half of the twenty-first century.[65] This group, which has been labelled "**Generation X**," "slackers," or "busters," was profoundly affected by the economic downturn in the first part of the nineties. In Canada, Generation X also includes 3.1 million baby boomers born between 1960 and 1966. Like the "true" baby busters, this subgroup feels the pressure of the economic recession and earns about 10 percent less than their parents did at the age of 30. However, unlike the younger members of Generation X, they are likely to be less well-positioned (e.g., with computer skills) to participate in the new economy.[66]

In the past, advertisers fell all over themselves trying to create messages that they hoped would not turn off the worldly Generation X cohort. Many of these efforts to put marketing messages in contexts that busters would identify with consisted of references to old TV shows, or vignettes featuring dishevelled actors in

← Using contrasting images of child-like whimsy and grown-up sophistication, this Quaker ad sends the message that taste in snack foods also grows up.
Courtesy of Pepsi QTG.

Teen Values, Conflicts, and Desires

As anyone who has been there knows, the process of puberty and adolescence can be both the best of times and the worst of times. Many exciting changes happen as individuals leave the role of child and prepare to assume the role of adult. These changes create a lot of uncertainty about the self, and the need to belong and to find a unique identity as a person becomes extremely important. At this age, choices of activities, friends, and "looks" are often crucial to social acceptance. Teens actively search for cues from their peers and from advertising for the "right" way to look and behave. Advertising geared to teens is typically action-oriented and depicts a group of "in" teens using the product.

Consumers in this age subculture have a number of needs, including experimentation, belonging, independence, responsibility, and approval from others. Product usage is a significant medium through which to express these needs. For example, many kids view smoking cigarettes as a status activity due to the numerous movies they've seen that glorify this practice. In one study, Grade 9 students watched original movie footage with either smoking scenes or control footage with the smoking edited out. Sure enough, when the young viewers saw the actors smoking, these images enhanced their perceptions of smokers' social stature and increased their own intent to smoke. (The good news: when kids were shown an antismoking advertisement before the film, the effects of this advertisement cancelled out.)[18]

→ Marketers often influence public policy by creating messages to influence behaviours like smoking or drug use. This mosaic was used to promote a smoking prevention program.
Courtesy of Lorillard Tobacco c/o Caroline Group.

The tribal phenomenon is perhaps most pronounced in Japan, where teenagers invent, adopt, and discard fads with lightning speed. Teenage girls in Japan exhibit what science-fiction writer William Gibson (who invented the term *cyberspace*) calls "techno-cultural suppleness"—a willingness to grab something new and use it for their own ends—matched by no other group on earth. According to one estimate, cell phones sit in the purses and pockets of about 95 percent of all Japanese teenage girls. Unlike North American phones, these devices are connected constantly to the internet and plug these girls into a massive network.[44]

Researching the Youth Market

Bill Bishop, managing director of Cossette Communication's Alias Urban Marketing, recommends frequent research to measure changes in trends among youth: "Their values are very consistent, [but] it's the expression of values that change."[45] Research and media firms are coming up with innovative ways to tap the desires of teens, many of whom don't respond well to traditional survey techniques. Pizza Hut invites teens into its boardroom to have lunch with company executives and to share their opinions about the perfect pie.[46] Some research companies give teens video cameras and ask them to record a "typical" day at school—along with play-by-play commentary to help interpret what's going on. Procter & Gamble goes to the web to learn what kids are thinking. The company built two teen community websites to identify emerging trends. One of them, *www.tremor.com*, recruits teen members and rewards them with merchandise for spreading the word about products.[47] Firms such as look-look employ **coolhunters**—kids in major markets like New York, Los Angeles, and London who roam the streets to report back on cutting-edge trends.[48]

turned-around baseball caps doing their best to appear blasé. This approach actually turned off a lot of busters because it implied that they have nothing else to do but sit around watching old television reruns. Subaru sponsored one of the first commercials of this genre. It showed a sloppily dressed young man who described the Impreza model as "like punk rock," while denouncing the competition as "boring and corporate." The commercial did not play well with its intended audience, and Subaru eventually switched agencies.

Perhaps one reason why appeals to Xers with messages of alienation, cynicism, and despair fail is that many busters turned out not to be so depressed after all! Generation Xers are actually quite a diverse group; they don't all wear reversed baseball hats and work on and off as burger flippers. One industry expert observed, "Today's Gen Xer is both values-oriented and value-oriented. This generation is really about settling down." Many people in this segment seem to be determined to have stable families after being latchkey children themselves. Xers tend to view the home as an expression of individuality rather than material success. More than half are involved in home improvement and repair projects.[68]

BABY BOOMERS

The **baby boomer** age segment (born between 1947 and 1966) consists of people (over 30 percent of the Canadian population) whose parents established families following the end of World War II and during the 1950s, when the peacetime economy was strong and stable. The sheer size of this age cohort has helped to make it the source of many fundamental cultural and economic changes.[69] Imagine a large python that has swallowed a pig; the pig moves down the length of the python, creating a moving bulge as it goes.[70]

As teenagers in the 1960s and 1970s, the "Woodstock Generation" created a revolution in style, politics, and consumer attitudes. As they aged, their collective will was behind cultural events as diverse as student power, Expo '67, Trudeaumania, and hippies in the 1960s, to grassroots democracy, employee empowerment, and yuppies in the 1980s. Now that the "pig in the python" has

↓ Stutz appeals to Generation X with edgy ads that have lots of 'tude.
Courtesy of Stutz.

hard
apple
cider

ƨTUTZ

SERVE CHILLED

Marketing Pitfall

Most baby boomers are still in their forties and have children at home,[75] with parents in their late sixties. In fact, they are today's "sandwich generation" and are the gatekeepers to medical and healthcare purchases for three generations, including themselves.[76] Still, some are thinking about retirement. Decima Research conducted a study for Investors Group of more than 2000 Canadians aged 45 to 54; the results show some interesting contrasts between the plans baby boomers have for their retirement and the lifestyles of current retirees.

	Current Retirees	Boomer Plans
Travel to a warm place for the winter	27%	56%
Purchase a vacation property, motor home, or boat	15%	28%
Devote time to hobbies	45%	59%
Participate in physical activities	64%	82%
Work on own or in consulting	22%	51%

However, most baby boomers (56 percent) have not even determined their retirement income needs, although about one-fifth of them have savings and investments worth more than $250 000; another one-fifth have saved between $100 000 and $250 000.[77]

moved into its forties to sixties, this age group continues to exert the most impact on consumption patterns.

Most of the growth in the market over the next decade will be accounted for by the boomers who have moved into their peak earning years. By the age of 30, older baby boomers (born between 1947 and 1959) were earning 30 percent more than their fathers did at that age.[71] As baby boomers grow older, they are moving up to more responsible and lucrative jobs. Thus, consumers on average are becoming older and wealthier. And now that some baby boomers are approaching retirement, they are starting to spend on luxury items, such as pleasure boats.

Levi Strauss (*www.levistrauss.com*) is a good example of a company that built its core business on the backs (or backsides) of boomers. More recently, though, the apparel maker faced the challenge of keeping aging baby boomers in their franchise as former jeans-wearing hippies got older and lost interest in traditional styles. Levi Strauss answered this challenge by creating a new product category called "New Casuals," which are more formal than jeans but less formal than dress slacks. The target audience is men aged 25 to 49 who have higher-than-average education and income and who work in white-collar jobs in major metropolitan areas. Yes, it's the Dockers line.[72] Although the Levi's image has suffered among younger consumers, the company's role in providing clothes for "Casual Fridays" work environments continues to thrive.

Consumers aged 35 to 44 spend the most on housing, cars, and entertainment; baby boomers have been "feathering their nests," accounting for the lion's share of all the money spent on household furnishings and equipment.[73] In addition, consumers aged 45 to 54 spend the most of any age category on food, apparel, and retirement programs. According to N.P.D. Canada, women aged 45 to 54 represent about $3 billion (and growing) of the $10-billion women's clothing market. Holt Renfrew, Sears, and La Senza continue to appeal to this segment. In addition, some conventional retailers are opening stores that provide a relaxing atmosphere and that cater to the group's need for fun but age appropriate clothing that fits. Examples include Forth & Towne (Gap), Josef's (Jacob's), and Yzza (Liz Claiborne Canada).[74]

→ Schneider's uses a humorous take on Einstein's image to connect with parents' concern for the healthy development of their children.
Schneider's Smart Lunch.

In addition to the direct demand for products and services created by this age group, these consumers have also created a new baby boom of their own to keep marketers busy in the future. Because fertility rates have dropped, this new boom is not as big as the one that created the baby boom generation; the new upsurge in the number of births can best be described as a *baby boom echo*. Many couples postponed marriage and parenthood due to the new emphasis on careers for women. They began having babies in their late twenties and early thirties, resulting in fewer (but perhaps more pampered) children per family. This new emphasis on children and the family created opportunities for products such as cars (e.g., the success of the "minivan" and SUV concept among "soccer moms"), services (e.g., daycare), and media (e.g., magazines such as *Today's Parent*).

THE MATURE MARKET

The old woman sits alone in her dark apartment while the television blares out a soap opera. Once every couple of days she slowly and painfully opens her triple-locked door with arthritic hands and ventures out to the corner store to buy essentials like tea, milk, and cereal, always being sure to pick the least expensive brand. Most of the time she sits in her rocking chair, thinking sadly of her dead husband and the good times they used to have together.

Is this the image you have of a typical mature consumer? Until recently, many marketers did. As a result they largely neglected these consumers in their feverish pursuit of the baby boomer market. But as our population ages and people live longer and healthier lives, the game is changing rapidly. A lot of businesses are beginning to replace the old stereotype of the poor recluse. The newer, more accurate image is of a mature consumer who is active, interested in what life has to offer, and who is an enthusiastic customer with the means and willingness to buy many goods and services.[78] This market is growing even as we speak![79]

Economic Clout

The **mature market** consists of approximately 6.8 million people aged 55 and older. For many purposes these consumers are classified as "senior citizens" when they reach the age of 65 and their Canada Pension Plan benefits begin.[80] The number of Canadians 65 and older more than doubled to 4.2 million over the last 25 years, composing about 13 percent of the population. Statistics Canada predicts that they will make up 19 percent of the population in 2021 and 25 percent in 2041. Among the provinces, Saskatchewan has the highest proportion of seniors, at almost 15 percent; Alberta has 10 percent, the lowest proportion, but this number is growing due to the attraction of fewer taxes and more benefits in that province. Yukon, Nunavut, and Northwest Territories have less than 7 percent of their populations in the 65-plus age group.[81]

Overall, the mature market is the second-fastest-growing market segment in Canada, lagging behind only the baby boomers. Such dramatic growth can be explained largely by improved medical diagnoses and treatment and the resulting increase in life expectancy. Given the economic clout of senior consumers, it's often surprising how many marketers ignore them in favour of younger buyers—even though they are among the most loyal of any segment. Older consumers repurchase a brand more frequently, consider fewer brands and dealers, and choose long-established brands more often.[82] This is certainly true in the world of television advertising, where most companies salivate to attract the segment of 18 to 34 year olds.[83] The over-50 market accounts for about 55 percent of discretionary spending power and 80 percent of personal wealth in Canada. However, less than 5 percent of advertising addresses this market, which represents less than 5 percent of respondents in marketing research.

Some important areas that stand to benefit from the surging mature market include exercise facilities, cruises and tourism, cosmetic surgery, skin treatments, toys for grandchildren, "how-to" books, and university courses that offer enhanced learning opportunities. Mature consumers spend more on gifts than those in younger age groups, and those aged 55 to 64 donate the most to charitable organizations. Co-op housing near Toronto's lakefront and the provision of a more leisurely shopping pace and personalized service are recent examples of a consumer-based approach to the mature market.[86]

Understanding Mature Consumers

Hallmark's marketing group thought it had found a gold mine. When it realized that about 78 million baby boomers would be hitting age 50, the company created boxes and boxes of friendship, birthday, anniversary, and thinking-of-you cards, all designed to subtly flatter the aging boomer's flagging middle-aged ego. The "Time of Your Life" line of cards was displayed in its own section and featured active mid-lifers looking youthful as they frolicked on beaches and dove into swimming pools. But Hallmark missed one tiny yet telling psychological detail: No self-respecting boomer wants to be seen shopping in the "old people's" card section. The Time of Your Life line was scrapped.[87] This debacle underscores the importance for marketers to work harder to probe the psyche of older consumers. Researchers have identified a set of key values that are relevant to mature consumers. For marketing strategies to succeed, they should be related to one or more of these factors:[88]

- *Autonomy:* Mature consumers want to lead active lives and be self-sufficient. The advertising strategy of Depends, undergarments made by Kimberly-Clark for incontinent women, is centred on a famous actress, June Allyson, who plays golf and goes to parties without worrying about her condition.

- *Connectedness:* Mature consumers value the bonds they have with friends and family. Quaker Oats successfully tapped into this desire with its ads featuring actor Wilford Brimley, who dispenses grandfatherly advice about eating right to the younger generation.

- *Altruism:* Mature consumers want to give something back to the world. Thrifty Car Rental (*www.thrifty.com*) found in a survey that more than 40 percent of older consumers would select a rental-car company if it sponsored a program that gave discounts to senior-citizen centres. Based on this research, the company launched its highly successful program "Give a Friend a Lift."

Perceived Age: You're Only as Old as You Feel

Market researchers who work with mature consumers often comment that people think of themselves as being 10 to 15 years younger than they actually are. In fact, research confirms the popular wisdom that age is more a state of mind than of body. A person's mental outlook and activity level have a lot more to do with his or her longevity and quality of life than does *chronological age,* the actual number of years lived.

A better yardstick with which to categorize mature consumers is **perceived age**, or how old a person feels. Perceived age can be measured on several dimensions, including "feel-age" (how old a person feels) and "look-age" (how old a person looks).[89] The older consumers get, the younger they *feel* relative to actual age. For this reason, many marketers emphasize product benefits rather than age appropriateness in marketing campaigns, because many consumers do not relate to products targeted at their chronological age.[90]

Segmenting the Older Market

The subculture of older consumers is an extremely large market: The number of Canadians 65 years and older is almost 4.2 million, and there are roughly another

3.0 million between the ages of 55 and 64.[93] Because this group is so large, it is helpful to think of the mature market as actually consisting of four subsegments: an "older" group (aged 55–64), an "elderly" group (65–74), an "aged" group (75–84), and finally a "very old" group (85 years and older).[94]

The older mature market is particularly well-suited for segmentation because older consumers are easy to identify by age and stage in the family life cycle. Most receive benefits from the Canada Pension Plan. Many belong to organizations catering to this segment. Some read magazines for mature consumers, such as *Good Times: The Canadian Magazine for Successful Retirement,* and have their interests (e.g., in benefits plans) represented by the Canadian Association of Retired Persons. Canadian women aged 65 years and older listen to about 23.5 hours of radio per week (compared to 8.5 hours per week for teens).[95]

In addition to chronological age, marketers segment older consumers along dimensions, such as the particular years a person came of age (his or her age cohort), current marital status (e.g., widowed versus married), and a person's health and outlook on life.[96] For example, one ad agency devised a segmentation scheme for women over the age of 65 on two dimensions: self-sufficiency and perceived opinion leadership.[97] The study yielded many important differences among the groups. The self-sufficient group was found to be more independent, cosmopolitan, and outgoing. They were more likely to read books, attend concerts and sporting events, and dine out.

Several segmentation approaches begin with the premise that a major determinant of marketplace behaviour of older mature consumers is the way they deal with aging.[98] **Social aging theories** try to understand how society assigns people to different roles across the lifespan. For example, when someone retires, he or she may reflect society's expectations for someone at this life stage—this is a major transition point when people exit from many relationships.[99] Some people become depressed, withdrawn, and apathetic as they age; some are angry and resist the thought of aging; and some appear to accept the new challenges and opportunities this period of life has to offer. Table 15–2 summarizes selected findings from one current segmentation approach called **gerontographics**, which divides the mature market into groups based on both level of physical well-being and social conditions, such as becoming a grandparent or losing a spouse.

Marketing to Mature Consumers

Most mature consumers lead more active, multidimensional lives than we assume. Many Canadians aged 55 years and older offer their services through voluntary organizations (***www.volunteer.ca***), and many more volunteer informally, visiting the sick and elderly, shopping or driving for others, and caring for children.[100] In 2005, 45 percent of Canadians 65 years and older spent 269 hours volunteering. About 20 percent look after children at least once a week.[101]

It is also crucial to remember that income alone does not capture the spending power of this group. Mature consumers are finished with many of the financial obligations that siphon off the income of younger consumers. Most consumers over the age of 65 own their own home, and most of those homes are mortgage-free. In addition, child-rearing costs are over. And, as evidenced by the popularity of the bumper sticker that proudly proclaims, "We're spending our children's inheritance," many seniors now feel better about spending money on themselves rather than skimping for the sake of children and grandchildren.

Still, outdated images of mature consumers persist. The editors of *Modern Maturity* reject about a third of the ads submitted to them because they portray older people in a negative light. In one survey, one-third of consumers over age 55 reported that they deliberately did not buy a product because of the way an older person was stereotyped in the product's advertising.[102] To address these negative depictions, marketers can provide more welcoming environments for mature

TABLE 15–2

GERONTOGRAPHICS: SELECTED CHARACTERISTICS

Segment	Percent of 55+ Population	Profile	Marketing Implications
Healthy Indulgers	18%	Have experienced the fewest events related to aging, such as retirement or loss of spouse, and are most likely to behave like younger consumers. Main focus is on enjoying life.	Looking for independent living. Good customers for discretionary services, such as home cleaning and answering machines.
Healthy Hermits	36%	React to life events, such as death of a spouse, by becoming withdrawn. Resent that they are expected to behave like old people.	Emphasize conformity. They want to know their appearance is socially acceptable and tend to be comfortable with well-known brands.
Ailing Outgoers	29%	Maintain positive self-esteem despite adverse life events. They accept limitations but are still determined to get the most out of life.	Have health problems that may require a special diet. Special menus and promotions will bring these consumers into restaurants seen as catering to their needs.
Frail Recluses	17%	Have adjusted their lifestyles to accept old age but have chosen to cope with negative events by becoming spiritually stronger.	Like to stay put in the same house where they raised their families. Good candidates for remodelling and for emergency-response systems.

Source: Adapted from George P. Moschis, "Life Stages of the Mature Market," *American Demographics* (September 1996): 44–50.

consumers. Wal-Mart hires older people as greeters to be sure their mature customers feel at home.[103]

The Adeg Aktiv Markt 50+ in Salzburg, Austria, is Europe's first supermarket designed for shoppers over the age of 50. The labels are big; the aisles are wide; the floors are nonskid, even when wet; and there are plenty of places to sit down. The lights are specially calibrated to reduce glare on older customers' more sensitive eyes. The shelves are lower so products are within easy reach. And, in addition to regular shopping carts, there are carts that hook on to wheelchairs and carts that double as seats for the weary; as soon as a shopper sits down, the wheels lock.[104]

PRODUCT ADAPTATIONS

Many consumer products will encounter a more sympathetic reception from mature consumers if packages are designed to be sensitive to physical limitations. Packages are often awkward and difficult to manage, especially for those who are frail or arthritic. Also, many serving sizes are not geared to smaller families, widows, and other people living alone, and coupons tend to be for family-sized products rather than for single servings.

Some mature consumers have difficulty with pull-tab cans and push-open milk cartons. Ziploc packages and clear plastic wrap are also difficult to handle. Packages need to be easier to read and should be made lighter and smaller. Finally, designers need to pay attention to contrasting colours. A slight yellowing of the lens in the eye as one ages makes it harder to see background colours on packages. Discerning between blues, greens, and violets becomes especially difficult. The closer identifying-type colours are to the package's or advertisement's background colour, the less visible they are and the less attention they will command.[105]

The needs of aging baby boomers and their parents are pushing changes in product design. The Canadian Standards Association developed voluntary "Design for Aging Guidelines" to help companies design better products, services, and environments for Canada's aging population. Cuisipro offers chic, user-friendly measuring cups and spoons designed by Canadian Helen Kerr.[106] Specialty hotels, such as the Point Pleasant Lodge chain located close to major health centres in Halifax, cater to people who need medical attention and their support persons. Some specially equipped rooms accommodate physically challenged guests.

Carmakers are at the forefront of adapting their products to the needs of the mature market. General Motors formed a group called the Paragon Team that studies the needs of aging car buyers, and Ford has a similar group of engineers and designers called the Third Age Suit. GM redesigned some Oldsmobile models to include bigger buttons and clearer dashboard displays, and Cadillac's rearview mirrors automatically dim when hit by headlights. The Lincoln Town Car (the average age of a Lincoln driver is 67) features two sets of radio and air-conditioning controls, one on the dashboard and one on the steering wheel, because older drivers have trouble shifting attention from controls to the road. Chrysler engineers are experimenting with collision control systems that sound an alarm when a driver is too close to another car.[107]

Mature Marketing Messages

Mature consumers respond positively to ads that provide an abundance of information. Unlike other age groups, these consumers usually are not amused or persuaded by image-oriented advertising. A more successful strategy involves advertising that depicts mature consumers as well-integrated, contributing members of society, with emphasis on expanding their horizons rather than clinging precariously to life. In 2005, for example, a Leger Marketing survey showed that their preferred images for RRSP and investment ads included grandchildren, travel planning, and regular people talking straight about investing.[108] Some basic guidelines have been suggested for effective advertising to mature consumers:[109]

- Keep language simple.
- Use clear, bright pictures.
- Use action to attract attention.
- Speak clearly, and keep the word count low.
- Use a single sales message, and emphasize brand extensions to tap consumers' familiarity.
- Avoid extraneous stimuli (i.e., excessive pictures and graphics that detract from the message).

Net Profit

Canadians are heavy internet users, according to two Canadian studies. Canada Online, a survey of 3000 people over the age of 18, revealed that adults spend about 14 hours per week surfing; a large majority are seeking information. One-third read internet news daily. Another study entitled "Young Canadians in a Wired World" showed a different profile for younger Canadians. The survey of more than 5000 Grade 4 to Grade 11 students revealed that they gravitate to user-created content that connects them with friends. While the internet has become part of the everyday routine of adults, it's become an extension of the lives of Canadian youth.[110] Interestingly, women over 40 are the fastest-growing segment among online gamers; they spend about 10 hours per week playing web games.[111]

Ipsos-Reid found that Canadians over the age of 55 are the fastest-growing and wealthiest segment online, thanks to improved accessibility from technological advances. Keeping in touch with their children and grandchildren who may be scattered all over the world is a great attraction. These consumers also seek information on health, travel, finances, retirement living, and even dating.[112] Sites related to genealogy, coupons, and news/research are also of interest.[113]

Marketing Opportunity

Some Canadian manufacturers are redesigning their products aimed at **all** age groups following feedback from mature consumers. For example, Tylenol's (**www.tylenol.com**) redesigned big red cap with ridges for easy turning is endorsed by the Arthritis Society of Canada. Minute Maid of Toronto has an Easy-Peel Ring on frozen-juice containers. Kraft Canada won an award for its package for Country Time iced-tea mix, which features legible type and a lid that is easy to open and doubles as a measuring container.[114]

CHAPTER SUMMARY

PEOPLE HAVE MANY THINGS IN COMMON WITH OTHERS MERELY BECAUSE THEY ARE ABOUT THE SAME AGE.

- Consumers who grew up at the same time share many cultural memories and belong to the same age cohort, so they may respond well to marketers' nostalgia appeals that remind them of these experiences. Four important age cohorts are teens, university students, baby boomers, and mature consumers.

TEENS ARE AN IMPORTANT AGE SEGMENT FOR MARKETERS. THEY ARE UNDERGOING MANY CHANGES THAT INFLUENCE THEIR BEHAVIOUR AS CONSUMERS.

- Teenagers are making a transition from childhood to adulthood, and their self-concepts tend to be unstable. They are receptive to products that help them to be accepted and enable them to assert their independence. Because many teens earn money but have few financial obligations, they are a particularly important segment for many non-essential or expressive products, ranging from chewing gum to clothing fashions and music. Due to changes in family structure, many teens are also taking more responsibility for their families' day-to-day shopping and routine purchase decisions. University students are an important but hard-to-reach market. In many cases they are living alone for the first time, so they are making important decisions about setting up a household. Tweens are an increasingly important market segment; children aged 9 to 14 who are making the

transition from childhood to adolescence are influential purchasers of clothing, CDs, and other "feel-good" products. Many young people belong to youth tribes that influence their lifestyles and product preferences.

BABY BOOMERS CONTINUE TO BE THE MOST POWERFUL AGE SEGMENT ECONOMICALLY.

- As baby boomers age, their interests, as well as marketing priorities, change. The needs and desires of baby boomers affect demand for housing, child care, cars, clothing, and many other products and services.

MATURE CONSUMERS WILL INCREASE IN IMPORTANCE AS A MARKET SEGMENT.

- As the population ages, the needs of mature consumers will also become increasingly influential. Many marketers traditionally ignored this age segment due to the stereotype that they are too inactive and spend too little. This stereotype is no longer accurate. Many older adults are healthy, vigorous, and interested in new products and experiences—and they have the income to purchase them. Marketing appeals to this age subculture should focus on consumers' self-concepts and perceived ages, which tend to be more youthful than their chronological ages. Marketers should also emphasize concrete benefits of products because this group tends to be sceptical of vague, image-related promotions.

KEY TERMS

Age cohort p. 435	Generation X p. 446	Perceived age p. 450
Baby boomer p. 446	Generation Y p. 438	Social aging theories p. 451
Connexity p. 441	Gerontographics p. 451	Tweens p. 442
Coolhunters p. 444	Mature market p. 449	

REVIEW QUESTIONS

1. What is an age cohort, and why is it of interest to marketers?
2. List three basic conflicts teens face and give an example of each.
3. How are Gen Y kids different from their older brothers and sisters?
4. Who are tweens, and why are so many marketers interested in them?

5. How do tribal gatherings represent a marketing opportunity?
6. What are some of the most efficient ways for marketers to connect with university students?
7. What is a reward car, and who buys this type of vehicle?
8. What are some industries that stand to benefit most from the increasing affluence and vitality of the mature market?
9. What are some effective ways to segment the mature market?

In addition to the direct demand for products and services created by this age group, these consumers have also created a new baby boom of their own to keep marketers busy in the future. Because fertility rates have dropped, this new boom is not as big as the one that created the baby boom generation; the new upsurge in the number of births can best be described as a *baby boom echo*. Many couples postponed marriage and parenthood due to the new emphasis on careers for women. They began having babies in their late twenties and early thirties, resulting in fewer (but perhaps more pampered) children per family. This new emphasis on children and the family created opportunities for products such as cars (e.g., the success of the "minivan" and SUV concept among "soccer moms"), services (e.g., daycare), and media (e.g., magazines such as *Today's Parent*).

THE MATURE MARKET

The old woman sits alone in her dark apartment while the television blares out a soap opera. Once every couple of days she slowly and painfully opens her triple-locked door with arthritic hands and ventures out to the corner store to buy essentials like tea, milk, and cereal, always being sure to pick the least expensive brand. Most of the time she sits in her rocking chair, thinking sadly of her dead husband and the good times they used to have together.

Is this the image you have of a typical mature consumer? Until recently, many marketers did. As a result they largely neglected these consumers in their feverish pursuit of the baby boomer market. But as our population ages and people live longer and healthier lives, the game is changing rapidly. A lot of businesses are beginning to replace the old stereotype of the poor recluse. The newer, more accurate image is of a mature consumer who is active, interested in what life has to offer, and who is an enthusiastic customer with the means and willingness to buy many goods and services.[78] This market is growing even as we speak![79]

Economic Clout

The **mature market** consists of approximately 6.8 million people aged 55 and older. For many purposes these consumers are classified as "senior citizens" when they reach the age of 65 and their Canada Pension Plan benefits begin.[80] The number of Canadians 65 and older more than doubled to 4.2 million over the last 25 years, composing about 13 percent of the population. Statistics Canada predicts that they will make up 19 percent of the population in 2021 and 25 percent in 2041. Among the provinces, Saskatchewan has the highest proportion of seniors, at almost 15 percent; Alberta has 10 percent, the lowest proportion, but this number is growing due to the attraction of fewer taxes and more benefits in that province. Yukon, Nunavut, and Northwest Territories have less than 7 percent of their populations in the 65-plus age group.[81]

Overall, the mature market is the second-fastest-growing market segment in Canada, lagging behind only the baby boomers. Such dramatic growth can be explained largely by improved medical diagnoses and treatment and the resulting increase in life expectancy. Given the economic clout of senior consumers, it's often surprising how many marketers ignore them in favour of younger buyers—even though they are among the most loyal of any segment. Older consumers repurchase a brand more frequently, consider fewer brands and dealers, and choose long-established brands more often.[82] This is certainly true in the world of television advertising, where most companies salivate to attract the segment of 18 to 34 year olds.[83] The over-50 market accounts for about 55 percent of discretionary spending power and 80 percent of personal wealth in Canada. However, less than 5 percent of advertising addresses this market, which represents less than 5 percent of respondents in marketing research.

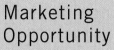

Marketing Opportunity

As the oldest members of the baby boom generation move into their late fifties, businesses are cashing in. Female menopause begins on average at the age of 51, and a new frankness about this life change has led to a boom in self-help books, estrogen supplements, and exercise classes.[84] Men are not immune to life changes, either, as many fall prey to so-called male menopause.

Marketers are eager to provide solutions to "menopausal" men's social anxieties. The Hair Club for Men (*www.hairclub.com*) has about 40 000 members who have received new heads of hair with the help of "hair-replacement engineers." Plastic surgeons also report a sharp rise in the number of men electing to have cosmetic surgery, including nose jobs and liposuction (see Chapter 5).

A popular stereotype in our culture is of the man who deals with a "mid-life crisis" by buying a sports car. Today, many women are joining the club by buying a car to mark their freedom from hauling kids around to soccer games. Sales of "reward cars" (as the industry calls them) among women over 45 are skyrocketing; the number who purchased cars in the niche known as "mid-sized sporty," which includes two-door models such as the Mazda RX-8 and the Chrysler Crossfire, is up 277 percent since 2000. Among women aged 45 and older who earn at least $100 000, sales of smaller luxury cars, such as the BMW 3 Series and the Audi A4, are up 93 percent. As one woman who just splurged on a snazzy Mercedes explained, "I'm just celebrating my life."[85]

Values are very general ideas about good and bad goals. From these flow **norms**, or rules dictating what is right or wrong, acceptable or unacceptable. Some norms, called *enacted norms,* such as the rule that a green traffic light means "go" and a red one means "stop," are explicitly decided upon. Many norms, however, are much more subtle. These *crescive norms* are embedded in a culture and are discovered only through interaction with other members of that culture. Crescive norms include the following:[7]

- A **custom** is a norm handed down from the past that controls basic behaviours, such as division of labour in a household or the practice of particular ceremonies.

- A **more** is a custom with a strong moral overtone. A more often involves a taboo, or forbidden behaviour, such as incest or cannibalism. Violation of a more often meets with strong punishment from other members of a society.

- **Conventions** are norms regarding the conduct of everyday life. These rules deal with the subtleties of consumer behaviour, including the "correct" way to furnish one's house, wear one's clothes, host a dinner party, and so on.

All three types of crescive norms may operate to define completely a culturally appropriate behaviour. For example, a more may tell us what kind of food is permissible to eat. (Note that mores vary across cultures, so a meal of dog may be taboo in Canada, while Hindus shun steaks and Muslims avoid pork products.) A custom dictates the appropriate hour at which the meal should be served. Conventions tell us how to eat it, including such details as the utensils to be used, table etiquette, and the appropriate apparel to be worn at dinner time.

We often take these conventions for granted (again, until we travel to a foreign country!), assuming that they are the "right" things to do. And it is good to remember that much of what we know about these norms is learned *vicariously* (see Chapter 3), as we observe the behaviours of actors and actresses in television commercials, sitcoms, print ads, and other popular-culture media.

Cultural differences show up in all kinds of daily activities. For example, when a Big Boy restaurant first opened in Thailand it had great difficulty attracting customers. After interviewing hundreds of people, the company found out why. Some said the restaurant's "room energy" was bad and that the food was unfamiliar. Others said the Big Boy statue (like the one Dr. Evil rode in the Austin Powers movies) made them nervous. One of the restaurant's executives commented, "It suddenly dawned on me that, here I was, trying to get a 3500-year-old culture to eat 64-year-old food." Now, after the company put some Thai items on the menu, business is picking up.[8] No word yet on the fate of the statue!

MYTHS AND RITUALS

Every culture develops stories and practices that help its members to make sense of the world. When we examine these activities in other cultures, they often seem strange or even unfathomable. Yet our *own* cultural practices appear quite normal—even though a visitor may find them equally bizarre.

To appreciate how "primitive" belief systems that some may consider irrational or superstitious continue to influence our supposedly "modern," rational society, consider the avid interest of many consumers in magic. Marketers of health foods, anti-aging cosmetics, exercise programs, and gambling casinos often imply that their offerings have "magical" properties that will ward off sickness, old age, poverty, or just plain bad luck. People by the millions play their "lucky numbers" in the lottery and carry rabbits' feet and other amulets to ward off "the evil eye," and many have "lucky" clothing or other items they believe will bring them good fortune. Software developers even supply "wizards" that help to guide the uninitiated through the arcane layers of their programs!

An interest in the occult tends to be popular when members of a society feel overwhelmed or powerless. Magical remedies simplify our lives by giving us "easy" answers. Even a computer is regarded with awe by many consumers as a sort of "electronic magician," with the ability to solve our problems (or, in other cases, to make data magically disappear!).[9] This section discusses myths and rituals, two aspects of culture common to all societies from the ancients to the modern world.

Myths

Every society possesses a set of myths that define that culture. A **myth** is a story containing symbolic elements that expresses the shared emotions and ideals of a culture. The story often features some kind of conflict between two opposing forces, and its outcome serves as a moral guide for people. In this way, a myth reduces anxiety by providing consumers with guidelines about their world.

Most members of a culture learn these stories, but usually we don't really think about their origins. Consider, for example, a story familiar to all of us: *Little Red Riding Hood*. This myth started as a peasants' tale in sixteenth-century France, where a girl meets a werewolf on her way to granny's house (there is historical evidence for a plague of wolf attacks during this time, including several incidents where men were put on trial for transforming themselves into the deadly but mythical animals). The werewolf has already killed granny, stored her flesh in the pantry, and poured her blood into a bottle. Contrary to the version we know, when the girl arrives at the house, she snacks on granny, strips naked, and climbs into bed with the wolf!

This story first appeared in print in 1697; it was intended as a warning to the loose ladies of Louis XIV's court (the author puts the story's lead character in red in this version because this colour symbolizes harlots). Eventually the Brothers Grimm offered their own version in 1812, but they substituted violence for sex in order to scare kids into behaving. And, to reinforce the sex-role standards of that time, in the Grimm version a man rescues the girl from the wolf.[10]

An understanding of cultural myths is important to marketers, who in some cases (most likely unconsciously) pattern their strategies along mythic structures. Consider, for example, the way that a company like McDonald's takes on "mythical" qualities.[11] The "Golden Arches" are a universally recognized symbol, one that is virtually synonymous with North American culture. They offer sanctuary to North Americans around the world, who know exactly what to expect once they enter. Basic struggles involving good versus evil are played out in the fantasy world created by McDonald's advertising, as when Ronald McDonald confounds the Hamburglar. McDonald's even has a "seminary" (Hamburger University) where inductees go to learn appropriate behaviours.

Corporations often have myths and legends as a part of their history, and some make a deliberate effort to be sure newcomers to the organization learn these. Nike

← Some advertisements borrow imagery from fairy tales to tell a story about a product. This Reebok ad substitutes an athletic shoe for a glass slipper in a twist on the Cinderella story.
Used with permission of Reebok.

designates senior executives as "corporate storytellers" who explain the company's heritage to other employees, including the hourly workers at Nike stores. They tell stories about the founders of Nike (***www.nike.com***), including the coach of the Oregon track team who poured rubber into his family waffle iron to make better shoes for his team—the origin of the Nike waffle sole. The stories emphasize the dedication of runners and coaches involved with the company to reinforce the importance of teamwork. Rookies even visit the tracks where the coaches worked to be sure they grasp the importance of the Nike legends.[12]

Myths serve the following four interrelated functions in a culture:[13]

1. *Metaphysical:* They help to explain the origins of existence.

2. *Cosmological:* They emphasize that all components of the universe are part of a single picture.

3. *Sociological:* They maintain social order by authorizing a social code to be followed by members of a culture.

4. *Psychological:* They provide models for personal conduct.

Myths can be analyzed by examining their underlying structures, a technique pioneered by the anthropologist Claude Lévi-Strauss (no relation to the blue jeans company). Lévi-Strauss noted that many stories involve **binary opposition**, in which two opposing ends of some dimension are represented (good versus evil or nature versus technology). Characters and, in some cases, products are often defined by what they are not rather than what they are (e.g., "This is not your father's Oldsmobile," and "I can't believe it's not butter").

Recall from the discussion of Freudian theory in Chapter 6 that the ego functions as a kind of "referee" between the opposing needs of the id and the superego. In a similar fashion, the conflict between mythical opposing forces is sometimes resolved by a *mediating figure* who can link the opposites by sharing characteristics of each. For example, many myths contain animals that have human abilities (e.g., a talking snake) to bridge the gap between humanity and nature, just as cars (technology) are often given animal names like Cougar, Cobra, or Mustang.

MYTHS ABOUND IN POPULAR CULTURE

Although we generally equate myths with the ancient Greeks or Romans, modern myths are embodied in many aspects of modern popular culture, including comic books, movies, holidays, and, yes, even commercials.

Comic-book superheroes demonstrate how myths can be communicated to consumers of all ages in order to teach a lesson about a culture. For example, Marvel Comics' Spiderman character tells stories about balancing the obligations of being a superhero with the need of his alter ego, Peter Parker, to do his homework.[14] Indeed, some of these fictional figures represent a **monomyth**—a myth that is common to many cultures.[15] The most prevalent monomyth involves a hero who emerges from the everyday world with supernatural powers and wins a decisive victory over evil forces. He then returns with the power to bestow good things on his fellow people.

Many blockbuster movies and hit television shows draw directly on mythic themes. Although dramatic special effects or attractive stars certainly don't hurt, a number of these movies perhaps owe their success also to their presentation of characters and plot structures that follow mythic patterns. Three examples of these mythic blockbusters are as follows:[16]

- *Gone with the Wind:* Myths are often set in times of upheaval, such as war. In this story, the American North (which represents technology and democracy) is pitted against the American South (which represents nature and aristocracy). The novel and movie depict a romantic era (the *antebellum* South) where love and honour were virtues. This era is replaced by the newer forces of materialism and industrialization (i.e., modern consumer culture). *Gone with the Wind* depicts a lost era when humankind and nature existed in harmony.

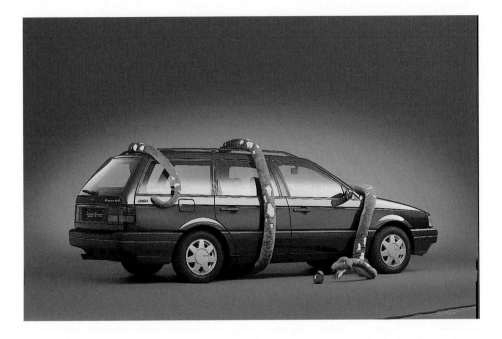

- *E.T.:* E.T. represents a familiar myth involving Messianic visitation. The gentle creature from another world visits Earth and performs miracles (e.g., reviving a dying flower). His "disciples" are neighbourhood children who help him combat the forces of modern technology and an unbelieving secular society. The metaphysical function of myth is served by teaching that the humans chosen by God are pure and unselfish.

- *Star Trek:* The television series and movies documenting the adventures of the starship *Enterprise* are also linked to myths, such as the story of the New England Puritans exploring and conquering a new continent— "the final frontier." Encounters with the Klingons mirror skirmishes with American Native peoples. In addition, the quest for paradise was a theme employed in at least 13 of the original 79 episodes filmed.[17]

Commercials can be analyzed also in terms of the underlying mythic themes they represent. For example, commercials for Pepperidge Farm ask consumers to "remember" the good old days (lost paradise) when products were wholesome and natural. The theme of the underdog prevailing over the stronger foe (i.e., David and Goliath) has been used by Chrysler and Avis.[18]

Rituals

A **ritual** is a set of symbolic behaviours that occur in a fixed sequence and that tend to be repeated periodically.[19] Although bizarre tribal ceremonies, perhaps involving animal or virgin sacrifice, may come to mind when people think of rituals, in reality many contemporary consumer activities are ritualistic. Just think of Whitney's daily "mental health" trip to Starbucks.

Rituals can occur at a variety of levels, as noted in Table 16–1. Some affirm broad cultural or religious values, while others occur in small groups or even in isolation. Market researchers discovered, for example, that for many people the act of late-night ice cream eating has ritualistic overtones, often involving a favourite spoon and bowl![20] And rituals are not always set in stone; they can be modified to change with the times. The custom of throwing rice to symbolize fertility at weddings is evolving. In recent years, many newlyweds have substituted soap bubbles or jingling bells because of the tendency of birds to eat the rice, which can then expand inside their bodies and cause injury or death. Some enterprising businesses

TABLE 16–1

TYPES OF RITUAL EXPERIENCE

Primary Behaviour Source	Ritual Type	Examples
Cosmology	Religious	Baptism, meditation, mass
Cultural values	Rites of passage	Graduation, marriage
	Cultural	Festivals, holidays (Valentine's Day)
Group learning	Civic	Parades, elections, trials
	Group	Business negotiations, office luncheons
	Family	Mealtimes, bedtimes, birthdays, Mother's Day, Christmas
Individual aims and emotions	Personal	Grooming, household rituals

Source: Dennis W. Rook, "The Ritual Dimension of Consumer Behavior," *Journal of Consumer Research* 12 (December 1985): 251–264. Reprinted with permission of The University of Chicago Press.

are springing up to work around this problem. One company sells a product called Bio Wedding Rice—reconstituted rice that dissolves in water and doesn't harm birds.[21] Another company, the Hole-in-Hand Butterfly Farm in Pennsylvania, ships newly hatched butterflies at $100 a dozen. They arrive in dark, cool envelopes that keep them in a resting stage until the package is opened, when they fly out in a crescendo of wagging wings.

Many businesses owe their livelihood to their ability to supply **ritual artifacts**—items used in the performance of rituals—to consumers. Birthday candles, diplomas, specialized foods and beverages (wedding cakes, ceremonial wine, or even hot dogs at the ball park), trophies and plaques, band costumes, and retirement watches are all used in consumer rituals. In addition, consumers often employ ritual scripts that identify the artifacts, the sequence in which they are used, and who uses them. Examples include graduation programs and etiquette books.

Perhaps one of the most successful and successfully exported ritual artifacts is the diamond ring for engagements and weddings. Until 1993, there was no such thing as a diamond wedding band or engagement ring in China. Then, with the slogan "Zuan shi heng jiu yuan, yi ke yong liu chuan," retail sales of diamonds in China reached $1.5 billion by 2004. The Chinese have become convinced that the jewellery purchase is a form of saving and are now spending an average of $600 on wedding diamonds.[22]

GROOMING RITUALS

Whether it is brushing your hair 100 strokes a day or talking to yourself in the mirror, virtually all consumers undergo private grooming rituals. These are sequences of behaviours that aid in the transition from the private self to the public self or back again. These rituals serve various purposes, ranging from inspiring confidence before confronting the world to cleansing the body of dirt and other profane materials.

When consumers talk about their grooming rituals, some of the dominant themes that emerge from these stories reflect the almost mystical qualities attributed to grooming products and behaviours. Many people emphasize a before-and-

Reality Check ✓

Rituals can provide us with a sense of order and security. In a study of the drinking rituals of university students, the researchers found that drinking imposed order in students' daily lives—from the completion of assignments to what and when to eat. In addition, ritualizing an activity such as drinking provided security and fellowship at a time fraught with confusion and turbulent change. Obviously, though, there's a dark side to drinking rituals. Indeed, although binge drinking is probably the most widely practised ritual among university students, it also has been described as the most significant health hazard on campuses today.[26]

What role does drinking play in the social life on your campus? Based on your experience, how does it fit into rituals of university life? Should these practices be changed? If so, how?

> Drinking plays a very important role in the social life here. Students enjoy a few pints after handing in a project, doing a presentation, or sitting an exam. It's seen as a type of reward for work done. It is particularly so when students feel under pressure, whether due to personal problems or college issues.... Students are proud of their drinking "talents" and "abilities" and often display empty bottles on the windowsill or build a wall of empty cans. Of course, it should not be like this, but it is practically impossible to change. Going to college is a rite of passage into young adulthood and drinking is one form of expressing this. Students are no longer living at home and have just reached the legal drinking age, which is 18 here in Ireland, so of course major drinking sessions are expected of them by fellow students.

Pamela Gillen, Dublin City University, Ireland

> Drinking does seem to be linked to ritualistic behaviour for many college students. Weekends begin Thursday nights and end on Saturday. For many, drinking has become a ritual by rewarding both achievements and failures. Many students drink after a hard week of exams, to celebrate a new job, or to relax after a stressful paper. It is often a time to build relationships and enjoy the freedom of college life.... The importance of having a sober ride, having fun at a party without alcohol, and the effects of peer pressure and drinking should be stressed to students. Drinking helps many students unwind and helps develop relationships with other students. Together, these make the student more successful in college. It may not be right for every student, but it's an important aspect of college life that would be difficult to remove.

Jennifer Freet, George Mason University, USA

> Drinking seems to be part of Japanese culture, which is not only practised by young college students but also by many of the businessmen of Japan. I think in Japanese culture there are not many times where people speak frankly about each other and about their thoughts. And in such situations alcohol plays an important role. What is a common ritual in Japan is, when you are served a drink from your elderly, you are not to refuse it. And when the elderly has nothing to drink, the others are to fill up their cup. And in each of these cases, not finishing a drink is considered to be rude. This is practised heavily among the sports clubs in Japanese colleges. This seems to increase the amounts of drinking, but by drinking, people are allowed to become frank to the elderly, which is not allowed when they are not drunk. This allows these people to have a better relationship than without drinks.

Ayano Yamada, Keio University, Japan

> Alcohol consumption plays a big role in the lives of many UAF students. Many view Fairbanks, Alaska, as an isolated and boring place to live with not much to do here. Students drink to socialize, make friends, and oftentimes just to get drunk. Not a single event goes by without drinking alcohol. Among the most popular drinking rituals is Case Day.... The Case Day ritual involves each individual drinking a case of beer in 24 hours (one beer per hour). During that day, most of the students on campus are "hammered." Many students even walk around with marks on their arms to prove, or keep track of, how many drinks they have had so far. I don't think the drinking rituals at the UAF campus should be changed. They don't hurt anyone. Sooner or later, most young people have this experience anyway. Most do realize there are more important things in life than "getting wasted" with friends. As for the ones that don't realize it, oh well, we all make choices in life.

Dmitri Batsev, University of Alaska, USA

after phenomenon, whereby the person feels magically transformed after using certain products (similar to the Cinderella myth).[23]

Two sets of binary oppositions that are expressed in personal rituals are *private–public* and *work–leisure*. Many beauty rituals, for instance, reflect transformations from natural states to the social world (as when a woman "puts on her face") or vice versa. In these daily rituals, women reaffirm the value placed by their culture on personal beauty and the quest for eternal youth.[24] This focus is obvious in ads for Oil of Olay Beauty Cleanser, which proclaim "And so your day begins. The Ritual of Oil of Olay." Similarly, the bath is viewed as a sacred, cleansing time, a way to wash away the sins of the profane world.[25]

GIFT-GIVING RITUALS

The promotion of appropriate gifts for every conceivable holiday and occasion provides an excellent example of the influence consumer rituals can exert on marketing phenomena. In the **gift-giving ritual** consumers procure the perfect object (artifact), meticulously remove the price tag (symbolically changing the item from a commodity to a unique good), carefully wrap it, and deliver it to the recipient.[27] In addition, making gifts or cards further personalizes the gift-exchange process.

Gift giving is viewed by researchers primarily as a form of *economic exchange,* in which the giver transfers an item of value to a recipient, who in turn is obligated to reciprocate. However, gift giving can also involve *symbolic exchange,* wherein the giver is motivated by unselfish factors, such as love or admiration, and does not expect anything in return. Some research indicates that gift giving evolves as a form of social expression; it is more exchange-oriented (instrumental) in the early stages of a relationship but becomes more altruistic as the relationship develops.[28] One set of researchers identified multiple ways in which giving a gift can affect a relationship. These are listed in Table 16–2.[29]

Every culture prescribes certain occasions and ceremonies for giving gifts, whether for personal or professional reasons. The giving of birthday presents alone is a major undertaking, and business gifts are an important component in defining professional relationships. Expenditures on business gifts are an important part of doing business, and great care is often taken to ensure that the appropriate gifts are purchased (sometimes with the aid of professional gift consultants). Most executives believe that corporate gift giving provides both tangible and intangible results, including improved employee morale and higher sales.[30]

TABLE 16–2

EFFECTS OF GIFT GIVING ON SOCIAL RELATIONSHIPS

Relational Effect	Description	Example
Strengthening	Gift giving improves the quality of a relationship	An unexpected gift such as one given in a romantic situation
Affirmation	Gift giving validates the positive quality of a relationship	Usually occurs on ritualized occasions such as birthdays
Negligible Effect	Gift giving has a minimal effect on perceptions of relationship quality	Non-formal gift occasions and those where the gift may be perceived as charity or too good for the current state of the relationship
Negative Confirmation	Gift giving validates a negative quality of a relationipn between the gift giver and receiver	The selection of the gift is inappropriate, indicating a lack of knowledge of the receiver; alternatively, the gift is viewed as a method of controlling the receiver
Weakening	Gift giving harms the quality of the relationship between giver and receiver	When there are "strings attached" or the gift is perceived as a bribe, a sign of disrespect, or offensive
Severing	Gift giving harms the the relationship between the giver and receiver to the extent that the relationship is dissolved	When the gift forms part of a larger problem, such as when threatening a relationship, or when a relationship is severed through the receipt of a "parting" gift

Source: Adapted from Julie A. Ruth, Cele C. Otnes, and Frederic F. Brunel, "Gift Receipt and the Reformulation of Interpersonal Relationships," *Journal of Consumer Research* 25 (March 1999): 385–402, Table 1, p. 389.

← Weddings are occasions for gift-giving rituals. Bass River offers a variety of solutions for gifts. *Courtesy of Bass River.*

The gift-giving ritual has three distinct stages:[31]

1. During *gestation,* the giver is motivated by an event to procure a gift. This event may be either *structural* (i.e., prescribed by the culture, as when people buy Christmas presents) or *emergent* (i.e., the decision is more personal and idiosyncratic).

2. The second stage is *presentation,* or the process of gift exchange. The recipient responds to the gift (either appropriately or not), and the donor evaluates this response.

3. In the third stage, known as *reformulation,* the bonds between the giver and receiver are adjusted (either looser or tighter) to reflect the new relationship that emerges after the exchange is complete. Negativity can arise if the recipient feels the gift is inappropriate or of inferior quality. For example, the hapless husband who gives his wife a vacuum cleaner as an anniversary present is asking for trouble, as is the new suitor who gives his girlfriend intimate apparel. The donor may feel the response to the gift was inadequate or insincere, or a violation of the **reciprocity norm**, which obliges people to return the gesture of a gift with one of equal value.[32] Both participants may feel resentful for being "forced" to participate in the ritual.[33]

In addition to expressing their feelings toward others through consumption, people commonly find (or devise) reasons to give themselves something as well. It is common for consumers to purchase **self-gifts** as a way to regulate their behaviour. This ritual provides a socially acceptable way of rewarding themselves for

→A Canadian Tire (*www.canadiantire.com*) gift certificate diminishes the giver's fear of buying inappropriate gifts, while at the same time offering diverse choices to the recipient.
Courtesy of Canadian Tire. Information presented represents historical information only.

How to say thank you 95,000 different ways

A simple thank you means a lot to your employees and valued customers. And when you show your appreciation with Canadian Tire Gift Certificates, it's like saying thank you 95,000 different ways. That's how many items Canadian Tire carries. With a selection like this, Gift Certificate recipients can choose the gift that suits them from a wide range of automotive, sports and leisure or home and hardware items.

Available in $5, $10, $25, $50 and $100 denominations, Canadian Tire Gift Certificates are welcomed at 430 Canadian Tire stores across the country. Gift Certificates are easy for your company to administer—there are no handling charges, redemption fees or mailing costs and there's no expiry date.

Canadian Tire Gift Certificates are easy to order. Ask about our volume discount.
Call us at **1-800-529-7092.**
Visit our website: www.canadiantire.ca
Or e-mail us at: giftcertificates@cantire.com

Still the right place

Net Profit

For better or worse, the web is transforming the age-old ritual of the buying of wedding gifts. Numerous online gift registries take the guesswork out of buying that perfect toaster for the new couple. These sites collect a referral fee from a retailer if a purchase is made.[34] Although registries have been around since the early 1930s, they used to be more subtle. Competition for the matrimonial market is fierce, so registry sites are scrambling to offer new incentives that will engage the engaged. At *www.theknot.com* the couple can even subsidize their honeymoon airfare: They earn frequent-flyer points for every dollar their guests spend on them. At *www.weddingchannel.com*, the lucky couple can create a personal wedding page where they post directions and pictures, plan toasts and seating arrangements, and tell stories about how they met. Guests pull up updated versions of a gift registry and purchase from retailers directly through the website. The Wedding Channel hopes to track its customers (assuming they stay married...) and create registries as they celebrate anniversaries and the arrival of babies (uh-oh, need another gift!). One of the site's executives says, "Once I have you, unless you stop me, you are a demographic dream."[35]

The proliferation of these registries is understandable, given that this business now takes in US$19 billion a year. The average wedding party includes 12 people (including six who get stuck with those awful dresses) plus 150 guests. On average, the bride and groom register for more than 50 products and receive an average of 171 wedding gifts.[36] About half the couples register at a place they have never shopped before, giving retailers a new customer base. According to the publisher of *Bride's Magazine*, "If you can hook this consumer when she is in this life stage, you will fundamentally brand her for life." Wedding registries continue to evolve; some couples have become so brazen they are requesting specific shares of stock (at *www.oneshare.com*), contributions to fund an around-the-world trip, or even mortgage payments on that new dream house.

Of course, there are downsides to this new efficiency: Because the wedding couple specifies exactly what they want in advance, the giver doesn't really have to know very much about the recipients. Part of gift giving should be developing or reinforcing a symbolic relationship, but now the process is much more automated. As one etiquette expert disdainfully points out, in the old days (pre-net) people were supposed to be "zealous with creativity" when selecting a gift. "Now, it's just gimme, gimme, gimme with a dollar amount attached." And in many cases the registry is listed on the invitation itself—a social no-no.[37] Registries also eliminate the likelihood of getting homemade or creative gifts.

The idea of sharing your specific material needs with friends and loved ones is expanding well beyond nuptials. Now a cottage industry of registries is springing up to enable consumers of all stripes to specify their desires online and then sit back to wait for the products to roll in. These registries include:[38]

> *www.twodaydreamers.com* for doll collectors
> All Nations Stamp and Coin for philatelists and numismatists
> The Wishing Well for motorboat parts and supplies
> Clinique, Prescriptives, and Bobbi Brown for lipstick and cosmetics
> Restoration Hardware and Goodwood for furniture and home supplies
> *www.officemax.com* for back-to-school shoppers who need to know what teachers require their students to have on the first day of class

good deeds, consoling themselves after negative events, or motivating themselves to accomplish some goal.[39] Indeed, retailers report that it is becoming increasingly common for people to treat themselves while they are ostensibly searching for goodies for others. As one shopper admitted recently, "It's one for them, one for me, one for them."[40]

The latest prenuptial ritual replaces balloons with beer. A visit to **www.daddytypes.com** reveals that the "man shower" is a hot chat-room topic. Instead of games, a man shower may have a backyard barbecue with the guys standing around the grill discussing the mysteries of the last trimester of pregnancy and the anxiety of becoming a father.[41]

HOLIDAY RITUALS

On holidays, consumers step back from their everyday lives and perform ritualistic behaviours unique to those times.[42] Holiday occasions are filled with ritual artifacts and scripts, and are increasingly cast by enterprising marketers as times for giving gifts. The Thanksgiving holiday is filled with rituals; these scripts include serving (in gluttonous portions) foods like turkey and cranberry sauce that may be consumed only on that day, complaints about how much one has eaten (yet rising to the occasion to somehow find room for dessert), and (for many) a post-meal trip to the couch for the obligatory video. On Valentine's Day, standards regarding sex and love are relaxed or altered as people express feelings that may be hidden during the rest of the year.

In addition to established holidays, new occasions are invented to capitalize on the need for cards and other ritual artifacts that will then have to be acquired.[43]

These cultural events often originate with the greeting-card industry, which conveniently stimulates demand for more of its products. Some recently invented holidays include Secretaries' Day and Grandparents' Day.

Most cultural holidays are based on myths, and often real or imaginary characters (e.g., Cupid on Valentine's Day) are at the centre of the stories. These holidays persist because their basic elements appeal to consumers' deep-seated needs.[44] Two of our holidays that are especially rich, both in cultural symbolism and in consumption meanings, are Christmas and Halloween.

The Christmas holiday is bursting with myths and rituals, from adventures at the North Pole to those that occur under the mistletoe. The meaning of Christmas has evolved quite dramatically over the last few hundred years. Few Canadians

← These costumes worn at the Renaissaince Ball in Tours, France, are among the consumer artifacts that bring the rituals of a bygone era to life.
Courtesy of Judith Zaichkowsky

Multicultural Dimensions

The importance of gift-giving rituals is underscored by considering Japanese customs, wherein the wrapping of a gift is as important as (if not more so than) the gift itself. The economic value of a gift is secondary to its symbolic meaning.[45] To the Japanese, gifts are viewed as an important aspect of one's duty to others in one's social group. Giving is a moral imperative (known as *giri*).

Highly ritualized gift giving occurs during the giving of both household/personal gifts and company/professional gifts. Each Japanese has a well-defined set of relatives and friends (usually 15 to 20) with whom he or she shares reciprocal gift-giving obligations (*kosai*).[46] Japanese tourists to Prince Edward Island, Banff, Whistler, and Victoria are serviced by stores opened and operated by Japanese nationals. It is not uncommon for tourists to purchase five to ten of the same items to take home to Japan.

Personal gifts are given on social occasions, such as funerals, to people who are hospitalized, to mark movements from one life stage to another (e.g., weddings and birthdays), and as greetings (e.g., when one is meeting a visitor). Company gifts are given to commemorate the anniversary of a corporation's founding or the opening of a new building, and they are a routine part of doing business, as when rewards are given at trade meetings to announce new products.

In keeping with the Japanese emphasis on saving face, presents are not opened in front of the giver, so that it will not be necessary to hide one's possible disappointment with the present.

→The Coca-Cola Company claims credit for inventing the modern image of Santa, which it distributed in its advertising in 1931. Until that time (the company claims) Santa was pictured as a cartoonlike elf. More likely, the modern image of Santa Claus was shaped by the nineteenth-century cartoonist Thomas Nast, whose rendering of Santa was related to his other drawings of "fat cats" like Boss Tweed and the Robber Barons, greedy capitalists who exploited the poor and lived in useless luxury. This Thomas Nast cartoon was published in 1881. Despite this figure's resemblance to Santa Claus, it is actually a caricature of a "fat cat" Robber Baron who had accumulated a horde of worldly possessions.

Source: T. Nast, "Merry Old Santa Claus," in Russell W. Belk, Journal of American Culture (Spring 1987): 88. NorthWind Picture Archives. Jerry Schwartz, "At Age 104, Coke Congratulates Itself," New York Times (August 11, 1990): C30.

know that Boxing Day is derived from old England, where the rich "boxed" their leftovers for the poor the day after Christmas. One of the most important holiday rituals involves Santa Claus, a mythical figure eagerly awaited by children the world over. In opposition to Christ, Santa is a champion of materialism. Perhaps it is no coincidence, then, that he appears in stores and shopping malls—secular temples of consumption. Whatever his origins, the Santa Claus myth serves the purpose of socializing children by teaching them to expect rewards when they are good and that members of society get what they deserve.

Halloween is a holiday that has evolved from a pagan religious observance to a secular event. However, in contrast to Christmas, the rituals of Halloween (e.g., trick-or-treating and costume parties) primarily involve non-family members. Halloween is an unusual holiday because its rituals are the opposite of many other cultural occasions. Contrasting with Christmas, it celebrates evil instead of good and death rather than birth, and it encourages revellers to extort treats with veiled threats of "tricks" rather than rewarding only the good. Because of these oppositions, Halloween has been described as an *antifestival*, in which the symbols associated with other holidays are distorted. For example, the Halloween witch can be viewed as an inverted mother figure. The holiday also parodies the meaning of Easter, by stressing the resurrection of ghosts, and of Thanksgiving, by transforming the wholesome symbolism of the pumpkin pie into the evil jack-o-lantern.[47] Furthermore, Halloween provides a ritualized, and therefore socially sanctioned, context in which people can act out uncharacteristic behaviours and try on new roles: Children can go outside after dark, stay up late, and eat all the candy they like for a night. The otherwise geeky guy who always sits in the back of class comes dressed as Elvis and turns out to be the life of the party.

Halloween observances among adults are booming, changing the character of this holiday. Halloween is now the second most popular party night for adults (after New Year's Eve), and one in four grown-ups wears a costume.[48] The holiday is now becoming trendy in Europe as well, where the French in particular have discovered it as an occasion for festivities, dancing, and the chance to show off new fashions.[49]

RITES OF PASSAGE

Examples of modern **rites of passage** are special times marked by a change in social status. Every society, both primitive and modern, sets aside times where such changes occur. Some of these changes may occur as a natural part of consumers' life cycles (e.g., puberty or death), while others are more individual in nature (getting divorced and re-entering the dating market).

Much like the metamorphosis of a caterpillar into a butterfly, consumers' rites of passage consist of three phases.[50] The first stage, *separation*, occurs when the individual is detached from his or her original group or status (e.g., the university student leaves home). *Liminality* is the middle stage, where the person is literally in between statuses (the new arrival on campus tries to figure out what is happening during orientation week). The last stage, *aggregation*, takes place when the person re-enters society after the rite of passage is complete (the student returns home for summer vacation as a university "veteran").

Rites of passage mark many consumer activities. A similar transitional state can be observed when people are prepared for certain occupational roles. For example, athletes and fashion models typically undergo a "seasoning" process. They are removed from their normal surroundings (athletes are taken to training camps, while young models are often moved to Paris), indoctrinated into a new subculture, and then returned to the real world in their new role.

Funeral ceremonies help the living to organize their relationships with the deceased; action tends to be tightly scripted, right down to the costumes (the ritual black attire, black ribbons for mourners, and the body in its best suit) and specific behaviours (sending condolence cards or holding a wake). Mourners "pay their last respects," and seating during the ceremony is usually dictated by mourners' closeness to the individual. Even the cortège (the funeral motorcade) is accorded special status by other motorists, who recognize its separate, sacred nature by not cutting in line as it proceeds to the cemetery.[51]

SACRED AND PROFANE CONSUMPTION

As we saw when considering the structure of myths, many types of consumer activity involve the demarcation, or binary opposition, of boundaries, such as good versus bad, male versus female, or even regular versus low calorie. One of the most important of these sets of boundaries is the distinction between the sacred and the profane. **Sacred consumption** involves objects and events that are set apart from normal activities and are treated with some degree of respect or awe. They may or may not be associated with religion, but most religious items and events tend to be regarded as sacred. **Profane consumption** involves consumer objects and events that are ordinary, everyday objects and events that do not share the "specialness" of sacred ones. (Note that profane does *not* mean vulgar or obscene in this context.)

Domains of Sacred Consumption

Sacred consumption events permeate many aspects of consumers' experiences. We find ways to set apart a variety of places, people, and events. In this section we'll consider some examples of ways that "ordinary" consumption is sometimes not so ordinary after all.

SACRED PLACES

Sacred places have been set apart by a society because they have religious or mystical significance (Bethlehem, Mecca, and Stonehenge) or because they commemorate some aspect of a country's heritage (the Kremlin, the Emperor's Palace in Tokyo, and the Statue of Liberty). Remember that in many cases the sacredness of these places is due to the property of contamination; that is, something sacred happened on that spot, so the place itself takes on sacred qualities.

Still other places are created from the profane world and imbued with sacred qualities. Graumann's Chinese Theater in Hollywood, where movie stars leave their footprints in concrete for posterity, is one such place. Even the modern shopping mall can be regarded as a secular "cathedral of consumption," a special place where community members come to practise shopping rituals. Theme parks are a form of mass-produced fantasy that take on aspects of sacredness. In particular, Disney World and Disneyland (and their new outposts in Europe and Japan) are destinations for pilgrimages from consumers around the globe. Disney World displays many characteristics of more traditional sacred places. It is even regarded by some as having healing powers. A trip to the park is the most common last wish for terminally ill children.[52]

In many cultures the home is a particularly sacred place. It represents a crucial distinction between the harsh, external world and consumers' "inner space." Consumers all over the world go to great lengths to create special environments that allow them to create the quality of homeyness. This effect is created by personalizing the home as much as possible, using such devices as door wreaths, mantle arrangements, and a "memory wall" for family photos.[53] Even public places, like Starbucks cafés, strive for a home-like atmosphere that shelters customers from the harshness of the outside world.

SACRED PEOPLE

People themselves can be sacred when they are idolized and set apart from the masses. Souvenirs, memorabilia, and even mundane items touched or used by sacred people become valuable. Many businesses thrive on consumers' desire for products associated with famous people. There is a bustling marketplace for celebrity autographs and objects once owned by celebrities. Whether Princess Di's gowns or John Lennon's guitars, these touched objects are often sold at auction for astronomical prices.

SACRED EVENTS

For many people, the world of sports is sacred and almost assumes the status of a religion. The roots of modern sports events can be found in ancient religious rites, such as fertility festivals (e.g., the original Olympics).[54] The sports pages are like the Scriptures (we describe ardent fans as reading them "religiously"); the stadium is a house of worship; and the fans are members of the congregation. Devotees engage in group activities such as tailgate parties and the "wave," where participants rise on cue and move their arms (as at a revival meeting), creating a wavelike motion around the stadium.

The athletes that fans come to see are godlike; they are reputed to have almost superhuman powers (especially superstars like Tiger Woods). Athletes are central figures in a common cultural myth: the hero tale. Often the hero must prove him or herself under strenuous circumstances (e.g., the situation where the starter is unexpectedly injured), and can achieve victory only through sheer force of will.

Tourism is another example of a sacred, non-ordinary experience of extreme importance to marketers. When people travel on vacation, they occupy sacred time and space. The tourist is continually in search of "authentic" experiences that differ from his or her normal world.[55] The tourism experience involves binary oppositions between work and leisure, and between being at home and being away; often norms regarding appropriate behaviour are modified as tourists scramble after illicit or adventurous experiences they would not dream of engaging in at home. This theme is reflected in Club Med's (*www.clubmed.com*) motto, "The antidote to civilization."

The desire of travellers to capture these sacred experiences in objects forms the bedrock of the souvenir industry, which may be said to be in the business of selling sacred memories. Whether a personalized matchbook from a wedding or Niagara Falls salt-and-pepper shakers, souvenirs represent a tangible piece of the consumer's sacred experience.[56]

In addition to personal mementos, such as ticket stubs saved from a favourite concert, the following are other sacred souvenir icons:[57]

- pictorial images (e.g., postcards)
- a "piece of the rock" (e.g., sea shells and pine cones)
- symbolic shorthand in the form of literal representations of the site (e.g., a miniature Eiffel Tower)
- markers (e.g., Hard Rock Café T-shirts)
- local products (e.g., pineapples from Hawaii)

From Sacred to Profane and Back Again

Just to make life interesting, in recent times many consumer activities have moved from one sphere to the other. Some things that were formerly regarded as sacred have moved into the realm of the profane, while other, everyday phenomena are now regarded as sacred.[58]

DESACRALIZATION

Desacralization occurs when a sacred item or symbol is removed from its special place or is duplicated in mass quantities, becoming profane as a result. For example, souvenir reproductions of sacred monuments (such as the Eiffel Tower) or artworks (such as the *Mona Lisa*), or clothing designers' adaptations of important symbols (such as the Canadian flag) eliminate their special aspects by turning them into unauthentic commodities, produced mechanically and possessing relatively little value.[59]

Religion itself has to some extent been desacralized. Religious symbols, such as stylized crosses or New Age crystals, have moved into the mainstream of fashion jewellery.[60] Religious holidays, particularly Christmas, are regarded by many (and criticized by some) as having been transformed into secular, materialistic occasions devoid of their original sacred significance. Even the clergy are increasingly adopting secular marketing techniques. Televangelists rely upon the power of television, a secular medium, to convey their messages. The Catholic Church generated a major controversy after it hired a prominent public relations firm to promote its anti-abortion campaign.[61]

SACRALIZATION

Sacralization occurs when ordinary objects, events, and people take on sacred meaning to a culture or to specific groups within a culture. For example, events like the Stanley Cup and people like Elvis Presley have become sacralized for some consumers.

Objectification occurs when sacred qualities are attributed to mundane items. One way that this process can occur is through *contamination*, where objects associated with sacred events or people become sacred in their own right. This explains the desire by many fans for items belonging to, or even touched by, famous people.

In addition to museum exhibits displaying rare objects, even mundane, inexpensive things may be set apart in *collections*, where they are transformed from profane items into sacred ones. An item is sacralized as soon as it enters a collection, and it takes on a special significance to the collector that in some cases may be difficult for an outsider to comprehend.

The contents of collections range from movie memorabilia, rare books, and autographs, to Barbie dolls, Beatles memorabilia, and junk mail.[62] Consumers are often ferociously attached to their collections. This passion is exemplified by the comment made in one study by a woman who collects teddy bears: "If my house ever burns down, I won't cry over my furniture, I'll cry over the bears."[63]

Collecting refers to the systematic acquisition of a particular object or set of objects, and this widespread activity can be distinguished from hoarding, which is merely unsystematic collecting.[64] Collecting typically involves both rational and emotional components, since collectors are frequently transfixed by their objects while also carefully organizing and exhibiting them.[65]

Some consumer researchers feel that collectors are motivated to acquire their "prizes" in order to gratify a high level of materialism in a socially acceptable manner. By systematically amassing a collection, the collector is allowed to "worship" material objects without feeling guilty or petty. Another perspective is that collecting is actually an aesthetic experience; for many collectors the pleasure emanates from being involved in creating the collection, rather than from passively admiring the items one has scavenged or bought. Whatever the motivation, hard-core collectors often devote a great deal of time and energy to maintaining and expanding their collections, so for many this activity becomes a central component of their extended self (see Chapter 5).[66]

CHAPTER SUMMARY

A CULTURE IS A SOCIETY'S PERSONALITY; OUR MEMBERSHIP IN A PARTICULAR CULTURE PLAYS A BIG ROLE IN SHAPING OUR IDENTITIES AS INDIVIDUALS.

- A society's culture includes its values and ethics and the material objects produced by its people. It is the accumulation of shared meanings and traditions among members of a society. A culture can be described in terms of its ecology (the way people adapt to their habitat), its social structure, and its ideology (including people's moral and aesthetic principles).

MYTHS ARE STORIES THAT EXPRESS THE SHARED IDEALS OF A CULTURE; IN MODERN TIMES MARKETING MESSAGES ARE USED TO HAND THESE STORIES DOWN TO MEMBERS OF A CULTURE.

- Myths are stories containing symbolic elements that express the shared ideals of a culture. Many myths involve some binary opposition, whereby values are defined in terms of what they are and what they are not (e.g., nature versus technology). Modern myths are transmitted through advertising, movies, and other media.

MANY OF OUR CONSUMPTION ACTIVITIES, INCLUDING HOLIDAY OBSERVANCES, GROOMING, AND GIFT GIVING, ARE BASED UPON DEEPLY INGRAINED RITUALS.

- A ritual is a set of symbolic behaviours that occur in a fixed sequence and that tend to be repeated periodically.

Rituals are related to many consumption activities that occur in popular culture. These include holiday observances, gift giving, and grooming.

- A rite of passage is a special kind of ritual that involves the transition from one role to another. These passages typically entail the need to acquire products and services, called ritual artifacts, to facilitate the transition. Modern rites of passage include graduations, initiations, weddings, debutante balls, and funerals.

WE CAN DESCRIBE PRODUCTS AS EITHER SACRED OR PROFANE; IT'S NOT UNUSUAL FOR SOME PRODUCTS TO MOVE BACK AND FORTH BETWEEN THE TWO CATEGORIES.

- Consumer activities can be divided into sacred and profane domains. Sacred phenomena are "set apart" from everyday activities or products. People, events, or objects can become sacralized. Sacralization occurs when sacred qualities are ascribed to products or items owned by sacred people. Objectification occurs when formerly sacred objects or activities become part of the everyday, as when "one-of-a-kind" works of art are reproduced in large quantities. Desacralization occurs when objects that previously were considered sacred become commercialized and integrated into popular culture.

KEY TERMS

REVIEW QUESTIONS

1. What do we mean by culture? How is it related to an individual's personality?
2. How do ideology, social structure, and ecology shape a culture? Give examples of different forms these may take.
3. Give examples of public versus private rituals. Name some ritual artifacts we use to perform these rituals.
4. What ritualistic functions does a bath perform?
5. Describe the three stages of the gift-giving ritual.
6. Define a rite of passage, giving two examples. Specify the stages involved.
7. What is the difference between sacred and profane consumption?
8. Are sports events sacred? Why or why not?
9. Describe the two processes of sacralization and desacralization, providing an example of each.
10. What is collecting, and how does it differ from hoarding?

CONSUMER BEHAVIOUR CHALLENGE

Discuss

1. We can think of culture as a society's personality. If your culture were a person, how would you describe its personality traits?
2. This chapter argues that not all gift giving is positive. In what ways can this ritual be unpleasant or negative?
3. For many people, Disneyland is a sacred place. Do you agree? Why or why not?
4. Describe the three stages of the rite of passage associated with graduating from university.
5. Have you ever given yourself a gift? If so, why did you do it and how did you decide what to get?
6. "Christmas has become just another opportunity to exchange gifts and stimulate the economy." Do you agree? Why or why not?
7. Bridal registries lay out very clearly the gifts a couple wants. How do you feel about this practice? Should people actually specify what you should buy for them, or should a gift be a more personal expression?

Experiential Exercises

8. The next time you go out on a first date, identify the set of crescive norms that are operating. Write a report (preferably when the date is over!) describing the specific behaviours each of you performed that made it clear you were on a first date. What products and services are affected by these norms?
9. Interview people you know about any "magic" items they own (e.g., a lucky charm, a St. Christopher's medal, or some other object hanging from their rear-view mirrors). Get them to describe their feelings about these objects and to explain how they acquired their magical properties. How would they feel if they lost these special items?
10. Identify modern-day myths that have been created by corporations. How do the companies communicate these stories to consumers?
11. Interview people you know who collect some kind of object. How do they organize and describe their collections? Do you see any evidence of sacred versus profane distinctions? (For example, people who collect matchbooks might have sets they'll actually use to light a candle, but other sets that can't ever be touched.)
12. Ask friends to describe incidents where they received a gift they thought was inappropriate. Why did they feel this way, and how did this event influence their relationships with the gift giver?

CBC 🍁 VIDEO VIGNETTE

CONCEPTS AT WORK FOR INTERNATIONAL BUSINESS

With increasing globalization, Canadians more frequently find themselves dining and doing business in other countries. Food and how it is consumed is one of the most pervasive conveyors of culture, so knowing how to eat soup as you go from country to country really does help to avoid embarrassment and build business relationships. Fortunately, etiquette experts, such as Adeo Czink, make manners their business. Czink can guide the novice through the confusion of dining abroad and the cross-cultural "dos and don'ts" of how to consume specific foods, how to use cutlery, how to clink wine glasses, and how to use one's hands when eating. So...how should you eat a bowl of soup in China? Do you have to eat that unusual food in front of you? How much sake should you drink?

Rules of etiquette also apply to making conversation and exchanging business cards in other countries. In some countries, for example, asking about the person's family must precede talking about business if you want to get off to a good start. The exchange of business cards in Japan compared to North America is very complex. Clearly, there is a lot to learn about navigating cross-cultural interactions, but even the smallest efforts on the part of a globe-trotting business person will go a long way toward building positive international business relationships.

Questions

1. What is the role of food in culture?

2. Why is it important to understand global table manners?

3. What are some of the rules of etiquette associated with international interactions?

4. Why is there a difference in table etiquette across countries? How can Canadians learn about these differences?

Resources: "International Dining," *Venture #764, CBC Air Date: November 14, 2000;* and "Japanese Name Cards," *Venture #782, CBC Air Date: April 10, 2001.*

NOTES

1. Bill McDowell, "Starbucks Is Ground Zero in Today's Coffee Culture," *Advertising Age* (December 9, 1996): 1 (2 pp.).

2. Louise Lee, "Now, Starbucks Uses Its Bean," *Business Week* (February 14, 2000): 92–94; Mark Gimein, "Behind Starbucks' New Venture: Beans, Beatniks, and Booze," *Fortune* (May 15, 2000): 80.

3. Clifford Geertz, *The Interpretation of Cultures* (New York, NY: Basic Books, 1973); Marvin Harris, *Culture, People and Nature* (New York, NY: Crowell, 1971); John F. Sherry, Jr., "The Cultural Perspective in Consumer Research," in *Advances in Consumer Research* 13, ed. Richard J. Lutz (Provo, UT: Association for Consumer Research, 1985), 573–575.

4. William Lazer, Shoji Murata, and Hiroshi Kosaka, "Japanese Marketing: Towards a Better Understanding," *Journal of Marketing* 49 (Spring 1985): 69–81.

5. Geert Hofstede, *Cultures Consequences* (Beverly Hills, CA: Sage, 1980). See also Laura M. Milner, Dale Fodness, and Mark W. Speece, "Hofstede's Research on Cross-Cultural Work-Related Values: Implications for Consumer Behavior," in *Proceedings of the 1992 ACR Summer Conference* (Amsterdam: Association for Consumer Research, 1992).

6. Daniel Goleman, "The Group and the Self: New Focus on a Cultural Rift," *New York Times* (December 25, 1990): 37; Harry C. Triandis, "The Self and Social Behavior in Differing Cultural Contexts," *Psychological Review* 96 (July 1989): 506; Harry C. Triandis et al., "Individualism and Collectivism: Cross-Cultural Perspectives on Self-Ingroup Relationships," *Journal of Personality and Social Psychology* 54 (February 1988): 323.

7. George J. McCall and J.L. Simmons, *Social Psychology: A Sociological Approach* (New York, NY: Free Press, 1982).

8. Robert Frank, "When Small Chains Go Abroad, Culture Clashes Require Ingenuity," *Wall Street Journal Interactive Edition* (April 12, 2000).

9. Molly O'Neill, "As Life Gets More Complex, Magic Casts a Wider Spell," *New York Times* (June 13, 1994): A1 (2 pp.).

10. Susannah Meadows, "Who's Afraid of the Big Bad Werewolf?" *Newsweek* (August 26, 2002): 57.

11. Conrad Phillip Kottak, "Anthropological Analysis of Mass Enculturation," in *Researching American Culture,* ed. Conrad P. Kottak (Ann Arbor, MI: University of Michigan Press, 1982), pp. 40–74.

12. Eric Ransdell, "The Nike Story? Just Tell It!" *Fast Company* (January/February 2000): 44(2).

13. Joseph Campbell, *Myths, Dreams, and Religion* (New York, NY: E.P. Dutton, 1970).

14. Jeff Jensen, "Comic Heroes Return to Roots as Marvel Is Cast as Hip Brand," *Advertising Age* (June 8, 1998): 3, 2.

15. Jeffrey S. Lang and Patrick Trimble, "Whatever Happened to the Man of Tomorrow? An Examination of the American Monomyth and the Comic Book Superhero," *Journal of Popular Culture* 22 (Winter 1988): 157.

16. Elizabeth C. Hirschman, "Movies as Myths: An Interpretation of Motion Picture Mythology," in *Marketing and Semiotics: New Directions in the Study of Signs for Sale,* ed. Jean Umiker-Sebeok (Berlin: Mouton de Guyter, 1987), pp. 335–374.

17. See William Blake Tyrrell, "Star Trek as Myth and Television as Mythmaker," in *The Popular Culture Reader,* eds. Jack Nachbar, Deborah Weiser, and John L. Wright (Bowling Green, OH: Bowling Green University Press, 1978), pp. 79–88.

18. Bernie Whalen, "Semiotics: An Art or Powerful Marketing Research Tool?" *Marketing News* (May 13, 1983): 8.

19. See Dennis W. Rook, "The Ritual Dimension of Consumer Behavior," *Journal of Consumer Research* 12 (December 1985): 251–264; Mary A. Stansfield Tetreault and Robert E. Kleine III, "Ritual, Ritualized Behavior, and Habit: Refinements and Extensions of the Consumption Ritual Construct," in *Advances in Consumer Research* 17, eds. Marvin Goldberg, Gerald Gorn, and Richard W. Pollay (Provo, UT: Association for Consumer Research, 1990), 31–38.

20. Kim Foltz, "New Species for Study: Consumers in Action," *New York Times* (December 18, 1989): A1.

21. "The Bride: Get Ready to Release a Swarm of Live Insects," *Wall Street Journal* (January 22, 1996): B1.

22. Robyn Meredith, "Wedded to the West," *Forbes* (March 28, 2005): 77–78.

23. Dennis W. Rook and Sidney J. Levy, "Psychosocial Themes in Consumer Grooming Rituals," in *Advances in Consumer Research* 10, eds. Richard P. Bagozzi and Alice M. Tybout (Provo, UT: Association for Consumer Research, 1983), 329–333.

24. Diane Barthel, *Putting on Appearances: Gender and Advertising* (Philadelphia, PA: Temple University Press, 1988).

25. Barthel, *Putting on Appearances.*

26. Debbie Treise, Joyce M. Wolburg, and Cele C. Otnes, "Understanding the 'Social Gifts' of Drinking Rituals: An Alternative Framework for PSA Developers," *Journal of Advertising* XXVIII, 2 (Summer 1999): 17–32.

27. Russell W. Belk, Melanie Wallendorf, and John F. Sherry, Jr., "The Sacred and the Profane in Consumer Behavior: Theodicy on the Odyssey," *Journal of Consumer Research* 16 (June 1989): 1–38.

28. Russell W. Belk and Gregory S. Coon, "Gift Giving as Agapic Love: An Alternative to the Exchange Paradigm Based on Dating Experiences," *Journal of Consumer Research* 20, 3 (December 1993): 393–417.

29. Julie A. Ruth, Cele C. Otnes, and Frederic F. Brunel, "Gift Receipt and the Reformulation of Interpersonal Relationships," *Journal of Consumer Research,* (March 25, 1999): 385–402.

30. Alf Nucifora, "'Tis the Season to Gift One's Best Clients," *Triangle Business Journal* (December 3, 1999): 14.

31. John F. Sherry, Jr., "Gift Giving in Anthropological Perspective," *Journal of Consumer Research* 10 (September 1983): 157–168.

32. Daniel Goleman, "What's Under the Tree? Clues to a Relationship," *New York Times* (December 19, 1989): C1.

33. John F. Sherry, Jr., Mary Ann McGrath, and Sidney J. Levy, "The Dark Side of the Gift," *Journal of Business Research* 28 (November 1993): 225–244.

34. Bob Tedeschi, "Letters to Santa Are No Longer Necessary," *New York Times on the Web* (November 15, 1999). For an exploration of the role of the bridal salon in the performance of wedding rituals, see Cele Otnes, "Friend of the Bride, and Then Some: The Role of the Bridal Salon in Wedding Planning," in *Servicescapes: The Concept of Place in Contemporary Markets,* ed. John F. Sherry (Lincolnwood, IL: NTC Press, 1998), pp. 228–258.

35. Wendy Bounds, "Here Comes the Bride, Just a Mouse Click Away," *Wall Street Journal Interactive Edition* (January 14, 1999).

36. Cyndee Miller, "Nix the Knick-Knacks; Send Cash," *Marketing News* (May 26, 1997): 1, 13.

37. Quoted in "I Do . . . Take MasterCard," *Wall Street Journal* (June 23, 2000): W1, 2.

38. Sherry Jr., "Gift Giving in Anthropological Perspective."

39. David Glen Mick and Michelle DeMoss, "Self-Gifts: Phenomenological Insights from Four Contexts," *Journal of Consumer Research* 17 (December 1990): 327; John F. Sherry, Jr., Mary Ann McGrath, and Sidney J. Levy, "Monadic Giving: Anatomy of Gifts Given to the Self," in *Contemporary Marketing and Consumer Behavior: An Anthropological Sourcebook,* ed. John F. Sherry, Jr. (New York: Sage, 1995): 399–432.

40. Quoted in Cynthia Crossen, "Holiday Shoppers' Refrain: 'A Merry Christmas to Me'," *Wall Street Journal Interactive Edition Edition* (December 11, 1997).

41. Tralee Pearce, "Guys Hit the Shower—The Baby Shower, That Is," *Globe and Mail* (June 18, 2005): L1, L8.

42. See, for example, Russell W. Belk, "Halloween: An Evolving American Consumption Ritual," in *Advances in Consumer Research* 17, eds. Richard Pollay, Jerry Gorn and Marvin Goldberg (Provo, UT: Association for Consumer Research, 1990), 508–517; Melanie Wallendorf and Eric J. Arnould, "We Gather Together: The Consumption Rituals of Thanksgiving Day," *Journal of Consumer Research* 18 (June 1991): 13–31.

43. Rick Lyte, "Holidays, Ethnic Themes Provide Built-In F&B Festivals," *Hotel & Motel Management* (December 14, 1987): 56; Megan Rowe, "Holidays and Special Occasions: Restaurants are Fast Replacing Grandma's House as the Site of Choice for Special Meals," *Restaurant Management* (November 1987): 69; Judith Waldrop, "Funny Valentines," *American Demographics* (February 1989): 7.

44. Bruno Bettelheim, *The Uses of Enchantment: The Meaning and Importance of Fairy Tales* (New York: Alfred A. Knopf, 1976).

45. Colin Camerer, "Gifts as Economics Signals and Social Symbols," *American Journal of Sociology* 94 (supplement 1988): 5180–5214.

46. Robert T. Green and Dana L. Alden, "Functional Equivalence in Cross-Cultural Consumer Behavior: Gift Giving in Japan and the United States," *Psychology & Marketing* 5 (Summer 1988): 155–168.

47. Theodore Caplow, Howard M. Bahr, Bruce A. Chadwick, Reuben Hill, and Margaret M. Williams, *Middletown Families: Fifty Years of Change and Continuity* (Minneapolis, MN: University of Minnesota Press, 1982).

48. Andrea Adelson, "A New Spirit for Sales of Halloween Merchandise," *New York Times* (October 31, 1994): D1 (2 pp.).

49. Anne Swardson, "Trick or Treat? In Paris, It's Dress, Dance, Eat," *International Herald Tribune* (October 31, 1996): 2.

50. Arnold Van Gennep, *The Rites of Passage*, trans. Maika B. Vizedom and Gabrielle L. Caffee (1908; London: Routledge and Kegan Paul, 1960); Michael R. Solomon and Punam Anand, "Ritual Costumes and Status Transition: The Female Business Suit as Totemic Emblem," in *Advances in Consumer Research* 12, eds. Elizabeth C. Hirschman and Morris Holbrook (Washington, DC: Association for Consumer Research, 1985), 315–348.

51. Walter W. Whitaker III, "The Contemporary American Funeral Ritual," in *Rites and Ceremonies in Popular Culture,* ed. Ray B. Browne (Bowling Green, OH: Bowling Green University Press, 1980), pp. 316–325. For a recent examination of funeral rituals, see Larry D. Compeau and Carolyn Nicholson, "Funerals: Emotional Rituals or Ritualistic Emotions" (paper presented at the Association of Consumer Research Conference meeting, Boston, October 1994).

52. Conrad Phillip Kottak, "Anthropological Analysis of Mass Enculturation," in *Researching American Culture*, ed. Conrad P. Kottak (Ann Arbor, MI: University of Michigan Press, 1982), pp. 40–74.

53. Grant McCracken, "Homeyness: A Cultural Account of One Constellation of Goods and Meanings," in *Interpretive Consumer Research*, ed. Elizabeth C. Hirschman (Provo, UT: Association for Consumer Research, 1989), pp. 168–184.

54. Susan Birrell, "Sports as Ritual: Interpretations from Durkheim to Goffman," *Social Forces* 60, 2 (1981): 354–376; Daniel Q. Voigt, "American Sporting Rituals," in *Rites and Ceremonies in Popular Culture*, ed. Ray B. Browne (Bowling Green, OH: Bowling Green University Press, 1980), pp. 125–140.

55. Dean MacCannell, *The Tourist: A New Theory of the Leisure Class* (New York: Shocken Books, 1976).

56. Belk, Wallendorf, and Sherry, Jr., "The Sacred and the Profane in Consumer Behavior. . . ."

57. Beverly Gordon, "The Souvenir: Messenger of the Extraordinary," *Journal of Popular Culture* 20, 3 (1986): 135–146.

58. Belk, Wallendorf, and Sherry, Jr., "The Sacred and the Profane in Consumer Behavior. . . ."

59. Belk, Wallendorf, and Sherry, Jr., "The Sacred and the Profane in Consumer Behaviorr. . . ."

60. Deborah Hoffmann, "In Jewelry, Choices Sacred and Profane, Ancient and New," *New York Times* (May 7, 1989).

61. "Public Relations Firm to Present Anti-Abortion Effort to Bishops," *New York Times* (August 14, 1990): A12.

62. For an extensive bibliography on collecting, see Russell W. Belk et al., "Collecting in a Consumer Culture," in *Highways and Buyways*, ed. Russell W. Belk (Provo, UT: Association for Consumer Research, 1991), pp. 178–215. See also Russell W. Belk, "Acquiring, Possessing, and Collecting: Fundamental Processes in Consumer Behavior," in *Marketing Theory: Philosophy of Science Perspectives*, eds. Ronald F. Bush and Shelby D. Hunt (Chicago, IL: American Marketing Association, 1982), pp. 85–90; Werner Muensterberg, *Collecting: An Unruly Passion* (Princeton, NJ: Princeton University Press, 1994); Melanie Wallendorf and Eric J. Arnould, "'My Favorite Things': A Cross-Cultural Inquiry into Object Attachment, Possessiveness, and Social Linkage," *Journal of Consumer Research* 14 (March 1988): 531–547.

63. Quoted in Ruth Ann Smith, "Collecting as Consumption: A Grounded Theory of Collecting Behavior" (unpublished manuscript, Virginia Polytechnic Institute and State University, 1994): 14.

64. Dan L. Sherrell, Alvin C. Burns and Melodie R. Phillips, "Fixed Consumption Behavior: The Case of Enduring Acquisition in a Product Category," in *Developments in Marketing Science* XIV, ed. Robert L. King (1991), pp. 36–40.

65. Belk, "Acquiring, Possessing, and Collecting."

66. For a discussion of these perspectives, see Smith, "Collecting as Consumption."

Amy is on vacation with her Aunt Judy in France. She is awed by the fashions in the stores. They seem so cool compared with what she has seen in the malls back home in Burlington. What particularly catches her eye are the shoes. She is determined to have a pair, even if it means using all the rest of her babysitting money and borrowing the balance from her aunt. There is nothing else she wants but these shoes.

As Amy tries on the shoes, she is envisioning the reactions of her friends when she returns to high school. All her friends read *Seventeen* magazine and talk about the latest styles. Amy knows she will be the envy of her classmates back in Canada.

CHAPTER → 17

The Creation and Diffusion of Culture

This chapter considers how the culture in which we live creates the meanings for everyday products and how these meanings move through a society to consumers. As Figure 17–1 shows, meaning transfer is largely accomplished by such marketing vehicles as the advertising and fashion industries, which associate consumer goods with symbolic qualities. These goods, in turn, impart their meanings to individual consumers who use these products to create and express their identities in their daily lives.[1] Recall that in Chapter 1 we learned that one of the fundamental premises of the modern field of consumer behaviour is that people often buy products not for what they do, but for what they *mean*. Thus, this closing chapter brings us full circle, back to the issues regarding the diverse meanings of consumption considered in Chapter 1.

CULTURAL SELECTION

Nipple rings, platform shoes, sushi, high-tech furniture, postmodern architecture, chat rooms, double decaf cappuccino with a hint of cinnamon: We inhabit a world brimming with different styles and possibilities. The food we eat, the cars we drive, the clothes we wear, the places we live and work, the music we listen to—all are influenced by the ebb and flow of popular culture and fashion.

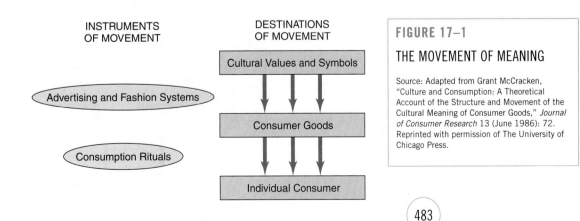

INSTRUMENTS OF MOVEMENT

DESTINATIONS OF MOVEMENT

Advertising and Fashion Systems

Consumption Rituals

Cultural Values and Symbols

Consumer Goods

Individual Consumer

FIGURE 17–1

THE MOVEMENT OF MEANING

Source: Adapted from Grant McCracken, "Culture and Consumption: A Theoretical Account of the Structure and Movement of the Cultural Meaning of Consumer Goods," *Journal of Consumer Research* 13 (June 1986): 72. Reprinted with permission of The University of Chicago Press.

Consumers may at times feel overwhelmed by the sheer number of choices in the marketplace. A person trying to decide on something as routine as a necktie has many hundreds of alternatives to choose from. Despite this seeming abundance, however, the options available to consumers at any time actually represent only a small fraction of the total set of possibilities.

The selection of certain alternatives over others—whether automobiles, dresses, computers, recording artists, political candidates, religions, or even scientific methodologies—is the culmination of a complex filtration process resembling a funnel, as depicted in Figure 17–2. Many possibilities initially compete for adoption, and these are steadily winnowed down as they make their way along the path from conception to consumption in a process of **cultural selection**.

Our tastes and product preferences are not formed in a vacuum. Choices are driven by the images presented to us in mass media, by our observations of those around us, and by our desire to live in the fantasy worlds created by marketers. These options are constantly evolving and changing. A clothing style or type of cuisine that is "hot" one year may be "out" the next.

Amy's emulation of European style described at the beginning of the chapter illustrates some of the characteristics of fashion and popular culture:

- Styles are often rooted in and reflect deeper societal trends (e.g., politics and social conditions).

- Styles usually originate as an interplay between the deliberate inventions of designers and business people and the spontaneous actions of ordinary consumers. Designers, manufacturers, and merchandisers who can anticipate what consumers want will succeed in the marketplace. In the process, they also help to fuel the fire by encouraging mass distribution of the item.

FIGURE 17–2

THE CULTURE PRODUCTION PROCESS

Source: Adapted from Michael R. Solomon, "Building Up and Breaking Down: The Impact of Cultural Sorting on Symbolic Consumption," in *Research in Consumer Behavior*, eds. J. Sheth and E. C. Hirschman (Greenwich, CT: JAI Press, 1988): 325–351.

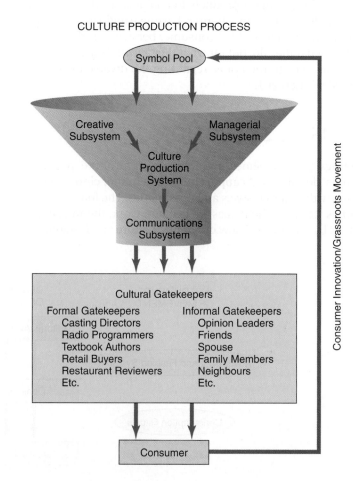

CULTURE PRODUCTION PROCESS

- These trends can travel widely, often between countries and continents. Influential people in the media play a large role in deciding which of these trends will succeed.

- A style begins as a risky or unique statement by a relatively small group of people, and then spreads as others become increasingly aware of the style and feel confident about trying it.

- Most styles eventually wear out, as people continually search for new ways to express themselves and marketers scramble to keep up with these desires.

Culture Production Systems

No single designer, company, or advertising agency is totally responsible for creating popular culture. Every product, whether a hit record, a car, or a new clothing style, requires the input of many different participants. The set of individuals and organizations responsible for creating and marketing a cultural product is a **culture production system (CPS)**.[2]

The nature of these systems helps to determine the types of products that eventually emerge from them. Important factors include the number and diversity of competing systems and the amount of innovation versus conformity that is encouraged. For example, an analysis of the country and western music industry has shown that the hit records it produces tend to be similar to one another during time periods when it is dominated by a few large companies, whereas there is more diversity when a greater number of producers are competing within the same market.[3]

The different members of a culture production system may not necessarily be aware of or appreciate the roles played by other members, yet many diverse agents work together to create popular culture.[4] Each member does his or her best to anticipate which particular images will be most attractive to a consumer market. Of course, those who are able consistently to forecast consumers' tastes most accurately will be most successful over time.

COMPONENTS OF A CPS

A culture production system has three major subsystems: (1) a *creative subsystem* responsible for generating new symbols or products; (2) a *managerial subsystem* responsible for selecting, making tangible, mass producing, and managing the distribution of new symbols or products; and (3) a *communications subsystem* responsible for giving meaning to new products and providing them with symbolic sets of attributes that are communicated to consumers.

An example of the three components of a culture production system for a record would be (1) a singer (a creative subsystem); (2) a company that manufactures and distributes CDs (a managerial subsystem); and (3) the advertising and publicity agencies hired to promote the CDs (a communications subsystem). Table 17–1 on page 486 illustrates some of the many *cultural specialists,* operating in different subsystems, who are required to create a hit CD.

CULTURAL GATEKEEPERS

Many judges or "tastemakers" influence the products that are eventually offered to consumers. These judges, or **cultural gatekeepers**, filter the overflow of information and materials intended for consumers. Gatekeepers include movie, restaurant, and car reviewers, interior designers, disc jockeys, retail buyers, and magazine editors. Collectively, this set of agents is known as the *throughput sector.*[5]

High Culture and Popular Culture

Do Beethoven and Diddy have anything in common? Although both the famous composer and the hip hop singer are associated with music, many would argue that the similarity stops there. Culture production systems create many diverse kinds of products, but some basic distinctions can be offered regarding their characteristics.

TABLE 17–1

CULTURAL SPECIALISTS IN THE MUSIC INDUSTRY

Specialist	Functions
Songwriter(s)	Compose music and lyrics; must reconcile artistic preferences with estimates of what will succeed in the marketplace
Performer(s)	Interpret music and lyrics; may be formed spontaneously, or may be packaged by an agent to appeal to a predetermined market
Teachers and coaches	Develop and refine performers' talents
Agent(s)	Represent performers to record companies
A&R (artist and repertoire) executive(s)	Acquire artists for the record label
Publicists, image consultants, designers, stylists	Create an image for the group that is transmitted to the buying public
Recording technicians, producers	Create a recording to be sold
Marketing executives	Make strategic decisions regarding performers' appearances, ticket pricing, promotional strategies, and so on
Video director(s)	Interpret the song visually to create a music video that will help to promote the record
Music reviewers	Evaluate the merits of a recording for listeners
Disc jockeys, radio program directors	Decide which records will be given airplay and placed in the radio stations' regular rotations
Record-store owner(s)	Decide which of the many records produced will be stocked or promoted heavily in the retail environment

→ Galeries Lafayette in Paris celebrates the influence of the Chinese culture at its flagship store in its New Year 2003 displays.
Courtesy of Rosemary Polegato and Judith Zaichkowsky.

One distinction can be made between arts and crafts.[6] An **art product** is viewed primarily as an object of aesthetic contemplation without any functional value. A **craft product** (e.g., a ceramic ashtray or hand-crafted fishing lures), in contrast, is admired because of the beauty with which it performs some function. A piece of art is original, subtle, and valuable, and is associated with the elite of society. A craft tends to follow a formula that permits rapid production. According to this framework, elite culture is produced in a purely aesthetic context and is judged by reference to recognized classics. It is high culture—that is, "serious art."[7]

HIGH ART VERSUS LOW ART

The distinction between high and low culture—high art versus low art—is not as clear as it may at first appear. In addition to the possible class bias that drives such a distinction (i.e., we assume that the rich have culture while the poor do not), high and low culture are blending together in interesting ways. In addition to selling appliances, tires, and cereals by the case, the warehouse club Costco now stocks fine art, including limited-edition lithographs by Pablo Picasso, Marc Chagall, and Joan Miró.[8] Popular culture reflects the world around us; this phenomenon touches both rich and poor. In Europe, for example, advertising is widely appreciated as an art form. Advertising executives are often public figures in Great Britain. In fact, TV commercials (which the British call "adverts") have become so fashionable that a satellite network called the Advert Channel shows them 24 hours a day.[9]

All cultural products that are transmitted by mass media become a part of popular culture.[10] Classical recordings are marketed in much the same way as Top 40 CDs, and museums use mass-marketing techniques to sell their wares.

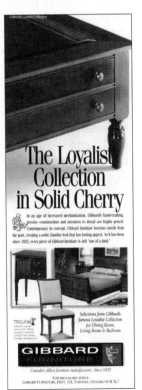

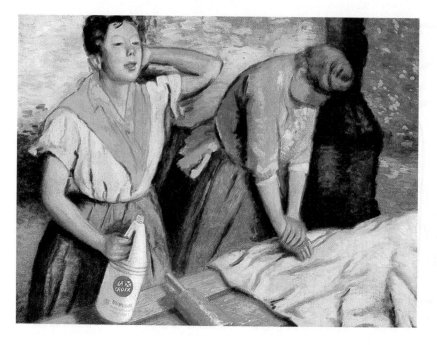

Marketers often incorporate high-art imagery to promote products. They may sponsor artistic events to build public goodwill or feature works of art on shopping bags.[11] When observers from Toyota watched customers in luxury-car showrooms, the company found that these consumers tended to view cars as art objects. This theme was then used in an ad for the Lexus with the caption: "Until now, the only fine arts we supported were sculpture, painting, and music."[12]

CULTURAL FORMULAE

Mass culture, in contrast, churns out products specifically for a mass market. These products aim to please the average taste of an undifferentiated audience and are predictable because they follow certain patterns. As illustrated in Table 17–2, many popular art forms, such as detective stories or science fiction, generally follow a **cultural formula**, where certain roles and props often occur consistently.[13] Romance novels are an extreme case of a cultural formula. Computer programs even allow users to "write" their own romances by systematically varying certain set elements of the story.

Reliance on these formulae also leads to a *recycling* of images, as members of the creative subsystem reach back through time for inspiration. Thus, young people watch retro shows like *Gilligan's Island* and remakes of *The Brady Bunch*; designers modify styles from Victorian England or colonial Africa; hip hop DJs sample sound bites from old songs and combine them in new ways; and the Gap (***www.gap.com***) runs ads featuring now-dead celebrities, including Humphrey Bogart, Gene Kelly, and Pablo Picasso, dressed in khaki pants. With easy access to CD burners, digital cameras, and imaging software, virtually anyone can "remix" the past.[14]

AESTHETIC MARKET RESEARCH

Creators of aesthetic products are increasingly adapting conventional marketing methods to fine-tune their mass-market offerings. Market research is used, for example, to test audience reactions to movie concepts. Although testing cannot account for such intangibles as acting quality or cinematography, it can determine whether the basic themes of the movie strike a responsive chord in the target audience. This type of research is most appropriate for blockbuster movies, which usually follow one of the formulae described earlier. In some cases research is combined with publicity, as when the producers of the Will Smith movie *Men in Black*

TABLE 17–2

CULTURAL FORMULAE IN PUBLIC ART FORMS

Element	Classic Western	Science Fiction	Hard-Boiled Detective	Family Sitcom
Time	1800s	Future	Present	Anytime
Location	Edge of civilization	Space	City	Suburbs
Protagonist	Cowboy (lone individual)	Astronaut	Detective	Father (figure)
Heroine	Schoolmarm	Spacegal	Damsel in distress	Mother (figure)
Villain	Outlaws, killers	Aliens	Killer	Boss, neighbour
Secondary characters	Townfolk, Indians	Technicians in spacecraft	Cops, underworld	Kids, dogs
Plot	Restore law and order	Repel aliens	Find killer	Solve problem
Theme	Justice	Triumph of humanity	Pursuit and discovery	Chaos and confusion
Costume	Cowboy hat, boots, etc.	High-tech uniforms	Raincoat	Regular clothes
Locomotion	Horse	Spaceship	Beat-up car	Station wagon
Weaponry	Sixgun, rifle	Rayguns	Pistol, fists	Insults

Source: Arthur A. Berger, *Signs in Contemporary Culture: An Introduction to Semiotics* (New York: Longman, 1984), p. 86. Copyright ©1984. Reissued 1989 by Sheffield Publishing Company, Salem, Wisconsin. Reprinted with permission of the publisher.

showed the first 12 minutes of the film to an advance audience and then let them meet the stars to create a pre-release buzz.[15]

Even the content of movies is sometimes influenced by consumer research. Typically, free invitations to pre-screenings are handed out in malls and movie theatres. Attendees are asked a few questions about the movie, and then some are selected to participate in focus groups. Although group members' reactions usually result in only minor editing changes, more drastic effects occasionally result, such as a change in the outcome of the story.

Reality Engineering

A promotional ploy for the hit show *Desperate Housewives* illustrates how art imitates life imitates art. ABC arranged to distribute about one million plastic laundry bags in Los Angeles and New York with the photos of the four principal cast members and the show's slogan, "Everybody has some dirty laundry." In a later episode of the show, one of the characters (played by Felicity Huffman) tries to help her husband succeed in selling his client's make-believe product, Spotless Scrub, by suggesting that they advertise on...dry cleaning bags![16] Many of the environments in which we find ourselves, whether shopping malls, sports stadiums, or theme parks, are composed at least partly of images and characters drawn from products, marketing campaigns, or the mass media. **Reality engineering** occurs as elements of popular culture are appropriated by marketers and converted to vehicles for promotional strategies.[17] It's hard to know what's real anymore; even "used jeans" are created by applying chemical washes or using sandpaper and other techniques to make a new pair of jeans look like they're ready for retirement. The industry even has a term for this practice that sums up the contradiction: *new vintage!*[18]

→ Art imitates life imitates art: ABC distributed laundry bags to promote the TV show *Desperate Housewives*. The idea became part of the plot in a later episode of the show.
Ambient Planet.

Elements of popular culture include aspects of everyday existence in the form of products appearing in movies, odours pumped into offices and stores, billboards, theme parks, video monitors attached to shopping carts, and even faked "documentaries" like *The Blair Witch Project*. This process is accelerating; historical analyses of Broadway plays, best-selling novels, and the lyrics of hit songs, for example, clearly show large increases in the use of real brand names over time.[19]

Media images appear to exert significant influence on consumers' perceptions of reality, affecting viewers' notions about such issues as dating behaviour, racial stereotypes, and occupational status.[20] Studies of the **cultivation hypothesis**, which relates to media's ability to distort consumers' perceptions of reality, have shown that consumers who watch a lot of television tend to overestimate the degree of affluence in the country; these effects also extend to such areas as perceptions of the amount of violence in a culture.[21] The media also tend to exaggerate or distort the frequency of behaviours like drinking and smoking.[22]

An analysis of two weeks of prime-time television programs and movies shown on six broadcast networks revealed several gaps between reality and fantasy. For example, the programs and movies showed a lack of working mothers and had fewer parents and more men than in the actual population. Only 13 out of 150 episodes showed a character dealing with stress caused by conflicts between the demands of a job versus family. Only 26 out of 820 adult television characters had any caregiving responsibility for an adult relative. Only 14 percent of adult television characters were over 50, compared with 38 percent of the actual population. Characters shown taking time off for personal problems encountered no resistance from their bosses. In real life, 34 percent of workers find it difficult to get time off to deal with personal matters.[23] Then again, maybe this kind of escape from reality is why people are watching in the first place!

Product Placement

Traditionally, networks demanded that brand names be "greeked" or changed before they could appear in a show. Nowadays, though, real products pop up everywhere.

It is quite common to see real brands prominently displayed or to hear them discussed in movies and on television. In many cases these plugs are no accident. **Product placement** refers to the insertion of specific products or the use of brand names in movie and television scripts. Perhaps the greatest product placement success story was Reese's Pieces; sales jumped by 65 percent after the candy appeared in the film *E.T.*[24]

The success of a product placement strategy in that movie opened the floodgates, and today most major releases are brimming with real products. Directors like to incorporate branded props because they contribute to the film's realism. When Steven Spielberg directed the movie *Minority Report*, he used such brands as Nokia, Lexus, Pepsi, Guinness, Reebok, and American Express to lend familiarity to the plot's futuristic settings. Lexus even created a new sports car model called the Maglev just for the film.[25]

The practice of product placement is becoming so commonplace (and profitable) that it's evolving into a new form of promotion called *branded entertainment*, where advertisers showcase their products in longer-form narrative films instead of commercials. For example, *SportsCenter* on ESPN showed installments of "The Scout, Presented by Craftsman at Sears," a six-minute story about a washed-up baseball scout who discovers a stunningly talented stadium groundskeeper.[26]

Some researchers claim that product placement can aid in consumer decision making because the familiarity of these props creates a sense of cultural belonging while generating feelings of emotional security.[27] One recent study found that consumers are more persuaded by the presence of embedded products when they are consistent with the plot.[28] On the other hand, a majority of consumers polled believed the line between advertising and programming is becoming too fuzzy and distracting (though, as might be expected, concerns about this blurring of boundaries rose steadily with the age of respondents).[29] But, for better or worse, products are popping up everywhere:

- Entire episodes of NBC's *The Apprentice* now revolve around one brand: Instead of selling lemonade or rickshaw rides (as the candidates used to do), the aspiring business tycoons now sell Mars's newest candy bar, hawk Crest toothpaste, and construct a new toy for Mattel.[30]

- In the movie *Shrek 2*, the ogre and his bride-to-be drive through a town that has a Baskin-Robbins storefront. Out in the real world, the ice-cream retailer created three flavours—"Fiona's Fairytale," "Puss-in-Boots Chocolate Mousse," and "Shrek's Swirl"—named for characters in the film.

- The U.S. Treasury Department tried to encourage citizens to use its redesigned $20 bill by getting writers on the CBS crime drama *CSI: Miami* to work the new currency into an episode.[31]

- A script for the ABC soap opera *All My Children* was reworked so that one of the characters could plug a new Wal-Mart perfume called Enchantment. Daytime TV stars eat Butterball turkeys, wear Nascar shirts, and use Kleenex tissue. The characters on *All My Children* have also been drinking a lot of Florida orange juice—and not because they're thirsty![32]

- A cartoon series on Comedy Central called *Shorties Watchin' Shorties* incorporates the names and products of sponsors into the animated action. Characters use branded products including Domino's Pizza, Red Bull energy drink, and Vans sneakers.[33]

Research shows that consumers are not bothered by product placement and that advertisers can use it to gain "share of mind." Decima Research asked viewers of popular TV shows to identify car brands seen on different programs through an

Marketing Pitfall ↘

One of the most controversial intersections between marketing and society occurs when companies provide "educational materials" to schools. In 1994 Pepsi-Cola signed an agreement with the Toronto Board of Education to be the official supplier of soft drinks in the school system through vending machines. The problem was that the Board did not realize that many schools already had vending machines for soft drinks and agreements with other suppliers. There were profound ideological differences over the concept of "selling" the school system in exchange for corporate sponsorship. There is now a 13-point checklist for school boards that tries to ensure that any corporate involvement "enhances the quality and relevance of education" for learners. The Board also wants to make sure that corporate sponsorship does not replace public funding of education.[34]

aided recall task. The results ranged from a high of 56 percent for the Hummer on *CSI Miami* to a low of 7 percent for the Camaro on *ER*.[35]

This is becoming a global advertising strategy, as the Chinese are jumping on the product-placement bandwagon as well. A talent show called *Lycra My Show* is partly funded by Invista, the maker of Lycra fabric, so contestants sing while wearing stretchy Lycra-based clothing. Ford produced a *Survivor* clone called *Ford Maverick Beyond Infinity*, where 12 contestants on a tropical island hunted for treasure in a Ford Maverick sport-utility vehicle, leapt onto rafts while wearing Nike clothing, and cooled off with Nestlé drinks. Ford's marketing director in China noted, "We really built the show around the product."[36]

In India, the booming Bombay film industry (known as Bollywood) is discovering the potential of movies to expose viewers to brand names. (Indian cinema attracts huge local audiences, especially in villages where television is not available.) Coca-Cola paid to have its local soft drink, Thums Up, prominently featured in a Hindi-language remake of the Quentin Tarantino classic *Reservoir Dogs*. To ensure the audience doesn't miss the placement, in one scene a number of slickly dressed gangsters flash each other the thumbs-up sign just before the bullets start flying.[37]

ADVERGAMING

If you roar down the streets in the "Need for Speed Underground 2" video racing game, you'll pass a Best Buy store and billboards hawking Cingular Wireless, Old Spice, and Burger King. DaimlerChrysler AG's Chrysler Group devotes 10 percent of its overall marketing budget to planting Chryslers, Jeeps, and Dodge cars in more than a dozen video games.[38]

Computer gaming isn't what it used to be. Not long ago, the typical players were scruffy teenage boys "shooting" at TV screens in their basements. But with the online gaming explosion of recent years, gamers have become a more sophisticated lot and are now more representative of the general population. More women are participating, as well as older people and professionals. In fact, today more than 41 percent of people who frequent gaming sites like ***www.gamespot.com***, ***wwwcandystand.com***, and ***www.pogo.com*** are women, and 43 percent are from 25 to 49 years old.[39]

As gaming goes mass market, many marketers are turning on to a new strategy called **advergaming**, where online games merge with interactive advertisements that let companies target specific types of consumers. Why is this new medium so hot? For one reason, compared to a 30-second TV spot, advertisers can get viewers' attention for much longer: players spend an average of five to seven minutes on an advergame site. Also, the nature of the game and the products in it can be tailored to the profiles of different users. For example, strategy games can be directed to upscale, educated users, while action games can be geared to younger users.

In addition, the format gives advertisers great flexibility, because game marketers are beginning to ship PC video games with blank spaces in which virtual ads can be inserted. This allows advertisers to change ads on the fly and pay only for the number of times the ads are actually seen by game players. With this method, there's great potential to track usage-and-conduct marketing research. For example, an inaudible audio signal coded into Activision's "Tony Hawk's Underground 2" skating game on PCs will alert a Nielsen monitoring system each time the test game players view product placements related to the Jeep brand within the game.[40]

THE DIFFUSION OF INNOVATIONS

New products and styles, termed **innovations**, constantly enter the market. These new products or services occur in both consumer and industrial settings. Innovations may take the form of a clothing style (e.g., skirts for men), a new manufacturing technique, or a novel way to deliver a service. If an innovation is successful (most are not), it spreads through the population. First it is bought or used by only a few people, and then more and more consumers decide to adopt it, until in some cases it seems that almost everyone has bought or tried the innovation. **Diffusion of innovation** refers to the process whereby a new product, service, or idea spreads through a population. The rate at which a product diffuses varies. For example, within 10 years after its introduction, cable television was used by 40 percent of households, compact discs by 35 percent, answering machines by 25 percent, and colour television sets by 20 percent. It took radio 30 years to reach 60 million users and television 15 years to reach this number. In contrast, within three years 90 million people were surfing the web.[41]

Adopting Innovations

A consumer's adoption of an innovation resembles the decision-making sequence discussed in Chapter 9. The person moves through the stages of awareness, information search, evaluation, trial, and adoption, although the relative importance of each stage may differ depending upon how much is already known about a product, as well as on cultural factors that may affect people's willingness to try new things.[42]

However, even within the same culture, not all people adopt an innovation at the same rate. Some do so quite rapidly, and others never do at all. Consumers can be placed into approximate categories based upon their likelihood of adopting an innovation. The categories of adopters, shown in Figure 17–3, can be related to phases of the product-life-cycle concept used widely by marketing strategists.

As can be seen in Figure 17–3, roughly one-sixth of the population (innovators and early adopters) are very quick to adopt new products, and one-sixth (laggards) are very slow. The other two-thirds are somewhere in the middle; these majority adopters represent the mainstream public. These consumers are interested in new things, but they do not want them to be too new. In some cases people deliberately wait to adopt an innovation because they assume that its technological qualities will be improved, or that its price will fall after it has been on the market a while.[43] Keep in mind that the proportion of consumers falling into each category is an estimate; the actual size of each depends upon such factors as the complexity of the product, its cost, and how much risk is associated with trying it.

Even though **innovators** represent only 2.5 percent of the population, marketers are always interested in identifying them. These are the brave souls who are always on the lookout for novel developments and will be the first to try a new offering. Just as generalized opinion leaders do not appear to exist, innovators tend to be category specific as well. A person who is an innovator in one area may even be a laggard in another. For example, a gentleman who prides himself on being at the cutting edge of fashion may have no conception of new developments in

FIGURE 17–3   TYPES OF ADOPTERS

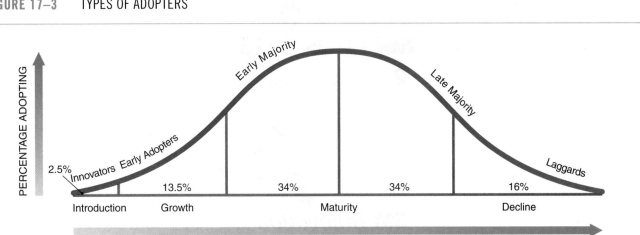

recording technology and may stubbornly cling to his phonograph albums even while he searches for the latest avant-garde clothing styles in obscure boutiques.

Despite this qualification, some generalizations can be offered regarding the profile of innovators.[44] Not surprisingly, for example, they tend to have more favourable attitudes toward taking risks. They also are likely to have higher educational and income levels and to be socially active.

Early adopters share many of the same characteristics as innovators, but an important difference is their degree of concern for social acceptance, especially with regard to expressive products such as clothing and cosmetics. Generally speaking, an early adopter is receptive to new styles because he or she is involved in the product category and also places high value on being in fashion. The style change has already been "field tested" by innovators, who truly took the fashion risk. Early adopters are likely to be found in "fashion-forward" stores featuring the latest "hot" designers. In contrast, true innovators are more likely to be found in small boutiques featuring as-yet-unknown designers.

Types of Innovations

Innovations can be categorized in terms of the degree to which they demand changes in behaviour from adopters. Three major types of innovations have been identified, though these three categories are not absolutes. They refer, in a relative sense, to the amount of disruption or change an innovation brings to people's lives.

A **continuous innovation** refers to a modification of an existing product, as when General Mills introduced a Honey Nut version of Cheerios or Levi's promoted shrink-to-fit jeans. This type of change may be used to set one brand apart from its competitors. Most product innovations are of this type; that is, they are evolutionary rather than revolutionary. Small changes are made to position the product, to add line extensions, or merely to alleviate consumer boredom.

Consumers may be lured to the new product, but adoption represents only minor changes in consumption habits, since innovation perhaps adds to the product's convenience or to the range of choices available. A typewriter company, for example, many years ago modified the shape of its product to make it more "user friendly" to secretaries. One simple change was the curving of the tops of the keys, a convention that is carried over on today's computer keyboards. The reason for the change was that secretaries had complained about the difficulty of typing with long fingernails on the flat surfaces.

← In a clever, direct way, this 3M ad illustrates how they have been continuous innovators in the tape category.
Used with permission of 3M company.

A **dynamically continuous innovation** is a more pronounced change in an existing product, as represented by self-focusing 35-mm cameras or Touch-Tone telephones. These innovations have a modest impact on the way people do things, creating some behavioural changes. When introduced, the IBM Selectric typewriter, which used a typing ball rather than individual keys, permitted secretaries to change the typeface of manuscripts instantly by replacing one Selectric ball with another.

A **discontinuous innovation** creates major changes in the way we live. Major inventions, such as the airplane, the car, the computer, and the television set, have radically changed modern lifestyles. The personal computer has supplanted the typewriter, and it has created the phenomenon of "telecommuters" by allowing many consumers to work out of their homes. Of course, the cycle continues, as new continuous innovations (e.g., new versions of software) are constantly being made for computers; dynamically continuous innovations, such as the keyboard mouse, compete for adoption, and discontinuous innovations like wristwatch personal computers loom on the horizon.

PREREQUISITES FOR SUCCESSFUL ADOPTION

Regardless of how much behavioural change is demanded by an innovation, several factors are desirable for a new product to succeed:[48]

- *Compatibility:* The innovation should be compatible with consumers' lifestyles. As one illustration, a manufacturer of personal-care products tried unsuccessfully several years ago to introduce a cream hair remover for men as a substitute for razors and shaving cream. This formulation was similar to that used widely by women to remove hair from their legs. Although the product was simple and convenient to use, it failed because men were not interested in a product they perceived to be too feminine and thus threatening to their masculine self-concepts.

- *Trialability:* Since an unknown is accompanied by perceived high risk, people are more likely to adopt an innovation if they can experiment with it prior to making a commitment. To reduce risk, companies often choose the expensive strategy of distributing free "trial-size" samples of new products.

- *Complexity:* The product should be low in complexity. A product that is easier to understand and use will be chosen over a competitor's. This strategy requires less effort from the consumer, and it also lowers perceived risk.

- *Observability.* Innovations that are easily observable are more likely to spread, since this quality makes it more likely that other potential adopters will become aware of its existence. The rapid proliferation of fanny packs (pouches worn around the waist in lieu of wallets or purses) was due to their high visibility. It was easy for others to see the convenience offered by this alternative.

- *Relative advantage:* Most important, the product should offer relative advantage over alternatives. The consumer must believe that its use will provide a benefit other products cannot offer. Two popular products demonstrate the importance of possessing a perceived relative advantage vis-à-vis existing products: Energizer Green Power Batteries are promoted as being better for the environment because they contain less mercury, and the Bugchaser is a wristband containing insect repellent. Mothers with young children like the Bugchaser because it is non-toxic and non-staining. In contrast, the Crazy Blue Air Freshener, which was added to windshield wiper fluid and emitted a fragrance when the wipers were turned on, fizzled: People didn't see the need for the product and felt there were simpler ways to freshen their cars if they cared to.

THE FASHION SYSTEM

The **fashion system** consists of all those people and organizations involved in creating symbolic meanings and transferring those meanings to cultural goods. Although people tend to equate fashion with clothing, it is important to keep in mind that fashion processes affect *all* types of cultural phenomena, including music, art, architecture, and even science (i.e., certain research topics and scientists are "hot" at a given time). Even business practices are subject to the fashion process; they evolve and change depending on which management techniques, such as total quality management or just-in-time inventory control, are "in vogue."

Fashion can be thought of as a *code,* or language, that helps us to decipher these meanings.[49] Unlike a language, however, fashion is *context dependent*. The same item can be interpreted differently by different consumers and in different situations.[50] The meaning of many products is *undercoded*—that is, there is no one precise meaning, but rather plenty of room for interpretation among perceivers.

At the outset, it may be helpful to distinguish among some confusing terms. **Fashion** is the process of social diffusion by which a new style is adopted by some group(s) of consumers. In contrast, *a fashion* (or style) refers to a particular combination of attributes. And to be *in fashion* means that this combination is currently positively evaluated by some reference group. Thus, the term *Danish Modern* refers to particular characteristics of furniture design (i.e., it is a fashion in interior design); it does not necessarily imply that Danish Modern is a fashion that is currently desired by consumers.[51]

Cultural Categories

The meaning that does get imparted to products reflects underlying **cultural categories**, which correspond to the basic ways we characterize the world.[52] Our culture makes distinctions between different times, between leisure and work, between genders, and so on. The fashion system provides us with products that signify these categories. For example, the apparel industry gives us clothing to denote certain times (e.g., evening wear, resort wear); it differentiates between leisure clothes and work clothes; and it promotes masculine and feminine styles.

These cultural categories affect many different products and styles. As a result, it is common to find that dominant aspects of a culture at any particular time tend to be reflected in the design and marketing of very different products. This concept is a bit hard to grasp, since on the surface a clothing style, say, has little in common with a piece of furniture or a car. However, an overriding concern with a value such as achievement or environmentalism can determine the types of products likely to be accepted by consumers at any time. These underlying or latent themes then surface in various aspects of design. A few examples of this interdependence demonstrate how a dominant fashion motif reverberates across industries:

- Costumes worn by political figures or movie and rock stars can affect the fortunes of the apparel and accessory industries. A movie appearance by actor Clark Gable without a T-shirt (unusual at that time) dealt a severe setback to the men's apparel industry, while Jackie Kennedy's famous pillbox hat prompted a rush for hats by women in the 1960s. Other cross-category effects include the craze for ripped sweatshirts instigated by the movie *Flashdance,* a boost for cowboy boots from the movie *Urban Cowboy,* and singer Madonna's legitimization of lingerie as an acceptable outerwear clothing style.

- The Louvre (***www.louvre.fr***) in Paris was remodelled to include a controversial glass pyramid at the entrance designed by the architect I.M. Pei. Shortly thereafter, several designers unveiled pyramid-shaped clothing at Paris fashion shows.[53]

- In the 1950s and 1960s, much of the United States was preoccupied with science and technology. This concern with "space-age" mastery was fueled by the

Russians' launching of the Sputnik satellite, which prompted fears that the U.S. was falling behind in the technology race. The theme of technical mastery of nature and of futuristic design became a motif that cropped up in many aspects of U.S. popular culture—from car designs with prominent tail fins to high-tech kitchen styles.

- At any point in time a small number of colours dominate the design world. Many companies actually buy colour forecasts from specialists such as Pantone that rank the top 10 fashion colours for each season (e.g., in Fall 2005 the top two were Moroccan Blue and Glazed Ginger). These charts influence mass-market fashion companies as well as other industries, such as automotive, home furnishings, and home appliances. A dominant colour often takes years to emerge. For example, when black was prominent during the 1980s and 1990s, designers snubbed brown as a "dirty" colour. Then, Starbucks began to take off—and espresso, latte, and other coffee colours began to seep into mass culture. In addition, consumers rediscovered gourmet chocolates like Godiva, and (at least in some circles) fur regained its popularity. Colour forecasts put brown back on the fast track. Sure enough, United Parcel Service now asks, "What Can Brown Do for You?"[54]

Remember that creative subsystems within a culture production system attempt to anticipate the tastes of the buying public. Despite their unique talents, members of this subsystem are also members of mass culture. Like the fashion magazine editors discussed earlier, cultural gatekeepers are drawing from a common set of ideas and symbols and are influenced by the same cultural phenomena as the eventual consumers of their products.

The process by which certain symbolic alternatives are chosen over others has been termed **collective selection**.[55] As with the creative subsystem, members of the managerial and communications subsystems also seem to develop common frames of mind. Although products within each category must compete for acceptance in the marketplace, they can usually be characterized by their adherence to a dominant theme or motif—be it "The Western Look," "New Wave," "Danish Modern," or "Nouvelle Cuisine."

Behavioural Science Perspectives on Fashion

Fashion is a very complex process that operates on many levels. At one extreme, it is a macro, societal phenomenon affecting many people simultaneously. At the other, it exerts a very personal effect on individual behaviour. A consumer's purchase decisions are often motivated by his or her desire to be in fashion. Fashion products are also aesthetic objects, and their origins are rooted in art and history. Thus, there are many perspectives on the origin and diffusion of fashion. Although these cannot be described in detail here, some major approaches can be briefly summarized.

PSYCHOLOGICAL MODELS OF FASHION

Many psychological factors help to explain why people are motivated to be in fashion. These include conformity, variety seeking, personal creativity, and sexual attraction. For example, many consumers seem to have a "need for uniqueness." These consumers want to be different, but not too different.[56] For this reason people often conform to the basic outlines of a fashion but try to improvise and make a personal statement within these guidelines.

One of the earliest theories of fashion proposed that "shifting **erogenous zones**" (sexually arousing areas of the body) accounted for fashion changes, and that different zones become the object of interest because they reflect societal trends. J.C. Flugel, a disciple of Freud, proposed in the 1920s that sexually charged areas wax and wane in order to maintain interest and that clothing styles change to highlight or hide these parts. For example, it was common for Renaissance-era

→ This ad for Maidenform illustrates that fashions have accentuated different parts of the female anatomy throughout history.
Copyright 1990 by Maidenform, Inc.

ISN'T IT NICE TO LIVE IN A TIME WHEN WOMEN AREN'T BEING PUSHED AROUND SO MUCH ANYMORE?

Women have spent the last ten centuries conforming to their lingerie. Fortunately, lingerie has finally gotten around to conforming to women.

MAIDENFORM

Marketing Pitfall

Large companies that try to stay on top of hot fashion trends face a disturbing paradox: Young consumers are drawn to happening street fashions like those produced by small entrepreneurs. For example, when Dina Mohajer was a student at the University of Southern California in 1995, she needed blue nail polish to go with her blue platform shoes, and so she mixed up her own batch. Her friends loved the idea, and she started Hard Candy with a loan from her parents. Soon Drew Barrymore, Cher, and even Antonio Banderas were wearing such Hard Candy colours as Trailer Trash, Jail Bait, and Fiend.[59]

However, as soon as these styles are "discovered" and mass produced, they are no longer cool. Even M.A.C. cosmetics is no longer the cool fashion statement of the times. In the old days, *couture* houses and major retailers set the styles, but with the advent of the web and numerous small 'zines produced by individuals or small companies, the big guys no longer have the final say on what is cool, and big brand names are distrusted. One way around this dilemma is to spin off a separate division and try to distance it from the parent company, as Levi Strauss did with its Silver Tab boutique label and Miller did with its boutique brewery Red Dog.

women to drape their abdomens in fabrics in order to give a swollen appearance, successful child-bearing being a priority in the disease-ridden fourteenth and fifteenth centuries. Interest in the female leg in the 1920s and 1930s coincided with women's new mobility and independence, while the exposure of breasts in the 1970s signalled a renewed interest in breast-feeding. Breasts were de-emphasized in the 1980s as women concentrated on careers, but a larger bust size is now more popular as women try to combine professional activity with child rearing. Some contemporary fashion theorists suggest that the prevalence of the exposed midriff reflected the premium our society places on fitness.[57] (Note that, until very recently, the study of fashion focused almost exclusively on its impact on women. It is to be hoped that this concentration will broaden as scholars and practitioners begin to appreciate that men are affected by many of the same fashion influences.)

ECONOMIC MODELS OF FASHION

Economists approach fashion in terms of the model of supply and demand. Items that are in limited supply have high value, while those readily available are less desirable. Rare items command respect and prestige.

Veblen's notion of conspicuous consumption proposed that the wealthy consume to display their prosperity, for example by wearing expensive (and at times impractical) clothing. As noted in Chapter 12, this approach is somewhat outdated, since upscale consumers often engage in *parody display*, in which they deliberately adopt formerly low-status or inexpensive products, such as Jeeps or jeans.

Other factors also influence the demand curve for fashion-related products. These include a *prestige-exclusivity effect*, wherein high prices still create high demand, and a *snob effect*, in which lower prices actually reduce demand ("if it's that cheap, it can't be any good").[58]

SOCIOLOGICAL MODELS OF FASHION

The collective selection model discussed previously is an example of a sociological approach to fashion. This perspective focuses upon the initial adoption of a fashion (idea, style, etc.) by a subculture and its subsequent diffusion into society as a whole. Such diffusion often begins with youth subcultures like the hip hop segment. Another example is the integration of Goth culture into the mainstream. This

fashion started as a mode of expressing rebellion by young outcasts who admired nineteenth-century romantics and who defied conventional styles with their black clothing (often including over-the-top fashion statements like Count Dracula capes, studded collars, and black lipstick) and punk music of bands like Siouxsie & the Banshees and Bauhaus. Today, Virgin Megastores sells vampire-girl lunch boxes, and mall outlets sell clunky cross jewellery and black lace. You can find a T-shirt that looks like a corset at Kmart. At the Hot Topic website, teen surfers can buy a "Multi-Ring Choker." Hard-core Goths are not amused, but hey, that's fashion for you.[60]

The **trickle-down theory**, first proposed in 1904 by Georg Simmel, has been one of the most influential approaches to understanding fashion. It states that there are two conflicting forces that drive fashion change. First, subordinate groups try to adopt the status symbols of the groups above them as they attempt to climb up the ladder of social mobility. Dominant styles thus originate with the upper classes and *trickle down* to those below. However, this is where the second force kicks in: Those people in the superordinate groups are constantly looking below them on the ladder to ensure that they are not imitated, and they respond to the attempts of lower classes to "impersonate" them by adopting even *newer* fashions. These two processes create a self-perpetuating cycle of change—the machine that drives fashion.[61] The integration of hip hop phrases into our vocabulary illustrates how people who set fashions often resist their adoption by the mainstream. The street elite shunned some slang terms like *bad*, *fresh*, and *jiggy* once they became too mainstream. The rap community even held a funeral (with a eulogy delivered by Al Sharpton) for the word "Def" once it was included in the *Oxford English Dictionary*.[62]

The trickle-down theory was quite useful for understanding the process of fashion changes when applied to a society with a stable class structure that permitted the easy identification of lower- and upper-class consumers. This task is not so easy in modern times. In contemporary Western society, this approach must be modified to account for new developments in mass culture:[63]

- A perspective based on class structure cannot account for the wide range of styles that are simultaneously made available in our society. Modern consumers have a much greater degree of individualized choice than they did in the past because of advances in technology and distribution. Just as an adolescent is almost instantly aware of the latest style trends by watching MuchMusic, *elite fashion* has been largely replaced by *mass fashion*, since media exposure permits many groups to become aware of a style at the same time.

- Consumers tend to be more influenced by opinion leaders who are similar to them. As a result, each social group has its own fashion innovators who determine fashion trends. It is often more accurate to speak of a *trickle-across effect*, where fashions diffuse horizontally among members of the same social group.[64]

- Finally, current fashions often originate with the lower classes and *trickle up*. Grassroots innovators typically are people who lack prestige in the dominant culture (like urban youth). Since they are less concerned with maintaining the status quo, they are more free to innovate and take risks.[65]

A "Medical" Model of Fashion

For years and years, the lowly Hush Puppy was a shoe for nerds. Suddenly—almost overnight—the shoe became a chic fashion statement even though the company did nothing to promote this image. Why did this style diffuse through the population so quickly? **Meme theory** has been proposed to explain this process using a medical metaphor. A *meme* is an idea or product that enters the consciousness of people over time—examples include tunes, catchphrases ("Is that your final

→ This Jim Beam ad illustrates the cyclical nature of fashion.
Courtesy of Jim Beam Brand Inc.

answer?"), or styles like the Hush Puppy. In this view, memes spread among consumers in a geometric progression, just as a virus starts off small and steadily infects increasing numbers of people until it becomes an epidemic. Memes "leap" from brain to brain via a process of imitation.

The memes that survive tend to be distinctive and memorable, and the hardiest ones often combine aspects of prior memes. For example, the *Star Wars* movies evoked prior memes relating to Arthurian legend, religion, heroic youth, and 1930s adventure serials. Indeed, George Lucas studied comparative religion and mythology as he prepared his first draft of the *Star Wars* saga, *The Story of Mace Windu*.[66]

The meme idea is itself catching on. A website called ***www.memepool.com*** is a pool for ideas that attracts 7000 users a day who post random thoughts that others may adopt.[67] More generally, the diffusion of many products in addition to Hush Puppies seems to follow the same basic path. The product initially is used by a few people, but change happens in a hurry when the process reaches the moment of critical mass—which one author has called the **tipping point**. For example, Sharp introduced the first low-price fax in 1984 and sold about 80 000 that year. There was a slow climb in the number of users for the next three years. Then suddenly, in 1987, enough people had faxes that it made sense for everyone to have one, and Sharp sold a million units that year. Cell phones followed the same trajectory.[68]

Cycles of Fashion Adoption

In 1996, Tickle-Me-Elmo dolls were all the rage among North American children. Faced with a limited supply of the product, some retailers reported near-riots among adults as they tried desperately to buy the dolls for their children. In Fredericton, New Brunswick, 300 parents sent a Wal-Mart employee to hospital after they rushed the store to grab one of the 48 Elmos on the shelves.[69] Although the Tickle-Me-Elmo craze lasted for a couple of months, it eventually died out and consumers moved on to other things, like Pokémon, which is now dead, too.

Although the longevity of a particular style can range from a month to a century, fashions tend to flow in a predictable sequence. The **fashion life cycle** is quite similar to the more familiar product life cycle. An item or idea progresses through basic stages from birth to death, as shown in Figure 17–4.

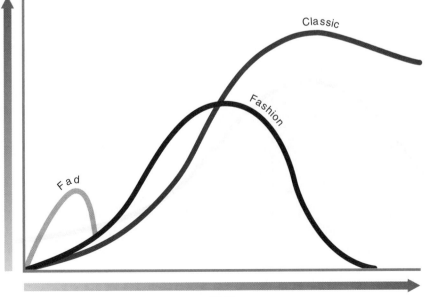

FIGURE 17–4

COMPARISON OF THE ACCEPTANCE CYCLES OF FADS, FASHIONS, AND CLASSICS

Source: Reprinted with the permission of Macmillan College Publishing Company from *The Social Psychology of Clothing* by Susan Kaiser. Copyright © 1985 by Macmillan College Publishing Company, Inc.

The diffusion process discussed earlier in this chapter is intimately related to the popularity of fashion-related items. To illustrate how this process works, consider how the **fashion acceptance cycle** works in the popular music business. In the *introduction stage* a song is listened to by a small number of music innovators. It may be played in clubs or on "cutting-edge" university radio stations (which is exactly how "grunge rock" groups like Nirvana got their start). During the *acceptance stage* the song enjoys increased social visibility and acceptance by large segments of the population. A record may get wide airplay on Top 40 stations, steadily rising up the charts "like a bullet." In the *regression stage* the item reaches a state of social saturation as it becomes overused, and eventually it sinks into decline and obsolescence as new songs rise to take its place. A hit number may be played once an hour on a Top 40 station for several weeks. At some point, though, people tend to get sick of it and focus their attention on newer releases. The former hit record eventually winds up in the discount rack at the local music store.

Figure 17–5 illustrates that fashions are characterized by slow acceptance at the beginning, which (if the fashion is to "make it") rapidly accelerates and then tapers off. Different classes of fashion can be identified by considering the relative length of the fashion acceptance cycle. Although many fashions exhibit a moderate cycle, taking several years to work their way through the stages of acceptance and decline, others are extremely long-lived or short-lived.

A **classic** is a fashion with an extremely long acceptance cycle. It is in a sense "antifashion," since it guarantees stability and low risk to the purchaser for a long period of time. Keds sneakers, introduced in 1917, have been successful because they appeal to those who are turned off by the high-fashion, trendy appeal of L.A. Gear, Reebok, and others. When consumers in focus groups were asked to project what kind of building Keds would be, a common response was a country house with a white picket fence. In other words, the shoes are seen as a stable, classic product. In contrast, Nikes were often described as steel-and-glass skyscrapers, reflecting their more modernistic image.[70]

A **fad** is a very short-lived fashion. Fads are usually adopted by relatively few people. Adopters may all belong to a common subculture; the fad "trickles across" members but rarely breaks out of that specific group. Some successful fad products include hula hoops, snap bracelets, and pet rocks. To learn more about these and other "must have" products, visit ***www.badfadscom***. Streaking was a fad that hit university campuses in the mid-1970s. This term referred to students running

---

FIGURE 17–5   A NORMAL FASHION CYCLE

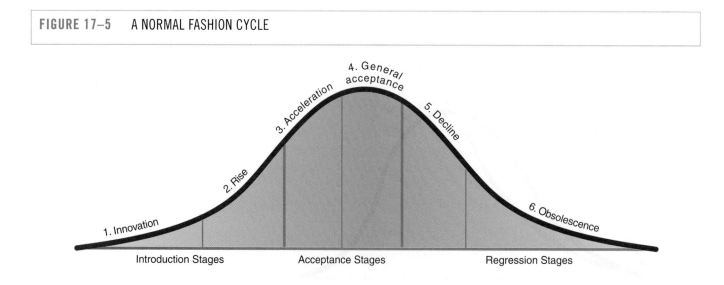

Source: Reprinted with the permission of Macmillan College Publishing Company from *The Social Psychology of Clothing* by Susan Kaiser. Copyright ©1985 by Macmillan College Publishing Company, Inc.

naked through classrooms, cafeterias, and dorms. Although the practice quickly spread across many campuses, it was primarily restricted to university settings. Streaking highlights several of the following important characteristics of fads:[71]

- The fad is non-utilitarian; that is, it does not perform any meaningful function.
- The fad is often adopted on impulse; people do not undergo stages of rational decision making before joining in.
- The fad diffuses rapidly, gains quick acceptance, and is short-lived.

FAD OR TREND?

In 1988, Clearly Canadian began selling a clear soft drink, and over the next few years others jumped on board. Colgate-Palmolive spent US$6 million developing a clear version of Palmolive dishwashing liquid; by 1992 Colgate was selling clear soap; Coors introduced a clear malt beverage called Zima; and consumers could even choose clear gasoline for their cars. Clear products were so ubiquitous that they were spoofed on *Saturday Night Live* in a fake commercial for Crystal Gravy: "You can see your meat!" It was clear that the beginning of the end was in sight and that the novelty was wearing off the "clear" fad. The comments of one 25-year-old participant in a research study of clear drinks sums up the problem: "When I first started drinking them, I thought they were interesting. But once it became a fad I thought, 'This isn't cool anymore.'"[72]

The first company to identify a trend and act on it has an advantage, whether the firm is Starbucks (gourmet coffee), Nabisco (Snackwell's low-fat cookies and crackers), or Taco Bell (value pricing). Although nothing is certain, some guidelines help to predict whether the innovation will endure as a long-term trend or whether it is just a fad:[73]

- Does it fit with basic lifestyle changes? If a new hairstyle is hard to care for, this innovation will not be consistent with women's increasing time demands. On the other hand, the movement to shorter-term vacations is more likely to last since this innovation makes trip planning easier for harried consumers.
- What are the benefits? The switch to poultry and fish from beef came about because these meats are healthier, so a real benefit was evident.
- Can it be personalized? Enduring trends tend to accommodate a desire for individuality, while styles like mohawk haircuts or the grunge look are inflexible and don't allow people to express themselves.
- Is it a trend or a side-effect? An increased interest in exercise is part of a basic trend toward health consciousness, while the specific form of exercise that is "in" at any given time will vary (e.g., low-impact aerobics versus in-line skating).
- What other changes have occurred in the market? Sometimes the popularity of products is influenced by *carry-over effects*. The miniskirt fad in the 1960s brought about a major change in the hosiery market, as sales of pantyhose and tights grew from 10 percent of this product category to more than 80 percent in two years. Now sales of these items are declining because of the casual emphasis in dressing.
- Who has adopted the change? If the innovation is not adopted by working mothers, baby boomers, or some other important market segment, it is not likely to become a trend.

TRANSFERRING PRODUCT MEANINGS TO OTHER CULTURES

Innovations know no country boundaries; in modern times they travel across oceans and deserts with blinding speed. Just as Marco Polo brought spice from

China and colonial settlers introduced Europeans to the "joys" of tobacco, today multinational firms seeking to expand their markets are constantly working to conquer new markets and convince legions of foreign consumers to want their offerings.

As if understanding the dynamics of one's own culture weren't hard enough, these issues get even more complicated when we take on the daunting—but essential—task of learning about the practices of other cultures. The consequences of ignoring cultural sensitivities can be costly. This oversight became evident, for example, during the 1994 soccer World Cup. Both McDonald's and Coca-Cola made the mistake of reprinting the Saudi Arabian flag, which includes sacred words from the Quran, on disposable packaging used in promotions. Despite their delight at having a Saudi team in contention for the Cup, Muslims around the world protested the use of sacred imagery, and both companies had to scramble to rectify the situation.[74]

In this section we'll consider some of the issues confronting marketers who seek to understand the cultural dynamics of other countries. We'll also consider the consequences of global culture, as Western marketers continue to export popular culture to a world full of increasingly affluent consumers, many of whom are eagerly waiting to replace their traditional products and practices with those of McDonald's, Levi's, and MTV.

Rather than ignore the global characteristics of their brands, firms must learn to manage those characteristics. This is crucial, because future growth for most companies will likely come from foreign markets. In 2002, developed countries in North America, Europe, and East Asia accounted for 15 percent of the world's population of 6.3 billion. By 2030, according to the World Bank, the planet's population will rise to 9 billion, with 90 percent of people living in developing countries.

Think Globally, Act Locally

As corporations increasingly find themselves competing in many markets around the world, the dialogue has intensified regarding the necessity of developing separate marketing plans for each culture. A lively debate has ensued about the need to "fit in" to the local culture. Let's briefly consider each viewpoint.

ADOPTING A STANDARDIZED STRATEGY

Proponents of a standardized marketing strategy argue that many cultures, especially those of relatively industrialized countries, have become so homogenized that the same approach will work throughout the world. By developing one approach for multiple markets, a company can benefit from economies of scale, since it does not have to incur the substantial time and expense of developing a separate strategy for each culture.[75] This viewpoint represents an **etic perspective**, which focuses upon commonalities across cultures. An etic approach to a culture is objective and analytical; it reflects impressions of a culture as viewed by outsiders.

Starbucks is becoming a household name in Japan (where it is pronounced STAH-buks-zu). Local outlets feature comfortable sofas, and hip hop and reggae tunes play in the background. The idea of hanging out in a coffee shop and knocking back an oversized gourmet coffee is new to most Japanese, who are accustomed to sipping tea from tiny cups in dimly lit shops. But Starbucks became an instant hit, and now there are well over 300 outlets buzzing with Japanese customers. In addition to the cachet associated with the chain, unlike most Japanese coffee shops (called *kisaten*), Starbucks does not allow smoking. This policy attracts young women, who do not smoke nearly as much as Japanese men.[76]

Starbucks is succeeding by exporting its recipe for success around the world. The company continues to confound local experts by bringing its version of the coffee experience to local cultures that (unlike Japan) have a long history of coffee snobbery. It's opening stores in San Juan and Mexico as part of a push into Latin America, where *café con leche* is part of the culture.[77] And talk about a brash move:

Now Starbucks is even opening in Austria, which already boasts one coffeehouse for every 530 citizens. These people take their coffee seriously. Again, although some aficionados who are used to ordering their coffee from waiters and drinking it out of china cups turned up their noses at this American intrusion, so far the new Starbucks stores are thriving.[78]

In 2004, Starbucks opened its first shop in France, hoping to spread "to go" coffee culture among Parisians long accustomed to waiting for their drinks and lingering for hours in one of the city's 2000 traditional cafés.[79] It costs more to drink your Starbucks coffee sitting down in France than if you were to take it away. Italy remains to be conquered by Starbucks; you won't find a single one in Milan. However, the more American tourists there are, the easier it will be for Starbucks to disrupt the local coffee culture.

Critics of the cultural consequences of standardization often point to Starbucks as an example of a company that succeeds by obliterating local customs and driving small competitors out of business. A recent in-depth study of patrons of local coffee shops in one American city examined the effect of the Starbucks phenomenon by looking at how consumers react to the influence of global brands on local culture. Many of the customers voiced strong negative feelings about Starbucks (note that these respondents are not Starbucks customers, whom we'd expect to have a somewhat different view). The authors of the study identify two distinct types of consumers who choose to give their business to local shops rather than to Starbucks:

- *Café flaneurs* view local coffee shops as dynamic public spaces and enjoy them primarily for the social spectacle of the crowd and for the feeling of artistic inspiration they gain from the ambiance.

- *Oppositional localists* view their choice of local coffee shops as a way to express solidarity with the local community.[80]

ADOPTING A LOCALIZED STRATEGY

Unlike Disney World in Orlando, visitors to the Walt Disney Studios theme park at Disneyland Paris don't hear the voices of American movie stars narrating their guided tours. Instead, European actors like Jeremy Irons, Isabella Rossellini, and Nastassja Kinski provide commentary in their native tongues. Disney learned the hard way about the importance of being sensitive to local cultures after it opened its Euro Disney Park in 1992. The company got slammed for creating an entertainment venue that recreated its American locations without catering to local customs (such as serving wine with meals). Visitors to Euro Disney from many countries took offense, even at what seemed to be small slights. For example, initially the park sold only a French sausage, which drew complaints from Germans, Italians, and others who believed their own local versions to be superior. As Euro Disney's CEO explains, "When we first launched, there was the belief that it was enough to be Disney. Now we realize that our guests need to be welcomed on the basis of their own culture and travel habits."[81]

Disney is applying the lessons it learned in cultural sensitivity to its new Hong Kong Disneyland. Executives decided to shift the angle of the front gate by 12 degrees after consulting a *feng shui* specialist, who said the change would ensure prosperity for the park. Disney also put a bend in the walkway from the train station to the gate, to make sure the flow of positive energy, or *chi*, did not slip past the entrance and out to the China Sea. Cash registers are close to corners or along walls to increase prosperity. The company burnt incense as it finished each building, and it picked a lucky day (September 12) for the opening. One of the park's main ballrooms measures exactly 888 square metres because the Chinese think eight is a number of fortune. And, since the Chinese consider the number four to be bad luck, you won't find any fourth-floor buttons in hotel elevators. Ironically, Disney may be trying *too* hard to cater to local customs: Activists raised a ruckus when the

→ JCDecaux, the second-largest outdoor advertising company worldwide, specializes in "street furniture" like these kiosks, newsstands, and public toilets. They represent an emic perspective because each is designed to reflect the local culture.

Courtesy of J.C. Decaux Advertising.

company announced it would serve the traditional Chinese dish of shark's fin soup at wedding banquets held in the park. The species is endangered, and one group distributed T-shirts showing Mickey Mouse and Donald Duck holding knives and leering over three bleeding sharks.[82]

Disney's experience supports the view of marketers who endorse an **emic perspective**, which focuses on variations within a culture. They feel that each culture is unique, with its own value system, conventions, and regulations. This perspective argues that each country has a national character and a distinctive set of behaviour and personality characteristics.[83] An effective strategy must therefore be tailored to the sensibilities and needs of each specific culture. An emic approach to a culture is subjective and experiential; it attempts to explain a culture as it is experienced by insiders.

Sometimes this strategy involves modifying a product or the way it is positioned to make it acceptable to local tastes. For example, the Chinese beer Tsingtao is trying to break into the Taiwanese market by airing a commercial featuring happy people kneeling on tatami mats while a woman in a kimono sings a traditional Japanese tune in Taiwanese dialect. This ad would never be accepted in Tsingtao's home market, where there is strong historical hostility toward Japan. In Taiwan, however, many associate Japanese culture with high status.[84]

In some cases, consumers in one place simply do not like some products that are popular elsewhere—or their different lifestyles require companies to adapt the way they make their products. IKEA finally realized that Americans weren't buying smaller European glasses because they add a lot of ice to their drinks. The Swedish furniture chain also figured out that, compared to Europeans, Americans sleep in bigger beds, need bigger bookshelves, and like to curl up on sofas rather than sit on them.[85] Snapple failed in Japan because consumers didn't like the drink's cloudy

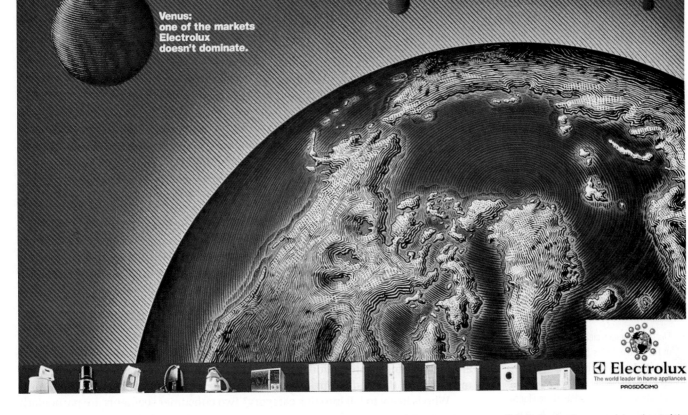

Venus:
one of the markets
Electrolux
doesn't dominate.

Electrolux
The world leader in home appliances
PROSDÓCIMO

↑ Globalization has become an integral part of the marketing strategy of many, if not most, major corporations.
Courtesy of Electrolux/Fabiana.

appearance or the stuff floating in the bottles. Similarly, Frito-Lay Inc. stopped selling Ruffles potato chips there (too salty) as well as Cheetos (the Japanese didn't appreciate having their fingers turn orange after eating a handful).[86] Cheetos are made in China, but the local version doesn't contain any cheese, which is not a staple of the Chinese diet. Instead, local flavours are available in varieties like Japanese Steak.[87]

CULTURAL DIFFERENCES RELEVANT TO MARKETERS

So which perspective is correct—the emic or the etic? To answer this question, perhaps it would be helpful to consider some of the ways that cultures vary in terms of their product preferences and norms regarding what types of products are appropriate or desirable.

Given the sizeable variations in tastes within Canada alone, it is hardly surprising that people around the world have developed their own unique preferences. For example, Europeans favour dark chocolate over milk chocolate, which they regard as suitable only for children. Sara Lee sells its pound cake with chocolate chips in the United States, with raisins in Australia, and with coconut in Hong Kong. Whisky is considered a "classy" drink in France and Italy but not in England. Crocodile bags are popular in Asia and Europe but not in the United States. Americans' favourite tie colours are red and blue, while the Japanese prefer olive, brown, and bronze.[88]

Marketers must be aware of a culture's norms regarding such sensitive topics as taboos and sexuality. Opals signify bad luck to the British, while hunting-dog or pig emblems are offensive to Muslims. The Japanese are superstitious about the number four. *Shi*, the word for four, is also the word for death. For this reason Tiffany sells glassware and china in sets of five in Japan.

Marketing Pitfall ↘

The language barrier is one problem confronting marketers who wish to break into foreign markets. Travellers abroad commonly encounter signs in tortured English, such as a note to guests at a Tokyo hotel saying, "You are invited to take advantage of the chambermaid," a notice at a hotel in Acapulco reassuring people that "The manager has personally passed all the water served here," or a dry cleaner in Majorca who urged passing customers to "drop your pants here for best results." One technique that is used to avoid this problem is back-translation, where a translated ad is retranslated into the original language by a different interpreter in order to catch errors. Some specific translation obstacles that have been encountered around the world include the following:[92]

> Electrolux vacuum cleaners were marketed in the United States by the Scandinavian manufacturer with the slogan: "Nothing sucks like an Electrolux."

> Colgate introduced a toothpaste in France called Cue, which also happens to be the name of a well-known porn magazine.

> When Parker marketed a ballpoint pen in Mexico, its ads were supposed to say, "It won't leak in your pocket and embarrass you." The translation actually said, "It won't leak in your pocket and make you pregnant."[93]

> *Fresca* (the name of a soft drink) is Mexican slang for *lesbian*.

> When spelled phonetically, *Esso* means *stalled car* in Japan.

> Ford had several problems in Spanish markets. The company discovered that a truck model it called *Fiera* means *ugly old woman* in Spanish. Its *Caliente*, a model sold in Mexico, is slang for *streetwalker*. In Brazil, *Pinto* is a slang term meaning *small male appendage*.

Does Global Marketing Work?

So, after briefly considering some of the many differences one encounters across cultures, what's the verdict? Does global marketing work? Perhaps the more appropriate question is, "*When* does it work?"

Although the argument for a homogeneous world culture is appealing in principle, in practice it has met with mixed results. One reason for the failure of global marketing is that consumers in different countries have different conventions and customs, so they simply do not use products the same way. Kellogg, for example, discovered that in Brazil big breakfasts are not traditional, and cereal is more commonly eaten as a dry snack.

In fact, significant cultural differences can show up within the *same* country. Advertisers know that when they target consumers in French-speaking Quebec, their messages must be much different from when they are talking to their fellow Canadians who speak English. Ads in Montreal tend to be a lot racier than those in Toronto, reflecting differences in attitudes toward sexuality between consumers with French versus British roots.[89]

Some large corporations, such as Coca-Cola, have been successful in crafting a single, international image. Still, even Coca-Cola must make minor modifications to the way it presents itself in each culture. Although Coke commercials are largely standardized, local agencies are permitted to edit them to highlight close-ups of local faces.[90] As the world's borders shrink because of advances in communications, many companies continue to develop global advertising campaigns.

To maximize the chances of success for these multicultural efforts, marketers must locate consumers in different countries who nonetheless share a common world view. This is more likely to be the case among people whose frames of reference are relatively more international or cosmopolitan or who receive much of their information about the world from sources that incorporate a worldwide perspective.

Who is likely to fall into this category? Two consumer segments are particularly good candidates: (1) affluent people who are "global citizens" and who are exposed to ideas from around the world through their travels, business contacts, and media experiences, and who, as a result, share common tastes; and (2) young people whose tastes in music and fashion are strongly influenced by MTV and other media that broadcast many of the same images worldwide.

A recent large-scale study conducted with consumers in 41 countries identified the characteristics people associate with global brands, measuring their relative importance to consumers when they buy products.[91] The study identified the following dimensions:

* *Quality signal*: Many assume that if a company has global reach it must excel on quality.

* *Global myth*: Consumers look to global brands as symbols of cultural ideals, buying these brands to help them "bond" with like-minded people around the world. As a Costa Rican participant commented, "Local brands show what we are; global brands show what we want to be."

* *Social responsibility*: People recognize that global companies wield extraordinary influence—both positive and negative—on society's well-being. They expect firms to address social problems linked to what they sell and how they conduct business.

The researchers also identified four major segments among consumers who evaluate global brands:

1. *Global citizens*: The largest segment (55 percent of consumers) uses the global success of a company as a signal of quality and innovation. At the same time, this group is concerned about whether companies behave responsibly on issues like consumer health, the environment, and worker rights.

2. *Global dreamers:* The second-largest segment, at 23 percent, consists of consumers who see global brands as quality products and who readily buy into the myths they author. They aren't nearly as concerned about a company's social responsibilities as are the global citizens.

3. *Antiglobals:* Thirteen percent of consumers are sceptical that transnational companies deliver higher-quality goods. They dislike brands that preach American values and don't trust global companies to behave responsibly. They try to avoid doing business with transnational firms.

4. *Global agnostics:* The remaining 9 percent of consumers don't base purchase decisions on a brand's global attributes. Instead, they evaluate a global product by the same criteria they use to judge local brands, refusing to regard its global nature as meriting special consideration.

The Diffusion of Consumer Culture

Coca-Cola is the drink of choice among young people in Asian countries, and McDonald's is their favourite restaurant.[94] The National Basketball Association sells US$500 million worth of licensed merchandise every year *outside* the United States.[95] Walk the streets of Lisbon or Buenos Aires and you'll be accosted by the sight of Nike hats, Gap T-shirts, and Levi's jeans at every turn.

The allure of consumer culture has spread throughout the world. In a global society, people are quick to borrow from other cultures, especially those they admire. For example, many Koreans are influenced by the cultural scene in Japan, which they view as a very sophisticated country. Japanese rock bands are more popular than Korean bands, and other exports such as comic books, fashion magazines, and game shows are eagerly snapped up. A Korean researcher explains, "Culture is like water. It flows from stronger nations to weaker ones. People tend to idolize countries that are wealthier, freer and more advanced, and in Asia that country is Japan."[96]

"I'D LIKE TO BUY THE WORLD A COKE . . ."

The West is a *net exporter* of popular culture. Many consumers have learned to equate Western lifestyles in general and the English language in particular with modernization and sophistication, and many American brands are slowly but surely insinuating themselves into local cultures. Indeed, a survey conducted by a marketing research firm in Beijing found that nearly half of all children under 12 think McDonald's is a domestic Chinese brand![97]

According to recent polls conducted by a market research firm, nearly 20 percent of consumers abroad say they will avoid U.S. companies and products like McDonald's, Starbucks, American Airlines, and Barbie dolls because of the U.S.'s unilateral foreign policies. And the more American a brand is perceived to be, the more resistance it encounters. For instance, almost half the survey respondents (including 1000 people from each of the G8 nations, excluding the U.S.) associate Mattel's Barbie with America, while only 10 percent make the same link with Kleenex tissues; 33 percent of respondents say they will avoid Barbie, but only 10 percent won't touch the tissues.[98] Indeed, some products have become so widespread that many people are only vaguely aware of their countries of origin. In surveys, consumers routinely guess that Heineken is German (it's really Dutch) and that Nokia is Japanese (it's Finnish). Nestlé, a Swiss brand, found itself on some Arab boycott lists of American products during the Iraq war, while few people know that Haagen-Dazs and Estée Lauder were actually born in the United States. Even where consumers can correctly identify the national origin of a multinational brand, they are more inclined to think of it as global rather than American or Japanese.[99]

American television also inspires knockoffs around the world. Some local shows "borrow" from American programs: A German hit called *Das Traumschiff* (the *Dream Ship*) is a remake of the old American hit *Love Boat*. In fairness, American reality-show hits like *Big Brother* and in-your-face game shows like *The*

Marketing
Opportunity !

The huge popularity of a humble local product traditionally worn by Brazilian peasants illustrates the diffusion of global consumer culture as consumers hunger for fresh ideas and styles from around the globe. The local products are simple flip-flops called *Havaianas* (pronounced ah-vai-YAH-nas)—the name is Portuguese for "Hawaiians." The lowly shoes, which sell for $2 a pair in Brazil, are associated so strongly with poor people in that country that the expression *pe de chinelo*, or "slipper foot," is a popular slang term for the downtrodden. The main buyers in Brazil continue to be blue-collar workers, but now fashionable men and women in cities from Paris to Sydney are wearing the peasant shoes to trendy clubs and in some cases even to work.

How did these flip-flops make the leap to fashion statement? In an attempt to boost profit margins, a company named Alpargatas introduced new models in colours like lime-green and fuchsia that cost twice as much as the original black- or blue-strapped sandal with a cream-coloured sole. Then, it launched newer styles, including a masculine surf model. Middle-class Brazilians started to adopt the shoes and even the country's president was seen wearing them. The fashion spread as a few celebrities, including supermodels Naomi Campbell, Kate Moss, and Brazil's own Gisele Bündchen, discovered the flip-flops. Company representatives helped fuel the fire by giving out free sandals to stars at the Cannes Film Festival. The result: Alpargatas' international sales zoomed from virtually zero to more than 5 million sandals sold around the world.[108]

Weakest Link started out as European concepts that were imported by U.S. producers.[100] A popular reality show in Europe is a Spanish production called *Operación Triunfo* (*Operation Triumph*). Similar to *American Idol*, it's being sold to TV networks in many countries including Russia, Italy, Britain, Greece, Mexico, Brazil, and Portugal.[101]

And, of course, the hit show *The Apprentice* is being reproduced all over the globe. As local versions spread rapidly across Europe, Latin America, and Asia, the Trump role is being assumed by such disparate taskmasters as a German soccer-team manager, a billionaire Arab entrepreneur, and the CEO of a Brazilian ad agency. Each local *Apprentice* show is tailored to the country's culture; contestants sell flowers in London, hot dogs in Frankfurt, and rolled fish in Finland.[102] Not everyone is treated quite as harshly as the American losers, either: In Finland, contestants are told, "You're free to leave."

Despite the proliferation of Western culture around the world, there are signs that this invasion is slowing. Political developments strongly influence the demand for American products, particularly in regions like the Middle East that oppose U.S. policies. When American warplanes began their bombing campaign in Afghanistan following the events of 9/11, thousands of protestors in Karachi marched through the streets chanting "Death to America" and setting fire to businesses linked to the U.S., including KFC restaurants (even though these are locally owned).[103] Coca-Cola estimates that it lost 40 million to 50 million cases of soft-drink sales in the Gulf, Egypt, and Saudi Arabia in 2002 alone as a result of an anti-U.S. backlash. Procter & Gamble even saw a big dip in sales of its Ariel laundry detergent after it was targeted by a pro-Palestinian boycott—because the brand shared the first name of Ariel Sharon, Israel's prime minister.[104] Critics in other countries—especially the French—deplore the creeping Americanization of their cultures. The French have even tried to ban the use of such "Franglais" terms as *le drugstore, le fast food*, and even *le marketing*, though this effort was recently ruled unconstitutional.[105] Resistance to the diffusion of American culture is best summarized in the words of one French critic who described the Euro Disney theme park as "a horror made of cardboard, plastic, and appalling colours—a construction of hardened chewing gum and idiotic folklore taken straight out of a comic book written for obese Americans."[106]

Opposition to a global fast-food culture also comes from groups like the Slow Food movement that was founded by an Italian journalist to protest the arrival of the first McDonald's restaurant in Rome. This group promotes what it calls "Slow Cities," which stress environmental policies that create public green spaces and encourage new ways to dispose of garbage. All members share a commitment to restoring older parts of their cities before agreeing to expand into new areas. They discourage chain stores and fast-food franchises, as well as the use or production of any genetically modified agriculture. Today, there are 30 Slow Cities, and 40 more towns have requested membership.[107]

EMERGING CONSUMER CULTURES IN TRANSITIONAL ECONOMIES

More than 60 countries have a gross national product of less than $10 billion, while more than 135 international companies had revenues greater than that. The dominance of these marketing powerhouses has helped to create a **globalized consumption ethic:** As people the world over are increasingly surrounded by goods and tempting images of them, a material lifestyle becomes more important to attain. Shopping evolves from a wearying, task-oriented struggle to locate even basic necessities to become a leisure activity, and possessing luxury items becomes a mechanism to display one's status (see Chapter 13)—often at great personal sacrifice.

After the downfall of Communism, eastern Europeans emerged from a long winter of deprivation into a springtime of abundance. The picture is not all rosy, however, since attaining consumer goods is not easy for many in *transitional economies,* where the economic system still is "neither fish nor fowl." Governments ranging from China to Portugal struggle with the difficult adaptation from a controlled, centralized economy to a free-market system.

Some of the consequences of the transition to capitalism include a loss of confidence and pride in the local culture, as well as alienation, frustration, and an increase in stress as consumers sacrifice leisure time because they have to work ever harder to buy consumer goods. The yearning for the trappings of Western material culture is perhaps most evident in parts of eastern Europe where citizens who threw off the shackles of Communism now have direct access to coveted consumer goods from the U.S. and western Europe—if they can afford them. One analyst observed, "As former subjects of the Soviet empire dream it, the American dream has very little to do with liberty and justice for all and a great deal to do with soap operas and the Sears catalogue."[109]

As the global consumption ethic spreads, rituals and product preferences in different cultures become homogenized. For example, Christmas is now celebrated among some urbanites in Muslim Turkey, though gift giving even on birthdays is not customary in many parts of the country. Christmas fever is gripping China's newly rising urban middle class as an excuse to shop, eat, and party. People there are snapping up Christmas trees, ornaments, and Christian religious objects (even though the street vendors peddling photos of Jesus and Mary can't always identify who they are). Chinese consumers are embracing Christmas because celebrating the holiday is seen as international and modern, not because it's a traditional Christian celebration. The Chinese government encourages this practice because it stimulates consumer spending. To make the holiday even merrier, China exports about $1 billion worth of Christmas products every year, and its factories churn out $7.5 billion of the toys that people worldwide put under their trees.[110]

Does this homogenization mean that in time consumers who live in Nairobi, New Guinea, or the Netherlands will all be indistinguishable from those in New York or Nashville? Probably not, because the meanings of consumer goods often mutate to be consistent with local customs and values. For example, in Turkey some urban women use ovens to dry clothes and dishwashers to wash muddy spinach. A person in Papua New Guinea may combine a traditional clothing style such as a *bilum* with Western items such as Mickey Mouse shirts or baseball caps.[111] These processes make it unlikely that global homogenization will overwhelm local cultures, but it *is* likely that there will be multiple consumer cultures, each blending global icons such as Nike's pervasive "swoosh" with indigenous products and meanings.

CREOLIZATION

In some cases the meanings of desired products are adapted to local customs and needs. **Creolization** occurs when foreign influences are absorbed and integrated with local meanings—just as modern Christianity incorporated the pagan Christmas tree into its own rituals. Creolization makes it unlikely that global homogenization will overwhelm local cultures; rather, there will probably be multiple consumer cultures, each blending global icons.

The creolization process sometimes results in bizarre permutations of products and services when they are modified to be compatible with local customs. Consider these creolized adaptations, for example:[112]

- In highland Papua New Guinea, tribesmen put Chivas Regal wrappers on their drums and wear Pentel pens instead of nose bones.

- The Japanese use Western words as a shorthand for anything new and exciting, even if they do not understand their meaning. Cars are given names such as Fair Lady, Gloria, and Bongo Wagon. Consumers buy *deodoranto* (deodorant) and *appuru pai* (apple pie). Ads urge shoppers to *stoppu rukku* (stop and look), and products are claimed to be *yuniku* (unique).[113] Coca-Cola cans say, "I feel Coke and sound special," and a company called Cream Soda sells products with the slogan, "Too old to die, too young to be happy."[114] Other Japanese products with English names include Mouth Pet (breath freshener), Pocari Sweat ("refreshment water"), Armpit (electric razor), Brown Gross Foam (hair-colouring mousse), Virgin Pink Special (skin cream), Cow Brand (beauty soap), and Mymorning Water (canned water).[115]

CHAPTER SUMMARY

STYLES ARE MIRRORS THAT REFLECT UNDERLYING CULTURAL CONDITIONS.

- The styles prevalent in a culture at any given time often reflect underlying political and social conditions. The set of agents responsible for creating stylistic alternatives is termed a culture production system. Factors such as the types of people involved in this system and the amount of competition by alternative product forms influence the choices that eventually make their way to the marketplace for consideration by end consumers.

WE CAN DISTINGUISH BETWEEN HIGH AND LOW CULTURE.

- Culture is often described in terms of high (or elite) forms and low (or popular) forms. Products of popular culture tend to follow a cultural formula and contain predictable components. On the other hand, these distinctions are blurring in modern society as imagery from "high art" is increasingly being incorporated into marketing efforts.

MANY MODERN MARKETERS ARE REALITY ENGINEERS.

- Reality engineering occurs as elements of popular culture are appropriated by marketers and converted to vehicles for promotional strategies. These elements include sensory and spatial aspects of everyday existence, whether in the form of products appearing in movies, odours pumped into offices and stores, billboards, theme parks, or video monitors attached to shopping carts.

NEW PRODUCTS, SERVICES, AND IDEAS SPREAD THROUGH A POPULATION; DIFFERENT TYPES OF PEOPLE ARE MORE OR LESS LIKELY TO ADOPT THEM.

- Diffusion of innovation refers to the process whereby a new product, service, or idea spreads through a population. Innovators and early adopters are quick to adopt new products, while laggards are very slow. A consumer's decision to adopt a new product depends on his or her personal characteristics as well as on characteristics of the innovation itself. Products stand a better chance of being adopted if they demand relatively little change in behaviour from users, are easy to understand, and provide a relative advantage compared with existing products.

MANY PEOPLE AND ORGANIZATIONS PLAY A ROLE IN THE FASHION SYSTEM THAT CREATES AND COMMUNICATES SYMBOLIC MEANINGS TO CONSUMERS.

- The fashion system includes everyone involved in the creation and transference of symbolic meanings. Meanings that express common cultural categories (e.g., gender distinctions) are conveyed by many different products. New styles tend to be adopted by many people simultaneously in a process known as collective selection. Perspectives on motivations for adopting new styles include psychological, economic, and sociological models of fashion.

FASHION FOLLOWS CYCLES.

- Fashions tend to follow cycles that resemble the product life cycle. The two extremes of fashion adoption—classics and fads—can be distinguished in terms of the length of this cycle.

PRODUCTS THAT SUCCEED IN ONE CULTURE MAY FAIL IN ANOTHER IF MARKETERS FAIL TO UNDERSTAND THE DIFFERENCES AMONG CONSUMERS IN EACH PLACE.

- Because a consumer's culture exerts such a big influence on his or her lifestyle choices, marketers must learn as much as possible about differences in cultural norms and preferences when marketing in more than one country. One important issue is the extent to which marketing strategies must be tailored to each culture rather than standardized across cultures. Followers of an etic perspective believe that the same universal messages will be appreciated by people in many cultures. Believers in an emic perspective argue that individual cultures are too unique to permit such standardization; marketers must instead adapt their approaches to be consistent with local values and practices. Attempts at global marketing have met with mixed success; in many cases this approach is more likely to work if the messages appeal to basic values and/or if the target markets consist of consumers who are more internationally rather than locally oriented.

KEY TERMS

REVIEW QUESTIONS

1. What is collective selection? Give an example.
2. Describe a culture production system (CPS) and list its three components. What is an example of such a CPS?
3. Define a cultural gatekeeper, giving three examples.
4. Describe the difference between arts and crafts.
5. What is a cultural formula? Give an example.
6. What is new vintage? How is this an example of reality engineering?
7. Define product placement and list three examples of it. How is this practice the same or different from branded entertainment?
8. What is advergaming? Give an example.
9. What is the diffusion of innovations?
10. Define innovators, early adopters, and laggards.
11. Describe the differences among continuous innovations, dynamically continuous innovations, and discontinuous innovations, providing an example of each. Which type are consumers least likely to adapt?
12. What is the difference among the terms "fashion," "a fashion," and "in fashion"?
13. What are cultural categories, and how do they influence product designs?
14. Summarize some of the major approaches to understanding fashion from the perspectives of psychologists, economists, and sociologists.
15. What is the trickle-down effect? List some reasons why it is no longer as valid as it used to be.
16. What is the difference between a fad, a fashion, and a classic fashion life cycle?
17. What is the difference between an emic and an etic perspective on globalization?
18. Define creolization and provide an example.

CONSUMER BEHAVIOUR CHALLENGE

Discuss

1. Watchdog groups have long decried product placements for blurring the line between content and advertising without adequately informing viewers. And the networks themselves appear to be divided on how far they want to open the gate. "You've got to wonder when it starts to destroy the entertainment value," asks one former television executive. How do you see the future of product placement? Will it get out of hand and create a consumer backlash, or is it a valuable alternative to traditional advertising?
2. Is advertising an art or a craft? Which should it be?
3. This chapter mentions some instances in which market research findings influenced artistic decisions, as when a movie ending was reshot to accommodate consumers' preferences. Many people would most likely oppose this practice, claiming that books, movies, records, or other artistic endeavors should not be designed merely to conform to what people want to read, see, or hear. What do you think?
4. Due to higher competition and market saturation, marketers in industrialized countries are increasingly trying to develop Third-World markets by encouraging people in underdeveloped countries to desire Western products. Asian consumers alone spend $90 billion a year on

cigarettes, and American tobacco manufacturers continue to push relentlessly into these markets. Cigarette advertising, often depicting glamorous Western models and settings, is found just about everywhere, on billboards, buses, storefronts, and clothing, and many major sports and cultural events are sponsored by tobacco companies. Some companies even hand out cigarettes and gifts in amusement areas, often to preteens. Should this practice be encouraged, even if the products being marketed may be harmful to consumers' health (e.g., cigarettes), or if they divert needed money away from the purchase of essentials? If you were a trade or health official in a Third-World country, what guidelines, if any, might you suggest to regulate the import of luxury goods from advanced economies?

5. Comment on the growing practices described as reality engineering. Do marketers "own" our culture? Should they?

6. If you worked in marketing research for a cosmetics firm, how might you apply the lead user concept to help you identify new product opportunities?

7. Many consumers around the world seem to be willing to suffer for the sake of fashion. Others argue that we are merely pawns in the hands of designers, who conspire to force unwieldy fashions down our throats. What do you think? What is and what should be the role of fashion in our society? How important is it for people to be in style? What are the pros and cons of keeping up with the latest fashions? Do you believe that we are at the mercy of designers?

Experiential Exercises

8. If you were a consultant to a toy company, what would you forecast as the next big trend in this market? Survey toy stores and watch what kids are playing with today to help you with your prediction.

9. How might the rise of peer-to-peer music sharing influence the structure of the music CPS? One hypothesis is that this method erodes the dominance of the big labels because listeners are more likely to access music from lesser-known groups. Survey your friends to determine if this is in fact happening. Are they listening to a wider variety of artists, or just downloading more of the big-time groups?

10. Read several romance or action novels to see if you can identify a cultural formula at work. Do you see parallels among the roles different characters play (e.g., the hero, the evildoer, the temptress, etc.)?

11. Watch 12 hours of TV shows and keep a log of all the product placements you see. What are the dominant products being inserted into the programs?

CBC ⊛ VIDEO VIGNETTE

CONCEPTS AT WORK FOR CASHING IN ON COOL

What's cool? What's in? What's out? These questions are always on the minds of entrepreneurs and established retailers alike. Even with the technology to truncate the lead times for production and distribution, plans need to be made that require picking some products over others and to allocate space and marketing communication dollars. Then, just when you get comfortable riding the wave of a winner in the marketplace, competitors step in and the market becomes saturated. The story of Muks is a case in point.

Muks are distributed by Harper Lee Worldwide Ltd., a company based in London, U.K. Canadian owners Jaime Cooke and Courtney Wise identified Mukluks as a unique product that would sell through exclusive retailers around the world. Although Jaime wore Mukluks as a young girl growing up in Canada, it was a pair that she received as a gift after she moved to London that started a worldwide trend. The path to establishing this global trend illustrates the complexities of the rise and fall of market dynamics. With the fashion cycle moving toward decline for Muks, Jaime and Courtney are asking, "What's next? What's hot?"

Questions

1. Describe the components of the cultural production system that leads to the success of a product.

2. Do Muks exemplify how a CPS works? Explain your answer.

3. Describe how Muks have and are moving through the fashion life cycle.

4. Identify trends that co-exist and may evolve from the marketplace success of Muks.

Resources: "Cashing in on Cool," Venture #7, CBC Air Date: January 30, 2006; **www.muklukstore.com**.

NOTES

1. Grant McCracken, "Culture and Consumption: A Theoretical Account of the Structure and Movement of the Cultural Meaning of Consumer Goods," *Journal of Consumer Research* 13 (June 1986): 71–84.

2. Richard A. Peterson, "The Production of Culture: A Prolegomenon," in *The Production of Culture*, ed. Richard A. Peterson, Sage Contemporary Social Science Issues (Beverly Hills, CA: Sage, 1976), p. 722.

3. Richard A. Peterson and D.G. Berger, "Entrepreneurship in Organizations: Evidence from the Popular Music Industry," *Administrative Science Quarterly* 16 (1971): 97–107.

4. Elizabeth C. Hirschman, "Resource Exchange in the Production and Distribution of a Motion Picture," *Empirical Studies of the Arts* 8, 1 (1990): 31–51; Michael R. Solomon, "Building Up and Breaking Down: The Impact of Cultural Sorting on Symbolic Consumption," in *Research in Consumer Behavior*, eds. J. Sheth and E.C. Hirschman (Greenwich, CT: JAI Press, 1988), pp. 325–351.

5. See Paul M. Hirsch, "Processing Fads and Fashions: An Organizational Set Analysis of Cultural Industry Systems," *American Journal of Sociology* 77, 4 (1972): 639–659; Russell Lynes, *The Tastemakers* (New York, NY: Harper and Brothers, 1954); Michael R. Solomon, "The Missing Link: Surrogate Consumers in the Marketing Chain," *Journal of Marketing* 50 (October 1986): 208–219.

6. Howard S. Becker, "Arts and Crafts," *American Journal of Sociology* 83 (January 1987): 862–889.

7. Herbert J. Gans, "Popular Culture in America: Social Problem in a Mass Society or Social Asset in a Pluralist Society?" in *Social Problems: A Modern Approach,* ed. Howard S. Becker (New York, NY: Wiley, 1966).

8. Martin Forstenzer, "In Search of Fine Art Amid the Paper Towels," *New York Times* on the Web (February 22, 2004).

9. Nat Ives, "All Commercials, All the Time," *New York Times* (July 26, 2004).

10. Michael R. Real, *Mass-Mediated Culture* (Englewood Cliffs, NJ: Prentice Hall, 1977).

11. Annetta Miller, "Shopping Bags Imitate Art: Seen the Sacks? Now Visit the Museum Exhibit," *Newsweek* (January 23, 1989): 44.

12. Kim Foltz, "New Species for Study: Consumers in Action," *New York Times* (December 18, 1989): A1.

13. Arthur A. Berger, *Signs in Contemporary Culture: An Introduction to Semiotics* (New York, NY: Longman, 1984).

14. Michiko Kakutani, "Art Is Easier the 2nd Time Around," *New York Times* (October 30, 1994): E4.

15. Nigel Andrews, "Filming a Blockbuster Is One Thing; Striking Gold Is Another," *Financial Times*, accessed via Simon & Schuster College Newslink (January 20, 1998).

16. Stuart Elliott, "Ad for Television Show Becomes Element of the Show," *New York Times on the Web* (November 26, 2004).

17. Michael R. Solomon and Basil G. Englis, "Reality Engineering: Blurring the Boundaries between Marketing and Popular Culture," *Journal of Current Issues and Research in Advertising* 16, 2 (Fall 1994): 1–17.

18. Austin Bunn, "Not Fade Away," *New York Times on the Web* (December 2, 2002).

19. T. Bettina Cornwell and Bruce Keillor, "Contemporary Literature and the Embedded Consumer Culture: The Case of Updike's Rabbit," in *Empirical Approaches to Literature and Aesthetics: Advances in Discourse Processes* 52, eds. Roger J. Kruez and Mary Sue MacNealy (Norwood, NJ: Ablex, 1996): 559–572; Monroe Friedman, "The Changing Language of a Consumer Society: Brand Name Usage in Popular American Novels in the Postwar Era," *Journal of Consumer Research* 11 (March 1985): 927–937; Monroe Friedman, "Commercial Influences in the Lyrics of Popular American Music of the Postwar Era," *Journal of Consumer Affairs* 20 (Winter 1986): 193.

20. George Gerbner et al., "Aging with Television: Images on Television Drama and Conceptions of Social Reality," *Journal of Communication* 30 (1980): 37–47.

21. Stephen Fox and William Philber, "Television Viewing and the Perception of Affluence," *Sociological Quarterly* 19 (1978): 103–12; W. James Potter, "Three Strategies for Elaborating the Cultivation Hypothesis," *Journalism Quarterly* 65 (Winter 1988): 930–939; Gabriel Weimann, "Images of Life in America: The Impact of American TV in Israel," *International Journal of Intercultural Relations* 8 (1984): 185–197.

22. "Movie Smoking Exceeds Real Life," *Asbury Park Press* (June 20, 1994): A4.

23. Lynn Elber, "TV Offers Fantasy Depiction of Real-Life Family, Work Life, Study Says," *Montgomery Advertiser* (June 11, 1998): B1.

24. Benjamin M. Cole, "Products that Want to Be in Pictures," *Los Angeles Herald Examiner* (March 5, 1985): 36. See also Stacy M. Vollmers and Richard W. Mizerski, "A Review and Investigation into the Effectiveness of Product Placements in Films," in *Proceedings of the 1994 Conference of the American Academy of Advertising,* ed. Karen Whitehill King: 97–102; Solomon and Englis, "Reality Engineering ...."

25. Wayne Friedman, " 'Minority Report' Stars Lexus, Nokia," *Advertising Age* (June 17, 2002): 41.

26. Nat Ives, "'Advertainment' Gains Momentum," *New York Times on the Web* (April 21, 2004).

27. Denise E. DeLorme and Leonard N. Reid (1999), "Moviegoers' Experiences and Interpretations of Brands in Films Revisited," *Journal of Advertising* 28, 2: 71–90.

28. Cristel Antonia Russell, "Investigating the Effectiveness of Product Placement in Television Shows: The Role of Modality and Plot Connection Congruence on Brand Memory and Attitude," *Journal of Consumer Research* 29 (December 2002): 306.

29. Claire Atkinson, "Ad Intrusion Up, Say Consumers," *Advertising Age* (January 6, 2003): 1.

30. Evelyn Nussenbaum, "Products Slide into More TV Shows, With Help from New Middlemen," *New York Times* (September 6, 2004).

31. Suzanne Vranica and Brian Steinberg, "The Robot Wore Converses—Chaos Reigns as Marketers, Media Scramble to Negotiate Product-Placement Deals," *Wall Street Journal Interactive Edition* (September 2, 2004): B1.

32. Brooks Barnes, "Good Soap Script Includes Love, Tears And Frosted Flakes: As Ratings Slip, Daytime TV Gets Generous with Plugs; A Kiss before Using OnStar," *Wall Street Journal Interactive Edition* (January 17, 2005): A1.

33. Stuart Elliott, "Product Placement Moves to Cartoons," *New York Times on the Web* (October 21, 2004).

34. Jennifer Lewington, "Pepsi Ignites Corporate Debate," *Globe and Mail* (March 27, 1997).

35. Rebecca Harris, "Brand Watchers," *Marketing Magazine* (May 15, 2006): 6.

36. Geoffrey A. Fowler, "New Star on Chinese TV: Product Placements," *Wall Street Journal Interactive Edition* (June 2, 2004): B1.

37. Gabriel Kahn, "Product Placement Booms in New Bollywood Films," *Wall Street Journal Interactive Edition* (August 30, 2002).

38. "Advertisements Insinuated into Video Games," *New York Times on the Web* (October 18, 2004).

39. Hassan Fattah and Pamela Paul, "Gaming Gets Serious," *American Demographics* (May 2002): 39–43.

40. Kevin J. Delaney, "Videogame Makers Borrow TV's Tactics for Selling Ads; 'Virtual' Billboards Allow Firms to Pitch Change-Ups; Rates Based on Eyeballs," *Wall Street Journal* (October 18, 2004): B5.

41. Robert Hof, "The Click Here Economy," *Business Week* (June 22, 1998): 122–128.

42. Eric J. Arnould, "Toward a Broadened Theory of Preference Formation and the Diffusion of Innovations: Cases from Zinder Province, Niger Republic," *Journal of Consumer Research* 16 (September 1989): 239–267; Susan B. Kaiser, *The Social Psychology of Clothing* (New York: Macmillan, 1985); Thomas S. Robertson, *Innovative Behavior and Communication* (New York: Holt, Rinehart and Winston, 1971).

43. Susan L. Holak, Donald R. Lehmann, and Fareena Sultan, "The Role of Expectations in the Adoption of Innovative Consumer Durables: Some Preliminary Evidence," *Journal of Retailing* 63 (Fall 1987): 243–259.

44. Hubert Gatignon and Thomas S. Robertson, "A Propositional Inventory for New Diffusion Research," *Journal of Consumer Research* 11 (March 1985): 849–867.

45. C.K. Prahalad and Venkatram Ramaswamy, "Co-Opting Customer Competence," *Harvard Business Review* (January/February 2000): 79–87.

46. Eric von Hipple, "Users as Innovators," *Technology Review* 80 (January 1978): 3–11.

47. Jakki Mohr, *Marketing of High-Technology Products and Services* (Upper Saddle River, NJ: Prentice Hall, 2001).

48. Everett M. Rogers, *Diffusion of Innovations*, 3rd ed. (New York, NY: Free Press, 1983).

49. Umberto Eco, *A Theory of Semiotics* (Bloomington, IN: Indiana University Press, 1979).

50. Fred Davis, "Clothing and Fashion as Communication," in *The Psychology of Fashion*, ed. Michael R. Solomon (Lexington, MA: Lexington Books, 1985), pp. 15–28.

51. Melanie Wallendorf, "The Formation of Aesthetic Criteria through Social Structures and Social Institutions," in *Advances in Consumer Research* 7, ed. Jerry C. Olson (Ann Arbor, MI: Association for Consumer Research, 1980), 36.

52. McCracken, "Culture and Consumption."

53. "The Eternal Triangle," *Art in America* (February 1989): 23.

54. Sally Beatty, "Fashion's 'It' Colors: How Runway Dresses, Cars—Even Washer-Dryers—Turned Shades of Blue, Brown," *Wall Street Journal Interactive Edition* (February 4, 2005).

55. Herbert Blumer, *Symbolic Interactionism: Perspective and Method* (Englewood Cliffs, NJ: Prentice Hall, 1969); Howard S. Becker, "Art as Collective Action," *American Sociological Review* 39 (December 1973); Richard A. Peterson, "Revitalizing the Culture Concept," *Annual Review of Sociology* 5 (1979): 137–166.

56. C.R. Snyder and Howard L. Fromkin, *Uniqueness: The Human Pursuit of Difference* (New York, NY: Plenum Press, 1980).

57. Linda Dyett, "Desperately Seeking Skin," *Psychology Today* (May/June 1996): 14; Alison Lurie, *The Language of Clothes* (New York, NY: Random House, 1981).

58. Harvey Leibenstein, *Beyond Economic Man: A New Foundation for Microeconomics* (Cambridge, MA: Harvard University Press, 1976).

59. Gregory Beals and Leslie Kaufman, "The Kids Know Cool," *Newsweek* (March 31, 1997): 48–49.

60. Nara Schoenberg, "Goth Culture Moves into Mainstream," *Montgomery Advertiser* (January 19, 2003): 1G.

61. Georg Simmel, "Fashion," *International Quarterly* 10 (1904): 130–155.

62. Maureen Tkacik, "'Z' Zips into the Zeitgeist, Subbing for 'S' in Hot Slang: Slang from the 'Hood Now Sells Toyz in Target," *Wall Street Journal Interactive Edition* (December 30, 2002).

63. Grant D. McCracken, "The Trickle-Down Theory Rehabilitated," in *The Psychology of Fashion*, ed. Solomon, pp. 39–54.

64. Charles W. King, "Fashion Adoption: A Rebuttal to the Trickle-Down Theory," in *Toward Scientific Marketing*, ed. Stephen A. Greyser (Chicago, IL: American Marketing Association, 1963), pp. 108–125.

65. Alf H. Walle, "Grassroots Innovation," *Marketing Insights* (Summer 1990): 44–51.

66. Robert V. Kozinets, "Fandom's Menace/Pop Flows: Exploring the Metaphor of Entertainment as Recombinant/Memetic Engineering," *Association for Consumer Research*, (October 1999). The new science of memetics, which tries to explain how beliefs gain acceptance and predict their progress, was spurred by Richard Dawkins who, in the 1970s, proposed culture as a Darwinian struggle among "memes" or mind viruses—see Geoffrey Cowley, "Viruses of the Mind: How Odd Ideas Survive," *Newsweek* (April 14, 1997): 14.

67. Janet Kornblum, "Everybody into the Mempool for Links to Some Very Odd Sites," *USA Today* (May 4, 2000): 3D.

68. Malcolm Gladwell, *The Tipping Point* (New York: Little, Brown and Co., 2000).

69. Petti Fong, "Trample Me Elmo to Arrive in Vancouver before Christmas," *Vancouver Sun* (December 18, 1996): B1.

70. Anthony Ramirez, "The Pedestrian Sneaker Makes a Comeback," *New York Times* (October 14, 1990): F17.

71. B.E. Aguirre, E.L. Quarantelli, and Jorge L. Mendoza, "The Collective Behavior of Fads: The Characteristics, Effects, and Career of Streaking," *American Sociological Review* (August 1989): 569.

72. Quoted in Kathleen Deveny, "Anatomy of a Fad: How Clear Products Were Hot and then Suddenly Were Not," *Wall Street Journal* (March 15, 1994): B8.

73. Martin G. Letscher, "How to Tell Fads from Trends," *American Demographics* (December 1994): 38–45.

74. "Packaging Draws Protest," *Marketing News* (July 4, 1994): 1.

75. Theodore Levitt, *The Marketing Imagination* (New York: Free Press, 1983).

76. K. Belson, "As Starbucks Grows, Japan, too, Is Awash," *New York Times on the Web* (October 21, 2001).

77. "Starbucks Plans 24 Stores in Puerto Rico, Mexico: Will Consumers Buy $5 Coffee in the Land of 50 Cent Cafe?" *Wall Street Journal Interactive Edition* (August 29, 2002).

78. Steven Erlanger, "An American Coffeehouse (or 4) in Vienna," *New York Times on the Web* (June 1, 2002).

79. Ariane Bernard, "New American Beachhead in France: Starbucks," *New York Times on the Web* (January 16, 2004).

80. Craig J. Thompson and Zeynep Arsel, "The Starbucks Brandscape and Consumers' (Anticorporate) Experiences of Glocalization," *Journal of Consumer Research* 31 (December 2004): 631–642.

81. Paulo Prada and Bruce Orwall, "Disney's New French Theme Park Serves Wine—and Better Sausage," *Wall Street Journal Interactive Edition* (March 12, 2002).

82. Laura M. Holson, "The Feng Shui Kingdom," *New York Times on the Web* (April 25, 2005); Keith Bradsher, "Disneyland for Chinese Offers a Soup and Lands in a Stew," *New York Times* (June 17, 2005): A1 (2).

83. Terry Clark, "International Marketing and National Character: A Review and Proposal for an Integrative Theory," *Journal of Marketing* 54 (October 1990): 66–79.

84. Jason Dean, "Beer's Taiwan Entry Tests Taste for Chinese Products," *Wall Street Journal Interactive Edition* (July 4, 2002).

85. Marc Gobé, *Emotional Branding: The New Paradigm for Connecting Brands to People* (New York: Allworth Press, 2001).

86. Norihiko Shirouzu, "Snapple in Japan: How a Splash Dried Up," *Wall Street Journal* (April 15 1996): B1 (2 pp.).

87. Glenn Collins, "Chinese to Get a Taste of Cheese-Less Cheetos," *New York Times* (September 2, 1994): D4.

88. Julie Skur Hill and Joseph M. Winski, "Goodbye Global Ads: Global Village Is Fantasy Land for Marketers," *Advertising Age* (November 16, 1987): 22.

89. Clyde H. Farnsworth, "Yoked in Twin Solitudes: Canada's Two Cultures," *New York Times* (September 18, 1994): E4.

90. Hill and Winski, "Goodbye Global Ads ...."

91. Douglas B. Holt, John A. Quelch, and Earl L. Taylor, "How Global Brands Compete," *Harvard Business Review* (September 2004): 68–75.

92. David A. Ricks, "Products that Crashed into the Language Barrier," *Business and Society Review* (Spring 1983): 46–50.

93. Shelly Reese, "Culture Shock," *Marketing Tools* (May 1998): 44–49.

94. Normandy Madden, "New GenerAsians Survey Gets Personal with Asia-Pacific Kids," *Advertising Age International* (July 13, 1998): 2.

95. "They All Want to Be Like Mike," *Fortune* (July 21, 1997): 51–53.

96. Quoted in Calvin Sims, "Japan Beckons, and East Asia's Youth Fall in Love," *New York Times* (December 5, 1999): 3.

97. Elisabeth Rosenthal, "Buicks, Starbucks and Fried Chicken, Still China?" *New York Times on the Web* (February 25, 2002).

98. Sean Gregory, "Anti-U.S. Backlash," *Time* (January 2005): A3.

99. Special Report, "Brands in an Age of Anti-Americanism," *BusinessWeek* (August 4, 2003): 69–76.

100. Suzanne Kapner, "U.S. TV Shows Losing Potency around World," *New York Times on the Web* (January 2, 2003).

101. Emma Daly, "In a Spanish Reality TV Show, Even the Losers Win," *New York Times on the Web* (December 4, 2002).

102. Laurel Wentz and Claire Atkinson, "Apprentice Translators Hope for Hits All over Globe," *Advertising Age* (February 14, 2005): 3, 73.

103. B. O'Keefe, "Global Brands," *Fortune* (November 26, 2001): 102–106.

104. Kevin J. Delaney, "U.S. Brands could Suffer Even before War Begins," *Wall Street Journal Interactive Edition* (January 28, 2003).

105. John Sherry, Jr., and Eduardo G. Camargo, "French Council Eases Language Ban," *New York Times* (July 31, 1994): 12.

106. Alan Riding, "Only the French Elite Scorn Mickey's Debut," *New York Times* (1992): A1.

107. Matthew Yeomans, "Unplugged," *Wired* (February 2002): 87.

108. Miriam Jordan and Teri Agins, "Fashion Flip-Flop: Sandal Leaves the Shower Behind," *Wall Street Journal Interactive Edition* (August 8, 2002).

109. Erazim Kohák, "Ashes, Ashes ... Central Europe After Forty Years," *Daedalus* 121 (Spring 1992): 219, quoted in Belk, "Romanian Consumer Desires and Feelings of Deservingness."

110. David Murphy, "Christmas's Commercial Side Makes Yuletide a Hit in China," *Wall Street Journal Interactive Edition* (December 24, 2002).

111. This example is courtesy of Professor Russell Belk, University of Utah, personal communication (July 25, 1997).

112. Eric J. Arnould and Richard R. Wilk, "Why Do the Natives Wear Adidas: Anthropological Approaches to Consumer Research," *Advances in Consumer Research* 12 (Provo, UT: Association for Consumer Research, 1985): 748–752.

113. John F. Sherry Jr. and Eduardo G. Camargo, "'May Your Life Be Marvelous': English Language Labeling and the Semiotics of Japanese Promotion," *Journal of Consumer Research* 14 (September 1987): 174–188.

114. Bill Bryson, "A Taste for Scrambled English," *New York Times* (July 22, 1990): 10; Rose A. Horowitz, "California Beach Culture Rides Wave of Popularity in Japan," *Journal of Commerce* (August 3, 1989): 17; Elaine Lafferty, "American Casual Seizes Japan: Teen-agers Go for N.F.L. Hats, Batman and the California Look," *Time* (November 13, 1989): 106.

115. Lucy Howard and Gregory Cerio, "Goofy Goods," *Newsweek* (August 15, 1994): 8.

Cases $\rightarrow$

Case	Main Chapter(s)	Other Relevant Chapters
1. Jake and the Bear: The Efforts of a Volunteer Organization	2, 4, 7, 8, 11	6, 17
2. Tomasino's Restaurant Ltd.	7, 8	3, 11, 15
3. Juul Møller Bokhandel A/S	9, 10, 11, 17	7, 8
4. Artventure: Children's Creative Art and Party Centre	12, 13, 14, 15	4, 6, 9, 10
5. Alessi: Italian Design and the Re-enchantment of Everyday Objects	2, 6, 16, 17	4, 5, 13, 14, 15
6. AtlanticRider.com	6, 8, 9	2, 4, 11

CASE 1: JAKE AND THE BEAR: THE EFFORTS OF A VOLUNTEER ORGANIZATION

↑ The Spirit Bear of British Columbia.
Courtesy of Charlie Russell.

Five years ago, Jake Yule joined the Sierra Club to help establish a protected habitat for the rare Spirit Bear of British Columbia. These efforts had been very successful, as indicated by the recent announcement of a coastal protected area including more than 200 000 hectares of Sprit Bear habitat,[1] plus the announcement that the Spirit Bear would become an official symbol of the province of British Columbia.[2] As Jake looked back over the Spirit Bear efforts, he wondered what lessons had been learned and what he should do next.

Early Days

Jake had graduated with a Bachelor of Engineering from the University of Saskatchewan and had been pleased to find a job with a major engineering firm in Vancouver. He had been to the west coast on holidays and had welcomed the chance to live in a different part of the country, away from Saskatchewan winters. Since moving to B.C., he had been spending more and more of his recreational time in the wilderness parts of the province and at the same time becoming more and more confused by his friends' conflicting views about logging and environmental issues.

He had always viewed the forests as a renewable resource and logging as a critical source of employment on the west coast. His "green" friends, on the other hand, always talked about the detrimental impact of forestry practices on salmon spawning rivers, threats to endangered species, biodiversity, and the rights of First Nations peoples. Because of these many conflicts Jake had read *Balancing Act* by Hamish Kimmins (see Exhibit 1-1) and had joined the Sierra Club, an organization he considered somewhat more balanced in perspective than some other environmental groups.

The Sierra Club of British Columbia

The Sierra Club was founded by naturalist and writer John Muir in 1892 to protect the wilderness of the Sierra Nevada. Over the years, the activities of the Sierra Club

[1] http://www2.news.gov.bc.ca/news_releases_2005-2009/2006AL0002-000066.htm
[2] http://www.climatecrisis.net/thescience

Exhibit 1–1 EXTRACTS FROM *BALANCING ACT*

> Both environmentalist and experienced field foresters should be members of a multidisciplinary team that contributes to the development of policies to guide the sustainable use and development of forests. For such a partnership to be effective, there must be agreement at the outset concerning the meaning of words used in discussions. Loaded terms such as "never" and "forever" would be best "checked at the door."…The environment is too important for us to go on arguing about it. All sides in the forestry–environment debate must enter a partnership to ensure sustainable development. We must base this partnership on social and environmental realities and our current scientific knowledge. We must use pictures and images that accurately portray the problems we face, and ensure that in our verbal and written communications we use our language in a way that accurately communicates our knowledge and goals.

Source: Hamish Kimmins, *Balancing Act: Environmental Issues in Forestry*, 2nd ed. (Vancouver: UBC Press, 1997) p. 287.

have expanded to include issues ranging from climate change and ozone depletion to toxic chemical contamination and loss of biological diversity. The Sierra Club has been active in Canada since 1969, working to influence public policy and environmental awareness. There were local chapters and working groups in every region of the country.

Literature provided by the Sierra Club of British Columbia positioned the forestry issue as follows:

> Ancient temperate rainforests are scarce, covering less than 0.2 percent of the Earth's land mass. Over 20 percent of the planet's remaining temperate rainforests are found in British Columbia. This highly productive, severely threatened forest supports one of the most abundant fisheries on earth.
>
> Coastal temperate rainforests once stretched in a thin, continuous band from northern California to southeastern Alaska. Today, almost all of the original ancient forest south of the Canada–U.S. border is gone, and very little remains intact in southern British Columbia and Vancouver Island. The few remaining large fragments in the south, such as the forest of Clayquot Sound, are still threatened with logging.
>
> The intact low- and mid-elevation forests on British Columbia's central coast contain some of the oldest and largest trees on earth. These forests provide a critical refuge for grizzly bears, salmon, and a rare white variation of the black bear called Kermode, or Spirit Bear.
>
> Protecting these species requires the preservation of large areas of contiguous ancient forest. Small areas of forest surrounded by clearcuts or parks that protect only mountain tops, meadows, and scrub cannot and will not prevent the extinction of these globally significant forests.

The Spirit Bear

The white bear mentioned above has been described by enthusiasts as:

> Powerful, yet gentle, an extraordinary wild creature. To scientists it is *Ursus americanus kermodei*. To the Tsimshian people of the Pacific Coast, it is moksgm'ol. [It is] not albino, but rather a subspecies with one in ten white and the rest black.

The only remaining habitat of the Spirit Bear is on British Columbia's remote mid-coast, the location of the proposed Spirit Bear Wilderness Park.

Preliminary Efforts

When Jake joined the Sierra Club, he had been asked to head up a task force of volunteers to develop an action plan for a "Spirit Bear Wilderness Park." His initial efforts had been to gather information about the issues associated with the park (Exhibit 1-2) and to identify other volunteer organizations interested in the Spirit Bear.[3] In addition, he realized that he had very little insight regarding what it takes to get people and organizations actively involved in environmental issues. As he addressed these initial efforts he had been faced with several interrelated questions:

1. Should we focus our energy on individuals, interest groups (such as tourism interests), corporations, or governmental organizations?

2. What can we hope to accomplish with each target group (i.e., donations, public support, political pressure)?

3. How will we convince each target group to participate (what messages, what media)?

What Next?

Jake felt very satisfied that the efforts of First Nations peoples and volunteer organizations had resulted in the establishment of protected habitat for the Spirit Bear. And yet he had to admit that the Spirit Bear habitat seemed like just a start. He had recently viewed *An Inconvenient Truth*, a film documentary on the Earth's climate crisis featuring Al Gore.[4] How could volunteer organizations have an impact on something as critical as global warming?

Exhibit 1–2   ISSUES ASSOCIATED WITH SPIRIT BEAR WILDERNESS PARK

- Ten parts of the province have been identified as "endangered rainforest areas soon to be lost to clearcut logging." The proposed Spirit Bear Wilderness Park was one of the ten areas.

- Concern that the provincial government may soon issue a permit to log the heart of the Spirit Bear's home range.

- Concern that forest industry interests dominate government actions.

- Importance of the proposed park in providing shoreline and mid-elevation habitat and in providing an important ecological link to a nearby inland mountain park.

- Importance of the park as the ancestral home of the Kitasoo people, who live within the proposed park in the small sea-village of Klemtu.

QUESTIONS

1. Why do people become involved in organizations like the Sierra Club?

2. What can a volunteer organization do to have an impact on global warming? Address this by answering Jake's three questions above.

---

[3]ForestEthics, *www.forestethics.org*; Greenpeace International, *www.greenpeace.org*; Valhalla Wilderness Society, *www.savespiritbear.org*; Spirit Bear Youth Coalition, *www.spiritbearyouth.org*
[4]*http://www.climatecrisis.net*

CASE 2: TOMASINO'S RESTAURANT LTD.

As saturated as the Halifax market area was with pizzerias, Thomas Vacon (owner and manager) and Leo Arkelian (business partner) felt they had found a niche for gourmet pizza pies. Unfortunately, another local entrepreneur also identified this niche; and while Tomasino's was still in the planning stage, Salvatore's opened on South Street with a very high-quality gourmet pizza.

However, this did not stop Mr. Vacon and Mr. Arkelian, who went ahead with their plans anyway. In November 1994 the partners decided to expand and move Tomasino's to a new location on South Street.

Strategy

Tomasino's Pizzeria opened for business in November 1989, initially as a takeout and delivery operation to test the market for gourmet pizza in downtown Halifax. The restaurant was located on McCully Street during the first five years, where the business developed a reputation as "one of Metro's best." This position was won by Tomasino's in a local newspaper's annual pizza contest. However, Tomasino's had plans from the start to expand into a full-service, licensed restaurant.

The move and expansion were financed with $10 000 from Tomasino's and a $25 000 small-business bank loan. An expansion budget was prepared but did not include costs associated with the actual move (Exhibit 2-1). The main reason for the move was to facilitate the addition of a restaurant to Tomasino's existing business. The eat-in service specialized in Italian pizza and Mediterranean foods, with a broader menu including pastas, soups, salads, and desserts.

Location

The new location on South Street was across from the Hotel Nova Scotia in a historical restaurant site (Exhibit 2-2). The previous occupant, Citadel Café, had sales exceeding $70 000 per month. Ironically, Tomasino's former closest competitor, Salvatore's, had been in the building adjacent to this new location. In 1993 they had gone bankrupt, blaming the recession and the Goods and Services Tax (GST) for their demise.

In comparison to Tomasino's McCully Street address, this new location was more visible and closer to the downtown core of Halifax. The proximity to office towers, hotels, hospitals, universities, and a dense residential area offered the potential for an eat-in restaurant, as well as expanded delivery sales in Halifax's south end.

Promotional Efforts

The owner believed in the old adage that "a good product will sell itself" and relied heavily on word-of-mouth advertising. Tomasino's tried television and newspaper advertising with little success. The primary promotional tool was direct mail flyers.

Exhibit 2–1 RESTAURANT EXPANSION BUDGET

Kitchen equipment (stove, oven)	$ 12 600.00
Tableware (dishes, silverware)	600.00
Furniture (tables, chairs)	3 200.00
Leaseholds (renovations, flooring, lighting)	8 600.00
Total budget	$ 25 000.00

Note: The above prices are based upon cost estimates of work, quoted prices for new items, and projected costs of used goods where available.

Source: Company Records

Exhibit 2–2 MAP OF HALIFAX

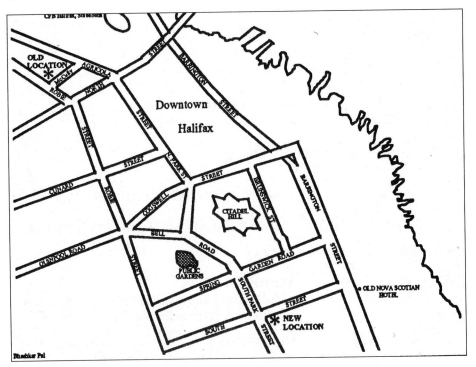

These efforts had been more effective, more convenient, less expensive, and easier to measure.

Tomasino's Restaurant was scheduled to open in April 1995. Coupon flyers (Exhibit 2-3) and other advertising methods were budgeted for the grand opening, which coincided with the G7 Conference in June and the return of the student population in September (Exhibit 2-4).

Cost Data

The projected cash flow statement (Exhibit 2-5) shows conservative growth in 1995 based on the following assumptions:

1. Restaurant income is calculated on seating for 70, with customer turnover of 1.25 per day and an average customer spending $6.50.

2. Takeout sales were projected from monthly historical variations, with eat-in sales varying in the same cycle.

3. Eat-in sales were factored downward for the initial start-up months.

4. Liquor sales were calculated as 35 percent of eat-in sales.

5. Variable costs were based on historical data and industrial averages.

6. The loan was assumed to be amortized over 60 months at 10.5 percent.

Personnel Data

Thomas Vacon is an Acadian from Yarmouth County, Nova Scotia. He holds a Bachelor of Arts degree in Economics and has been working directly in the food and beverage industry for more than 10 years. Most of the employees working at Tomasino's also have a university degree or are pursuing their studies.

The staff at Tomasino's are not only well-educated, but also very professional and well-trained. They are more courteous, more polite, and more efficient than the industry standards—virtues noticed and liked by the customers. Both the owner and employees of Tomasino's take great artistic pride in their work. "Making or creating a Tomasino pie is not a mechanical process but one that stems from the heart. Our dough is the canvas we use to create a culinary work of art," says Mr. Vacon.

Exhibit 2–3 COUPON FLYER FOR GRAND OPENING

TOMASINO'S CELLAR RISTORANTE

5173 South Street–Halifax–Tel: 425-7111

GRAND OPENING LUNCH SPECIALS

Buy One 7" Luncheon Pizza–Get One Free (11am–4pm)

SAMPLES FROM OUR MENU

FOCCACIA BREAD
(asiago, mozzarella, and parmesan with fresh
basil and a light brushing of olive oil. Serves four)

ACADIAN SEAFOOD CHOWDER

CAESAR SALAD (TOMASINO'S FAMOUS)

SPINACH SALAD
(with our delicious poppyseed dressing)

GREEK SALAD
(tomato, Spanish onion, and kalamata olives on a
bed of romaine, sprinkled with feta)

PENNE PUTINESCA
(penne, sundried tomatoes, black kalamata olives,
and capers in an olive oil herb mixture)

FETTUCCINI ALFREDO
(with smoked ham or vegetarian)

CHICKEN PESTO FUSILLI

**SMOKED SALMON & PEPPERS ON
ANGEL HAIR PASTA**

HALF-9" PIZZA WITH CAESAR SALAD

CAESAR SALAD WITH CHICKEN BREAST

PIZZAS

VONGOLE
(baby clams and artichoke hearts, topped
with fresh garlic and parmesan cheese)

NEW YORK
(mozzarella, parmesan, and feta)

AMBROSIA
(sautéed mushrooms, soin, and Italian
sausage)

EOS
(feta cheese, black kalamata olives, Spanish
onions, and tomatoes)

LOS ANGELES
(pesto, sundried tomatoes, and feta cheese)

LIGHT CHOCOLATE GRAND MARNIER

SORBET
DAILY CHEESECAKE

Exhibit 2–4 PROPOSED ADVERTISING BUDGET

MONTH AMOUNT IN $	Jan.	Feb.	Mar.	Apr.	May	June	July	Aug.	Sept.	Oct.	Nov.	Dec.
	100	3000	100	100	100	1000	100	100	1500	100	100	100

Source: Company Records

Exhibit 2–5 PROJECTED CASH FLOW SUMMARIZED STATEMENT JANUARY TO DECEMBER, 1995

CASH INFLOWS		CASH OUTFLOWS	
		Capital costs	$ 25 000
Takeout sales	$ 153 200	Accounting & legal	1 800
Eat-in sales	197 306	Advertising	6 400
Liquor sales	63 074	Bank charges	2 700
Loan	25 000	Business taxes	2 100
		Delivery costs	27 576
Total:	$ 438 580	Food purchases	94 637
		Insurance	1 800
		Interest	1 725
		Liquor purchases	31 537
		Loan repayment	4 170
		Miscellaneous	1 200
		Office supplies	900
		Rent	34 000
		Repairs & maintenance	1 440
		Telephone	3 900
		Utilities	5 400
		Wages	134 000
		Total	$ 380 285

Source: Company Records

QUESTIONS

1. How would you segment the market for Tomasino's pizza?
2. Suggest appropriate marketing mix strategies for each of Tomasino's potential target markets.
3. If you were responsible for approving the small-business loan based on the data provided in the case, would you have granted Tomasino's the money? Why or why not?
4. Evaluate the promotional efforts practised by the business. Should more be invested in advertising the move and expansion? Explain your answer.

CASE 3: JUUL MØLLER BOKHANDEL A/S

In April 1996, Dag Juul Møller, owner and president of Juul Møller Bokhandel A/S, a medium-sized bookstore company (in Norwegian terms) located in Oslo, Norway, was sitting in his home office contemplating a new challenge to the industry. He had just finished a telephone conversation with Dagfinn Nettland, a young master of management student at the Norwegian School of Management with a passion for computers. Dagfinn had helped him set up his home office.

Dagfinn had spent the Easter break surfing the internet and writing his term paper for a course called GRA2329, "IT in Global Business." The assignment was to take an existing company and analyze how it could use the internet as an information and sales channel for products and services. The students in GRA2329 chose a wide variety of businesses and organizations. Dagfinn was a member of a group that had worked with Norsk Rikstoto, the company administering nationwide equestrian sports gambling. What interested Dag, however, was another aspect of the course: when GRA2329 started, the required books were not yet available in the bookstore; they first started arriving several weeks into the course.

Normally, in situations like this, the professor would have postponed the discussions over the delayed literature until later in the course. However, for GRA2329, things had been different. Several of the students had bought the course literature over the internet from Amazon.com. Some of the students had also tried Blackwell's, a bookstore website in England, but had been less satisfied. Dagfinn found it impressive that these book shops could deliver American and English literature in as little as four days, at prices close to those of Juul Møller. One student had also tried to buy other products, such as Levi's jeans, over the internet, but had been less successful. Although he had received the product, and the price was somewhat below what it would have cost to buy the jeans in Norway (he had to pay both customs and sales tax), the increased complexity and time meant that it was better to just buy them in a regular store.

Dagfinn, who wanted to continue working with Juul Møller once he had passed his remaining exams, was a bit worried that the students would cease to buy their books from Juul Møller and start buying only from the internet.

Norli—A Cautious Pioneer

After talking to Dagfinn, Dag decided to call a colleague in another bookstore to discuss the matter with him. He poured another cup of coffee, opened his connection to the internet, and located a telephone number in the *Yellow Pages* of Telenor, Norway's recently privatized national telecommunications provider. Rolf Olsen in Norli, one of Norway's largest chains of bookstores, was an amiable person who was willing to discuss his experiences with the internet.

"We started about 18 months ago," said Olsen, "when we were approached by Forlagssentralen, maybe you remember that initiative? They have set up an internet service for bookshops called Boknett. In the beginning, all we could do was set up static webpages, presentations of the company and such, but in the spring of 1996 they started offering a service where the customer could order books over the internet from the individual bookstore. Forlagssentralen is the biggest book distributor in Norway; they have all the large publishers except Cappelen, so it looked like a good option for us. We have a few pages on their server..."

"I remember that now," said Dag. "We got some offers from a number of foreign publishers as well—Springer was one of them—about being on their homepages."

"That makes the whole process rather simple," continued Olsen. "We don't have to do anything technical; we just upload the pages and, of course, we have to handle the page design and maintenance. The latter has been a bit sporadic. We started with a flourish, but since then only some parts of it have been maintained, particularly the computer books. There we have one guy from the computer book department who has taken ownership of the pages and keeps them current with comments and new books all the time."

"How is it? Do you get any customers out of that?" asked Dag.

"Well...kind of hard to say, because we haven't done any monitoring of it, but I think we get about six to seven orders every day," Olsen ventured. "Some of it is from Norwegians abroad, some within computer books. Not a lot, but we still think this has a future. We are actually about to hire a person in a 50 percent position to be responsible for the web effort, evolving it into something more substantial. We have been very inspired by Akers Mic, that big music CD shop on the Oslo waterfront, which has done a great job and invested a lot of money in its website. They sell CDs and stereo equipment for millions of kroner per year..."

"What do you think about the rest of our industry?" Dag wondered.

"Well…," Olsen said, "except us, I suppose Bruns Libris up in Trondheim is the most active. They started cooperating with a local ISP—that is, an internet service provider. We are the largest user of Forlagssentralen's services, but there are some other bookshops that have started as well. Then there are some authors who have started communicating over the net. Most of the action is in the U.S., of course; Amazon.com is a real competitor to the larger bookstores there, such as Borders and Barnes & Noble. Both are large chains with huge multi-storey bookshops, but they seem to feel competitive enough to start their own initiatives on the internet. I think the real action is going to be in university and schoolbooks. But how about you, what have you done so far?"

"Not much," said Dag. "As you know, we have plenty of computer experience, but I have been busy lately. But I think I am choosing to view this as an opportunity rather than a threat. Anyway, thanks for filling me in!"

Background

Juul Møller Bokhandel had about 25 employees at four locations: a large store at a busy pedestrian street in the centre of Oslo, and three stores at the Norwegian School of Management (NSM), Norway's largest business school with 14 000 students. Of these three stores, one was at the main campus in Sandvika, one in the biggest branch campus in the centre of Oslo, and a small store at a small branch campus outside Oslo. About five people worked in the store in Sandvika, although this number varied considerably with highs in the beginning of each semester.

The relationship between Juul Møller and NSM went back a long way. Dag's father had started supplying books to NSM in the late forties, when NSM had just started and was housed in a large villa in Oslo. Dag was a graduate of NSM himself, from the mid-sixties. He had not planned to become a bookseller, but started working in ANSA, an organization for Norwegian students abroad, after graduation. However, in 1957 his father died suddenly, and Dag was the only one who could take over the family-owned firm. The company had evolved with the NSM: as the school grew to become one of the largest business schools in Europe, Juul Møller had maintained a close relationship with both the school and the student union, and had become the largest dealer in business administration books in Norway. NSM (and its students) was Juul Møller's largest customer.

It hadn't always been like that. Juul Møller had had similar agreements with the Norwegian School of Banking, the Norwegian School of Marketing, and Oslo Business School, but during the first half of the 1990s, NSM had acquired these schools, and Juul Møller found itself dealing with one large school.

The business relationship was regulated by an agreement, called the Bookseller Agreement, which was negotiated roughly once every five years between Juul Møller, NSM, and the student union. The main feature of the agreement was that Juul Møller was awarded the right to have stores in NSM's locales as well as early access to the literature specifications for the school's courses. In return, Juul Møller paid fixed rent for the store locations to the school and a percentage of sales to the student union, making Juul Møller the union's largest single source of income.

This agreement was unique in Norway. At other schools and universities, the bookshops were either run by the student unions as cooperatives (as was done at the University of Oslo), or the students bought their books in regular bookshops located off campus. The last time the agreement was negotiated, the student union had tried to interest other booksellers in it. Several had been interested, but Juul Møller was the only bookseller willing to take the terms, and the only store with strong experience and competence in business and management literature.

Ironically, the most visible face of Juul Møller—the store in Sandvika—was something of a problem for the company. Even though Juul Møller made a profit on its total relationship with NSM, the store in Sandvika was expensive due to a relatively high number of personnel, high rent, and relatively little sales outside course books. Another problem was that students often vented their frustrations on the staff, and finding people who had both the competence and the inclination to work in Sandvika could be difficult.

An important aspect of the relationship with NSM was the competence Juul Møller gained, both from being a large importer and distributor of foreign-language books and from knowing what books were used for the various courses. Due to this competence, Juul Møller could advise both individuals and companies that required literature on various aspects of business and management. An important market was comprised of the former students of the school, many of whom kept Juul Møller as their primary source of business literature after graduation, frequenting the store in the centre of Oslo.

Ordering Books

The part of Juul Møller's business that demanded the most managerial attention was ordering books: the situation was complicated, leading to the unavailability of books that Dag wanted.

The faculty at NSM specified books for each course, normally through the course catalogue, which was available a few months before the year started. For each course, there would be some books that were required, and some that were recommended as additional reading material. Unfortunately for Juul Møller, many specifications came too late or were unreliable; some faculty members might at the first course meeting announce that one or more of the books would not be important for the examination. Some faculty had been known to change the required literature, or switch a book from recommended to required status, without bothering to inform the bookstore.

Pricing the books was tricky: if the books were priced too high, very few would be sold. In some concentration courses, where a book could cost 800 to 900 kroner, sometimes only two books would be sold—"one for the library and one for some affluent student whose daddy picks up the tab," according to one observer. However, given the size of its operations, Juul Møller was sometimes able to negotiate substantial discounts. One example was a textbook for a large basic statistics course, where Juul Møller's standard price would have been 490 kroner. After discussions with the professor, Dag had talked to the publisher directly and reduced the price to 295 kroner. A large number of books was sold; Juul Møller was the largest seller of this particular book in Europe, and all parties were satisfied.

Except for grade-school textbooks, neither publishers nor distributors would normally allow returns of unsold books. Grade-school textbooks were usually a substantial source of revenue for Norwegian booksellers, but Juul Møller stayed out of that market, concentrating on university-level books.

The Distribution Chain

Book distribution varied widely. Typically, foreign-book orders within Europe were handled by distribution centres in England, or sometimes on the continent. The large publishers had cooperative distribution agreements. For instance, books from Harvard Business School Press were distributed in Europe by McGraw-Hill. If Juul Møller wanted, say, 30 books from HBS Press, the order would normally be sent by fax or electronic mail to McGraw-Hill's distribution centre in Maidenhead, England.

If the book was out of stock, a message to that effect could take as long as two weeks to arrive; so if there was little time, it was normally a good idea to call ahead by telephone to check availability. The automated inventory of the distributors and publishers could be very imprecise; for instance, books were frequently flagged as "out of stock" if the inventory fell below 100. If Juul Møller needed only 30, a telephone call could fix the problem. These calls were done by a few of Juul Møller's employees, as well as Dag himself. After many years, the company had forged relationships with a number of people at publishers and distributors and knew the suppliers' internal routines and whom to call to get precise answers and good service. Persistence was important—one time, Dag had tried calling a publishing house but got only voice mailbox answers. He then started dialing telephone numbers close to the one he had called, increasing the number by 10 every time. After one hour, he got through to someone who could help him.

If the books were in stock, the order would normally be shipped by boat from England and would reach Juul Møller in eight days, depending somewhat on which day of the week the order was sent. More often than not, however, the situation was more complicated than that. If McGraw-Hill in Maidenhead, England, had, say, only two books in stock, the rest would have to be ordered from the main publisher in the U.S. If McGraw-Hill could get the remaining books within the next eight to ten days, it was normally best to wait for the regular delivery from England. "Drop shipment" (that is, direct airfreight from the U.S.) was an option, but was costly, meaning that although Juul Møller could supply the books, it would be without profit (or, as had happened, at a loss).

If the books had to be ordered directly from the publishers, the situation became more complicated. Delivery from McGraw-Hill could then take more than six weeks (with considerable variance), partly because the publisher would take some time and partly because, to minimize transportation cost, orders were consolidated in New York so that whole containers of books could be sent across the Atlantic. Juul Møller had much experience in judging the students' propensity to buy books and would choose how to order based on that. For example, if there was a need for 300 copies of a book and there were 100 in stock, Juul Møller would order the 100, order the rest from further up the chain, betting that the first 100 would suffice until the rest arrived.

If the publishers could not deliver, either because they were temporarily out of stock or because the book was out of print (a fact that did not always make it into the publishers' catalogues), things became more difficult. The first action was then to call other distributors or bookshops. As a last resort, Juul Møller could photocopy the book and sell the copy, after first getting permission from the publisher.

Occasionally, the distribution chains became very complicated. Once, Juul Møller ordered some books from Prentice-Hall's distribution centre in England. It turned out that the remaining copies of the books were in a warehouse in Singapore, and after a lot of back and forthing, the books were sent to Norway. Ironically, the books were to be used for NSM's activities in Fudan in China. Since bureaucracy and transportation was complicated there, the professor ended up packing the books as personal luggage on his plane from Oslo.

Information Technology at Juul Møller

Of Juul Møller's 25 employees, two worked primarily with information technology, either with system maintenance or data capture. Most development and operations were performed by an external company. The software used was regular office software, some industry-specific databases, and a proprietary inventory and order system. The hardware was mainly Windows-based workstations. Both the company and Dag himself had internet connections.

Juul Møller's computer background was rather idiosyncratic, thanks to Dag. In 1977, Dag had started investigating the use of computers in helping to run the bookshop, but the existing mini-computer-based systems were too expensive. Instead, Dag and his friend Michael Wittwer started experimenting with microcomputers, which at that time were little more than printboards and single parts. After much fiddling and programming in Dag's home, they had a simple, multi-user operating system, probably one of the world's first, for a Zilog 80 (Z80) processor. Then they built programs for use in the bookshop, starting with invoicing. Michael Wittmer was the technician and programmer, and Dag was the user representative who "had all the stupid questions." They even made some hardware themselves, such as the I/O-card. The system was a success, and Wittwer started a company called GC Data, with Dag as one of the principal shareholders. GC Data was first located in the basement of Dag's house, and developed and sold industry solutions to other companies based on the first bookshop system. One of the first customers was Norli, who bought the software in 1978.

During the 1980s, GC Data grew and obtained a number of customers for its transaction-oriented systems. Nixdorf, a large German-owned computer company, bought the software and enhanced it. When the Norwegian Post Office implemented new teller systems, they were supplied by Nixdorf, with development assistance from GC. Another large customer was Kreditkassen, Norway's second-largest bank. Eventually, GC Data had 12 employees and had outgrown Dag's basement. In the fall of 1995, the company moved to new offices in the centre of Oslo. Just before the Christmas of 1996, Dag sold all his shares in GC Data to Tieto, a Finnish computer corporation with 3400 employees. Michael Wittmer carried on as CEO. GC was changing its products toward network-based software, and the products seemed to have a lot of promise: their intranet solution was nominated for the Rosing prize (a highly regarded quality award) in February 1997. Another product was Intershop, an electronic commerce software package.

The Future

Dagfinn can relax, thought Dag. *I have been thinking a lot about what to do with the internet, but I want to do something substantial, not just another corporate brochure about who we are and what we offer. Most students are really like Dagfinn—they don't see the big picture.* Dag was thinking of some articles about the new bookseller agreement in *INSIDE*, the student newspaper. Some students seemed to think that Juul Møller made a profit of over 100 kroner per book, which was certainly not the case! Most students did not know about the close links between Juul Møller, NSM, and the student union. Dag was even a "Høker," an honorary member of the student union.

On the other hand, thought Dag, *it won't do to point at a long history of co-operation and service when the students can go outside the system and buy their books directly. But it is not in their interest to have Juul Møller disappear either. I have to look at this more systematically...*

QUESTIONS

1. Which consumer markets does Juul Møller serve? How do these consumers make book-buying decisions?
2. Who, besides consumers, has a stake in how Juul Møller distributes books?
3. Is Amazon.com a threat to Juul Møller?
4. Should Juul Møller become involved in e-distributing?

CASE 4: ARTVENTURE: CHILDREN'S CREATIVE ART AND PARTY CENTRE

In May 1999, Eileen Walfish and Tina Diamant—the owners and only employees of Artventure—were reviewing the results of their first year of operation. Although they were satisfied with the results, they were concerned about the years ahead. They expected significant challenges due to increased operating expenditures (especially wages), increased competition, and the introduction of new programming, such as a proposed summer camp for 1999. Their challenge was to develop a long-term strategic plan for Artventure that would ensure the continued growth and profitability of the business.

Artventure is a creative and educational centre. Through a wide variety of activities and specialized programs, it provides artistic and educational stimulation to children between the ages of eight months and 12 years. Artventure is not a daycare centre. Artventure's mission is "...to enhance the creativity and self-esteem of young children and preteens through various activities centring around the arts, as well as entertaining and coordinating children's birthday parties, catering to every parent and child's needs." The owners aim to develop children's love for the arts and sciences in a pleasant, well-supervised environment. They also want to foster children's intellectual growth, interpersonal and artistic skills, and self-esteem through a broad range of programs and activities. Artventure's services include photography, dance, animated music, and cognitive games, as well as children's birthday parties. There are 100 party packages from which parents can choose.

Background

Eileen and Tina have no previous business management experience; however, both have training in early childhood education, as well as practical experience working with children. Eileen began working with children at the age of 12, at a day camp. She had experience putting on puppet shows and plays. She also organized activities for children between the ages of two and eight years. In the summer of 1992, Eileen became the program director and counsellor-in-training, where she gained supervisory experience. Subsequently, she became involved in creating and teaching different activities, such as swimming, dance, music, art, nature, and science for children between two and eight years. In addition, she organized graduation ceremonies, birthday and other children's parties, and holiday shows, and had conducted private art workshops in the homes of clients.

Eileen has a D.E.C. in literature and arts from Marie Victorin College[1] in Montreal and a Bachelor's degree in Education and Religion from Concordia University. During her educational years, she received Good Citizenship Awards, Good Sportsmanship Awards, and Achievement Awards in physical education and drama.

Klimentina (Tina) has a degree in education from the University of Sarajevo. Prior to her arrival in Canada in 1993, she was director and coordinator of a youth theatre specializing in the field of puppetry and in the design and creation of marionettes. She was also responsible for scenery and costume design for various plays in which she had acted. In Sarajevo, that experience netted her new positions in children's television, cartoon animation, and as a TV show host.

In Canada, she maintained a strong interest in early childhood education and earned a D.E.C. in education. She worked as an early childhood educator at a nursery, where she was responsible for planning, programming, and managing activities in creative art, dance, and shows. She also had experience coordinating special events for parents. In 1997, she became the art and jewellery specialist at a day camp, where she organized and conducted innovative and creative projects for children aged 3 to 12.

In their past positions, the owners had developed strong relationships with clients, children, and parents, earning them an excellent reputation in the Jewish community in Côte St Luc, Hampstead, and Westmount (see Exhibit 4–1).

---

[1]In Quebec, a student makes the following progression through the educational system: Kindergarten, primary, secondary, CEGEP, and university. Marie Victorin College is a CEGEP, and students normally attend for two years. CEGEP is an acronym for Collège d'enseignement général et professional.

Exhibit 4–1 THE LOCATION OF ARTVENTURE AND MAIN COMPETITORS

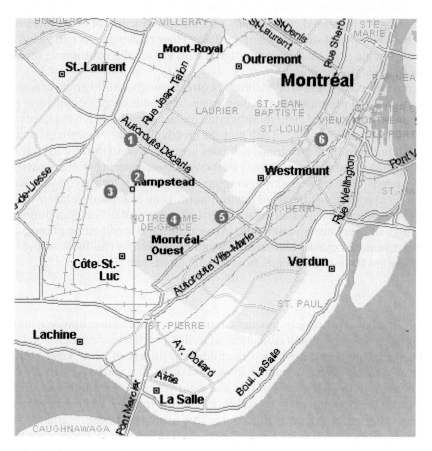

1. Artventure
2. Adath Israel Kiddie Korner
3. Crayons Art and Party Centre
4. Kidnasium
5. Le Castelet
6. Concordia University

The Centre

Eileen and Tina believe that activity centres are needed to provide extended entertainment and education for children. The market, according to the owners of Artventure, needs centres that provide ongoing, creative, and innovative projects that challenge and enhance the child's creative talents and cater to the needs of parents. Since parents have little time to spend with their families, these centres can act as "added parents" by providing education, creative stimulation, and fun during the hours when it is difficult for parents to provide supervision.

Artventure commenced operations on May 3, 1998, and is located at 6900 Decarie Square, a shopping centre in Montreal, Quebec. At this location, parking is plentiful and free. Decarie Square lies next to Highway 15, a major north–south highway running through the city of Montreal (Exhibit 4-1). This location makes it very convenient to drop off and pick up children at the centre. Artventure has 1120 square feet of available space, which is more than enough to run its programs. Decarie Square, however, is not an upscale shopping centre; much of the space is unoccupied, and there is low customer traffic. Although Artventure is nicely decorated, which clearly indicates to mall traffic that it is a children's centre, one space next door is empty and the space on the other side is a clothing repair shop. Opposite to Artventure, a fruit shop and a home decoration store can be found. Recently, however, some companies, such as Aldo, Stokes, and Au Coton, have established liquidation outlets at this shopping centre.

Eileen and Tina see Artventure as a provider of high-quality programs aimed at systematically developing the whole child. Artventure offers creative, stimulating, and entertaining activities such as original art activities, puppet shows, and drama plays for small children; enjoyable food and refreshments for children and parents; and cognitive games and animated music activities. Eileen and Tina believe that constant variation in activities allows for new and exciting experiences and that this variety is an effective method of capturing the attention of young children as they explore their creative spirits.

Artventure's Programs

Artventure offers four programs:

1. **Creative Junior Tots** is for children between the ages of 15 months and 4 years. This program is subdivided into two age categories (both run for a period of four weeks): Mom and Tot, offered on Tuesdays and Thursdays, includes art, music, live animals, drama, stories, and creative movement; Junior Tots, offered on Mondays, Wednesdays, and Fridays, includes science, music, and dance. For both programs, peanut-free kosher snacks are served. The chart below shows the two categories, as well as their times and prices. These two programs generate approximately 30 percent of Artventure's annual revenue.

CREATIVE JUNIOR TOTS

Age Category	Classes per Session	Duration of Classes	Clases per Week	Price per Session	Children per Group
15 to 24 months	8	9:30 to 11:00	Tuesday & Thursday	$192	Min: 6 Max: 10
2 yrs to 4 yrs	12	9:00 to 12:00	Monday, Wednesday & Friday	$288	Min: 6 Max: 10

2. **Photography Fun** is intended for children four years and older. This program involves picture taking and development. More specifically, this program allows children to see the results of their creativity. Artventure believes that Photography Fun is a great way for children to discover themselves and develop self-esteem. Children can also show family and friends the pictures they have taken. The cost for a seven-class session is $112.

3. **Funky Dance** is for children aged five years and older. This program introduces the participants to modern dance techniques and fosters body coordination. It also incorporates costumes and props, such as wigs, thereby enhancing the creative element. Upon completion of the program, Artventure invites parents to watch a dance recital performed by the participants. The cost for a seven-class session is $95. Funky Dance and Photography Fun together compose 20 percent of Artventure's revenue.

4. **Children's Birthday Parties** includes a creative and original atmosphere where children aged 4 to 12 can celebrate their birthdays. Artventure offers theme parties or specialized parties. The theme parties focus on things like the child's favourite sport, TV show, super hero, or toys. Dramatic plays, puppet shows,

treasure hunts, art activities, and many other cognitive activities capture the children's imagination while they participate in an original and zestful birthday party. The specialized parties focus on areas such as art, drama, jewellery, music, dance, photography, and video production.

Artventure provides juice, paper crafts, toys, specialized birthday cards, party surprises, art materials, decorations, and animators for the children, as well as coffee for the parents. Additionally, the parties have a unique style and emphasize an unlimited amount of fun. The parties last for two hours, from four o'clock to six o'clock, Monday to Friday, and, by special appointment, any time during the day on weekends. The price is $200 for 20 children or fewer and $5 for each child thereafter. Artventure derives 50 percent of its revenue from birthday parties.

Customers

Eileen and Tina feel that more young parents are seeking early educational development for infants and toddlers, thus creating a high demand for parent and tot programs. Furthermore, social interaction and a strong sense of the arts and culture for preschoolers and preteens make extracurricular activities a must during school hours and on weekends.

They also observe that parents increasingly hold their children's birthday parties outside of the home. In the last six years, the popularity of this concept has grown as more mothers continue to join the workforce. In addition, many parties have up to 40 guests so that all classmates, relatives, and outside school friends can be invited. In sum, they feel that there is a strong demand for this service.

Artventure identifies their potential clientele as families with children aged 8 months to 12 years. These families are affluent: many parents are university graduates and have careers in fields such as medicine, law, finance, and business ownership (jewellery, insurance, manufacturing, retail, import/export, and stockbrokerage). Although Artventure welcomes all religious, ethnic, and racial groups, the owners have built a strong reputation within the Jewish community and are trusted and known by many in that community. Ninety-five percent of the children attending Artventure are from Jewish families. The other 5 percent are Italians, Greeks, and Francophones. In fact, one of Artventure's desires is to increase the number of children from other ethnic groups.

Eileen and Tina describe the parents as those with a strong interest in recreational activities, a high regard for the arts (dance, drama, and creative arts), and a strong belief in education that enhances self-esteem and the intellectual growth of their children. Parents also want attractive, clean, spacious, and safe environments with innovative programming where their children can have fun. Eileen and Tina believe that parents appreciate the involvement of the owners in the day-to-day activities of the centre and the children. Price, available equipment, quality of the programming, and small classes are important considerations for parents. They look for style to keep up with other members of the community and for the "latest trends." They are loyal to a service if it impresses them. The parents are also helpful and supportive, especially when they are more familiar with the business owners. They are potential promoters of the business when they are satisfied with the services offered.

Due to Eileen and Tina's experience and reputation in the Jewish community, this community was their major target. Until the 1970s, Montreal was the most important Jewish centre in Canada. Since the mid-1970s, however, a large percentage has moved to other areas in Canada, especially Ontario. By 1999, Toronto had replaced Montreal as the home of the largest Jewish community. There are, however, more than 100 000 members of the Jewish community in Montreal. In Montreal, 60 percent of Jewish children go to Jewish primary schools and 30 percent go to Jewish high schools. Artventure identified Côte St Luc, Hampstead, Town of Mount Royal, and Westmount as their principal markets. Exhibit 4-2 provides demographic data on these and neighbouring cities.

Exhibit 4–2 CITY DEMOGRAPHICS

	Côte St-Luc	Hampstead	Westmount	Mtl-West	Mt-Royal
Pop 1991	30 126	7 219	20 239	5 180	18 212
1996	29 705	6 986	20 420	5 254	18 282
Total Male	13 280	3 310	9 200	2 565	8 610
0–4 years	640	225	435	210	475
5–9 years	710	205	520	220	570
10–14 years	710	220	590	235	615
Total Female	16 425	3 675	11 220	2 690	9 670
0–4 years	590	205	420	140	455
5–9 years	665	225	500	225	525
10–14 years	680	215	540	185	515
Mother Tongue					
English	15 205	4 615	12 035	3 655	3 655
French	3 300	835	4 065	465	7 215
Home Language					
English	20 265	5 520	14 245	4 370	7 190
French	2 920	835	3 745	330	7 400
Jewish Population	19 395	4 935	4 345	825	2 625
Undergraduate or Higher	6 190	2 520	8 850	1 715	6 640
Number of Families	8 075	1 930	5 235	1 455	5 005
Median Family Income	$51 099	$93 855	$101 525	$81 156	$90 983
Family Income					
< $10 000	380	85	160	30	120
$10K–19 999	680	85	240	60	220
$20K–29 999	990	70	250	100	275
$30K–39 999	995	95	305	95	370
$40K–49 999	905	145	255	80	310
$50K–59 999	760	105	240	95	400
$60K–69 999	540	130	280	140	335
$70K–79 999	460	110	270	105	180
$80K–89 999	490	95	320	95	265
$90K–99 999	325	80	240	65	205
$100 000 +	1 555	920	2 670	590	2 320

Source: Adapted from Statistics Canada, *Profiles of Census Divisions and Subdivisions in Quebec* (data products: area profiles; 1996 Census of Population), Catalogue 95-186.

Eileen and Tina know that demand for their various offerings varies depending on the season. During the summer, for example, parents enroll their children in outdoor day-camp programs. Therefore, afternoon art classes from June to August are quiet periods. Not all camps accept children younger than three years, so Artventure is planning to design a day-camp program for children aged two to five years, while continuing to offer their Parent and Tots Program for children aged 15 months to 24 months. Many camps have half-day programs from nine o'clock to noon for children aged three to five years, so the owners want to offer special art classes to this age group from one o'clock to three o'clock. For birthday parties, June to August is slow since many families are on vacation, hold pool parties, or choose to wait for the school year to start to invite classmates. October to May is the busiest time for parties.

Eileen and Tina interviewed 50 families in the Hampstead and Côte St Luc areas and found that they had spent an average of $600 or more on birthday parties for their children. Given the income levels of their target market, the owners believe that these families, even in a recession, would continue to use these centres, especially for parties, since parents would find it difficult to deny their children birthday parties.

Competition

Eileen and Tina believe that the industry of children's recreation and party centres is in a period of growth. In 1992, there was only one private play and party centre that catered to families with children from one to six years old, in areas such as Hampstead, Côte St Luc, Westmount, Town of Mount Royal, St Laurent, and even the West Island (Exhibit 4-1). In 1999, however, similar centres could be seen in many areas, such as Kidnasium Gym & Party Centre in NDG, Neverland in the West Island, Crayons Art & Party Centre in Cavendish Mall, Artfolie in the Monkland area, and Adath Israel Kiddie Korner in Hampstead (Exhibit 4-1). Even the City of Westmount, at its Greene Avenue Centre, as well as Concordia University, offer activities for children. Other centres, such as Bedrocks, Coconuts in the West Island, and Enfantastique Drop Off & Party Centre in Place Vertu, and Carrefour Angrignon, which had sprung up to meet the demand, ceased operations in 1998. Tina and Eileen identified three centres they consider direct competitors:

1. **Le Castelet**, an artistic awakening centre, is a preschool located about three to four kilometres from Artventure, on Sherbrooke Street, one of the major arteries in Montreal (Exhibit 4-1). This centre is divided into three rooms, two of which are designated for artistic and intellectual usage. The third and largest room is used for dance and physical play. The centre is located directly across from a municipal park that is easily accessible. The goal of Le Castelet is to provide an atmosphere of interaction that will prepare children for their entrance into primary education.

   The programs of Le Castelet centre around music, theatre, dance, and arts and crafts. It designs these activities to encourage children to interact with other kids and to instill a sense of learning and openness. This centre specializes in the artistic environment and tries to implant a taste for the arts. The courses are conducted mostly in French. The instructors can communicate in English, but there is greater emphasis on communicating in French. The hours of operation and prices are as follows:

   > Morning Sessions: 8:30 a.m. to 12 p.m. @ $16.75 per morning.
   > Full-Day Sessions: 8:30 a.m. to 5:30 p.m. @ $24.50 per day.

On a monthly basis, the costs are as follows:

> 2 mornings/week = $134
> 3 mornings/week = $201
> 4 mornings/week = $268
> 5 mornings/week = $335

These programs follow the school calendar of the regular elementary schools. The year, therefore, is from September to June. There is also a summer day-camp program that focuses more on outdoor activities, such as playing in the park. The price for the summer day camp is the same as the school-year program. The classes are divided into groups of eight per instructor. The age group for instruction is from two to five years old.

The school also has theme days every other week. These are used to teach the children about art, nature, and other subjects of interest. An example of a theme day is Forest Day, whereby children learn about the different kinds of trees and animals in the forest. Parents supply all food, such as snacks and lunches. The school supplies fruit drinks. Birthday parties are celebrated for the children who attend Le Castelet (parents supply the cakes).

2. **Kidnasium** is a 6000-square-foot facility that opened its doors approximately two years before Artventure. It enjoys fair success. The facility is divided into two parts: the indoor playground, with foam floor surface and playground equipment, and the gym. The goal of this centre is to provide children aged one month to six years with non-competitive programs in a group setting.

   This centre is located at the corner of Somerled and Grand Blvd in NDG and offers four programs. They are as follows:

   - A gym program that includes an instructor. The instructor teaches the children aerobic-type gym skills, as well as tumbling and coordination. This program runs for fifteen 45-minute sessions at a cost of $225 per child, tax included. There is a maximum number of 12 children per group.

   - The dance program, "Tooney Loonz," runs for fifteen 45-minute sessions at a cost of $215 per child, tax included. Two reputable instructors entertain children with animated performances using, for example, guitars and sing-alongs.

   - The open gym program does not include an instructor. The price is $6 per child, $10 for two children.

   - The last type of program is birthday parties. Playground parties for 20 children cost $225 each. For 30 children or more, the cost is $285. A gym party costs $300 for 20 children or fewer, and $385 for more than 20 children. Both parties last for two hours and include paper products, balloons, fruit juice for the children, coffee for parents, and instructors for the gym activities. Extra costs for the birthday-party program, which can run up to an additional $400, include food for guests, cakes, loot bags, and entertainment such as music, clowns, and magicians.

   The location of this centre is not very central for the important market areas of Hampstead, Westmount, Town of Mount Royal, Côte St Luc, and the West Island or St Laurent. Moreover, parents must also supervise their own children due to the high risk of injury in the gym area. The limited variety of programming for parties also forces parents to hire entertainment to please party-goers.

3. **Crayons Art and Party Centre**, situated in Cavendish Mall, Côte St Luc, has been in existence for about 18 months. It is a drop-off centre, which means that there are few scheduled activities. Anyone, at anytime, can walk into the centre and participate in the art class of the day. The centre serves children over the age of three. It also offers art programs to senior citizens. The fee for drop-off is $10 per person, per hour. A special six-week program is available at a cost of $90. This program concentrates on only one area of art, such as painting, drawing, and so on. Crayons offers these programs at hours that do not coincide with regular school hours, so this program is geared more to adults and senior citizens. Thus, Eileen and Tina believe that this centre is not a significant threat to Artventure.

   Crayons is strictly an arts and crafts centre and does not offer any programs in other areas of the arts. It does, however, offer birthday parties. These parties cost between $140 and $210, with a choice of a party in jewellery or pottery. All materials are included, as well as juice, paper products, and coffee for parents. The variety of parties is limited and does not capture the attention of party-goers for the full two hours. This centre is also physically small (about 800 sq ft)—it tends to get very crowded when there are many children present.

Exhibit 4-3 is a comparison of Artventure's birthday party offerings with those of two competitors. In addition to the three competitors described so far, there are other potential competitors.

Adath Israel Kiddie Korner, for example, offers morning classes for two to five year olds. It also offers specialty activities, such as ballet, creative movement, and computers. Furthermore, there is a Mom and Tots group with programs for children aged 18 months to 24 months from 9 o'clock to 10:45 a.m. and for children aged 12 months to 17 months from 11 o'clock to noon. This centre also offers "Music with Tooney Loonz" on Tuesdays, Wednesdays, and Fridays. The City of Westmount, at its Greene Avenue Centre, offers children's programs that include "Magical Fun" from 11 o'clock to 12:30 p.m., "Tumbling Tots Indoor Playground" from 9:30 a.m. to 11:30 a.m. for preschoolers, and "After School Home Away from Home" from 3:30 p.m. to 6 o'clock for kindergarteners to six year olds. Concordia University's Department of Education offers "Children and Parents Learning Together" for three and four year olds on Tuesdays, Wednesdays, and Thursdays, from 9 o'clock to 11:30 a.m. Parents and teachers discuss child rearing on Thursday mornings.

Babysitters are also an ongoing competitive threat to any centre. Many parents prefer dealing with people they know and trust. Babysitters and domestics provide the service of "watching over" your children.

The Environment

In spite of the growth in activity centres for children, Tina and Eileen believe that the market is large enough for another successful centre. Their reasoning is that each centre focuses on different age groups and activities, and that they are all situated in different locations. They estimate that some centres average $84 000 per

Exhibit 4–3 BIRTHDAY PARTY GRID

Birthday Centre	Parties Offered	Services/Party Materials	Costs	Extra Costs
Artventure	Theme parties: Physical, cognitive, and artistic activities. Parties in music, drama, jewellery, dance	Entertainment: Specifically designed decorations, party animators, party favours, paper products, juice, coffee, birthday cards, balloons, birthday crowns	$200–$250	Food $40–$100
Crayons	Art and jewellery parties	Art materials, coffee, juice, paper products, monitors	$140–$210	Food, loot bags, entertainment up to $400
Kidnasium	Gym and playground parties	Instructor, juice, paper products, balloons	$225–$385	Food, loot bags, entertainment up to $400

year in birthday parties alone. They believe that in the Montreal region there is plenty of room for new players who cater to party-goers aged 6 to 12 years. The major centres do not offer services to this age group. They are also limited in their offering of different types of recreational activities other than art.

The owners of Artventure believe that as long as high-income families continue to cater to their children's desires and mothers are in the workforce, party centres will have a strong place in the market. The industry is growing rapidly due to a new generation of parents with healthy incomes who have no time or energy for being entertainers and creative specialists in their children's lives. These concerned parents, therefore, seek outside assistance. With the increasing number of families where both parents are in the workforce, proper child care plays a critical role in the everyday lives of families. These trends, plus a genuine love of children, prompted the creation of Artventure.

Eileen and Tina are concerned, however, that at some point, government regulations might make the business less appealing. For example, the government may enforce more rigorous safety requirements or require that all centres carry high levels of insurance. They also feel that the ongoing political debate about the possible separation of Quebec from Canada make conditions increasingly difficult for the business. They fear that many English-speaking families, Artventure's target market, will relocate outside of Quebec. Other possible administrative threats lie in the Quebec laws and regulations governing the use of language on all signs and mailings. Artventure may, in the future, face the prospect of bilingualization—both to comply with government regulations and to increase the pool of prospective clients.

Promotion and Strategy

Artventure relies primarily on word of mouth and print media to generate awareness. Eileen and Tina believe that their attempts at advertising have been unsuccessful. In trying to increase growth in the number of clients, Artventure advertised in a weekly newspaper, *The Suburban*. *The Suburban*, delivered at no cost to residents, has a circulation of 101 000, with approximately 41 000 copies distributed to homes on the West Island. The remainder is distributed in the other English sectors of Greater Montreal. Artventure feels, however, that the cost is relatively high compared to the results obtained. A quarter-page advertisement costs $600. Artventure also advertised in the weekly *Canadian Jewish News*. The circulation of the Montreal edition of this newspaper is 18 735 households, and 96 percent are paid subscriptions. A quarter-page ad costs $320 for a maximum of four insertions. Beginning in November 1998, Eileen and Tina placed advertisements in each issue of *Montreal Families* at a cost of $400 per insertion. *Montreal Families*, like *The Suburban*, is distributed free of charge at pick-up points every other month in both the West Island and the English-speaking sectors of Greater Montreal. Circulation for *Montreal Families* is 25 000. Artventure also uses a mailing list of about 300 families.

Artventure's strategy is to provide top-quality creative programs and parties at a price that "will not burn a hole in parents' pockets." The activities they offer—drama, art, dance, and music—do not require expensive apparatus. Expensive apparatus does not necessarily capture a child's attention, Eileen and Tina believe. In addition to their advertising in *The Suburban*, Artventure also offers discounts of up to 15 percent on the price of its programs to those parents who register their children early or who bring a friend. The service component of their strategy is to develop strong relationships with parents, subcontractors, suppliers, and the children who participate in the activities. They take into consideration the different schedules and needs of the various age groups and design programs to suit clients. Services are unique and non-repetitive, and entertainment services are included in party packages. Exhibits 4-4 and 4-5 show Artventure's income statement and balance sheet, respectively. (In the first year of operation, Eileen and Tina did not take a salary from the business.

Exhibit 4–4[1]   ARTVENTURE INCOME STATEMENT FOR THE YEAR ENDED APRIL 30, 1999

Sales		**$46 633**
Less: Cost of sales		23 841
Gross Operating Profit		**$22 792**
Less: Sales expenses	5 014.00	
Less: Rent	17 592.00	
Less: Administrative Expenses	4 200.00	$26 806
Net Profit (Loss)		**($4 014)**

[1] In their first year of operation, Eileen and Tina were paid an "off-balance-sheet" salary by an agency of the provincial government. This subsidy, designed to promote entrepreneurship and small business in the province, was available to them for only their first year of operation.

Exhibit 4–5   ARTVENTURE BALANCE SHEET AS AT APRIL 30, 1999

Assets		
	Current Assets	
1.	Bank account	$ 5 000
2.	Start-up expenses	0
3.	Deposit-rent	2 800
4	Total current assets	$ 7 800
	Fixed Assets	
5.	Incorporation	$ 610
6.	Betterment	4 000
7.	Art equipment and accessories	9 028
8.	Office equipment	1 265
9.	Party equipment	3 180
10.	Computer equipment	4 000
11.	Less: Accumulated depreciation	($2 000)
Total Assets		**$27 883**
Liabilities		
	Current Liabilities	
12.	Accounts payable	$ 0
13.	Current portion of long-term debt	3 000
	Long-Term Liabilities	
14.	Long-term debt	$ 0
	Total Liabilities	**$ 3 000**
Equity		
15.	Young Promoters grant	$12 000
16.	Capital investment	16 897
17.	Loss from operations	(4 014)
Total Equity		**$24 883**
Total Liabilities and Equity		**$27 883**

Their 1999 salary was paid by an agency of the provincial government, in the context of a program designed to encourage small business and entrepreneurship.)

At this point, Eileen and Tina have completed one year of operation and are wondering whether they are on the right track. They had heard about the planned opening of Childzplay Party Centre in October, in the same shopping centre where they are located. This venture, a entertainment haven with an area of 3000 square feet "will be replete with all number of attractions for kids under 10, including in-line skating, floor hockey, dance, jewellery making, magic, cartooning, animals, slides, a magic store, an earth ball, and a multitude of fun-filled activities. Childzplay will also be "mommy friendly, with a café bistro where tired parents can sip on a cappuccino or nibble on a dessert while watching the kids explore the centre." Eileen and Tina wonder about the possible effects this new arrival will have on their business, and what else they should be doing to ensure the long-term survival of Artventure. Should they, for example, take their activity centre to schools and cruise ships?

What they do not want to do is develop their centre into a computer games arcade. A computer games strategy is not part of their vision. They also believe that these games do not stimulate the creativity and self-esteem that they want to develop in children. They believe that they have a winning formula with their services, but they wonder whether they have a sustainable strategy.

QUESTIONS

1. What is the nature of Artventure's market? What are the important environmental factors?
2. What are the characteristics of Artventure's customers?
3. How does Artventure compare relative to the competition?
4. Is Artventure viable? If so, what marketing program should they develop? If not, what should they do?

CASE 5: ALESSI: ITALIAN DESIGN AND THE RE-ENCHANTMENT OF EVERYDAY OBJECTS

One of the main characteristics of a consumer society is the serialization of objects and their subsequent loss of uniqueness, distinctness, and authenticity due to their ever-increasing reproduction and diffusion. The fact that objects are repeatedly produced leads to a fade-out of meaning of most everyday objects—they become mere commodities and, thus, lose their substance. This loss of meaning of most consumer objects is partly due to a societal shift from craftsmanship to industrialization, leading to the serialization of objects. It is also partly due to a marketing approach based on the design of objects that responds closely to consumer needs and, therefore, excludes a surprise effect. This phenomenon inevitably leads to an impoverishment of sensory experience and a loss of a relationship with objects. Consider the fact that at the beginning of the nineteenth century, a four-person, average-income family was surrounded, at most, by only 150 to 200 objects (including crockery and clothes), and that nowadays, a similar family owns between 2500 and 3000 objects, including electrical appliances and decorative objects. Today, a person is said to come into daily contact with approximately 20 000 products. Thus, consumers often seem to be immersed in an uncontrolled number of signs and confronted with the well-known phenomenon of semiotic pollution.

As a result, designers have to invent products and create signs that can survive in a consumption and societal environment saturated with a tremendous and ever-increasing number of products and signs. Design, therefore, has an essential role in giving meaning to objects through the use of shapes, colours, and materials. Also, the penetration of science and technology into our daily environment has eliminated most technical barriers to the production of objects. New forms and functions can now be used, thus enlarging the field of possibilities and the creative abilities of designers.

One of the most remarkable examples of this will to poetize life through object design is the Italian company Alessi, founded in 1921 by Giovanni Alessi. The first articles produced were coffee pots and trays; they were soon followed by a large series of accessories for table service. The company, now in its fourth generation, is headed by Alberto Alessi, who has recruited renowned industrial designers and architects to create signature products for the company. This venture has been extremely successful—many objects have become cult objects, such as Aldo Rossi's conical kettle, Philippe Starck's juicer, and Michael Graves' bird kettle. At present, the production is grouped under the trademarks Alessi (mass production, mainly of steel and plastic), Officina Alessi (small- or middle-series production in different metals: silver, nickel-silver, titanium, brass, stainless steel, iron, tin-plate), Tenentes (porcelain), and Twergi (wood). Alessi designers and products can be viewed at *www.alessi.it*.

Officina Alessi is extremely representative of a design tradition that focuses more on existential values than on the mere utilitarian approach to objects. This Alessi trademark was introduced in 1983 to identify an aspect of the company's activity, which in the past had remained in books of blueprints or at the prototype stage. Their objective is to research and experiment with innovative forms, styles, functions, and methods of manufacture, free from the limits usually imposed by industrial mass production. The company wants to offer a wide range of products that combine both sophisticated industrial technology and traditional handicraft processes to a keen and culturally curious public. In particular, the use of "historical" metals such as nickel-silver, brass, copper, silver, and tin are chosen not only for their intrinsic value, but also to match the characteristics of each design (Presentation Catalogue of Officina Alessi, 1994). According to the circumstances, the results take the form of standard production or a limited series, or even unique pieces. For instance, Officina Alessi launched a series of Tea and Coffee Piazzas that were commissioned from 11 internationally recognized architects. The 11 sets were each produced in limited editions of 99 and were priced individually at about £12 000. In 1983, galleries in Milan and New York simultaneously hosted their launch, thus reinforcing the cultural status and economic exclusivity of the objects.

What this example of design innovation illustrates is that, even though the shape of an object usually follows its function, the shape of an object may by far overlap its function. There is always a degree of freedom that gives the designer the opportunity to disconnect (sometimes quite radically) from form function. If the shape of the object always more or less indicates its use, it also adds an inescapable aesthetic dimension that may contribute to a real redefinition of the object. Therefore, design really means "to illustrate, to clarify, to modify, to dignify, to dramatize, to persuade, and perhaps even to amuse" (Rand, 1993: 3). This definition, given by an American designer, points out two approaches to design that refer to two distinct traditions in Europe. The first approach considers design as a way to clarify and to persuade. This approach may be said to be characteristic of German and Nordic designs, of which companies like Braun and Bang & Olufsen may be considered representative. In these countries, design appears to be more functional in the sense that it aims to express the mere function of the object. The approach to the object is essentially seen as utilitarian because the object designed has to convince the user that it serves particular functions. The role of design is to convey an impression of effectiveness and solidity through appropriate features, colours, and materials.

The second approach, which is usually more representative of Southern European countries (Italy, Spain, partly France), tends to develop objects with stronger existential connotations, such as emotional values (the object design has to arouse feelings and affective states), ludic values (the object is considered as a potential game), and epistemic values (the ability of the product to arouse curiosity and to provide novelty). This approach to design refers to consumers' need to live new experiences through the use of products that provide innovative combinations of shape, material, colours, and so on. The importance of these existential values in the choice of products and brands, and therefore in the way consumers perceive the design of products, is also related to hedonistic consumption, which is a very important paradigm of consumption of these countries.

The design philosophy promoted by Alberto Alessi is highly representative of this second approach, in the sense that it aims at overcoming technological marketing constraints that dominate the actual production of consumer goods and result in a world of anonymous and impassive objects. The company's mission is hence seen as a way to literally poetize everyday objects. At the same time, the company is also preoccupied with the functional dimension of objects, as illustrated by this quote from Alessandro Mendini (who designed the Falstaff pots for Alessi):

> With their simple elegance, the Falstaff pots seek to present a group of utensils that harmonise with the kitchen surroundings and at the same time enhance the practice of that supreme cosmetic culinary art of gastronomy...They are model pots of the latest generation, a design intended as a multiple art form, a kitchen landscape with pots...At work and at rest, they form a bouquet of reflectively polished, convex objects, discreetly present; sometimes slightly invisible; sometimes brilliantly present perhaps poetic kitchen sculptures. Actors perhaps, that tell us mysterious tales while they cook...Stressing the idea of play, of magic, invention and ritual, present today in the pleasure of performing numerous ancient actions that are no longer a chore but actually fun—for example, the act of cooking itself. (Presentation Catalogue of the Falstaff collection)

The implicit objective is to transform everyday consumer objects into objects of aesthetic contemplation through the application of colour, pattern, and additional elements. It also means that there is no single meaning assigned to an object; on the contrary, there is a plurality of meanings. An object is different from a tool in the sense that it does not necessarily boil down to a mere utilitarian function. The objective of a brand like Alessi is to break the conventional codes of representation of the object to transform an apparently boring practice (cooking) into a joyous and pleasant activity.

This leads to a real exploration of the communicative boundaries of design illustrated by the juicer designed by Philippe Starck, which looks like a rocket, or the conical kettle designed by Michael Graves. These objects propose totally new approaches to familiar objects. By breaking the usual codes of representation, the designer opens the object to a multitude of meanings, which contribute to re-semantizing the objects beyond their functional purposes. Thus, the design of any object implies two dimensions: (1) an *endophoric* dimension, which guarantees that the object belongs to a certain class and organizes the invariable elements, and (2) an *exophoric* dimension, which allows for radical formal innovation in the object category. On the one hand, the endophoric axis limits, crystallizes, and adjusts; it is more or less related to utilitarian values. On the other hand, the exophoric axis invents, diffuses, and disorients. The first axis makes the object recognizable and has a reassurance function, whereas the second axis destructures the object and responds to new expectations. Consider, for instance, the kettle designed by Michael Graves for Alessi. This object is strongly exophoric: its very cone shape destabilizes the idea of a kettle, while the little bird sitting on the spout conveys the idea of lightness and defies the geometric rigidity of the object. Looking at the kettle for the first time, one is disoriented by an object whose identity as a kettle is seriously questioned, and searches for a new identity outside the functional aspect. Playing with the exophoric dimension, the designer does nothing less than break the endophoric codes in order to open the object to new interpretations. One could even say that such objects may be considered as postmodern objects, in the way Robert Venturi defines them:

> … elements which are hybrid rather than "pure," compromising rather than "clear," distorted rather than "straightforward," ambiguous rather than "articulated," perverse as well as "impersonal," conventional rather than "designed," accommodating rather than "excluding," redundant rather than "simple," vestigal as well as "innovating," inconsistent rather than direct and clear. (Venturi, 1966, quoted in Woodham, 1997: 191)

The other interesting phenomenon is that, despite the fact that Alessi's objects seem at first glance to be very much culturally bound, they have met wide success in most European countries and some large American cities. Furthermore, the growing success of such objects leads to the notion of a "New International Style," which initially emerged in the 1980s due to the influence of such designers as Ettore Sottsass and Andrea Branzi from Italy, Hans Hollein from Austria, Michael Graves from the United States, Xavier Mariscal from Spain, and Philippe Starck from France. During the 1980s, exhibits of the group work were held in major museums in capital cities around the world and the products were marketed under the banner of the "New International Style." This notion indicated the commodification of particular concepts within a global concept (Woodham, 1997: 161). This notion of "design as art" was generally collected for its visual identity and implicit cultural values rather than any premium on function or practicality. Specializing on what has been termed the "tabletop industry" or "micro-architecture," companies like Alessi focused on the commissioning of small-scale pieces of decorative arts by well-known architects and designers. Most products were exposed in museums all around the world—this indicated a collapse of the boundaries between art and everyday life. This phenomenon has been said to be very representative of the postmodern condition, as Mike Featherstone emphasizes it as "the effacement of the boundary between art and everyday life... a general stylistic promiscuity, and playful mixing codes" (Featherstone, 1991: 65).

QUESTIONS

1. How would you explain the fact that, despite its focus on intangible and aesthetic product features, Alessi's objects are successful in nearly all European countries? Can you identify key target markets based on gender, age, income, or lifestyle?
2. To what extent would you agree with the idea that objects represent communication devices?
3. Do you think consumers from various European countries, the United States, and Canada would be willing to pay a price premium to get a product from one of Alessi's collections? Why or why not?
4. Alessi's objects are said to be very postmodern. To what extent would you agree with this assertion?

REFERENCES

Alessi, various promotional material.

Bernard Cova and Christian Sventfelt, "Societal Innovations and the Postmodern Aestheticization of Everyday Life," *International Journal of Research in Marketing* 10 (1991): 297–310.

Mike Featherstone, *Consumer Culture and Postmodernism* (London: Sage, 1991).

Benoit Heilbrunn, "In Search of the Lost Aura: The Object in the Age of Marketing Re-Illumination," in Stephen et al (eds), *Romancing the Market* (London: Routledge, 1998).

Laur Pilinoro, *L'officina Alessi* (F.A.O. spa, Crusinello, 1989).

Paul Rand, *Design, Form & Chaos* (New Haven & London: Yale University Press, 1993).

Robert Venturi, *Complexity and Contradiction in Architecture* (New York: Museum of Modern Art, 1996).

Jonathan M. Woodham, *Twentieth-Century Design* (Oxford University Press, 1997).

CASE 6: ATLANTICRIDER.COM

"Opportunities are always there. But only people who are prepared get them. If you are prepared, you are lucky. If you are not prepared, you are unlucky." —Jane Savoie, U.S. Olympic Equestrian Athlete

AtlanticRider.com has established itself as the most popular website for horse enthusiasts in Atlantic Canada. In the first 10 days of 2004, the Riders' Forum alone hosted more than 85 000 page views by its 1129 registered members and other visitors (considered "lurkers" because they visit, but don't post). This is an amazing accomplishment for a site with a target market of approximately 3851 participants who ride and drive about 18 000 horses. The present challenge for the CEO of AtlanticRider.com is to overhaul the site in a way that meets current challenges and ensures future success (see Exhibit 6-1).

The Initial Business Model

AtlanticRider.com is a web portal serving horse enthusiasts in Atlantic Canada and beyond (see Exhibit 6-2). The site was launched in October 1999 after several

Exhibit 6-1 ATLANTICRIDER.COM STATISTICS

Site Traffic in Page Views, October 1999 to December 2003

Year	Average/Month	Year Total
1999 (Fourth Quarter only)	66 024	198 072
2000	224 701	2 696 421
2001	298 896	3 586 763
2002	906 347*	10 876 164*
2003	1 286 279	15 435 350

* Estimated due to problems with monitoring software.

Detailed Statistics as of January 2004

86 373 page views (first 10 days in 2004)
9 forums
1129 registered members
223 paid classified subscribers
25 paid hyperlinks from front page ($120 each)

Exhibit 6-2 ESTIMATED NUMBER OF HORSES PER PROVINCE

Province	Estimated # of Participants	Average # of Horses per Owner	Estimated # of Horses	% of National Total	Horses on 1996 Census Farms	% of National Total
Canada	110 574	—	886 431	100%	443 889	100%
British Columbia	19 754	5.74	113 387	12.79%	49 305	11.11%
Alberta	20 101	15.38	309 146	34.88%	149 960	33.78%
Saskatchewan	13 035	9.47	123 441	13.93%	66 372	14.95%
Manitoba (adjusted for PMU farms)	7 143	5.99	70 786	7.99%	68 783	15.5%
Ontario	36 875	5.12	188 800	21.30%	76 553	17.24%
Quebec	9 815	6.42	63 015	7.11%	25 108	5.70%
New Brunswick	2 183	4.89	10 677	1.20%	2 757	0.62%
Prince Edward Island	346	4.43	1 534	0.17%	1 869	0.42%
Nova Scotia	1 083	4.60	4 982	0.53%	2 907	0.65%
Newfoundland and Labrador	239	2.78	664	0.07%	275	0.06%

Source: Adapted from 1998 *National Horse Industry Study/Étude de l'industrie canadienne du cheval 1998* (Table 3.3: Estimated Number of Horses per Province). Accessed at www.equestrian.ca/EC/EC_HIC_IR_1998Study_Table3-3.shtml on January 26, 2004.

months of planning and development. With a newly acquired MBA (in electronic commerce and international business) and 20 years of horse-industry experience, the founder and CEO, Diana Swain, recognized the need for an Atlantic Canadian horse site. She expected it to be well received, based on the rapid growth of the World Wide Web and the striking similarities in demographics of internet users and horse owners (see Exhibit 6-3).

Initially, the portal blended paid and free services to appeal to individual horse enthusiasts, as well as horse-related businesses (such as stables, tack and equipment stores, insurance agents, and others). Free services to individuals included a discussion board, classified ads, weekly newsletter, featured riders, tributes, and listings of events. Free web design and hosting (five-page sites) were offered to non-profit horse clubs within the region. There were also free reciprocal hyperlinks for those with existing sites to increase the visibility and traffic of AtlanticRider.com.

The initial business model offered web design and hosting services to horse-related businesses. In 1999, very few horse-related businesses had existing websites, and only the early adopters were motivated to navigate the information highway. As the site grew, however, business owners began to feel the pressure to affiliate with the site, whether they chose a hosting package with AtlanticRider.com or purchased a hyperlink to their existing site. As a result, the number of purchased hyperlinks to existing websites began to grow. The hyperlink package offered (and continues to offer) a link from the front page, a link from the business's free directory listing, and a profile in the regular e-zine, called *e-Rider* (see Exhibit 6-4). Stallion owners were offered the opportunity to promote their stallions on the site through a customized "one-page site" that included up to two photos, an extended pedigree (ancestry), text, and contact information. Finally, business owners could choose to advertise on AtlanticRider.com's front page in the form of a banner or block ad (see Exhibit 6-5).

Exhibit 6-3 DEMOGRAPHIC CHARACTERISTICS OF HORSE OWNERS

The Canadian Horse Industry (1998 Equine Canada Study)

- 880 000 horses in Canada with 110 000 owners
- More than 1.3 million people ride each year (riding lessons, competition, trail rides, etc.)
- Average investment of $1700 per horse
- Average investment in tack and equipment: $1500 per horse
- 77 percent female
- Median age: 40–49 years
- 60 percent attended college or university
- Usually more than one rider per "horsehold"
- 83 percent have been riding/driving for 10+ years
- 93 percent own another pet
- 68 percent to 70 percent own a computer
- 47 percent use the internet; 86 percent of those research horse-related information
- Estimated total economic impact: $2.1 million–$4.7 billion
- "Normal" household incomes for horse owners: $40 000–$60 000 per year

Exhibit 6-4 NUMBER OF E-RIDER SUBSCRIPTIONS

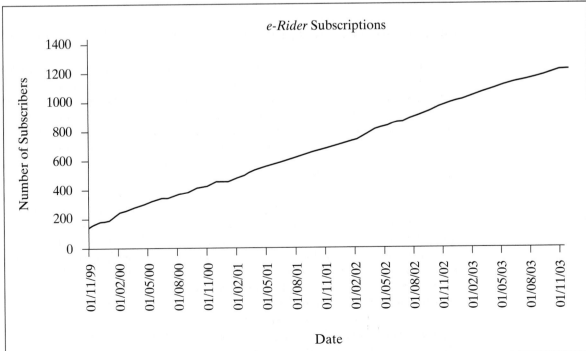

Exhibit 6-5 PRICE SCHEDULE FOR ADVERTISING

Front-page ad (one month)	$150.00
Same ad (subsequent months)	$100.00
Hyperlink from front page (yearly)	$120.00
Stallion advertising (yearly)	$120.00
Website hosting (yearly)	$300.00
Domain forwarding (yearly)	$120.00
e-Rider sponsorship (issue)	$50.00
Classified subscription (yearly)	$24.50

The website itself was designed with best practices in mind. A professional appearance, ease of navigation, and simplicity of design were of paramount importance to attract visitors who were new to the web. Frequent site updates and changes were implemented to keep visitors coming back, and the weekly e-zine kept visitors apprised of upcoming events, new classified ads, and news that had been added to the site. The initial components of the site included Rider of the Week; Show Results; Upcoming Events; Local, National, and International News; a weekly e-zine (*e-Rider*); Kids' Pages; a directory of horse-related businesses in the region; Tributes; Photo Gallery; and Stallion Barn.

The success of AtlanticRider.com can be attributed in large part to the marketing strategy that was employed even before the site launched in October 1999. The choice of name was strategic and aimed to appeal to an Atlantic Canadian audience, while not conflicting with any existing business in Canada to facilitate national incorporation. A graphic artist was hired to create a logo that would not exclude any type of rider or riding discipline.

The promotion strategy began with ads in the "Horses & Equipment" and "Livestock" sections of major newspapers in the four Atlantic provinces (New Brunswick, Nova Scotia, Prince Edward Island, and Newfoundland) and was supplemented with other promotional activities. Registration with search engines was a key element in ensuring that surfers could find the new site. (The site was optimized for search engines through strategic choice of design features and keywords.) Free components, such as classifieds and horse-club sites, also helped to generate traffic.

These efforts were augmented with participation at trade shows and the creation of a booth that included a cart, banner, and computer with the new site available for surfing. Promotional materials distributed at these events included business cards, notepads, and tri-fold brochures—each with the site address and benefits clearly identified. Contests at trade shows and on the site included draws for AtlanticRider.com baseball hats, horse-oriented books, and a toy stable.

Changes to AtlanticRider.com

The skeleton of the site has remained essentially stable since its initial launch, with minor changes that included discontinuing the kids' pages, which were not receiving significant traffic. Software has been added to the site to make it more user-friendly for visitors and site administrators; automated classified ad software (to replace the original practice of posting ads manually with one that allows users themselves to post ads, including photos); bulletin-board software; newsletter distribution service; and a real-time chat room. A domain-forwarding service has been employed so that hosted sites can choose their URLs (for example, *www. mystable.com*), while still enjoying the benefits of hosting within AtlanticRider.com. The weekly schedule for *e-Rider* has been changed to a monthly schedule to reduce the time required for publication, and Rider of the Week has been changed to Rider of the Month. The most recent change to the business model occurred in September 2002, when the site began charging for classified subscriptions. Advertisers now pay a yearly fee to post their ads on the site.

Current Challenges

The company is now facing a number of challenges to its continued success. After four years, the site is in need of an overhaul—a new look and feel to keep it fresh. Keeping the content current is very labour intensive and challenging, especially for a company of this size. The company must constantly battle the persistent attitude that services on the internet should be free, and it faces potential competition from sites offering free classifieds.

QUESTIONS

1. What is the nature of the market segment(s) served by AtlanticRider.com?
2. How well does AtlanticRider.com serve its market segment(s)? How much is this service worth to the segment(s)?
3. How well does AtlanticRider.com do relative to its competitors?
4. What must AtlanticRider.com do to overhaul the website?

APPENDIX I

Sources of Secondary Data

Many organizations in the government and private sector collect information on consumer buying patterns.

A selected list of other secondary data sources and indexes that are particularly useful to consumer researchers follows. Many of these sources are available in the reference section of your library.

COMMERCIAL SOURCES

- *ABI/Inform Ondisc.* Ann Arbor, MI: University Microfilms International. These are abstracts (on compact disc) of articles from business journals.

- *Aging America: Trends and Projections.* Washington, DC, Government Printing Office: U.S. Senate Special Committee on Aging and the American Association of Retired Persons. This gives data on demographic characteristics and growth projections on the elderly over the next 30 years.

- *American Marketing Association International Directory & Marketing Services Guide.* Chicago: American Marketing Association. This complete directory of AMA members includes both individual and corporate listings and a guide to marketing research firms, by area of specialization (published annually).

- *Ipsos Reid Group Inc.* Many syndicated studies are available for purchase. The cost of the surveys depends on their age.

- *BAR/LNA Multi-Media Service.* New York: Leading National Advertisers. This is a listing of advertising expenditures for media and specific brands (updated quarterly).

- *Business Information Sources.* Berkeley: University of California Press. Listed are sources of information about market research and statistical data.

- *Business Periodicals Index.* New York: H.W. Wilson Company. This is an index of business periodicals (updated monthly).

- *Communication Abstracts.* Beverly Hills, CA: Sage Publications, Inc. This is an index of articles and books on topics related to advertising and marketing (published quarterly).

- *Directory of Online Databases.* Santa Monica, CA: Cuadra Associates, Inc. The directory lists databases that are accessible by computer.

- *Dissertation Abstracts International.* Ann Arbor, MI: University of Microfilms International. This is an index of doctoral dissertations, including relevant studies in the Humanities and Social Sciences section, from major universities (updated monthly).

- *Encyclopedia of Information Systems and Services.* Detroit: Gale Research Company. The encyclopedia is a source of information about producers of various databases.

- *Financial Post Canadian Markets.* Toronto: Maclean-Hunter. Contains forecasts for consumer spending along with economic and demographic information.

- *FINDEX: The Directory of Market Research Reports, Studies, and Surveys.* Bethesda, MD: Cambridge Information Group. This international guide to reports is produced by research companies.

- *Guide to Consumer Markets.* New York: The Conference Board. Data on consumer spending and income is published (annually) in this guide.

- *Print Measurement Bureau Production Profile Guide.* This is product data in a two-year database from a sample of more than 20 000 respondents (1-800-PMB-0899).

- *Social Sciences Citation Index.* Philadelphia: Institute for Scientific Information. This is an index of articles in social science periodicals (updated three times a year).

- *Standard Directory of Advertisers.* Wilmette, IL: National Register Publishing Company. This directory is a guide to companies whose advertising spending exceeds US$75 000 and includes information such as their agencies, types of media used, and specific products advertised.

ACADEMIC, INDUSTRY, AND NON-PROFIT SOURCES

Statistics Canada
R.H. Coats Building
Tunney's Pasture,
Ottawa, Ontario K1A OT6
(613) 951-7277

Center for Mature Consumer Studies
College of Business Administration
Georgia State University
University Plaza
Atlanta, GA 30303
(404) 651-4177

The Conference Board
Consumer Research Center
845 Third Avenue
New York, NY 10022
(212) 759-0900

Marketing Science Institute
1000 Massachusetts Avenue
Cambridge, MA 02138–5396
(617) 491-2060

INTERNATIONAL SOURCES

The Roper Center for Public Opinion Research
P.O. Box 440
Storrs, CT 06268
(203) 486-4440

Center for International Research
U.S. Bureau of the Census
Washington, DC 20233
(301) 763-4014

Population Institute
East-West Center
1777 East-West Road
Honolulu, HI 96848
(808) 944-7450

European Society for Opinion and Marketing
Research (ESOMAR)
Central Secretariat
J.J. Viottastraat 29
1071 JP Amsterdam
Netherlands
31-20-664-21-41

Euromonitor
87–88 Turnmill Street
London ECIM 5QU
England
0171-251-8024

The European Community
2100 M Street, NW
Suite 707
Washington, DC 20037
(202) 862-9500

Latin American Demographic Centre (CELADE)
Casilla 91
Santiago, Chile
011-56-2-485051

The Organization for Economic Cooperation and
Development
2001 L Street, NW
Suite 700
Washington, DC
20036-4905

Population Reference Bureau, Inc.
1875 Connecticut Avenue, NW
Suite 520
Washington, DC 20009
(212) 483-1100

United Nations
Public Inquiries Unit
Public Services Section
Department of Public Information
Room GA–057
New York, NY 10017

The World Bank
1818 H Street, NW
Washington, DC 20433
(202) 473-2943

MAJOR WEBSITES

- *www.statcan.ca*: a comprehensive list of data available from Statistics Canada
- *www.guideline.com*: this commercial service performs regular industry analyses and provides one-page industry profile summaries online
- *www.fuld.com*: a competitive intelligence service with corporate information online
- *www.pmrs-aprm.com*: Canadian Professional Marketing Research Society

- *www.ama.org*: American Marketing Association online
- *www.amic.com*: advertising media internet centre; information about internet commerce; a link to the Advertising Research Foundation; a link to Georgia Tech web-user survey; plus many more links
- *www.acnielsen.ca*
- *www.kpmg.ca*
- *www.ipsos.ca*
- *www.surveysite.com*: the websites for research firms that sell summaries of reports on various topics
- *www.colorinstitute.pantone.com*
- *www.sric-bi.com*
- *www.angusreidstrategies.com*
- *www.visioncritical.com*

E-commerce Sites

- *www.nua.ie/surveys*: summaries of surveys about the internet
- *www.intelliquest.com*: a consulting firm specializing in internet commerce; report summaries available online
- *www.ecc.ca*: Electronic Commerce Canada
- *www.birks.com*: gift advisor
- *www.decoratingden.com*: quiz
- *www.landsend.com*: virtual model

Careers in Consumer Research

An understanding of consumers is of course essential in virtually every aspect of marketing. To prepare for a career in a consumer-related field, consider getting involved in relevant research that one of your professors may be doing. In addition to your consumer behaviour course, be sure to take as many courses as possible in other aspects of marketing. Also, try to achieve proficiency in statistics and computer skills. Courses in the social sciences, particularly psychology and sociology, are also helpful.

CAREER PATHS

The following list identifies aspects of marketing where knowledge of consumer behaviour is particularly valuable.

- *Marketing research:* Researchers define problems and collect information needed to resolve them. They typically design projects, analyze data, present findings, and make recommendations to management. Researchers may be employed by corporations that maintain their own market research staffs, or they may work for independent market research firms, trade organizations, advertising agencies, the government, or non-profit organizations.

- *Brand management:* Managers direct marketing efforts for a specific product or line of products. They oversee all aspects of product strategy, including research, packaging, sales, promotion, and forecasting.

- *Customer affairs:* A customer affairs representative acts as a liaison between the firm and its customers. He or she handles complaints and may act as an advocate for the customer within the company.

- *Global marketing:* As firms globalize their operations, they need managers who understand the importance of cultural differences and who can adapt strategies to foreign markets.

- *Advertising copywriters:* Copywriters translate a brand's positioning strategy into concrete form by creating words and visual images that convey this imagery. They need to understand the target market in order to employ imagery that will create the desired response.

- *Advertising account executives:* An account executive supervises the development of a marketing plan and makes sure that the agency's clients understand and are happy with the plan. This job requires knowledge about all aspects of marketing, including an understanding of target markets.

- *Retail managers and merchandisers:* A department or store manager must make decisions about such factors as the store's sales force and how merchandise is displayed in the store. He or she must understand the factors that add to or subtract from the quality of the customer's experience while in the store.

- *Retail buyers:* A buyer purchases merchandise for a store. A good buyer is always "tuned in" to upcoming trends and fashions and is sensitive to the wants and needs of the store's clientele.

- *Public relations:* A public relations specialist is responsible for maintaining positive public awareness of the firm and minimizing negative reactions to company activities. Knowledge of how people's perceptions are influenced by the media is integral to this job.

THE INDUSTRY ROUTE

Many entry-level jobs are available to a competent person with a bachelor's degree (though in some fields it is increasingly difficult to get hired without at least a master's degree). A typical starting position for a university graduate in a marketing research firm, for example, would be as an assistant project manager. This person assists in the design and administration of studies and ensures that they are enacted within the prescribed budget. The beginner may also be assigned to supervise field operations, overseeing the actual collection of data and perhaps coding and analyzing it.

Over time the person would move up to a supervisory position with increasing responsibility. Eventually the person might attain the position of vice-president of marketing research, where he or she would be responsible for the entire company's marketing research efforts and be part of senior management. Chances of moving up tend to improve greatly if the individual received advanced training in statistics, experimental design, and other aspects of consumer psychology.

THE ACADEMIC ROUTE

Another alternative is to consider training to become a scholar in the field of consumer behaviour. Many major business schools offer doctoral programs in marketing, where it is possible to specialize in consumer behaviour research. In addition, some psychology departments offer doctoral programs in consumer psychology. The typical doctoral program involves from four to seven years of intensive study, where the student is trained in both theoretical and technical aspects of consumer research. Many doctoral students in business have already earned an MBA, though this is not always the case.

Most consumer behaviour Ph.D.s who did not obtain their degrees in marketing were trained in psychology. Other possible fields of study—as the discipline's perspective continues to widen—include sociology, anthropology, economics, history, English, human ecology, and others.

These individuals may take faculty positions in a business school, where they conduct research that is published in such academic journals as the *Journal of Consumer Research*. They may also work as consultants to corporations, advertising agencies, and the government. In addition, those with Ph.D.s are in demand in full-time non-academic positions, such as in consulting firms and "think- tanks," or in advertising agencies, manufacturing companies, trade groups (e.g., the Wool Bureau or the Conference Board), or government agencies (e.g., Statistics Canada).

For further insight on these possibilities, consider asking your professor about his or her educational background and research activities.

Glossary →

20/80 rule a rule of thumb in volume segmentation, which says that about 20 percent of consumers in a product category (the heavy or frequent users) account for about 80 percent of sales

Absolute threshold the minimum amount of stimulation that can be detected on a sensory channel

Accommodative purchase decision the process of using bargaining, coercion, compromise, and the wielding of power to achieve agreement among a group whose members have different preferences or priorities

Acculturation the process of learning the beliefs and behaviours endorsed by another culture

Acculturation agents friends, family, local businesses, and other reference groups that facilitate the learning of cultural norms

Activation models of memory approaches to memory stressing different levels of processing that occur and activate some aspects of memory rather than others, depending upon the nature of the processing task

Actual self a person's realistic appraisal of his or her qualities

Adaptation the process that occurs when a sensation becomes so familiar that it is no longer the focus of attention

Advergaming a marketing strategy where online games merge with interactive advertisements featuring real products

Affect the way a consumer feels about an attitude object

Age cohort a group of consumers of the same approximate age who have undergone similar experiences

Agentic goals goals that favour the advancement of the individual

AIOs (activities, interests, and opinions) the psychographic variables used by researchers in grouping consumers

Allocentrics individuals who have a group orientation and receive something of value

Androgyny the possession of both masculine and feminine traits

Animism the attribution of conscious life to inanimate objects

Anticonsumption the actions taken by consumers that involve the deliberate defacement or mutilation of products

Archetype a universally shared idea or behaviour pattern, central to Jung's conception of personality; archetypes involve themes, such as birth, death, or the devil, that appear frequently in myths, stories, and dreams

Art product a creation viewed primarily as an object of aesthetic contemplation without any functional value

Aspirational reference group high-profile athletes and celebrities used in marketing efforts to promote a product

Atmospherics the use of space and physical features in store design to evoke certain effects in buyers

Attention the extent to which processing activity is devoted to a particular stimulus

Attitude a lasting, general evaluation of people (including oneself), objects, or issues

Attitude object (A_o) anything toward which one has an attitude

Attitude toward the act of buying (A_{act}) the perceived consequences of a purchase

Attitude toward the advertisement (A_{ad}) a predisposition to respond favourably or unfavourably to a particular advertising stimulus during a particular exposure occasion

Autonomic decisions those purchase decisions that are made almost exclusively by one spouse or the other

Avatar a cyberspace presence represented by a character whose movements you control inside a visual, graphical world

B2C commerce businesses selling to consumers through electronic marketing

Baby boomers a large cohort of people born between the years of 1947 and 1966 who are the source of many important cultural and economic changes

Balance theory a theory that considers relations among elements a person might perceive as belonging together, and people's tendency to change relations among elements in order to make them consistent or "balanced"

Behaviour a consumer's actions with regard to an attitude object

Behavioural economics the study of the behavioural determinants of economic decisions

Behavioural influence perspective the view that consumer decisions are learned responses to environmental cues

Behavioural learning theories the perspectives on learning that assume that learning takes place as the result of responses to external events

Binary opposition a defining structural characteristic of many myths, where two opposing ends of some dimension are represented (e.g., good versus evil, nature versus technology)

Blog (or *weblog*) an online posting of a person's thoughts about some topic

Blogging a frequent chronological publication of personal thoughts and weblinks online

Blogosphere the name given to the universe of active weblogs

Body cathexis a person's feelings about aspects of his or her body

Body image a consumer's subjective evaluation of his or her physical self

Boomerang kids grown children who return to their parents' home to live

Brand community a set of consumers who share a set of social relationships based upon usage or interest in a product

Brand equity a brand that has strong positive associations in a consumer's memory and commands a lot of loyalty as a result

Brand loyalty a form of repeat-purchasing behaviour reflecting a conscious decision to continue buying the same brand

Brand personality the set of traits people attribute to a product as if it were a person

Business ethics the rules of conduct that guide actions in the marketplace; the standards against which most people in a culture judge what is right or wrong

Buzz word of mouth that is viewed as authentic and generated by customers rather than companies

C2C commerce consumer-to-consumer activity through the internet

Census family a housing unit containing at least one family (a husband and wife, married or living common law, or lone parent of any marital status, with or without children who have never married and are still living at home)

Chavs young, lower-class men and women who mix flashy brands and accessories from big names, such as Burberry, with clothing like track suits

Classic a fashion with an extremely long acceptance cycle

Classical conditioning the learning that occurs when a stimulus eliciting a response is paired with another stimulus that initially does not elicit a response on its own, but will cause a similar response over time because of its association with the first stimulus

Co-branding strategies when two or more companies team up to jointly promote related products

Cognition the beliefs a consumer has about an attitude object

Cognitive learning theory the perspectives on learning that assume that learning takes place as the result of internal mental processes: people actively use information from the world around them to master their environment and solve problems

Collective selection the process by which certain symbolic alternatives tend to be jointly chosen over others by members of a society

Collectivist culture a society that encourages people to subordinate their personal goals to those of a stable in-group; values such as self-discipline and group accomplishment are stressed

Communal goals goals that favour the well-being of the group or community as a whole

Communications model a framework specifying that a number of elements are necessary for communication to be achieved, including a source, message, medium, receivers, and feedback

Comparative advertising a strategy in which a message compares two or more specifically named or recognizably presented brands and makes a comparison of them in terms of one or more specific attributes

Comparative influence the process whereby a reference group influences decisions about specific brands or activities

Compatibility matching an innovation or product with the consumer's lifestyle

Compensatory decision rules a set of rules that allow information about attributes of competing products to be averaged in some way; poor standing on one attribute can potentially be offset by good standing on another

Complexity the level of product difficulty to understand or use

Compulsive consumption the process of repetitive, often excessive, shopping used to relieve tension, anxiety, depression, or boredom

Conditioned response a new or modified response elicited by a stimulus after conditioning.

Conditioned stimulus (CS) a stimulus that causes a response due to a learned association

Conformity refers to a change in beliefs or actions as a reaction to real or imagined group pressure

Connexity 20-somethings who place high value on being both footloose and connected

Consensual purchase decision a decision in which the group agrees on the desired purchase and differs only in terms of how it will be achieved

Consideration set those products already in memory plus those prominent in the retail environment that are actively considered during a consumer's choice process

Conspicuous consumption the purchase and prominent display of luxury goods to provide evidence of a consumer's ability to afford them

Consumer addiction the physiological and/or psychological dependency on products or services

Consumer behaviour the processes involved when individuals or groups select, purchase, use, or dispose of products, services, ideas, or experiences to satisfy needs and desires

Consumer confidence the state of mind of consumers relative to their optimism or pessimism about economic conditions; people tend to make more discretionary purchases when their confidence in the economy is high

Consumer hyperchoice an overabundance of choices for the consumer

Consumer satisfaction/dissatisfaction (CS/D) the overall attitude a person has about a product after it has been purchased

Consumer socialization the process by which people acquire skills that enable them to function in the marketplace

Consumer tribe a group of people who share a lifestyle and who can identify with each other because of a shared allegiance to an activity or a product

Consumption communities web groups where members share views and product recommendations online

Continuous innovation a product change or new product that requires relatively little adaptation by the adopter

Conventions norms regarding the conduct of everyday life

Coolhunters kids in major cosmopolitan markets who roam the streets to report back on cutting-edge trends

Corporate paradox the more involved a company appears to be in the dissemination of news about its products, the less credible it becomes

Country of origin the country in which a consumer good was produced

Craft product a creation valued because of the beauty with which it performs some function; this type of product tends to follow a formula that permits rapid production and is easier to understand than an art product

Creolization the process whereby foreign customs are integrated into a local culture, producing a blend of foreign and local practices

Cult products items that demand fierce consumer loyalty and devotion

Cultivation hypothesis a perspective emphasizing the media's ability to distort consumers' perceptions of reality

Cultural capital a set of distinctive and socially rare tastes and practices

Cultural categories the grouping of ideas and values that reflect the basic ways members of a society characterize the world

Cultural formula a sequence of media events where certain roles and props tend to occur consistently

Cultural gatekeepers individuals who are responsible for determining the types of messages and symbolism to which members of mass culture are exposed

Cultural selection the process where some alternatives are selected over others by cultural gatekeepers

Culture the values, ethics, rituals, traditions, material objects, and services produced or valued by the members of a society

Culture jamming the defacement or alteration of advertising materials as a form of political expression

Culture production system (CPS) the set of individuals and organizations responsible for creating and marketing a cultural product

Custom a norm that is derived from a traditional way of doing things

Cybermediary an intermediary that helps to filter and organize online market information so that customers can identify and evaluate alternatives more efficiently

Database marketing the process of creating a database of consumers and their purchases through tracking programs, and then customizing marketing appeals to suit these different customers

Decay structural changes in the brain produced by learning decrease over time

Decision polarization the process whereby individuals' choices tend to become more extreme (polarized), in either a conservative or risky direction, following group discussion of alternatives

De-ethnicitization the process whereby a product formerly associated with a specific ethnic group is detached from its roots and marketed to other subcultures

Deindividuation the submerging of individual identities within a group

Demographics the observable measurements of a population's characteristics, such as birth rate, age distribution, and income

Desacralization the process that occurs when a sacred item or symbol is removed from its special place, or is duplicated in mass quantities, and becomes profane as a result

Determinant attributes product features that are essential to final choice

Differential threshold the ability of a sensory system to detect changes or differences among stimuli

Diffusion of innovation the process whereby a new product, service, or idea spreads through a population

Discontinuous innovation a product change or new product that requires a significant amount of adaptation by the adopter

Discretionary income the money available to a household over and above that required for a comfortable standard of living

Divestment rituals the act of "freeing up" objects as they are passed from one owner to another

Drive the desire to satisfy a biological need in order to reduce physiological arousal

Dynamically continuous innovation a product change or new product that requires a moderate amount of adaptation by the adopter

Early adopters people receptive to new styles because they are involved in the product category and place high value on being in fashion

E-fluentials people who act as opinion leaders on the internet

Ego the system that mediates between the id and superego

Elaborated codes the ways of expressing and interpreting meanings that are more complex and depend on a more sophisticated world view and that tend to be used by the middle and upper classes

Elaboration likelihood model (ELM) the approach that one of two routes to persuasion (central versus peripheral) will be followed, depending upon the personal relevance of a message; the route taken determines the relative importance of message contents versus other characteristics, such as source attractiveness

Emic perspective an approach to studying cultures that stresses the unique aspects of each culture

Encoding the process in which information from short-term memory is entered into long-term memory in a recognizable form

Enculturation the process of learning the beliefs and behaviours endorsed by our native culture

Erogenous zones areas of the body considered by members of a culture to be foci of sexual attractiveness

Ethnic subculture a self-perpetuating group of consumers held together by common cultural ties

Ethnocentrism the tendency to prefer products or people of our own culture over those from other countries

Ethos a set of moral, aesthetic, and evaluative principles

Etic perspective an approach to studying cultures that stresses commonalities across cultures

Evaluative criteria the dimensions used by consumers to compare competing product alternatives

Evoked set those products already in memory plus those prominent in the retail environment that are actively considered during a consumer's choice process

Exchange the process whereby two or more organizations or people give and receive something of value

Exchange theory the perspective that every interaction involves an exchange of value

Expectancy theory the perspective that behaviour is largely "pulled" by expectations of achieving desirable outcomes, or positive incentives, rather than "pushed" from within

Experiential perspective an approach stressing the gestalt, or totality, of the product or service experience, focusing on consumers' affective responses in the marketplace

Exposure an initial stage of perception where some sensations come within range of consumers' sensory receptors

Extended family traditional family structure where several generations live together

Extended problem solving an elaborate decision-making process, often initiated by a motive that is fairly central to the self-concept and accompanied by perceived risk; the consumer tries to collect as much information as possible and carefully weighs product alternatives

Extended self the definition of self created by the external objects with which a person surrounds him or herself

Extinction the process whereby a learned connection between a stimulus and response is eroded so that the response is no longer reinforced

Fad a very short-lived fashion

Family financial officer (FFO) the individual in the family who is in charge of making financial decisions

Family life cycle (FLC) a classification scheme that segments consumers in terms of changes in income and family composition and changes in demands placed upon income

Fantasy a self-induced shift in consciousness, often focusing on some unattainable or improbable goal; sometimes fantasy is a way of compensating for a lack of external stimulation or for dissatisfaction with the actual self

Fashion the process of social diffusion by which a new style is adopted by some group(s) of consumers

Fashion acceptance cycle the diffusion process of a style through three stages: introduction, acceptance, and regression

Fashion life cycle the "career" or stages in the life of a fashion as it progresses from introduction to obsolescence

Fashion system those people and organizations involved in creating symbolic meanings and transferring these meanings to cultural goods

Fear appeal an attempt to change attitudes or behaviour through the use of threats or by highlighting negative consequences of noncompliance with the request

Figure-ground principle the gestalt principle whereby one part of a stimulus configuration dominates a situation while other aspects recede into the background

Flow state a condition of absorption that consumers enter when they are truly involved with a product, an ad, or a website

Foot-in-the-door technique based on the observation that a consumer is more likely to comply with a request if he or she has first agreed to comply with a smaller request

Frequency marketing reinforces regular purchasers by giving them prizes with values that increase along with the amount purchased

Functional theory of attitudes a pragmatic approach that focuses on how attitudes facilitate social behaviour; attitudes exist because they serve some function for the person

Gemba the one true source of information

Gender-typed traits characteristics that are stereotypically associated with one gender or the other

Generation X the cohort of consumers in their twenties who were affected by the economic downturn in the first part of the nineties; also, this term refers to those born between 1967 and 1979

Generation Y those born between 1980 and 1995—also referred to as the baby boom echo

Geodemography techniques that combine consumer demographic information with geographic consumption patterns to permit precise targeting of consumers with specific characteristics

Gerontographics divide the mature market into groups based on both level of physical well-being and social conditions, such as being a grandparent or spouse

Gestalt psychology a school of thought that maintains people derive meaning from the totality of a set of stimuli, rather than from any individual stimulus

Gift-giving ritual the events involved in the selection, presentation, acceptance, and interpretation of a gift

Globalized consumption ethic the global sharing of a material lifestyle including the valuing of well-known multinational brands that symbolize prosperity

Goal a consumer's desired end state

Green marketing a marketing strategy involving an emphasis on protecting the natural environment

Guerrilla marketing promotional strategies that use unconventional locations and intensive word-of-mouth campaigns to push products

Habitual decision making the consumption choices that are made out of habit, without additional information search or deliberation among products

Habitus a status-marking force that causes consumption preferences to cluster together

Halo effect the transfer of the original impression to other associated categories

Hedonic consumption the multisensory, fantasy, and emotional aspects of consumers' interactions with products

Heuristics the mental rules of thumb that lead to a speedy decision

Hierarchy of effects a fixed sequence of steps that occurs during attitude formation; this sequence varies depending upon such factors as the consumer's level of involvement with the attitude object

High-context culture group members who tend to be tightly knit and who generally infer meanings that go beyond the spoken word; symbols and gestures, rather than words, carry much of the weight of messages

Homeostasis the state of being where the body is in physiological balance; goal-oriented behaviour attempts to reduce or eliminate an unpleasant motivational state and return to a balanced one

Home shopping parties a gathering where a company representative makes a sales presentation to a group of people who have gathered in the home of a friend or acquaintance

Homogamy the tendency for individuals to marry others similar to themselves

Host culture a new culture with which a person comes in contact

Hype corporate propaganda planted by companies to create product sensation—dismissed as inauthentic by customers

Hyperreality refers to the "becoming real" of what is initially simulation of "hype"

Id the system oriented toward immediate gratification

Ideal of beauty a model, or exemplar, of appearance valued by a culture

Ideal self a person's conception of how he or she would like to be

Idiocentrics people having an individualist orientation

Impulse buying a process that occurs when the consumer experiences a sudden urge to purchase an item that he or she cannot resist

Individualist culture a society that encourages people to attach more importance to personal goals than to group goals; values such as personal enjoyment and freedom are stressed

Inertia the process whereby purchase decisions are made out of habit because the consumer lacks the motivation to consider alternatives

Information search the process whereby a consumer searches for appropriate information to make a reasonable decision

Innovation a product or style that is perceived as new by consumers

Innovators people who are always on the lookout for novel developments and will be the first to try a new offering

Instrumental conditioning the process by which the individual learns to perform behaviours that produce positive outcomes and to avoid those that yield negative outcomes

Instrumental values those goals that are endorsed because they are needed to achieve desired end states, or terminal values

Interference a process whereby additional learned information displaces the earlier information, resulting in memory loss for the item learned previously

Interpretant the meaning derived

Interpretation the process whereby meanings are assigned to stimuli

Interpretivism a research perspective that produces a "thick description" of consumers' subjective experiences and stresses the importance of the individual's social construction of reality

Invidious distinction the display of wealth or power (e.g., through product consumption) to cause envy in others

Involvement a person's perceived relevance of an object based on inherent needs, values, and interests

JND (Just Noticeable Difference) the minimum change in a stimulus that can be detected by a perceiver

Kansei engineering a Japanese philosophy that translates customers' feelings into design elements

Kin-network system the rituals intended to maintain ties among family members, both immediate and extended

Knowledge structures organized systems of concepts relating to brands, stores, and other concepts

Laddering a technique for uncovering consumers' associations between specific attributes and general consequences

Lateral cycling a process where already-purchased objects are sold to others or exchanged for other items

Latitudes of acceptance and rejection formed around an attitude standard; ideas that fall within a latitude will be favourably received, while those falling outside this zone will not

Lead user an involved, experienced customer who is very knowledgeable about the field

Learning a relatively permanent change in a behaviour, caused by experience

Lifestyle a set of shared values or tastes exhibited by a group of consumers, especially as they are reflected in consumption patterns

Limited problem solving a problem-solving process in which consumers are not motivated to search for information or to evaluate each alternative rigorously; they instead use simple decision rules to arrive at a purchase decision

Long-term memory the system that allows us to retain information for a long period of time

Looking-glass self the process of imagining the reaction of others toward ourselves

Low-context culture group members who tend to be rather loosely connected and who generally are quite literal; words, rather than symbols and gestures, carry much of the weight of messages

M-commerce buying or selling of goods and services through wireless handheld devices

Market beliefs the specific beliefs or decision rules pertaining to marketplace phenomena

Market maven a person who often serves as a source of information about marketplace activities

Marketing segmentation identifies groups of consumers who are similar to one another in one or more ways, and then devises marketing strategies that appeal to one or more groups

Masked branding the strategy of deliberately hiding a product's true origin

Mass class global consumers who have a high level of purchasing power that enables them to afford high-quality products, except for big-ticket items such as higher education, housing, and luxury cars

Mass customization the ability of the customer to purchase goods that are to their personal specifications

Match-up hypothesis the theory that the dominant characteristics of a product should match the dominant features of the communications source

Materialism the importance consumers attach to worldly possessions

Mature market consumers aged 55 years and older

Meme theory an idea or product enters the consciousness of people over time, starting off small and steadily increasing its presence

Memory a process of acquiring information and storing it over time so that it will be available when needed

Mental accounting a principle which states that decisions are influenced by the way a problem is posed

Metaphor the use of an explicit comparison ("A" is "B") between a product and some other person, place, or thing

Metrosexual an urban male who has strong aesthetic sense and spends a great deal of time and money on his appearance and lifestyle

Microculture communities of consumers who participate in or otherwise identify with specific art forms, popular culture movements, hobbies, and so on

Monomyth a myth with basic characteristics that are found in many cultures

More a norm with strong moral overtones

Motivation an internal state that activates goal-oriented behaviour

Motivational research a qualitative research approach, based on psychoanalytic interpretations, with a heavy emphasis on unconscious motives for consumption

Multi-attribute attitude models those models that assume that a consumer's attitude (evaluation) of an attitude object depends on the beliefs he or she has about several or many attributes of the object; the use of a multi-attribute model implies that an attitude toward a product or brand can be predicted by identifying these specific beliefs and combining them to derive a measure of the consumer's overall attitude

Myth a story containing symbolic elements that expresses the shared emotions and ideals of a culture

Negative reinforcement the process whereby the environment weakens responses to stimuli so that inappropriate behaviour is avoided

Negative word-of-mouth the passing on of negative experiences involved with products or services by consumers to other potential consumers

Neuromarketing assessing brain function through an MRI to develop advertising strategy

Non-compensatory decision rules a set of simple rules whereby a brand with a low standing on one attribute can make up for this position by being better on another attribute

Normative influence the process in which a reference group helps to set and enforce fundamental standards of conduct

Norms the informal rules that govern what is right or wrong

Nostalgia a bittersweet emotion where the past is viewed with sadness and longing; many "classic" products appeal to consumers' memories of their younger days

Nuclear family a contemporary living arrangement comprising a married couple and their children

Object the product that is the focus of the message

Observability level of product visibility

Observational learning the process in which people learn by watching the actions of others and noting the reinforcements they receive for their behaviours

Opinion leaders those people who are knowledgeable about products and who are frequently able to influence others' attitudes or behaviours with regard to a product category

Paradigm a widely accepted view or model of phenomena being studied

Parental yielding the process that occurs when a parental decision maker is influenced by a child's product request

Parody display the deliberate avoidance of widely used status symbols, whereby the person seeks status by mocking it

Perceived age how old a person feels rather than his or her true chronological age

Perceived risk the belief that use of a product has potentially negative consequences, either physical or social

Perception the process by which stimuli are selected, organized, and interpreted

Perceptual selectivity a process in which people attend to only a small portion of the stimuli to which they are exposed

Permission marketing the strategy of first asking consumers to indicate interest in receiving information about a product or service to ensure that they will pay attention to the promotional messages they will then receive if they agree

Personality a person's unique psychological makeup, which consistently influences the way the person responds to his or her environment

Persuasion an active attempt to change attitudes

Pleasure principle the belief that behaviour is guided by the desire to maximize pleasure and avoid pain

Point-of-purchase (POP) stimuli the promotional materials that are deployed in stores or other outlets to influence consumers' decisions at the time products are purchased

Popular culture the music, movies, sports, books, celebrities, and other forms of entertainment consumed by the mass market

Positioning strategy the place a brand name occupies in the consumer's mind with regard to important attributes (such as functional features) and competitive offerings

Positive reinforcement the process whereby rewards provided by the environment strengthen responses to stimuli

Positivism a research perspective that relies on principles of the "scientific method" and assumes that a single reality exists; events in the world can be objectively measured; and the causes of behaviour can be identified, manipulated, and predicted

Principle of closure the gestalt principle that consumers tend to perceive an incomplete picture as complete

Principle of cognitive consistency the belief that consumers value harmony among their thoughts, feelings, and behaviours and that they are motivated to maintain uniformity among these elements

Principle of similarity the gestalt principle that describes how consumers tend to group objects that share similar physical characteristics

Problem recognition the process that occurs whenever the consumer sees a significant difference between his or her current state of affairs and some desired or ideal state; this recognition initiates the decision-making process

Product complementarity the view that products in different functional categories have symbolic meanings that are related to one another

Product placement the process of obtaining exposure for a product by arranging for it to be inserted into a movie, television show, or some other medium

Product signal communicates an underlying quality of a product through the use of aspects that are visible only in the ad

Profane consumption the process of consuming objects and events that are ordinary or of the everyday world

Progressive learning model the perspective that people gradually learn a new culture as they increasingly come in contact with it; consumers assimilate into a new culture, mixing practices from their old and new environments to create a hybrid culture

Prospect theory a descriptive model of how people make choices that finds that risk differs when the consumer faces options involving gains versus those involving losses

Psychographics the use of psychological, sociological, and anthropological factors to construct market segments

Psychophysics the science that focuses on how the physical environment is integrated into the consumer's subjective experience

Punishment the learning that occurs when a response is followed by unpleasant events

Purchase momentum an increase in the likelihood of buying after initial purchases are made

Queuing theory the mathematical study of waiting lines

Rational perspective a view of the consumer as a careful, analytical decision maker who tries to maximize utility in purchase decisions

Reactance a "boomerang effect" that sometimes occurs when consumers are threatened with a loss of freedom of choice; they respond by doing the opposite of the behaviour advocated in a persuasive message

Reality engineering the process whereby elements of popular culture are appropriated by marketers and become integrated into marketing strategies; examples of this phenomenon include infomercials and product placement

Reciprocity norm a culturally learned obligation to return the gesture of a gift with one of equal value

Reference group an actual or imaginary individual or group that has a significant effect upon an individual's evaluations, aspirations, or behaviour

Relationship marketing the process of creating, maintaining, and enhancing strong, value-laden relationships with customers

Relative advantage the benefits a product can provide over other competing products

Resonance a literary device, frequently used in advertising, that uses a play on words (a double meaning) to communicate a product benefit

Response bias a form of contamination in survey research where some factor, such as the desire to make a good impression on the experimenter, leads respondents to modify their true answers

Restricted codes the ways of expressing and interpreting meanings that focus on the content of objects and that tend to be used by the working class

Retail theming a strategy involving the creation of imaginative store environments that transport shoppers to fantasy worlds or provide other kinds of stimulation

Retrieval the process whereby desired information is accessed from long-term memory

Retro brand relaunched historical brands with new features

Risky shift a willingness by a group to consider riskier alternatives than those favoured by individual group members

Rites of passage sacred times marked by a change in social status

Ritual a set of multiple, symbolic behaviours that occur in a fixed sequence and that tend to be repeated periodically

Ritual artifacts items (consumer goods) used in the performance of rituals

Role theory the perspective that much of consumer behaviour resembles actions in a play

Sacralization a process that occurs when ordinary objects, events, or people take on sacred meaning to a culture or to specific groups within a culture

Sacred consumption the process of consuming objects and events that are set apart from normal life and treated with some degree of respect or awe

Salience the prominence or level of activation of a brand in memory

Schema an organized collection of beliefs and feelings represented in a cognitive category

Self-concept the attitude a person holds toward him or herself

Self-gifts buying something for one's self as a reward

Self-image congruence models the approaches based on the prediction that products will be chosen when their attributes match some aspect of the self

Self-perception theory an alternative explanation of dissonance effects; it assumes that people use observations of their own behaviour to infer their attitudes toward some object

Semiotics examines the correspondence between signs and symbols and their role in the assignment of meaning

Sensation the immediate response of sensory receptors (eyes, ears, nose, mouth, fingers) to such basic stimuli as light, colour, and sound

Sensory memory the temporary storage of information received from the senses

Shaping the learning of a desired behaviour over time by rewarding immediate actions until the final result is obtained

Shopping orientation a consumer's general attitudes and motivations regarding the act of shopping

Short-term memory the system that allows us to retain information for a short period of time

Shrinkage the loss of money or inventory due to shoplifting and employee theft

Sign the sensory imagery that represents the intended meanings of the object

Silent commerce a new trend that enables transactions and information gathering to occur in the background without any direct intervention by consumers or managers

Skin a graphical interface that acts as both the face and the control panel of a computer program

Sleeper effect the process whereby differences in attitude change between positive and negative sources seem to diminish over time

Social aging theories theories on how society assigns people to different roles across the life span

Social class the overall rank of people in a society; people who are grouped within the same social class are approximately equal in terms of their social standing, occupations, and lifestyles

Social comparison theory the perspective that people compare their outcomes with others' as a way to increase the stability of their own self-evaluation, especially when physical evidence is unavailable

Social judgment theory the perspective that people assimilate new information about attitude objects in light of what they already know or feel; the initial attitude acts as a frame of reference, and new information is categorized in terms of this standard

Social marketing the promotion of causes and ideas (social products), such as energy conservation, charities, and population control

Social mobility the movement of individuals from one social class to another

Social power the capacity of one person to alter the actions or outcome of another

Social stratification the process in a social system by which scarce and valuable resources are distributed unequally to status positions that become more or less permanently ranked in terms of the share of valuable resources each receives

Sociometric methods the techniques for measuring group dynamics that involve the tracing of communication patterns in and among groups

Source attractiveness refers to the source's perceived social value

Source credibility a communications source's perceived expertise, objectivity, or trustworthiness

Spreading activation A meaning can be activated indirectly; energy spreads across nodes of varying levels of abstraction. As one memory node is activated, other nodes associated with it also begin to be triggered. Meaning thus spreads across the network, bringing up concepts including competing brands and relevant attributes that are used to form attitudes toward the brand

Stage of cognitive development the ability to comprehend concepts of increasing complexity as a person ages

Status crystallization the extent to which different indicators of a person's status (income, ethnicity, occupation) are consistent with one another

Status hierarchy a ranking of social desirability in terms of consumers' access to such resources as money, education, and luxury goods

Status symbols products that are purchased and displayed to signal membership in a desirable social class

Stereotype a knowledge structure based upon beliefs not necessarily supported by evidence

Stimulus discrimination the process that occurs when behaviour caused by two stimuli is different, as when consumers learn to differentiate a brand from its competitors

Stimulus generalization the process that occurs when the behaviour caused by a reaction to one stimulus occurs in the presence of other, similar stimuli

Storage the process that occurs when knowledge entered in long-term memory is integrated with what is already in memory and "warehoused" until needed

Store image a store's "personality," composed of such attributes as location, merchandise suitability, and the knowledge and congeniality of the sales staff

Subculture a group whose members share beliefs and common experiences that set them apart from other members of a culture

Subliminal perception the processing of information presented below the level of the consumer's awareness

Superego the system that internalizes society's rules and that works to prevent the id from seeking selfish gratification

Surrogate consumer a professional who is retained to evaluate or make purchases on behalf of a consumer

Symbol in semiotic terms, a sign that is related to a product through either conventional or agreed-upon associations

Symbolic interactionism a sociological approach stressing that relationships with other people play a large part in forming the self; people live in a symbolic environment, and the meaning attached to any situation or object is determined by a person's interpretation of these symbols

Symbolic self-completion theory the perspective that people who have an incomplete self-definition in some context will compensate by acquiring symbols associated with a desired social identity

Syncratic decisions those purchase decisions that are made jointly by both spouses

Synoptic ideal a model of spousal decision making where both partners take a common view and act as joint decision makers, assigning each other well-defined roles and making mutually beneficial decisions to maximize the couple's joint utility

Terminal values end states desired by members of a culture

Theory of cognitive dissonance the perspective that cognitive discomfort results from an individual holding logically inconsistent beliefs about an object or event. The consumer is motivated to reduce dissonance through changing his or her beliefs and evaluations about the object or event

Theory of reasoned action an updated version of the Fishbein multi-attitude theory that considers such factors as social pressure and A_{act} (the attitude toward the act of buying a product), rather than attitudes toward just the product itself

Time poverty the feeling that one is more pressed for time than ever before

Tipping point the moment of critical mass

Total fertility rate (TFR) the number of births per woman aged 15 to 49 years

Trade dress colour combinations that come to be strongly associated with a corporation or brand

Traits the identifiable characteristics that define a person

Trialability the ability of consumers to try a product before they purchase it

Tribal marketing linking a product to the needs of a consumer group defined by shared allegiance to a lifestyle

Trickle-down theory the perspective that fashions spread as the result of status symbols associated with the upper classes "trickling down" to other social classes as these consumers try to emulate those with greater status

Tweens 2.4 million Canadian children aged 9 to 14 years

Two-factor theory the perspective that two separate psychological processes are operating when a person is repeatedly exposed to an ad: repetition increases familiarity and thus reduces uncertainty about the product, but over time boredom increases with each exposure, and at some point the amount of boredom incurred begins to exceed the amount of uncertainty reduced, resulting in wear-out

U-commerce the use of ubiquitous networks, for example, wearable computers or customized advertisements beamed to us on our cell phones

Unconditioned stimulus (UCS) a stimulus naturally capable of causing a response

Uses and gratification theory the perspective that the consumer uses the media to meet more than strictly information needs

Value an enduring belief that a specific mode of conduct is personally or socially preferable to an opposite mode of conduct

Value system a culture's ranking of the relative importance of values

Values and Lifestyles (VALS2™) a proprietary psychographic segmentation system used to categorize consumers into clusters, or "VALS Types"

Variety seeking the desire to choose new alternatives over more familiar ones

Vigilante marketing the power of common consumers to affect change in the marketplace

Viral marketing the strategy of getting customers to sell a product on behalf of the company that creates it

Virtual community of consumption a collection of people whose online interactions are based upon shared enthusiasm for and knowledge of a specific consumption activity

Voluntary simplifiers people who reduce their consumption due to a belief that once basic material needs are satisfied additional possessions do not add to happiness

Want the particular form of consumption chosen to satisfy a need

Weber's law the principle that the stronger the initial stimulus, the greater its change must be for it to be noticed

Word-of-mouth communication (WOM) the information transmitted by individual consumers on an informal basis

Index ⊝→